Practical Problems in Organizations

Practical Problems in Organizations

Cases in Leadership, Organizational Behavior, and Human Resources

James G. Clawson

The Darden Graduate School of Business Administration
University of Virginia

Prentice
Hall

Upper Saddle River, New Jersey 07458

Library of Congress Cataloging-in-Publication Data

Clawson, James G.
 Practical problems in organizations: cases in leadership, organizational behavior, and human resources/James G. Clawson.
  p. cm.
 Includes index.
 ISBN 0-13-008389-5
 1. Leadership—Case studies. 2. Organizational behavior—Case studies. 3. Personnel management—Case studies. I. Title.
HD57.7.C546 2002
658—dc21

2001055415

Executive Editor: David Shafer
Editor-in-Chief: Jeff Shelstad
Acquisitions Editor: Melissa Steffens
Editorial Assistant: Kevin Glynn
Senior Marketing Manager: Shannon Moore
Marketing Assistant: Christine Genneken
Managing Editor (Production): John Roberts
Production Editor: Kelly Warsak
Permissions Coordinator: Suzanne Grappi
Associate Director, Manufacturing: Vincent Scelta
Production Manager: Arnold Vila
Manufacturing Buyer: Michelle Klein
Cover Designer: Bruce Kenselaar
Composition: BookMasters, Inc.
Full-Service Project Management: BookMasters, Inc.
Printer/Binder: The Lehigh Press, Inc.
Cover Printer: RRDonnelley

Pearson Education LTD.
Pearson Education Australia PTY, Limited
Pearson Education Singapore, Pte. Ltd
Pearson Education North Asia Ltd
Pearson Education, Canada, Ltd
Pearson Educación de Mexico, S.A. de C.V.
Pearson Education—Japan
Pearson Education Malaysia, Pte. Ltd

10 9 8 7 6 5 4 3 2 1
ISBN 0-13-008389-5

Contents

■ v ■

Contents of Feature Topics

Women in Management

Managing Diversity

International Settings

Cases with Related Video or CD-ROM Materials

Preface

This volume organizes and presents 42 field-based cases in leadership and organizational behavior. The cases are organized roughly according to the general leadership framework included in *Level Three Leadership,* Second Edition, by this editor and as shown below. Briefly put, the model suggests that effective leadership is a function of many elements including characteristics of the individual leader, that person's strategic view of what tasks to select and pay attention to, that person's ability and willingness to influence others toward that vision, and that person's ability to design and implement organizational forms and systems that unlock the potential of its members. These four leadership initiatives—strategic thinking, influencing others, designing high-performance organizations, and leading change—are represented by the northeast, northwest, north-south, and southeast axes, respectively, in the model in Figure 1. The collection of cases presented here is intended to allow students to explore practical realities of leading on each of these axes.

This model assumes that conversations about leadership are really about leading strategic change. My premise is straightforward: One cannot talk about leadership and not talk about strategy without asking, "Leadership for what and to what end?" Likewise, one cannot talk about leadership without talking about leading change, because if there is no change, there is no leadership. These and related ideas and concepts are laid out in detail in *Level Three Leadership.*

The cases all revolve around leadership and related issues in organizational behavior—managing people in organizations. The cases were chosen in part to represent a variety of industries, protagonist gender, diversity, international settings, and level in organizational hierarchy. Many of the cases are new. Some that reflect classic issues and have proved themselves in the classroom have more dated copyrights. While we acknowledge that many business problems today are unique and require fresh perspective, we also note that human

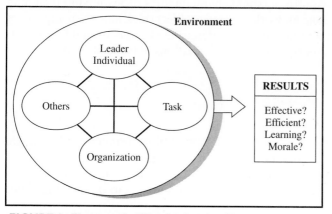

FIGURE I Elements in Effective Leadership

behavior has enduring qualities. One challenge in managing people is to use what we have learned over the last century and to augment our understanding of human behavior as it occurs in the modern context. This array of cases should allow one to do that.

Instructors may or may not wish to use *Level Three Leadership,* Second Edition, as a companion text with the cases presented here. Both volumes can be used independently. One may use the text with a different set of cases (indeed, we often use a variety of cases from other schools to augment our curricula), and one may use this case book with other conceptual frameworks to illustrate and explore the practical realities of leadership in organizational settings.

The merits of case method instruction have been debated over the last 50 years. Traditional researchers tend to discount the value of case method instruction, preferring to rely on theory introduction, memorization, and application. We assert, again, that case method is not atheoretical; rather, it provides the same dilemma that confronts a researcher—real-world phenomena and the challenge to deal with them. Further, the high level of involvement that open-case discussions engender in students raises their energy and retention levels significantly. Although one might use the cases in this volume without any theoretical overlay as a means of introducing the students to real problems in managing people in organizations, I believe in a balanced approach—introducing conceptual frameworks in *Level Three Leadership,* Second Edition, and practical situations in this volume. Instructors can use either or both in whatever depth and degree they are most comfortable. When examining cases, we can include high levels of student involvement and participation, dealing with the realities of business issues, a bias toward action, and the gentle distillation of experience and wisdom that comes from wrestling with real problems repeatedly.

The cases in this volume are assembled into sections, roughly correlating with the general model of leadership shown in Figure 1. I will not give a synopsis here of the cases and their usual focus in class because such summaries might focus readers' attention artificially on some aspects of the cases at the expense of others. Most cases can be taught and used from a variety of perspectives. Notes about how to do this are contained in the instructor's manual meant to accompany this volume.

LEADER/SELF

This section contains cases that explore personal characteristics of leadership including energy management, visioning, balancing work and family life, ethics, and other aspects of one's personal profile. The section also includes cases describing leaders from different cultures to provide some international perspective on the variations in leadership style around the globe.

STRATEGIC THINKING

This section presents several cases that one might use to explore principles of strategic thinking. Although the list is neither long nor by any means comprehensive enough for a course in strategy, it can, and in our experience does, introduce students to the relationship between leadership and strategy and set up a clear need for students to be thinking about how to develop their strategic thinking skills.

INFLUENCING OTHERS

These cases revolve around leadership and management situations in one-on-one and group/team settings. Sometimes the issues at hand are performance issues, sometimes human relations issues, sometimes ethical issues, and sometimes diversity issues. All of these and other issues are well represented in the cases provided in this section.

DESIGNING ORGANIZATIONS

A key leadership role demand is designing organizations and their systems. The cases in this section allow readers to explore the practical realities of organizational design and their impact on employees.

LEADING CHANGE

Leaders initiate change. Effective leaders understand the change process, are masters at guiding others through it, and can make an extraordinary difference where others bog down in history and tradition. The cases in this section offer a rich opportunity to explore the challenges of designing, implementing, and capitalizing on organizational change efforts.

CONCLUSION

I acknowledge the comments, suggestions, contributions, and ideas of many of my colleagues at the Darden School in the compilation of this volume. Paul McKinnon and I first discussed this project more than a decade ago. Bill Zierden, Alex Horniman, Jack Weber, Lynn Isabella, Ted Forbes, Joe Harder, and Martin Davidson have all contributed in a variety of ways—including cases they have written. Our collective hope is that by reading, discussing, and wrestling with the issues, problems, and challenges presented here, readers will become better managers and better leaders of human behavior in organizations.

James G. Clawson
Charlottesville, Virginia
April 2002

Case 1   Astral Records, LTD., North America

The date was August 24, 1993, and Sarah Conner felt overwhelmed and more than a little disoriented. Only 2 days ago, she had rushed from her office at Bendini, Lambert & Locke (BLL), a well-known venture-capital firm, to board the company jet for Knoxville, Tennessee, where she would assume operating control of Astral Records, Ltd., North America (Astral NA). One week earlier, Astral NA's president and chief executive officer, Sir Maxwell S. Hammer, had been killed in a tragic hunting accident. As the owner of 60 percent of the company, BLL had felt an immediate need to protect its investment. Accordingly, BLL's managing director, T. J. Lambert, had asked Conner to run the company while the firm planned its next moves. He had assured her that she would be in Pigeon Forge, Tennessee, for at least a year.

Conner was the obvious choice. After graduating from Wellesley College in 1982 with a degree in classical music, she had gone to work for Galaxy Records, first in marketing and later in production. In 1987, she was admitted to the Darden Graduate School of Business Administration, where she was president of the Entrepreneurs Club, a Shermet scholar, and, upon graduation, a recipient of the Faculty Award for academic excellence. Hoping to combine her love of music with her business acumen, she joined BLL as assistant manager of the entertainment portfolio. That BLL was acquiring new music-industry companies made it the perfect, and first, choice among her several job offers.

Conner had progressed quickly during her four years at BLL. Nevertheless, she was rather surprised at how quickly she had been asked to assume operating control of one of the fastest-growing compact-disc (CD) manufacturers in the world. In two weeks, she was scheduled to meet with BLL's principals. They wanted a status report, a set of recommendations, and an action plan for the next year. She knew that a number of important issues were likely to need attention in the wake of Sir Maxwell's death.

CD INDUSTRY

In principle, CD technology was an evolutionary refinement of records and tapes. Under the old technology, music and voice were converted into electronic impulses that were then embedded in a medium such as vinyl or magnetic tape. These impulses were then decoded and amplified to reproduce the original music. CDs, however, represented a huge technological leap forward. Sound was converted into digital code that could then be decoded by a laser to reproduce exactly the original digital information.

(UVA-OB-0443)

This case was prepared by Lynn A. Isabella, Associate Professor of Business Administration, and Ted Forbes. This case was written as a basis for class discussion rather than to illustrate effective or ineffective handling of an administrative situation. Copyright © 1993 by the University of Virginia Darden School Foundation, Charlottesville, VA. All rights reserved.

CDs were produced in two steps. First, a master was made. An extremely flat, glass master disc received an adhesive and a thin (0.12 micron) layer of light-sensitive photoresist on one side. The photoresist was then exposed to a 100-milliwatt laser beam that applied the sequence of coded digits in real time to the photoresist. After an alkaline bath removed unwanted resist, a pattern of micropits was left. A nickel impression, known as the father, was made from the glass master. The positive mothers that were produced from the negative father were used to make the stampers of the polycarbonate substrate.

Because the photoresist was damaged when it was developed, the exposed glass master could normally be put to use only once. Four or five nickel mothers were usually made from a single father. Another four or five stampers could be sputtered in metal from each mother, for a total of up to 25 stampers from the single master disc. Each stamper, in turn, could be used to make up to 10,000 discs. The master could thus become the source of up to 10,000 discs per stamper, or 250,000 CDs.

In the second step, a mold received polycarbonate resin that was stamped to make the hard, transparent CD wafer. A vaporized metal layer, usually aluminum, was applied in a vacuum chamber as the surface that reflected the laser beam for player reading. Then came another hard, protective resin layer, the printed label, automatic inspection, and packaging.

CDs were first mass-produced in 1980. Since then, CD technology had seen mostly refinements rather than breakthroughs. For example, in 1989, CD-production cycle times were 13 seconds; now those times were less than 7 seconds, and leading-edge technology produced CDs in less than 5 seconds. The machinery was more efficient and less expensive than the old equipment, with the cost of a new, small plant in the range of $8 to $10 million.

Although industry dynamics had stabilized in recent years, predicting volume and designing appropriate capacity were as much art as science. "Correct capacity, either annually or monthly, is like an Indiana spring. It's only two or three days a year. You're either over or under capacity. If we weren't talking about being over capacity, we'd be talking about a shortage; it's never correct for very long," stated Robert McGee, executive director of ComDisc, a trade association.

Quality had improved dramatically over the past 10 years. In most plants, quality control was completely automated. The implementation of statistical process controls had a tremendous impact. In 1986, industry reject rates were approximately 12 percent. By 1993, rates were as low as 1.5 percent. "The discs coming off the machines today are simply better quality. Because of our knowledge and machine consistency, inspection is made easy," said Billie Holliday, director of Quality for Celestial Records.

As the technology matured, producers discovered that cover art was increasingly important in selling CDs. Many CD replicators now had five-color capacity. Most CD producers used silk-screen printing, and the large operations used offset printing. Over the years, packaging was standardized around the jewel box, a hard, plastic case used to hold the CD and accompanying liner notes. Efforts to move toward environmentally friendly packaging had not succeeded.

Wholesale prices for finished product averaged $1.30. Packaging costs were approximately 23 cents per disc, and the finished disc itself cost approximately 90 cents. Industry analysts asserted that price competition among disc replicators had come down to pennies and half pennies, as opposed to differences of 15 to 25 cents in the late 1980s. "When the business is soft and you establish a price, it's very difficult to establish a higher price once business picks up. The gross margins on CDs have eroded tremendously over the past 5 years. I don't see there's any more maneuvering left on the price," said Eleanor Rigby, record-industry analyst with Sergeant and Pepper Investments.

Record labels contracted with manufacturing facilities to produce the finished product. The labels then sold, either directly or through a distributor, to the retail outlets. Sales from label/distributor to retail outlets were on a consignment basis. Continued Rigby,

> Although quantity discounts are available, most labels are placing smaller orders and then reordering on a more frequent basis to keep inventory at manageable levels. There are only so many returns a label can take and still turn a profit, so we're seeing labels be a bit more cautious about their opening orders and then coming back for more in a shorter turnaround period than before.

Recent advances in laser technology had opened up the market in both the computer and video arenas. Because the technologies were essentially the same, audio CD manufacturers could easily produce CD-ROM discs for computers or laser discs for video. Sam Cooke, vice president of Marketing and Sales, Galaxy Records, asserted,

> Quality of the CD in the industry is fairly standard now. A disc we stamp is the same quality as any of the other major houses. What might set a company apart, though, is what we do on the terms of fulfillment services, packaging and design, and drop shipping. Customer service has definitely become the buzz word among replicators for the '90s.

COMPANY HISTORY

Astral Records was founded by Count Francisco Smirnov, a Franco-Russian nobleman, in 1967 in Wollaston-on-Heath, England. Smirnov was a professional musician who had a vision of building a new kind of record company. Appalled by the quality of records at that time, Smirnov set out to construct a studio whose sole purpose would be to produce classical-music record masters of a quality greater than that of any other company in the world. The count had been disappointed to learn that the long-playing records made from his masters were little better in sound quality than most others on the market. Undaunted, he decided to move into manufacturing.

Smirnov's vision was of a utopian musical village, where classical musicians and company directors would reside in luxury and elegance. The count wanted nothing to impede the creative process: "Beautiful music can only happen in beautiful surroundings. If society continues to ignore the high arts, then society will be led into a barbarian condition."

In 1975, Astral purchased a 50-room Georgian mansion on 187 acres near the top of the Cynwyr Valley not far from Wales. Each step in the production process would be carried out on site. The ballroom was turned into one of the most elegant recording studios in the industry. The count and five of the seven managing directors continued to live the vision, residing in the exquisitely furnished headquarters and taking all their meals together. Key business decisions were often made casually over lunch and dinner. Recording musicians were invited to live on the grounds for as long as they needed to complete their projects.

Astral Records might well have continued to operate in this idyllic setting, but for a major technological breakthrough. The count was captivated by the emerging compact-disc technology. He immediately saw the medium's potential for producing virtually flawless recordings. The combination of pure digital sound and laser technology became the count's obsession, even though he would be going up against the industry giants.

Instead of simply licensing CD technology from the giants, the count and his researchers decided to develop their own process. In 8 months they developed production capabilities that not only saved them millions in royalty fees, but also won them a Queen's Award for technological achievement. Astral Records was the first company in the United Kingdom to produce CDs, 2 years ahead of its major competitors. By the mid-1980s, more than 50 record labels were using Astral's facilities to record, produce, and manufacture CDs. Astral's own labels constituted a mere 10 percent of the company's sales.

Astral's bold, yet whimsical, business decisions had been wildly successful. In 1980, Astral Records, Ltd., U.K., employed 27 people and grossed 600,000 pounds. By 1992, the company had 500 employees and turned a pretax profit of £2.7 million on sales of £20 million.

ASTRAL RECORDS, LTD., NORTH AMERICA

In 1986, the count entered into negotiations with Bendini, Lambert & Locke to secure capital for a planned expansion into the U.S. market. The market for CDs was booming, and the plant in England was struggling to keep pace with demand. One night, Smirnov had a vision of the new facility: It would be nestled among mountains and streams surrounded by lush pastures. In 1987, in exchange for 60 percent ownership of the U.S. operation, BLL financed the construction of a $14 million plant on 265 acres in Pigeon Forge, Tennessee. The count chose Sir Maxwell S. Hammer, an English aristocrat and hunting partner, to run the U.S. operation. "I shall endeavor to carry the mission of Astral Records to the States," Sir Maxwell stated.

Astral Records, Ltd., N.A., was predominately a manufacturing facility, capable of pressing 100,000 CDs per day. Ninety percent of its business was producing CDs for a variety of other record labels. Diverging from the Astral, U.K., core business and classical tradition, Sir Maxwell had begun to explore recording and producing CDs beyond Astral's classical catalogue, which contained 300 titles. Sir Maxwell's wide-ranging interests ran from classical to blues to rock and roll to new age to rap. Having seen the phenomenal sales of many of the artists whose CDs Astral manufactured under contract, Sir Maxwell entered into negotiations with a variety of country, world-music, and new-age artists to bring them under Astral's own labels.

Under Sir Maxwell's leadership, Astral Records quickly became known as the premier CD manufacturer in the United States. Astral's stringent quality-control standards were far higher than those set by its competitors. Within the industry, an Astral CD was widely believed to be playable without error on any CD player. "It's quality. I think if we lost that, then the company would be truly adrift. Music and all the arts are extremely fragile creations, and it's quite simple to lose that very thing after which you are chasing," said Mr. Kite, Astral's celebrated music director.

Sir Maxwell built a reputation as an innovator in the industry. Astral invented multisonic recording, a method of capturing reverberated sounds from the rear of the orchestra. Astral also pioneered the use of new packaging systems that used recycled paper. The company's current research focused on creating the ability to compress feature-length motion pictures onto a standard 5-inch disc. In his last interview before his death, Sir Maxwell stated, "People no longer want to just hear music; they want to see it. Video is the future."

He also had embarked on a path of expansion in order to increase capacity in a growing market. In 1991, the company completed a $3 million capital project that increased capacity by 40 percent.

Production lines were expanded from five to eight, and two new mastering systems were added. Astral represented the latest in CD-manufacturing systems.

Sir Maxwell ran the U.S. operation as though it were his own colonial outpost. "Sir Max," as his employees called him, affectionately referred to his top managers as "toppers." He quickly established a reputation as a demanding taskmaster, and he insisted on being involved in every aspect of the business. He oversaw every major decision. Not surprisingly, therefore, the managers and employees at Astral were feeling adrift in the wake of Sir Maxwell's death.

SARAH CONNER TAKES CHARGE

At 8:00 A.M., Sarah Conner sat in the walnut-paneled conference room overlooking the great Smoky Mountains. Sir Maxwell's office was elegant, but Conner did not feel comfortable in it yet. In front of her was an assortment of memos, phone messages, faxes, and other correspondence that had accumulated, mostly over the past week. Conner believed she needed to deal with all of these papers and also begin preparing the report for the upcoming meeting with the partners from BLL. The next couple of weeks promised to be interesting. ∎

TO:	All Astral Toppers
FROM:	Sir Maxwell S. Hammer
DATE:	August 16, 1993
SUBJECT:	Staff Meeting

Please join me for high tea in the boardroom on August 24th at 3:00 P.M.

EXHIBIT I-I   Astral Records, LTD., North America

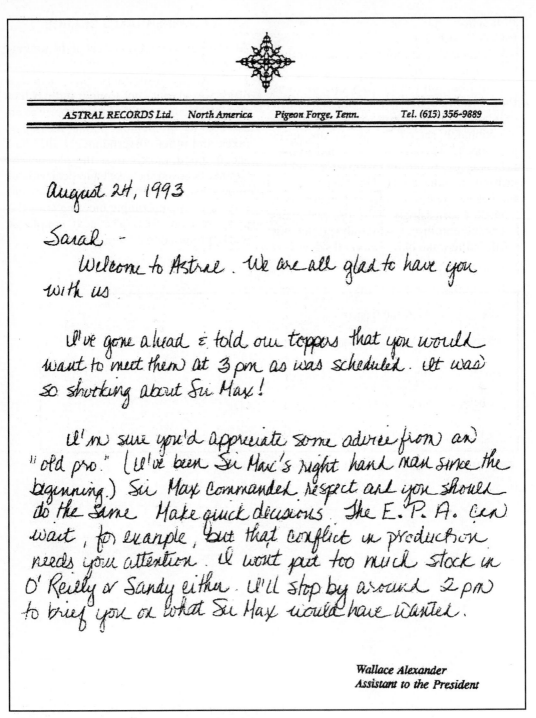

ASTRAL RECORDS Ltd.　North America　Pigeon Forge, Tenn.　Tel. (615) 356-9889

August 24, 1993

Sarah -

Welcome to Astral. We are all glad to have you with us.

I've gone ahead & told our toppers that you would want to meet them at 3 pm as was scheduled. It was so shocking about Sir Max!

I'm sure you'd appreciate some advice from an "old pro." (I've been Sir Max's right hand man since the beginning.) Sir Max commanded respect and you should do the same. Make quick decisions. The E.P.A. can wait, for example, but that conflict in production needs your attention. I won't put too much stock in O'Reilly or Sandy either. I'll stop by around 2 pm to brief you on what Sir Max would have wanted.

Wallace Alexander
Assistant to the President

EXHIBIT I-2　Astral Records, LTD., North America

To _Ms Conner_

Date _8/23_   Time _10:03_   ☒ AM ☐ PM

WHILE YOU WERE OUT

M _Prof Calhoun_

of _Univ of Tennessee_

Phone (_____) _____

| Area Code | Number | Extension |

TELEPHONED	✓	PLEASE CALL	✓
CALLED TO SEE YOU		WILL CALL AGAIN	
WANTS TO SEE YOU		URGENT	
RETURNED YOUR CALL			

Message _Confirming student
visits tomorrow @ 10 AM —
final count — 50 MBA
students for tour & mgmt
briefings. Look forward to
continuing relationship with_

Operator

AMPAD
EFFICIENCY®

Astral REORDER
#23-008

EXHIBIT I-3   Astral Records, LTD., North America

August 20, 1993

TO: Bart O'Reilly   FROM: Roberta Prospect
        V.P. Operations   District Sales Manager
        Astral NA

CC: Sir Maxwell S. Hammer

FAX: 804-555-1234   FAX: 212-458-0000

URGENT ACTION REQUEST!!!!!!!

Purchasing personnel from Republic Music Distributors, Inc., are on their way to see us once again, and we need your help. Can you meet with me on Wednesday, August 25, to help us figure a way out of the current order backlog—particularly since Republic is my largest customer. Currently, we have a production run that is out of spec on color and electrical properties, but Republic is still willing to take it. Our plant manager is balking at shipping anything out of spec.

The new equipment still has problems. The plant manager and the staff have been working around the clock, it seems, to get the utilization promised by the equipment manufacturers. They have made great progress in stabilizing the production processes, particularly in view of the new technology in the NCC-1701A equipment, but there are still problems.

My issue at the moment is the plant's unwillingness to be a bit flexible in what it ships out to Republic. Here is the latest incident. This afternoon, I called our shipping department to verify that the Republic order would be picked up by Smith's Transfer. We had promised a ship date of Tuesday of this week, and I have been reassuring Republic's purchasing agent all week that this shipment would be made by the week's end.

When I found out the products were being scrapped, I really hit the ceiling. I felt like this action would be the last straw with Republic. We will lose all credibility if we don't get product to them by next Thursday. There is no way to meet their needs if we start a new production run. I was able to get the current run placed on hold by the QA (quality assurance) manager. The plant manager promises a new run from NCC-1701-A by next Friday afternoon. Even if this run goes perfectly and we airship, the product will arrive too late for Republic to meet its customer ship date.

I proposed to the plant manager and quality assurance manager that the plant work overtime on Monday and Tuesday, sorting the products on electrical properties conformance. The purchasing people at Republic said they would be willing to accept "sorted-product." Moreover, for this *one order* they would allow off-specification occurrences for the color schemes on the various outside graphics. (We will have to process all of the 8,000 units through the certifier to sort "good/bad" on electrical properties. There are nine critical electrical performance attributes that must meet specifications.) Then the color consistency must be checked visually by our people. This visual check is a manual process and will take a lot of labor, particularly because the visual check requires a tricky disassembly step to remove the protective shield covering the minted surface.

So, I can get the purchasing people at Republic off my back with this one-time stop gap sort and yet the plant manager refuses to schedule the overtime. He says that my proposal and the plant's TQM (total quality management) initiative don't go hand in hand. Their TQM activities have been underway for eight months, so I don't see how the actions would impact his TQM implementation. We need to be more customer focused at Astral.

Please call me later today and give me some help on this one. Thanks.

EXHIBIT I-4   Astral Records, LTD., North America

ASTRAL RECORDS Ltd.	Wollaston-on Heath	England	Tel. 098-765-54

AUGUST 22

Dearest Sarah,

Alas, I wish the circumstances surrounding your arrival were more joyous. Sir Max was a dear friend and a valued associate.

The Directors and I would like to formally welcome you into the company. We will hold a Fox Hunt here at the compound on September 7. The hunt will be in your honor. Please plan to arrive on the fifth, and stay through the tenth.

We eagerly anticipate your arrival!

Count Francisco Smirnov #
P.O.R. ; R.G.G. ; R.D.G.

EXHIBIT I-5   Astral Records, LTD., North America

Bendini, Lambert & Locke, P.A.
39 Beale Street
Memphis, TN

FACSIMILE TRANSMISSION

TO:	Sarah Conner	FROM:	T. J. Lambert
	Astral Records, NA		Partner, BLL

DATE: August 24, 1993

MESSAGE:

Sarah. . . . Welcome to Astral. Hope your flight on the Lear was enjoyable. Just wanted to once again let you know that we are expecting great things from you. This Astral Records affair has cost us a great deal more money than we had anticipated. Arthur and I know that you will work your magic on Astral in short order. Let's get this company straightened out.

As we set up before you left, Arthur, Helen and I will be coming to Astral on September 7th to meet with you. Please arrange appropriate accommodations for us. You know what we like.

By the way, we have been unable to locate the financial model you built for the TechnoWiz deal. As I recall, this was an extremely complex spreadsheet. Celia, your former secretary, left unexpectedly last Friday and no one can find her files. Can you build it for us again by the end of this week as we hope to complete this deal immediately?

Look forward to seeing you in two weeks. Best of luck.

EXHIBIT I-6   **Astral Records, LTD., North America**

"We cover the world with chemicals."

Polycarbonate SubStrate Inc.
R. D. # 3
Box 4788
Kenner, Louisiana

TO:	Sir Maxwell S. Hammer
FROM:	J. Cash
	Accounts Receivable Manager
DATE:	August 9, 1993
SUBJECT:	Overdue Account

This is to notify you that Astral Records, North America, is more than 90 days overdue in its payment to us. You currently owe us $27,914.22.

If payment is not received by August 26, 1993, we will not deliver the next shipment of resins. Thank you for your prompt attention to this matter.

EXHIBIT I-7   **Astral Records, LTD., North America**

To _Ms Conner_

Date _8/23_ Time _1:43_ ☐ AM ☒ PM

WHILE YOU WERE OUT

M _Bea Walters_

of _BILLBOARD MAGAZINE_

Phone (____)

Area Code	Number	Extension

TELEPHONED		PLEASE CALL	✓
CALLED TO SEE YOU		WILL CALL AGAIN	
WANTS TO SEE YOU		URGENT	
RETURNED YOUR CALL			

Message _____

Would like interview
ASAP regarding management
transition.

Operator

AMPAD
EFFICIENCY®

REORDER
#23-008

EXHIBIT 1-8   Astral Records, LTD., North America

TO: Sir Max

CC: Bart O'Reilly
Vice President, Manufacturing

CC: Safety Committee

FROM: Mr. and Mrs. Richard Clark
Shipping Department

DATE: August 16, 1993

As you may know, the September 1993 Safety Day plans are almost finished. We had a chance to see the last working document that was prepared by the Plant Safety Committee. We are really upset and want to see you ASAP. Can we schedule ourselves into one of your "open doors" later this week.

For the fourth year in a row, there will be a Safety Day exhibition on Home Safety. We applaud Home Safety as one of the key themes. However, this year's focus on "CONSTRUCTION OF A DEER STAND: SAFETY AND SAFE HUNTING" is offensive to many of us. First, it is a fact that 38 percent of our plant employees are female, and they have no interest in hunting, particularly shooting deer from a stand placed off the ground in trees somewhere on the company's property. Certainly, you understand this point personally. Second, we think it is time to step up to the environmental issues and get our employees involved with recycling (newspapers, aluminum cans, plastic bottles, glass). Can't you order the Safety Committee to drop the Deer Stand Construction exhibition? After all, we think productivity/absenteeism and quality suffer at the opening of deer season every year. It is time, we think, to de-emphasize hunting and get people to stay focused on what they are paid to do.

EXHIBIT I-9 Astral Records, LTD., North America

TO: Sir Max

CC: G. Scott Herron
V.P., Marketing and Sales

FROM: Larry Taylor, Account Manager

DATE: August 13, 1993

SUBJECT: Unauthorized Return of Merchandise

Harris' Sound Machine, the largest chain of retail music stores in New York City, has informed me they intend to return 1,252 CDs with the title "Buddy Holly's Greatest Hits" and are asking for a full refund. They claim the CDs arrived damaged. The one they sent me looks like it was cut with a knife used to open the shipping cartons. Since this is a slow seller, I am somewhat doubtful about how the CDs were damaged. Please let me know what to do.

EXHIBIT I-I0 Astral Records, LTD., North America

Y U R B A N K
"Serving Pigeon Forge's Families and Businesses Since 1929"
2300 Main Street
Pigeon Forge, TN

TO: Sir Maxwell S. Hammer

FROM: C. Hewitt Farmington
           Senior Relationship Manager
           YurBank

DATE: July 1, 1993

SUBJECT: Renewal of Revolving Credit Agreement

Sir Max, this is to remind you that your revolver with the bank is due for review and renewal at the end of this month. As it currently stands, the bank is committed to lend you up to $500,000 at LIBOR + 1 percent with a 0.5 percent fee on the unused portion of the commitment. In light of the growth of last year's sales and your expectation of future growth, I recommend that we increase the commitment to $600,000. I do not expect the pricing structure to change before the end of this month.

Our understanding is that the line is used for seasonal working capital needs, and as such your company will be out of the bank loan for at least 45 days during the next 12 months. Part of the purpose of the review is to see if the financial condition of the company has changed substantially since last year. Historically, your peak loan needs have occurred from September through December. My back-of-the-envelope calculations show that increasing the revolver will not violate the debt-to-equity covenant of the term loan unless equity is unexpectedly low prior to or during your peak seasonal need.

Is the early part of next week too early for your people to get the financials prepared so we can discuss things? I'll check back with you in a day or so to confirm.

EXHIBIT I-II   **Astral Records, LTD., North America**

```
To _Astral Records_
Date 8/23  Time 8:00   ☒ AM
                        ☐ PM
WHILE YOU WERE OUT
M _Tony Witherspoon_
of _Environmental Protection_
            _Agency_
Phone (____) _____
    Area Code    Number    Extension

| TELEPHONED      | ✓ | PLEASE CALL      |   |
| CALLED TO SEE YOU |   | WILL CALL AGAIN  |   |
| WANTS TO SEE YOU | ✓ | URGENT           | ✓ |
|        RETURNED YOUR CALL        |

Message
Fish kill in local river
downstream of plant.
E. P. A. requests full site
inspection, Wed AM - Aug 25

                    Operator

AMPAD
EFFICIENCY®              REORDER
                        #23-006
```

EXHIBIT 1-12   Astral Records, LTD., North America

TO: Sir Max

CC: G. Scott Herron
           V.P., Marketing & Sales

FROM: John Henry, Account Manager
           Mississippi See Dee

DATE: August 10, 1993

SUBJECT: Contract Negotiation 1994/1995

Mississippi See Dee's has a fast growing collection of Delta Blues. (They own the rights to much of John Lee Hooker's, Jimmy Reed's, and Lightnin' Hopkins's titles).

Larry Johnson, their purchasing agent, says he is willing to increase our share of their business from 15 percent to 20 percent if we can guarantee 2-week delivery of titles and reduce prices by 5 percent. I think this is a great opportunity to increase sales.

EXHIBIT 1-13   Astral Records, LTD., North America

TO: Richard & Emma Clark

CC: Sir Max
         Bart O'Reilly, Vice President, Manufacturing

FROM: Maggie May

DATE: August 17, 1993

Will you two get off it! Who do you think you are suggesting that women don't enjoy hunting? I'll have you know I've been hunting since I was six when my daddy let me load his gun. I won't miss deer season, and believe me, these safety reminders are important. Not all women want to join your sewing circle, Emma. So stop writing memos to the VP and accusing us of not doing our work. If you are writing memos, how can you be doing your own jobs!

EXHIBIT 1-14   Astral Records, LTD., North America

EXHIBIT 1-15   Astral Records, LTD., North America

TO:	Sir Max
CC:	Bart O'Reilly, V.P., Manufacturing G. Scott Herron, V.P., Marketing & Sales
FROM:	Phil Kreutzman, Purchasing
DATE:	August 11, 1993
SUBJECT:	Proposal for New Plastic Packaging Material

As you know, our packaging costs are substantial. I have a new plastic supplier who can cut our total COGS by 20 percent. Eventually, costs might be even lower.

The advantage of this company's new formula is that it is *completely* biodegradable in 10 years. The disadvantage is that the package will no longer be serviceable after 3 to 5 years of normal usage. Should we pursue this project?

EXHIBIT 1-16   Astral Records, LTD., North America

TO:	Sir Maxwell S. Hammer
FROM:	Richard Cory, Treasurer
DATE:	July 3, 1993
SUBJECT:	Approval of New Packaging Equipment

Below is a summary of the analysis we have been conducting on some new packaging equipment. Based on a discounted cash flow analysis, we estimate that the $1 MM investment will increase firm value by $200,000. If we order by the end of this month, we should have the equipment installed and running in time for the increase in production that always occurs around October. The supplier will accept installment payments of $400,000, $300,000, and $300,000 over the next 3 months as payment. Since we are currently out of the bank, we could use the revolver line to make the $400,000 initial payment.

I hope the numbers on the attached sheet help show the merits of the new system. Frankly, Sir Max, it is rare that such a good opportunity comes around. The sooner we start using it, the better.

EXHIBIT 1-17   Astral Records, LTD., North America

CASH FLOW ANALYSIS
New Packaging Equipment

Initial investment: $1.0 MM

Projected annual savings:[1] $160 M

Corporate tax rate: 34%

Economic/depreciable life: 7 years

Cash flow summary ($000):

Year==>	0	1	2	3	4	5	6	7
Investment	(1,000s)							
After-tax savings		106	106	106	106	106	106	106
+Depreciation		143	143	143	143	143	143	143
Total after-tax								
cash flows	(1,000s)	248	248	248	248	248	248	248

Net present value = $209,000

Internal rate of return = 16.1%

Payback = 4 years

_____
[1]After depreciation, before taxes.

EXHIBIT I-18   Astral Records, LTD., North America

Y U R B A N K
"Serving Pigeon Forge's Families and Businesses Since 1929"
2300 Main Street
Pigeon Forge, TN

TO: Sir Maxwell S. Hammer

FROM: C. Hewitt Farmington
           Senior Relationship Manager
           YurBank

DATE: August 10, 1993

SUBJECT: Renewal of Revolving Credit Agreement

Things have changed. The credit review committee has put your company on its credit watch list because of our increasing exposure and the growth-induced strain on your balance sheet. They do not want to renew the revolver unless you can give us some sort of indication of how you are going to manage the growth of the firm going forward. Frankly, there is a general concern that your company is growing beyond its financial capabilities and that we might find ourselves with a bad term loan and very little usable collateral.

I spent the better part of an hour arguing with the credit committee, and I can tell you that these people are serious. This is all part of the tightened credit standards that were instituted following the S&L crisis. The only way I can see us doing business in the future is for you to strengthen the balance sheet with an equity infusion. The investment banking folks here would be interested in helping you take the company public. I think you should consider it. The equity markets are strong these days, and you may not be able to get a better price in the near future if this bull market turns bearish.

Sorry to catch you with this news with such little notice, but there was nothing I could do. I will meet anytime you are available. Obviously, time is of the essence.

EXHIBIT 1-19   Astral Records, LTD., North America

TO: Sir Maxwell S. Hammer

FROM: Abby McDeere
           Chief Legal Counsel

DATE: July 17, 1993

SUBJECT: Lawsuit Against Astral

Please be advised that MasterVision Associates of Burbank, California, has filed suit in the Los Angeles Superior Court against us. They are a worldwide optical disc licensor. They charge that some of our CD manufacturing equipment infringes on their patents. They are seeking unspecified "substantial damages" and note that there is still litigation pending from 1988 when they accused us of two other optical disc patent violations.

The resolution of these charges is uncertain. I will keep you advised.

EXHIBIT 1-20   Astral Records, LTD., North America

TO:	Sir Max
FROM:	Sandy Bien-Fait Human Resource Manager
DATE:	August 16, 1993
SUBJECT:	Hiring

Sir Max -

We can't afford to lose any more time addressing the issue of hiring. The increase in production has strained the existing shift personnel. And, as I mentioned last week at our weekly tea, the surrounding area just doesn't have the numbers of workers we need. Either we have to pay more or get them from somewhere else. I need authorization to hire 20 shift workers immediately.

Also, Sir Max, I think it is time to eliminate playing a musical instrument as a hiring criteria. We have simply run out of musicians in the community.

EXHIBIT 1-21   Astral Records, LTD., North America

TO:	Sir Max
FROM:	Margaret Lee Public Relations
CC:	Bart O'Reilly V.P., Operations
DATE:	March 7, 1993
SUBJECT:	CD Rot

There have been an increasing number of articles in the trade press describing a phenomenon known as "CD Rot." If the CD Rot stories are true, certain CDs may begin to self-destruct within 8 to 10 years because the ink used for labeling begins to eat into the protective lacquer coating. This in turn can oxidize the aluminum layer, resulting in an unplayable CD.

Although we have not yet had any inquiries or returns due to "CD Rot," we should nevertheless be prepared to respond to this possible crisis.

EXHIBIT 1-22   Astral Records, LTD., North America

TO: Sir Max

FROM: Carl Christie, Ph.D.
            Research and Development

DATE: August 16, 1993

SUBJECT: Project FutureVision

We are at the breakthrough stage on Project FutureVision. Compression technologies are progressing at an acceptable rate, and we anticipate being able to place full-length motion pictures with Dolby Surround Sound tracks on a 5-inch disc within the next 6 months.

I don't need to tell you about the commercial possibilities. However, the lab is feeling the pinch financially right now. My people have estimated that we need another $3.5 million within the next month in order to complete our work. Because you have been so generous in the past, I know that we can count on your continued support.

EXHIBIT I-23   Astral Records, LTD., North America

TO: Sir Maxwell S. Hammer

FROM: Abby McDeere
            Chief Legal Counsel

DATE: August 10, 1993

SUBJECT: Lawsuit Against Astral

On August 7th, I met with Richard Milhous, Chief Legal Counsel for MasterVision. After protracted discussion and negotiation, they have offered a settlement for all litigation pending against us.

They have offered to settle for either a one-time cash payment of $5 million or a 4 cent-per-disc royalty over the next 10 years of production.

We must respond by the 24th of August. Please advise me of your decision.

EXHIBIT I-24   Astral Records, LTD., North America

TO: Sir Max

FROM: Bruce Park-Asbury
Shift Supervisor

CC: Sandy Bien-Fait
Human Resource Manager

DATE: August 17, 1993

SUBJECT: Employee Reprimand

This is the third time that I have had to reprimand Sonny Barger for being insubordinate. I am at my wit's end with him and don't know what to do.

On February 7, Barger refused to clean up his work area, and I gave him a formal reprimand. On March 23, Barger was found taking an unauthorized cigarette break and was again reprimanded. On August 16, Barger left his station 15 minutes before quitting time to run to his car to turn on the air-conditioning, I suppose so it would be cool when he got out. I wrote him up for this incident. He told me to watch out, that he was going to get me and "the whole damn company."

I honestly believe that Barger is trying to undermine my authority as shift supervisor. If something doesn't change, I may have to leave Astral.

EXHIBIT I-25   Astral Records, LTD., North America

Crosby, Sells, Cash, and Young
Certified Public Accountants
Knoxville, TN

TO: Sarah Conner

FROM: Janet Young

SUBJECT: Audit Planning Meeting

DATE: August 23, 1993

I wanted to make sure that you were aware of the planning meeting to discuss our audit of Astral's financial statements for the fiscal year ended December 31, 1993, that is scheduled for 10:00 A.M. on Friday, September 10. We hope to begin our preliminary audit work on Monday, September 27.

Please be advised that we intend to continue our discussion about Astral's contingent environmental liabilities. We told Sir Max last year that the 1993 financial statements would likely contain at least footnote disclosure of environmental issues and, perhaps, even reflect actual environmental liabilities. Please be prepared to bring us up to date on all environmental matters.

Also, we just heard about the "CD Rot" problem. This could have a material effect on Astral's financial statements. We are anxious to learn more about it from your production personnel. Finally, we will need current information about actual and pending litigation. What is happening regarding the MasterVision case?

I look forward to meeting you. If you need to reschedule our meeting, that's OK, but we don't have a lot of flexibility. Please let me know ASAP.

EXHIBIT I-26   Astral Records, LTD., North America

TO: Sir Max

FROM: Ed Heath
Foreman, Waste Disposal Unit

SUBJECT: Equipment Maintenance

DATE: August 13, 1993

The PCB filtration actuators are breaking down regularly these days. We really need to replace these units. I know replacements are expensive, but this stuff is really toxic and these units are almost to the end of their serviceable life. It won't take much to cause a major problem. In fact, just yesterday, one of our technicians knocked the master valve loose and it took us almost 3 hours to clean up the spill.

I've talked with the finance people a number of times about getting replacements, but I can't seem to get an answer. We need to move on this soon.

EXHIBIT I-27 Astral Records, LTD., North America

DECEMBER

August 17, 1993

Sir Maxwell S. Hammer
President and CEO
Astral Records, NA
Pigeon Forge, TN

Sir Max:

DECEMBER is thrilled that Astral Records in interested in placing them under contract. Plans are well underway for the signing party and free concert in Pigeon Forge on the 26th.

I know this will be the beginning of a successful relationship. Attached is our sketch for the cover art of our first CD.

Regards,

Matthew D. Booth
Business Manager, DECEMBER

Attachments: 1

EXHIBIT I-28 Astral Records, LTD., North America

ASTRAL RECORDS Ltd.   *North America*   *Pigeon Forge, Tenn.*   Tel. (615) 356-9889

Sir Max,

You should know that Roberta Prospect was seen leaving Arnold Smither's house yesterday morning at six a.m.! Smither is the purchasing manager at Republic records. Aren't they one of our biggest customers? I think this is just scandalous.

Your faithful employee.

(sorry but I can't sign my name)

EXHIBIT 1-29   Astral Records, LTD., North America

TO: Sarah Conner

FROM: Richard Cory, Treasurer

DATE: August 24, 1993

SUBJECT: Capital Structure Summary

In response to your request, I am summarizing Astral's current financial structure below. Note that the line of credit and 5-year term loan are with YurBank and that the 15-year subordinated debt is a loan obtained at a favorable rate from BLL in 1987. As you can see, we have just about reached our debt limit. We probably should discuss this at your convenience. However, the sooner the better.

Capital Structure ($ millions)

Line of credit	0.5
Term-loan	3.0
Subordinated debt	10.0
Equity	6.5
Total	20.0

EXHIBIT I-30   Astral Records, LTD., North America

Case 2 Paragon Corporation and Its Flight Department

David Brooks drove toward Manhattan one rainy spring morning, absorbed in his thoughts. Underlying them all was a sense of amazement at how much his life had changed in a single year. He had been a pilot for a major airline not long ago, with 20 years under his belt and 20 just like them stretching ahead. Then came a conversation in an airport with a corporate executive named Trent Fillmore, the mailing of a résumé, and a string of interviews. Suddenly, he was director of Flight Operations for Paragon Corporation, facing issues and challenges he'd never imagined.

Paragon Corporation was headquartered in New York, but its business operations spanned much of the globe, making the frequent use of corporate aircraft a necessity. Its Division of Flight Operations consisted of three units: the North American Flight Center (NAFC) in New Jersey, the European Flight Center in Paris, and the Asian Flight Center in Hong Kong. Each center had three aircraft. Paragon was committed to the global diversity of its workforce, and much of the staff at its two overseas flight centers consisted of European and Asian nationals. The company traditionally promoted from within, so the hiring of an outsider such as David Brooks to oversee the entire Division of Flight Operations was a comment on the numerous problems that had plagued the division of late.

Business difficulties, as well as a shift in the geographic focus of Paragon's operations, had made adjustments and cost cutting necessary across the organization, and Flight Operations was no exception. It was, however, a special case in the eyes of headquarters: They felt the division had become a sort of renegade—or three renegades, more accurately—that was barely answerable to New York. When Trent Fillmore brought David on board, he was frank about how inscrutable the aviation culture seemed to senior management. "I don't understand pilots—how they think, what they want. Same goes for the mechanics and crew. They're as much a mystery as the symbols and signs on the runway."

As director of Flight Operations, working out of New York headquarters and reporting to Trent Fillmore, David ultimately would be answerable for the performance— in the air and on the balance sheet—of all three flight centers. A sense of immediacy hung over this role, with worldwide business showing some softness and all of Paragon's divisions under increasing pressure to perform. In addition, as a liaison between the aviators and the corporate executives, David was expected to help build mutual understanding between the two cultures. And indeed, though they sat together in planes on a regular basis, the pilots understood the executives no better than the executives did the pilots.

As he neared the George Washington Bridge, David tried to decide where to begin addressing his numerous challenges. It would be best, he thought, to consider each flight center separately, though he

UVA-OB-0668

This case was prepared by Greg Bevan, under the supervision of James G. Clawson. This case was written as a basis for class discussion rather than to illustrate effective or ineffective handling of an administrative situation.

sensed that the underlying problems would not be so easy to isolate.

NORTH AMERICAN FLIGHT CENTER (NAFC)

The brightest spot in Paragon's business these days was Canada. Earnings there were up 20 percent versus the prior year and showed signs of sustainable growth. However, if all was well in the marketplace, such was not the case at the North American Flight Center, headed by North American flight operations manager (FOM) Allan Sedgwick (an old friend of Trent's). Allan had been in his position hardly any longer than David had been in his, and so far his tenure had seen some difficulties. David could identify several distinct problems, though he had no clear idea how they might be solved.

The most long-standing source of trouble in the center was dissatisfaction with pay. David had seen figures that showed that employees at all three Paragon flight centers had historically been paid well under the industry average. Discontent had been building, especially at the NAFC under former FOM Curtis Gearhardt, whom subordinates had described as "Mussolini with a toothache."

At that time the NAFC had its current fleet of two *Falcon 50s* and a *Citation Ultra*, each with its own crew. The compensation issue came to a head when Paragon instituted a new policy—with the NAFC as the "pilot" location—of requiring each crew to get type-rated for both types of aircraft. Greater crewing flexibility was the objective, but what the changes amounted to were a significant increase in responsibility, for which the crews did not receive any added compensation. Shortly thereafter, two pilots left the company, naming compensation as their main grievance. "To Paragon," one of them reportedly said, "a plane is just a bus with wings."

The company made some minor changes in its compensation plan, took the additional step of offering early retirement to Curtis Gearhardt, and promoted Allan Sedgwick to FOM. Allan, who had been a pilot at the NAFC, had a more conciliatory style than his predecessor. However, he was also one of the only dissenters on the compensation issue. He later told David that he thought Paragon's new compensation scheme was competitive with the industry: Pilots could earn an incentive bonus, based on company results, of up to 50 percent of their annual salary. Nonetheless, another pilot soon defected over the compensation issue. Allan later discovered that he had gone to work for a company that offered lower annual pay—because of a less lucrative bonus structure—but higher weekly pay.

Compensation problems at the NAFC were being aggravated by an interpersonal issue, too. When Curtis Gearhardt had retired, chief pilot Mel Tanner had expected to win the FOM post—only to find Allan Sedgwick leapfrogging over him to fill the vacancy. Mel's resentment of this state of affairs was sharpened by the widespread knowledge that Allan was a close personal friend of Trent Fillmore, and also seemed to have no real grievance with the compensation status quo. For these reasons, among others, Allan had limited credibility in the flight department, a problem Mel exacerbated by complaining about him to the other pilots and crew members.

Discontent was spreading through the department, and morale was beginning to suffer. David, who had enjoyed Allan's complete loyalty and support, needed to act. Senior management looked favorably on Allan, but the pilot staff was backing Mel. What, David wondered, could be the solution?

As he piloted his car down the West Side Highway, the Manhattan skyline like a bar graph in his window, his thoughts began to drift overseas. Paragon's European business had dropped off, which meant that the director of Flight Operations had another set of challenges to examine.

EUROPEAN FLIGHT CENTER

When David thought of the European Flight Center (EFC), he immediately pictured Claude Marteau. The day David had met him in Paris, the veteran FOM had eyed his new boss as if trying to decide whether to keep him or throw him away. Claude had been with Paragon for 25 years and had seen four CEOs come and go. Senior management had long respected him for the punctual, immaculate operation he ran, but David could see thàt his subordinates found him haughty and authoritarian. One of them described his leadership technique with a French phrase that David, thumbing through his Larousse later on, translated as "management by ego."

Whatever the name for it, this style had created friction between the EFC and headquarters before. A particular episode from a few years ago occurred to David. Although it had happened before he joined Paragon, he had heard all of the details.

At that time, the EFC had its current fleet of two *Challenger 601-3As* and a *Dash 8-100,* all of which Paragon had purchased on Claude's advice. During one European flight, the CEO mentioned to the crew his desire to purchase a used *Falcon 50.* Upon landing, the crew passed along this information to Claude, who may have felt that his unofficial decision-making role on the purchase of aircraft was being threatened.

Claude immediately began to criticize the CEO's idea in front of the crew, punctuating his speech with rapid puffs on a cigarette. He then set to work crunching numbers to demonstrate the error of the CEO's ways. He had always wanted a bigger, newer aircraft in his hangar, and this may have seemed the perfect opportunity to

make such a pitch as an alternative to the CEO's used-aircraft idea. At that time, Falcon was unveiling a new, long-range plane, the *Falcon 9000,* with two engines, a range of 6,400 nautical miles, and a price tag of $30 million.

For two months, Claude prepared his *Falcon 9000* presentation for the Paragon Executive Committee. The work paid off handsomely: The committee deferred to his expertise once again, approving purchase of a *Falcon 9000* for the coming year. Claude felt validated.

But the year began ominously: Paragon Europe faced a revenue shortfall of $500 million. As a result, the company had to make some hard budget-cutting decisions, and Claude's pet plane was one of the casualties. Several alternatives were under consideration—delaying purchase of the plane for two years, as well as buying a used *Falcon 50* as the CEO had suggested—but none would pacify Claude, who made it clear to David at their first meeting that he saw the shelving of his plan as a slap in the face. "My years of authority, my *expertise:* These mean nothing?"

David had gathered that Claude's subordinates at the EFC, who had always felt that their suggestions to him went unheeded, saw something vindicating about this turn of events. It seemed proof that ego was indeed the driving force behind Claude's management style. The ongoing challenge for David was to treat the FOM in a way he would find fair—he was still a favorite of Paragon executives for the professionalism of his flight center—while at the same time addressing the concerns of his subordinates, whose morale was beginning to suffer.

In further conversations, David had begun to suspect that Claude's anger at headquarters could not be chalked up entirely to insufficient ego gratification. In part, he was expressing frustration with what he believed to be Paragon's view of flying aircraft: a cost to be controlled and nothing more. Indeed, David's own position as director of Flight Operations had been created largely with the corporate balance sheet in mind. He and Claude were both former pilots, and he could sympathize with Claude's feelings that there were aspects of running a flight department—all kinds of hard-to-quantify operational requirements—that the people in finance could not understand.

At the EFC, David was faced with another dilemma; his name was Chet Chisholm. Chet was the chief pilot in Paris, second-in-command behind Claude Marteau, and considering his career history, his high rank was understandable. For more than 20 years, Chet had been one of Flight Operations's star performers. A veteran of countless international missions, he had worked as a pilot/manager in the Far East for most of that time, and his knowledge of world aviation was unmatched in the company. His brash, charismatic personality had enabled him to succeed in unfamiliar environments that would have daunted more cautious American pilots, and part of the credit for Paragon's meteoric rise in Asia over the last two decades was legitimately his.

In hopes of bringing some of that initiative and achievement closer to home, Paragon had given Chet the chief pilot position at the EFC and often invited him to corporate headquarters in New York as a kind of special advisor on flight operations-related matters. David did not feel threatened by this arrangement: Chet had no burning managerial ambitions, and David felt he could learn a lot from Chet about corporate aviation. However, his chief pilot position in France and his many visits to New York brought Chet into frequent contact with corporate staff, and it was here that problems arose. While in the Far East, he had grown accustomed to the treatment that Asian nationals working for Paragon afforded him: deference, admiration, and

unquestioning respect. His word was the last word, but when he set foot in corporate headquarters, he didn't seem to realize that the rules were different.

Chet would stride into the Manhattan offices, as stubble faced as a bomber pilot after a dozen sorties, and issue what sounded like orders to the suit-and-tied corporate staff. Headquarters expressed to the EFC its feeling that Chet was a renegade who was unwilling to cooperate with others, to which the reply was, "You should try working with him every day." The Paris staff felt his time on the corporate frontier had left Chet far too coarse and unrefined for the French capital, and female coworkers in particular found his locker-room manner offensive.

In decades past, Chet's interpersonal style simply might have been overlooked. However, as a modern corporation with worldwide concerns, Paragon was committed to the diversity of its workforce, which put Chet's manner directly at odds with the company's mission. David was faced, then, with a dilemma: Were Chet's contributions as a pilot overshadowed by the damage he was doing to the corporate culture—and if so, what to do?

Turning inland, David cruised through the heart of midtown Manhattan toward Paragon's headquarters. A vacant office flashed by, and for a moment David could see workers inside putting up drywall. Renovation: It turned his thoughts immediately to the Far East.

ASIAN FLIGHT CENTER

In the 1980s, Asia had been a hot growth area for Paragon, and the Asian Flight Center (AFC) had seen heavy use. Under the management of FOM Li Huang and the piloting leadership of Chet Chisholm, the AFC became an active hub for executive travel across the Far East.

The Hong Kong facility itself did not keep pace with this expansion though. Li complained periodically about the outdated equipment and cramped quarters, but the AFC—out of sight around the globe from Paragon's New York headquarters—never saw budgeting for a renovation until early last year. That was when David, in the first weeks of his tenure as director of Flight Operations, stopped by for a close look at the meager facility, which consisted of a rusty storage hangar and an attached office trailer. At that time, construction was underway on Hong Kong's new, state-of-the-art international airport, which would be the AFC's new home, and David thought the time was right to take Li's case to New York. As long as the flight center was being moved, he suggested, why not bring it up to date? Senior management bought into the idea, and a new, improved AFC was now being constructed.

There were a number of changes—most importantly the installation of a new computer system, modeled after the system at the North American Flight Center, to replace the antiquated one the AFC had been using for close to 20 years. Cost and schedule targets were being met, and yet David had two big concerns. One was Paragon Asia's sluggish business in the wake of the Asian financial crisis, which now had senior management eyeing the cash outlays at the AFC closely, though they had pledged to allow the modernization to go forward. The other was the Hong Kong staff, on whom the task of updating the AFC would largely rest. David knew Li was

enthusiastic about the money being spent, but on his visits he had sensed that the rest of the AFC was somewhat indifferent and tradition bound. Tucked away for years in their office trailer, all but forgotten by the company, the staffers had developed work habits and routines that would not adapt easily, or perhaps even willingly, to new company mandates.

It was a question of cultural differences, David thought to himself, his car sliding into the darkness of the Paragon parking garage. What was remarkable was that although Paragon did business around the globe and employed people of many nationalities, the cultural differences in this and every other case before him did not run along national borders. The Hong Kong renovation, the dissent in New Jersey, the Chet Chisholm and Claude Marteau situations—all of them illuminated a cultural gap between Paragon's flight centers and the corporation itself. It was this gap that David had been charged with bridging, and his drive to the office had left him more certain than ever that the task would not be an easy one.

It also left him full of a sense of possibility of a sort he had not known during his years as a commercial pilot. Unfamiliar problems called for inspired solutions, and as he climbed out of his car and headed for the elevator, David hoped inspiration would strike soon. ■

Case 3   John Wolford (A)

John Wolford, a vice president and general manager for Eurotech-USA, awoke with a start and looked with disbelief at his clock radio.

"Damn it!" he mumbled to himself in a rush of anger. He had carefully set the alarm for 5:00 A.M. It was now 10 minutes after 6 o'clock.

It was Wednesday morning and his mind raced with the hundreds of details he had to attend to that day. A meeting with his boss. A funeral. A briefing from his controller. A 3-day trip to London to prepare for. Bags to pack. Plane reservations to confirm. Personal bills to pay. To complicate matters, he would be attending a 6-week residential management development program almost immediately upon his return. He felt overwhelmed.

JOHN WOLFORD'S BACKGROUND

John Wolford was 41 years of age. He was born in Los Angeles and grew up there. After graduating from the California Institute of Technology with a degree in mechanical engineering, John accepted a position with Hewlett-Packard, an electronics company in the San Francisco Bay Area.

After working for Hewlett-Packard in design engineering for 5 years, John got married, bought a house in Los Altos Hills, and began attending evening courses in management. Shortly thereafter, he accepted an engineering management position with Precision Instruments, Inc.

During the next 10 years, Wolford held various engineering management positions at Precision Instruments. When the company was acquired by Eurotech Ltd., a European multinational, John was named vice president and general manager of the Precision Instruments Division.

In that position, Wolford was responsible for more than 800 people and $118 million in annual sales. His division consisted of one plant and six regional sales offices and was organized along simple functional lines with the heads of manufacturing, sales, engineering, personnel, quality control, and finance and administration reporting to him. In addition, he had an administrative assistant, Jack Short, a recent MBA graduate from a prestigious Eastern business school.

Although Wolford formally reported to Lutz Boehm, president of Eurotech-USA, located in nearby San Francisco, he felt a stronger sense of responsibility to the managing director of the parent company in London with whom Wolford negotiated the annual objectives for his division. However, beyond an annual estimate meeting every December and a periodic profit review at corporate headquarters, John was able to function autonomously.

Outside of work, Wolford had numerous interests, although his 12-hour days and full briefcase every evening left him little

UVA-OB-0167

This case was prepared by R. Jack Weber. This case was written as a basis for class discussion rather than to illustrate effective or ineffective handling of an administrative situation. Copyright © 1981 by the University of Virginia Darden School Foundation, Charlottesville, VA. All rights reserved.

time to pursue any of them. He frequently described himself as an engineer at heart and loved to tinker with mechanical devices, especially vintage cars. What little spare time he had he devoted to working on restoring a 1958 Austin Healey roadster.

John was proud of his three children and wished he had more time with them. However, since they had become teenagers, he rarely saw his two daughters, Mary and Elizabeth. He also found it increasingly difficult to communicate with his 10-year-old son, Frank, who was going through what Wolford described as a rebellious phase.

WEDNESDAY MORNING

John could feel his heart racing as he jumped out of bed and grabbed a report to read while he brushed his teeth. Wolford was to meet his boss at 9 o'clock and had planned to use the extra hour preparing for the president's questions. "I'll *never* get through this by then," he thought.

The report that he skimmed showed that his division had fallen more than $400,000 short of its quarterly profit plan. "What a jerk I was to have given them so much freedom," he thought to himself, reflecting on the operating management team he had entrusted with day-to-day operating authority only months before.

Although Wolford had demonstrated his mettle as a "hands-on manager," he had decided earlier in the year to remove himself from daily operating decisions. He had done so partly because of complaints from his subordinates about his being too involved and partly because he wanted to devote more time to new product development. Although he had thoroughly enjoyed spending more time in the engineering laboratory, the manufacturing function had experienced substantially decreased profitability.

Wolford made himself a cup of coffee and dressed hastily. He knew his family would be waking up soon, and he wanted to spend some uninterrupted time analyzing the quarterly results. He looked at his watch. It was already 6:30.

At 7:00 he awoke his wife and three children, poured another cup of coffee, and returned to his study to analyze the report. At 7:50, his wife, Pat, opened the door to his study and the following conversation ensued:

Pat: Frankie missed the school bus.
John: So what else is new? (irritated) I already yelled at him 20 times this morning. I told him he'd be late if he didn't hurry up. What am *I* supposed to do about it?
Pat: I thought you could take him to school on your way to work.
John: I've got too much to do to drive him.
Pat: But you're dressed.
John: (angrily) So what! You can take him or he can walk. I used to walk *much* further than that when *I* was in fifth grade.
Pat: You never do anything around here! (slamming door) Come on Frank, Mommy will drive you.

John felt guilty and wished he hadn't been so abrupt. However, he didn't have time to apologize, and he certainly didn't have time to drive his son to school. The plant was nearly 30 miles away and it would be a "close call . . . even without the detour," John thought.

On the way to the plant, John stopped at McDonald's, a fast-food restaurant, and got two sausage and egg biscuits and a large coffee to take out. It was a morning ritual. He also managed to dictate several memos while driving over the San Mateo bridge. Wolford vowed silently that he would never buy another car without automatic speed control.

As he pulled into the company parking lot, Wolford was surprised that several of his hourly people were handing out leaflets to fellow employees who were leaving the third shift. The flyer urged hourly employees to boycott the Employee Attitude Survey that was being conducted that morning at Wolford's request.

John had initiated the survey, at the president's request, as a way of maintaining contact with his people. Yet the memo alleged that the survey data would be used against the union in the forthcoming contract negotiations.

"Those bastards!" Wolford mumbled angrily to himself. He had worked especially hard to involve the union officers in the design of the survey, and he suspected that this was a power ploy on the part of the dissident faction to undermine the authority of the elected leadership.

"How dare they impugn my motives!" he thought to himself. At times like this, he was convinced he would have been better off staying in engineering.

As he entered the plant, he was cornered by Jim Kerns, one of his top salespeople. After exchanging pleasantries, Jim asked Wolford to prevail upon the plant manager to alter the production schedule to get out an order of test equipment for a preferred customer.

Wolford said he would look into it and headed for his office. John resented Jim at times and vowed to review Kerns's sales compensation plan. With sales commissions, Kerns earned more than anyone in the company, including Wolford.

The meeting with the president in Wolford's office went smoothly. Wolford was going to England that evening to review the quarterly results with the managing director and his staff, and Boehm wanted to be briefed.

As he was leaving, Boehm asked Wolford to prepare a brief report on the preliminary results of the Employee Attitude Survey. Boehm explained that he was meeting with the company's legal counsel and a visitor from the corporate personnel staff on Monday morning to review some Equal Employment Opportunity (EEO) discrimination charges and expressed his hope that there would be "some data in the survey that would be relevant."

Wolford reminded Boehm that he would be in the office only for a couple of hours on Monday morning and that he would be leaving almost immediately for a 6-week management development program at the University of Virginia. However, he told Boehm that if Boehm could get one of his staff members to computer analyze the data, he, Wolford, would have Jack Short, his administrative assistant, prepare a written report for their joint review on Monday morning.

After the meeting, John looked for Jack Short. Unable to find Short, he scribbled a note requesting the report by Monday and rushed across the bay to a funeral. The wife of one of his first-line supervisors had died precipitously the day before, and he felt obliged to go. He hated funerals. Ever since he had turned 40, he had become more and more aware of his own mortality. Funerals made the fact impossible to ignore.

On his way back to the plant, John stopped at Taco Bell, another fast-food restaurant, and ordered two beef burritos and a large coffee to go. Because he didn't have time to stop, he ate as he drove.

As Wolford passed a favorite men's store, he wished he had time to stop and shop. He needed some new sports clothes for the forthcoming executive program. However, he had put on so much weight in the past few years that he just didn't enjoy shopping as much as when he was slimmer. John had a 32-inch waist when he graduated from Cal Tech, and he was now up to nearly 38 inches. He still wore size 42 suits and 36-inch slacks, but he felt "like a sausage" in them and had been jogging sporadically. John vowed to lose some pounds at the management school.

Thinking of school reminded him of the advance assignment that he had been asked to complete for the program. He had been asked to have someone at work who knew him well write a one-page description of him as a manager and as a person. When he returned to his office, he asked Ann Marshall, his secretary, to write a confidential description of him and return it to the management program staff. Her response is shown in Exhibit 3-1.

The rest of Wolford's day was filled with meetings and fire fighting: a conversation with the sales manager on the burgeoning accounts receivable, discussions with the

---

MEMO

Personal and Confidential

TO: Executive Program Staff

From: Ann Marshall, Secretary to Mr. Wolford

Subject: Mr. John Wolford

Mr. Wolford is a very intense manager. He is bright, perfectionistic, and driven. His office is a mess. I can't keep it organized, although *he* is very organized. In fact, he is ruthless in his attention to details. He checks up on everything.

He is always in a hurry. Always. He sees himself as "available," but others don't see him that way at all. In fact, most of them feel guilty about bothering him. He likes to keep his door closed when he is working alone or in a conference. He has a conference table in his office, although most of his meetings are with individuals, not groups. He still has a cubicle in the engineering lab and spends quite a bit of time down there.

Mr. Wolford is somewhat introspective but doesn't seem to have a very accurate self-image. He sees himself as warm and understanding. I see him that way, but most others view him as cold and impatient. He also sees himself as a good delegator. Although he doesn't spend much time in the plant, others still feel he makes most of the decisions. Publicly, he encourages people to make decisions, but the fact is that he makes most of the important decisions himself. Or people do what they think *he* would do. It drives people nuts, especially the plant manager, when someone says, "Well, John says. . . ."

Mr. Wolford is impatient and often harried. He walks fast, eats fast (frequently in his office), and talks fast. One quirk that annoys me is that he often interrupts me in the middle of a sentence or finishes sentences for me. I told him about it and he's doing better, but I still find it irritating when he skims a report or looks around while I'm talking to him. He always seems to be doing two things at once. For example, when he's dictating a letter, he might also be skimming the *Wall Street Journal* or looking up a telephone number in his Rolodex.

He eats an enormous amount of food and nibbles on snacks constantly. He also drinks eight to ten cups of coffee a day. He has been trying to quit smoking ever since I have known him. He smokes only in his office and in his car. He doesn't smoke at home or in the plant. I guess he must feel guilty about it.

EXHIBIT 3-1   Description of John Wolford

plant manager on his plans for handling employee turnover on the third shift, a brief appearance in the company training room during an orientation program for new employees, and a 2-hour meeting with some outside consultants who were designing a new scheduling system.

When the first shift had left for the day, John began dictating responses to the enormous pile of memos and letters that had accumulated in his in basket during the past few weeks. Before he was a quarter of the way through it though, it was 7 o'clock and he realized that he had only 2 hours to drive home to Los Altos, pack his bags, and get back up to San Francisco International Airport for his flight to London.

THE TRIP TO LONDON

John arrived in London on Thursday morning at 9:00 A.M. local time. It had been a virtually sleepless flight. The company required its executives to fly coach class, and John had the misfortune to get seated in the last row of a *Boeing 747* jumbo jet next to a family of restless and noisy children. He was met at Heathrow by a driver and taken to Eurotech's International Management Centre in Wimbledon, a suburb outside of London.

While at the Centre, John averaged only 2 or 3 hours of sleep each night because of time changes. He usually went to bed at midnight at home, but midnight in London was only 4:00 P.M. San Francisco time. As a result, he would toss and turn until the middle of the night before getting up at 6:00 A.M. local time to work on his presentations. It was an exhausting few days and ended with a talk by the chairman on Saturday afternoon.

Although top management had asked a lot of tough questions, John's presentations had gone well. Because there were no flights to San Francisco that evening, John got a ticket to a theater near Covent Garden and rewarded himself with dinner

and a play in London before returning to his room in Wimbledon around midnight.

SUNDAY MORNING

As during the past few nights, John had difficulty getting to sleep. Nevertheless, he set his alarm for 7:00 A.M. to give himself time for a jog in Wimbledon Common and a quick swim in the Centre's indoor swimming pool. Even though he completed his morning exercise routine by 8:00 A.M., he was still in a hurry.

John showered and began packing his bags for the trip. He had a lot to do before his car arrived at 10 o'clock: expenses to submit, thank-you notes to write and distribute to the Centre housekeeping staff, a 220-to-110-volt conversion transformer to return to the house steward, and several phone calls to make to friends in Greater London.

John had completed most of the tasks and was stuffing his bathing suit, now wrapped in a plastic cleaning bag, into the outside compartment of his new leather suitcase when his bell rang. A moment later the steward announced through the closed door, "Mr. Wolford, your car is here."

"Damn it!" John mumbled to himself. "What is he doing here 20 minutes early?"

"Tell the driver I'll be down at 10 o'clock," he shouted through the door. Then he opened the door and added, "Thanks, Cliff. I ordered the car for 10 o'clock and my flight doesn't leave until 11 o'clock."

John hurriedly completed his notes of acknowledgment and one of his calls to a friend. He then grabbed his bags and rushed down the stairs to his waiting car.

It was a beautiful, crisp, sunny day, and he wished he could stay. One of Eurotech's sales executives from Wales had offered him tickets to the New Zealand-Wales rugby match at Cardiff Arms Park. It was like a chance to go to the Super Bowl, but he *had* to get home that evening to California so that he could get ready for his trip to the University of Virginia on Monday afternoon. It was going to be a close call.

John cursed silently to himself again as he noticed that the car provided to take him to Heathrow Airport was a dented old Rover. Jaguar XJ-12s were normally provided for company executives visiting London. John got even more upset when he noticed his wet bathing suit beginning to leak through the fine leather skin of his new suitcase.

John handed his bags to the driver, unconsciously walked around to the right side of the car, and started to open the front door, having forgotten the English convention on the placement of the steering wheel.

"Are you going to drive, sir?" the driver joked. John was embarrassed and shook his head as he climbed into the back seat.

John looked nervously at his watch. It was 10:06 A.M. "Thirty minutes for the trip," he thought, "and 20 minutes to check in." Suddenly he remembered that it was an international flight, and he would have to go through passport control. It was going to be tight.

THE TAXI RIDE

As the 1973 Rover left behind the manicured lawns and gardens of Eurotech's International Management Centre, the following conversation ensued between the driver and John Wolford:

Driver: I've never made this trip before.
Wolford: You mean out here to the Centre?
Driver: No, I meant the airport.
Wolford: (With incredulity) You've never been to Heathrow?!
Driver: A long time ago . . . but not from Wimbledon. I only started driving 2 days ago.

Wolford: (Leaning forward in his seat and noticing the driver's hand shaking as he strips the gears) You've only been driving for 2 days?
Driver: (Laughing) No, I've been driving for 40 years.
Wolford: (Feeling reassured, but confused) Looks like a lot of traffic today.
Driver: Yeah. Something going on in London. By the way, do they usually take you over the Kingston-Thames bridge?
Wolford: (Looking at his watch and thinking, "What in the hell is he asking *me* for?") Yes, I think so.
Driver: (As the car crosses the bridge) Does this look familiar?
Wolford: (Reassured by the familiarity of the round-about) Yes, it does. You said you've only been driving for 2 days?
Driver: Yes. I've been repairing radios and tellies since the war.
Wolford: Why did you change jobs?
Driver: I had a nervous breakdown . . . (Pause) . . . Do you know where we are?
Wolford: (Trying to contain his anxiety) No, I've never seen this road before.
Driver: (Looking at a map and almost running into a refuse lorry) I wrote the names of the streets on the inside cover.
Wolford: (Thinking, "At least he did some homework," and taking the map from the driver) Here, I'll read the

names to you: "London Road to Queen's Way to Ravenswood Drive to Uxbridge Road."

Driver: What road are we on?

Wolford: (Looking for a street sign as they drive at least 2 miles along a long wall enclosing a park on one side) Yes! There's a sign. We're on Warren Road. (Looking in map index and seeing three Warren Roads and four Queen's Ways in Greater London, John begins to get angry but controls himself.) I don't know where in the hell we are! Why don't you stop and ask that man walking his dog.

Driver: (Stops) Excuse me. How do we get to Uxbridge Road? (Note: The stranger gives directions three times. Each time the driver repeats them back mistakenly.)

Wolford: (Angrily looking at his watch and noting that it is 25 minutes until 11 o'clock, John begins to have an upset stomach.)

Driver: (Turns left and starts heading back on the other side of the park in the direction whence they had just come)

Wolford: (Thinking, "Damn it! This jerk is driving us around in circles!") Could we radio Wimbledon Cars and order another car? I really *have* to make this flight.

Driver: Yes, sir. But they haven't installed a radio yet . . .

you're nervous, aren't you, sir?

Wolford: You're damn right I'm nervous! We've only got 21 minutes and all the other flights are booked and I've *got* to be in San Francisco by tonight!

Driver: (Excitedly) There's Uxbridge Road! (Turning right)

Wolford: I'm pretty sure we should have gone left. (Thinking, "How could they possibly send a driver who had never been to Heathrow before?" and "That dumb jerk. Why didn't he read the damn map while he was waiting?")

Driver: I think we're going in the right direction, sir. But do you want me to turn around?

Wolford: (Notices the driver's hand shaking badly on the gear shift) No, let's drive on a bit . . . Isn't this more nerve-racking than repairing television sets?

Driver: Aye. The last 2 days have been *much* worse, sir! I especially hate driving in central London at night. I made a trip to the Royal Opera House last night and thought I would get killed.

Wolford: Did you get there on time?

Driver: No, but it wasn't my fault.

Wolford: (Looking at his watch again) Were the people upset?

Driver: I didn't have people. I was delivering some new curtains.

Wolford: (Thinking, "Geezus! They hire *this* turkey to deliver curtains to the Royal Opera House?!" . . . Then, shouting jubilantly) There's a sign! "Heathrow-A4 . . . 5 miles." Hang a left and step on it!

Driver: Oh, Lord. I feel relieved.

Wolford: We have 13 minutes until flight time. (His heart is racing.)

Pan American flight 125 was delayed for 2 hours while a spare part was flown in from Amsterdam. John was furious and spent nearly an hour composing a letter to the president of the airline.

John finally settled down and began reading one of his management program advance assignments. "We are what we do . . . and may do what we choose," the essay asserted. "Oh, yeah?" John reflected. "I sure as hell can't 'do what I choose' right now." He was still upset at the flight delay and found it difficult to concentrate. ◼

Case 4   Hassan Shahrasebi: The Golden Boy

In early March of 1993, the executives at Iran Office Machines Center Company Ltd. (IOMCo) were very busy. Office machines sales were at a peak before the end of the Iranian calendar year as government agencies rushed to spend the last of their remaining budgets. In addition, IOMCo's own fiscal year closed at the end of March, which put the Accounting Department under extra pressure to close the books for the year. That particular day, however, was exceptionally frantic because the company's chief financial officer, Hassan Shahrasebi, had been in a serious car accident the previous night.

Around 9:30 P.M., Hassan, like usual, was the last one to leave the office building. He said good night to the guard, entered his company car, and started driving home. Passing over a highway bridge, Hassan dozed off and the car veered into the bridge's outside barrier at high velocity. The barriers deflected the car, which then rebounded for a second and a third impact. Immobilized with shock, Hassan was dragged out of his car by passing motorists. Hassan was lucky that the car had not flipped off the bridge or caught on fire. He escaped the incident with a few minor cuts and bruises even though the car was damaged beyond repair. This was Hassan's second accident in 6 months. The first one involved his wife and 1-year-old son, who also had escaped disaster with a few cuts and bruises.

Despite the accident, Hassan was the first one at work the next morning. He himself informed the other executives about the previous night's incident. The chairman, CEO, and president of IOMCo each spent time talking with Hassan that morning, expressing relief and concern at the same time—relief because he had escaped harm and concern because he was working himself too hard.

IRAN OFFICE MACHINES CENTER CO. LTD.

Iran Office Machines Center Co. Ltd., a closely held family company established in 1964, was the oldest and largest office machines company in Iran. IOMCo represented in Iran exclusively a number of international manufacturers of office machines. Exhibit 4-1 provides the list of IOMCo's suppliers and the list of products marketed by IOMCo.

IOMCo imported, marketed, sold, and serviced the office equipment of the companies it represented, selling directly to the government using a network of approximately 750 dealers to distribute nationwide, and employing a direct sales force for its private customers. The company provided after-sales service through 120 service dealers and its own team of 125 technicians. Exhibit 4-2 shows IOMCo's installed machine population and service coverage channels. In all, the company employed 280 personnel, and revenues from local operations reached a record $45.4 million in 1992.

IOMCo survived the Iranian revolution of 1978 and had maintained its leadership in

UVA-OB-0590

This case was written by Amir Massoud Amiri under the supervision of James G. Clawson. Copyright © 1995 by the University of Virginia Darden Business School Foundation, Charlottesville, VA. All rights reserved.

SHARP CORPORATION—Osaka, Japan: Since 1964.
  * Photocopy Machines
  * Calculators
  * Cash Registers
  * Facsimile Machines
  * Bank Teller Machines (Government orders only)

GLORY CO., LTD.—Osaka, Japan: Since 1986.
  * Banking and Cash-Handling Equipment (Government orders only)

SEIKO EPSON CORPORATION—Tokyo, Japan: Since 1991.
  * Epson brand of computer printers.

OLIVETTI S.P.A.—Ivrea, Italy: Since 1991.
  * Personal Computers
  * Notebook Computers
  * Banking Systems
  * Electronic Typewriters

MITSUBISHI PENCIL CO.—Tokyo, Japan: Since 1980.
  * Writing Instruments

EXHIBIT 4-1 **IOMCo's Exclusive Agencies/Distributorships for the Iranian Market**

Product	Installation 1985–1993	IOMCo Serviced (%)	Dealer Serviced (%)
Copiers	50,000+	40	60
Facsimiles	11,600	60	40
Printing Calculators	210,000	35	65
Other Calculators	2,400,000	30	70
Cash Registers	3,000	70	30
Electronic Typewriters	1,700	0	100
Bank Teller Terminals	8,300	100	0
Bank Note Counters	5,800	100	0
Personal Computers	17,000	90	10
Notebook Computers	1,900	90	10
Printers	29,000	95	5

EXHIBIT 4-2 **IOMCo's Installed Machine Population and Service Coverage Channels**

Iran's turbulent environment since then by being innovative and flexible. For example, throughout the 8-year Iran/Iraq war when the import of nonessential products was restricted, IOMCo maintained its own critical flow of supplies and spare parts (especially for photocopiers) by using airline passengers as carriers from Dubai (The United Arab Emirates). Because the process was costly, margins were low and the risk was high. Most competitors opted to cease operations altogether, and a few limited their transactions to sporadic government orders only. The result was that IOMCo's SHARP brand copiers were the only operational copiers in Iran for 8 years. Although IOMCo made no substantial profits during this period, it seized a leading market share in key products. When restrictions for imports were lifted in April of 1989, IOMCo had firmly established a 750-strong dealer network and developed a leading market share for nearly all of its products. By 1993, IOMCo held an 85 percent share of the Iranian copier market, was more than triple the size of its closest competitor, and was the only company selling a complete line of office machines in Iran.

HASSAN SHAHRASEBI

Hassan Shahrasebi was 37 years old, married, and had a 1-year-old son. He had joined IOMCo as assistant manager of accounting in 1980. After working for 3 years, he had taken a leave of absence for 2 years to earn an MBA in the United States at the University of Texas. Upon completion of his MBA, he returned directly to IOMCo where he had remained. His honesty, deep concern for the company, and consistent hard work led to rapid promotions to his present post of chief financial officer, the number-four position after the president. The joint owners of the company—the founding chairman and his brother, the CEO—held Hassan in the highest esteem and considered him one of the central pillars of the company. They privately referred to him as the "Golden Boy."

Hassan was responsible for all of IOMCo's financial activities. These included IOMCO's internal accounting, 750 dealer accounts, currency purchases, import administration, bank relationships, and all receivables and payables. His signature was required on every company check. He had six people reporting to him directly from the Accounting Department. Hassan also supervised the Warehousing and Shipping Departments with managers of each department reporting directly to him. In addition, he personally supervised the computerization of the Accounting Department by overseeing the design and implementation of the system by an outside software company. Hassan held a seat on the board of directors and worked closely with the chairman, CEO, and president in devising the growth and expansion strategies of IOMCo.

Hassan's work habits had become a legend in the company. He was always the first person at work, arriving at around 7:00 A.M., and the last one to leave, departing at around 9:30 P.M. He had refused to take a vacation in more than 3 years and spent most weekends at the office. The chairman, CEO, and president had each asked him to take a vacation on numerous occasions, but Hassan invariably refused to do so. There were always projects that needed his attention or tasks too delicate for others to handle.

Hassan always had a number of important projects going on at the same time. In addition, he was a perfectionist. He had to work on a project until it was perfect. The computerized accounting system was a case in point. In 1989, IOMCo decided to computerize its accounting system in order to maintain its speed and flexibility amidst its rapid growth. After reviewing existing software, Hassan chose a bookkeeping package and decided to enhance it by developing a parallel information system with an outside software company. The information system was designed to record every sales transaction and maintain a current database on all dealer accounts and individual products. This was a formidable task considering that IOMCo distributed 600 different products through 750 dealers nationwide (excluding spare parts). The copier department alone ordered and distributed more than 70,000 items monthly. Spending many weekends and late nights, Hassan saw that the comprehensive computer system was operational within 1 year. He then continued refining it for the next 3 years, adding networking capabilities and countless other specifications.

The computerized information system became instrumental to management's continuous speed and agility requirements. The system itself, however, had become so complex that only Hassan and two programmers from the outside software company could maintain it; the software design had not been documented during its development. Some managers from the Computer Department expressed concern about the obsolescence of the underlying database engine used in the system, but Hassan dismissed these concerns as unfounded. Incidents of software crashes and inaccurate information, however, had increased as IOMCo's operations continued to expand.

The information system also had become a crisis trigger for Hassan. If receivables were stretched or products turned over too slowly, Hassan would wage a battle cry against that particular evil and immediately warn other executives about the imminent dangers. Then, managers of the related department would be pressured continually to resolve the problem as soon as possible.

These crises became obsessions for Hassan. For example, when the calculator inventory reached the equivalent of 7 months of sales one December, Hassan declared that calculators had dramatically reduced the liquidity of the company and that their liquidation was a top priority. He had taken it upon himself to press the product manager of the Calculator Department to sell, sell, sell and not order anything more. The product manager obliged although he reported to the president and not to Hassan.

The other executives did not interfere with Hassan's crisis management style, but they were never as alarmed as he was. In that particular case, for example, calculators represented only about 5 percent of IOMCo's sales. The executives would joke that every

time they asked Hassan how he was doing, he would reply, "These calculators—I don't know what to do with them! I dream about the damn things at night!"

Hassan always seemed to be facing a number of crises at once. During the calculator inventory buildup, he began to worry about low margins on computer printers. The fact that the chairman of the company was responsible for the Computer Department did not stop Hassan from confronting him directly. He walked into the chairman's office and asked angrily "Why don't you want to make money on printers? It's your company, but you might as well just put the budget of printers in the bank and earn interest on it! Why bother paying salaries if you don't plan to make money?"

After calming Hassan down, the chairman would explain that he was trying to penetrate the market preemptively and secure the best dealers before other competitors could do so. In addition, they were under the constraint of a minimum quantity contract with the manufacturers, and so on. Eventually, Hassan would leave the room, shaking his head and saying, "I don't know. It's your department, but I don't know . . ." The chairman knew that Hassan would be back again in a week but what could he say when someone showed so much concern and dedication toward the company? He would smile and shake his head, thinking that Hassan was the only person in the whole company who raised his voice with him.

Despite Hassan's temper, everyone in the company liked him. The reason was his unconditional dedication to the company and his genuine concern for employees. Several months earlier during a late night major delivery to the warehouse, one of the employees unloading the trucks had fainted. Hassan, who was helping supervise the unloading that night, had rushed the employee to the hospital himself. By the time they reached the hospital, the employee had regained consciousness, but

Hassan insisted that he would stay at the hospital for the night. In addition, he was to be given a complete checkup the next day. The result of the checkup and the doctor's recommendation were to be sent directly to Hassan, and the company would bear all expenses. Later that night, Hassan returned to the warehouse and personally filled in for the position of the hospitalized employee. Actually, it wasn't uncommon to see Hassan help unload trucks on busy nights.

Hassan's dedication to the company even seemed to precede that to his family. About 4 months after his son was born, Hassan dropped by the office one morning to say that their refrigerator had broken and that he had to go buy a new one urgently. He said he would be back in the office as soon as he had the refrigerator delivered to his home. As he walked out of the office, he noticed a loose tile hanging above the fifth floor of the office building. He went back into the office and gave instructions that the tile had to be fixed immediately as it could break loose with the slightest wind and injure someone on the sidewalk. A manager volunteered to take care of it, but Hassan insisted on making the arrangements himself. He called a contractor who then had to secure scaffolding in order to reach the damaged area. The repair took 3 days, during which time Hassan oversaw everything while continuing his usual daily chores. After 3 days, Hassan himself joked that "I fixed the office building, but my wife and child are still without a refrigerator at home."

Over the last 2 years, Hassan had developed a number of unusual health problems. Despite his young age, he had high blood pressure; his skin flared up occasionally with rashes; and he complained about a runny nose, headaches, and backaches. In the beginning, Hassan associated these problems with the two packets of cigarettes he smoked daily. After a few attempts, he managed to quit smoking completely and hadn't smoked for more than a year. After quitting, he put on some weight but claimed that generally he felt much better. However, although the headaches had diminished, he still had high blood pressure, and most of the other symptoms remained. Hassan believed that the remaining symptoms were a result of his sporadic eating habits. He said he now was trying to reduce the fat in his diet.

Contrary to Hassan, the chairman and president believed that some of Hassan's health problems were due to excessive work. They insisted that he should take vacations and at one point banned him from coming to the office on weekends. Hassan had not cooperated with any of the above attempts, however, and continued his hard work behavior. The chairman had even threatened to reduce Hassan's lucrative bonuses if he didn't take a vacation, but he never followed through on this as it seemed counterintuitive to reduce someone's bonuses for doing exceptional work. Everyone had given up changing Hassan—until that morning after the accident.

NEXT STEPS

The thought of losing Hassan shocked the executives. Hassan himself was perturbed about the incident. After some earnest discussions during the day, Hassan had agreed, for the first time, to take a 2-week vacation with his wife and son as soon as he had completed some pending projects. He also agreed to leave the office at 8:00 P.M. every evening at the latest and stay away from work on weekends.

That afternoon, the chairman, CEO, and president talked among themselves after they sent Hassan home. The general consensus was that the accident had been a blessing in disguise for it had convinced Hassan to work less and relax a bit. That evening the executives went home relieved that all was well and everything would be back to normal. ■

Case 5   Jackie Woods (A)

Jackie is like the first firecracker lit in a package of firecrackers . . . there is this constant energy, this constant edge. Once she is lit, she lights everything else around her. It becomes contagious, just like a package of firecrackers; one right after the other, they just start to go. Once she has accomplished something, there is this huge explosion around it.

In May 1992, Jackie Woods, vice president of Business Marketing for Ameritech Services, was walking down the hall in the east wing of the new Ameritech office building in Hoffman Estates, Illinois. Jackie had been asked recently to participate on a task force of 100 senior managers from throughout Ameritech that was charged with exploring significant strategic issues facing the company, including how the company should be organized to face the next century. The task force also had the responsibility of designing a structure that would allow Ameritech to reduce the layers of supervision for its 70,000-person workforce. The duties of the task force were expected to span a period of at least 6 months. To be included in such a significant task force was a source of deep satisfaction to Jackie and signaled just how favorably she was viewed by Ameritech executives. As Jackie turned a corner, she bumped into Bob Brown, a colleague on the reorganization task force.

"So, Jackie, when are you going to tell the family?"

"Tell them what, Bob?"

"You know, about the committee and the work we're going to be doing this summer. I know that you've planned a vacation to Europe with your family. I'd planned to take what we considered a once-in-a-lifetime trip to Belize this summer, but given the hectic schedule for the task force, I had to go back

and cancel it. It wasn't easy. How are you going to break it to the girls?" Jackie smiled and made a pleasant comment before continuing down the hallway. She and her husband, Jack, had been planning a trip to Europe with their two daughters. In fact, they had already paid for the trip before Jackie was assigned to the task force. She grimaced as she remembered the earnestness in her daughters' eyes as they anticipated the trip and in Bob's eyes as he expressed his empathy for Jackie's dilemma.

BACKGROUND

The major milestones in Jackie's life are shown in Exhibit 5-1. Jackie, born in Cleveland, Ohio, in 1947, was the only child of Jack and Gladys Dudek. She first left home to attend Muskingum College in southern Ohio. During the summer between her junior and senior years, she met Jack Woods, a student at the University of Akron. She graduated in 1969 with a double major in communications and psychology; within a few months, she and Jack were engaged.

Two months before the big day, however, Jack was drafted into the army and sent to basic training at Fort Polk, Louisiana, interrupting both his new career at B.F. Goodrich and the couple's wedding plans. Jack and Jackie were married in December 1969 when he came home on leave. In

UVA-BP-0330

This case was prepared by Catherine M. Lloyd, MBA '93, under the supervision of James G. Clawson. This case was written as a basis for class discussion rather than to illustrate effective or ineffective handling of an administrative situation. Copyright © 1993 by the University of Virginia Darden School Foundation, Charlottesville, VA. All rights reserved.

Summer 1968	Jackie Dudek meets Jack Woods.
September 1969	Jackie gets job at Ohio Bell.
November 1969	Jack gets drafted.
December 1969	Jack and Jackie get married.
Mid-1978	Jack is transferred to Philadelphia, and Jackie accepts job with Bell of Pennsylvania.
January 1982	Jackie accepts sales job at Ohio Bell.
June 1984	Divestiture puts Jackie in autonomous subsidiary.
January 1989	President tells Jackie that she needs headquarter's experience; she accepts CFO position in Chicago (family moves); Jack gets job in procurement at Ameritech.
August 1990	Jackie moves back to marketing.
December 1991	Jack and Jackie plan European trip for family.

EXHIBIT 5-1 Milestones

March 1970, Jack was shipped out to Vietnam, where he spent the next 2 years.

This turn of events had made it necessary for Jackie to look for a job. In September 1969, she started working in the Ohio Bell business office, where she was responsible for customer ordering and billing operations in the Cleveland area:

> All of it started right then [when Jack was drafted]. Would my career ever have played out this way if Uncle Sam hadn't taken Jack away for the first 3 years of our marriage or would I have worked a few months and said, "I don't think that the career life is for me?" So when people say to me, "How did you decide to have a career?" I say, "It just happened, at least a little bit, because of the war." If you would have asked me at the time whether I was going to have a 20-year career [and reach this level of success], I would have told you most likely not.

At that time, Jackie noted, many employers required their female workers to submit signed statements declaring that they would not get pregnant within the first 2 years of their tenure at the company. Noncompliance was grounds for dismissal.

Jack returned from Vietnam in 1971 and went back to work for B.F. Goodrich. Jackie chose to continue working with Ohio Bell, and they continued to live and work in Cleveland. Then, in 1978, B.F. Goodrich told Jack that he would have to move in order to advance his career and assigned him to a petrochemical facility in Philadelphia, Pennsylvania. Because they had lived all their lives in Ohio and now had a 6-month-old daughter, Nicole, their decision was incredibly difficult. Nevertheless, they left their families and friends behind as they made the joint decision to move to Pennsylvania to pursue Jack's early career goals.

Originally, Jackie thought she would not work after the move:

> I agreed to sacrifice—if that is the appropriate word—my career for my husband's at that point . . . and I did not intend to work. I said, "Well, I've had a nice career here for 7 or 8 years. I'll tend to my family now and not do this."

Much appeared to be changing in Jack and Jackie's lives. Jackie's relationship with the Bell System seemed to be a source of stability in their lives, however, so when they got to Philadelphia, Jackie decided to pursue a job with the local telephone company:

> I interviewed at Bell of Pennsylvania and decided to go ahead and pursue a career with them just to see how it would work. We moved to Philadelphia, [and I] worked in public relations, public affairs, and then moved to marketing.

Jackie's new job required her to take a step down not only in salary, but also in management responsibility. Although such a reversal can be extremely frustrating for anyone, Jack and Jackie were confident that she would do a good job and move up quickly. Furthermore, the job allowed her some flexibility to spend more time with Nicole.

THE WOODS RETURN TO CLEVELAND

Four years later, in 1982, Jack was transferred back to B.F. Goodrich's corporate headquarters in Cleveland. With Nicole and now Stephanie, ages 4 and 2, Jack and Jackie gladly headed back to Ohio. Jackie went back to Ohio Bell and found a job in sales. Ironically, she was not given the same level of management responsibility that she had enjoyed before she left the company in 1978. The transfer to sales, however, added another dimension to her professional experience. Reflecting on her move into sales, Jackie noted:

> My recommendation to young people starting in careers—and I would say this to men or women—is to get into highly measurable jobs. Sales is one of those. If you are in a position that is subject to someone's decisions about you and based on pretty subjective criteria, you can sit and wonder what you could have

done, would have been, if there hadn't been this personality conflict or this difference in management style. If you get into a highly measurable job, the results speak for you.

Despite the general reality that women in the telephone industry seldom went beyond first-line management, Jackie's work at Ohio Bell was punctuated by a series of promotions. While her success was driven by her management skills, her career path was certainly influenced by her multicompany experience and geographical moves.

DIVESTITURE TRANSFORMS AN INDUSTRY AND A CAREER

In June 1982, federal Judge Greene directed American Telephone and Telegraph (AT&T) to divest itself of its local telephone operations, which comprised 22 operating companies, of which Ohio Bell was one. The reorganization of the Bell system created seven regional Bell operating companies (often referred to as RBOCs). The five Bell companies serving Michigan, Indiana, Illinois, Ohio, and Wisconsin became a part of American Information Technology Corporation (Ameritech). The divestiture also greatly enhanced the importance of the sales and marketing functions in the telephone companies nationwide. Under AT&T's service orientation, sales and marketing had been relatively quiet; these departments now had major responsibilities for revitalizing and building the new phone companies. The sales departments of the five Bell companies in Ameritech were consolidated into a single, unregulated organization, Ameritech Services, that was allowed to operate with little interference from its regulated telephone sibling.

In 1986, Jackie was made president of Ohio Bell Communications, the sales subsidiary of Ohio Bell. In this capacity, she oversaw a wide variety of functions including finance, human resources, quality, vendor relationships, labor negotiations, sales, and marketing:

> I found that customers that were going to spend a substantial amount of money, whether it be $40,000 or $1 million, wanted to see the president. They wanted somebody that would come out and sit there and say, "Your business is important and I'm going to make sure that this team cares about your business and delivers the service to you that we're committing to in this contract."

FAMILY AFFAIRS

Jackie's aging parents were living with the Woods family at this time. When Jackie's mother went into a nursing home, Jackie found herself balancing visits to day-care schools to see the two girls and to the nursing home to see her mother. This routine continued for 8 months until her mother passed away. Jackie's father, Jack, continued to live with them:

> The thing that helped [him], at least according to my dad, was that we had small children who provided a great deal of joy and entertainment. He would frequently say to us that [if it weren't for the girls], living there with my husband and me would be just terribly boring because we came home late at night if we had work to do. We weren't any fun.
>   We met with the pediatrician [about this time] and had a family conference about the role my father would play. He's a very strong kind of domineering guy, but the role he chose to play was one of unconditional love with the children. He would do no disciplining. He left that up to Jack and me.

Jackie went on to explain the additional support that she and Jack received in raising their children and managing the house:

> I have always had someone that helped me with the children even if it was picking them up from day care or working in the house, and that directly influenced how well things went. If this person worked well with us and got along well, our family life was much easier.

BACK TO BUSINESS

In 1988, Ed Bell, the president of Ohio Bell, told Jackie that her current position within the company would be the highest she would ever achieve if she chose to stay in Cleveland. He advised her that she needed experience at Ameritech headquarters in Chicago. Jackie agreed to think about it, and within a matter of months, she was offered the job of chief financial officer of Ameritech Services Division. The family now was faced with a decision similar to the one it had encountered when Jack was transferred to Philadelphia. Jack had been doing well since his transfer back to Cleveland (see Exhibit 5-2), and Nicole and Stephanie, now 11 and 9, faced the possibility of separation from friends and family. The girls expressed resistance to the move. Jackie had her own misgivings:

> At Ohio Bell Communications I was really running a microcosm of a large company like Ohio Bell. And it was a very successful operation. We *enjoyed* it. When the time came to leave, it was sad because the company was doing very well, and I very easily could have stayed. In addition, we had a home we loved to live in. My children loved their school and their friends. My husband loved his career; he'd done very well since we had come back from Philadelphia and was moving ahead.

Nevertheless, after considerable discussion with Jack and the girls, they agreed, now, to support Jackie's career. The family moved to Chicago in January 1989. As it turned out,

Jack also took a position at Ameritech Services in the Information Technology Department managing the procurement and deployment of computers within the firm.

Jackie's new job increased her responsibility, allowed her to expand her technical and analytical skills, and gave her additional exposure at the corporate offices. She found, however, that she disliked the job:

> It was an awful job, I mean a *boring* job. You know, they all wore navy blue suits and were wringing their hands all the time. It was just terrible! And here we were coming out of sales where you did things that mattered, where you got a lot of reinforcement from your customers when you were successful with them! And to go into something where all you heard about was if you did something wrong—and something always went wrong.

WRENCHING CHANGES AT HOME AND OFFICE

Soon after Jackie's arrival in Chicago, Ameritech faced some difficult market conditions and began a series of serious reorganizing efforts that included unprecedented cutbacks in the corporate workforce. Many people who had supported Jackie's move to headquarters were no longer with the firm, which caused Jackie some concern:

> We came here, and [shortly thereafter] the company changed its focus and actually fired some of our top management— people who had made commitments to me to bring me here. So, the rug was really pulled out from under us. [They] were redesigning the corporation so the kinds of jobs that I would typically look

to as my next move were being done away with.

The increasing competition and speed of technological change forced Ameritech and the other RBOCs to reexamine their basic decision-making processes. Jackie explained that, in the past:

> we were an industry that could make decisions on substantial analytical data that was gathered over a period of time. You could go back and reassess that data before you actually had to decide. It was almost no risk to delay the decision versus making an incorrect decision by moving quickly. Well, today, in the competitive marketplace, you can't do that. So, you have to make decisions on minimal amounts of data that you assess maybe once—and a lot of feeling about your customers.

In August 1991, Jackie moved over to marketing at Ameritech Services[1] (still in Chicago) and was given the responsibility for all of Ameritech's business customers in a five-state region. Her new department, however, was not immune to the substantial reductions in force occurring throughout Ameritech. The layoffs signaled a change in culture at the company:

> If you started with the telephone company and you did a good job, you were recognized and you were promoted and, I don't know if I'd say that you had a lifelong career, but you certainly had an extensive career. That isn't how it is today. We're really changing the design of how one succeeds in the business, so I need to go and build [my department's] morale at this point.

---

[1]Ameritech Services provided planning, development, management, and support for the Ameritech Bell Companies to help achieve common marketing and operational goals.

As a part of Ameritech's downsizing efforts, all employees were evaluated according to a variety of skills that the company believed were crucial to its future success. Many individuals were identified as not having the necessary qualities to continue with the company. Jackie commented on the serious changes people were experiencing:

> Now some of those people could retire, so the changes were a pretty easy move for them. Some of them, in their thirties and forties who couldn't retire, viewed it as a betrayal on the part of the company—changing the way we deal with them, the contract, as they call it. To them, we had literally broken the contract. But instead of deserving a job or believing that it's your right to have the job, we believe you have to *earn* the job every day. And you earn it through customer service. As a result, we took the bottom tier of people and moved them out of the business. It was a *very* painful thing to do.
>
> I think the real signal, though, is to people who were on the *next* tier. We've said to them, "We don't know if we're ever going to have to do this again, but if we do, you're at risk and here's why."

The upheaval caused by the downsizing prompted Ameritech officers to think carefully about how news of the restructuring was communicated to the 70,000-person workforce. Jackie commented on the approach:

> [Traditionally,] we let our employees read something in the newspaper or trade journals [about changes] that they should have understood and had explained to them before it appeared in print. Now, sometimes things just happen if there wasn't any planning, but there *are* other things we can do. We're working right now to figure out a decentralized communications process which says that the head of each unit would be able to [communicate the message] the way they want to. But the communication would be coordinated and prepared in documents from a centralized point of view.
>
> What we have found was that if each of us explains why the corporation is downsizing, we each kind of ad-lib why we think that's happening. And then we communicate that to 100 people who each kind of ad-lib to others. The message needs to be very clear. Now, whether I decide to do that over videotapes and you decide to have small group sessions and talk about it will be your decision. These messages require conversation and interactive discussion while others are able to be communicated, maybe, in print. So, what we're trying to balance now is the centralized message and the information around it, but with a decentralized distribution system. That isn't how we've done it to date. We've had one answer for everybody. We're going to send this out in print, it'll be distributed to 70,000 employees, and you'll read about it like everyone else.

As she examined her new job and the changes occurring in her markets, Jackie began to make what others called revolutionary changes for a telephone utility:

> One thing I've done here is reach down and create a multilevel reporting structure so that I have some people who would come to my staff meetings who, in our hierarchy, might be several levels below someone else but they are an expert in their field. Now the people feel honored because they're being recognized for their expertise and the role they're playing and are thrilled to come! What people began to realize was that the reason they were being brought in

was that in this meeting we were going to make decisions that required very specific operational information about very specific projects. So, you couldn't have some [who were] representing it who didn't understand the project or we'd probably make the wrong decision. We invite them to the meetings based on what the subject matter is. So, you get to attend a meeting based on what your role is and what's going to be discussed and your contribution, not because of your approved "right" to attend something because of the job you hold. So, the job doesn't necessarily convey the authority in power as much anymore as the individual and what they are responsible for.

The number of wrenching decisions that were being made and the daily increasing demands of marketing in a broad, five-state area with stiffening competition placed an enormous load on Jackie. Because the challenges of reorganizing her department were offset only partially by the excitement of working with corporate customers, Jackie was concerned about her experience at Ameritech Services. She missed the direct responsibilities of the line jobs she had had at Ohio Bell and, frankly, missed her roots and relationships in Ohio (see Exhibits 5-1 and 5-3). Further, the changes in management made her wonder if the kind of guidance given by those who had talked about and coordinated her move to Chicago had disappeared. She wondered how long and in what capacity she might stay in Chicago.

With those thoughts in mind, she and her husband began to talk about other options. Should they look for other jobs in other firms back in Cleveland? (Jackie's and Jack's resumes appear in Exhibits 5-2 and 5-3.) How long should they wait to see if their decision to follow Jackie's career would prove to be a dead end? How could they tell if the executives at Ameritech were

aware of and interested in their situation? (Comments about Jackie by some of her peers and subordinates and some of her own views on various topics are included in Exhibit 5-4.) As they discussed their thoughts, Jackie and Jack decided early in 1992 to wait another 2 years to see what would happen. Then, if nothing materialized, they would begin to consider other options:

> Our mind-set was probably [oriented toward] the beginning to middle of 1994. We didn't say, "We're gonna ride this out and we'll see how it is in 2 months." I mean, I had invested 20 years at Ameritech! It seemed worth it to invest 15 months more. We had decided that we would ride this out and see—with the feeling that if it did not play out by that point, we would both reassess where we wanted to be.

EUROPEAN VACATION PLANS

Meanwhile, in December 1991, Jackie and Jack had decided to plan a big European family vacation for July 1992. They wanted their children to have the experience of seeing Europe firsthand, something they considered an essential part of the girls' education. In the months following the decision to go, everyone—including Nicole, 14, and Stephanie, 11—spent a considerable amount of time planning all aspects of the trip. They paid for all of the travel and lodging arrangements in advance. Although the package was expensive, the Woods felt good about the itinerary and the experience it would be for the family. Their plans were complicated somewhat by Ameritech's restructuring announcement in May 1992 and by Jackie's subsequent assignment to the reorganization task force. Jackie viewed the assignment with mixed feelings. Although it signaled to her that she was not forgotten, it also conflicted directly with the planned family vacation:

Jack's Resume

Education

University of Akron	Akron, OH
Graduated May 1964	
B.S. in Business Administration	

Experience

1992–Present	Ameritech Services—Asset Management Director	Chicago, IL
1990–1992	Ameritech Services—Supplies Management Director	Chicago, IL
1989–1990	Ameritech Services—Procurement Director	Chicago, IL
1988–1989	B.F. Goodrich—Chemical Purchasing Director	Cleveland, OH
1985–1987	B.F. Goodrich—Procurement and Materials Management Director	Cleveland, OH
1984	B.F. Goodrich—Plant Purchasing General Manager	Cleveland, OH
1981–1983	B.F. Goodrich—Plant Purchasing Regional Manager	Philadelphia, PA
Outside Activities	Shelter, Inc.—Director; American Legion; Computer Dealers/Lessors Association—Customer Advisory Council	

EXHIBIT 5-2   Jack's Resume, June 1992

We had been working with the travel agent since January, and we very specifically picked someone here in town so on Saturday morning you could go up to town, stop at the corner store and get coffee and a doughnut, and go in and sit down and chat with this lady. We laid out maps. The girls went and ate bagels over her desk, and everybody talked about where we were going and had a very vested interest. The girls got to pick places they thought would be interesting. Jack and I contributed. Everybody had read the tour books and, about June, with everything pretty well paid for and arranged, [Ameritech] said, "Well, maybe you'd better not go."

Bob Brown's comment in the hallway heightened Jackie's concern about the trip. Clearly, that summer would be an important time in the history of the company. Decisions would be made that could shape the future of Ameritech—and of the Woods family. ■

Jackie's Resume

Education

Northwestern University	Chicago, IL
Executive Education Program	
Muskingum College	Muskingum, OH
Graduated May 1968	
B.A. in Psychology	
B.S. in Communications	

Experience

1990–Present	Ameritech Services—Business Markets	
	General Manager and Vice President	Chicago, IL
1989–1990	Ameritech Services	
	Vice President of Finance and Administration	Chicago, IL
1986–1989	Ohio Bell Communications	
	President and Chief Executive Officer	Cleveland, OH
1982–1984	Ohio Bell Communications	
	Vice President of Marketing	Cleveland, OH
1978–1982	Bell of Pennsylvania	
	Public Affairs Office	
	Marketing Department	Philadelphia, PA
1970–1978	Ohio Bell Communications	
	Public Affairs District Manager	
	Public Relations Manager	
	Business Office Supervisor	Cleveland, OH
Outside Activities	United Way, Muskingum College Alumni Association, Chicago Junior League, Chicago Executive Club, Chicago Easter Seals	

EXHIBIT 5-3   Jackie's Resume, June 1992

Jackie on Networking

I also find it interesting that men have had a very strong network, so it has been easier [for them] *to make decisions based on fact. You could go ask some of your buddies or your boss or the president, "Here's what I see happening, is that how it's going to be?" Women and minorities spent a lot of time guessing because they either didn't have the network or they were afraid to ask. What we're seeing now is that these new networks are being built. There are women's groups; there are minority groups. There is a formal network within their firms so that people can get better information to understand the alternatives.*

Jackie on Balancing Work and Family

That is the trade-off. If you are going to say, in a business environment, that you want to have so much more, that these are the jobs that I want to have, then you need to understand what it is going to take to get there. And if that's not what you are willing to do, then you have to take the responsibility for that, as well.

A Colleague's Observation of Jackie

Jackie is probably one of the most complete managers that I have encountered throughout my career with Ameritech. She has an incredible amount of energy, an outstanding ability to retain information and absorb detail. She tends to encourage and motivate her staff effectively, as well.

Jackie on Being Close to Employees and Customers

What I found was that if you go out and talk to people and spend your time with both your employees and your customers, it becomes easy to understand how to integrate their input into company operations. Employees need to know they have your support, and customers need to know the top executives draw on what's going on at the front line.

Jackie on Setting Priorities

Even if there are things that are very important to the business, basic tenets that the business is built on, you really need to question them. Let me give you an example: the pricing philosophy of how we price service. Maybe my customer data tells me that [the current way] *isn't the way we are going to be able to do that in the future. And my competitive data tells us that we are going to have to change. Well, pricing is something very basic to this business. Changes are going to have millions of dollars of impact. That isn't something I am going to bring up offhandedly in a meeting and expect to have resolved. I am going to evaluate the data, get more facts, and I am going to listen to people's positions on it, and I am going to, as you might say,* **work** *the issue.* [Anything] *that could have immediate impact to our customers is something to fight for that. So, having that sense of balance of how big this* [issue] *is to the corporation and customers is important to determining how quickly we need to act.*

Jackie's Colleague on Her Consensus-Building Skills

The Bell Operating Companies [in Ameritech's five-state region] *do not want us here. They would prefer to continue to run their own organizations, manage their own budgets, develop their own strategies, and do it in five different ways. So, we go out to the state operating companies and talk to the sales and support vice presidents about our plans, and the minute we walk into the room with the presidents and vice presidents, the guns are loaded. But by the time we leave that meeting, Jackie has really gotten a consensus on every issue that she has gone there with, and everyone feels like they have won at the end of the meeting. It's incredible how she builds the whole win-win situation.*

(continued)

EXHIBIT 5-4 Comments from and About Jackie Woods

Jackie on Management Fads

I think that American management has to have a lot of confidence in what they do real well. We sometimes decide that someone else is good at something and all of a sudden we drop everything we do. We read this book or we heard in this country they do this, so let's drop what we are doing. American management has to develop its own style. Certainly we should utilize things from other cultures, but we should build on a framework of what we really believe in this country and on what we really want to do in managing our businesses. We can't decide quality, for example, is the program for the day! And so now all the CEOs are going to walk out and talk about quality, and all are going to have a quality advisor and in a few months we are going to decide well quality isn't it anymore. I mean, quality has to be in the very basic way that we approach the business and every decision we make.

EXHIBIT 5-4   (continued)

Case 6   The Life and Career of a Senior Executive Officer (Tom Curren)

He tried to calculate it. He would drop 10 feet if the pin held, and he could extricate himself easily enough. But if it didn't, he'd go 40 feet, hit the ledge 20 feet below John, and probably be killed. Perhaps 15 minutes had gone by and he hadn't moved. Years of rock climbing were working in his head—he just didn't know whether or not he could make this last section.

There seemed to be a tiny flake at knee level on the steep wall. Was that another 6 feet above it? Eyes inches from the rock, the hand caresses over it. Yes! A ripple perhaps 1/32 of an inch . . . but a ripple. Somewhere inside him the move is being weighed: "You've stood on as small things before . . . I know, but that was on boulder problems 4 feet off the ground. Why do I come up here anyway?"

He stood on tiptoe feeling secure on the half-inch ledge. Strange, when he'd first reached it he was apprehensive about stepping onto it. Now, 20 minutes later, it felt like a truck stop.

He was clothed only in shorts, thin socks, and climbing shoes. He dipped his hand into the bag of gymnastic chalk hanging from his waist, dried the moisture off his fingertips, and dusted off the little hold.

Far down in the valley, a crow glided. Eight hundred feet below, little toy cars wove their way through the valley floor. Without a conscious decision to start, but rather attracted as a magnet, the left foot went up, weight shifting carefully to the tiny hold. As he straightened his left leg, the right foot moved up, tapping the smooth granite. Now 10 inches from the truck stop . . . 15 inches. Don't come off now left foot! Please don't come off now. Warnings exploding in his head and he knows, absolutely, that the piton will not hold the fall. You're committed, it's only 15 inches to the truck stop, but there is no going back.

Tom Curren's mind snapped back, his eyes refocusing on the picture in front of him on his desk. That was 6 years ago. Today, he was sitting in his office in Marriott World Headquarters, talking about his life and background. (See Exhibit 6-1 for his resume.)

TOM CURREN'S EARLY LIFE

"I am basically an only child, in that my mother didn't remarry till I was about 10. Mom was married during the war. My father went off, and then they separated when he came back, so I never lived with my father and never really developed a close relationship with him. So, I was raised by my mother and my grandmother.

"My mother remarried when I was 10 and had three more children. There was also a daughter by my stepfather's first marriage, so there were five of us in all. With all the other half brothers and stepbrothers, there was quite a family.

UVA-PACS-0023

This case was prepared by James G. Clawson. Copyright © 1989 by the Darden Graduate Business School Foundation, Charlottesville, Virginia. All rights reserved. The introduction was adapted by Tom Curren from an article entitled "Sometimes You Know—Sometimes You Don't" by Jim Sinclair, printed in the *Canadian Alpine Journal,* 1974, revised 8/96.

A. Thomas Curren

EDUCATION

Wharton Graduate Division   **University of Pennsylvania**
MBA Degree, 1967
Top 10% Directors Honor List

Trinity College   **Hartford, Connecticut**
BA Degree in Economics
Honors Thesis, Deans List, President of Fraternity

EXPERIENCE

ALLEN-CURREN ELECTRONICS
President (1967–1968) *Entrepreneur* — Cofounder of small venture which designed, manufactured and marketed industrial lighting controls for nightclubs, discotheques, and theaters. Distributed nationally through theatrical lighting houses in NYC. Made mistakes and learned from them. Military duty forced dissolution of the company.

U.S. NAVY, Lt. Comdr. Ellis
Officer (1968–1971) *Operations Management.* Responsible for all food service operations at Naval Station, Norfolk, VA. Managed 150 civilian and military personnel, $2.8 million budget. Introduced fast-food menu, cut inventories, won approval for $1.2 million in new facilities. Awarded 4.0 in all areas of performance evaluation, selected for accelerated promotion.

COMPTON ADVERTISING, Paul Paulson
Account Executive (1971–1973)
Marketer. Responsible for Procter & Gamble advertising of Cascade detergent in the United States and Canada.

MCKINSEY & CO., NYC, Tom Wilson
Engagement Manager (1973–1977)
Consultant. Managed study teams of two to four in order to solve strategic, marketing, and operational problems.

MARRIOTT, Gary Wilson
Director Corporate Planning (57) (1977–1981)
Strategic Planning. Believed to have played a significant role in the following decisions: revised FSM strategy (1977), OVA establishment of In-Flite RMT, acceleration of hotel growth, development of Hotel manpower program, shift to 3 EVP, sale of Dinner House, Farrell's, World Travel, repurchase of Marriott stock, establishment of 4x coverage policy, shift to International In-Flite management contracts, Roy Rogers/Gino's eastern strategy, disposition of Rustlers, Santa Clara Land sale, improved hotel pricing SOPs, post-acquisition integration of Host, new Casa Maria prototype, development of Courtyard, pursuit of Health Care/Elderly service opportunities.

MARRIOTT, Gary Wilson
VP — Corporate Planning (61) (1981–Present)
Business Development. Assumed MBO for new hotel product line on 5/80. Hired Washburn on 8/80. First five units approved by Board of Directors on 5/82. Forecast 10,000 to 18,000 rooms by year-end 1988.

Marketing Services. Took over CMS on 1/81. Felt that department was not maximizing its potential despite widespread satisfaction with existing organization. Replaced 70 percent of people and shifted emphasis from technically exotic research to providing basic, ongoing information. Staffed department with people who have advancement potential within Marriott.

(continued)

EXHIBIT 6-1   Resume as of 1984

Hotel Feasibility. Took over Feasibility on 10/81. Rebuilt department after departure of William, Webb, Moulton with emphasis on marketing/strategy capabilities (Isaac, Lavin, Eiseman). Created professional development programs, expanded use of computer, improved decision-making process.

Executive Development. Curren has recruited and developed six managers at the grade 55 level (Sid Laytin, Don Washburn, Tony Isaac, Larry Murphy, Frank Camacho, Bill Eggbeer). Most of these executives have the potential to advance to substantial leadership roles in the company in the mid-1980s.

EXHIBIT 6-1 **(continued)**

"I think I was a pretty quiet kid, serious, fairly introverted, and probably . . . you know, I would characterize [me] as a late bloomer. I never did particularly well in school; my grades were always middle of the class at best, and I never participated in a lot of extracurricular activities, never did much in the way of athletics. I had a few friends but was basically sort of floating through life.

"I went to private school up in Connecticut at a boarding school called Hotchkiss. Then I went directly into Trinity College in Hartford. I wanted to take some pictures in college, and so this other guy and I, we shot pictures all year and did our own darkroom work and published our own yearbook. I built an underwater camera case for my camera. I dated a model; I thought that was a big deal. She was on the cover of everything. I was pretty active socially.

"I graduated in 1965 with a degree in economics, went directly to Wharton, got my MBA in 1967, then went into the military in 1968 as a supply officer in the Navy. I got married in 1970, got out of the Navy in 1971, went to New York, lived and worked in Manhattan for 8 years—first working for an advertising agency, 1971 to 1973, then for McKinsey's New York office, 1973 to 1977, and in 1977 came to Marriott where I have been for the last 11 years. (See Exhibit 6-1.)

"I can't think of a setback I had other than being fairly withdrawn in the early part of my life. In the early part of college, things

just sort of began opening up for me. I began doing more and more and accomplishing more and more. I went through the beginning part of college, like, middle of the class and then shifted majors from math to economics. Toward the end of my senior year, I became more active. I became president of my fraternity, my grades picked up, and I decided to go on to graduate school.

"I went to Wharton. I was in the top 10 percent of my class there. I started a company when I was there, a little venture company, Allen-Curren Electronics. For some reason, I became interested in business. It was more of an intrinsic interest in the problems and the problem solving, and I just pursued that interest.

"Then, I did a stint in the military, which was tremendously helpful. Coming out of that I was 24. Although I felt like I'd 'lost' 3 years in the military, it was a great experience. I was at sea for 9 months, an officer on a ship, one of 12 officers with 300 crew. I stood watches at night, ran a ship. I loved the ocean, loved being at sea, loved operating in the Philippines and Japan and Vietnam—just a tremendous experience. It was an oiler; we refueled surface ships."

BUSINESS EXPERIENCE

"I was interested in marketing, and I was trying find a way to learn marketing, package-goods marketing, as fast as I could. The choice came down to either learning from the brand-management side at Procter & Gamble or General Foods or from the agency side working on a Procter or General Foods account. I went the agency route and went to work for an advertising agency in New York, working on Procter business. Again, it wasn't the agency I was picking, it was the account, because there was another agency, whom I thought was a better agency, but they wouldn't guarantee what account I would be on. I might have been on Camel cigarettes, and I wouldn't work on cigarette advertising.

"So I worked on Procter soap and detergent business for 20 months and was very successful. I was promoted from assistant account executive—to account executive, working on Cascade, which is a dishwashing detergent that 'Fights drops and spots. Leaves glasses virtually spotless!' That was a terrific experience. Cascade was a great learning brand; Procter had 33 sales districts, and something was going on in every one of them. We were defending against Palmolive in six districts, running a copy test in three districts, competing in low-phosphate districts, rolling out a 65-ounce size in some districts, lemon fresh in other districts, testing a 'media heavy up' in one district, and using two more districts as controls. *All* of this stuff going on. It was just *tremendous* learning.

"I took the brand through a budget cycle (this was 1971 to 1973), but I knew that I wasn't interested in the agency business *per se*. I didn't like selling advertising, although I liked the business itself. I really identified more with the Procter people than I did with the agency people; I viewed myself as their partner and got involved in a lot of aspects of their business and was pretty highly regarded by them.

"Anyway, after about 20 months, McKinsey called me up and said they were following up on a Wharton campus interview from several years earlier. I had my military commitment then, but they were inter-

ested in me and had put me in a 'look up' file for later. So they tracked me down (this was all in New York; I was living in Manhattan), and they said, 'Why don't you come to our New York office in the marketing practice?' So I did and spent 4 years there.

"I guess the summary of all the career decisions I made early on was, in retrospect, really looking at what job I could learn the most at. Certainly that was true with the first two jobs. With the Marriott job offer, I said I've learned a bunch of stuff and here's a place I think I can apply it, and I found it was *time* to apply it. But everything else was not driven by money or any long-term view of where I was going to be. It was more 'what can I get out of the next 2 or 3 years here?' Now, I never went to those places knowing I was going to leave, but I was not making a long-term commitment to advertising or to consulting; I was saying, 'Yeah, that's open-ended, but what I am sure I can get out of the next 3 years is a lot of learning experience.'"

WORKING AT MARRIOTT

"Between my third and fourth years at McKinsey, my learning was peaking out: I knew I did not want to be a consultant long term, for all the usual reasons: travel, lack of continuity in studies, lack of continuity in people, and so forth. So it was a two-step process: I decided to leave, and then I had this typical, systematic search and screened all these companies. Marriott missed the screens totally, but they were searching for somebody, and when I began to find out about the situation, it fit perfectly.

"Gary Wilson, who was chief financial officer here at the time, had planning responsibility for the company at that time, which consisted of senior management getting together once a quarter or every 6 months and talking about the issues. Somehow, he knew a McKinsey person could do planning, so Marriott retained a search firm and recruited several senior McKinsey people, but they weren't interested. They thought it was, I don't know, too risky because the function had never been done at Marriott, but I thought it was terrific, 'cause I thought this was a great company and I've got what they need—which was basically a very disciplined approach to thinking. I knew I didn't have a lot of operational experience, but they didn't need that. The company was full of operators and strong finance people, but they really lacked 'planning,' particularly a marketing approach to planning. I don't think Bill Marriott knew what he was hiring. I think he thought I was going to be some sort of corporate marketing officer; I don't think Gary knew either. He wanted me to take minutes at these [quarterly or semiannual planning] meetings, but *I* knew.

"I was there a couple of months, and Bill Marriott finally called me and said, 'We've got a problem with this business. It's got a new general manager, and I want you and the general manager to go figure it out.' That was in early 1978, and I sort of ushered in the era of very 'issue-based planning' as opposed to a planning process. Even to this day, we spend less than 20 percent of our time on process; 80 percent of our planning time is issue driven. Some of the issues are acquisition related, some are business start-up, and some are existing business strategy.

"So I started in July 1977. I was hired in as director of Corporate Planning with no staff (which is why some of the most senior McKinsey people turned it down), a new function, and no structure as to what it's going to be. I guess I never looked toward the risks, just saw the possibilities. It was great because I knew they had gone after more senior people, so I could negotiate a big step up in salary. So I got a bump [up in salary]. After about a year, I hired somebody, a young consultant out of Booz-Allen. So we had a two-man department, and then a three-man department. We did basic strat-

egy diagnostics in many of our major businesses. I just stayed doing the same job, and it became more senior and influential within the company. Finally, the job was regraded up to vice president.

"Around 1981, I got in the new-business start-up game. Then, we started developing other products. We wanted to get into the whole elderly area. Bill Marriott had an interest in that, but it wasn't well defined. We hit on 'life care' early on, but we weren't sure about it, so we said, 'Okay, let's survey the whole category ranging from hospital management to psychiatric hospitals to day care to life care,' etc. So we did what we would call 'a category assessment.' We did it inside our planning department and used a hospital-management consultant firm up in New York to give us some industry expertise. We did the category overview and said 'life care' is what we want and created what we now call our Senior Living Services Division. We worked similarly with time-sharing and some other products that segmented the lodging market. We did that all up here in Corporate Planning.

"So my job began to take on a new-business-development component. Then it began to take on an acquisition aspect when we acquired about a half dozen companies, the largest of which was Saga [a large food-services company]. Most of these deals were closely related; they were businesses that we were in, so our work wasn't entering a new category so much as it was me and my department being the strategic conscience of the company—basically, saying, 'Does this business make sense? Are we overvaluing it?' So the job brought me into the new-acquisition-strategy business.

"The next evolution was I began decentralized strategy development. When a division becomes large enough to support the caliber of strategic resources that we sustain at corporate, we set up strategic planning in the division. We have a group in hotels, we have a group in food-service management, and we have a group out at Host. Those are dotted-line relationships to me and solid lines to a senior operating person.

"Today [1988], I've got a Corporate Planning Department of about a dozen people. I have the Central Market Research group, which has about 40 people in it (we do about $6 million worth of consumer research), and then I have a dotted-line relationship to three division-level planners.

"In terms of influence, stature, and compensation and so forth, I think I am among the top ten people in the company. I am one of the six voting members of the Finance Committee that approves projects over $1 million or any change in strategy. My influence varies depending upon the decision. If it is how a financial deal is structured, I have no say and don't pretend to have any say. If it's a strategic decision (Should we be in this business? Is it correctly positioned? Is the pricing right? Do we understand what the customers want? How much should we pay for this company?), I am one of those handful of votes."

ON STRATEGIC PLANNING SKILLS

"When I hire people, I look for three qualities, and I think this has accounted for a large part of my success. First, I look for people that can do what we call 'integrated business analysis.' That is, they can take complex business problems, break them down, and solve them. We look for people that can do that fundamentally from a marketing standpoint as opposed to a financial standpoint. They have to be comfortable in all the disciplines, but their depth has to be marketing. When I say *marketing,* I don't mean tactical marketing. They don't have to have worked at PG Procter & Gamble and know all about in-ad coupons and all that. They have to fundamentally think of busi-

ness problems in terms of segmentation, targeting, and positioning; understand how to use consumer research; and basically approach problems in their stomach from a marketing standpoint.

"In junior people coming right out of school, we look at their resume, but more, we ask the case questions (and we team interview), we draw out that ability. We also hire people at a more senior level, and we look at their resume and see if, in fact, they have being doing that for the last 5 years. We also ask them case questions. So we look for problem solvers.

"Secondly, as I said, they have to do it from a marketing perspective, because our finance people are so strong, and we are very team oriented here within the company.

"Thirdly, I look for a set of personality traits that are very pragmatic, not elitist, not overly academic. We're not interested in anybody that can really, really get excited by correlation analysis and r-squares and plotting little things, you know. We want people to have a line aptitude, an action aptitude, toward their work, people that have values that fit in with the values and style of the company. This is this clean-living and hard-working, Midwestern almost, type of work ethic; it's cultural. And we need people that are aggressive and yet are team oriented at the same time. So it's a difficult blend we all struggle with. We want a little bit of perfectionism, but we also want a tolerance in people—to know how far they can push and how to build consensus. We really are looking for champions, for people that can take a point of view, drive things through and, you know, make things happen.

"There is a spectrum of things I don't like in subordinates. I've had people that were strong but couldn't recognize anybody's priorities but their own. They were too narrow. And then I have had another person that was so nice and friendly and empathetic that that person really couldn't push through their own agenda. Again, it's that middle ground of aggressiveness—you know, being a team player, knowing how to make things happen."

TOM CURREN, THE PERSON

"I am a pretty serious person. I mean I am pretty interested in getting results. I'm becoming more and more interested in people, the people side. I have always been interested in developing people and, in fact, have. One of the things I am proudest about is the people I have brought into this company and what they have done. One of my objectives is to have sponsored or brought in a substantial proportion of the top 100 people in this company. That's personally rewarding. Also, I think I reflect a point of view and an emphasis that's complementary to what is the natural inclination of some of the other people.

"I think I am a caring person; I think I am a sensitive person. I think I am aggressive. I am very strong in conceptual integration; the way my mind works, I can synthesize concepts very easily. I am always looking at concepts. I am primarily a visual person, so I am a concept synthesizer. I am less interested in the details.

"I am interested fundamentally in being on the leading edge of whatever we are doing. I think we've now developed our ability to develop new businesses fairly well. I think the edge at this point is the culture of the company and the human-resource management of the company. So I find myself working more closely with human-resource people and line people on human-resource issues. And more and more of the work we are doing is taking all the strategy and marketing work we've worked on and applying it to the human-resource side. We have done that in several businesses, and now we are looking to do that at corporate level."

TOM CURREN'S PHILOSOPHY OF LIFE

"I am looking for balance between my objectives at work, in my family life, in my intimate relationships, and for myself and the things I do for myself. Work can be all consuming, particularly my position in a company that is aggressive in its growth goals and requires as much as this one. I have objectives in all those areas and am constantly working on all of those. I live my life out of intensity and learning. I think if you had to distill it down to the one thing I am about, it is 'commitment.' Commitment and excellence.

"I think if you want to accomplish anything, (1) you need the commitment and (2) you need to find a coach, find a series of resources from which you could learn. To me, it doesn't matter what you are committed to, so long as you make that statement and you live your life out of that commitment. Myself, I am constantly working on the balance between commitments to myself, to my relationships, and to my work. Obviously, they all overlap, and the more you can integrate them, the more effective you are in all of those areas. I *work* on that balance.

"My mother and grandmother were middle class. They were not wealthy. I think a lot of the values I learned I learned from my grandmother: thrift and hard work, save your pennies, and learn your multiplication tables, and . . . just sort of the *basics* seem to be there."

ON MARRIAGE

"I've been married twice. I met my first wife while I was down in Supply Course School in Athens, Georgia. We had two children, two girls that are in New York whom I see quite frequently. They are terrific, both teenagers now.

"I think in my first marriage I never developed the depth of the relationship or the commitment that I have with my current wife or, in fact, many of my current relationships. There were reasons that weren't necessarily good, but we got married, and we sort of drifted along. I had my job, we had some children, and we were committed to our children. In terms of *our* relationship, there really wasn't anything there. We began to drift apart; there just wasn't much of an investment. We finally said, 'This isn't working.'

"Work provided a smoke screen almost for what was going on at home. I became more aware in the later years of how little we had in the marriage, but I didn't invest in saving it. Knowing what I know today, I would keep the investment in *any* person I was with. I would not say, 'This person has all these faults, and I am going to find a better person.' I would say 'Am I committed to this person?' And I would just make the commitment, and I would make it work.

"It isn't so much a matter of finding the ideal person. But I did, in fact, find somebody that, as I said, I have this visceral attraction to and who also is very interested in learning and in growing together. We both are pretty high-strung people and not the easiest people to be around, but we are forging something that is really strong, and I am very committed to that.

"I don't know what criteria it takes to make a commitment to another person, and that doesn't matter. All that matters is the commitment. You are either in a state of commitment or you're not. The reason it doesn't matter is because, once you commit, you're committing in the face of any circumstance and any reason. You're not 'well I am committing to this relationship as long as it works out,' or 'I am committing to this job as long as it is not a problem.' You commit! Who knows how you commit? Now, it's important that you choose your commitments carefully. When you commit, that's it, you do it. I don't mean you should live so

rigidly that you've got all these commitments and when you break them you feel bad, but you take those things seriously.

"Now the area of commitment that I am struggling with is, psychologically, my concept of myself within the concept of a relationship. The more intimate a relationship is, the more joyful and also the more potential for pain with a separation. I have been learning not to run when the going gets rough. When I run, I don't mean leave the house in the middle of an argument, but I mean 'shut down,' withdraw. Just to stay in there and battle it out—to me, that is commitment.

"I came to Washington in 1977 and met Judy 6 months later. We dated for about 3 years, then she went off to Stanford Business School and got her MBA out there, and I went out and visited her every 6 weeks for 2 years. She's a native Californian, and we had a great time doing outdoor and active things that we like to do. She came back East in 1982, and we were married in 1984.

"We have no children from that marriage. We live with her children from her first marriage—a son that is just going off to Stanford this fall and a daughter that will be a sophomore in high school—then my two children—a sophomore in high school and one entering eighth grade: four children total, two children in the house full time and four children every fourth weekend or week together at the shore or whatever. My children are in New York most of the time."

ON PARENTING

"I think, first of all, that when I came down here and my wife and children stayed in New York, I wanted to make sure that they didn't have the same experience I had when my father left me and my mother and rarely saw me. I am estranged from my father.

"And I am very careful about that [not giving his daughters the same kind of experience], so I continued to go up to New

York every third weekend and see them and have them down here for a month at a time for the summer and so forth. Basically, we have kept up that pattern for about 11 years. They come down once a month now rather than every third weekend. So I stayed close enough to them so that I knew what was going on. It wasn't one of these relationships where you take them to the circus, and you don't really have any feel for them.

"They were 2 and 4 when Cathy and I split, so they were pretty young. I have had to accept it that I am not the primary parent, but I kept involved and feel comfortable with that. I don't know how, psychologically, it's been on the kids.

"I have tried to teach them a sense of humor and a love of the outdoors. I had the kids rock climbing when they were 4, in Central Park. They know my 'three rules' of rock climbing: Use your hands, no knees, and little steps. They scramble over those rocks. I took them around on the back of my bike. I taught them a sense of humor, sensitivity toward people, I think also a seriousness of purpose—although I don't know if they have gotten that yet; it is hard to tell when they are teenagers. I think they are very clear about my love for them and my interest in their well-being and development."

A TYPICAL WORKWEEK

"I am generally up before 6:00 every morning, either to run or work out early in the morning or get to work early. So I get up early. I make fresh orange juice for the whole family. We have a big commercial juicer, and we buy oranges by the carton. I get breakfast set for everybody. I am generally at work by, it varies, between 7:00 and 8:30, although what I am trying to do is block 2 days a week where I have open time in the morning till 10:00. I find that I need that, because my work, the rest of my life, is so heavily scheduled.

"So I am managing to put in those blocks of time. I am generally at work here till 6:30 P.M., not through any specific intent, but usually there's so much to do, and I get involved and look up, and it's 6:00 and 6:30 by the time I wrap things up. Occasionally I work weekends but not that often. I think the last time I figured it, I put 50 hours a week directly into work. My travel schedule is fairly light; I might average three or four overnights a month. It really is what I want to make it be.

"I read at night, between 11:00 and 12:00 (See Exhibit 6-2.) in bed. I read a little on the weekend. It takes me a long time to read a book. It took me 6 months to read *Chesapeake.* I just don't put that much time into reading. When I read something [nonfiction], I'll read it, I'll underline it, I'll re-read it, I'll read sections, reread, I'll underline it, and then I'll take notes on it. So I have summarized on maybe four pages the key things I got out of a book. And then I'll go back periodically and read it and underline it. I think what I've got is some pretty good study habits. I don't know where I developed them. I noticed that in graduate school I would be very thorough about studying things, and I would then retain things that way.

"I put a fair amount of time into exercise. I exercise five or six times a week—running, racquetball, and weights. I put a lot of time into personal development. I would say I spend 5, at least 5, hours a week doing some forum or course on leadership or seeing a consultant or applying something.

"Weekend activities are either doing projects around the house, doing things with my wife or the kids, doing active things. I got into rock climbing for about 5 or 7 years, then I stopped that. The thing I am particularly interested in now is windsurfing. I have a board, and Judy has a board, and we have a place down on the Eastern Shore on the water. I am learning that—and it's like anything—if you want to get good at it, you get a coach and get commitment. I found an

In January 1987, Tom Curren attended a *MoreTime* seminar on time and personal management. He counted it as a milestone in his life (see below). Here are some excerpts from his personal-management binder that was associated with that seminar and that Mr. Curren continues to maintain.

GOALS

Personal Development

Family
1. Define and be a couple.
2. Establish a close circle of mutually supporting friends and coaches.
3. The family of man.

Work
1. Help people realize their potential in some impactful way.
2. Obtain and keep the flexibility and resources of financial independence.
3. Experience, challenge, fun, and excitement.

Self
1. Time and place to experience adventure, action, in nature, wind, and water.
2. Time and place to experience simplicity, reflection, and regeneration (drawing, poetry, and meditation).
3. Appreciate myself and richness in life and spirit.

Mr. Curren said that he reviewed these goals and their attributes and weekly expressions (past, current, and planned for next) at least once every 2 weeks. He also noted that he had longer-term objectives, but that they didn't have the power of the weekly goals.

EXHIBIT 6-2   Excerpts from and Commentary About Tom Curren's *MoreTime* Book

instructor in the D.C. area, and he is giving me some lessons. I am just learning to do it. It is tremendously exhilarating."

THE EMOTIONAL SIDE OF TOM CURREN

"For a long while, I had a tremendous lack of self-confidence and self-awareness. I viewed myself as this kid who was lonely and who really, in many ways, wasn't encouraged to express his feelings, to express anger, or to be in a lot of activities. I got a lot of things, I developed a lot of good core values, but I think I didn't really . . . it was something in my early life that really seemed to me that I was within this box, and it created a very limited view of myself. I developed this view that I was different, primarily in a negative way.

"Most people would say, 'Oh, you're pretty good! You succeed at this, you succeed at that, you do this, you take up rock climbing, you're a 5.8 lead climber, you take up this sport and that activity.' People tell you how good you are, and you get all this money and stuff. Yet I had this Mr. Magoo type of view, that I was just bumping through life.

"Finally, after about 20 years of this (I am 45), when I was 40, I began to look at the last 20 years and say, 'There isn't much evidence for this view of myself as sort of a wimpy loser.' Psychologically, I had to develop the self-confidence and a sense of being and awareness.

"Early on I was very careful not to compete head-on. I think that that's accounted for a lot of my success, because I've chosen areas that others didn't have staked out. I chose a niche in Marriott, for example. Nobody had this area staked out, and I just did it and sort of expanded it. Now, if you talk to people here, the senior executives that have worked for me will cite as a strength that I get along with everybody. I am clearly a team player, because I don't have line-management ambitions. I'm not jockeying for their jobs or involved in the politics of that. So, by being different I am sort of in a different game. It's almost an internal game.

"All this money and stature—I didn't seek this. It was a by-product of what I intrinsically wanted to do. And for a long time, I was naive about what I had. Now I am a little more responsible in terms of recognizing my position and the obligations it entails. I have to be careful of what I say. You can say something to a junior person, and they take it to heart. I didn't understand that at first but evolved into that.

"I think psychologically one of the things that I have been working a great deal on is anger. How to handle anger. I used to think anger was a bad thing. The idea of the positive uses of anger was totally new. I've been working on some things there."

ON FINANCES

"When my mom remarried, she married somebody whom I view as a successful businessman. I don't know whether he would be middle class or upper middle class. We had a nice house, we had some horses. He commuted into New York. We could take vacations. We weren't wealthy, but comfortable. It was comfortable enough to send me off to private school and so forth. I think to the extent that I thought about money, I thought, 'Well, that's a nice lifestyle; I would like to make that much money.' I've made more money than I ever expected to. Money is great because you can do things with it. I've learned not to talk about it because being well-off is something that has

a tendency to isolate you from other people because there's a jealousy, a resentment, and so forth. But it is nice to be able to not worry about money and essentially to live your life free of money worries.

"I have never been centered on having the material things; have always been centered on having experiences. More and more, that is where my life is centered. It is easy to say the BMW and the nice houses and everything don't matter; I can do it. Sure, I like those, but that doesn't seem to be where the action is.

"For me it was luck. Just luck. I mean *luck!* I picked Marriott, the first options on the stock were $2, now the stock is at $40. I have made a lot of money on stock options. That is how you become wealthy. I became well-to-do because I am one of the top ten people in the tenth biggest employer in the country. So it is a big, successful company, and they pay competitively."

THE PHYSICAL SIDE OF TOM CURREN

"I haven't always been physically active. Up until college, I wasn't. In college, I became a little more active. I played some intramural things. But I didn't put much energy into that and didn't imagine myself as much of an athlete. I think after working in New York 4 or 5 years, I was 29 years old, and I realized: I am not getting any exercise. If this trend continues, this isn't so good. I met a doctor at a party who said he ran. Back then, in 1971 or 1972, running was not a big thing. We lived up next to Central Park. He ran around the reservoir, which is 1.6 miles on a cinder track, and so he said, 'Try running.' There weren't any running shoes out then, you just went out. So for about 2 years, I ran this one lap, and I sure wasn't going to try a second lap, and I thought, 'Running a mile! The whole concept seems so long. What happens if I get tired and stop on the West Side? I'll be late for work!' Then, one day I just ran the second lap. 'Hey, this is no big deal!'

"When I think in terms of fitness, I have always run. I have enjoyed running, and I haven't let it get into a big competitive thing. I run maybe three times a week. I ran 5 miles this morning. I run 4 to 6 miles. Last winter, I thought I'd push my running times to see how fast I could run. I thought, 'If I am going to be out here, I might as well see how fast I can run.' I noticed my times were just, for me, phenomenally fast times. Running 6 miles at a 6.52 pace. For me, really fast. So I entered some 10Ks [10-kilometer races]. I did it more as a socialization thing, to run with a friend. I am trying not to get caught up in competitive running and running becoming something where I've got to work on my times and everything else.

"I've always been interested in the mountains. The first time I went to Switzerland, I saw the mountains, and I said, 'This is where I've got to be.' I dropped everything and found a mountain-climbing school and spent a couple of weeks in Switzerland and learned some basics of climbing, how to cut ice steps in glaciers and basic mountaineering. I really liked that.

"Clearly, in technical climbing you get in situations where, if you slip, you are dead. You don't consciously seek those situations, but you reach dicey points where you basically can only go forward rather than back. And the level of concentration and thrill of operating at that level is just . . . you are alive then, and it's almost like your sense of . . . your visual acuity and sensual acuity dial up tenfold, and you can see things and you are aware of things that you are not aware of in everyday life. That is the part of rock climbing that I really enjoy."

Nutrition

"One of the things I began doing was I started changing my health habits. In the last 2 years, I have started changing what I eat and drink. Two years ago, September 1986, I shifted to fruit in the morning. That's all we have in the morning is fruit and fresh orange juice. And I stopped drinking coffee. And I found the combination of those two things just made a huge difference in my energy level and just general sense of aliveness and well-being. It is just amazing.

"I've realized that I can't do anything in moderation. I am all gas and no brakes. So, in terms of things like drinking, it is hard for me to drink in moderation. When I drink, I like to drink. So, when I open wine with dinner, I will drink the whole bottle of wine. If I am at a party, I'll drink martinis as fast as I am drinking Seven-Up. I am not one of these people that sip on it. So what I found myself doing was constantly putting in rules that I could live by: I won't drink during the week this and that. Then I found I was always struggling with exceptions to the rules. So finally, May 10, 1988, I just stopped drinking, because it was too much of a concern. I was drinking with concern. So I stopped. I don't miss it at all. The problem is I have been a wine freak for the last 20 years, so I have this cellar of all this Bordeaux that's pretty good stuff. Maybe for a great wine I will have a sip. I would like to learn moderation and balance, and I don't do that very easily.

"Judy and I are pretty much together on our view on health. She switched over to fruit. I dropped coffee, then she dropped coffee. She still drinks; she probably has two drinks a week. You know, again, there is a technology solution. You can get those things that inject nitrogen into the wine bottles, and it will store the wine for months at a time. We got one of those, so you open a bottle of wine, put this thing in it that shoots nitrogen in it. You can buy an expensive wine and just keep it, and it will last months. I found for me to try to limit the drinking—and saying what are the rules—didn't work. I have tried that. I slowly creep back into more and more, so I found that the thing I wanted to do is not drink.

"It's like smoking. I started smoking in college (and I didn't smoke in high school because I was in boarding school). By the beginning of sophomore year, I was up to three packs of Luckys a day. I was smoking two packs, and then during [fraternity] rush weeks, I was up to three packs. I was lighting three packs, I wasn't smoking them all. I remember I would smoke a cigarette before I got out of bed. So again, I quit, I only meant to quit for a week to be back to two packs. But after a week, I said what the heck, I'll stay off it. So, what I found is, I found myself eliminating coffee, I found myself going to fruit in the morning, I found myself cutting down drinking and then eliminating it entirely.

"I didn't intend to, in the sense of writing it down as a goal. So the goal was fitness and making choices and being 'available.' If I have a half bottle of wine on a Wednesday night and it's 9:00 P.M., I am shot for the night. I am shot whether I want to work, I am shot whether I want to watch television, you know. I wanted more control over my life. I wanted to make the choices and found that those things limited my energy. I also found I need a lot of energy for what I want to do. I want to be resourceful. I want to not take in a lot of stuff that hinders that."

WORKING IN THE COMMUNITY

"I have never had much of a feeling that I have to, that I want to, give anything to society at large or to the community at large. I have always had a very strong belief in personal ethics and treating people that I come in contact with well. But world hunger, the bigger issues, I just never had a feeling for, although this is beginning to change somewhat. It's not because of my values as a human being and that I don't care about them. Maybe it's that I don't see that I can do anything about it, or it doesn't touch me the way it does some people. But individuals, people I can see and work with, yes, I work with them."

COSMOLOGY

"I have always found religion in nature—in the stars, in the water, in the rock. Sunday night, I was down on the Eastern Shore, and a gale came through. I went out on our dock, and it was mind blowing. I don't know what the wind was; it must have been 40 miles an hour; it was enough to knock over heavy furniture. It was blowing through, and the waves! It was just like the Red Sea was about to part! The lightning and the waves! I get a real sense of being in a relationship to that.

"I went out in it and put my fists up— you know, 'I'm ready to take you on!' Yeah, I really relate to that. I feel a power. If you go to Yosemite, if you go to the bottom of El Capitan. (El Capitan is the largest exposed piece of granite in the world, 3,000 feet straight up.) You go up, and you put your hand on that rock. I can feel the power in that rock. Maybe that's why I like to climb.

"I think in a religious sense I was very influenced by Scott Peck and his book *The Road Less Traveled.* And I was particularly affected by his section on 'Grace.' In fact, I was reading and rereading it on the plane this last January. I finished that section on grace and realized I was a Christian. Up until that time, this business of Christ and . . . you know, I couldn't understand it. The Son of Man thing never made any sense to me, and I realized then 'grace,' and I realized what the human spirit is trying to be and how it relates, and all of a sudden it hit me. But I'm not a member of an organized religion."

ON LEADERSHIP

"Having the vision, and then knowing what it takes, having the skills to enroll people in your vision or in your commitment; figuring out what needs to be done to get everyone going in the same way—that's leadership. Five years ago, I would have just said, 'It's all in my head, and I'll sort of figure it out. I'll do the technical work, and I'll figure it out.' I like figuring it out. But I have realized now I can see some things before other people sometimes—see them—and that's a very powerful thing: to enroll people in the vision and get them aligned so that all the arrows are going the same way."

ON BEING ORGANIZED

"I am pretty organized, and I spend time constantly working on devices to facilitate that. I hope the intent of these systems is to free me for the other more important areas of my life. You don't want people to get hung up in correlation analysis just because they like r-squares. I don't want to get hung up with the systems that get in the way of everything else. Nevertheless, I find myself investing a lot in and constantly developing and refining systems. I found, for me, the *MoreTime* system—and others I presume are comparable—was literally revolutionary. (I've since converted to Franklin Planner.) It was for me partially a calendar-management system, but what it really was was an energy-management system. The issue wasn't time; it was energy.

"The biggest drag on energy is an incomplete thought. So what you want to do is decrease the cycle time from the time you have a thought till it's dealt with. And it is dealt with either by writing it down, by setting a date to deal with it, by completing it, or by dropping it. You don't want to have anything left around uncompleted. It's like a computer with stuff in its core and it should be dumped into archive. You don't want to have anything in your mind that you are thinking about that you haven't resolved. That was the principle I got out of that.

"So I took *MoreTime* [a time and life management seminar]. (See Exhibit 6-3.) Affiliated with that was working through some goals and exercises in terms of incom-plete things in your life, things you meant to do and haven't been doing—people you meant to talk to, things you meant to say, and ways you want to be, etc. Once you go through that, you dump that out and just handle it. Now, again, it doesn't mean that you have to be compulsive and do it all that week, but I lost 10 pounds 6 months after I took *MoreTime* and dropped 2 hours sleep a night. I used to think I needed 7 hours sleep. It was an attitude, so that if I would wake up in the morning and only have 6½ hours of sleep, I'd say, 'I've only had 6½ hours of sleep; I must be tired.' [In this *MoreTime* program] you basically shift to a different attitude, so that, after the seminar, I would get only 4, 5, or 6 hours.

"I would be up at 1:00 in the morning working on these principles [of getting rid of the unnecessary], carrying old clothes out and throwing them in the Dumpster, suits that I had bought and never worn. You open your closet and you say, 'I wish I hadn't bought that suit,' you know. Get rid of it! Throw it away! So I did a lot of that, a lot of letters to people—things I wanted to say to them. I cleaned a lot of things out.

"I found a guy now that is doing some custom programming work—in effect, computerizing a *MoreTime* system. I'll be going on that in August. (See Exhibit 6-2.) So I'm always looking for devices that facilitate. (See Exhibit 6-3.) These [devices] are not just task oriented. I realized that there are about 100 people in this company I need to talk to on a regular basis. Some I need to talk to, like Bill Marriott, on a 2-week cycle and some on a 9-month cycle. So I have that list of people and try to schedule eight a week. I don't always make it, but I am always pushing out.

"What I do in those interviews is I let them know they are important and valued. I let them know what I am doing. I take the opportunity almost serendipitously to talk to them. It's incredible the amount of

Here are a list of the more prominent books, programs, and tapes that Tom Curren had either read recently or kept in his office for close reference. He starred the ones he especially recommended.

INFLUENTIAL BOOKS

*1. *Unlimited Power, the New Science of Personal Achievement,* Anthony Robbins, Simon & Schuster.
*2. *A Book for Couples,* Hugh and Gayle Prather, Doubleday.
*3. *The Road Less Traveled,* Scott Peck, Simon & Schuster.
*4. *The Franklin Time Control System,* Franklin Institute, 801-975-1776.
 5. *Designing Quality and Balance into Your Life, Work and Play,* Jack Riley, Wilderness Press.
 6. *A Brief History of Time,* Stephen W. Hawkins, Bantam.
 7. *Precision, a New Approach to Communication,* McMaster and Grinder Precision Models.
 8. *The Emotional Hostage, Rescuing Your Emotional Life,* Leslie Cameron-Bandler, Future Pace.
 9. *The Power of Myth,* Joseph Campbell with Bill Moyers, Doubleday (Also a PBS series.)
10. *Influencing with Integrity,* Genie Z. LaBorde, Sytony Publishing.
11. *Use Both Sides of Your Brain,* Tony Buzan, E.P. Dutton.
12. *The New Rational Manager,* Kepner and Tregoe, Princeton Research Press.
13. *Staying Supple: The Bountiful Pleasures of Stretching,* John Jerome, Bantam.
14. *Getting to Yes: Negotiating Agreement Without Giving In,* Roger Fisher and William Ury.

INFLUENTIAL SOFTWARE

*1. *Max Think, Idea Processor,* Neil Larson, 415-428-0104.
*2. *Manage Your Money,* Meca Ventures, Inc., 203-222-9087.

INFLUENTIAL TAPES

 1. Erickson Institute, Berkeley, California 415-526-6846, ask for catalogue. I recommend Self-Hypnosis, Deep Self Appreciation.

EXHIBIT 6-3   Devices That Facilitate

serendipity that comes up in these interviews. Both between me and them, or me getting an idea from one person and then from an interview later in the week; I am seeing somebody entirely different and get that same idea. So I found it helped from a business standpoint."

ON BURNOUT

"I burn out all the time. I become overwhelmed and get myself in a position where the world seems like there's all this that has to be done now, and I am the only one that can do it, and I can't do it all, and I am not getting anything out of it. And you hit burnout, you hit 'overwhelm.' There're different layers and approaches to managing that. There is an immediate way, which gets you out of it, and then you have to do some longer-term things.

"The immediate things you do are, first, you have to go through a mental shift and move from things that must be done and ought to be done to things that you want to do. You have to shift from things that should be done yesterday to extending the time frame. Then, you say, 'I haven't done this yet, I'm not yet there.' You shift from a point where you are seeing what you haven't done to fully appreciating what you have done. You look at your schedule and

> "I have a little project management system here [in his *MoreTime* book], which is a modification of a Focus program. I put into it different projects, and it automatically sorts them by priority, by date, by whose the lead responsibility is, and then up to ten people that are involved. I print them out all different ways—by priority, by date. If I am going in to see Bill Marriott or another executive, I just print out the printout that has all the things that would involve him—an automatic little checklist; it's a real fast facilitator. I give one to my direct reports so they will know where I am and what the priority is. And when they are complete, I mark them complete, and then they go into archive, and I can print them out. I can print out everything I have done in the last 6 months, 12 months, and look at it. So that's a tool that helps."

Conceptual Notes from Books and Other Sources

(In this section, Tom had summary notes from the better books he'd read.)

EXHIBIT 6-4   Project-Management System

reblock things. You relook at what you're delegating; you go back to your core values.

"I get overwhelmed at least once a month, but what I am able to do, now, because I'm doing so much work now in the technical structure of emotions (you know, What is anger? What is loneliness? What is feeling overwhelmed?) that I put in gear neurolinguistic programming. You take the problem, you separate from it, you send it to the moon—you slingshot it. I am trying to reach the point where I can mentally make shifts.

"Now, longer term what you do is you step back and you say, 'I'm taking on too much.' One of the things I am trying to do with this Tuesday and Thursday morning thing is to protect some blocks of time. Patty [his secretary] is better at that than I am, because I schedule stuff in there. But she will protect those two mornings, and that is very important for me. So I just, you know, have some time with nothing to do."

ON HIS WIFE

[Talking about his wife, Mr. Curren's voice wavered, his eyes misted over.] "With regard to Judy . . . I think that is emotional for me because it is such an important relationship to me, such an important relationship to both of us—and not always an easy one. I've found the problems in personal life are more difficult than the problems at work, because there is more emotional investment in my personal relationships. The closer you are to somebody—and the more you get out of it—the more they can hurt you. There's a personal intensity in that relationship that's like no other relationship I have.

"One of the things I have realized is she tends to be cynical about things, and rather than that being a negative, I recently discovered how useful that is, because it is always good to have somebody to tell you what's wrong with something. Then she will come around and think of the positive. But she will always hit with the mismatch rather than the match.

"How to describe Judy? This is one of these questions where I can do all this work on intellectualizing her personality traits, and I can tell you what her Myers Briggs [a common personality test] is and this and that and about perfectionism and all the tendencies and scales. But when it comes down to it, I just, I don't know . . . I'm just viscerally attracted to her. There's something about her components, physically, and her personality that I am just *attracted* to."

ON BUSINESS SCHOOL EDUCATION

"I agree with the general notion that work prior to business school makes the academic experience much more helpful. In fact, I

In his *MoreTime* book, Tom Curren maintained a list of milestones, events that he thought significant in his life. This list was begun in 1986 and is shown below with excerpts from his commentary shown in parentheses.

September 1986   Read Tony Robbins, *Unlimited Power.* (Probably is the most influential single book I have ever read. Basically, Robbins is a popular packager of a lot of these sort of self-development ideas. In one book, he hits diet, neurolinguistic programming, all these positive ways of thinking about things. I found it really tremendous.)

September 1986   Began Fit-for-Life Diet. [See "The Physical Side of Tom Curren" in text for detail.]

October 1986   Stopped drinking in October 1986 and went back on again, went off again. Then, finally off completely on May 10, 1988.

January 1987   Took *MoreTime* seminar. (I literally dropped 2 hours a night out of sleep. That was just mind boggling!)

March 1987   Judy resigned from Marriott. (She worked at Marriott for a while. She was a very successful executive, vice president of marketing. She took *MoreTime* and said, 'Heck this [working at Marriott] doesn't fit my goals,' so she quit, and we went to China for a month. We said, 'Let's go somewhere,' so we went to China. It was just great. We spent a month in mainland China.)

October 1987   Got reading glasses. (I have contacts, and if I take my contacts out, I don't need either. But when I have my contacts in, I need them.)

October 1987   Bought Oxford house. (We decided to buy a house in Oxford on the Eastern Shore, which Judy just renovated. It is a tremendous haven.)

November 1987   Had a big burnout. (Regrouped and recovered from that.)

November 1987   Ran 6 miles at a 6:52 pace. (I thought that was pretty good.)

January 26, 1988   Grace. (Got the concept of 'grace,' amazing grace, and really became a Christian.)

March 1988   Acupuncture. (I tried acupuncture five times. Didn't do much as far as I can tell.)

March 1988   Forum. (I took the Forum. It involves two weekends. Sponsored by Werner Erhard, an outgrowth and improvement on his EST program. If you take Robbins's seminar, take his weekend seminar. You will walk on fire, you'll walk on hot coals. I mean, I know I can walk on hot coals! I didn't need to prove that. The Forum has more power than that.)

EXHIBIT 6-5   Milestones

would say work experience and travel experience during college are things I certainly am going to encourage my kids to do. A semester abroad, not to go right from senior year into college or not go right from college into work. To take that time off is really important—and particularly if you are committed to something. I don't care whether you are committed to being a rock musician or you're committed to the world hunger project or you're committed to washing cars, so long as you want to have the best car finish in the country. Go and pursue it and, particularly, break up that academic experience.

"I would use business school as a time to—if there is any science to business, don't forget to learn the science while you are in business school. In other words, don't forget to take a basic statistics course. Don't forget to do work in how to think or clear writing, basic economics, or basic finance. You need a fundamental liberal arts part to the curriculum.

"In terms of looking for a job, I'd give the advice that I gave myself, which is, fundamentally, look for opportunities where you can learn. Have flexibility in as many areas of your life as you can. Drop any preconceived notions about certain industries. If you have the advantage of being willing to move and live in a lot of different countries, including lousy cities, think of what is really important—and if learning is really important, both learning from the people that you will be with and from the context that you will be with, you know, *go* for that. That's what I would go for. Forget about the money and everything else. Don't paint yourself in a box, in that you learn some specialty in a dying industry, but in your area of interest, ask how you're going to learn and what job will give you the most learning, and look at it realistically as a 2- to 3-year time commitment. That's the way I look at things."

IN CONCLUSION

"I think I am a person that is interested in solving problems and developing people, and my current job is a context in which I can do that and have done that very successfully. I am a person that is struggling with spiritual issues and psychological issues and recognizing that, as Peck says, 'Life is difficult because it is fundamentally overcoming a series of problems.' And there's no life without problems. But once you have recognized that, it's no longer a problem. [Laughter.] That's what it's about, you know.

"I'll try anything that I think will help me develop. Yeah, I'll try anything. I have always done risky stuff; in college I did skydiving. I just do it for the experiences . . . I don't know.

"I did this interview for three reasons. One, I am interested in developing people and if this is a way that some of the things I have done can be useful, match or mismatch, negative role model or positive, then good. Some of the things I have done I think could be useful to other people.

"Two, I'm interested in learning about myself, and frequently you don't learn about yourself unless you articulate it. Seeing it and getting it in play, you learn about yourself.

"Three, I've sort of got an ego. It's not a bad idea to make a movie about you and sort of hope, on balance, it's positive." ∎

Case 7   Peter Woodson (A)

Professor Ben Dempsey listened intently to his friend and client. Peter Woodson was not hard to listen to, because his style of talking was quite engaging. The topic of the evening's discussion, which the two men were having during the 1989 Milford Electronics annual conference, was Woodson's perceptions of his 25-year career with Milford Electronics—a career that led Woodson to the inner circle of company key executives.

Milford Electronics had been created by Franklin Milford, the father of the present chairman, Marshall Milford. Many considered Marshall Milford one of the most innovative and focused executives in the entire country. Milford Electronics was an industry leader in technology, innovation, and quality. The success of the company in the quality area was such that leaders of organizations around the United States visited the company on a regular basis to learn about the Milford quality process.

Milford Electronics was a privately held company, and the energies and aspirations of Marshall Milford clearly dominated company culture. Marshall Milford had been the chairman of Milford for well over 40 years. During that time, he had reinvested most of the profits of the organization into research, development, technology, and facilities. He expected competence, dedication, and loyalty from his employees. In return, they were well paid and provided with the best possible support equipment and facilities.

Peter Woodson's career clearly had been one of continuous success. He had joined Milford right out of college, and with a brief interruption for military service, had spent his entire career with the company. Woodson's personality and that of Marshall Milford fit well together, and it was not long before he became noticed in the company. Like others in the company, Woodson had been moved from line to staff and back to line positions on a regular basis. He had always performed well.

A few years before the current conversation with Dempsey, Woodson had considered himself to be the logical candidate to become Milford's president. That possibility ended, however, when Marshall Milford selected another executive, Sam Mills.

Woodson was hurt by the decision, because he believed that his efforts and abilities were more than sufficient to warrant his promotion to the presidency. He also was aware that his decision to divorce and remarry had violated Marshall Milford's expectations of how senior officers in the company should behave. This event may well have eliminated his chances for further promotion in the company. Somehow, he felt these private decisions should not have made a difference, but he believed they had been the issue.

Woodson recounted all this background information to Dempsey as they talked. He also commented on how much he had enjoyed being the Human Resource vice president and the contributions he thought his organization had made during the past few years. Just before the evening conversation ended, Woodson said, "I have

This case was written by Alexander B. Horniman, Professor of Business Administration. This case was written as a basis for class discussion rather than to illustrate effective or ineffective handling of an administrative situation.

really loved the past few years, but somehow not making it to the top troubles me. Oh, I know I am one of the trusted 'inner circle,' but it's not the same as being the president. Now don't get me wrong, I think Sam has done a great job. But!

"You know I'm 50 years old, and I'm not getting any younger. Maybe I should retire. I'm sure I could go out and do a number of things. What do you think? Is it time for a change?" ■

Case 8   Greenland

In May 1991, four Norwegians crossed the island of Greenland from Angmagssalik on the east coast to Søndre Strømfjord on the west coast, a trek of 650 km (394 miles), unsupported[1] and in only 13 days. The team broke an unofficial record of crossing this particular track by more than 10 days. The *average* time for this track without support of any kind had been 42 days. The expedition carried food for 20 days, and fortunately, at the beginning, experienced the finest weather one can expect in May in Greenland: sunny skies, $-5°C$ (28°F), and no wind. During the crossing, however, the expedition was exposed to the normal harsh environment of Greenland. Cold temperatures and high winds brought the windchill factor to as low as $-61°C$ ($-78°F$). Snow and whiteouts made the days endlessly long and tiring. What follows is a description of what happened, why these four young men went on this expedition, and what they learned from it as seen through the eyes of one of them.

Greenland, the largest island in the world, is more than three times larger than Texas and longer than the distance from New York City to Denver. The island is bowl-shaped with a low inland plateau surrounded by coastal mountains. A sheet of permanent ice covers the plateau, which occupies 1,833,900 square kilometers or more than 80 percent of the island.[2] The coldest region of Greenland is at the center of the plateau ice cap, where temperatures average $-47°C$ ($-53°F$) in February and $-11°C$ (12°F) in July. Because of the climate, the inland ice cap is totally deserted; no human or animal life exists. More people have climbed Mount Everest than have successfully crossed Greenland unsupported. Exhibit 8-1 shows previous expeditions from Angmagssalik to Søndre Strømfjord.

COMMITMENT AND PLANNING

The expedition began forming in late summer of 1990. Initially, seven or eight persons were interested in participating. As plans progressed, the number dropped to four:

Odd Harald Hauge (35), chief financial editor of Norway's largest newspaper, *Aftenposten*. Born in 1956 in Kristiansand. Finished gymnasium[3] top of class. Served his mandatory military service in the Coastal Artillery, top of class. M.B.A. from one of Norway's best business schools, Norges Handelshøyskole, in 1980. Journalist and later chief editor of one of Norway's biggest financial magazines, *Kapital,* from 1980–1991. Director of corporate finance in Merchant Bank FIBA in Oslo, 1991–1993. Chief financial editor of *Aftenposten* from 1993. Has written two unauthorized biographies of some of Norway's richest and most

UVA-OB-0581

This case was written by Morten Lie. Copyright © 1994 by the University of Virginia, Darden School Foundation, Charlottesville, VA. All rights reserved.

[1]In arctic expeditions, *unsupported* means "without any help from the outside and also without any support from dogs, sails, airdrops or anything else." All the equipment for the whole expedition is carried by the members from the start.

[2]708,760 square miles.

[3]Gymnasium: A secondary school that prepares students for university. Gymnasium is a 3-year education after the compulsory 9 years of school.

Year	Country	Number of days	Comments
1931	ENGLAND	63	DOGS
1966	SCOTLAND	36	SAILS, FIRST WOMAN
1966	FINLAND	38	DOGS
1968	NORWAY	24	DOGS
1973	NORWAY	23	DOGS
1975	JAPAN	53	
1980	USA	50	
1981	FINLAND/NORWAY	26	SAILS
1982	ENGLAND	44	
1983	NORWAY	26	PARACHUTES
1984	CZECK	40	
1986	SPAIN	42	
1987	ENGLAND	30	SAILS/PARACHUTES
1988	SPAIN	26	
1988	SWEDEN	41	
1990	NORWAY	26	DOGS
1991	NORWAY	30	
1991	NORWAY	13	(The present expedition)
1991	NORWAY	15	VEGARD ULVANG (Also May 1991)

Average Time for First 17 Expeditions: 36 days
Average for Unsupported Expeditions: 42 days
(Before our expedition)

EXHIBIT 8-I Greenland Crossing Expeditions: Angmassalik—Søndre Strømfjord

influential businessmen. After Greenland, Harald was the first to cross the island of Spitsbergen from north to south. He plans to lead an expedition to the South Pole with a physically disabled Norwegian (Cato Zahl Pedersen) in 1994. Harald has been married twice to the same woman (divorced in Greenland in 1991). One child.

Ivar Erik Tollefsen (30), an entrepreneur. Born in 1961, grew up in Asker, a suburb of Oslo. Found school to be boring and too slow for him. After he started his own public company in 1980, he did not have time to finish gymnasium and dropped out when he had 3 months left. At 24, he sold his company for $3 million. Went bankrupt when he was 27, with

$1 million in debt. In 1986, one of his British suppliers got involved in organized crime in Britain. Ivar was kidnapped and held for ransom. He managed to escape and became the prosecutor's key witness. The accused were found guilty, and the group was broken up. During this period, Ivar and his family received threats on their lives, so he had police protection and personal bodyguards from the antiterrorist police for more than a year. After Greenland, Ivar organized two other expeditions. He climbed five mountains, each the highest on its continent, in April 1992. In December 1993, he went on to climb several previously unclimbed mountains in Queen Mauds Land in Antarctica. Ivar is divorced with two children from that marriage and has another child from a second broken relationship.

Bård Stokkan (31), an IBM operator and customer-support representative. Born in 1960 in Trondheim. After a short stay in Stockholm, his family moved to Asker. After the compulsory 9 years of school, Bård mustered on the Norwegian full-rigged school ship, *Christian Radich.* After serving 6 months on the ship, he got a "temporary" job at IBM that lasted 17 years. Bård did his mandatory military service in the Royal Norwegian Air Force as a radar operator in northern Norway. Bård accompanied Ivar on his two expeditions after Greenland. Bård is unmarried with no children.

Morten Lie (28), a lieutenant commander in the Royal Norwegian Navy. Born in 1962 and grew up in Asker. Father died when Morten was 14 years old. Exchange student in Sacramento, California, from 1978–1979. After graduating from gymnasium in 1982 at the top of his class, he was accepted into the Royal Norwegian Naval Academy. After graduating from the academy in 1986 (third in his class) with a major in economics, he served as supply officer and substituting executive officer on fast patrol boats for 2 years, as a financial officer in NATO for 18 months, and at Norwegian Defense Headquarters for 12 months. Based on merit, he was a special appointee with temporary rank of naval commander to a federal Strategic Defense Study in 1991, where he worked as a strategic analyst. He held this position until entering Darden in 1992. He got his M.B.A. in 1994. Unmarried, no children.

Our first preparation for Greenland was to find a climbing instructor who could teach us as much as possible in a short time.

All advertised climbing courses were booked, so we had to get a friend to teach us. During a couple of weekends, we made great progress. We felt ready to take on the Norwegian mountains. Every other weekend we took off right after work and were usually not back before early Monday morning. Winter days in Norway are short; the sun rises at 9 A.M. and sets at 3 P.M. We managed with headlights to average 12 to 15 hours a day, most of which were in the dark. We climbed close to 50 mountains that winter. Looking back, this may have been the greatest key to our success. We got used to long hours and long days. The Norwegian winter can be extremely severe. The weather during some of these trips was far more dangerous and harsh than we were ever going to experience in Greenland, and hands, faces, and feet all got frostbitten. We learned to take care of our bodies and also to take care of each other. Frostbite on your face is one example of something a friend can detect easier than you can.

We also got the chance to test a lot of equipment during these trips. We were extremely humble. We asked friends and strangers who had any arctic or polar experience about equipment, routes, techniques, and anything else we could think of. We never took any advice as more than advice. We tested equipment and found some to be unusable and some to be adequate. We invented other equipment and techniques ourselves.

Navigation in polar regions is unique. You cannot use your compass efficiently owing to the closeness of the magnetic poles, and, especially in Greenland, you cannot navigate optically by looking at the landscape. A global positioning system (GPS) was borrowed from the U.S. Navy.[4] It would

---

[4]GPS is a system built and operated by the U.S. Navy. The system consists of 24 satellites in orbit. At any time, 21 are supposed to be operational. By receiving signals from three satellites at the same time, a GPS receiver—the size of a calculator—can give you exact position, plus or minus 30 feet.

prove to be highly successful after we made some modifications to the power supply.

The preparations took time. Permits had to be collected. Insurance and guarantees (for rescue operations) had to be obtained. Tickets and equipment had to be purchased and tested. Finally, we had to answer all the questions from friends, colleagues, and family as to why we were doing this. No one believed we could pull it off. Not even the most optimistic person thought that the four of us could do it. Crossing Greenland is an accomplishment in itself. Most people fail. Our goal was not only to cross it, but to do it faster than anyone else had. Initially, the goal had been around 20 days. The previous record for an unsupported crossing was 26 days (23, supported). During the summer of 1990, someone had almost managed to cross the inland ice cap in 12 days, but had to turn back and be rescued before reaching the west coast. In our own minds, we knew that the inland ice cap could be crossed in 20 days and possibly less.

In retrospect, I learned how important proper preparations are. Roald Amundsen—a Norwegian polar explorer, the first to navigate the Northwest Passage (1903–1906), the first to reach the South Pole (1911), and the first to fly over the arctic basin and the North Pole—once said, in a comment about Robert Scott (whom he beat in the famous race to the South Pole and who faced starvation and death on the way back, whereas Amundsen and his men put on weight and even fed their dogs chocolate on the return): "Victory awaits those who have everything worked out. It is called luck. Defeat is a sure consequence for those who have failed to take the necessary precautions in time. It is called misfortune."

What Amundsen is referring to is his extensive preparations. Scott failed to pre-

pare so well. Amundsen taught the world a lesson in polar expeditions that the world will never forget. He showed the world what could be achieved through careful preparations and a professional attitude toward challenges. In taking on a challenge, preparation is the key. Preparing for polar expeditions, as in all other tasks, means to prepare for the unexpected. It is leaving room for flexibility to alter the course of action if something happens. To try to find multiple uses for all your equipment and to still leave room for more flexibility. However, careful preparation must not be done in such a fashion that it paralyzes your action. Preparation and action together get results. You will not reach your goals if you neglect either of these.

During this period, I also learned how important it is to stick to one's goals. Since most people had doubts about our expedition, it would have been easy to pull out, save face, and get on with my life. The reason I kept on was the challenge. It is easy to go through life without sticking your neck out, but you do not gain much. Going through with the expedition meant sticking out my neck with the risk of getting it cut off. It meant possibly taking a blow to my ego and to my reputation. The expedition was as much about receiving recognition from others as it was for building my personal ego. Taking a risk means that you also have to face the possible downside. The question becomes whether you, in time, can face the downside and keep on going. In retrospect, we got the recognition. We boosted our egos. In the future, it will be easier to once again stick our necks out. It will also be easier to face the possible downside and failure. In order to get something, you have to take a chance. Something worth having seldom comes "floating on a piece of wood."

GREENLAND

We arrived in Angmagssalik, Greenland, on May 1, 1991. Our plan was to stay for a couple of days before being flown to our starting point. The village of Angmagssalik is the only major village on the east coast of Greenland. It has about 2,000 inhabitants and is mostly managed by Danes.

When we started planning for the trip, our original idea was to start our expedition from Angmagssalik, but in order to get to the inland ice, we had to cross a fjord 25 km wide. This year the weather had caused the fjord to be full of pack ice.[5] If it had been frozen, we could have skied across it. Had it been open water, we could have taken a boat. The pack ice prevented us from doing either, however, and our only transportation across would be by helicopter.

The year 1991 had seen a record number of expeditions trying to cross Greenland. Seven expeditions had received the necessary permission from the local authorities and police. We were the sixth expedition out. Before us, only one had been successful, completing the trek in 30 days. Three had been rescued under dramatic circumstances. We did not want to become the fourth.

The day we arrived, the weather turned against us, and we ended up spending 16 days stuck in Angmagssalik. Finally, on May 16, we got lucky. The weather improved, and we flew to our starting point.

More polar bears are shot on the east coast of Greenland than anywhere else on Earth, so our chances of meeting a polar bear were greater here than anywhere else on our route. In our permit from the local police to cross the ice, it was specifically stated that we could not bring any hand weapons into Greenland. The only firearm we would be allowed to bring to protect us against polar bears was a rifle. Because we thought that a rifle would be too heavy to carry across the ice, we had decided to take the chance and not bring anything. Ivar, who was the first to be flown to our starting point, had to wait for almost 3 hours for the rest of us. He was a little alarmed being in polar-bear country alone without a gun or rifle. Nothing was spotted, however, and we all camped safely after a hike of 15 km (9 miles) to our jumping-off point.

During those 15 km, we learned a valuable lesson. Throughout our training during the winter, we had tested the equipment for almost everything. Yet during those short 15 km, two of our sledge carabiners[6] broke. We had used the carabiners throughout the winter without any accidents. Now we were stuck with two broken ones. We fixed them with some climbing rope we had brought along in case one of us were to fall into any crevasses along the way. The improvised solution worked well for the rest of the trip.

If anything can go wrong, it will. Something unplanned will always happen. A plan must therefore be flexible enough for adjustments, and one must be prepared and willing to leave the plan in order to reach goals. A plan is just a draft of what one predicts the trail toward a goal will be. One also has to be willing to improvise, to encourage creative thinking, and to accept less than 100 percent solutions in order to reach goals and move on.

---

[5]Pack ice is a large area of floating ice, consisting of pieces that have become massed together.
[6]Sledge carabiners are used to attach the sledge and its pulling device to a backpack. They are like single chain links that can be opened, hooked onto something, and then locked.

MAY 17

The inland ice from Angmagssalik on the east coast to Søndre Strømfjord on the west coast is approximately 600 km (364 miles) wide. An additional 50 km (30 miles) on land has to be crossed on the west coast. The ice cap itself starts at about 800 to 1,200 meters (2,580 to 3,900 feet) above sea level on both sides. In the middle, the ice reaches altitudes of up to 3,000 meters (9,750 feet). Exhibit 8-2 shows a cross-sectional profile of our route.

The first day of our real journey finally had arrived. We were at sea level. Above us, the ice began at an altitude of about 1,000 meters (3,240 feet). The hardest part of the trip would be the first day or two. We were underway at 8 A.M. We chose an unplanned route. Our original route had crevasses, and because of poor weather and visibility in the morning, we chose a harder but safer route. By choosing a route with fewer crevasses, we also could traverse without being tied to a rope, which makes it easier to ski and move. To our delight, we have

not heard of anyone, either before or after us, who has taken this route. We may have been the first.

The day turned out to be beautiful and warm. After hiking for 12 hours, we camped at 1,200 meters. I was completely exhausted, and that day, I was definitely the weakest. I had leg cramps that would stay with me for the next 2 days. Physically, the last 600 meters was a walk through hell. Mentally, I felt pretty bad, too. I had not considered myself the weakest before we left. The first day had proved otherwise. I was feeling down but tried to cheer up by reminding myself that no one had ever traversed this glacier up to 1,200 meters in only 1 day. I should be allowed to be exhausted. Harald and Ivar did a fantastic job up front. They broke tracks the whole day. To this day, I have no idea where they found the energy to do so.

Our first real camp on the ice was established on May 17, Independence Day in Norway—a big celebration back home. Up here, there also would be one. All the guys

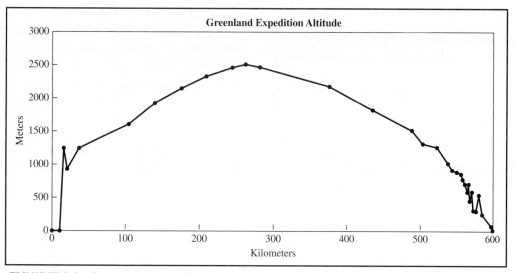

EXHIBIT 8-2   Greenland Expedition Altitude

had slipped a couple of beers into the sledge,[7] and they were consumed with dignity. A half bottle of cognac also was brought out. It had been classified as "medicine" by our excellent medicine man, Bård. Carefully, a shot the size of the cork was given to each one and a toast to Norway was given.

MAY 18

The weather couldn't have been worse; we were faced with a total whiteout.[8] This made it unsuitable to traverse through terrain that might have crevasses. Luckily, we had made enough progress the day before for us to feel fairly safe that we were out of the edge areas of the glacier, where there were too many crevasses. Owing to my leg cramps, we had to camp after only 20 km — a good day for other expeditions but behind schedule for ours. Again, I was disappointed by my own performance.

MAY 19

Up early. We decided to start the day earlier and possibly make up what we lost yesterday. Our equipment seems to be functioning perfectly. All sledges, including the repaired ones, are working as expected. Everyone had his own sledge. Because we expect that the last 50 km on the west coast will be without snow, we have to bring along a backpack.

Managing weight was an important part of our success. In order to save weight, we had modified the backpacks so we could pull our sledges with them; that way, the backpacks did not represent deadweight for the majority of the trip. This saved us

265 grams (0.58 pounds). Before leaving Norway, everyone had told us to take skis with steel edges because they increase the skis' strength. Only days before we left, however, Ivar had argued that skis without steel edges would be better because of better cross-country-skiing rhythm and because the terrain on the inland ice was almost flat, which would reduce significantly the chances of breaking or damaging a ski. We all agreed, and the skies functioned perfectly the whole trip: an excellent choice.

We also had done the same with our ski poles. Instead of steel poles that you can do almost anything with, we brought glass-carbon racing poles that are half the weight of steel poles. We did have to be more careful with them than we normally would be. They, too, worked out flawlessly throughout the expedition. You especially feel the benefits in your arms after 30 to 40 km a day of cross-country skiing. Instead of lifting 400 grams every other second, you lift only 200 grams, a big difference after 12 hours of skiing.

Taking on a new task, it is easy to follow in the footsteps of those who have done it before you. In order to do it better than the former, one must think "outside the box." Step back and think about the rationale behind what you are about to do. Peak performance comes from creative thinking.

Our food was also somewhat different from that of other expeditions. Breakfast consisted of a combination of high-energy cereal and infant formula mixed in water. The infant formula was brought along because it contained more vitamins and

---

[7]A sledge is a light, fiberglass frame drawn after you for transporting people or goods over snow.

[8]Whiteout is a weather condition well known to climbers and mountaineers, when everything around you turns white. You are not able to distinguish between heaven or earth. It is like walking in total darkness except that it is white instead of black. You lose your natural balance. In order to compensate, your muscles are much more tense, and you no longer are able to use your skiing skills efficiently. Also, everything around you changes shape and you feel like you are walking in a white canyon.

more minerals than dried milk. Lunch consisted of biscuits and chocolate bars. Dinner was dried food cooked together with a half pound of butter in order to get enough calories. The unusual food was the potato chips and the peanuts. Containing more fat and more calories than most people would like to think about, they were perfect for us even though we had to eat them with a spoon at the end of the expedition. We also mixed our water with high-energy sugar that turned the water into a sport drink similar to Gatorade. This gave us quick energy during the day.

MAY 20

We all have diarrhea, more or less. The last couple of days of extremely hard work have gotten to us all. The steep snowdrifts are not making it easier. They are constantly pulling us back, and the abdominals are taking a beating. Both Bård and I were forced to change underwear. We did not plan to bring extra underwear, but in our fast departure from Angmagssalik, we all forgot to take the extra pairs out of our backpacks. Now we are happy we did. In 10,000 years, maybe some archaeologist will find them and go crazy trying to figure out what people were doing up on the ice cap. Other than that, though, we have almost no garbage. In order to save weight, all the food was taken out of the boxes and, if possible, rewrapped in lighter material.

It is getting colder and colder as we move up the ice cap. The winds are picking up and the breaks are getting shorter and shorter. The cold is not too harsh when we are walking, which makes the skiing fairly comfortable. You move on the edge between being cold and sweating. As soon as you stop, you feel the cold, but it is important not to sweat. If you do, you freeze instantly upon stopping. It is a fine balance. The last 2 hours every day, we slow down in order to make sure that our clothes are not wet at the end of the day. By slowing down somewhat, the body heat helps to dry the inner clothes. We use the breaks to stretch out, answer the call of nature, and eat. Our backs are turned up against the wind to make it somewhat more pleasant. The breaks are down to 10 to 15 minutes every 2 hours.

As it gets colder and colder, it takes me longer and longer to get my feet warm in the morning. In the sleeping bag my feet are fine, and in the tent they are OK, but as soon as I put them in my boots, they feel like they will freeze into solid ice. For the rest of the expedition, it usually took me between 3 and 5 hours every day to get any feeling back into them.

MAY 21

Everyone is starting to get into the expedition. Even though we were together throughout last winter practicing and training, it takes some time to get everything to work perfectly. The team's spirit is high. We have been making major progress during the last few days, and we are back on a schedule of 20 days. The tone of our conversation is also fairly good. We don't say much during the day, but whenever we get a chance, we at least try. Everyone is fairly worn out when it comes time for camp. All we have time for is eating and getting as much sleep as possible in order to be back in shape for the next morning. Sleep is important. During the day, you wear your body down. Sleep and enough food help you recover somewhat during the night.

We lose some strength every day and start off each new day weaker than the day before. What else can you expect? Up here it is like running a marathon every day, 20 days in a row. At the end of a day, none of us is looking particularly pretty. Our eyes are like glass. Sallow and swollen. A clear sign of low blood sugar. In fact, our faces are swollen and sore. But who cares? We have adopted a couple of slogans for the expedition. One of them is, "This is not a beauty contest." Another is, "No time for tenderness."

A team is never stronger than the weakest component. At this point in the expedition, getting enough sleep is a question of safety. At the end of an expedition, you can always allow yourself to tap the last resources of your body because you know that you are near the end and that the possibility of unexpected events has decreased. At an early stage of any task, however, you have to make sure that the team will have enough strength and resources to finish.

We are taking turns cooking, and it's my turn. Cooking means less sleep and more work, but it also means you can take about 1.5 kilos off your sledge to make dinner. (Nothing comes for free.) We also have to melt enough snow for 12 to 15 liters of water to prevent dehydration. We need 3 to 4 liters every day. By urinating at least 1 liter a day, we know that we are drinking enough. This is an old, golden rule known to high-altitude climbers.

MAY 22

Most of the guys are starting to run out of toilet paper. The diarrhea has been bad. From now on, we have to use ice blocks instead of paper.

We also had our first conflict. We argued about how fast we should walk. I belive that the time frame is too tight and that we are not allowing ourselves enough sleep to recover from day to day. The probability of serious injuries also is increasing. Ivar thinks we can keep up the same speed. He is not as concerned about safety as I am. The argument is brief. Maybe 5 to 10 minutes. However, the ice is broken. Is this a

warning of something to come? I have never read about an Arctic expedition that didn't have some sort of conflict. Arctic expeditions place people in one of the worst physical conditions on Earth. The difficulties caused by terrain, weather, and isolation call for both physical and mental strength. The mental strain usually results in opposing views. We all knew that before we left. We had talked about it. Now, it was a reality. As it turned out, however, this was the first and the last argument we would have. The rest of the expedition we grew away from each other, but we did not have any more arguments.

The argument may have been a result of the members starting to tire out and injuries that were starting to show. When people are getting tired and worn out, their mental condition also worsens. Putting people under pressure physically will eventually also put them under pressure mentally. In a team, it is important to talk about the possibility of opposing views and conflicts that are likely to occur. Some conflict can be very good in order to get some mental "relief." Suppressed mental conditions can be lethal to team results and are possible "time bombs" that may explode and destroy all team spirit. It is better to let off the pressure a little at a time to avoid blowing your top. Discussing possible conflicts beforehand enables the team to deal with them in a more rational way when they occur. A mutual understanding that conflicts are not necessarily bad and that conflicts are seldom personal will make it easier for the team to overcome them.

All the talk about women also is gone. The first days, it was the favorite subject. Now, it is only occasional. I guess the body has shut down the production of testosterone. Survival is more important than reproduction.[9]

MAY 23

We talked to Bård's mother on the radio. She was on her way to the United States with Bård's father to attend Bård's brother's wedding. Bård was supposed to be his best man. We all felt the emotions flowing when we finally heard her voice over the radio. The plane was 350 km away, but the radio was working perfectly. It was the only time during the expedition that we had radio contact with the rest of the world. Behind us, we knew that Vegard Ulvang, three-time gold-medal winner in the Olympics, had started his expedition. No need to give him our position. He might speed up if he knew how fast we were progressing over the ice.

We also started to throw away some of the food today. A couple of breakfast rations each. We had made great progress over the last couple of days, and now we were on a schedule for 18 days: 162 km out of 600 were done. We knew that when we passed the top of the ice, the going would be easier. Eighteen days was within reach. We kept the dinner rations for the two extra days in case something were to happen and we needed backup.

It still is getting colder and colder, and being the last to enter the tent becomes more and more of a nightmare. Between the time the first one enters and the last one enters may take up to 20 to 25 minutes. The tent is not big enough for all of us to organize ourselves at the same time and if we all were to enter at the same time, the tent probably would be filled with snow. We do not want

that to happen. Exhibit 8-3 shows the temperatures we encountered during the trip.

I'm also getting closer and closer to Harald. Somehow, we have a lot to talk about. Then again, a lot is relative up here. We all sleep in and, once again, we all agree that it has been a good day.

In a team, beware of the subteams that may be formed. They can be devastating. We did not form subteams, but the right environment for subteams existed.

MAY 24

The guys are getting more and more tired. Harald is not a pretty sight anymore. His eyes look like the eyes of a deep-sea fish that has been dragged to the surface too fast. Then again, I realize that I probably do not look any better. I have had nosebleeds for a couple of days. I keep asking the guys if I have any blood on my face. They keep telling me no. Not until I saw my face in the mirror at the hotel in Søndre Strømfjord would I realize that they had been lying for the last 10 days.

MAY 25

I have finally managed to remember "Our Father." I have been trying to remember it for 2 days. Now I say it 20 times a day. My hip has been sore for the last 2 days. That is the reason for trying to remember the prayer. I have never been a frequent visitor to the church. I think I need some religion, however, in order to restore my hip to health.

---

[9]Unlike many other expeditions, ours did not have any scientific purpose. On an expedition on Greenland in 1988, a Norwegian doctor concluded that the production of testosterone was extremely low during the last part of the expedition. The conclusion is that the body is using that energy elsewhere. After returning to Norway, at least some of the guys in our expedition disappointed their girlfriends for a couple of days.

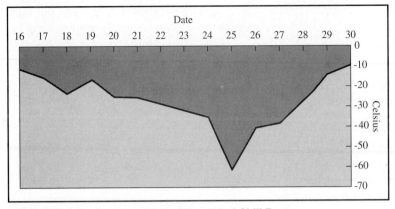

EXHIBIT 8-3   Greenland Expedition Wind Chill Factor

The weather is getting worse and worse. The last couple of days have been a nightmare. Whiteouts, increasing winds, and colder weather. Our faces are taking the worst beating. Our lips are breaking up, and the wind and the cold make our faces blow up. But again, "This is not a beauty contest."

The days are beginning to look alike. We get up. Take an hour to pack, eat, and get dressed. Then 2 hours on skis with 15 minutes each in front. Doing the front job is the hard part. Breaking the tracks can be hell if the snowdrifts are steep and the snow is deep. Being the number-four guy after you have been breaking tracks for 15 minutes is a relief. A 10 to 15 minute break. Then another 2 hours. We are usually on skis almost 10 hours every day. We are making very good progress, and some of the dinner rations are donated to scientific discovery down the road. We passed the top of the ice cap today. At least it looks like it on our GPS. The maps of Greenland are not very good. First of all, they are *all white.* All they show are some topographical contours, but the company that made them specifically states on the map that the contours are so bad, it takes no responsibility for their correctness. All in all, the maps are not reliable.

Harald and I stepped outside of the box today. Normally, we all walk in a straight line in order to save some energy. We took the time off, however, and walked next to each other for quite awhile. I guess the time for tenderness had come. I am never going to forget those moments. Definitely the best ones I had. "Stepping out" to care a little about people and feeling that someone wants to talk to you felt good.

When you are all worn out and tired, it is hard to take time off and sacrifice strength in order to take care of each other. But it is important. It builds the team. It builds confidence and trust in each other.

In the last 2 hours of the day, the weather cleared up. Almost no wind and no whiteout. With the clear weather, however, comes the cold. The temperature dropped to −30°C (−22°F) without the windchill, and the wind was not completely gone.

MAY 26

An awful day. The wind has picked up again, and we figure it to be a full storm. The whiteout is also back. Luckily, the wind comes from behind; that makes it a little better. Robert Scott once wrote about the South Pole in his diary, "God, what an awful place this is." I want to say the same about the inland ice as of today: "God, it's an awful place." The windchill factor drives the effective temperature down to −61°C (−78°F). Not a place meant for human beings.

At noon we discovered that our tent poles were missing. We had lost them. We debated for a couple of minutes. We decide to push on.[10] The rest of the day we tried to come up with solutions for how to put up an "igloo-shaped" tent with skis and ski poles.[11]

After the best day we had on the ice (almost 100 km or 61 miles), we camped. We decided to dig a hole and somehow get the tent up. It didn't look pretty once it was up, and it sure as hell would not be good to sleep in. It is my turn to cook, and I end up spilling the dinner on everyone else. But the dinner is scraped up and eaten with delight.

It is easy to try to find scapegoats when something goes wrong. On the ice, however, we never thought about that. We did not even mention it. I think we all realized that there was nothing any one of us could do about it. Instead of wasting time determining who had left the tent poles and picking on the chosen scapegoat, we all directed our energy toward finding a solution.

MAY 27

Harald wakes me up in the middle of the night. We are all hyperventilating. The snow has gathered on top of the tent, and now we are stuck under it, suffocating. The opening is hard to find. All the snow on top is blocking the midnight sun from getting in. It is almost pitch dark. Harald spent the rest of the night digging out. He is the only one who can move. We are all hyperventilating because of lack of oxygen. A scary moment.

If Harald had not woken up, we might all have been dead. With the lack of oxygen, you just do not wake up. No pain, but again, no fun. In the morning, we all agree it had been a close one, and we all want to get the hell out of this place as fast as possible. We conclude that by expanding the day from 24 to 30 hours, we may be able to walk 12 to 15 hours a day and get down from the ice in 3 days. We still have the option of trying to reach the abandoned U.S. radio station. I'm the only one who mentions this option. The other guys do not want to do it. The station is approximately 50 km (23 miles) to the south-southeast. It will cost us an extra day. After a short discussion, we decide to forget the station and head straight down the ice. The sledges are cleaned up. Again, we are donating some food to nature.

I think that one suppresses fear when one is in the middle of it. Looking back on the tent episode, I cannot believe that we were as calm as we were. Danger and fear may seem far away when you are in the middle of it. It is the closest call I ever had.

Bård is playing with the thought of what would happen if the inland ice cap suddenly melted. He calculates that the oceans would rise 6 to 7 meters and that we would free-fall for more than 55 seconds before hitting the earth. The inland ice is so heavy that it has pressed the land underneath to below sea level. The only thing that holds it in place is the mountains along the coast of Greenland.

We have changed our schedule. Instead of 2-hour stints, we are now doing 3-hour stints with the same man in front the entire

---

[10]We had a choice of trying to reach an abandoned U.S. radio station about 50 miles to the south of us. We knew it was abandoned back in 1988, but we had heard rumors that two U.S. scientists were living there for the spring and summer in order to conduct some tests. In any case, we might be able to find some material that we could use as tent poles.

[11]The tent was a North Face, Himalaya Hotel model.

stint. Ivar got the first stint, followed by Harald, myself, and Bård.

The weather is still horrible. The day started out with high winds and low temperatures, but fairly good visibility. Now, visibility is zero. Bård and I are doing our stints in total "darkness." We even get some sympathy from Harald and Ivar. It is definitely not weather to ski in. We were trying to live by the rule that no weather was too severe to ski in and that no weather should be bad enough to keep us inside our tent for a day or two. The weather always looks worse from inside your sleeping bag than when you actually start skiing. Then, you realize that it "ain't that bad after all." This is bad weather, but we do not have time to lie down and wait for anything better. Back home we would have been classified as criminals and severely insane if we had skied in this kind of weather. We have a plane to catch on Friday morning and today is Monday. The next flight out of Greenland is the next Monday if we do not make the Friday flight.

The day also is spent trying to come up with better solutions for the tent. We all have seen how our sledges are seldom snowed down in the morning. The snow is always piled up behind the sledges. Our theory at the end of the day is that if we put the tent up right on top of the ice, the wind will blow the snow off. We decide to try this theory, and it turns out to be correct. The remaining days, we do not run into the same problem we had the first night in our improvised tent. Looking back, we should have realized this the first night. Back home, however, we are used to digging in if the weather becomes too severe. The terrain is different up here, where the wind and the snow seem to act differently. We are lucky to have figured that one out before it was too late.

We have the wind at our back now. We are going downhill. In the middle of the inland ice cap and on top, severe low-pressure weather is formed. The cold air picks up speed as it moves down the ice. The winds in Greenland can reach incredible speeds. The falling winds are locally called *piteraqs*. Luckily, we do not run into one of those. They say piteraqs make hurricanes look like breezes. But the winds also help us now that we are over the top. We can now almost certainly expect winds from behind just as we almost certainly could expect head winds on the first stage of the expedition.

The expansion of the day is working. We are now on a 30-hour schedule. We can see the end, and when you are close to it, you also are more willing to wear down your body. The safety margins are reduced. In the beginning, we had to make sure to get enough sleep to reenergize our bodies. Now, we can afford to wear them down. We have "only" 190 km (115 miles) left on the ice and another 50 km (30 miles) on foot hiking to Søndre Strømfjord.

We make good progress. The GPS is showing 59 km since the beginning of the day. Good. With this speed we will be down in 2 days. With no sleep the last night, this means only 2 more days in our improvised tent. We are going for it. This is not a beauty contest.

Earlier in the trip, we were concerned about getting enough sleep in order to let our bodies "recharge." The end is close, however, and we do not need the same safety margin we did earlier in the trip. The whole team is in on it. We all bring out forgotten and hidden energy to finish this one. I think this is the truth with a lot of jobs and projects. It gets hectic in the end. All the team members must be willing to put in something extra at the end.

MAY 28

The weather is much better. However, we are all "beaten up" by the last day's speed. Harald and I are not showing the right team spirit. We are speeding up our stints to an insane speed without thinking of the others. Bård gets in trouble. His leg has had an infection the last 8 or 9 days so that one of his legs is twice the size of the other. I admire him. No whining, no tears, no complaints.

A team is never stronger than the "weakest." In the beginning, I was the weakest. I have picked up. Now, I may be one of the strongest. My self-confidence is returning. I feel bad, however, when some of the guys are complaining about the speed I maintain while in front.

Always take care of the team. Never forget that it is a team performance and that no medals are awarded to individuals, only to the team. I do not know why I speeded up. It may have been to restore my self-confidence and my respect among the others owing to my miserable performance the first couple of days.

If there is something I will remember from Greenland, it will be the light. It is the most unique and beautiful light I have ever seen. It is a combination of colors, shades, and movement that I think is unique to the polar regions. Unfortunately, the light played a little joke on us today. Bård and I were certain that we had seen another tent on the ice and that there had been a pack of 12 to 14 wolves in front of us. We almost convinced Harald and Ivar, too, before we realized that it was all due to the ice and the light.

The slight hallucination was a clear sign that we were starting to get worn out. We were pushing ourselves to the limit. We did not take it seriously at this point. We were so close to the finish. It is important, however, to take action if one team member starts to hallucinate or in other ways show signs of fatigue. It is normally time to slow down.

We stopped early today. We did not completely finish the last stint. Harald and Bård had accidentally gotten some fuel in their food last night, and both were feeling rather sick at the end of the day. However, not a bad day overall: 52 km (31 miles) is good on any day. We camped at 6 A.M. While Harald and Ivar are getting the tent together, Bård and I are watching the sun. The midnight sun is beautiful. We also grab a shot of "medicine" that Bård still has left.

Tomorrow will be the day. We can almost feel the end of the ice. When we arrived in eastern Greenland in the beginning of May, the police told us that getting down from the ice on the west coast would be a problem. It is an art in itself. Because of the weather, the ice is melting. All the melting forms big rivers and lakes. If you get caught in a labyrinth like that, it is almost impossible to get down. Huge crevasses make it even harder. Before leaving Norway, we had ordered an aerial photo of the area. Based on the photo, we had tried to pick a route with fewer crevasses. We then plotted the route into our GPS. In order to get down, we had decided to descend from the ice during the night. That way, the snow would be harder because of less intensive sunlight; there was also the possibility of finding frozen lakes during the night.

Now, we were camped at 6 A.M., planning to get underway again at 1 P.M. to reach the descent area around midnight. With luck, we could be down in 24 to 30 hours, or Thursday morning. Then, only 50 km on foot would separate us from the flight back on Friday.

MAY 29

Our expedition had been all about risk assessment. We had managed to maintain high speed because of low starting weight. You can guard against anything when you plan. Our theory was that with low starting weight, we would manage to maintain high speed, and high speed means safety in itself. Our starting carrying weight was less than 60 kilos (132 pounds) each. Other expeditions have had starting weights twice ours and even more. Low weight also meant sacrificing safety equipment. We had only brought along one extra ski, two ski poles, an extra pair of windproof mittens, and an extra windproof hood. The only spare equipment we had to use was the extra ski. Ivar broke one of his yesterday. The binding froze,[12] and while trying to bend his boot out of it, the whole ski split in two. Looking back, some may criticize us for not bringing enough equipment along. Yes, that may be true. We did miss some extra tent poles, but who brings extra tent poles? We did not miss anything else, and for us, that was enough.

The day passed. We did get some downhill skiing at the end of the day. The joy was enormous when we discovered mountains on the horizon. We had made it! Now, only the last 20 km were left—getting down from the ice. Our plan proved to be an excellent one; it was probably the fastest descent in history. The GPS, the aerial photo, and Bård unroped in front proved to be an unbeatable recipe. (We always sent Bård in front. He was the lightest and easiest to get up from a crevasse. We were pretty sure where the big crevasses were, and because visibility was great, the chances of hitting a crevasse were extremely low.) Two hundred meters to each side of us, we could see areas with huge crevasses that would have taken days to get through. We had managed to find the "highway" down.

We reached the hilltop named 660, which marks the end of the ice, in the morning (Thursday) around 7 A.M. We had completed our expedition in the incredible time of 12 days and 23 hours. Faster than anyone before. We had used half the time the second-fastest unsupported expedition had needed.

I expected the joy to be greater. We all felt, however, that it was an anticlimax. It is always better to be underway than to arrive. But it is over; we did it. The ecstasy might have been greater if we had all arrived at 660 at the same time. Unfortunately, Harald's sledge broke 300 meters from the hilltop. Instead of repairing it, he repacked everything into his backpack. He arrived an hour later. We should have waited for him and arrived together as a team.

For me, the journey is what I will remember. Not the arrival. As with many things in life, it is the "arrival" that gives you recognition from others. For the one who does it, the "journey" is what gives you self-respect and self-recognition. I guess that goes for many things in the business world as well. It is the results that give you the recognition and the promotions, but it is the actual work that makes you believe in yourself and that makes you perform time after time. After awhile, the actual arrival is nothing more than the beginning of a new journey, a new task, a new job.

We sat down for 3 hours and cooked the last dinners we had. All the food was gone except for two dinner rations each. We ate 7,000 calories each that morning, enough to keep me going for 4 days back home. We were all thinner, too. The best "diet" you can do is a polar expedition! I lost 5 kilos (11 pounds) in 13 days. Not bad,

---

[12]We knew about the problems with the bindings before leaving Norway. The binding was constructed in such a way that when exposed to harsh weather, it had a tendency to accumulate snow, and in the end it froze. The manufacturers of the binding had reassured us that the problems were taken care of and that the new binding we got from them was of a better design. The new design, however, did not work. That night, we all took the bindings of our skis, cleaned them, and came up with a solution to the problem that would prove to be very effective: We simply removed two parts from the binding.

but far less than most people lose. We had just started to take off body fat. It takes some time before the body actually begins to do this. Again, this was a safety issue we had calculated. The faster we walk, the less food we need each day. The body needs more than the 5,000 calories a day that we had brought with us. With high speed, however, we had calculated that we could make it on 5,000 a day plus what the body could give us and still not lose too much weight.

We packed everything we had in our backpacks. No more snow to drag the sledge on. They were left on the edge of the ice. Even though they were made of fiberglass, they were too heavy to carry home on our backpacks. The backpacks already weighed around 30 kilos (66 pounds). We did not want the extra 8 kilos (18 pounds) that the sledges represented. We hope someone will pick them up, or that we will be lucky and someone will ship them to us later. What a trophy to put on the wall of your cabin! After some joking remarks from Bård, Harald, and me, Ivar decides he is going to try to carry his sledge back. He needs another challenge!

Getting off the skis and starting to walk on our feet proved to be more difficult than we had thought. Our feet swelled up. The backpacks were also incredibly heavy. This was not a good sign. It was already noon, and we had only some 24 hours before the plane left. After slow progress for about 4 hours, we decided to split up. Ivar and I would go in front, reach Søndre Strømfjord, and try to get a four-wheel-drive vehicle to pick up Harald and Bård.

We did it again. We split up the team. In retrospect, I regret it. Splitting up the team so near the goal may deprive someone of feeling like a team member when you reach the goal that all have worked so hard for. This is not a good idea. Later in life, I hope I learn from this incident. I will try never again to leave my teammates right before the team reaches its goal. Again, no "medals" are awarded for individual performance on a team. As a team, I think we failed to accomplish this. At the end of the trip, we totally failed to act and perform as a team.

We reached Søndre Strømfjord at midnight. We realized that no four-wheeler in the world could get inland to our comrades. We talked to the local police officer, who was quite surprised to see us. He had not expected us for another 10 days. At first, he thought we were with Vegard Ulvang's expedition. We borrowed two three-wheel motorbikes that the police officer promised us would make it in the tough terrain. By 7 A.M. after a long and eventful night, all four of us were finally gathered in the local cafeteria. We had been on the move for the last 42 hours and had walked about 120 km (73 miles).

After showering twice and putting on fresh underwear we were lucky enough to buy at the local store, we returned to the transit hall of the airport. We were the local heroes around the bar. After another 12 hours' air time, we were back in Norway.

We were all in pretty good shape. Bård had a leg infection, and Harald had a swollen and sore knee. Besides that, the only real injuries were some sore and slightly frostbitten feet. I could not wear my own shoes for the next 4 or 5 days. My feet, normally size 9, were swollen to size 12. We all had lost around 5 kilos, and our faces were dark and weather-bitten after 13 days on the ice.

Seven days after we walked off the ice, Vegard Ulvang arrived in Søndre Strømfjord. We had beaten a three-time Olympic champion by 2 days.

During the whole trip, we kept up an extreme discipline (not military discipline). Every day, we walked. Every day, we went through the same proven routines, however boring and tiring they may have been. Discipline in the sense that everyone is working toward the same goal and discipline in the sense that everyone is willing to do their share of the work will lead to success. Without discipline, we would never have been able to beat Vegard Ulvang.

Why did we do it? I think we all had different reasons for doing it. Ivar had stated it was on impulse. Bård, too. I did it because I wanted the challenge. I needed the challenge. Deep inside, however, I think we all wanted to gain some respect from others. People never do expeditions like this just for self-respect or for themselves. They want some foundation on which to build their image.

Most of all, I learned something about myself. I learned my limits, but I also moved some. These days, crossing Greenland doesn't get much attention in Norway. The Norwegians are far too spoiled by Arctic and Antarctic expeditions. We have our national heroes in Frithjof Nansen (an Arctic explorer and a winner of the Nobel Peace prize) and Roald Amundsen. We also have some contemporary exceptional Arctic explorers who do things far more spectacular than crossing Greenland. I have proven myself enough to get the recognition I need to go on. To once again take on a challenge. ■

Case 9   Ray Hagen (A)

"From the loading dock in back of my company's warehouse, I watched George Perrilli, assisted by his wife, walk slowly across the street. George had suffered a heart attack 6 months earlier, and I knew that he was coming to my office to ask for his old job back. I wasn't sure what I should say." Ray Hagen leaned back in his chair as he described a difficult situation he had faced not long ago.

RAY HAGEN'S BACKGROUND

"But first, let me give you a little background to the story. When I graduated from the University of Notre Dame, I went to work for a family-owned company, a large company, in Louisville. We manufactured equipment for the chemical and food-processing industry. I was hired by the man who was the sales manager—he had been sort of a family friend for a number of years—and went to work for them in the sales capacity. I guess you might say I got on the fast track and achieved some success in the company.

"We were a company of 275 employees doing approximately $6 million in sales. About 1970, the man who was the president of the company, one of the family owners, passed away. Now that the president was gone, other family members from the parent corporation—people who had never taken a strong interest in the company—suddenly started to become involved. The man I had worked for was sort of shoved off to the side, and they brought in a new man. He was from Westinghouse, and he'd been exposed to 1960 methods of running a business: managing and forecasting.

"So all of a sudden I was answering to a man who was asking me for reports and asking me to forecast what I was going to do, and I had never been asked to do these kinds of things. It had been a sort of—not a loose corporation—but not as tight a ship as the new situation, and I guess I wasn't totally comfortable with that, but I did respect that type of discipline and began to see its merits. My boss was not a warm person in his dealings with the salesmen. He split the company into three regions—three profit centers—and I was made the regional manager in Atlanta. While there I worked very hard, but I never could seem to get the total job done, all the reporting and the paperwork of the business. Basically, that's because I'm a salesman.

"So I began to look around for opportunities either to go to another company or to have my own business. I had an opportunity in 1974 to go in with another man and buy an old company—the oldest distributorship of its kind in Louisville. I knew nothing about the business, absolutely nothing, except that I was a little bit familiar with the products that the company handled because they were used on some of the equipment that we built. During the negotiations, I learned that the lady (an older woman of about 60) who was selling knew something about the man I was going in with that I didn't know, and she didn't want to have anything to do with him because of some almost illegal things he had done. I decided to make her an offer on my own.

UVA-OB-0262

This case was prepared by James G. Clawson. Copyright © 1983 by the University of Virginia Darden School Foundation, Charlottesville, VA. All rights reserved.

"So, while living in Atlanta, and traveling to Louisville for meetings or conferences or something, I was also negotiating to purchase this company, and I did in October 1975. I moved back to Louisville, and although I knew nothing about the business, all of a sudden one day I'm the chief operating officer and responsible for everything in the company. I looked at the situation and told myself that the most important thing I needed to do was learn about the products—who buys them, why they buy them, and what they are used for. Again, sort of a salesmen's mentality, not worrying about the other parts of the business.

"There were only five employees when I bought the company: the woman who had owned the business, three men, and an old maid bookkeeper upstairs who paid the bills. I was the sixth employee. I had no outside salesman, so I felt that in order to pay for this company as soon as possible, I had to work hard.

"We closed out 1975 with just a little under $500,000 in sales. It took me about 10 to 12 months to get a grasp of the business—what the products were, who they were sold to, the companies that we were distributor for, the people who worked for them. And I learned that the only business this company had was the business that came in off the street or that came in over the phone.

"The name of my company was Louisville Power Transmission, and I was a distributor for what was called power transmission equipment—things that make machinery go, big V-belts and motors and chains and gears and gearboxes. In my business, I was a buyer, a middle man, if you want to call it that. I bought from maybe 20 different companies, and I inventoried those products. I had about $500,000 of inventory. Then I turned around and sold them to basically two classes or two types of accounts: industrial users that had machinery in operation—a bakery, a concrete plant, or a plastic plant making plastic bottles. I also sold to what we called the OEM accounts, original equipment manufacturers. My business was divided up about 70 percent to the first group and the balance to OEM accounts.

"My strategy was to keep that type of mix as close as I could because, needless to say, I got a lot of small orders with big margins on the one end, and big volume and low margins on the other end, so a proper mix was important. Working with the OEM accounts enhanced my buying position. In other words, I could go to the manufacturer and instead of buying 100 widgets, I could buy 1,000 widgets because I knew that I could move volume to the OEMs, but when I sold it to the industrial user, I got a bigger margin because I bought it on volume."

RECRUITING

"I took one of the young men who was working in the back putting up stock, making deliveries, and I said, 'I don't know a great deal about this business, I'm not an engineer' (some of the products required some technical expertise in their sales), 'but if you teach me about the business and how these products are used, I'll teach you about selling.' He said 'okay,' so I sent him to a sales training program in Atlanta and then I worked with him, and we began to get some business.

"I called on some of the people that I'd known from years past—they became my customers, and the business started to grow. About the early part of 1977, I thought maybe I should get another salesman outside, particularly somebody who knows the business, has some technical expertise, and maybe is known around the city because he's sold these products. In other words, maybe I should go pirate somebody. So, I looked around. My competitors didn't really worry too much about me, because they had heard that I didn't know anything about the business. They knew something about the old business that I bought, and it was just a mom-and-pop grocery store sort of operation.

"I did meet one fellow who was with a competitor, and he impressed me, and I thought, 'maybe this is my man.' In the spring of 1977, I called him and said, 'If you are downtown, why don't you stop by some evening—I would like to talk to you about possibly going to work for me.'

"Now, one of the reasons I told you about my background was because I'm basically a salesman. I didn't know about good management practices, and I didn't recognize all the responsibilities of a chief operating officer or of a general manager of a company, so I was handling things with the same mentality as the guy who had come in from Westinghouse and became my boss. I placed most of my emphasis on getting to know a guy. I felt like I was a good judge of people and if this particular fellow was a good guy, I would worry later about what talents he had. He seemed like a nice enough fellow, so I offered him a job, and he accepted. It wasn't very long after that I regretted my decision.

"He started raising hell with a lot of people. He was always bitching, 'You don't make my deliveries, you're not talking nice to my customers, you're not handling them like you handle the other customers, you charge them too much, you people really don't know the business—if you only knew half of what I knew, it would be easy for you.' Saying this to my inside people. And, he would say these things openly in the office. You know, he would be speaking to one fellow, but he'd say it loud enough so everybody could hear. So, I'm getting all of these vibrations. The other employees would say, 'Just get that guy away from me.'

"Then he would come in and raise hell and yell at one of the delivery boys: 'I told you that you should always take that to the back of that guy's store' or 'You give these items to me so I can deliver them, because that's how I get in the back door.' He used to do a lot of what they call 'back-door selling.' In other words, this guy would take the delivery and when he did, he would go in to see the customer. There's not anything really wrong with that, but it makes some customers uncomfortable. They don't like people wandering around in their plants. I heard from a couple of customers that, if possible, they'd prefer the deliveries to be sent UPS or by truck because they didn't want this guy wandering around in their plants."

COACHING

"But, I said, maybe I could work with him. I will be kind to him because one of the things he was telling me was that everybody had dumped on him everyplace he'd been. And you know, I have always been sort of dumped on, and I thought, well, maybe I could turn that around—maybe if I'm kind to him and if I'm nice to him, show some interest in him, just do a few nice little things for him, give him a few perks, maybe he'll turn around.

"About 2 months after he came to work for me, I received a call from a customer who said George had passed out and looked like he'd had a heart attack, and that he was being taken by the rescue squad to the hospital. I immediately went to the hospital. George was in intensive care, but the doctor said he didn't think it was a heart attack. They weren't sure what had happened. They kept him there for a couple of days.

"He came back about a week later. He said that his blood pressure had dropped down to a very low point. I guess the symptoms of very low blood pressure are like a heart attack. At least, that's what the doctor said.

"He had had a history of heart problems. In 1968, he had gone to work for a company out of Indianapolis and had started a branch in Louisville. He had worked very hard but never was really productive. That is, he didn't manage his time properly, and he worried too much about things that he didn't need to worry about. As a result, he had a very serious heart attack and was out of work for about 6 to 7 months.

"I made a real conscientious effort to work with the guy and to put up with his idiosyncrasies. This went on for several years. I hired several other salesmen, and they saw how I was coddling this guy and trying to be nice to him, and they became a little upset with me. They told me, 'You shouldn't let that guy run you around like that.' One instance I remember very vividly. Every fall I would get the salesmen and the nonsales people together, and we'd talk about what had happened that year, and what we'd look for next year, and what things we wanted to do the coming year. Basic, simple planning—setting up some objectives. This one dinner in October turned into a shouting match—all of a sudden, things that had been boiling just under the surface came out. This fellow, George, called another guy an 'SOB,' who then called him an 'AH.' You know, right then and there. I just ended the meeting.

"I really didn't know what to do. I felt like I should terminate the man, but he was bringing me some business, and I was growing. I was getting a lot of pressure, particularly from the general manager inside, a young guy in charge of sales and the warehouse. He kept saying, 'You have just got to get rid of this guy; he's causing too damn much trouble around here, raising hell.' And I was saying, "Well, he's bringing me some orders.' But it concerned me that we weren't a real profitable business, and George was not a good salesman. He tried to sell his technical expertise where in a lot of cases, people didn't want it. Then he would just cut the price. His approach to selling was that if he came in to see you, he would say, 'How much do you pay for these items?' And somehow he would get it out of you, and say, 'Well, I'll sell them to you for 10 percent less.' Arbitrarily, without consulting me, without saying whether we were even in the business—it could have been

products that we didn't even handle as a distributor! It put us in a difficult position. But he *was* bringing us some business, and I was going through some very heavy growth years. I closed out in 1979 with about $2.5 million in sales.

"George was 55 years old then, and he had a history of moving from company to company. That was another thing I learned—about my naïveté. I didn't know that the man had had three jobs before he came to me. I also didn't know that at two of the places, he had been asked to leave. Sometime later, one of the managers of the company from whom I hired him told me that they were sure glad that I took him off their hands because they didn't know what the hell they were going to do with him. He said they'd been telling the people in headquarters that they needed to get rid of him because he was such a problem in the business."

GROWTH AND OTHER CRISES

"I was reaching a point where I couldn't do it all. There was just no way. I mean, I couldn't be the bookkeeper, I couldn't be the sales manager, I couldn't be the floor sweeper, I couldn't be it all. I began to recognize that I had to get some people in to help me.

"Meanwhile, George had had a heart attack at Christmas of 1979. A *bad* heart attack. He was 58. In January of 1980, I began looking around for a man to help me manage some of the other salesmen, someone who had technical expertise and had good accounts of his own but who could help me assume some of the responsibilities managing the men. So, I hired Bob Dreyer in January. He was to come in as sort of a sales manager, but he was really to be more of a shepherd to take care of the salesmen and to help me.

"So, I said to the staff, 'Mr. Dreyer isn't in here as a true sales manager; he's going to help us get organized. If I need to get a plan put through the sales area, I hope that he'll get that message to you so we can implement it. George is in the hospital in intensive care for about 3 weeks, so we really won't know what his condition is until the end of January. We spoke to his wife, and she indicated that he would probably be in the hospital for another month to 6 weeks, and then there'll be a period of 3 or 4 months' recuperation. They still don't know how severe the heart damage is—his doctor wouldn't give us any indication about his future—whether he could ever go back to work again, whether he might require surgery. He might be out for another 6 or 8 months.'

"As it turned out, while George was gone, the company suddenly started working smoothly. Everybody was getting along well, and people were happy. We were experiencing tremendous growth. I was getting some positive feedback from customers. I had to have the general manager and Dreyer take over George's accounts, and we were generating new sales from these companies. They liked Dreyer, and it looked like they would probably do more business with us.

"About the first of April, I had a conversation with George's doctor, who said George might be able to come back to work in June, but he wasn't sure. George was resting at home then. He couldn't drive a car; if he had to go somewhere, his wife took him.

"This last time, the doctor told me that the earlier low-blood-pressure episode was in fact a heart attack, though a very slight one. I guess they can tell through tests, you know, how many times the heart has been injured or damaged. They found evidence of this first serious one and then of the tiny little one that happened in September."

RAY'S FATHER'S CASE

"Now, my father died when he was 52 years old. I don't know whether I've ever totally gotten over that. I remember my mother being so upset about it—upset with the men that he'd worked for. My father had several heart attacks and when he had the third one, I remember the men from the company coming to visit my father and asking him to help them with something or give them some advice, and asking, 'When are you coming back to work?'

"My father was a conscientious guy, and he went back to work. I can remember my mother in tears at the funeral, screaming at the president and the executive vice president of the company, 'You killed my husband! You made him come back to work, and you've killed him, and here I am with these seven young children! If you hadn't made him come back . . .' When I thought about my father, deep down, I guess I didn't want the responsibility of having George come back to work for me.

"I remember that when George had the slight heart attack, he was anxious to come back immediately. I didn't want the responsibility then, either. So, now I wondered if I were using responsibility to cover up my real feelings—maybe I just didn't want him back. But after thinking about it seriously, I really believed that I didn't want the responsibility of his coming back to work."

GEORGE'S VISIT

"I had talked to George on the telephone occasionally. He'd been telling me that the doctor really doesn't want him to come back to work, but that if George says he's okay, then the doctor will agree. So, he's sort of telling the doctor, 'I'm okay, I want to go back to work.' The doctor isn't totally sure, but if he's the patient and he's telling the doctor that he's okay and he wants to go back to work, then I guess you sort of have to give him the benefit of the doubt.

"I knew I had to face this problem. I hadn't seen George in 6 months when I asked him to come down and talk to me. It was a warm June day—the doors were all open in the back on the dock, and I was talking with one of the warehousemen. I looked across the street. George and his wife—she was driving—pulled up in the parking lot. He had a tough time getting out of the car, and his wife helped him cross the intersection. She wasn't exactly holding him up, but she was just sort of guiding him as you would guide an older person. I told him to go upstairs. It took him 5 minutes to go up two flights because he had to stop and rest before he could go on. So, we went up to talk in the office.

"I asked how he was feeling and what he wanted to do, and this was when he told me, 'I'll be ready to come back to work in 3 weeks. I'm getting stronger every day, and I know I can come back to work. My wife might have to drive me around a little bit, but I think I can start back on at least a 3-day basis.'" ■

Case 10   Phil Charles (A)

Phil wasn't certain just what was going on, but something was causing the S&A Chemicals stock to move in a dramatic way on January 28, 1999. The S&A Chemicals stock had been dormant for months, and suddenly the stock price had gone up more than 50 percent in 1 day. Little did Phil realize that this stock activity marked the beginning of a year-long period of personal change.

Phil was 38 years old at the time of this activity, and he had spent the previous 11 years at S&A Chemicals. Prior to that period, he had spent 6 years at MCF Chemicals. MCF Chemicals was a much larger, full-time competitor of S&A Chemicals. While at MCF Chemicals, he had covered the same accounts in the same territory that he began covering with S&A Chemicals. Phil left MCF Chemicals because he concluded that due to his educational limitations, his career aspirations were being threatened. Phil had graduated from North Carolina State with a bachelor of arts in communications in 1982. At the time of his graduation, MCF Chemicals was hiring nontechnically trained graduates to sell. However, in l987, the decision was made to hire technically trained people to sell and MBA graduates to manage. Because Phil had neither, he decided to seek out a smaller company that would afford him more opportunity for growth, development, and contribution.

S&A Chemicals fit Phil's need well. Although they were not a strong competitor to MCF Chemicals, they did provide many opportunities for growth and development. They lacked the sophistication of MCF, which had provided Phil with a valuable learning opportunity. Phil was eager to succeed and quick to volunteer to work on bringing the sales force up to speed by piloting a home computer and a cell phone for his use. He also brought better training and more contacts to S&A Chemicals. Three years after joining S&A Chemicals, he was promoted to a regional manager's position. Two years later, he was asked to consider an operational assignment, as materials manager. Two years after accepting his operational assignment he was asked to become the national sales manager for a newly formed sales force in the Specialty Chemicals business. This new position required managing highly technical individuals located in home offices across the country. However, Phil discovered that the challenges of managing these technical people were similar to his previous sales force experience. He was more than up to the challenge.

After 2 years in this position, Phil grew tired of the constant travel. When the opening for the director of Material Management occurred, Phil applied for the position. In January of 1998, Phil was selected for the role of director, Materials Management. The scope of this position was expanded to include all of North and South America, and it included all purchasing, logistics, and facilities management. Phil was looking forward to the challenges in his new position, and for the first time in a long time he felt comfortable in his assignment.

UVA-OB-0729

This case was prepared by Charlie Flocco and Professor Alexander B. Horniman. This case was written as a basis for class discussion rather than to illustrate effective or ineffective handling of an administrative situation.
Copyright © 2000 by the University of Virginia Darden School Foundation, Charlottesville, VA. All rights reserved.

A YEAR OF TURMOIL

A week after the S&A Chemicals shares movement began on the London Stock Exchange, news broke that Albertson Chemicals had made a friendly bid to take over S&A Chemicals, purchasing 14 percent of the outstanding shares. Once S&A Chemicals was "in play," per stock exchange rules, Albertson had 60 days to purchase a controlling interest, and other companies had that same time period to offer new bids. Two days prior to the end of the 60-day period, the French chemical giant Roussell Chemicals announced that they were offering a higher price for the S&A Chemicals shares. Roussell Chemicals quickly acquired 15 percent of the S&A Chemicals shares.

During this hectic period, Phil was in close contact with his colleagues in the United Kingdom. Because Phil reported directly to the president of S&A Chemicals, Americas, he had an opportunity to meet all senior managers in Asia, Europe, and the Americas. Phil discovered that there were many people he could keep in contact with at this time, and they were very helpful.

Based upon the information from his many contacts, Phil learned that it appeared that Albertson Chemicals would make a counterbid and secure the shares of the single largest shareholder, thereby ensuring the successful purchase of S&A Chemicals. Phil knew a number of people at Albertson Chemicals and had strong reason to believe that they would close their office in Louisiana and move the headquarters to S&A Chemicals offices in Virginia. Phil thought that given this likely chain of events, there would be little change, except the name on the door.

Albertson Chemicals did make a counterbid, but they were not able to obtain the 24 percent of the shares held by the major stockholder. As a result, many other shareholders held onto their stock, waiting to see if Roussell Chemicals would make a higher offer. Not much transpired in the ensuing 60 days, and then at the last minute Roussell Chemicals did come in with another offer. The offer held and S&A Chemicals came under the control of Roussell Chemicals, subject to European and American government approvals.

Several months went by and not much changed. The Federal Trade Commission (FTC) approval was expected to take 2 to 3 months, and Roussell Chemicals expected to fully integrate S&A Chemicals by the fall of 1999.

During this time of uncertainty, Phil kept busy working on the integration planning and trying to pick up any signals he could about what Roussell Chemicals would do about their American headquarters. At the time of the takeover activities, Roussell Chemicals had U.S. headquarters in central New Jersey. The facilities were old, outdated, and expensive to maintain at capacity. Recognizing these issues, Phil set to work with the Virginia Economic Development Council to create a proposal that VEDC could make to Roussell Chemicals to encourage them to move part or all of their headquarters to Virginia. At the time, this activity seemed to be worthwhile, but in hindsight the fact that Roussell Chemicals might have to abandon S&A Chemicals's $12 million lease was small potatoes in the grand scheme of a $1.6 billion deal.

Phil became concerned, despite what his boss was saying, when he heard that the Roussell Chemicals consultant for integration was asking questions about building leases, departmental head counts in staff areas, and related questions. Phil had done some merger work in the past and was aware of what these inquiries meant.

QUESTIONING THE FUTURE

The possibility of change in Phil's life began to trouble him. He had lived in Virginia for almost 9 years and had become accustomed to the work and lifestyle. The thought of moving back to New Jersey did not excite him. When he and his wife had moved to Virginia in 1991, he was able to purchase a much larger, custom-built home for the equivalent money, his wife was able to stay at home after the birth of their first child, and they joined a private golf club.

Phil, his wife, and soon two children enjoyed their home and neighborhood. Their children were in one of the best public elementary schools in the region, and they were delighted with their church.

About the time of the initial Roussell Chemicals activity, Phil's 7-year-old daughter began having difficulty at school. The teachers informed Phil and his wife that their daughter was upset and worried that her father might lose his job; she thought that if her father lost his job, they would have to move away. This issue did not make Phil feel any better. He was aware that his own concerns were affecting his family, and this troubled him.

As Phil contemplated what the future might hold in store, he decided to rekindle a once-close relationship with Mike Delavan, the executive vice president at the S&A Specialty Chemicals business. Phil had worked for Mike as his first national sales manager, and most of Phil's purchasing and logistics work was done for Mike's division. Phil and Mike shared a great deal in common and over the years had become good friends. It was Mike's view that his division would stay located in Virginia because the R&D labs were there; Roussell Chemicals didn't have any similar business and would need the people and the labs at least in the short run.

Summer became fall and the FTC had not made their decision known. They also decided that Roussell Chemicals and S&A Chemicals should cease all integration activities.

The FTC news stimulated the rumor mill to shift into high gear. One of the most common rumors was the good chance that

the merger would break up because the government was demanding that Roussell Chemicals sell off the most profitable part of its business.

Phil had not really given serious thought to what would happen if he should be required to move or, worse yet, be out of a job. Because the job market was tight, he wasn't concerned about finding a job, but he was concerned about having to move. Phil began to network with colleagues at other chemical companies. After all, the chemical industry was all Phil knew. The only real chemical business activity in Virginia was S&A Chemicals. Everything else was located out of state. Phil put out a few feelers to his friends from the golf club, but at the end of the day he was reasonably sure that Mike Delavan would find a spot for him in Virginia.

Fall turned to winter and still the FTC had not ruled on whether the Roussell Chemicals deal could go through. During the fall Phil rekindled an old friendship with Jim March, the national sales manager for Roussell Chemicals. Phil and Jim spoke to each other frequently during the "blackout period" and kept each other informed about the latest rumors. It was Jim's belief that Roussell Chemicals would not close the Virginia facility immediately. He also was convinced that Phil would have a place within the organization. He had heard Phil's name mentioned for several different jobs. Phil was relieved to hear this, but he made it clear that he wasn't excited about moving back to New Jersey.

Just after the start of the New Year 2000, the FTC allowed Roussell Chemicals and S&A Chemicals to continue with their nonbusiness integration discussions. These discussions could include conversations about people, office sites, and the like, but not include suppliers, prices, customers, plants, or production processes.

A week after the discussion decision had been clarified, Roussell Chemicals executives were in Virginia meeting with S&A Chemicals executives. Jack Ulrich, vice president of Purchasing and Logistics, called Phil to set up an appointment.

A NEW LOOK

Toward the end of 1999, Phil was searching the National Association of Purchasing Managers Web site. He discovered a job listed in the Virginia area for a group sourcing manager at Qual Card. Qual Card's headquarters were in Virginia, and at the time they were the seventh-largest credit card issuer in the country. Qual Card was regarded as one of Virginia's best employers. In fact, they were considered one of the nation's best companies for employment. Most of the job opportunities that Phil had seen previously were for call center-type jobs. So when Phil saw the group sourcing posting, he made some calls to people he knew at Qual Card.

Toward the end of November 1999, Phil sent his resume to a recruiter at Qual Card. He did so "just for the heck of it." Three weeks later he received a follow-up phone call from a Qual Card representative. This call led to several others.

Jack Ulrich's visit and the meeting with Phil were scheduled for the third week of January. As it turned out, Phil's first in-person interview with Qual Card was scheduled for the following week.

Phil's meeting with Jack Ulrich was candid, and it dealt with the people who would move, those who wouldn't, and what the future held for Phil. Phil made it clear he would prefer not to move, but if the right situation were created he would consider it. Phil also was aware that Mike Delavan had been positive about him keeping his position in Richmond "for at least a couple of years." From Phil's standpoint, this meant the least change and bought him more time to survey the job market in Virginia and in the chemical industry.

The next week Phil interviewed at Qual Card. It was an exhaustive affair with six interviews and two tests. He was reasonably sure the interviews had gone well, but he was concerned about the tests.

THINGS BEGIN TO CHANGE

On February 8, the president of Roussell Chemicals North America, Myron Goldsmith, visited S&A Chemicals's Virginia office to meet employees and to update them on the status of the FTC investigation and some of the decisions that Roussell Chemicals had made. Goldsmith indicated that the S&A Chemicals Virginia office would be closed as soon as possible after the final FTC decision. The Specialty Chemical Division would remain in Virginia for a short period and then be relocated to New Jersey no later than August of 2001. Most of the people anticipated the news, but when it was actually spoken by Myron Goldsmith it seemed to have a chilling effect on everyone. Phil still felt pretty safe and assured of his position.

Qual Card invited Phil back for a second round of interviews in February, but Phil failed to respond. It took Phil until March to respond to Qual Card.

During the time between Phil's first set of interviews and his delayed second set, several events occurred. More Roussell Chemicals executives began showing up in Virginia; in particular, Michel Marsul, the vice president of Integration, and Dave Eckles, the president of New Divisions, which would include S&A Chemicals. Phil knew Dave Eckles because they had both worked at MCF at the same time and had known each other through business activities.

Phil interviewed with Michel Marsul, who indicated that there were opportunities for Phil but that these would be in a shared service environment and not working for Mike Delavan in a division role. Marsul also asked Phil if he would consider moving.

Phil, feeling somewhat comfortable and self assured, indicated that unless the opportunity was right he saw no reason to move. Marsul was taken aback and asked what options Phil had available. Phil responded that options were always available, even if not all his first choice. As he was saying these things to Marsul, he quickly ran several options through his head.

He could walk away from Roussell Chemicals and take his $55,000 severance package and find another job.

He could take the package and go back to school and get his MBA. He concluded his heart really wasn't in the MBA.

He could hope things would work out at Qual Card. Although he knew nothing about the credit card industry, he did like what he had seen and learned about Qual Card.

The problem was that he knew chemicals and knew them well. He was pretty sure he could find work, even if it did mean a move. . . . But! ■

Case 11   Robert J. O'Neill, Jr. and the Fairfax County Government (A)

Fairfax County Executive Robert O'Neill, Jr., was sitting in his office one morning in September of 1999, overlooking the county's vast office complex and contemplating his upcoming performance evaluation with the county's board of supervisors. Given the way the board had handled conflicts with the county executive in recent years, O'Neill was not sure just what to expect at his performance evaluation. When O'Neill was hired in August of 1997 as Fairfax's third county executive in 7 years, the board wanted steady tax rates and an ambitious plan to reorganize the unwieldy, 11,000-employee bureaucracy. The government's problems had less to do with its size than with the unresponsive and inefficient form it had taken. Chairman of the Board of Supervisors Katherine Hanley said the county and the new executive had three challenges to confront: One was to do something about the structural deficit in the budget. Second, there was a need to be a more flexible and responsive government for changing times. Lastly, the government had to become more customer oriented.[1]

Addressing these three issues would not be an easy task. According to *The Washington Post,* the size and culture of Fairfax's bureaucracy had never been challenged because no leader existed to take it on.[2] When O'Neill was hired, he set out to create a vision for county employees and to paint a compelling picture of what the county should look like. He wanted to model a different behavior and a different way of making decisions in Fairfax County government.

His first year in office was a success, and his first evaluation last October went well. Agreeing with the resounding support he had from citizens' groups, the chamber of commerce, and the media, the board praised O'Neill's early efforts to streamline the bureaucracy and rated his overall performance "outstanding"—the highest available evaluation grade—and raised his salary. Unfortunately, his second year had been different. Many of his recent efforts to initiate change and institute sweeping reforms, including those to merge duplicate county functions and hire new top managers, were resisted by county employees, interest groups, and ultimately, the board, and he found himself being second-guessed by some of the very people who were previously demanding results.

FAIRFAX COUNTY, VIRGINIA

Fairfax County is a 399-square-mile county in suburban Washington, D.C. It is located approximately 14 miles west of Washington in northern Virginia, and was home at the

UVA-OB-0702

This case was prepared by Lindsey Houser (MBA '00) under the supervision of James G. Clawson, Professor of Business Administration. This case was written as a basis for discussion rather than to illustrate effective or ineffective handling of an administrative situation. Copyright © 2000 by the University of Virginia Darden School Foundation, Charlottesville, VA. All rights reserved.
[1]Charles Mantesian, "Frustrated in Fairfax," *Governing, December 1999, 34.*
[2]Michael D. Shear, "Fairfax Debates a Push for Power," *The Washington Post,* November 29, 1999, B4.

time of this writing to more than 975,000 residents, making it the most populous county in the Washington metropolitan area and the largest municipality in Virginia.[3] The county's median household income was $90,937, the highest of any in the country, and its crime rate was one of the lowest of any jurisdiction its size.[4]

Along with neighboring Loudoun County, Fairfax had become a hub for technology companies (both counties encompass the Dulles Corridor). Fairfax was home to approximately 2,000 technology companies— one of the highest concentrations in the United States—employing 60,000 people, and also 114 foreign-owned companies employing 8,500 people.[5] Tysons Corner and Reston accounted for the bulk of the county's 79 million square feet of office space—the fifth-largest inventory in the United States.[6] The county had a $2.1 billion operating budget, with more than half of that amount allocated to the public school system, which had an enrollment of about 151,000 students and was consistently ranked one of the nation's best.[7]

The county's finances were among the most stable in the country, as evidenced by its AAA bond rating, something only 22 municipalities in the country had.[8] Nonetheless, revenue growth had slowed considerably during the past 15 years, forcing the county to take a long look at its fiscal priorities. The main source of revenue for the county was

real estate taxes, and the real estate boom of the 1980s provided what seemed at the time to be an endless stream of revenue to fund its operations. According to Supervisor Michael Frey, a Republican representing fast-growing western Fairfax County, "There was so much revenue that the county could simply throw money at any problems. The easy success of the '80s caused the board to lose its focus."[9] The 1990s, on the other hand, were a different story. The county's population continued to soar and became more and more diverse. In 1980, for example, 12.9 percent of the population was black, Asian, or Hispanic, but by 1998, the total had risen to 30.8 percent. There were almost as many households with incomes less than $25,000 as there were with incomes greater than $150,000.[10] These changing demographics created new tensions as new services were in demand.

Two budget crises, one in the spring of 1992 and the other in the spring of 1996, highlighted the fiscal challenges facing the county. The latter was particularly alarming because the county's budget was running a deficit even at a time when the nation's overall economy was doing well. Virginia's tax structure was partly to blame. Local governments in Virginia did not collect income taxes and were unusually reliant on property taxes. This posed a particular hardship on Fairfax when real estate values began to level off. So although Fairfax

[3]Fairfax County, Virginia, FY2001, Advertised Budget Plan.

[4]Michael D. Shear and Tom Jackman, "Fairfax Boom Leaves Little Room for Poor," *The Washington Post,* March 14, 2000, A1. Kenneth Bredemeier, "Fairfax Grows More Affluent; County First to Achieve $90,000 Median Income," *The Washington Post,* June 10, 2000, A1.

[5]Fairfax County Economic Development Authority.

[6]Ibid.

[7]Fairfax County, Virginia FY2001, Advertised Budget Plan, Fairfax County Public Schools, Summary, Annual Report for the Fiscal Year Ended June 30, 1999.

[8]Chairman's Address, Inauguration 9th Urban Board of Supervisors and Constitutional Officers, December 20, 1999.

[9]Interview with Supervisor Michael T. Frey.

[10]Fairfax County General Economic and Demographic Overview, Fairfax County Web site.

boasted an unemployment rate of 1.5 percent and a wealth of high-paying jobs, the county treasury failed to reflect a similar picture of economic well-being.

Katherine Hanley, chairman of the board of supervisors, stated that during the second budget crisis, the board acknowledged that some changes were needed in the basic structure of the government. Citizens had become dissatisfied with the slow, inflexible, and unresponsive nature of their local government, and the board knew that it had to do something to bring the government's structure into alignment with fiscal constraints. Services like police, fire, and child care would need to expand, but the bureaucracy would not be able to grow in proportion to the population growth. Senior-level managers admitted that the government had gotten too complacent about change and the need to adapt to changes in the community. According to Hanley, "Internally, we finally recognized that things would never be the same again."[11]

FAIRFAX COUNTY GOVERNMENT

Fairfax County, with approximately 11,000 employees (excluding the public school system), was governed by the urban county executive form of government, one of several forms authorized in the Commonwealth of Virginia. The powers of government were vested in an elected board of supervisors consisting of nine members elected by district, plus a chairman elected at large. Board members were elected for 4-year terms; in September of 1999, there were six Democrat supervisors, including the chairman, and four Republican supervisors. The board established county policy, passed resolutions and ordinances, approved the budget, set tax rates, and approved land use plans

and zoning amendments. It also appointed the county executive—the administrative head of the county government. The board of supervisors was analogous to a public corporation's board of directors, and the county executive was analogous to a chief executive officer (CEO), but without the simple and clean definition of responsibilities of the corporate model.

Fairfax's government structure was different than that of many other localities, including those in neighboring suburban Maryland, where the system of governance was patterned after the federal model, which separated executive (i.e., administrative) and legislative functions. In Fairfax County, however, there was no defined separation of power—the legislative and administrative bodies were the same.

Two characteristics made governing in Fairfax County challenging. First was the relationship between the executive and the board of supervisors. Unlike many other counties that elected their executive, in Fairfax the executive was appointed by the board of supervisors. In Montgomery County, Maryland, for example, the elected executive crafted and presented the budget, hired and fired top managers, and could unilaterally implement new policies and procedures. The Fairfax County executive had little formal authority to do any of that; he or she hired many of the top managers and department heads—but only with consent of the board majority, and only the board could fire them. Likewise, the chairman of the board of supervisors—the top *elected* official in the county—had less formal authority than many small-town mayors.

In fact, real power in Fairfax was shared by the executive, the board, and hundreds of advisory committees and commissions.[12] As a result, neither the chairman nor the execu-

[11]Interview with Chairman Katherine K. Hanley.
[12]Shear, "Fairfax Debates a Push for Power," B1.

tive had both the mandate *and* the responsibility to lead. Thus, there had been a tendency to defer to committees, to avoid resolving major issues, and to not have anybody take a position and try to lead. This lack of a system of strong leadership had contributed to unfocused decision making in such areas as school funding, land development, and county finances.[13]

Second, the state was heavily involved in local decision making, especially on fiscal matters. Virginia was a Dillon rule state, which referred to a legal principle that limited local government powers to those expressly granted by the state legislature, necessarily implied in or incident to expressly granted power, or essential to accomplishing the declared objects and purposes of the local government. Therefore, the county executive was limited by what changes he or she could enact without first receiving permission from the Virginia General Assembly.

THE FAIRFAX COUNTY EXECUTIVE

The county executive in Fairfax led the administrative body of the county's government. The executive reported to the board, was responsible for strategic planning, crafted and presented the budget, and executed all resolutions and orders of the board. In fact, one supervisor believed that the executive's role was largely that of a bureaucrat who merely carried out the wishes of the board of supervisors. Rather than work under a contract with specific terms, the executive signed an appointment agreement and had a salary of approximately $145,000 per year, among the highest in the country for a similar position.[14]

One of the executive's most important and difficult tasks was proposing the county's operating budget. The process began in August when agencies submitted their budget requests to the Department of Management and Budget, which reviewed the requests, met with the department heads, and delivered a draft budget to the county executive in December. The executive then submitted the proposed budget to the board in February. After many reviews and public hearings, the board adopted a formal budget plan in April for the fiscal year that would begin in June.

Fairfax had lacked consistency in its top governing position in recent years, and at times the transition phases between two executives were somewhat ugly. Longtime County Executive J. Hamilton Lambert retired in December 1990 and was replaced by Dick King on an interim basis. King's immediate task was to resolve the budget shortage caused in part by the national recession. After that was resolved, the county began its search for a permanent replacement. The board had its first GOP majority in 10 years and was chaired by Republican Tom Davis. Bill Leidinger from Richmond, Virginia, was hired as county executive in January of 1993.

When Tom Davis resigned his position to run for Congress in 1995, the Democrats retook control of the board, and it became evident that they wanted a different style of leadership from what Leidinger had been providing. In the spring of 1996, the county found itself in yet another budget crisis, which forced Leidinger to make some difficult financial decisions, many of which the board disagreed with. According to Supervisor Frey, several Democrat supervisors then began to look for reasons to get rid of Leidinger. They announced in May that they had the votes to fire him, thereby greatly reducing his job security. In October

---

[13]Ibid.
[14]Mantesian, "Frustrated in Fairfax," 33.

of 1996, Leidinger went to a board meeting where they were working on his evaluation, and the board terminated his contract on the spot. No transition and no closure took place. Supervisor Frey added, "The board did not say, 'We think we need different direction; thank you, Bill.'" Instead, members cited a contract overrun on a consulting service as the reason.[15]

This history deeply soured relations among the board members and began a partisan period that the new executive would have to face. Deputy County Executive Anthony Griffin assumed the county executive position on an interim basis while the board turned its attention to finding a permanent replacement for Leidinger. Chairman Hanley said that they wanted to find someone who had experience in managing change in local government. In the summer of 1997, the board of supervisors (with a Democrat majority) embarked on a 3-month-long search for a new county executive. Eventually, the board narrowed the field to three candidates: interim County Executive Anthony Griffin; a consultant to the Washington, D.C. Control Board, Camille Barnett; and Robert O'Neill.

Robert O'Neill was an attractive candidate because of his successful record of revitalization at Hampton and the way he had transformed the city's traditional bureaucracy. The board felt that it had found in O'Neill someone who could effectively lead much-needed change in Fairfax County.

The final vote to hire O'Neill was eight votes in favor, one vote (a Republican) opposed, and one (another Republican) abstention. The views of Supervisor Frey, in particular, revealed some of the partisan mood that surrounded O'Neill's candidacy. Ideologically, Frey found it odd that the board would even look to an appointed

bureaucrat for strategic vision. In addition, when faced with a choice of hiring a candidate who had held the number one position at a smaller jurisdiction or the number two position at a large jurisdiction, Frey preferred the latter. Moreover, he was not overly impressed with O'Neill's revitalization efforts in Hampton because, according to Frey, they were funded largely with federal grants. He also was concerned with how O'Neill would manage the divided board in Fairfax County. While in Hampton, O'Neill worked with a non-partisan city council whose seven members were elected on an at-large basis to serve the entire city. Ultimately, even though Frey had some concerns, he felt O'Neill was a safe choice, and he did not want to add additional fuel to the partisan environment.[16] Nonetheless, O'Neill was viewed as the Democrats' candidate.

Amid this partisan squabbling, the board offered O'Neill the job of Fairfax County Executive in the summer of 1997. Cathy Chianese, assistant to the county executive, summarized the general feeling about the announcement:

County employees were generally unfamiliar with Bob O'Neill. Some were aware of his reputation as an innovator in Hampton but wondered what he could offer Fairfax County. And there was a general feeling among employees that Tony [Griffin] had done a great job as deputy county executive and did a great job as acting county executive. Employees were uncertain as to what the board was looking for in a new county executive. The board was quoted in the papers as saying that they were interested in making changes in the organization and hoped that the new

---

[15]Interview with Supervisor Michael T. Frey.
[16]Ibid.

executive would look at, among other things, the consolidation of activities and the elimination of positions. . . . and those are some of the reasons why they chose Bob O'Neill. Of course, as a county employee, those are not the messages you want to hear. There was a lot of unease and apprehension.[17]

O'Neill viewed the county executive position at Fairfax as the premier management challenge for someone in his field. He had peaked at Hampton, and he figured he either had to move on now or stay at Hampton for the rest of his career. Was he heading to the right place though? Former Fairfax County Public School Superintendent Dr. Robert Spillane had been quoted as saying that Fairfax's structure of government discouraged the type of decisive leadership that put O'Neill on the map in Hampton.[18] There were other questions: Would the same strategy that worked in Hampton also work in much larger Fairfax? He would not be able to reinvent Fairfax County by himself, so were Fairfax's employees ready for empowerment? How much time would he have? There had been absolutely no stability in the executive position in recent years, but perhaps Fairfax simply was not hiring the right type of leader. Despite these concerns, Robert O'Neill accepted the position of Fairfax County executive in August of 1997.

ROBERT O'NEILL

Robert O'Neill had been the city manager of Hampton, Virginia, since 1984. Prior to that, he was a director for Coopers & Lybrand for 3 years and a regional manager for the

Management Improvement Corporation of America for 2 years. During his 13 years as city manager and 4 years as assistant city manager for administrative services in Hampton, O'Neill gained regional and national recognition as one of the best public administrators in Virginia.

When O'Neill took the helm in Hampton, which had a government roughly 15 percent the size of Fairfax's, it was a troubled city: The population level was stagnant; taxes were among Virginia's highest; home values and per-capita income were low; the budget was out of balance; and the city was losing business to nearby communities.[19] O'Neill was hired to make the government there more innovative, flexible, cheaper, and more responsive to the community's needs. According to Mayor James Eason, he and city council wanted an "entrepreneurial government."[20]

Hampton's turnaround depended to a large extent on changing the way city government did its business. O'Neill recognized that he had to radically change the government's deep-rooted culture, and the values, beliefs, assumptions, and attitudes of its employees. In essence, entrepreneurial instincts would have to replace bureaucratic instincts. He started by creating a new vision for Hampton—to become the most livable city in Virginia—a vision that was even printed on employees' paycheck stubs.

O'Neill was recognized by various publications and associations for what he called a "major reinvention" of the Hampton city government. In addition to his success in changing the structure and operations of the government, O'Neill also won praise for directing a massive revitalization of the city's urban area, which had been neglected

---

[17]Interview with Cathy Chianese.
[18]Shear, "Fairfax Debates a Push for Power," B4.
[19]David Osborne and Peter Plastrik, "The O'Neill Factor," *The Washington Post Magazine,* July 13, 1997, W08.
[20]Ibid.

for years. O'Neill graduated summa cum laude from Old Dominion University and attended The Executive Program (TEP) at Darden in 1984.

COMING TO FAIRFAX

O'Neill was responsible for mapping the strategic direction for change within Fairfax's government. The board had a view that the organization needed to change—be more responsive, more customer oriented, quicker, less hierarchical—but those were fairly general wishes, and no clear set of priorities was articulated within the context of those needs. One of the first questions O'Neill posed to the board was, "What is your threshold of pain?" Depending on whom he talked to, he got a different response. O'Neill realized that he would need to take some time to assess where the organization was and where it needed to go. It was clear to him on day one that on a technical basis, the workforce was gifted and there was no fiscal crisis . . . at least not then. He talked about his agenda:

> I needed to figure how to build capacity within the organization so that it could adapt over time to what was going to be a relatively flat revenue stream, and still do the additional things that were going to be required by the changing population. What was going to have to change in the organization so that we could respond to these different stimuli?

O'Neill's strategy early on was to "engage my ears rather than my mouth." He took a step back to assess the strengths and weaknesses of the policies, processes, and people, and then he met with every agency head and organized small employee group meetings to ask questions, talk about what he saw, and get feedback on how employees viewed the organization. He sought out employees at satellite offices,

many of whom had never been visited by anyone from the executive's office. He also spent a considerable amount of time outside the walls of the county office buildings meeting with civic organizations, chambers of commerce, and other groups to listen to how others viewed county government. These listening efforts helped O'Neill figure out what needed to be done. The challenge he saw was how to get 11,000 employees all moving in the same direction. He could mandate change, but he knew he would have to engage people so that the organization would have the capacity to accept and deal with change on a continual basis. He wanted to "increase the number of ambassadors of the change effort."

One of O'Neill's first initiatives was to create 15 task forces with a cross section of employees on a wide range of topics including compensation, internal communication, performance evaluation criteria, and dealing with the new e-environment that was starting to dominate business in Fairfax County. He met with these task forces and gave them a charge (with respect to their specific topic) to figure out: (1) Where are we? (2) What are the dominant issues we face? and (3) What do you suggest we do? For the first time, department heads and staff people began working together. They cited this as evidence of how O'Neill had set about to change people's minds.

O'NEILL'S LEADERSHIP STYLE

O'Neill saw his primary role as that of a visionary—someone who could provide a vision of what the possibilities were and what the potential of the organization could be. Cathy Chianese agreed, adding:

> Bob's leadership style is very unique. I have never worked under someone like him before. He truly is the visionary . . . the strategic thinker . . . the person who moves this organization forward with-

out directing the things that need to happen on a day-to-day basis. You know from listening to him for just 5 minutes what his vision is, but he's not going to sit down and tell you the exact things he wants done and how he wants them done.[21]

According to O'Neill, "that would simply reinforce the hierarchical model that I was trying to change." O'Neill chose not to be terribly directive, preferring to say, "This is where we need to go." This new leadership style was especially important in his new role as executive because there was a perception that he was coming to Fairfax to fix something that was broken. However, to O'Neill, that was not the issue.

Whether or not it was broken did not really matter. What we were really about was what we would have to do as an organization tomorrow . . . the best predictors of future failures are past successes because the more successful you are, the more unlikely it is that you are going to be receptive to the stimuli that say you need to change.

Many employees wondered, "Why is it again that we have to change?" O'Neill admitted that it was hard to watch people do things differently than he would do them, but he persisted that it would be wrong for a leader to say, "Get out of my way and let me do this." Much of O'Neill's leadership style was new to employees of Fairfax County. Cathy Chianese commented, "Remember, if you have an organization that was used to being told what to do, you have a very interesting dynamic occurring when all of a sudden you have his leadership style."[22]

O'Neill's general process was to listen to the board's collective expectations, combine that with what he was hearing from the community and the task forces, and attempt to address those issues. When he needed the board's approval, he would attempt to get them comfortable enough with his plan to garner at least six votes. Sometimes this worked, sometimes it did not, and other times it produced mixed results.

One area of success was in changing the role of the executive's office. O'Neill felt that the office should be involved more in strategic issues and providing support to the entire organization. He wanted the day-to-day business of the county done at the department level, not dictated from his desk. He eliminated one of the deputy county executive positions, which acted as an intermediary between the agencies and the county executive, and created two additional assistant positions. As a result, the department heads were much more responsible and accountable for what their agencies were doing, and they had more autonomy to make decisions without calling the executive's office to ask for permission.

A second initiative he dealt with was merit pay for county employees. O'Neill never dictated that the county should change its pay system; rather, the recommendation and basic shell for the plan came from the work of one of the task forces. He agreed that it was important to add a pay component to recognize those who performed extraordinarily well, but the challenge was to get broad-based support among all employees who would be rewarded for performance over seniority.

Moreover, there were some unique challenges to installing a merit pay system in the public sector. For example, how

---

[21]Interview with Cathy Chianese.
[22]Ibid.

would one measure the bottom line? Were adequate support systems in place? O'Neill said that no one was going to get rich and he did not expect huge changes in behavior because of this variable pay element. However, it would allow a supervisor to recognize superior performance, and therefore, he felt there was inherent value well beyond the money. Unfortunately, the fresh memories of an unsuccessful attempt to institute performance bonuses for the county's public school teachers concerned the board, and the merit plan was not immediately adopted.

Because there was no clearly stated mandate from the board on what it wanted O'Neill to accomplish, there ended up being ten different expectations of what was going to be done. During his first year, these differences did not surface and the board supported most of his early initiatives. Unfortunately, in his second year, this support started to decline. It was an election year, and he soon heard rumblings from some supervisors: "So . . . when are you going to start?" Clearly, he had started, but O'Neill admitted that much of his first year was spent listening, gathering information, and carefully crafting his reform agenda. However, supervisors wanted tangible results to include in their reelection campaigns. Because they didn't want to risk alienating local constituencies, they wanted to take credit for O'Neill's successes without any of the blame for his mishaps. Over the course of his second year, O'Neill lost support for his reform agenda. When it came time to make tough decisions involving the most politically active constituencies, the board balked.

O'Neill reflected that in Fairfax, "There was an engrained culture of having done business a certain way for so long, and rela-

tionships and constituencies were built around the structure that was in place." This was evident in a plan he presented to merge the Department of Community and Recreation Services (DCRS) and the Park Authority. Many of the functions of those two departments either overlapped or were confusing or wasteful. For example, DCRS scheduled the ball fields, but the Park Authority owned and maintained them. A citizen was unable to register for Park Authority classes at one of the county's recreation centers. This seemed like a good opportunity to consolidate county services. However, O'Neill was unaware of the deeply embedded tensions between the two departments. For example, one thing that was important to the Park Authority and many citizens was open-space preservation. Chairman Hanley stated that:

> DCRS thought the Park Authority was the devil incarnate, and the Park Authority had a green team, which included people who thought that parkland should not all be athletic fields. Finding a balance between those two ideologies had always been an enormous problem for the county.[23]

Moreover, the citizen representation on the Park Authority board (the Park Authority board was appointed by the board of supervisors and did not report to the county executive) protected that balance. Functionally, not many people argued over O'Neill's plan; it was just that those two departments would *never* merge. The board rejected his plan.

O'Neill also learned that in Fairfax, supervisors—especially the four-member GOP minority—often were not willing to cede much authority to the executive's office.[24] Even an issue as straightforward as

---

[23]Interview with Chairman Katherine K. Hanley.
[24]Michael D. Shear and Patricia Davis, "Fairfax County Executive to Resign," *The Washington Post,* October 11, 1999, A1.

the selection of a new police chief presented a political minefield. It also represented the first time a disagreement between the executive and the board was made public, and it became a lightning rod for the press. Supervisors embarrassed O'Neill by forcing him to restart the search for the new police chief after Republican members criticized the initial search as being sloppy and producing finalists with weak credentials.[25] However, few within the organization were surprised. They said the board was going to have direct involvement in the selection of three individuals—the police chief, the fire chief, and the county attorney—regardless of who the county executive was. Quite simply, the four GOP members were not going to vote for O'Neill's selection. Chairman Hanley added that her decision to restart the selection "was not about Bob as a manager. . . . it was about politics. I was not going to hire a new police chief on such a partisan vote."[26] In the end, the board hired J. Thomas Manger, O'Neill's preferred candidate, but O'Neill's credibility already was damaged.

The board was not the only source of frustration for O'Neill. The politics of reform in Fairfax County also included thousands of civic groups, many of whom wanted to make policy decisions without actually running for office. O'Neill's revitalization plan provided a good example of these dynamics. The competing demands of the fast-growing portions of the county and the older, struggling areas forced O'Neill to tread carefully on economic development matters. Many within the government still thought of Fairfax as a brand-new county that was still developing. Consequently, nobody

was paying much attention to the older communities (mostly in the southern sections of the county). O'Neill suggested a revision of certain ordinances and the development review process to deal with the different needs and restrictions of older communities. He also created resource teams that would be available in the major revitalization areas to answer concerns and help guide new business owners through the approval process. However, newer communities would not sit quietly; they demanded equal treatment— they saw a dollar given to older areas as a dollar taken away from them.[27]

Although O'Neill had never stated this publicly, many observers said privately that he became frustrated by the lack of support he was receiving from the board.[28] On the other hand, most of the county's political, civic, and business leaders—especially the chamber of commerce and Fairfax County Federation of Citizens Associations— continued to support him. Chairman Hanley was one of his biggest supporters and was quick to point out that many forms of major reorganization were underway but were not getting any attention. Referring to his level of success, Hanley said, "If a baseball player batted what Bob had, he would be in the Hall of Fame."[29] Internally, Cathy Chianese said that the changes O'Neill made in his first 2 years were "incredible," and that there was "a complete turnaround in how we think about what we do and how we do it."[30]

O'Neill summarized his thoughts as he reflected on the past 2 years:

> I believe that the path we have taken in the past 2 years has been in the right direction and at the right pace. Yet I

[25]Ibid., A12.
[26]Interview with Katherine K. Hanley.
[27]Mantesian, "Frustrated in Fairfax," 35.
[28]Ibid., 33.
[29]Interview with Katherine K. Hanley.
[30]Interview with Cathy Chianese.

discovered that it is very difficult to build consensus on a broad set of objectives among nine people whose principal interests are what happens in his/her district. As a result, when we moved cautiously toward reform, we came under fire for moving too slowly. When we offered more ambitious plans, we were told we were changing too much.

Earlier that week, O'Neill received an interesting phone call. Without solicitation, he was offered the position of president of the National Academy of Public Administration (NAPA), a nonprofit government think tank in Washington, D.C. The job offered a national stage to give lectures on local government reform. His decision, as well as the timing of any announcement, was important. The top position at NAPA opened up about once every 10 years and NAPA historically had not offered the president's post to someone with only a local government background. Therefore, in his mind, this was a once-in-a-lifetime offer. However, O'Neill did not yet have the luxury of seeing his reforms through. His performance evaluation with the board was 2 weeks away, and he felt that if he decided to resign and move on to NAPA, it would be best to announce the decision prior to his evaluation.

Would he be cutting off his accomplishments too soon by leaving now and taking the job at NAPA? He did not feel that his work in Fairfax was finished, and it could hardly be said that he had come close to achieving what was predicted for him or reaching the goals that he himself outlined at the beginning of his tenure. The board of supervisors election would be over in 2 months, and he could then finally get their full attention. Perhaps the election would be a referendum on the supervisors who had been the most vocal against his policies. But had he accomplished about as much as he was going to? Could he be an effective change agent if he were to stay at Fairfax? The police chief incident was another reminder of the constituencies O'Neill had to answer to, the bullets he had to dodge, and the restrictions placed on his ability to change the face of county government. Perhaps the political dynamics in Fairfax County were too much for any appointed executive to master . . . even for Bob O'Neill. He wondered whether to stay or take the job at NAPA, and how to make and announce his decision. ■

Case 12   Japanese Leadership: The Case of Tetsundo Iwakuni

In 1993, a national survey revealed that Tetsundo Iwakuni,[1] mayor of Izumo City, was the most popular of Japan's 656 mayors. Based on his strong, positive, national image, as well as his brief but remarkable term as mayor, by the spring of 1995 Iwakuni was running for the national Diet seat from Setagaya. His decision to do so testified to his varied and interesting career as a domestic businessman, as an international investment banker, and as a local politician with national prominence. His story sheds light on the nature of Japanese leadership and the challenges facing it today.

CHILDHOOD

Iwakuni's story begins on the southern coast of Honshu in the Kansai Region. Iwakuni was born in Osaka in July 1936. In December 1943, in the midst of World War II, Iwakuni's father passed away: Iwakuni was only 7 years old. In later years, Iwakuni would remember his father as a generous man who had taken him on business trips and to baseball games. After Iwakuni's father passed away, Iwakuni's mother determined to escape the imminent threat of Allied bombing of Osaka by taking Iwakuni and his younger sister westward across the central mountain range to her ancestral home in Izumo City, Shimane Prefecture.

Izumo held a central place in Japanese history. According to ancient legend, Japan was formed by gods who gathered together scattered land to create islands. These gods and their relatives resided in Izumo (located on the west coast of the big island, Honshu). As the gods proliferated, they gradually settled on the other islands, but they returned to Izumo every October to pay their respects to their ancestral gods, or *kami*. From ancient times, then, Izumo was considered Japan's spiritual capital. Even in modern times, Izumo retained this distinction: In all prefectures except Shimane, October was known as *kanna-zuki,* the "month with no gods"; in Shimane, however, October was known as *kamiari-zuki,* the "month of the gods." Thus, despite the fact that Izumo was a small rural town of 85,000, far removed from Tokyo, it figured prominently in Japanese culture and history.

Iwakuni remained in Izumo for the duration of World War II. He remembered the day the war ended. He saw soldiers standing in a circle and crying while an officer explained something that Iwakuni could not hear. He knew that something disastrous had happened, because soldiers never cried. When he heard the emperor announce on the radio that Japan had been defeated, however, he understood. After the war, the young Iwakuni worked hard helping his mother. He cultivated land for growing tomatoes, cucumbers, squash, and other vegetables. By the time he was in the fifth grade, he was working part-time delivering newspapers and milk. Although it was unusual for a boy his age to work, he did not

UVA-OB-0627

This case was prepared by Maki DePalo and James G. Clawson. Copyright © 1996 by the University of Virginia Darden School Foundation, Charlottesville, VA. All rights reserved. Rev. 8/97.

[1]Japanese vowels are all pronounced the same: a = ah, I = ee, u = oo, e = eh, and o = oh. Hence, Mr. Iwakuni's name is pronounced, tets-oon-doh ee-wah-koo-nee. Likewise, Shimane = shee-mahn-eh and Izumo = ee-zoo-moh.

feel burdened. His father's early death meant that his role, as the oldest son, was to become the leader of the family. Although he sometimes cried himself to sleep recalling his father, he accepted his obligation to support his mother and to take care of his younger sibling.

Even though Japanese people, especially in the countryside, tended to keep a distance from strangers or newcomers, Iwakuni made friends with ease. He had a knack for drawing and enjoyed teaching the other kids to play baseball. He spent all his spare time playing baseball. "I played baseball all the time, probably because it made me feel closer to my father and would remind me of my days with him," he recalled. "I had a dream to be a teacher like my father. I was also interested in becoming a journalist or politician. Inspiring people by pen or organizing society through politics was attractive to me."

Iwakuni worked hard in school, and after taking the competitive Japanese entrance exam, was admitted to the best high school in Izumo. He commuted 2 hours each way to and from school. His schedule meant that he had to give up baseball, but he continued working part-time. He also studied diligently, finishing the advanced curriculum a year early. No one was surprised when he passed the entrance exam for Tokyo University, the best university in Japan. Armed with four scholarships, Iwakuni left Izumo for Tokyo.

COLLEGE LIFE

Tokyo University offered a powerful experience for the country boy from Shimane. If Japanese universities were famous for stiff entrance examinations, they were also notorious for lax academic discipline among admitted students. As a freshman, Iwakuni fell into this pattern and did little but play baseball. He skipped all his German classes for 2 years until he realized that the law program he intended to enter in his junior year required German. He petitioned the school administration to allow him to take all the required German tests for the 2-year curriculum. Fortunately, the administration authorized him to do so and set the test date for a week later. "I studied like a madman all day long for a week. It was quite fortunate that I passed all the tests. Naturally, I forgot everything I had learned within a week," he later recalled.[2]

At Tokyo University, Iwakuni met many talented people who eventually figured prominently in Japan's business and political arenas. One of these happened to be Hiromasa Ezoe, a founder of the Recruit Corporation, who later gained notoriety for his role in the Liberal Democratic Party's (LDP) bribery scandal, an incident that ultimately brought the curtain down on 36 years of LDP-controlled government. Iwakuni commented:

He, Hiromasa Ezoe, showed business talent while in university. He would gather notes from all our subjects and print them to sell to students who skipped classes. Frankly, I sold a couple of notes to him and it helped ease my financial burden a lot. It's still hard for me to be angry at him for the bribery scandal.[3]

Iwakuni's desire to become a teacher had diminished by the time he was ready to graduate and choose a career. He considered taking the public service exam

[2]Iwakuni, Tetsundo. "When a Man Makes a Decision," *PHP Laboratory,* October 1990, 136–139.
[3]Ibid., 141–143.

and entering one of the Ministries of the national government. He explained:

> I could have taken the exam to become a public servant, but to take the exam, I would have had to stay in Tokyo for the summer. However, I longed to return to Shimane to see my family. It was a family tradition to have a summer get-together, and my mother usually prepared a big feast for us. I could not resist this family tradition and opted not to take the exam.[4]

He also had considered becoming a journalist. However, after speaking with an alumnus of Tokyo University who had become an executive of Nikko Securities, Iwakuni decided to enter the world of finance.

Right after graduation, Iwakuni married a classmate from Izumo High School. "Initially, ours was not a passionate love; we were more like high school buddies. In fact, we did not even date while in high school. Since Ginko also went to college in Tokyo, we started to get together and gradually fell in love. It was more like a natural process that we got married," he explained.

Iwakuni noted that he expected that his career would occupy most of his time and there would not be any chance to build and maintain a relationship with Ginko if he had not married her at that time. He commented, "I remember that I told her a few conditions for our marriage, which were very old-fashioned ideas. As I expected, I devoted myself to my work and often did not make it back home. I was probably not a good husband at that time."[5]

CAREER AT NIKKO SECURITIES

Early in his career at Nikko, Iwakuni was asked to go to New York. Even though he could not speak Engish, his boss's considerable support and encouragement convinced him to take the assignment, and he and his wife moved to New York. For a while, he was a little disoriented at his new office; as much as possible, he avoided speaking English. When the telephone rang, he hoped someone else would take the call. Eventually, however, he saw that people spoke English with pride even if they were not fluent. He realized that people spoke Spanish-English, French-English, and Italian-English, so he might as well speak Japanese-English. This realization helped Iwakuni learn English.

Iwakuni became addicted to the dynamic business activities in New York, and later in Europe, and worked harder and harder. He became an acting branch manager in London and then played an important role in opening a new branch office in Paris. He successfully lobbied for a building in a prime location in Paris and then persuaded Nikko's president to invest in it. That building eventually became the standard for Japanese security companies in Paris, because other Japanese security firms followed Nikko's lead and established offices nearby. Soon, Iwakuni became branch manager of the Paris office. His career in Europe was also impressive. After he had created innovative financial products, including a tax-free, small-sum savings system and bond-investment trusts in Tokyo, he successfuly introduced a completely new convertible bond with options in the Middle East market.

Ginko was a supportive wife. She followed Tetsundo wherever his career led. They had two daughters, Mari and Eri, both of whom did their schooling in London and Paris. In addition to learning English and French, the children had to master their native Japanese, something that was

---

[4]Ibid., 143–144.
[5]Ibid., 144–148.

difficult to do while not living in Japan. Whenever Iwakuni visited the head office in Japan, he brought back videotapes of popular TV programs to help the girls in their Japanese studies. Because he'd lost his father early in life, Iwakuni paid as much attention to his family as he could. Although his weekdays were full until late with business, he spent every weekend with his family. He often arranged for them to travel together around Europe.

Then, quite unexpectedly, in 1977 Iwakuni received an order to return to Japan to manage the Ginza Branch in downtown Tokyo. By that time, both 15-year-old Mari and 13-year-old Eri had their own dreams of attending Cambridge University and Oxford University, respectively, to pursue their studies, and Iwakuni worried about interrupting their international experience. He also was concerned about the fact that Japan's educational system was less than accommodating for students who had been educated abroad. He saw four available options. First, he could go back to Japan alone. Second, the whole family could go back to Japan and Mari and Eri could attend the American School there. Third, the whole family could go back to Japan and Mari and Eri could attend Japanese school there. Fourth, he could resign from Nikko Securities and stay in London.

His family meant too much for Iwakuni to choose the first option. Taking the second and third options would put Mari's and Eri's dreams at risk. Iwakuni seriously considered the fourth option. Resigning from Nikko Securities, however, could be a fatal career choice. In Japan, where lifetime employment was given and expected, the strong conflict between company loyalty and family ties was usually resolved in favor of the company. Iwakuni had never imagined the possibility of resigning from Nikko Securities when he took their original offer. He was wracked by the implications of the

decision facing him and realized that no matter which option he chose, it would affect his career and the lives of his children in major ways. He recalled this time as one of most stressful periods in his life.

Iwakuni chose the fourth option. He resigned from Nikko Securities and stayed in London, even though he had no idea whether or not he could find another job. He chose to announce his decision to resign from Nikko and remain in London at his farewell party. Although he normally should have spoken with his superiors first, he knew they would have persuaded him to remain with Nikko and to transfer back to Japan. Although shocked by both Iwakuni's announcement and his forum, Iwakuni's boss understood that his decision was firm and did not try to talk him out of it. Iwakuni later wrote a long letter to the Human Resources Department, explaining that his situation was influenced heavily by his daughters' future educational needs. The Human Resources Director replied that in the future the firm would weigh such factors more heavily when changing assignments for other executives.

Subsequently, however, rumors began to circulate that Iwakuni had left Nikko Securities not to support his daughters' education but to further his personal career in Europe. There was also speculation that Iwakuni had regarded the assignment to the Ginza Branch office in Tokyo as a downgrade. In his book, Iwakuni described this episode:

I understood the company's concern about my career development. They realized that my lack of experience in Japan would hurt my career as I climbed the ladder at Nikko Securities. The Ginza branch office had a good reputation and solid customers and could provide a great opportunity for me to learn the Japanese market. I really appreciated their consideration.

To quell speculation that he had left Nikko for personal gain and not because of family obligations, Iwakuni hesitated before actively undertaking a job search. He eventually received an offer from the investment bank Morgan Stanley.

INTERNATIONAL CAREER

Ironically, Morgan Stanley soon required Iwakuni to return to Japan. Ginko and Tetsundo went back to Japan and left their daughters in Britain to continue their education. Whenever Mari and Eri visited them in Japan, Ginko and Tetsundo would meet them at the airport. On the way to the airport, Tetsundo's heart would dance thinking about Mari and Eri: How tall had they grown? How beautiful had they become? On the other hand, when he and his wife would see Mari and Eri off at the airport for the return trip to England, Tetsundo would feel his heart sink in despair.

One day, while driving back from the airport, Tetsundo asked Ginko, "Shall we go back to New York so that we could live together as before?" Eager to reunite his family, in 1984, Iwakuni left Morgan Stanley and joined Merrill Lynch in New York. He soon became the chairperson and president of Merrill Lynch Japan. In 1987, Iwakuni became the first Japanese senior vice president of Merrill Lynch Capital Markets (the parent company of Merrill Lynch Japan).

As a new international leader, Iwakuni was the subject of many journalistic inquiries. He repeatedly explained his career and his responsibilities during many interviews. He also was asked often to discuss racial issues. He recalled one incident at a train station when a stranger accosted him and accused Japanese soldiers of cruelty during World War II. Iwakuni tried to explain the Japanese side of the situation, but the gentleman remained angry. Iwakuni asked, "What do you think about Germany, then?"

"It's OK because they are Christian," replied the man. The incident left Iwakuni with a sense of the deep underlying racial distance still lying between the East and the West.[6]

Many Japanese people looked up to Iwakuni as one of only a handful of Japanese who had become truly international businessmen. Iwakuni, too, felt the significance of his rare accomplishment. He once said to an interviewer, "Sometimes in this office, viewing the scenery of Manhattan, I feel personal pride for achieving this position as an internationalist. Then I just bubble up with Enka, the popular music of my generation." The interviewer closed the article by noting, "It could be his being a Japanese country potato that made him [so successful as] an international business man."[7]

In 1988, the University of Virginia's Darden Graduate Business School asked Iwakuni to become a visiting professor and to give lectures occasionally at the university. Because one of his earliest childhood dreams was to become a teacher, Iwakuni accepted this offer. Typically, he visited Darden once or twice a year and lectured on current business and political affairs in Japan, answering questions afterward. He found that one of the benefits of being a professor was learning how the new generation viewed the world. Though his experience at the university was generally uplifting, Iwakuni recalled one sad incident. Students there were normally positive and asked questions even after the lecture. One day, however, he observed that African-American students were keeping away from him. This was shortly after an inconsiderate

[6]Minoru Sato, *President* (Tokyo, Japan, 1987), 292–305.
[7]Ibid., 292–305.

Japanese politician had made some ridiculous racial comments about black people. It was a time and circumstance Iwakuni regretted.

In September of 1988, Iwakuni received a phone call from an influential friend in Japan who asked him to run for mayor of his hometown, Izumo City. After that, the number of telephone calls increased each day. (For some of the people of Izumo, it was their first experience making an international telephone call.) Iwakuni received many enthusiastic calls asking him to become the mayor; a few voiced opposition to the idea. Those against the idea said that becoming the mayor of Izumo was too small a task for Iwakuni and if he wanted to enter politics, he should consider becoming a Diet member.

Iwakuni was overwhelmed by the political passion of the people in Izumo. He knew that becoming mayor would mean that he would have to return to Japan and live there. Mari and Eri were attending Stanford University and Harvard University, respectively, and the family would again be separated. Iwakuni faced a tough decision. Sensing his frustration, his wife reminded him that they could come back to New York again someday, but Iwakuni knew that despite these kind words, they probably never would return to New York if they left. Nevertheless, after much thought, he decided to run for mayor of Izumo.

MAYORAL ELECTION

Some people said that Iwakuni's bid for the mayorship in Izumo would merely prove to be a short-term stepping stone to the Japanese Diet. Iwakuni, however, viewed the mayorship as a 4-year commitment—an opportunity to satisfy his public service calling—and so did not look beyond the immediate term.

Iwakuni did not satisfy any of the four generally accepted tacit requirements for the mayor's job. The mayor in Izumo was supposed to be a person who had been born in Izumo, had grown up in Izumo, had been living in Izumo, and intended to live in Izumo afterward, as well. Iwakuni's intention to enter the race was a new experience for himself and for the people of Izumo.

At the outset, Iwakuni identified some conditions on which he wanted to conduct his campaign. First, he wanted to win the mayoral position in an open and fair election. In the countryside, it was not unusual to perform "spade work" prior to an election and effectively appoint a mayor by discouraging other candidates from running. Secondly, he demanded that he would not be limited only to Liberal Democrat Party (LDP)[8] policy recommendations. He wanted to receive recommendations from all other parties. Finally and most importantly, he made it clear that he would run his campaign in his own way.

During the campaign, Iwakuni walked all around his electoral district to see as many people as possible. He wanted to understand their hopes, as well as develop his policies. He was surprised and impressed at the level of support for and involvement in the election from the people of Izumo. Sometimes their enthusiasm went too far. For example, Iwakuni refused to use a Daruma doll, a traditional election symbol in Japan.[9] It was a custom in Japan that when politicians or businessmen set a goal such as running for office or improving

---

[8]LDP was the dominant political force in Japan following World War II; it was Iwakuni's supporting party at the time.
[9]Daruma dolls are papier-mâché replicas of Buddha, usually painted in red with large white eyes and no pupils. The dolls are bottom heavy so that if you knock them over, they return to a standing position, a sign of relentlessness. They are thought to be a good luck charm.

profits, they would purchase a large Daruma doll and paint in one of the eyes to symbolize the goal. When the goal was achieved, they would paint in the other eye as a symbol of success. Iwakuni's supporters thought that even though he did not like it, it would be necessary to have a Daruma doll to win the election, so they prepared the doll behind his back. When Iwakuni found the big, one-eyed Daruma doll in his office, he was shocked and gathered his people to set forth his philosophy again. He explained that whenever he saw Japanese politicians use this doll, he felt embarrassed for handicapped people. So many one-eyed Daruma dolls are thrown away after every election, he said; the practice reminded him of society's treatment of handicapped people and it bothered him a lot. His supporters then came to understand his thinking; the Daruma disappeared and did not return again.

Iwakuni won the Izumo City mayoral election on March 26, 1989.

MAYOR IWAKUNI

By all accounts, Iwakuni's service as mayor of Izumo was remarkable. He introduced a number of practices that reenergized and transformed municipal governments not only in Izumo but by example in numerous other cities, as well. He had an unorthodox style, creative ideas, and a curious tendency to break precedents while still maintaining a strong traditional belief in the Japanese people. Personally, he was rather shy, not given to emotional outbursts, and projected a professional but reserved presence both on and off camera. His creative thinking, however, was evident from his first day on the job.

As soon as Iwakuni won the election, his staff began planning the traditional first-day ceremony, which was always held at 9:30 or 10 o'clock in the morning of the first business day that the new administration took office.

Iwakuni, however, decided to have the ceremony between 7:50 and 8:20 A.M., so that city office staff could start service at their regular hour of 8:30 A.M. He felt that the municipal office should be considered one of the biggest and best service industries in Japan, and he didn't want to inconvenience the citizens with a celebration in the middle of regular service hours.

After the celebration, on his first day in office, Iwakuni outlined many of his plans for the city. He notified his staff that he would reorganize the whole organizational structure within 2 years in order to make it more responsive to citizen needs. This plan was a major undertaking because Iwakuni would have to learn the existing system and also give the municipal workers the opportunity to review their own practices.

He also declared that in order to minimize exposure to bribery attempts, senior officers, including himself, should resist attending wedding ceremonies, funerals, and other unofficial receptions. Traditionally, Japanese politicians were invited to these family events and given envelopes with "contributions" in them in return for favors. To further support his staff in adhering to this new policy, Iwakuni personally committed publicly not to attend any of these family occasions for anyone with any connection to his region during his tenure in office. He also made sure that Izumo City would not consider the recommendations of influential citizens when it came to hiring practices. Iwakuni wanted to wipe away the unfair custom of using personal influence to find a government job.

He also outlined plans to improve the quality of service to the citizens. Many city employees, who were used to doing just the minimum needed to get by, considered these changes overwhelming. Eventually, his policies designed to reduce bureaucratic overhead and improve service came to be known as "Small Office, Big Service." He felt that this concept was easier for citizens to understand than the more technical terms used in the newspapers, like *gyousei kaikaku,* "administrative reform."

Iwakuni had three immediate goals: improving citizen orientation, increasing efficiency, and maintaining commitment to deadlines. He felt that city government should be the model of high-quality service and began applying business procedures and processes in city hall. Iwakuni claimed that nobody at the municipal office should use the previously common expression, "We are giving it some thought," which often ended up meaning, "We are not going to do this." He permitted only two answers to a citizen's request: either "We will answer by this date" or "We cannot do it." This policy put a large amount of pressure on workers who were used to the more leisurely pace of the traditional bureaucracy.

As a part of this quality-improvement program, Iwakuni also launched a "man-power dispatching system" that borrowed personnel from large companies such as Mitsubishi Chemical and Yamaha Motors for short periods and employed them in city hall. These short-term employees set examples for and motivated municipal office workers.

As a part of his citizen focus, in May 1989, Iwakuni initiated a plan to develop a high-tech social-service card system. The card would use an integrated circuit chip that would contain all necessary social-service information. For example, the card would include administration, benefit, and health information that would ensure swift medical treatment in case of an emergency. Iwakuni planned to target the citizen ID card first to senior citizens and then to all Izumo citizens.

One of Iwakuni's most shocking propos-als had to do with making municipal services available during nonbusiness hours. Most Japanese work Monday through Friday and half days on Saturday. Because city hall was open during the same hours, it was difficult for working citizens to conduct their munici-pal business. People who wanted to obtain municipal documents or handle other city business had to coordinate their schedules to go down to the municipal office on week-days. Iwakuni felt, however, that this was tremendously inconvenient, especially given the increasing numbers of working women. His proposal to open branch offices of the city office building in shopping malls during weekends stunned people in Izumo City and earned nationwide attention.

Of course, many complaints came from municipal office workers at the beginning of this new procedure because they did not want to work on weekends. Iwakuni's plan to alleviate employee resistance turned out to be not only acceptable to his staff but innovative. He established several groups of five people. Each group was assigned just one Saturday and one Sunday a year at the weekend service center. In the end, his idea to locate the desk in shopping centers was welcomed by everybody—citizens and em-ployees alike—in Izumo.

Iwakuni also had a strong belief that the Japanese people had a close connection to nature and its resources. For example, in contrast with Chinese architecture, Japanese architecture was simple and used little orna-mentation and paint. Out of respect for nature, artists would intentionally leave a flaw in their work to show their regard for the original that they were imitating. The national religion, Shinto, taught that the gods, *kami,* lived in various places and dens of nature. Building on this theme, Iwakuni announced plans to rebuild the public schools out of wood and to construct an all-wood, all-weather, domed sports arena.

Many thought these ideas odd. At the time, most schools in Japan were two- and three-story concrete structures with exter-nal hallways overlooking all-dirt playing fields. The typical school design was reminis-cent of the thousands of modern, concrete blockhouse *danchi* or apartment buildings throughout the country. Iwakuni, however, believed that Japanese culture was based on paper and wood and that these features were reflected in traditional architecture and construction materials. He noted elements like *washi* paper, *shoji* doors, *fusuma* paper room dividers, post-and-beam construction, *kotatsu,* and other features of premodern Japanese houses. Iwakuni maintained that the concrete blockhouse construction of the modern schools desensitized students to their rich national culture and inured them to the fine arts. He wanted the citizens and students of Izumo to be encouraged rather than alienated by their surroundings. He instituted regulations that all new school buildings were to be designed and built with a much larger wood content than before.

Iwakuni's love of natural materials and his belief that the Japanese people had a close association with trees and wood extended to his concern for the environment in general. He established a "tree doctor certificate" and a tree service so that anybody could inform the municipal office of a sick or dying public or private tree. He gave licenses to six "tree doctors" and charged them with keeping the district's trees healthy. The idea took root, so to speak, and gained rapidly in popularity. Other municipalities began calling to find out about the program, and the national news media picked up the story and made it a national public interest story. Even Iwakuni was surprised at the number of inquiries received from all over Japan. It soon got the attention of the Ministry of Agriculture and Forestry and became a national project.

Based on his living experience in Paris, London, New York, and Tokyo, Iwakuni also was concerned with the problem of waste disposal. Several talks with women's groups resulted in a new measure for garbage treatment in Izumo. In order to decrease the amount of garbage the citizens of Izumo produced, the municipal office decided to adopt a fee system. Each January, the municipal office provided 100 garbage bags to every household. If those bags were not enough, households could purchase additional bags. By the same token, the city would repurchase leftover bags at the same price. It was mandatory to use these specially designed bags and to write the household name on them. Though the name requirement was controversial at first, after just 6 months, 80 percent of Izumo citizens approved of the policy.[10]

Iwakuni was as interested in his constituency as he was in trees and the environment. He wanted to know as many people in Izumo as he could. He frequently visited elderly centers. Those who lived in nursing homes usually didn't have much influence in politics and didn't understand how their city was changing. Iwakuni wanted to remedy that. As he visited, he explained what he was doing and encouraged residents to participate in city affairs. One example of his concern for the elderly centered around a great-grandmother and her famous son. On Respect-for-the-Aged Day, Iwakuni visited the oldest woman in Shimane Prefecture to pay his respect. As it turned out, she was the great-grandmother of a famous baseball player in Japan.

She was proud of her great-grandson and often talked about him to her friends. Though her great-grandson kept in touch, she had not seen him for a long time. Iwakuni was so taken by her story that he promised, out of the blue, to bring her great-grandson back to Izumo so that she could see him. After he left the center, Iwakuni began to worry because he had no way of getting this famous person to Izumo. Bound by his promise, however, he was determined

---

[10]Saburo Nagao, *Friday,* Tokyo, Japan: 48–51.

to do his best. Using every connection of which he could think and despite great difficulty, Iwakuni reunited the great-grandmother and her famous great-grandson in January of 1990. She passed away peacefully a year later.

Iwakuni participated in community group meetings as much as possible. He found that women's study groups and organizations were tremendously innovative and often developed interesting ideas. Because Iwakuni was actively involved in the women's participation movement, whenever he could he worked with women's groups instead of groups consisting of mainly men. He even went as far as discriminating against men in some ways so that he could have more time to exchange ideas with women. He wrote in his weekly magazine article, "Women tend to be more verbal than men. They constantly communicate with their children or mothers . . . They are more responsive as well. . . . Women are the majority, too. Fifty-two percent of Izumo citizens are women and 53 percent of the eligible voters are women as well . . ." He also gave higher-level positions to women in the municipal office. He called it manpower expansion without hiring. Although there were no women in upper management when he became mayor, during his tenure Iwakuni saw to it that more women obtained promotions; his policy was that women's careers should advance according to their talent.

Iwakuni also tried to have close contact with children. He visited many elementary schools and high schools to encourage the children to think about Izumo City's future. He would explain things as plainly as possible so that the children could understand. In his book he described their enthusiasm:

They listen to my stories with their eyes wide, openly showing their curiosity about what is happening in their city. Often, they would write a letter to me after the lecture. Even though their letters are not that sophisticated and their writings were somewhat hard to read, reading their letters is one of my favorite activities.[11]

Although he knew that his practice of visiting children would have little if any political benefit, he wanted to make certain that they had a clear vision for the future. Whenever he visited schools, Iwakuni brought a pair of red and white dogwood trees so that the children could learn about beautiful flowers and trees. He truly believed in the significance of trees and dreamed that the city would one day be full of beautiful trees and flowers.

By July of 1990, most of Iwakuni's plans were in full swing. Many of his programs had multiple purposes: to build on Japanese culture and cultural values, to teach, and to benefit the citizenry. For example, he promoted a national event, a 42.195-kilometer footrace, in Izumo. He called the race "Izumo Kamiden" (the "god marathon") to invoke the ancient myth and held it in October, the month when legend held that the gods congregated in Izumo. The race enabled people to remember their national heritage, to learn more about Japanese culture and about Izumo, and also to undertake a healthy exercise program preparing for the run.

Another manifestation of Iwakuni's appreciation for Japanese culture was his instruction to limit the number of English-based terms used in public office. Japanese borrowed many foreign terms and even had a script, *katakana,* set aside just for foreign terms. Iwakuni set the example and invited others to avoid using these *gairaigo,* or foreign terms, as another means to build

---

[11]Tetsundo Iwakuni, "Three Promises II," *Yomiuri Newspaper,* July 14, 1993, 239–243.

national pride. Paradoxically, Iwakuni also believed that residents of rural Japanese cities should know more about world affairs.

Rural cities in Japan like Izumo tended to have a primarily domestic orientation and were generally ignorant of international affairs. This was, in many respects, a holdover from the isolationist policies of the Tokugawa government that had kept Japan separated from the rest of the world for 300 years. Thus, many rural Japanese were unaware and distrustful of foreign affairs, people, and customs. However, Iwakuni, because of his experience, saw the importance of introducing world events to his district. He felt that the lack of international exposure in the countryside accelerated the movement of young, ambitious people to Tokyo, a phenomenon that had been encouraged by the national government since World War II and which had deprived the outlying prefectures of youthful talent. To change this myopic focus, Iwakuni energetically promoted the existing "Sister City" program with Santa Clara, California.

He also changed the official calendar from the traditional Japanese calendar (which counted the years of each emperor's reign) to the Western calendar. Izumo was the only municipality in Japan to do this. He then organized a goodwill trip to China. Iwakuni found it fascinating that housewives were open-minded about this trip and enthusiastically attended, in part based on their respect for him, saying, "There is nothing to worry about because Mayor Iwakuni is here with us."

Education was one of Iwakuni's most important community platforms. As mentioned, young people frequently left Izumo to attend colleges or 4-year universities in Tokyo. This was in part because of a shortage of higher-education opportunities in the countryside. Tokyo absorbed not only the Izumo labor force, but also its young scholars, leaving for the most part only children and senior citizens. Iwakuni launched a plan to establish a women's junior college in the Izumo region.[12]

Iwakuni also was concerned about the traditional Japanese educational system. The existing Japanese educational system emphasized a series of annual exams that determined advancement and further educational opportunities. Regardless of what did or did not happen during the school year, students knew they would have to pass the annual exams if they wanted to progress. This situation had led to the development of a tutoring school industry throughout Japan and created some conflict in educational circles. Students tended not to learn such subjects as world history because they knew these subjects did not have much significance in the national college entrance exams. At the same time, the world was becoming smaller and smaller, and the need to understand global affairs was increasing. Iwakuni believed that learning another country's history was the first step in understanding its culture and spirit. To give credence to his ideas, Iwakuni declared that anybody who did not study world history in school would not be eligible to become a municipal officer in Izumo.

REACTIONS

Most of the reactions to Iwakuni's innovations in Izumo were positive. Not only did local citizens applaud his efforts, but news reporters and municipal officials from other cities constantly contacted him for more information on his new approaches. Not all of the reactions were positive, however. One journalist who attended a meeting at

---

[12] The college was completed in March 1995.

the Izumo municipal office in September 1990 wrote the following critique:

> One attendee questioned a project's budget and progress report to Tetsundo. Accordingly, Tetsundo made a detailed inquiry. His staff hurried to find and assemble the requested information. Tetsundo stated that the information was not enough for him to see the contractor in question. He even asked, "why don't you try to do this job by yourself?" . . . Workers were exhausted and there was no capacity for them to accomplish any more. There was a general lack of ideas among the staff to find a way out of their predicament. . . . Especially for those low achievers who were not used to working at their best, changes initiated by Tetsundo could be a little too overwhelming. Thirty-four workers resigned from the office within a year. . . . Izumo City's budget was increasing. . . . In his first year as mayor, the budget was $219 million; a 13.1 percent increase from the previous year's budget. This year's budget reached $251 million; a 14.7 percent increase from the previous year's budget . . .[13]

This column was one of only a few articles that gave a somewhat negative opinion of Iwakuni's work. The majority of the articles were positive or expressed appreciative opinions.

Iwakuni's popularity grew quickly throughout Japan. In his first year, he lectured more than 150 times around the nation. He was a frequent guest on TV and radio programs. In March of 1991, Izumo City was given the "Marketing Excellence" award by Japan's *Noritsu Kyokai* as one of the best service organizations among prestigious electronics, automobile, and cosmetics companies. It was the first and only time a governmental agency had received the award. By this time, Iwakuni had been appointed to several other national governmental committees. Subsequently, he also was nominated to the Provisional Council for the Promotion of Administrative Reform, an advisory committee to the Prime Minister.

By April 1991, most of Iwakuni's projects were reaching fruition. The IC social-service card system had been introduced and was the first of its kind in the nation. The Izumo Cultural Museum was established with the mandate of passing on Japan's precious traditions to future generations. Plans for a senior citizens' exercise facility were well underway. In 1992, the Izumo all-weather athletic dome was completed. It was the world's biggest wooden dome, reaching 48 meters high and equaling the legendary height of the original Izumo shrine. The dome, which was designed to glow at night when lit from the inside, received an award for the beauty of its lighting. To celebrate the city's growth and innovation, the Prince of Japan even paid a goodwill visit.

Although many city office staff members struggled with Iwakuni's new policies and procedures, as the office improved service the staff's attitude also improved. Nobuo Hanya, a blind man, for example, expressed his intention to participate in the annual Kunibiki Marathon race, and the municipal staff was initially at a loss as to what to do. Blind people had to run accompanied by a co-runner. No one in the city had received training to be a co-runner for the blind runner. After some discussion among themselves, the staff came up with a solution. Five workers volunteered to run with Mr. Hanya, each runner staying with him for 2 kilometers. The group of five started to practice their transitions that very

---

[13]Kazuko Takai, *Seiron* (1990), 172–179.

night. The next year, 48 city staff members signed up to assist eight blind runners.

In the elections in March of 1993, Iwakuni garnered 87 percent of the vote and was reelected Izumo City's mayor. The vote clearly demonstrated that the people of Izumo approved of Iwakuni's policies. Soon after the election, a group of people from Tokyo, who recognized and supported Iwakuni's innovative political policies and were impressed by his strong knowledge of the economy and his international experience, requested that he run in the Tokyo mayoral election in 2 years. During this time a survey conducted by a popular magazine revealed that Iwakuni was regarded as one of the top eight people likely to become Japan's Prime Minister in the twenty-first century.[14]

Iwakuni's political ideas concerning Japan at the national level were well recognized; they became even better known when his co-author, Morihiro Hosokawa, became the first non-LDP Prime Minister in 36 years. When Hosokawa was governor of Kumamoto Prefecture, Iwakuni and he had written a book, *Hina-no-ronri*, outlining their views on national policy. In their book, Iwakuni and Hosokawa discussed what they considered to be government misconduct; they were particularly concerned about the central government's heavy-handed control over local municipal offices. They claimed that projects with strictly local impact were severely mired in central government red tape. For example, they needed to wait forever for government approval to move a bus stop just a few feet away from its original position in order to make the bus stop more convenient. One theme of the book was that the central government discouraged local offices from doing anything unusual or creative. Hence, Iwakuni and Hosokawa argued, much of

the centralization that had taken place during the last 100 years should be reversed by moving many national government powers to outlying local authorities. This, they argued, would be healthier for the country and would revitalize the rural areas outside Tokyo and Osaka.

Iwakuni was widely recognized as one of the main advocates of decentralization. At the Tenth Congress of Secretaries in Asia, he remarked:

> In the postwar period, Japan accomplished remarkable economic growth by centralizing all of our economic and political control in Tokyo. We, the local governments, now advocate decentralization. We need more autonomy in terms of authorization for decision making in our respective cities and towns, rather than having to always rely on Tokyo. Tokyo is not Japan. The same things that dictate policy in Tokyo cannot, by any means, dictate an effective policy for local governments in rural Japan . . . Japan's energy is thoroughly concentrated in Tokyo. The burden on the capital has reached a dangerously high level. In the 47 years since World War II, Tokyo has developed into what it is today because short supplies made centralization extremely efficient. During that period, Tokyo grew at the expense of outlying areas. Now that Japan is rebuilt and wealthy, development along the same lines can no longer be justified. Therefore, I would like to develop from the local area.

NEXT STEPS

Recounting the successes of his 5 years of service, Iwakuni noted, "I have not approved any plans to build schools based on concrete construction. The tree doctor system,

---

[14]Shuichi Kondo, *Weekly Post*, May 1993, 62–63.

adopted in 1989 in Izumo, was extended to a national program in 1991."

In 1994, Izumo City was chosen as the best city in Japan for the second year in a row. The "best city" award was based on 15 criteria including security and convenience. Iwakuni took pride in saying that the award was won by combining Izumo's natural resources with the efforts and contributions of the municipal office's staff and leadership. Moreover, Iwakuni was named the most popular mayor in Japan.

About this time, Iwakuni wrote another book, *Rin Toshite Nihon,* about the reforms that he thought were necessary to move Japan into the twenty-first century. The list of some 70 recommendations that he put forth in the book are shown in Exhibit 1.

Meanwhile, in Izumo, Iwakuni announced that he would not run in the next mayoral election. He believed that nobody should be in a public office for more than 10 years because 10 years should be more than enough time to achieve whatever one set out to accomplish. If a leader could not reach all of his or her goals within that period, that leader should recognize his or her incompetency and step down, he said. In addition, Iwakuni noted, because in the next 10 years the world would change dramatically it was appropriate to pass the leadership on to a younger generation, who would breathe new life into the government. Finally, Iwakuni stated that he was satisfied with his service

and believed that all the projects he had planned had been realized.

Shortly thereafter, Iwakuni declared himself a candidate for the office of mayor of Tokyo. The mayor of Tokyo enjoyed a large public forum, influence among the vast majority of the country's business leaders, and close connections with the national government, and Iwakuni thought this might be the appropriate next step in his endeavors to reform Japanese institutions. Thus far, Iwakuni's career had been a series of surprising, major changes, and if he were able to win the mayor's post in Tokyo, this pattern would continue. In the spring of 1995, Iwakuni established his residence in Tokyo and began an intense, 1-month campaign.

As it turned out, a television comedian won the office from among a dense field of candidates. A similar result in Osaka, where another comedian won the mayor's job, was taken by most observers as a statement of how little respect and trust Japanese had for their established political community. Scandals relating to bribery, paybacks, indecision during the Gulf War, and other events had undermined the public trust. Iwakuni was heartened, though, that he was able to win 820,000 votes during the short campaign period. In early 1996, he announced his plans to run for the Diet seat from Setagaya-ku, one of the 23 *ku* or districts in the Tokyo metropolitan region. In October, he was elected with a wide margin. ■

**Reforms Proposed
by Tetsundo Iwakuni**

As found in his book, *Rin Toshite Nihon* (*A Mature Japan Pursuing Real Wealth for Coexistence*)
Translated by Yuichi Kamoto, edited by Jim Clawson

Economic Reform
1. Disassemble the ministry of finance and redefine its role into clear and smaller functions.
2. Protect depositors' rights from financial crisis and disclose full information on financial institutions to general depositors.
3. Apply disciplines of capitalism to banks.
4. Put the Japanese version of SEC under the jurisdiction of ministry of justice.
5. Japanese companies relocating headquarters could solve trade friction and the rise of yen.
6. Allow Japanese companies to buy back their own stock so that the companies would restore the confidence of investors and so that the companies would have more alternatives in carrying out their capital-structuring strategies.
7. Develop and invigorate small- and medium-sized companies that contribute more to the development of the local economy.
8. Allow easy transaction of real estate and land in order to make full use of these for economic activities by loosening and tightening relevant taxes.
9. To invigorate Japanese economy,
    1. create fixed annual salary system for compensating business people.
    2. reintroduce stock option plans.
    3. deregulate and delegate powers to local governments.
10. Detach the triangle relationship among politicians, bureaucrats, and businesses. Japanese exporting companies are actually buying yen, which raises the value of yen. Japanese importing businesses get the benefits of high-valued yen and keep its products' and services' price high by regulations.
11. Arrange the return of the U.S. base at Yokota and turn it into the Japanese international airport, then establish three hub airports (Yokota, Narita, and Haneda).
12. Merge Tokyo and Saitama prefecture into one entity to realize the New Capital Area Plan.

Immediate Anti-Recession Policies
13. Elect a prime minister and minister of finance who understand economics and the stock market.
14. Save agricultural association financial institutions with public funds because of its importance and the emergence of the issues.
15. Do not lower real property tax (tax imposed on land). Rather raise it in order to increase the flow of land.
16. Lower the land sales tax.
17. Establish a public "Land Bank" in order to stabilize the rapidly falling land prices.
18. Acquire lands worth 300 trillion yen for the next 10 years (until year 2004).
19. Lower taxes related to buying and renovating housing.
20. To invigorate smaller- and medium-sized companies,
    1. zero housing-loan interest
    2. zero the increase rate of public utilities rates (postal service, telephone, highway, etc.)
    3. zero the consumer tax (sales tax).

In Harmony with Bureaucrats
21. Stop "Amakudari" (literally, "angels descending from heaven," bureaucrats finding jobs in subsidiary organizations after forced retirement from major institutions). This happens way before they become 60 years old.

(continued)

EXHIBIT 12-1　Iwakuni's Proposed Reforms

22. Do not elect bureaucrats and ex-bureaucrats to the administrative reform committees. If this reform proposal cannot be kept, do not set up the committees. Use anonymous votes in the decision-making processes in the committees so that bureaucrats would not know who voted what.
23. Set up systems where Diet representatives can control the bureaucrats.
24. Business leaders should say "good-bye" to politicians and bureaucrats.

Agricultural Reforms
25. Government should help establish large-scale agricultural business by owning lands and leasing them. Financial resources should come from zero-coupon bonds.
26. Support farmers who are financially weak and small, but contribute to preventing natural disasters such as floods and landslides. (Japan is a mountainous country.)
27. Invest in agricultural business in spite of the fact that Japan will not be able to feed itself, because this business is not only important for national security, but also a benchmark for how friendly our country is to nature.
28. Establish a "Rice Bank" in Japan and make it the center for production and sale of rice in the world. Start helping to solve food-shortage problems in the world.
29. Help Japanese farmers farming abroad and exchange agricultural know-how.

In Harmony with the Rest of the World
30. Introduce referendums for major issues and speed up decision-making process in our country.
31. Elect a prime minister directly.
32. Amend the Constitution, especially the ninth article (which renounces war and prohibits Japan from establishing its own military forces).
33. Clearly state our right to defend our country with our military force.
34. Decrease the number of both Upper and Lower Diet members by 50 percent.
35. Diplomacy, defense, education, and culture should be solely under the jurisdiction of the Upper house.
36. Voters should have multiple and negative votes to elect representatives to reflect their opinions more precisely.
37. Introduce an electric voting system that allows voters to cast votes anywhere.
38. Apply more rigid discernability criteria against economic criminals. Do not give them leeway to escape from indictment by letting them say, "I was not aware of the situation, or the regulation."

Correct Things That Are in the Way of This Harmony (Coexistence) Process
39. Establish a sound monetary administration and transparent disclosure system of company performance.
40. Build up grass-roots relationships on the municipal levels such as prefecture-state and city-sister-city relationships. This would contribute greatly to Japan's national security.
41. Build water pipelines covering the African continent to prevent famine, poverty, and war in the continent with Japan's technology and financial might.
42. Establish an International Peace Squad in Japan for peace-keeping operations in the world.
43. Japan has, from its own historical experience, an obligation to contribute to world peace by making its economic might and technological know-how available to the world.
44. Establish "Terakoya" all over the world. Japan should help countries all over the world set up schools for the general public and help them invest in education in their country. This would lead these countries to be more stable and help them understand more about Japan.
45. Invest in cultural exchange. Accept workers and students from foreign countries in Japan.

Create Happy Community
46. Give financial incentives (zero or minus loans) for families in big cities to build three-generation houses (grandparents, parents, and children) and financial incentives for families who live close to their parents (for example, within a 500-yard radius). This would help reduce the health-care cost for elderly citizens by saving the huge cost of construction and maintenance of aged people's accommodations by local government.

EXHIBIT 12-1   (continued)

47. Establish an elderly care system where neighbors can mutually take care of elderly families.
48. Introduce Personal Identification Cards for every citizen. This would help identify the person if he or she cannot identify himself or herself in an emergency, such as Great Hanshin Earthquake.
49. Establish a police organization that covers interprefectural, nationwide, and international crimes such as Oum Group.
50. Establish "anti-disaster" headquarters to develop and implement rigid and reliable contingency plans for disasters.
51. Eliminate vending machines of alcohol and adult magazines on the streets.
52. Introduce deposit system for merchandise such as automobiles, soda cans, batteries, and so forth.
53. Eliminate regulations that are causing the high consumer prices in Japan.
54. Make donations deductible for income tax.

In Harmony with Women, Elderly Citizens, and Children
55. Staff government and public offices with 30 percent women.
56. Intertwine volunteerism to reduce the health-care cost, especially for elderly citizens.
57. Introduce a Comprehensive Welfare Card for each citizen (medical information, blood type, pension history, insurance, and so forth).
58. Utilize elderly citizens' skills and experience in business and social contexts by establishing seminars and schools to support these intellectual and social assets.
59. Fight against discrimination (discrimination against foreigners, disabled citizens, voting rights, women).
60. Introduce curriculum for religion that does not advocate one specific religion, but does facilitate students understanding religions in their historical contexts. This would prepare young Japanese people to make better judgments on their beliefs.
61. Make senior high school education mandatory. Unleash students from "examination hell" and focus on real education that prepares them to be global citizens.
62. Emphasize and ask continually where we are from, historically and culturally. One of the ways to do this is to realize how close we are to trees and tree cultures (wooden schools, houses, and buildings).
63. Set up "Green-Keeping Operations" for the world.

Locals Coexist with the National
64. Create a small, central government and large, local governments.
65. Encourage local governments and businesses to import from the United States and the other parts of the world to solve trade deficit issues.
66. Hand over many authorities to the local governments except policies such as defense, diplomacy, and monetary policies. These authorities would promote soliciting and developing businesses in the areas of local, employment, welfare, environmental, and education policies.
67. Slim down local government and reduce costs, as well.
68. Impose restrictions on terms for mayors and governors.
69. Design a Japan that consists of 300 City States as seen in ancient Greece. (Japan now consists of 3,300 cities, towns, and villages.)
70. Maintain the current pricing system whereby any person anywhere in Japan can purchase newspapers and books at the same price. This system would help keep our education stable and equal throughout Japan.

EXHIBIT 12-1   (continued)

References

Be a strong and gentle corporate worker. 1994. *Tokai,* 15 May.

Iwakuni, Tetsundo. 1988. *New Japan from Wall Street.* Tokyo: Kodansha Publishing.

Iwakuni, Tetsundo. 1990. *When a Man Makes a Decision.* Tokyo: PHP Laboratory.

Iwakuni, Tetsundo. 1991. *A Message from the Mayor of Izumo—New Regionalism.* Tokyo: NHK Publishing.

Iwakuni, Tetsundo. 1991. *Current & Surges: Is Any Breakthrough of the Status Quo Possible for Japan?* Tokyo: World Culture Publishing.

Iwakuni, Tetsundo. 1992. Three promises. *Yomiuri Newspaper,* July.

Iwakuni, Tetsundo. 1993. Creating new generations. Gakushu Kenkyu sha, April.

Iwakuni, Tetsundo. 1993. *Changing Our Way in Japan.* Tokyo: NHK Publishing.

Iwakuni, Tetsundo. 1993. Three promises II. *Yomiuri Newspaper,* July.

Iwakuni, Tetsundo. 1994, 1995. Another textbook of mine. *President,* July 1994: 94–97, III 1994, IV 1995.

Iwakuni, Tetsundo. 1995. *Rin Toshite Nihon.* Tokyo: Kobunsha.

Iwakuni, Tetsundo and Morihiro Hosokawa. 1991. *Theory of Region.* Tokyo: Kobunsha Publishing.

Kondo, Shuichi. 1993. Tetsundo Iwakuni runs for Tokyo mayoral election? *Weekly Post,* 7 May, 62–63.

Nagao, Saburo. Tetsundo Iwakuni. *Friday,* 48–51.

Nakayama, Masaiko. 1989. International businessman coming down to a mythical country. *Weekly Current Topics,* 29 April, 38–41.

Otani, Kiyoshi. 1994. Tetsundo Iwakuni. *Nikkei Business,* 30 May, 60–63.

Sakai, Koichiro. 1990. Tetsundo Iwakuni—Mayor of Izumo. *Nikkei Business,* 4 June, 82–86.

Sato, Minoru. 1987. Tetsundo Iwakuni's my fight. *President,* June, 292–305.

Takai, Kazuko. 1990. "Applause and conflict: Mayor of Izumo. *Seiron,* September, 172–179.

Taki, Ken. What should current leaders do? *Pinnacle,* 3–14.

Case 13   Stewart-Glapat Corporation (A)

On June 7, 1985, during the 9-hour drive from Charlottesville, Virginia, to Zanesville, Ohio, William Tanner Stewart had lots of time to consider what he would do upon his arrival; on Monday, June 10, he would take over operating control of his family's business, Stewart-Glapat, Inc., a maker of conveyor systems. Tanner had been away from the business for 10 years pursuing a career in engineering and business education before deciding to return to the company his father had founded and which his brother had run for the 7 years since his father's death.

Tanner had a number of concerns as he drove along. Although the company had been profitable, competition was stiffening considerably from domestic and international companies; production efficiency was not nearly what Tanner thought it should be; sales volume was bumping along without the kind of steady growth Tanner believed the company needed to survive in an increasingly competitive environment; the plant seemed dirty to him—always congested and cluttered with stacks of steel stock and subassemblies—and the bathrooms were filthy; the equipment was old and generally worn out; new products were needed to augment the company's basic line; and the workers complained of the heat in the summer, the cold in the winter, and the poor air quality in the plant. He also could not see the kind of management teamwork that he felt was needed. Many of the management processes in the firm seemed to Tanner to be nearly as old and dilapidated as much of the equipment upon which the firm depended. Perhaps the most significant of these was the lack of formal production schedules.

Through the hills of West Virginia, Tanner reflected on the advice of his brother Charlie (currently the chairman and chief executive officer): "Don't try to change too much at once," he said. "Move into your office next to mine, nose around a bit, just get to know the situation here. Get to know the people and how we do things now before you start changing things." It seemed incongruous to Tanner to have made the major career decision to leave the University of Virginia where he had been a tenure-track associate professor of operations, come "home" to the family business, and not do anything. Not only was he going to have to change his lifestyle and his daily work routine to make this change, he also was going to have to change his name: All of his Zanesville friends, including the people at the plant, knew him as "Bill," but he had gone by "Tanner" while in academe. Changing his name seemed symbolic of the magnitude of the change he was now a part of. Tanner mumbled, "That's not my style. I grab it by the throat. If I don't want to live with it, I get it resolved. Some people say I try to move too fast, but I've got to make a difference, or these people won't have jobs in 5 years."

Tanner wondered what his Dad would have done, and as he did, became a bit sad. He had never been close to his father, but he respected and admired his engineering genius greatly.

UVA-OB-0348

This case was written by James G. Clawson as a basis for class discussion rather than to illustrate effective or in-effective handling of an administrative situation. Copyright © 1987 by the University of Virginia Darden School Foundation, Charlottesville, VA. All rights reserved.

C. T. STEWART AND THE FOUNDING OF STEWART-GLAPAT

Charles Thomas Stewart's first job after receiving his degree in mechanical engineering from Massachusetts Institute of Technology was as an industrial engineer for the Heisy Glass Company in Newark, Ohio. Stewart moonlighted, designing glass equipment on the side, because the company discouraged his experimentation. He invented several pieces of glass-handling equipment, including machinery that made glass goblets, polished glass, and loaded glass cases into trucks. He could not put his name on his inventions because he was employed by Heisy, so he registered the patents under the name Glapat for "glass patent." The first telescoping conveyor Stewart made was not used for loading and unloading trucks, but for putting glass ingots into a furnace.

In 1942, Stewart disagreed with the Heisy Company's marketing manager about whether or not to trim the company's product line from 2,000 to 500 items; as a result, he was fired. With his father, C. O. Stewart, Stewart (or "C.T." as he was sometimes called) started his own company making glass-handling equipment. Taking the lead from his patents, he named the company Stewart-Glapat, Inc.

Stewart liked to tinker and invent. Tanner mused aloud as he remembered days spent with his father:

My dad was one of the most brilliant design engineers I ever met. He had great spatial perception, in terms of visual kinematics. He could envision complicated pieces of machinery in his head, and that was a gift. He made the very first airplane loader. They took a telescoping conveyor and put it on a Jeep. I remember as a child out at the local airport here. We went out one night, I rode on the Jeep, and they flew

in a TWA DC3, and he had to load it for them. It turned out that nobody wanted it. He made the very first extendable package conveyor. I can remember as a small child, 5 or 6 years old, being out in the older part of the plant and sitting on a telescoping conveyor at night when my dad was running it in and out, playing with me. That is as vivid as if it had just happened.

My dad was an entrepreneur in the sense that he would never run away from an engineering challenge. In fact, as a young college student, I would travel with him during the summer. We would go to various customers. I knew a good bit about our product, since I had worked in our plant when I was younger. We would go out and look at an application. And he would say, 'Yeah, we can do that and here's what it will cost you.' The guy would give him an order. I would be sitting in the car, and I would say, "Dad that looks like a damned complicated thing you're going to do. I've never seen us do that." He would say, "Well, we've never done it, but we will figure out a way." And 95 percent of the time he would. And 5 percent of the time, we would end up in a lawsuit.

Dad got involved in opening bags automatically—something nobody had ever successfully done. Bags of asbestos and chemicals and other harmful stuff. He built a fully automatic bag opener that never really worked. He kept building and selling them and always got into problems. We built one of these for Romania, but the ship sank on the way to Europe. We got paid in full from the insurance company, and they never ordered another one. We don't build those anymore. If you think about the liability of having workers around an asbestos machine that you claim is dust-proof, you'd have to put a gun to my head to do that. And yet dad was doing it off the cuff: "No problem! Sure we will do that." He just didn't really envision the risk.

Back in those days, it was a very single-dimensional company, in that dad made all the big decisions. People just did what he told them to do.

Mr. Stewart was a remarkable engineer and inventor; he was not, however, as accustomed to managing the financial side of the business. He was eager to accept engineering challenges even when the financial return was not immediately apparent. One employee who used to travel extensively with him on road trips noted that one customer, who had been a classmate of Stewart's at MIT, asked him, "How's Charlie's little toy laboratory doing?" The comment seemed to fit Stewart's interest in tinkering in the shop and building new machines. The employee noted:

> Charlie [senior] was a genius. He was always thinking about how he could do it better, redesigning a machine he'd seen in his head. He was not a practical man, though, not a business manager. The plant was like his personal lab: He'd want to try something out, we'd build it for him, and then he'd go on to the next idea. On the road, he'd treat you like a king, but in the plant you worked for him: He'd say little needling things to keep you in line. He was in here 7 days a week.

When he passed away of a heart attack in 1978 on a business trip to Germany, Stewart left a company recognized by most to be on the brink of bankruptcy. Employees walking down the street in Zanesville would be asked if their jobs were still intact. Some thought that Mr. Stewart's passing would mean a large layoff, even the demise of the company.

CHARLIE, JUNIOR

When Stewart died, his eldest son, Charlie Jr., took control of the company. Charlie had played football in college and was, some said, more interested in sports than the family business. Many were surprised when he joined the business after graduating from Denison University in 1966, but Charlie began as purchasing agent, and in 1971 was elected vice president. When his father died, Charlie Jr. became president. Tanner was pursuing his engineering doctorate at The Ohio State University.

Charlie had little interest in the engineering features of the machines the company built and seldom went out on the shop floor. As a sportsman, his philosophy was what he called the "team concept." He assembled the best people he could find to run sales, design, machine shop and assembly, and the finances of the firm and let them do their work. He did review the financial results periodically and would become animated if the firm was not making money on each project. He refused to bid for or accept any projects that were not profitable, a practice substantially different from his father's.

Charlie coached little league football in Zanesville. He noted with pride in 1985 that in the 16 years he had coached, his teams failed to win the league championship only twice. Charlie's office was different from the rest of the Stewart-Glapat company space, which was austerely functional. Charlie's office looked and felt like the head coach's office of a major college football program—carpeted floor, leather couches and chairs, built-in bookcases filled with trophies, team pictures, autographed footballs, certificates, and other sports memorabilia.

Charlie also sponsored a Division B American Softball Association slow-pitch softball team that won many trophies and even took the national championship in

1984. Because only a few of the players worked for Stewart-Glapat and the cost of supporting the team was substantial, it caused some controversy among the family and employees. The old drafting room in the basement under the machine shop was filled with 58 softball trophies, some of them 6 feet tall.

Under Charlie's tutelage, the firm paid off its debts and became profitable. Bill mused aloud about Charlie's administration of the company:

> When dad died and I was gone, something happened to the company that was very important. My brother was not an engineer and was faced with 'What do I do? Do I go coach football 'cause that is my education, or do I still try to maintain this company?'
>
> He decided to maintain the company. We were in terrible financial difficulties. Basically, what happened was the company decided to do only what it knew how to do well, which was telescoping conveyors, and tried to beef up the product, to make it a better product, and to learn how to sell it better. Those things paid off. We became a very prominent, profitable small company.
>
> In the years that my brother was in charge, basically, he paid the people very good salaries, tremendous benefits, kept the key people here, and then muddled through.

According to Dutch Lewis, the sales manager, so long as the bottom line was okay, Charlie Jr. didn't get involved in department policy:

> As long as he had competent people heading up each department, he would keep his hands out of those departments. He would be a very close observer of performance levels, but generally, he was the type of boss, as long as the bottom line was coming out, then

that was good enough. He did not get involved in departmental policy. If the bottom line was not what he liked to see, then he would get involved, and we would have our sessions—our management sessions—and discuss policy. And it would be a joint effort. We got along well and worked together well. He did oversee all of our price changes, too.

One manager described Charlie Jr. this way:

> Everybody thought that since C.T. died, we'd go under. If he'd *lived,* we'd have gone under! After 3 weeks, Dutch got rolling, moved us in a different direction. He said, "Let's market this exclusively." And Charlie agreed. Charlie trusted us. He had the personnel around him; he didn't know what we were doing, but he believed we were working for the benefit of the company. He got the work rolling through here. He was like a coach, walking the sidelines, watching, while we did the work. But he is very moody. You don't know what will happen with him. Charlie'd put decisions back on the team, though.

Another employee described Charlie as "more of a businessman. He left all the engineering and design to the departments, and the money kept coming in. If it wouldn't make money, Junior wouldn't touch it."

During this period, the management team assembled by Charlie became accustomed to having autonomy in their jobs. Each manager developed his own systems and managerial style.

THE MANAGEMENT TEAM

Charlie's team consisted of Dave Redman, plant manager; Dutch Lewis, sales manager; Ronald Bachelor, engineering manager; Jack Rutherford, materials manager; and David Shaeffer, office manager (see Exhibit 13-1).

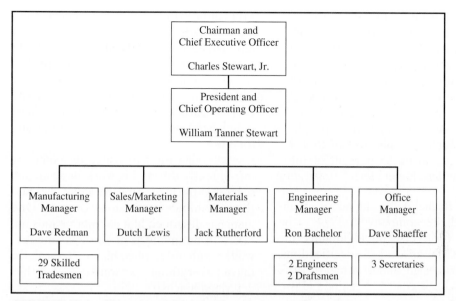

EXHIBIT 13-1   Abbreviated Organization Chart as of June 1985

Dave Redman, the plant manager, joined the company in 1961 when he finished high school and had supervised plant operations since 1966. His responsibilities included building the company's products to the specifications of the Engineering Department; supervising the machine shop, assembly, and paint crews; managing cost reduction; and managing the flow of the work through the factory.

Dutch Lewis, the sales manager, received his Juris Doctor (J.D.) degree at The Ohio State University, where he and Bill were roommates for a brief period, and then worked in Columbus in real estate. He came to Stewart-Glapat when Bill invited him to come and manage the company's sales efforts. As the sales manager, Dutch was responsible for identifying and bidding on new business—in essence, managing the revenues of the firm. The bidding process was a key part of the company's success: Because most of the machines were custom designs, Dutch had to estimate what the machine would cost to build, often without any company experience on that machine,

and then price the bid competitively against the rest of the industry.

Before Dutch joined the company, Stewart-Glapat had a difficult time selling its products. Dutch joined the company in May 1976 and was trained by Bill in the basic product and manufacturing knowledge of the firm. When Bill left 3 months later to pursue his doctorate, Dutch made several changes in the way the company went to market. He decided to concentrate on civilian contracts, because the company hadn't been successful in getting and maintaining government contracts. He concentrated on preengineered, more standardized extendable conveyors that would be cheaper to make and easier to bid. Dutch also was able to have Stewart-Glapat products listed in the materials-handling catalogues of Litton and Rexnord, two major industry sales tools.

By 1985, Dutch did not have to travel a lot. He reported:

I don't have to make cold calls. I would do it if we got some major house accounts, but we don't want to step on the toes of our distributors, reps, and major OEMs [original equipment manufacturers]. I do proposals, answer phone calls, do contract administration on our work with the government, keep track of what bids are being let out, and participate in marketing policy. I talk to people, keep in touch, and because of that, I guess we are in on 95 percent of the extendable bids that are let.

Ronald Bachelor, the engineering manager, joined the company in 1974 to be responsible for overseeing all engineering activities—such as design specifications, rework, parts design, and drafting. In 1985, Ron's team consisted of two senior and two junior designers.

Prior to joining Stewart-Glapat in 1981, Jack Rutherford, the materials manager, was inventory controls and materials manager for Schrader-Bellows, a division of Scovill, for 14 years. Jack received a bachelor's degree in economics from Wittenberg University in 1966. His responsibilities included materials procurement and supervision of the shipping employees.

David Shaeffer, the office manager, received an associate's degree in accounting from Columbus Business University and worked as an accountant and cost controller for several companies (primarily 12 years with United Technologies) before joining the Stewart-Glapat management team in 1982. His responsibilities at Stewart-Glapat included managing the office (with three secretaries); overseeing the billing, collecting, and correspondence of the company; and preparing the financial statements.

And now as part of the team, of course, there was Bill, who with his wife and four children was going back to Ohio to be the president and chief operating officer. The younger Stewart son had been active in the company as vice president of engineering from 1969 (upon his graduation from

MIT) until 1976, so many of the managers in the firm had some experience working with him. He earned a Ph.D. at The Ohio State University and became an assistant professor at Purdue University for 4 years, after which he was an associate professor at The Colgate Darden Graduate School of Business Administration at the University of Virginia for 3 years.

Although Bill had visited the company infrequently during his work in academe, several of the managers and employees had formed initial impressions of him. One manager described him as "more hands on, likely to be involved in all departments," while another described him as "radical. He takes everything personally." Another described him as:

moody. He can be very sarcastic when you ask him a question. I don't like it. It's a bunch of BS. He feels like he's too smart for the people around here. It's obnoxious. . . . He's been around college too long. You need that attitude there, but not in dealing with the people here. There's a difference between asking and telling.

His approach is to go off the deep end. He doesn't think things out rationally. Charlie, on the other hand, wants to work things back and forth until you get an answer. If Bill doesn't get what he wants, he says, "G– – =t, then let's just send someone else!" He doesn't think things through rationally. If I need to talk to him about a problem, he just says, "Why can't *you* handle that? That's not my job."

Another employee stated:

Bill's more like his dad, lots of intelligence; smart, but not too practical. He doesn't understand life from a working man's point of view; he's never had to live like we do. A lot of guys don't like his overbearing attitude. He comes out with his stopwatch and clipboard and times the cutters to see how long it takes to cut angle iron. They don't like it.

Another employee noted:

Bill doesn't listen well. There's not much communication between the men and him. He has a certain sarcastic manner. He wants it done his way or else. He thinks that if somebody doesn't like it, he can quit. Or if he doesn't like it, we'll fire him.

STEWART-GLAPAT IN 1985

By 1985, Stewart-Glapat had grown in size and volume but remained a small, family owned business. The number of all employees including about 10 managers and office staff had hovered around 25 to 30 during C.T.'s administration. For one brief, 18-month period, C.T. had hired an additional 100 people, but when anticipated business did not materialize, the workforce was cut back to its previous level. Under Charlie's guidance, the number of employees grew gradually to fluctuate from 33 to 35.

During the period when Charlie was in operating control, the company had focused on relatively few markets: newspaper companies, retail distribution, and units for the U.S. Postal Service. The latter, however, had not proved to be a stable market. At one time, Dutch secured a contract with another company to market the Stewart-Glapat machines under its own name. The stability and widespread markets served by this company helped revive Stewart-Glapat's financial health to the point that sales began to average $3 million per year, and profits substantially exceeded the 4.28 percent of sales average of other firms like Stewart-Glapat.

The building had been extended significantly from when the company opened for business, yet there was sufficient land surrounding the plant to more than double its size. Prior to 1972, the plant had been added on to three times, twice by extending it directly back from the original building (see Exhibit 13-2) and once by pushing out sideways from the machine shop. Of that addition, one employee noted, "The worst thing they did was build the new Engineering Department. We used to get a draft, a breeze across the plant, but that [addition] blocked the big windows, so now we get no breeze. And it's so hot in here in the summer."

Even with floor space of more than 47,000 square feet, Bill was concerned that the production scheduling and manufacturing flow was not what it should be. Most of the machinery in the plant was original and showing severe signs of wear. Scheduling was done ad hoc. Several jobs would be in the assembly process at any one time. If a job couldn't be completed because of delays in parts or subassemblies, it was simply pulled aside and left standing until the necessary parts were ready. Similarly, jobs had no completion deadlines. When the jobs were done, the machines were shipped. Customers were given a general idea about shipping but seldom firm dates.

Even with plenty of space, there was an irritatingly unkempt appearance about the shop floor: Parts, scrap, partially assembled machines, and raw inventory stocks of steel in various shapes and sizes littered the shop floor from the office door to the raw materials dock at the back. During his visits, Bill had attempted to get employees to clean the plant, but he was met with explanations that it could not be done with the kind of work they were doing.

Overall, though, most employees seemed to like working at Stewart-Glapat. Mr. Earl Rupe, the union steward, commented on what it was like:

Working here is decent money, including the 5 hours on Saturdays. It's not steady

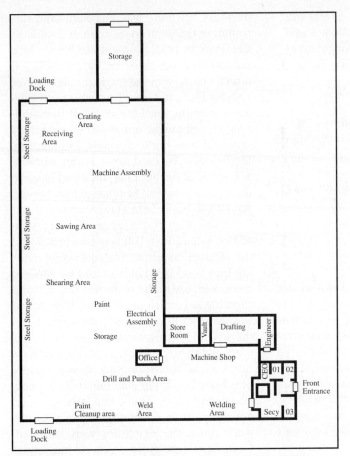

EXHIBIT 13-2 **Abbreviated Floor Plan as of June 1985**

work; they lay off and add on, and the working conditions are fair to poor. It should be cleaner here. The money is better than average, but not the best in town. On July first, they announced a new retirement plan that was negotiated. The plan came out of the International Association of Machinists where they contribute $3 a week if you haven't missed any time that week.

ADJUSTOVEYOR

The Stewart-Glapat Corporation manufactured and sold extendable conveyor belts under the name of Adjustoveyor. (See Exhibit 13-3 for an example of the company's product brochure.) The company's main product since 1950, extendable conveyor belt systems were used to load and unload trucks—typically at warehouses or shipping terminals where the task was performed dozens of times a day. The name "Adjustoveyor" came from the ability of the conveyor belt to extend and retract. A typical Adjustoveyor had a simple set of hand controls on the leading edge of the cantilevered boom, so that a single person could unload a semitrailer by extending the boom into the truck as he or she worked.

ADJUSTOVEYOR offers you a new era in truck loading/unloading productivity

- Labor savings through productivity improvement ● Economic payback of one year or less
- Fast turnaround of vehicles ● Reductions in product damage
- Smooth, continuous product flow ● Load rating of 65 lbs. per lineal ft.

The model 2580T triple boom Adjustoveyor was developed to offer industry improved material handling productivity for loading and unloading the longer over-the-road vehicles which are widely used today. With a seven foot dock leveler and a 48' trailer, a full 55' of cantilevered extension is required to serve the entire vehicle. Previous designs often fell short when confronted with these new requirements. But no longer! The Model 2580T features a 25' closed length, extending to an overall length of 80 feet, thus providing the full 55' of powered cantilevered extension required.

Adjustoveyor is shown installed in a large midwestern distribution center where it is used to rapidly strip inbound vehicles of product needed for shipments to catalog sales customers. This unit is self-propelled and serves two dock locations. The unit was designed for around-the-clock duty and for the severe operating conditions often encountered in dock areas. The live load rating of 65 pounds per lineal foot is the highest in the industry and provides that extra margin of safety and reliability for long and continuous service. This customer had used a smaller Adjustoveyor for three years and specified the new larger model for a new system addition due to the increased use of 48' vehicles.

EXHIBIT 13-3   Sample Product Brochure as of June 1985

The unit unloads inbound trailers and connects with a takeaway system which conveys product to a sortation station, prior to placing the goods in inventory. The lifeblood of the total system is the smooth, uninterrupted flow of product from the producers, through the Distribution Center, and on to the final customers. Bottlenecks cannot be tolerated and with a requirement for JUST-IN-TIME inventory management, product cannot sit in a trailer or linger on a dock, while a customer is told the item is out of stock. COMPETITIVENESS IS BUILT ON PERFORMANCE, AND THE ADJUST-OVEYOR HAS ALWAYS BEEN A KEY PLAYER IN OVERALL SYSTEM EFFICIENCY.

Many truckloads have both conveyable products and palletized loads which must be quickly unloaded. To accommodate forklift movement, dock levelers are used to gain access to trailers of differing heights. The typical 7' dock leveler requires that the Adjustoveyor be set back from the door opening, thus reducing the effective reach into the vehicle. The Model 2580T is designed to extend over the dock leveler and still reach the end of a 48' trailer. Since the unit is fully cantilevered, no support in the trailer is necessary.

Write or phone us for full information.

Your employee working on the loading dock controls the flow of your operation. Once material reaches your facility, you cannot afford to impose delays on that needed material. The Model 2580T is designed with the safety and productivity of your employees clearly in mind. All controls are located on the front end of the unit for easy access. A safety bar protects the operator from extensions beyond safe limits. All pinch points are guarded and operator safety is stressed in a videotape provided with each unit. The Adjustoveyor provides the link between your employees on the dock and overall system productivity. Don't saddle your employees with shorter units which hinder their efforts to be fully productive in longer trailers.
ADJUSTOVEYOR IS YOUR BEST LONG-TERM CAPITAL INVESTMENT!

"Where new ideas originate"

STEWART-GLAPAT Corp.
P.O. Box 2486 • 1639 Moxahala Avenue • Zanesville, OH 43701-6406 • 614-452-3601

Designed and manufactured by American workers in the U.S.A.

Litho in U.S.A.   5M-11-85

EXHIBIT 13-3   (continued)

Because most applications of its product line required special features, Stewart-Glapat was essentially a custom job shop. The company made most of its own parts to specification from the design group (two senior designers and two apprentice designers) in the company machine shop. Lately, however, the firm had been subcontracting many of the higher-volume parts, because the Stewart-Glapat wages could not meet the low costs of the dedicated machine shops.

By 1985, Stewart-Glapat had built the largest extendable, cantilevered conveyor system in the world, a machine with a 36-inch-wide belt that would extend through three steel booms 55 feet into a truck trailer and carry 65 pounds per linear foot of belt. These large machines rested on railroad-like tracks set in a warehouse floor and could roll back and forth to service several doors. The company also built smaller machines.

STRATEGIC PLANNING

As Tanner, becoming more and more "Bill," drove down to the flatlands of Ohio, he thought about the future of the company, he was convinced that it needed to expand its volume and manage its costs to become the low-cost, volume producer of extendable conveyors in order to bid successfully against the growing tide of competitors. Shipping costs for the large machines were exhorbitant, yet the company recently had lost contracts to overseas producers. This worried Bill, and he wondered how he might build the volume of the company's plant so that it could pass on the cost savings to customers through the bidding process. One way would be to introduce a new product that would revolutionize the industry. A conveyor that would load and unload pallets automatically would be such a machine, but so far the technical aspects of this project had been insurmountable. Other ways,

he thought, would be to increase sales and add a second shift, or to increase the efficiencies of the plant, or both.

The second shift alternative raised the questions of the local labor market and Stewart-Glapat's reputation in it.

ZANESVILLE, OHIO

The Stewart-Glapat Corporation was located in Zanesville, Ohio, a small town, rich in history. It had been formed by Ebenezer Zane in 1797 when he and a group of woodmen cut a path in the wilderness from Wheeling, [now West] Virginia, through Ohio to Maysville, Kentucky. One clearing that they made was called the Zane's Trace, which, in becoming a gateway to the West, formed the nucleus of what later became Zanesville.

In 1985, Zanesville was the county seat of Muskingum County and boasted 150 manufacturing and processing establishments. Some of the principal products produced in Zanesville were agricultural machinery, alloys, batteries, boilers, cement, ceramic products, conveyor systems, corrugated fiber shipping containers, dairy products, egg solids, electrical sheet steel, electronic components, meat products, radiators, tile transformers, pet food, bakery goods, and carpets. Even though Zanesville had a diversity of industry, so employment was not concentrated in any one, it had an unemployment rate of 12.5 percent in 1985, when the Ohio average was 8.9 percent and the national average was 7.2 percent.

Despite these statistics, Bill wondered if the company could attract the people for a second shift. Stewart-Glapat had a reputation for hiring short term to meet contract needs and then laying off shortly thereafter when the contract expired. In addition, if he could find the business to support a second shift (and he thought he could) and then be able to hire one, he wondered who would supervise it; he felt sure that none of the current managers would be willing to work

3:30 P.M. to midnight. Bill reached this conclusion in part because of an earlier effort to institute change at the company.

While still at the University of Virginia, Bill succeeded in getting the company to buy two microcomputers. One was assigned to the design department and was attached to a modern, computer-aided-design (CAD) software package and a wide-carriage plotter. The other was assigned to the front office for use in managing accounts receivable, correspondence, billing, and other office functions. Bill knew by the time he was driving home that neither of these computers was being well utilized and that, in fact, some managers were refusing to try to learn how to use them. The CAD machine had sat idle for the 10 months it had been in the design office, and the office machine was ignored by all but one of the other officers and secretaries.

MANAGEMENT TEAMWORK

Remembering that incident brought Bill's mind to another concern: the ability of the Stewart-Glapat management team to work together. Because they had all been working independently for the last 10 years, Bill was concerned that in many areas of interaction among the various departments, the company was wasting time, energy, and financial resources. Sometimes subcontracted parts were not available when the assemblers were ready; other times designed parts did not fit the machine under assembly. Accounts receivable were building up, and no one seemed to worry much about the increasing competition.

Bill wanted to build a strong sense of cooperative teamwork, but he was aware that the managers had been operating as autonomous individuals for a decade. During this time, they had developed a set of common beliefs. Bill noted that many of these perceived sacred cows limited company growth. He had heard many of them repeated in the past few months:

> "If our costs aren't competitive, we should get out of that market."
> "You can't find good enough welders. There are only five people in Zanesville who can weld our equipment."
> "There is a fixed market volume for our product. Whatever it is, it is."
> "If there is a problem, it must be somebody's fault."
> "This place has always been messy and always will be because our workers are slobs."
> "The unit will be shipped when it is done. We cannot predict when that will be."
> "Computers are a waste!"
> "Put off telling the boss about a problem. He'll just get mad."

Bill did not believe any of these, but he knew his vision for the company would be tarnished by each and every one of them.

In the middle of these reflections, Bill realized that he was crossing the Muskingum River in Zanesville. The next exit was his; he was home. As he circled down the ramp into his hometown, he began to lay his plans for the following Monday morning. He also was eager to get out of the car and stretch his legs on his usual daily, 5-mile run. ■

# PART 3

STRATEGIC THINKING

Case 14   Secom Company, Limited

In January 1989, a Secom Company, Limited, advertisement in the major Tokyo daily newspapers declared:

> Secom has built a system structure that enables its information network to establish a new 'social system' society. Describing the future of Secom is the same as seeing the twenty-first century. In the near future, the Secom system will be a necessity for building modern towns, cities, and even culture. Keep your eye on the future of Secom Company!

Reading the advertisement in his office, the charismatic chairman of Secom, Makoto Iida, sighed and murmured:

> We have built excellent hardware in our 27 years of operation. Our information network system is the best in Japan. We will have several new business opportunities by fully utilizing the network system. Our human resources, however, may not be skillful enough to support the system and capture the opportunities.

HISTORY

Secom Company, founded in 1962 by Makoto Iida and Juichi Toda, was the first security service company in Japan. After graduating from university, where he set up an American football club, Iida followed his dream of forming his own company. He chose the security industry because no one else had. The basic concept of a security service firm at that time was to provide customers with safety and peace of mind by dispatching guards to watch their premises. Secom called this a "static guard system." When Secom was founded, few Japanese were interested in the service, mostly because there was little felt need in Japan for safety systems; the new business did not match Japanese cultural realities. Despite aggressive sales efforts by Iida and Toda, Secom was unable to sign a single customer contract in the first 6 months of business. The two men tried to persuade potential customers by pointing out that their service was less expensive than hiring full-time employees to protect their tangible assets.

The 1964 Olympic Games, however, boosted Secom onto the public stage and made it a medium-sized, fast-growing company. Secom was hired by the Japanese Olympic Committee to guard the athletes' villages. Secom's success at this job dramatically improved its corporate image and increased the number of corporate clients. Because the "static guard system" was labor intensive, an increase in the number of employees was unavoidable when the

UVA-OB-0741

This case was written by Toshimasa Yashima and Bing Shui, MBAs, International University of Japan, under the direction of James G. Clawson while he was a visiting professor at IUJ. This case was written as a basis for class discussion rather than to illustrate effective or ineffective handling of an administrative situation. Copyright © 2001 by the University of Virginia Darden School Foundation, Charlottesville, VA. All rights reserved.

number of customers rose. Correspondingly, the number of employees increased from two in 1962 to 300 in 1964. Iida, president of the firm since its inception, thought at the time, though, that it would soon be impossible to manage the growing number of employees, and that it was crucial for Secom to develop an electronic security system so that the firm could operate more efficiently.

THE NEW ELECTRONIC SECURITY SYSTEM

Consequently, in 1966 Secom developed a new electronic security system called the SP Alarm System (SPAS). The system consisted of four parts: first, electronic sensing devices installed at a customer's location that could detect gas leaks, fire, or intrusion of burglars; second, the transmission of the information generated by the electronic sensors to a control center through telephone lines; third, the analysis of that information by operators in the control center and then the dispatch of guards, called beat engineers (BEs), to the customer; and fourth, the decisions and actions of the BEs at the customer location to rectify the situation. Either the operators or the BEs could contact the police or fire stations if necessary. This centralized system enabled Secom to reduce the number of guards required by the static guard service. SPAS enabled Secom to provide much cheaper security service than allowed by the static guard system. Iida said:

> Although the SP Alarm System was an excellent system, some of our sales managers were opposed to adopting the system because the static guard service was beginning to sell well. I could understand their resistance. They were focused

on the current situation, and customers were satisfied with the current service. They did not like the dramatic change caused by the introduction of the SP Alarm System. They thought this might force them to work much harder. I rejected their views not merely because the SP Alarm System improved our operations but because I wanted managers to devote more serious time to their future career development.

Secom's sales and operations managers found getting customer acceptance of the SP Alarm System to be a difficult task. First, the reliability of the electronic sensing devices on SP Alarm System was not high when the system was launched. Control center operators were barraged constantly by incorrect information sent from the devices. The efforts caused by the low reliability of the devices tired both operators and BEs, and increased operating expenses. Secom had neither its own manufacturing facilities nor a research and development laboratory at that time; however, by working closely with suppliers, Secom was able to increase gradually the reliability of the hardware, and thereafter, the number of customers using the SP Alarm System.[1]

By 1970, the number of customers exceeded 1,000. At a company conference of directors and department managers (*kacho*) that year, Iida said:

> Extending the SP Alarm System all over Japan will contribute to the future success of our company. We will have a strong weapon by having an information network system based on our security service.

Because the Secom managers could not imagine a nationwide information network

---

[1]In 1975, Secom acquired a factory to produce its electronic devices and established a laboratory called "The Technical Center" or "TE center" to develop and raise the reliability of new security systems.

system, few managers understood what Iida said. The 1,000 customers at the time were simply not enough for them to imagine the size and scope of such a system. Secom continued to concentrate on the diffusion of the SP Alarm System by increasing both sales and the number of telephone lines that connected Secom and its customers. The increase in the number of telephone lines contributed to the building of the information network system. As a result, sales increased dramatically from ¥4.8 billion in 1970 to ¥18.5 billion in 1975.[2]

THE COMPUTER SECURITY SYSTEM

In 1975, Secom introduced a new product, the Computer Security System (CSS). With the previous system, SPAS, the control center operators had to monitor customers' sensor data by looking at lights on a console. CSS took the next step by gathering the information sent from the electronic devices, analyzing the information by computer, and displaying the information in more understandable forms. Because the operators did not need to concentrate heavily on the "lamp board," errors in their judgment were reduced greatly by this new system. Secom now was able to provide customers with a much more accurate and high-quality service. In what was now characteristic fashion, Iida noted:

CSS is merely a milestone for our big picture. In the future, CSS, which is currently a regional computer system, will be integrated into one big, nationwide network system. It is apparent that we cannot deal with the increasing number of customers by using the current CSS. A centralized computer system will be a necessity for us to pursue operating efficiency and cost

reductions. Establishing that system will be our next target.

At the same time Secom introduced CSS, the company also introduced a computer information system for its office management in the Tokyo area. Later, Secom expanded its management information and control system (MICS) all over Japan, so that it could establish a corporate-wide database for management. Clerical operations such as accounting, material distribution, and customer control were greatly enhanced through MICS.

When the number of customers reached 150,000 in 1982, Secom integrated CSS and MICS into one network system. The new system was called "Secom Net" and was immediately the second-largest information network system in Japan. (See Exhibit 14-1.) At the press conference called to announce the completion of Secom Net, Iida said:

Secom Net excels in its advanced backup system. Regional processors can substitute for the host computer when the host is down and vice versa. Moreover, our customer database is important. We have integrated the host and regional processors to maintain and build the confidence of our customers.

In 1988, Secom sales, riding an annual growth rate of 10 percent, exceeded ¥90 billion ($753,846,000). (See Exhibit 14-2.) The number of employees surpassed 8,000. Secom had gained more than 50 percent of its market in Japan. As a proportion of total sales, the static guard security service, Secom's original service, had decreased to 12.4 percent. More than 70 percent of sales came from the electronic security services. (See Exhibit 14-3.) Customers ranged from small households to New Tokyo International

---

[2]$36,923,000 and $142,308,000, respectively, at $1 = ¥130.

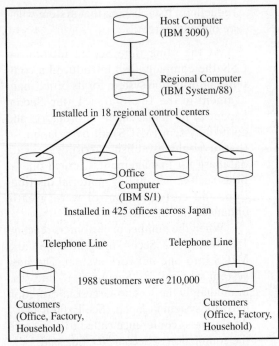

Host Computer
(IBM 3090)

Regional Computer
(IBM System/88)

Installed in 18 regional control centers

Office
Computer
(IBM S/1)

Installed in 425 offices across Japan

Telephone Line

Telephone Line

1988 customers were 210,000

Customers
(Office, Factory,
Household)

Customers
(Office, Factory,
Household)

EXHIBIT 14-1   Basic Concept of Secom Net

airport. Exhibit 14-4 shows Secom product lines in 1988. One director of Secom said:

> As Maslow's hierarchy of needs indicates, people are pursuing security needs when the physiological needs are satisfied. It is not an exaggeration to say that

all Japanese are satisfied with food, air, water, and shelter, however. Secom has provided Japan with the most sophisticated security service by establishing Secom Net. There is no doubt that Secom will continue to grow its security business. We may not need to search for

EXHIBIT 14-2   Sales and Income of Secom

| | *(Million Yen)* | | | |
	1982	**1983**	**1984**	**1985**
Sales	55,000	61,000	65,500	71,000
Income (before tax)	10,500	11,500	13,000	13,700
Profit Ratio	0.19	0.19	0.20	0.19

	1986	**1987**	**1988**	**Growth Rate**
Sales	77,500	85,000	95,000	9.5%
Income (before Tax)	15,000	15,800	19,000	10.3%
Profit Ratio	0.19	0.19	0.20	

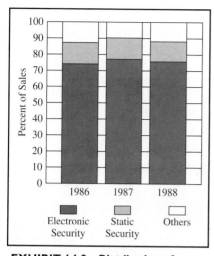

EXHIBIT 14-3 Distribution of Sales 1986–1988

management relied heavily on Iida for strong leadership. He had committed to corporate-level decision making at the foundation of the firm. The introduction of the SP Alarm System, which made Secom a leader in the Japanese security business, was a product of his endeavor and insight. It was, however, critical for Secom to grow future managers who fit the organization. In Japan the tendency among new university graduates was to select their new employers not by the nature of their business but by their corporate image and public awareness. Because Secom's corporate image had been low and the business was not well known until the introduction of CSS, Secom had had to work hard to recruit skillful workers from other companies rather than from among the ranks of university graduates. Secom's recruiting philosophy was that technical skills were taught more easily than personal and interpersonal attitudes, so it sought candidates who had group skills, communication skills, and problem-solving skills rather than technical skills. Furthermore, Secom had invested more than ¥1.0 billion a year ($7.7 million) in training new employees. Even later, when Secom could have recruited the graduates relatively easily because of its increasing external corporate awareness, the company maintained its

new business opportunities as long as our electronic service has a strong competitive edge. But, Secom Net should not be our only asset for a single business. We must have a clear image of what can be the next business of Secom.

RECRUITING AND TRAINING OF WORKFORCES

Secom management's second priority was internal training for its labor force. Secom

EXHIBIT 14-4 Electronic Security Service Lines of Secom in 1989

Name	*Target*
Secom Home Security	Households
Secom SX System	Small shops and offices
Secom MX System	Large factories and buildings
Secom BT System	Tenant buildings
Secom TX System	Hotels and other lodgings
Secom MS-1 System	Small and medium-sized mansions (apartment buildings)
Secom MS-2 System	Large-sized mansions
Secom Museum System	Museums
Secom "Hanks" System	ATM, CD systems of banks
Secom Totax System	Total systems for small communities

criteria for recruiting and its emphasis on internal training for the newcomers.

The training for newcomers was typically Japanese. The newcomers were sent to the training center owned by Secom and were trained for 6 days by trainers from headquarters. The training began with an orientation about the philosophy of Secom and included various kinds of lectures on government regulations relating to the security industry, the basic methods of handling electronic devices, and the introduction of Secom Net. The newcomers were required to work as BEs or guards for the static security service for at least 6 months in order to understand the concept of the field operations that generated sales for Secom. These field assignments were considered a key part of the training.

CORPORATE CULTURE

The most important aspect of Secom's corporate culture, as emphasized by Iida, was an active and flexible organization. Although Iida was seen as a charismatic leader, he promoted skillful employees to important positions according to their talent and assigned them essential tasks aggressively. All employees were motivated by the constant growth of their company, relatively high salaries, the flexible organization, and Iida's charismatic leadership. One BE in the Yokohama office said:

More than 200 customers are in my assigned area. I am very busy, but I am proud of providing my customers with safety. I am motivated not only by my salary but by my job, which gives me excellent delight for achievement.

Iida, at an entrance ceremony for the graduates from universities, said:

The most important thing for Secom is not to satisfy my expectations, but to meet your expectations of your own performance. In other words, it is significant for Secom whether or not 1 year later you feel joining Secom was a right decision. Your satisfaction will lead Secom to become a much more excellent company. Take care of yourself. Grow yourself as much as possible.

INTRODUCTION OF THE NEW ORGANIZATION

Secom's personnel system including recruitment and promotion seemed to work well, but Iida complained with alarm about the organization of 1988. The organization consisted of more than 50 regional offices, each of which had ten to 15 local offices. Headquarters controlled every function of each regional and local office. Consequently, the managers of the branches had learned not to take initiative, but rather to wait for commands from headquarters. The resultant burden on headquarters exceeded its capacity. Some managerial conflict between headquarters and the regional offices occurred because the functional managers at headquarters could not respond to the increasing needs of the regions as the corporation grew. Some managers in headquarters could not understand the needs of the regional and local managers, who were focusing on increasing customer service.

In October 1988, Iida introduced a new organization that consisted of 19 regional departments. (See Exhibit 14-5.) Each department became a profit center, and the role of headquarters shifted dramatically to that of support rather than decision maker. Secom Net contributed to the establishment of this organization because it enabled the departments to improve the efficiency of clerical and managerial work by providing the regions with simple application forms of software necessary for each administrative job. In other words, the clerical work was almost automated through Secom Net. The

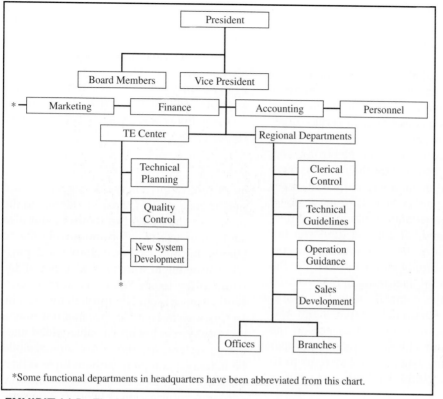

*Some functional departments in headquarters have been abbreviated from this chart.

EXHIBIT 14-5 The New Organization Introduced in 1988

objectives that Iida saw for Secom Net in this new role were as follows:

- Raise and maintain the morale of employees.
- Upgrade the quality of operations and obtain the trust of the local community.
- Maximize sales and profit by increasing market share.
- Keep the organization more efficient and active.

This new organization was oriented toward field operations and had the objective of making the field organization more active in generating and building the business. Iida intended also that the organization motivate field workers by giving them more autonomy in decision making. This new organization required each regional and local manager to consider, analyze, and solve the problems relating to their operation and organization. Iida said:

I was most afraid that the large, centralized organization would damage the active corporate culture we had built so far. I strongly hope that the new departments, which I consider as independent organizations, will work well and maintain our originality. Moreover, I hope the managers who have to work hard in their regions will obtain excellent knowledge about both operations and management. They will be candidates for the future managers who will build the future of Secom at headquarters. The new organization presents those future managers a good training opportunity.

In the new organization, each department head (regional and local) could determine target sales and profit figures, the number of new customers they would capture, and the number of new field workers such as guards and sales representatives that they would need. In order to maintain corporate-wide consistency of service quality, they were not, however, allowed to change the content of the electronic services Secom provided for their customers.

Some departments remained at headquarters but only in support of the regional offices. The personnel function was different, though, and left not as a supporter but as a controller of the labor force at the corporate level. Equity was believed to be the most important factor in managing and motivating the centrally recruited workforce. The Personnel Department was charged with managing all aspects of the labor force and with developing the proper organizational structure and systems to fit the corporate culture and business strategy of Secom.

One regional manager said:

I understand the concept and principle of our new organization. I do my best to achieve my goals as determined in advance. But field operations are too busy. My subordinates are working very hard to provide our existing customers with safety, to acquire new customers, and to train newcomers. We do not have enough time to consider new business as senior management emphasizes. If we are stressed much more than the current situation, it is very doubtful for me that we can manage ourselves. Do we *need* to create new business? We can expand the size of Secom as long as we continue our current business!

NEW BUSINESS OPPORTUNITIES

The new business opportunities facing Secom varied widely. Although Secom Net was the second-largest telephone network system in Japan, it relied heavily on the largest, Nippon Telephone and Telegraph (NTT), which dominated the Japanese telephone market. Whatever Secom's new business would be, NTT would have to play a key role in the new business development. One possibility was a Value Added Network service, or VAN.

VAN Service

VAN referred to a network system that not only transmitted information relating to the nature of the system to its users, but also sent other useful information relating to clients' businesses. For example, a department store might want to send a special discount offer to all Secom customers currently using Secom Net through the system. In this way, Secom Net became not only a security system but also a value-added marketing system. Another VAN service could be helping a company with multiple offices on Secom Net to establish its own internal corporate information network system similar to the way that Secom used Secom Net for its own information management. In the marketing example, each customer who received the special offer from the department store would need a visual display or printer. In the latter case, Secom would be required to design new software and develop new telephone digital exchange machines to add internal network system capability to Secom Net. Iida said:

We do not know the market potential in this system. There is no doubt, however, that two of our customers can contact each other through Secom Net even if one lives in Hokkaido and another lives in Kyushu. The amount of data which is presently transmitted from each customer to each assigned control center is only a fraction of what we can transmit. It takes less than 1 minute to send all the information necessary for our operation when nothing unusual is happening. In other words, we are not fully utilizing the system at all. Some customers may need information about travel arrangements we could provide through Secom Net. One problem is cost. We would have to invest huge amounts in Secom Net to develop new systems which would conform to customers' needs. The customer would have to pay additional charges to use new services. Another problem is the workforce. We have excellent engineers who developed Secom Net, but we do not have skillful workers who have experience in marketing this kind of business.

Emergency Medical Service

Secom also was interested in emergency medical service as a possible new business opportunity. In Japan, ambulance service was mainly furnished by municipalities. The services available in the municipal ambulances were severely restricted. Ambulances were not allowed to make medical treatments beyond basic first aid. As a result, many persons heavily injured in traffic accidents or suffering heart attacks lost their lives in ambulances. Some people, referring to the highly advanced ambulance service system in the United States, criticized this incomplete medical service system. One person from the Ministry of Health and Welfare (MHW) said:

Since Japanese ambulance service is free, anyone can use the service when he or she needs it. We would have to lose this advantage if we adopt the U.S. approach. It will cost much more to dispatch a doctor in every ambulance or to train drivers of the ambulances so that they will be able to make more sophisticated medical treatments. Furthermore, it is much more difficult to maintain the quality of the service at satisfactory

level [when it is dispersed among so many care providers].

Secom had tried to penetrate this service earlier when the company estimated that the market potential was enormous, but it was unable to move ahead because of stringent MHW regulations and the lack of internal medical know-how. Secom management thought that if they could combine a new medical service with its existing security service, it could attract many more new customers. With this combination, Secom could provide its customers with total security service by not only dispatching BEs in an emergency but also by providing superior medical care and thus reducing clients' worries about disease and accident.

The problems surrounding entry to the emergency medical service industry were very similar to those related to the VAN service. Secom's lack of employees with enough medical experience was serious. Moreover, because government regulations were extremely limiting under current regulations, Secom would not be allowed to start this service even if it could find qualified personnel and develop the necessary supporting organization.

Artificial Intelligence System

Secom also was investigating an Artificial Intelligence System (AI System) in an intelligent systems laboratory installed in the TE center from 1986. AI systems could be applied to more advanced electronic devices, which could identify people who were registered in advance according to their voice, pupils, and fingerprints. Secom tried to develop a new entry system with the highest reliability for highly restricted areas such as nuclear plants, military plants, and corporate computer rooms. The company also studied an AI system that could accumulate information about the daily activities of operators and BEs and give them appropriate hints or suggestions when they faced complicated problems. Although this system was aimed at streamlining internal operations, Secom management believed that the know-how gained from developing this system could be applied to software development that would help a wide range of customers increase their operational efficiencies. Another AI option was the development of a security robot. Secom tried to make a robot that could guard a customer's house by prioritizing information from the electronic sensors and then communicating with Secom central operators, BEs, police, and/or the fire station according to the indicators from the sensors. The manager of the AI laboratory said:

> The products or software currently being researched here seems to be useless for the future business of Secom because of the uncertainty of market potential and completion dates. The research has just begun. However, it is too early to gauge the result of our research. The knowledge accumulated here through our research may be a good weapon for our future even if the products are not launched.

MIXED OPINIONS

Some negative opinions were voiced about the development of Secom's new business opportunities. Two employees confessed their opinions candidly. One BE answered a question about the future business:

> I know what kinds of business Secom is trying to do through our corporate newspaper. I have no ideas about them, since I am heavily squeezed by my current job. I do not know what will happen to Secom in the future. What I have to do is not to consider the future of Secom but to manage to deal with my current tasks, isn't it?

One sales representative of a regional department said:

> I am in charge of sales expansion of our security system. I am not sure whether our customers are asking for more sophisticated service such as VAN or the emergency medical treatment service. I doubt if the market is matured enough to accept our new systems. Our approach may be beyond the expectation of our customers.

JANUARY 1989

Secom was about to become a $1 billion company. The firm had accumulated state-of-the-art know-how in the security business, developed a huge customer base, owned an almost unparalleled asset in Secom Net, and had perfected various software and hardware technologies. Thus far, Chairman Iida's insight and vision for the security business was always right, and those who believed in him still supported him firmly. Although the size of Secom exceeded the dimension where one person could supervise the whole company, most employees felt that the Secom culture that defined the firm as one family remained.

In January 1989, a discussion of the new strategy Secom should follow began at corporate headquarters. The options included the following:

- Secom should concentrate on the existing services instead of finding new business opportunities. The number of employees in each regional department should be increased to meet current demand.
- Secom should take as the first priority forming a new department or subsidiary that would deal with VAN service exclusively and hire new employees necessary for the service.

- Secom should delay penetrating Emergency Medical Service because the time for the move had not yet arrived.
- Secom should change the training system for newcomers to match their background so that more specialists in each functional area would be developed.

At the meeting, Iida described his enthusiasm for a "social system industry" and Secom as follows:

It is very difficult to identify the exact meaning of the social system industry. I think the new businesses combined with our current security business can be one example of the industry. The security business itself may not be able to satisfy the real customer's needs, because their needs fluctuate very widely according to the increase in the present uncertainty. VAN service and the emergency medical service are good candidates for the industry. I know the market potential of both systems is very ambiguous, but I am sure developing VAN service is the right strategy for Secom and will hit the hearts of our customers in the near future. Secom is always looking for the business chances others are not willing to take. If the regulations of the MHW which prevent us from introducing the emergency medical treatment service are tight, we should make efforts to change them. I know my subordinates are working very hard to let our security system penetrate more, and haven't the time or energy to think of the image of the social system industry. But we have to make our organization more energetic. If we concentrate on current tasks, we cannot make us more active. Secom was always energetic, and we must keep the vigor in future. ∎

Case 15   Disney Productions: The Walt Years (A)

I just want to leave you with this thought that it's just been sort of a dress rehearsal . . . so if any of you start resting on your laurels, I mean, just forget it, because . . . we are just getting started.

— WALT DISNEY, QUOTED IN *THE DISNEY MANAGEMENT STYLE*

Almost 50 years after the company's founding, manicured lawns and ethereal quiet conveyed a campuslike atmosphere at Walt Disney Productions in Burbank, California. Executives still arrived at work wearing Mickey Mouse polo shirts, animators still played the volleyball games Walt Disney encouraged on a studio lawn, Disney's favorite chili remained on the menu, and everyone still went by first names, but behind the facade was a very different company from the one Walt Disney left behind.

In early 1984, Raymond L. Watson, the new chairman of Walt Disney Productions, and Ronald Miller, the president, were faced with serious problems. Earnings had been sliding; for the company's fiscal 6 months ending March 31, although revenues had increased to $648.3 million, income declined 34 percent to $31.3 million. In the second quarter, the company's stock price, after reaching $84 the previous year—still a far cry from the heady days of the 1970s when it sold at 80 times earnings—had dropped to $51. In some brokerage houses, the stock had been downgraded from a "buy" to a "hold." To make matters worse, many prominent business and news publications were reporting the possibility of a takeover.

COMPANY HISTORY

Melville Bell Grosvenor, former editor of *National Geographic,* said in a 1966 edition:

> When future historians sit down to choose a Hall of Fame for our time, there will be trouble over the name of Walt Disney. Some judges will list him as an artist; others will call him an educator. Still others may insist that Disney belongs with the inventors, and some will argue that he was a naturalist. Each, in my view, will have a point, for Walt Disney is all these things. But on one question the historians are bound to agree: Walter Elias Disney was a genius who brought laughter and knowledge to the world in a distinctive American way.

Animation

Walt Disney lived the American dream. Born in Chicago in 1901 and raised in rural Missouri, by the age of 10, he rose every morning at 3 A.M. to deliver newspapers in the suburbs of Kansas City. At home, he drew pictures of animals, only to have his father tear them up. Later, while working as a cartoonist for the *Kansas City Tribune,* he used some of his free time to make a few short movies that combined live characters

UVA-BP-0332

This case was revised by Jeanne M. Liedtka, Associate Professor of Business Administration. The original case was written by William E. Fulmer and Robert M. Fulmer. In addition to the publications mentioned in this case, a selected bibliography is given in the teaching note. Copyright © 1993 by the University of Virginia Darden School Foundation, Charlottesville, VA. All rights reserved.

and animation. In 1923, he moved to Hollywood with $40 and a head full of ideas.

In the fall of 1927, Disney traveled to New York with his wife Lillian (called Lilly) to negotiate a new contract for an animated series called *Oswald the Rabbit*. The distributor stole the series and hired Disney animators away. It was a doleful trip back; Disney needed a whole staff of animators, and he also needed a new character—fast.

The idea for Mickey Mouse was born on that return train trip. "I've got it," Walt told Lilly. "I'll do a series about a mouse. I'm going to call him Mortimer Mouse." Lilly liked the idea but thought "Mortimer" sounded "too dignified for a mouse." Walt responded, "All right, we'll call him Mickey Mouse. Mickey has a good friendly sound."

In Hollywood, Walt, his brother Roy, and chief animator Ub Iwerks began work on Mickey Mouse. That first Mickey cartoon, *Plane Crazy,* was a bit of nonsense inspired by the Lindbergh flight. When Disney took the movie to New York, film distributors were not interested. Nor were they interested in a second Mickey film, produced while Disney was traveling.

About this time, sound was being introduced in films. Disney and Iwerks rigged a homemade radio with a microphone, put up a white sheet as a screen, and with two helpers, stood at the mike behind it with noisemakers, a xylophone, and a harmonica played by Wilfred Jackson, a newly employed animator. For 6 hours, Roy projected a short bit of animation from *Steamboat Willie,* the third Mickey film. The "sound crew" watched the image and whanged away. The result was ragged, but Disney was convinced that sound was for cartoons.

He hurried to New York with the film to complete the *Steamboat Willie* sound track. During the process, he had to wire Roy for more money. To raise it, Roy sold, among other things, one of Walt's proudest possessions, his Moon Cabriolet, an automobile

with red and green running lights. The additional capital, however, enabled Disney to add sound to the first two "mouse films."

Suddenly the talking mouse was the darling of distributors. Now they came to Disney, asking him what he wanted to do and what they could do to help him. They got only part of the answer they were hoping for. He did plan to go on making Mickey Mouse cartoons, but he did not want to sell the film outright. Remembering his earlier experiences, he insisted on retaining complete control of his product. He signed Pat Powers as exclusive distributor for the Mickey Mouse cartoons on a 1-year contract with no guaranteed option for renewal.

By the time Disney left New York in 1929, he had a package of four Mickey Mouse films ready for release: *Plane Crazy, Gallopin' Gaucho, The Opry House,* and *Steamboat Willie.* The reception when these films went into national distribution was so positive that he decided to attempt an animated short without Mickey or Minnie. He created *The Skeleton Dance,* the first of the Silly Symphonies.

The Skeleton Dance had no story and no "characters." It was set in a graveyard in the smallest hours of the night, when the skeletons emerged from their graves and vaults, danced together for a few minutes, and then, with the coming of dawn, climbed back into their resting places. One distributor told Disney it was simply too gruesome, and Pat Powers told him to stick to mice.

Disney was beginning to suspect that his deal with Pat Powers was not working out, however. Powers would send them occasional checks for $3,000 to $4,000 from New York, which were enough to keep them going but not nearly what the Disneys believed they should be receiving for their widely acclaimed series. Walt and Roy were unable to get a full financial report on distribution revenues, and Powers, they discovered, had a somewhat shady business reputation. An even more disturbing rumor suggested that Powers was trying to make off with Ub Iwerks.

Roy and Walt casually mentioned to Powers that they needed additional cash. To indicate his goodwill, and in hopes of a tighter contract, Powers wrote a check for $5,000. Disney stalled him until the check cleared, then broke off contract negotiations. The Disneys made no attempt to retain the immensely talented Iwerks who, with Powers' backing, set up a new shop to produce a series called Flip the Frog. Flip did not catch on, because Iwerks lacked the one talent Disney had in abundance—that of story editor. Within a few years, Iwerks was back at work for Disney on a strictly businesslike basis. Witnesses reported that when passing Iwerks on the lot, Disney carefully looked the other way or, at best, spoke to him in monosyllables. Iwerks's technical genius was of enormous value to Disney, but his moment of disloyalty was never forgotten.

Disney continued to work with the Silly Symphonies because of their diversity and challenge. Because they were free of the script demands of Mickey and his gang, the Symphonies allowed more freedom to experiment with new concepts and techniques.

His next project involved Technicolor's new three-color process for film. Although a Silly Symphony called *Flowers and Trees* was already fully photographed in black and white, he decided to remake it in color. It was a gamble, because Technicolor was extraordinarily expensive, but the color version of this Silly Symphony caused a revolution in the animated-cartoon industry. In 1932, it became the first cartoon to win an Oscar.

Donald Duck made his first sputtering appearance in 1934. *The Wise Little Hen* made Donald an immediate hit. He went on to surpass Mickey as the star of the Disney stable. According to Disney:

We're restricted with the mouse. He's become a little idol. The duck can blow his top and commit mayhem, but if I do anything like that with the mouse, I get letters from all over the world. "Mickey wouldn't act like that," they say.

As the pictures were cranked out, the art of animation progressed. Characters were given more dimension and perspective than the first, flat figures, but Disney was never satisfied with the status quo. "I knew locomotion was the key," he once said. "We had to learn to draw motion. We had to learn the way a graceful girl walks, how her dress moves, what happens when a mouse starts or stops running." Disney set up an elaborate school for his artists. "It was costly, but I had to have them ready for things we would eventually do." Even during financial difficulties, Disney maintained his commitment to the studio's extraordinary art school, where classic art and the Old Masters were studied.

His next dream was to make *Snow White and the Seven Dwarfs,* as the world's first feature-length cartoon. When word of this project got around Hollywood, many movie people said Disney was making his biggest mistake.

While his artists were training, Walt had technicians working on a new kind of camera he planned to use for *Snow White.* He was no longer satisfied with just round figures; now he wanted the illusion of depth in the scenes. To achieve it, he developed the radically different "multiplane" camera—and won an Academy Award for it. In photographing animated films, three separate drawings were usually involved, each done on a sheet of transparent celluloid. One showed the foreground, one the animated figures, and the last the background. Before the multiplane camera, the three celluloids were simply stacked together and the camera shot through them all, giving a flat image. With the multiplane, more than three celluloids could be used, and they could be placed in different planes, sometimes as much as 3 feet apart. The camera could focus in and out among these planes to give an effect of depth and motion.

Snow White cost $1.5 million. When the bankers became nervous about the costs, Disney reluctantly showed their representative the unfinished product to try to retain their confidence. He reported:

> We needed a quarter of a million dollars to finish the picture, so you can guess how I felt. He sat there and didn't say a word. Finally, the picture was over and he walked to his car, with me following him like a puppy dog. Then he said, "Well, so long. You'll make a lot of money on that picture." So we got the money.

Snow White and the Seven Dwarfs went on to make cinema history and brought many honors to Disney. In 1938, Yale gave him an honorary master of arts. The same year brought honors from Harvard and the University of Southern California.

The immediate manifestations of this euphoria were the studio at Burbank (which cost $3.8 million) and the animated films *Pinocchio* ($2.5 million), *Bambi* ($1.7 million), and *Fantasia* ($2.3 million). The Disneys were soon heavily in debt. According to Roy Disney, "Success is hard to take."

Walt's intensity in pursuit of quality reached into every aspect of the studio, and his animators were known for their talent as artists in the truest sense of the word. The great English political cartoonist, David Low, said of Disney:

> I do not know whether he draws a line himself. I hear that at his studios he employs hundreds of artists to do the work. But I assume that his is the direction, the constant aiming for improvement in the new expression, the tackling of its problems in an ascending scale and seemingly with aspirations over and above mere commercial suc-

cess. It is the direction of a real artist. It makes Disney, not as a craftsman but as an artist who uses his brains, the most significant figure in graphic art since Leonardo.

The making of *Fantasia* was a perfect example of the Disney style: innovation and the "constant aiming for improvement." *Fantasia,* released in 1940, started out to be a kind of super Silly Symphony for Mickey Mouse, with Leopold Stokowski directing a full orchestra in "The Sorcerer's Apprentice." Walt built it into much more, a brilliant combination of animation and fine music—from Beethoven's "Pastoral Symphony" to Stravinsky's "Rite of Spring." *Fantasia* introduced stereophonic sound 15 years before it was generally used in motion pictures.

Fantasia was released at a time when Disney was losing much of his freedom to experiment. The company's heavy debts and the war in Europe, which knocked out the lucrative foreign market, had forced him to go public. In 1940, Walt Disney Productions issued 155,000 shares of 6 percent convertible preferred stock at $25 a share, raising $3.5 million. Walt and Roy received employment contracts with the company, but they were never again to run the firm with the same freedom and creativity as before. *Fantasia,* the high point of Disney's experimentalism, had to be released in an abbreviated version. "The bankers panicked," said Disney. "*Fantasia* was never made to go out in regular release. I was asked to help cut it. I turned my back. Someone else cut it." It failed at the box office.

In the summer of 1941, the studio was hit by a jurisdictional strike, an event that so dismayed Walt Disney that he wept. With one catastrophe after another, the Disney stock slumped to $3 a share. According to Roy, "More than once I would have given up, had it not been for Walt's ornery faith that we would eventually succeed."

The crisis in the company was overshadowed over the next 4 years by war. The wartime public showed little interest in animated films. People wanted live action. Just before Pearl Harbor, Disney converted to war work, and soon about 94 percent of his efforts involved making training and propaganda films. There was little profit, but this war work helped reduce the company's bank loans to $500,000.

While Disney prints brought in some money and helped ease the company's debt problems, wartime production simply postponed the firm's other problems. "We had to start all over again," Walt said. The old freewheeling, free-spending days were over. Roy commented, "When you go public it changes your life. Where you were free to do things, you are bound by a lot of conventions—bound to other owners."

True-Life Adventure Films

The nature films had begun with the animated *Bambi,* but after the war, Disney began looking for new kinds of films to make. He decided that "to get closer to nature we had to train our artists in animal locomotion and anatomy." He introduced live animals into the studio—deer and rabbits and skunks:

> But they were not good. They were just pets. So we sent the artists out to zoos, and all we got were animals in captivity. Finally I sent out some naturalist-cameramen to photograph the animals in their natural environment. We captured a lot of interesting things and I said, "Gee, if we really give these boys a chance, we might get something unique!"

Disney sent Alfred Milotte and his wife Elma to Alaska. They sent back miles of film. In reviewing it, Disney stumbled on one of the great stories of nature: the saga of the fur seals coming up from the sea to crowded island beaches in the Pribilofs to mate and calve. The film was *Seal Island,* which won an Oscar as 1948's best two-reel subject.

For another film, Walt kept cameraman-naturalist Milotte in the wild for more than a year, photographing the beaver's life habits. Out of Milotte's footage came an Oscar for *In Beaver Valley.* Other Oscar-winning films in the True Life Adventure series were *Nature's Half-Acre, Water Birds, The Alaskan Eskimo, The Living Desert, Bear Country, The Vanishing Prairie,* and *White Wilderness.* Between 1950 and 1960, more than a dozen films were produced in this series.

The True Life Adventures were sometimes criticized for being subjective and emotional. Because the producers anticipated the audience's tendency to identify with the animals on an emotional level, animal behavior was interpreted in human terms. The films were designed for the enjoyment of a mass audience—what Disney called the "big family."

Live-Action Films

Live-action feature-length films were a greater challenge than nature filming: "I had to grow with them," Disney said. "I couldn't make a live-action feature until I had experience." This came after the war as a result of money the company had impounded abroad. Disney went to England to use some of those funds and decided to experiment there with live action. "I struggled with it. I kept playing around. I couldn't decide what kind of live action I should do, what would please that big family." The format finally crystallized in the early 1950s with *Treasure Island, The Story of Robin Hood and His Merry Men, The Sword and the Rose,* and *Rob Roy, The Highland Rogue.* They were immensely popular films with the public, and Disney knew he could succeed with live action.

Meanwhile, he was working on another animated feature. It took him more than 2 years to make it, but he hit the jackpot with it. *Cinderella* grossed more than $4 million domestically, and Walt Disney Productions (WDP), which had been in the red for 2 years, was solvent again.

The company's position was further strengthened in the 1950s by a rising tide of affluent youngsters and by further diversification, this time into ventures other than motion pictures. Roy Disney established a profitable film-distribution subsidiary in 1953, the Buena Vista project, which gave the company control of its film releases and reduced distribution costs from 30 percent of gross rentals to an estimated 15 percent.

Television

The motion picture industry had no clear notion of how to cope with television in the mid 1950s. Most studios were fearful. Roy Disney commented, "When the industry was cussing television and trying to ignore it, Walt moved in and worked with it and made it work for him."

Disney's strategy was simple enough. With the opening of Disneyland in the works, he started *The Wonderful World of Disney* in 1954. The series ran for two decades on NBC-TV. He also developed a *Mickey Mouse Club* television show. Television made a modest profit for Disney, but more importantly, it provided free advertising for Disneyland, Disney motion pictures, and Disney himself. The TV productions went into the company's film library and were wholly owned by WDP.

Disney's ability to relate to his audiences was exemplified by the process of choosing kids for the *Mickey Mouse Club* show. Disney told producer Bill Walsh, "Don't get me those kids with the tightly curled hairdos—tap dancers—get me children who look like they're having fun. Then later we can teach them to tap dance or sing or whatever." He suggested going to ordinary schools and watching kids at recess, because "pretty soon there would be one we would watch—whether he was doing any-

thing or not—because that would be the one we'd be interested in. And that would be the kid we'd want for the show." They used the technique and found Annette and Darlene and Cubby and the bunch—and they all became popular.

Along with launching *The Wonderful World of Disney* in 1954, the studio also released *20,000 Leagues Under the Sea*, the most ambitious live-action picture in company history. It was a big-budget movie using major Hollywood stars (Kirk Douglas, James Mason, Paul Lukas, and Peter Lorre) and spectacular special effects. The film combined fantasy and adventure with an excellent script and direction; it won two Oscars. It was followed by *Swiss Family Robinson, The Shaggy Dog, The Absent-Minded Professor, Son of Flubber, Pollyanna,* and *The Parent Trap.* In 1964, *Mary Poppins* became one of the greatest hits in the history of the industry and captured five Academy Awards.

The studio was now enjoying success with a wide variety of live-action productions and animation. The outlook for Disney was bright, partly because of the decision to move into television rather than hoping it would not interfere with the movie business. Most other major studios experienced a sharp decline in their fortunes.

Disneyland

Walt Disney had been thinking about Disneyland for 15 or 20 years before it became a physical reality. The idea of sinking millions of dollars into an amusement park, even Disney's kind of amusement park, seemed so preposterous that he did not mention it to anyone for a long time. He just quietly began planning. "I had all my drawing things laid out at home, and I'd work on plans for the park, as a hobby, at night."

He borrowed $100,000 against his life insurance policy to finance the planning of Disneyland. To find a proper site for it, Disney called in the Stanford Research

Institute, which recommended three locations as alternatives. Disney picked Anaheim because it had 5 inches less rain a year than the San Gabriel or San Fernando Valley sites. It also happened to be in the population center of Southern California and only 26 miles from Los Angeles. Disney purchased 244 acres of land, mostly orange groves, with his own money. To finance Disneyland, he brought in three investors: WDP, ABC, and Western Printing and Lithographing Company.[1]

Disney wanted a park that adults could enjoy (adult guests outnumbered children three and a half to one). According to Dick Nunis, the boss of outdoor recreation, Disney believed, "Everyone's a kid at heart—all you have to do is let him find a way to be one." Disney people were also quick to point out the educational aspects of theme parks, but Disney had said, "I'd rather entertain and hope people learn than teach and hope they are entertained." He always maintained that his audience was "honest adults."

In the park, Disney was a stickler for quality, authenticity, and attention to detail. There were 700 varieties of plants from all over the world. (It took 30 gardeners to care for them.) The trash bins cost $150 each to paint and were designed to be highly visible without clashing with their surroundings. Audio-Animatronic figures were so lifelike that they often invoked arguments as to whether they were real. An air jet was put in front of every porthole in the submarine, because fewer people suffered from claustrophobia if they had moving air and something to see.

The Matterhorn was 1/100 the height of the real one. It contained 500 tons of structural steel, and almost no two pieces were the same length, size, or weight. Disney designers studied hundreds of pictures of the rugged peak to create as close a copy as they could. Roy Disney opposed building the Matterhorn because of the $7 million cost, but when Roy was away on a trip to Europe, Walt called an executive meeting. "We're going to build the Matterhorn and when Roy gets back from Europe, let him figure out how to pay for it." Walt had once commented, "The folks who win financially are the ones who don't worry about money."

Disneyland characters and entertainers underwent several days of training before meeting the public. They were to be neat, friendly, and courteous. No stone was to be left unturned to ensure people an enjoyable and hassle-free escape from the troubles of everyday life.

At the opening in July 1955, Disney said, "Disneyland will never be completed. It will grow as long as there is imagination left in the world."

Mineral King Project

"The fun is in always building something," Disney said. "After it's built, you play with it a little and then you're through. You see, we never do the same thing twice around here. We're always opening up new doors."

The next new door came out of Walt's personal interest in skiing. The Forest Service asked for bids to develop the Mineral King area into a year-round recreational area. An Alpine-like area, with its peaks rising as high as 12,400 feet in the Sequoia National Forest, Mineral King is about halfway between Los Angeles and San Francisco.

The most ambitious of the six bids submitted was by WDP. Disney's successful bid called for the construction of permanent

---

[1] Disneyland in 1989 was owned solely by Walt Disney Productions, which began buying out the other investors in 1957. For example, Disney bought out ABC's interest for $7.5 million and took over the food services as soon as the leases could be terminated.

housing with 2,400 beds plus temporary summer units with 4,800 beds; a 2,600-car parking area; and an Alpine Village from which cars would be excluded. Ski lifts would be designed to handle 15,000 to 20,000 skiers on the slopes at one time. A 25-mile road, part of it through the Sequoia National Park and over some of the most rugged terrain in the Sierra Nevada mountains, was planned.

Disney's plan, and particularly the road, was opposed by the Sierra Club, a national organization of conservationists with considerable strength in California. Disney, surprised at the strength and tenacity of the Sierra Club, was ultimately forced to abandon the Mineral King project.

Walt Disney World

In October 1965 (approximately the same time as the Mineral King project was announced), Disney announced "the biggest thing we have ever tackled." The project (eventually Walt Disney World and EPCOT) involved building two cities, one called "Yesterday" and one called "Tomorrow," in central Florida. These cities would include an airport, hotels, motels, convention facilities, industrial exhibits by U.S. corporations, shopping centers, camping grounds and facilities, curio and gift shops, service stations, golf, swimming, boating, a game refuge, power generators, and possibly even a movie studio. The project required 7 years of planning and $600 million to build.

WDP firmly resolved to avoid repeating the principal business error made in the development of Disneyland: allowing hundreds of motels and other businesses to spring up around the periphery of the park. Calling them "honky-tonks," Disney believed they detracted from the park's image. Also, hotels in the vicinity of the park were grossing $300 million a year at a time when Disneyland grossed only $65 million. E. Cardon "Card" Walker, then executive vice president of WDP, said, "We were determined that if we ever did it again, we would

buy enough land to control the complete environment."

In the early 1960s, the company's real estate agents purchased 27,443 acres in about 18 months at an average cost of just under $200 an acre under the company names of Tomahawk and Compass East. In October 1965, an announcement was made that the entire tract was owned by subsidiaries of Walt Disney.

Perhaps Disney's biggest coup in the project was the enabling legislation won from the state of Florida. It gave the company the powers of a county. It could establish its own building code and zoning regulations, form its own improvement district, and finance improvement with municipal bonds. It established two municipalities, Reedy Creek and Bay Lake, in which top Disney people were councilmen. The company also got Florida to ban the use by others of any Disney characters in a business name anywhere in the state, and no business could advertise itself as being so many miles from Disney World.

Disney also worked out an impressive agreement with 17 building trade unions that contained no-strike, no-lockout clauses and provisions for handling grievances, including binding arbitration. When it became clear that the Florida management could not attract the number of attractive, personable young people it needed, the company decided to hire 1,200 students to rotate in 300 jobs. By working with colleges, they were able to hire 300 students each quarter in jobs related to their majors. Some colleges even gave credit for the experience. Although few inside opportunities to advance beyond entry-level positions existed, Disney created an outplacement program that brought employees who did not want to remain in park-related jobs together with corporations that did business in the park.

Work on the landscaping began 3 years before the park was built. The Jungle Cruise had to have real African flora, and Liberty

Square had to have a 32-ton Liberty Oak. In all, 55,000 trees and shrubs were brought in from all over the world—not for planting but for testing.

CULTURE AT THE THEME PARKS

The "service-through-people" theme at the Disney parks started with a special language. There was no such thing as a worker at Disney. The employees out front were "cast members," and the personnel department was "casting." Whenever someone worked with the public, he or she was "on stage." Red Pope (a longtime Disney observer and writer) noted this phenomenon when two of his children, ages 16 and 18, were hired by Disney World to take tickets. For this seemingly mundane job, four 8-hour days of instruction were required before they were allowed to go "on stage." They learned about Guests—not lowercase "c" customers, but uppercase "G" Guests.

When Pope asked his children why it had taken 4 days to learn how to take tickets, they replied:

What happens if someone wants to know where the rest rooms are, when the parade starts, what bus to take to get back to the campgrounds? We need to know the answers and where to get the answers quickly. After all, Dad, we're on stage and help produce the Show for our Guests. Our job every minute is to help Guests enjoy the party.[2]

People were brought into the Disney culture early. All of the parks had a grooming and behavior code. Men had to have their hair cut above their ears and collars and be clean-shaven. Women had to be "natural" and not wear large earrings, eye shadow, or noticeable makeup. Employees were to be pleasant and helpful at all times and not eat, drink, smoke, curse, or chew gum while working with the public. Everyone had to attend Disney University and pass "Traditions I" before going to specialized training. According to Red Pope:

Traditions I is an all-day experience where the new hire gets a constant offering of Disney philosophy and operating methodology. No one is exempt from the course, from VP to entry-level part-timers. Disney expects the new CM (cast member) to know something about the company, its history and success, its management style before he actually goes to work. Every person is shown how each division relates to other divisions—Operations, Resorts, Food and Beverage, Marketing, Finance, Merchandising, Entertainment, etc. and how each division "relates to the show." In other words, "Here's how all of us work together to make things happen. Here's your part in the big picture."

Employees were well indoctrinated with the 11 characteristics of "The Disney Management Style": (1) we're a friendly, informal organization, (2) we work as a team, (3) it's all "our responsibility," (4) we're a Disney Democracy, (5) we communicate openly, (6) we make mistakes, because we're human, (7) we have a sense of humor, (8) we're creative people, (9) we're curious people, (10) we're business people, and (11) we're not only dreamers, but doers.

The systems support for people on stage was also impressive. For example, hundreds of phones were hidden in the bushes as hot lines to a central question-answering service. The amount of effort put into the daily cleanup amazed even the most calloused outside observers.

---

[2]The comments by Red Pope are reported in Thomas J. Peters and Robert H. Waterman, Jr., *In Search of Excellence* (New York: Harper & Row, 1982), 167–68.

Intense management involvement in the parks was highlighted at Disney by an annual weeklong program called "cross-utilization." As Pope described it, this program entailed Disney executives leaving their desks and their usual business garb to "don a theme costume and head for the action." For a full week, the boss would sell tickets, popcorn, dishes of ice cream, or hot dogs, load and unload rides, park cars, drive the monorail or the trains, and take on any of the 100 onstage jobs that made the entertainment parks come alive.

TRANSITIONS

In the midst of all this activity of the mid-1960s, Walt Disney was diagnosed as having cancer. According to Roy Disney, "I heard him refer to this cruel blow only once. 'Whatever it is I've got,' he told me, 'don't get it.'"

Having resigned all official positions in the company as early as 1960, Walt now was encouraging others to take on more responsibility. He claimed that his "greatest accomplishment was that I built an organization of people that enable me to do the things I wanted to do all my life." He had given his seven top producers an opportunity to share financially in the success or failure of their projects. He hoped that one of them would emerge as a clear successor. None had.

He was asked in 1963, "What happens when there is no more Walt Disney?"

Every day I'm throwing more responsibility to other men. Every day I'm trying to organize them more strongly. But I'll probably outlive them all. I'm 61. I've got everything I started out with except my tonsils, and that's above average. I plan to be around for a while.

He died on December 15, 1966, 2 weeks after his 65th birthday.

Walt Disney's death left a creative void at Disney. Because he was such a catalyst for ideas, talented men and women had been willing to work for him. "When Walt was alive, he was the leader because he was a creative cyclone," said Roy.

Red Pope commented:

How Disney looks upon people, internally and externally, handles them, communicates with them, rewards them, is in my view the basic foundation upon which five decades of success stand. I have come to observe closely and with reverence the theory and practice of selling satisfaction and serving millions of people on a daily basis successfully. It is what Disney does best.

He was a genius, but a moody genius. If he liked an idea, he was lavish in his praise, but if he disliked an idea, he could be abrupt, curt, and bitingly critical. He had no patience with anyone who would settle for second best. As a result, Disney people sometimes worked with butterflies in their stomachs trying to come up with "what Walt wants."

Roy Disney, at age 74, tried to replace his brother's distinctive brand of creative leadership with management by committee. Working with Roy to carry on were William H. Anderson, production vice president; Donn B. Tatum, assistant to the president; Card Walker, marketing vice president; and Ronald W. Miller, Walt's son-in-law and a board member. Roy explained:

I know a committee form is a lousy form in this business, but it's the best we've got until someone in the younger crowd shows he's got the stature to take over the leadership. If the chips are down, I've got the decisions. My way is to compromise, and I admit that that isn't a sound basis. But, I think I would do even more damage trying to make creative decisions the way Walt did.

Walt left a legacy of products. Five brand-new movies were all but in the can. Disneyland had just undergone an expansion, and Disney World was well along in the planning stages. Just weeks before his death, he first sketched EPCOT on a napkin and described it in a film as a model city, "a working community with employment for all." According to Roy:

We've never before had this much product on hand. Walt died at the pinnacle of his producing career in every way. The big thing that is bugging American industry is planning ahead. We've got the most beautiful 10-year plan we could ask for.

As CEO, Roy Disney supervised the completion of Florida's Walt Disney World, which opened in October 1971, and later that year, he died at the age of 78.

Now the leadership passed to Card Walker. Walker, who had joined the company in 1938 as a mail clerk, possessed an encyclopedic knowledge of the business that had made him invaluable to the Disneys. He was very close to their families, a good friend, and an enthusiastic supporter. He tried to continue the Walt Disney spirit. He once remarked, "Walt's in this room. He'll always be in this room. We know what he would think is right or wrong, and that's good enough for us."

EPCOT

The immediate success of Walt Disney World spurred the decision in the mid 1970s to proceed with the Experimental Prototype Community of Tomorrow, EPCOT. Walt's original model-city concept, however, with a dome controlling the climate of the central city and office buildings that would be orbited by residences, schools, and green space, was too ambitious for even the most loyal Walt Disney followers. Disney management abandoned it as too expensive to keep technologically up-to-date and too difficult to control. Furthermore, the idea for 20,000 people to live and work in the community was scrapped. Instead, EPCOT evolved into two theme parks—"Future World," to showcase past and future technologies and the expression of human imagination, and "World Showcase," which simulated the cultures of nine nations (more to come) in a sort of permanent world's fair. It was a $1.2 billion project, and more than its predecessors, Disneyland and Disney World, EPCOT was aimed primarily at grown-ups.

As with all Disney endeavors, the logistics strained the imagination. Some 54 million tons of earth were moved; 16,000 tons of steel were used; and 500,000 board feet of lumber went into construction of the sets alone. Around the 40-acre man-made lagoon, 70 acres of sod were laid, and 12,500 trees and 10,000 shrubs were planted. More than 1.5 million feet of film were shot in 30 different countries and edited for more than 4 hours of shows. An entire 3-D camera and projection system was invented for the 360-degree wraparound show in the Imagination pavilion.

Money from corporate tie-ins was crucial to Disney's ability to finance EPCOT, by generating more than one third of the total cost. Large corporations paid up to $25 million each for the privilege of affixing their names to individual pavilions.

Just before EPCOT opened in the fall of 1982, Disney officials were surprised when Disney World characters voted 45 to 41 to be represented by the Teamsters. Although Disney had defeated earlier efforts by characters to join the stagehands' union, management accepted Teamster representation quietly. The Teamsters became the seventeenth union at Disney World and EPCOT. (Disneyland had 28 unions.) According to *Forbes*, "There had already been enough bad publicity from employees—evading the Disney ban on talking to the press—complaining anonymously to reporters about hot and dirty costumes, abusive child customers, and low wages." (The wage base for Disney World employees, many of whom were food-and-beverage or sanitation workers, in 1983 was $4.60 to $6.00 per hour, resulting in a payroll of $4 million per week.)

Tokyo

In April 1983, after 2 years of construction involving 3,000 workers, the biggest Disneyland of them all at that time opened on 202 acres of landfill in Tokyo Bay. Oriental Land Company, the Japanese real estate company that built and owned the park, had begun reclaiming the land almost 20 years earlier. For this desolate mudflat land, they paid $70 per 3.3 square meters. By 1984, those 3.3-square-meter parcels were worth more than $2,000 each. With 300 acres still undeveloped, Oriental Lands stood to clear $740 million on resale, more than enough to cover the $673 million borrowed from Japanese banks to build this Disneyland.

Walt Disney Productions had started talks with Oriental Land in 1974, but a final agreement was not reached until 1979. Disney had zero cash investments in the project, and therefore risked only its name. For the use of the name and the Disney know-how, Disney received 10 percent of the entrance gross and 5 percent on all food and souvenirs sold in the park. WDP retained "theme supervision" for the life of the project, which meant everything had to be done "Walt's way." Except for signs, which had Japanese subtitles under larger English words, there was little that was distinctly Japanese about the park. Only two of the park's 27 restaurants sold Japanese food, and they served only sushi and bento, basically an oriental box lunch. A weatherproof skylight covered the entire World Bazaar

complex (Main Street USA). Sheltered queue areas, walkways, and enclosed patios were also provided. Most of the electronic show and ride designs represented the latest in Disney technology and were more advanced than similar attractions at U.S. Disneyland and Disney World.

One third of Japan's population lived within 90 minutes of the site, and first-year attendance was projected to be 10 million visitors, but the project was not without problems and risks. The weather was the most obvious difficulty. Tokyo averages 58.52 inches of rain and 108 rainy days every year. It snows every winter in Tokyo, and the park lies squarely in the path of the famous Pacific typhoons. This double threat obliged Disneyland's gardeners to provide gas heating for the park's 300,000 newly planted trees, and to tie every one down with four solid guy wires. Furthermore, Japanese children put in 6, and sometimes 7, days per week at school, with only a week of vacation in May and two more in August.

* * * * *

Card Walker stepped down as chairman of WDP in May 1983 at the age of 68. He was succeeded by real estate developer Raymond L. Watson, a long-time Disney board member. President of California's Irvine Company for 4 of his 17 years there, Watson was credited with much of the planning for the development of 60,000 acres that included the entire city of Irvine and sections of five adjacent cities.

The 57-year-old Watson was described as an "analytical planner with a conservative management track record" who was unlikely to tamper with the Disney heritage or "The Disney Way of Leadership" (Exhibit 15-1). According to Watson, "You don't come to a tradition-minded company and say, 'I'm going to change everything.' The employees would run you out of town."

Another element of our management style is our strong belief in our people-oriented approach to leadership.

A Disney Leader Gets Results Through People

Simplified, this means that a Disney leader is a people specialist. He does not get results by doing his own thing . . . he works with other people and helps them put on a good show. It is a known fact that leadership is a science and can be learned like any other skill, but you have to work at it every day. There are some key skills important to the Disney Way of Leadership.

Human Relations Skills

Good human relations is a basic cornerstone of the Disney people philosophy. The success of our organization depends on the way we deal with people, and it begins with the way we deal with our employees.

Our ability to work positively with people lies in continually putting to practice some key points.

- Set the example . . . it starts with you.
- Encourage a positive attitude.
- Get to know your employees . . . treat them as individuals.
- Be with your team . . . provide encouragement and attention.
- Use empathy . . . look at the other person's point of view.
- Have respect for others.
- Be objective . . . be firm, fair, and consistent.
- Give recognition for a job well done.
- Maintain your sense of humor.
- All problems are not the same . . . treat each individually.
- If an employee has a problem . . . help solve it.
- If a promise is made . . . keep it.
- See that your employees have good working conditions.

Communications Skills

One of the most valuable and important skills of the Disney leader is his ability to effectively communicate. All of the positive human relations techniques available today are virtually useless without effective communication.

Since communication means getting ideas across and finding out what other people have to say, we stress the following points in the Disney Way of Leadership.

- Communicate clearly . . . get your message across.
- Let your employees know how they're doing.
- Encourage upward and downward communications.
- Listen to what employees have to say.
- Keep an open door and an open mind.
- Tell employees how they fit in . . . explain the big picture.
- Let your employees feel like they belong.
- Communication should be direct, open, and honest.

Training Skills

Training is the method of developing the basic skills to create an efficient work group, and is the responsibility of every Disney leader.

An efficient operation can never come about as the result of a "happy accident." Each employee must have a clear-cut idea of what they are expected to accomplish and how to achieve it with the greatest proficiency.

Some key training points to remember:

- Be sure your employees receive the proper training which they need for doing their job.
- Provide for your employees' future growth and development.
- Give employees a chance to learn and participate.
- Encourage new ideas and creative contributions.

Other Leadership Skills

In addition to the aforementioned skills, the Disney leader also needs to be aware of and skillful in areas of planning, organizing, directing, and controlling his/her team's efforts.

Planning is really just looking ahead. Once objectives are understood, the means necessary to achieve them are presented in plans. Organizing is the process of putting all the resources together to carry out the plan. Directing involves the process of carrying out the plan using all the resources gathered. Controlling measures performance in relation

(continued)

EXHIBIT 15-1   The Disney Way of Leadership

to expected standards of performance.

The Disney Way of Leadership stresses arranging work into a logical and workable manner to insure its successful completion. Keep in mind these helpful points.

- A plan of action is the best control to make sure we get there.
- Don't over-structure a plan . . . stay flexible.
- Set clearly defined priorities and completion schedules.
- Be realistic with target dates . . . but set them.
- Don't assume . . . follow-up on assign-

ments and requests.
- Organize around jobs and people.
- Find the right person for the job.
- Issue effective and understandable instructions and directions.
- Establish effective controls to get things done in a timely manner and by priority.

In summary, the Disney Way of Leadership actually integrates all of these skills, applies them as appropriate at the point of action. For it is only through daily application and practice that we "fine tune" the essential skills of effective leadership.

Source: From *The Disney Management Style,* Walt Disney Productions, 1977, pp. 32–34.

EXHIBIT 15-1   (continued)

Also in 1983, Ronald W. Miller, the 50-year-old one-time tight end for the Los Angeles Rams, was named president. Miller had joined the Disney studios 3 years after marrying Walt's eldest daughter in 1954. (They were separated in 1983.)

At least since the 1970s, company observers had voiced concern for the future of Walt Disney Productions. Some wondered whether the company had the creativity needed to capture new markets. Many of the "new" plans were leftover ideas of Walt Disney's. Top managers suggested that if their plans seemed to fit a strategy of attracting older audiences, that was merely a coincidence. "What we are doing is intuitively based on a hell of a lot of experience," explained Card Walker. "More important than planning and research is the combination of experience we get from a lot of segments of the company." According to a former senior executive with Disney, "The company is creatively burned out. All those guys [top management] are so square you can't roll them downhill." A research analyst described current management as being "very businesslike and competent, but . . .

squelching creativity." (For a list of the company's management team, see Exhibit 15-2.)

A REVIEW OF OPERATIONS

Movie Division

The crisis facing Disney was most visible in the film division. In 1979, it had accounted for 20 percent of pretax earnings. In 1982, films lost $33 million. Part of the problem was demographics. Disney films had always appealed to a young (under 14) audience. That group comprised 14.7 percent of the population in 1950, 18.2 percent in 1960, 15 percent in 1970, and 13.6 percent in 1980.

The traditional Disney audience had indeed shrunk, but as Card Walker saw it, the problem ran even deeper: "Young adults today want a more sophisticated point of view, with more sex and violence. We don't ever want to go that far." Ron Miller, who served as executive producer throughout the decade of the 1970s, described the situation in personal terms. "We were not reaching that broad audience. I saw it with my own children. The moment they turned about 14 or 15, I would run a

Disney film at home and they'd look and say, 'Oh God, not that corn again.'" Miller had been frustrated by being unable to bid for scripts like *Kramer vs. Kramer* and *Raiders of the Lost Ark* because of the Disney image.

The reluctance of freelance Hollywood talent to adapt to Disney's narrow range and stingy compensation deals had often kept Miller's instincts from bearing fruit. According to a former Disney executive, "Card [Walker] would listen but not hear. Ron would listen but not act." Reportedly, Miller had eagerly pursued Michael Eisner, president of Paramount Pictures (*Raiders of the Lost Ark, Saturday Night Fever, Flashdance, Terms of Endearment,* and three *Star Trek* movies) for the Disney studios, but *Business Week* reported:

> Industry experts assume that Eisner would have wanted more control than Disney was prepared to give. Says a key executive at a rival studio: "Disney's movie division is relatively small. Even though they are beefing up production, they will release only about seven films a year. The majors each release more than 15. The movies are a small part of Disney's total business. Any heavy-weight would want some control of the theme-park operations. That would upset too many longtime Disneyites." And he adds: "People still doubt that Disney wants to—and can—change its image."

In recent years, there had been a talent drain, some of which was the result of the retirement of longtime animators. Don Bluth, a talented animator who produced the well-received film *The Secret of NIMH,* walked out of Disney in 1979 with two colleagues. They were soon followed by 14 more. As Bluth repeatedly told the press, his goal was to return to the "classic" Disney techniques of *Snow White* and *Pinocchio.*

Recent write-offs in the movie division included:

Something Wicked This Way Comes	$21.0 million
Night Crossing	10.5 million
The Watcher in the Woods	6.8 million
Midnight Madness	4.5 million
Condorman	$20.5 million

Not all of the movies in recent years had been losers. *The Rescuers,* an animated film, surpassed 1964's *Mary Poppins* in revenues. This fact escaped the attention of most Disney observers, however, because a large portion of the gross came from West Germany, where the movie was the biggest hit of all time. *The Fox and the Hound* cost $12 million to produce and earned $50 million. *The Black Hole* was disappointing but was expected to break even.

The Disney film library was another important company asset. Valued at $60 million and with annual amortization costs of approximately $66 million, it was estimated by some to be worth $400 million to $600 million. The library contained 650 titles ranging from classics such as *Mary Poppins* and *Snow White* to lesser films such as *The Shaggy D.A.* and *The Bootniks.* In 1983, *Snow White* was rereleased and brought in $20 million.

In 1981, Thomas Wilhite, who had been the company's publicity director, was given responsibility for all film production. Wilhite, then 27 and the company's youngest vice president, represented youth and a fresh approach. He was a film buff but had never produced a picture. Wilhite's first film, *Tron,* did not do well (a $10.4 million write-off) despite enormous advance publicity. Wilhite's next venture was *Tex,* a $5 million production about a teenager growing up in Oklahoma. It was favorably reviewed but drew small audiences.

In March 1983, Richard Berger, senior vice president for Worldwide Productions at

Board of Directors

Caroline Leonetti Ahmanson*†
Businesswoman, civic leader, and philanthropist

William H. Anderson
Independent producer

Robert H. B. Baldwin†§
Chairman—Advisory Board, Morgan Stanley, Inc. (investment bankers)

Roy E. Disney*
Chairman of the Board, Shamrock Holdings, Inc. (radio and television broadcasting)

Philip M. Hawley†§
President and Chief Executive Officer, Carter Hawley Hale Stores, Inc. (retail merchandising)

Ignacio E. Lozano, Jr.*†
Publisher, LA OPINION (newspaper publishing)

Ronald W. Miller‡
President and Chief Executive Officer

Richard T. Morrow
Vice President—General Counsel

Richard A. Nunis
Executive Vice President—Walt Disney World/Disneyland

Donn B. Tatum‡§
Chairman of the Finance Committee

E. Cardon Walker‡
Chairman of the Executive Committee

Raymond L. Watson‡
Chairman of the Board

Samuel L. Williams
Senior Partner, Hufstedler, Miller, Carlson & Beardsley (law firm)

Corporate Officers

Ronald W. Miller
President and Chief Executive Officer

Raymond L. Watson
Chairman of the Board

E. Cardon Walker
Chairman of the Executive Committee

Michael L. Bagnall
Executive Vice President—Finance

Carl G. Bongirno
Executive Vice President—Administration

Barton K. Boyd
Executive Vice President—Consumer Products and Merchandising

Ronald J. Cayo
Executive Vice President—Business Affairs and Legal

James P. Jimirro
Executive Vice President—Telecommunications

Jack B. Lindquist
Executive Vice President—Marketing

Richard A. Nunis
Executive Vice President—Walt Disney World/Disneyland

Martin A. Sklar
Executive Vice President—WED Creative Development

John J. Cornwell
Vice President—Management Information Systems

Jose M. Deetjen
Vice President—Tax Administration and Counsel

Dennis M. Despie
Vice President—Entertainment

Robert W. Gibeaut
Vice President—Studio Operations

Luther R. Marr
Vice President—Corporate and Stockholder Affairs

Richard T. Morrow
Vice President—General Counsel

Howard M. Roland
Vice President—Construction Contract Administration and Purchasing

Doris A. Smith
Vice President and Secretary

Frank P. Stanek
Vice President—Corporate Planning

Donald A. Escen
Treasurer

Bruce F. Johnson
Controller

Leland L. Kirk
Assistant Secretary–Treasurer

Neal E. McClure
Assistant Secretary

Alvin L. Shelbourn
Assistant Treasurer

Donald E. Tucker
Assistant Treasurer

Douglas E. Houck
Assistant Controller

Joe E. Stevens
Assistant Controller

Corporate Management Committee

Ronald W. Miller, Chairman; Michael L. Bagnall, Richard L. Berger, Carl G. Bongirno, Barton K. Boyd, Ronald J. Cayo, James P. Jimirro, Jack B. Lindquist, Richard A. Nunis, Martin A. Sklar

(continued)

EXHIBIT 15-2 Management Team

Principal Domestic Divisions (*) and Subsidiaries with Chief Operating Executives

Buena Vista Distribution Co., Inc.
Charles E. Good, President

Buena Vista International, Inc.
Harold P. Archinal, President

Canasa Trading Corporation
Harold P. Archinal, President

The Disney Channel
James P. Jimirro, President

Disneyland*
Richard A. Nunis, President

Disneyland, Inc.
Richard A. Nunis, President

Lake Buena Vista Communities, Inc.
Richard A. Nunis, President

MAPO*
Carl G. Bongirno, President

Reedy Creek Utilities Co., Inc.
Ronald J. Cayo, President

United National Operating Co.*
Barton K. Boyd, President

Vista Advertising*
Jack B. Lindquist, President

Vista Insurance Services, Inc.
Philip N. Smith, President

Vista-United Telecommunications
(a Florida partnership)
James Tyler, General Manager

Source: From 1983 annual report.

Walt Disney Educational Media Company*
James P. Jimirro, President

Walt Disney Music Company
Gary Krisel, President

Walt Disney Pictures
Richard L. Berger, President

Walt Disney Telecommunications and Non-Theatrical Company
James P. Jimirro, President

Walt Disney Television*
William Brademan, President

Walt Disney Travel Co., Inc.
Jack B. Lindquist, President

Walt Disney World Co.
Richard A. Nunis, President

WED Enterprises*
Carl G. Bongirno, President
Martin A. Sklar, Executive Vice President

WED Transportation Systems, Inc.
Richard A. Nunis, Chairman and President

Wonderland Music Company, Inc.
Gary Krisel, President

Foreign Subsidiaries with Principal Marketing Executives

Belgium
Walt Disney Productions (Benelux) S.A.
Andre Vanneste

Canada
Walt Disney Music of Canada Limited

James K. Rayburn

EXHIBIT 15-2 (continued)

20th Century Fox, was made president of a new Disney subsidiary, Walt Disney Pictures. Eight months later, Wilhite quit, claiming "the film company is big enough for only one head of production." According to *Variety*:

> With unusual candor for a departing exec, Wilhite said that "Richard Berger and I didn't see things the same way. We disagreed on the viability of 'Splash,' which he'd turned down at Fox. He never fulfilled his promise to bring staff salaries and titles up to industry standards. Everyone who came from the outside got the good salaries, but not those already here. I think my exit has been inevitable, one way or the other, for some time."

Consumer Products

The consumer products division was responsible for collecting royalties on the Disney name and characters. Every item that carried the name of Disney or any of its characters generated revenue—everything from Mickey Mouse ears, books, watches, and T-shirts to Tokyo dolls with Mickey wearing a kimono. On divisional assets of $37 million and revenues of $111 million, consumer products earned income of $57 million in 1983. In 1979, its pretax earnings were nearly a 200 percent return on assets. Some analysts had valued the consumer products division at $350 million.

Cable Television: The Disney Channel

TV revenues had declined from $44.4 million in 1982 to $27.9 million in 1983. The company that had produced *The Wonderful World of Disney* and *The Mickey Mouse Club* for network television no longer had any hit shows on the air.

To counter the decline, the Disney Channel was formed in April 1983, with an initial programming investment of $45 million. Offering a 16-hour-a-day schedule, 7-days-a-week, the Disney Channel, 6 months later, had more than 532,000 basic subscriber homes and had signed agreements with 1,123 cable systems offering the service to 9.9 million homes in all 50 states. By March 31, 1984, the number of subscribers was 916,000. This record established the Disney Channel as the fastest growing and most successful new pay-television service in history and put it on target toward its projected breakeven of 2 million subscribers by the end of 1985.

Subscribers paid between $7 and $11 a month for Disney's family-oriented programming. The foundation for this service was the Disney library of feature films, cartoons, true-life adventures, educational shorts, and television shows. The channel also acquired exclusive pay-television rights to 12 classic Charlie Chaplin features and purchased films such as *Can Can* and *Guys and Dolls* from other studios. In addition, Disney announced that 25 production crews were working on 658 shows (all 1/2-hour and 4-hour series) in Los Angeles, Orlando, and a dozen other sites throughout the United States.

If objectives were met, pay-TV services could generate profit margins of 25 percent. According to Jim Jimirro, president of Walt Disney Telecommunications, "The number of viewers who are interested in family entertainment has been very underestimated. There is every evidence that those people will reach vigorously for our type of product." More than 80 percent of the subscribers gave the channel high marks, and 21 percent of those surveyed never before had subscribed to any pay service (20 percent of the subscribers did not have children under the age of 13). Still, Jimirro admitted in 1984, "We have not yet reached our projected penetration levels." Only 7 percent of the homes that could get the channel were taking it. He had anticipated 15 percent.

In the first quarter of 1984, the Disney channel lost $11 million. The projected loss was cut from $15 million to $9 million in the second quarter by producing and acquiring less programming, cutting marketing expenditures, and amortizing some programming costs more slowly.

Some cable operations complained that management was too rigid in its marketing strategies. One reported, "They don't know the cable business, and they don't listen. We wanted to give the channel away free for 2 weeks to create a viewing habit among children so the parents would buy. But it was a tough struggle to finally convince Disney to do it."

Another complaint came from the National Coalition on Television Violence. After monitoring the channel for 2 weeks in 1984, the organization reported an average of nine violent acts per hour on real-life programming and 18 per hour on cartoons, nearly as high as on the three networks. The coalition described the level of violence as "quite troubling," and its chairman, a University of Illinois psychiatrist, claimed the violence could be harmful to children.

Theme Parks

In early 1984, concern also was being expressed about Disney's theme parks. Attendance had been virtually flat for the past decade. Disney World and Disneyland generated 87 percent of total 1983 income. EPCOT attendance rose in 1983 but fell 8 percent in the quarter ending December 31, 1983. Early 1984 attendance was off 19 percent. According to an analyst with Wertheim & Company, "The 19 percent drop was a big disappointment. It raises a real question about whether EPCOT Center has the growth potential the investors expected."

Some of the attendance drop could be attributed to the harsh Eastern winter, but Disney World's decline was greater than neighboring attractions such as Cyprus Gardens and Sea World. According to Watson, "We think we may be losing the young marrieds, for example, because we are not marketing the resort and recreational aspects of the park."

According to one entertainment analyst, "The increment to the theme park's operating earnings from Disney's $1.2 billion investment probably did not exceed $80 million before taxes. After charging itself taxes, Disney is left with about $45 million. That represents less than a 4 percent return on EPCOT. If Disney had invested in Treasury bills, it could have done better." In 1983, depreciation on the amusement parks was $88 million. Total revenues were approximately $1 billion.

Attendance at California's Disneyland rose 10 percent in the first and second quarter of 1984 because of Disney's $45 million investment in rebuilding Fantasyland. Response to Tokyo Disneyland had been strong, with 1983 royalties estimated to be $10 million to $20 million.

Because of the Tokyo experience, top management was considering the desirability of building a Disneyland in Latin America or Europe. Another project being debated was a series of mini-Disney entertainment parks throughout the United States. If such projects were undertaken, some Disney executives thought the parks should be in urban centers; others championed suburban sites near popular shopping malls. Other executives feared such parks would cheapen the Disney name. According to Watson, "The idea has been around for years. I've told Ron [Miller, president] we should either decide on it or stop talking about it." Another option was to buy other amusement parks and add Disney's distinctive touch. Theme parks in North Carolina, Virginia, Texas, and Ohio recently had sold for just under two times revenue.

Real Estate

Outsiders expected Ray Watson to bring his expertise to Disney's real estate holdings, including approximately 40 underdeveloped acres at the California Disneyland site. In Orlando, Disney owned 28,000 acres—a tract twice the size of Manhattan. According to Watson, "If we've used up more than 3,000 acres of that I'm surprised." There had been talk about more hotels and Disney ventures such as shopping centers, residential housing, or industrial parks. Although some of the Florida property would be hard to develop, analysts estimated that its value would range from $1,000 to $1 million an acre. In addition to its central Florida land, the company also owned about 40 acres of undeveloped Florida coastal property. Disney's total Florida landholdings were estimated to be worth $300 million to $700 million.

* * * * *

By February 1984, Roy E. Disney's personal shareholdings had dropped from $96 million in 1983 to $54 million because of the declining value of Disney stock. As Disney examined the latest financial reports for the company (Exhibits 15-3 through 15-7), he wondered what could be done to restore the value of the assets that the Disney brothers had built. ■

	1983	*1982*	*1981*	*1980*	*1979*
Entertainment and Recreation					
Walt Disney World					
Admissions and rides	$ 278,320	$ 153,504	$ 139,326	$ 130,144	$ 121,276
Merchandise sales	172,324	121,410	121,465	116,187	101,856
Food sales	178,791	121,329	114,951	106,404	95,203
Lodging	98,105	81,427	70,110	61,731	54,043
Disneyland					
Admissions and rides	102,619	98,273	92,065	87,066	75,758
Merchandise sales	72,300	76,684	79,146	72,140	60,235
Food sales	45,699	44,481	44,920	41,703	35,865
Participant fees, Walt Disney Travel Co., Tokyo Disneyland royalties and other	83,044	28,502	29,828	28,005	26,843
Total revenues	$1,031,202	$ 725,601	$ 691,811	$ 643,380	$ 571,079
Theme park attendance					
Walt Disney World	22,712	12,560	13,221	13,783	13,792
Disneyland	9,980	10,421	11,343	11,522	10,760
Total	32,692	22,981	24,564	25,305	24,552
Motion Pictures					
Theatrical					
Domestic	$ 38,635	$ 55,408	$ 54,624	$ 63,350	$ 49,594
Foreign	43,825	64,525	76,279	78,314	57,288
Television					
Worldwide	27,992	44,420	43,672	19,736	27,903
Home video and nontheatrical					
Worldwide	55,006	37,749	22,231	10,565	9,273
Total revenues	$ 165,458	$ 202,102	$ 196,806	$ 171,965	$ 144,058
Consumer Products and Other					
Character merchandising	$ 45,429	$ 35,912	$ 30,555	$ 29,631	$ 24,787
Publications	20,006	20,821	24,658	22,284	18,985
Records and music publishing	30,666	26,884	27,358	23,432	16,129
Educational media	10,259	15,468	21,148	21,908	19,967
Other	4,327	3,453	12,704	1,905	1,768
Total revenues	$ 110,697	$ 102,538	$ 116,423	$ 99,160	$ 81,636

Source: From 1983 annual report.

EXHIBIT 15-3   **Revenue by Major Groups (000)**

Year Ended September 30	*1983*	*1982*	*1981*
Revenues			
Entertainment and recreation	$ 1,031,202	$ 725,610	$ 691,811
Motion pictures	165,458	202,102	196,806
Consumer products and other	110,697	102,538	116,423
Total revenues	1,307,357	1,030,250	1,005,040
Costs and expenses of operations			
Entertainment and recreation	834,324	592,965	562,337
Motion pictures	198,843	182,463	162,180
Consumer products and other	53,815	54,706	65,859
Total costs and expenses of operations	1,086,982	830,134	790,376
Operating income (loss) before corporate expenses			
Entertainment and recreation	196,878	132,645	129,474
Motion pictures	(33,385)	19,639	34,626
Consumer products and other	56,882	47,832	50,564
Total operating income before corporate expenses	220,375	200,116	214,664
Corporate expenses (income)			
General and administrative	35,554	30,957	26,216
Design projects abandoned	7,295	5,147	4,598
Interest expense (income), net	14,066	(14,781)	(33,130)
Total corporate expenses (income)	56,915	21,323	(2,316)
Income before taxes on income	163,460	178,793	216,980
Taxes on income	70,300	78,700	95,500
Net income	$ 93,160	$ 100,093	$ 121,480
Earnings per share	$2.70	$3.01	$3.72

Source: From 1983 annual report.

EXHIBIT 15-4   Consolidated Statements of Income (000)

September 30	1983	1982
Assets		
Current assets		
Cash	$ 18,055	$ 13,652
Accounts receivable, net of allowances	102,847	78,968
Income taxes refundable	70,000	41,000
Inventories	77,945	66,717
Film production costs	44,412	43,850
Prepaid expenses	19,843	18,152
Total current assets	333,102	262,339
Film production costs—noncurrent	82,598	64,217
Property, plant, and equipment, at cost		
Entertainment attractions, buildings, and equipment	2,251,297	1,916,617
Less: Accumulated depreciation	(504,365)	(419,944)
	1,746,932	1,496,673
Construction and design projects in progress		
EPCOT Center	70,331	120,585
Other	37,859	39,601
Land	16,687	16,379
	1,871,809	1,673,238
Other assets	93,686	103,022
	$ 2,381,195	$ 2,102,816
Liabilities and Stockholders' Equity		
Current liabilities		
Accounts payable, payroll, and other accrued liabilities	$ 187,641	$ 210,753
Taxes on income	50,557	26,560
Total current liabilities	238,198	237,313
Long-term borrowings, including commercial paper		
of $118,200 and $200,000	346,325	315,000
Other long-term liabilities and noncurrent advances	110,874	94,739
Deferred taxes on income and investment credits	285,270	180,980
Commitments and contingencies		
Stockholders' equity		
Preferred shares, no par		
Authorized—5,000,000 shares, none issued		
Common shares, no par		
Authorized—75,000,000 shares		
Issued and outstanding—34,509,171 and 33,351,482 shares	661,934	588,250
Retained earnings	738,594	686,534
	1,400,528	1,274,784
	$ 2,381,195	$ 2,102,816

Source: From 1983 annual report.

EXHIBIT 15-5   Consolidated Balance Sheets (000)

Year Ended September 30	1983	1982	1981
Cash provided by operations before taxes on			
income (see below)	$308,369	$309,431	$316,949
Taxes paid (received) on income, net	(28,987)	34,649	106,144
Cash provided by operations	337,356	274,782	210,805
Cash dividends	41,100	39,742	32,406
	296,256	235,040	178,399
Investing activities			
EPCOT Center, net of related payables	250,196	566,428	285,651
Other property, plant, and equipment	83,542	47,988	47,756
Film production and programming costs	83,750	52,295	55,454
Rights to the Walt Disney name	(3,640)	40,000	
EPCOT Center and The Disney Channel pre-opening			
and start-up costs	18,253	19,170	1,907
Long-term notes receivable and other	11,406	26,881	4,023
	443,507	752,762	394,791
	(147,251)	(517,722)	(216,392)
Financing activities			
Long-term borrowings	137,500	205,000	110,000
Reduction of long-term borrowings	(99,925)		
Common-stock offering	70,883		
Common stock issued (returned) to acquire rights			
to the Walt Disney name and certain equipment	(3,640)	46,200	
Participation fees, net of related receivables	11,169	23,867	24,745
Collection of long-term notes receivable and other	35,667	2,030	7,646
	151,654	277,097	142,391
Increase (decrease) in cash and short-term investments	4,403	(240,625)	(74,001)
Cash and short-term investments, beginning of year	13,652	254,277	328,278
Cash and short-term investments, end of year	$ 18,055	$ 13,652	$254,277

The difference between income before taxes on income as shown on the "Consolidated Statements of Income" and cash provided by operations before taxes on income is explained as follows:

Income before taxes on income	$163,460	$178,793	$216,980
Charges to income not requiring cash outlays:			
Depreciation	90,184	41,917	38,886
Amortization of film production and			
programming costs	65,575	64,868	55,222
Other	15,526	9,950	9,449
Changes in:			
Accounts receivable	(25,863)	1,077	(18,591)
Inventories	(11,228)	(6,944)	(5,125)
Prepaid expenses	(1,691)	(2,754)	(3,960)
Accounts payable, payroll, and			
other accrued liabilities	12,406	22,524	24,088
	144,909	130,638	99,969
Cash provided by operations before taxes on income	$308,369	$309,431	$316,949

Source: From 1983 annual report.

EXHIBIT 15-6   Consolidated Statements of Changes in Financial Position (000)

	1983	*1982*	*1981*	*1980*	*1979*
Statements of Income					
Revenues	$1,307,357	$1,030,250	$1,005,040	$ 914,505	$ 796,773
Operating income before					
corporate expenses	220,375	200,116	214,664	231,300	205,695
Corporate expenses	42,849	36,104	30,814	25,424	20,220
Interest expense (income), net	14,066	(14,781)	(33,130)	(42,110)	(28,413)
Taxes on income	70,300	78,700	95,500	112,800	100,000
Net income	93,160	100,093	121,480	135,186	113,788
Balance Sheets					
Current assets	333,102	262,339	457,829	506,202	484,141
Property, plant, and equipment,					
net of depreciation	1,871,809	1,673,238	1,069,369	762,546	648,447
Total assets	2,381,195	2,102,816	1,610,009	1,347,407	1,196,424
Current liabilities	238,198	237,313	181,573	145,291	119,768
Long-term obligations, including commercial paper of $118,200 (1983) and $200,000 (1982)	457,199	409,739	171,886	30,429	18,616
Total liabilities and deferred credits	980,667	828,032	442,891	272,609	235,362
Total net assets (stockholders' equity)	1,400,528	1,274,784	1,167,118	1,074,798	961,062
Statements of Changes in Financial Position					
Cash provided by operations	337,356	274,782	210,805	204,682	182,857
Cash dividends	41,100	39,742	32,406	23,280	15,496
Investment in property, plant, and equipment	333,738	614,416	333,407	149,674	56,629
Investment in film production and programming	83,750	52,295	55,454	68,409	44,436
Per Share					
Net income (earnings)	2.70	3.01	3.72	4.16	3.51
Cash dividends	1.20	1.20	1.00	.72	.48
Stockholders' equity	$ 40.58	$ 38.22	$ 35.99	$ 33.22	$ 29.76
Average number of common and common-equivalent shares outstanding during the year	34,481	33,225	32,629	32,513	32,426
Other					
Stockholders at close of year	60,000	61,000	60,000	62,000	65,000
Employees at close of year	30,000	28,000	25,000	24,000	21,000

Source: From 1983 annual report.

EXHIBIT 15-7 Selected Financial Data (000)

Case 16　　Stewart Glapat Corporation vs. Caljan (A)

As he hung up the phone, William Tanner Stewart shuddered with the realization that for the first time, his company had a real and dangerous competitor. For more than 40 years, Stewart Glapat Corporation had been the major manufacturer of long, structural-steel telescoping conveyors in the United States. But a procurement officer for Federal Express, one of Stewart Glapat's most valued customers, had just told Bill that Federal Express had qualified a competitor for supplying its telescoping conveyor belts. After having used Stewart Glapat exclusively for the past 5 years, Federal Express had suddenly decided to consider Caljan as a qualified, additional supplier.

In recent years, Stewart had not considered that he might have a major competitor in his primary market niche. He knew Caljan: a Danish company that manufactured short telescoping conveyors, primarily for the European market, with some sales in the United States. Now Stewart had just learned that Caljan, having expanded its operations in the United States, had designed a lower-priced, long conveyor that apparently met the needs of Stewart Glapat's customers. In the midst of his surprise, Stewart contemplated his options for response. He had always considered competing on price—rather than on quality, service, and track record—as a form of failure. Now, however, he might be forced to lead his small design and manufacturing company into a price war with Caljan, a large corporation.

BACKGROUND

In 1985, Bill Stewart left his teaching career at the Darden Graduate School of Business Administration, University of Virginia, to return to Zanesville, Ohio. Bill was to succeed his brother, Charlie, and become president and chief operating officer of the business that their father had started in 1941. Charlie was to become chief executive officer. Before this transition, Stewart had pursued a career in engineering and business education. After graduating from MIT in 1969, he earned a Ph.D. at The Ohio State University. He taught as an assistant professor at Purdue University for 4 years before moving to the University of Virginia, where he became an associate professor of operations at the Darden Graduate School. From 1969 to 1976, he had also served as vice president of engineering for Stewart Glapat. Bill, his brother Charlie, and their mother were sole owners of the business after their father died in 1978.

Leaving academics to run the family business had been a major career decision for Stewart. Although he enjoyed the academic lifestyle, he wanted to help the family business grow and to actually manage something. The firm was struggling at the time, and Stewart wanted to make changes at Stewart Glapat that would improve its financial health. As president, he began to apply the principles that he had been teaching to his business students. Stewart became

UVA-OB-0628

This case was prepared by Andrew Spreadbury and Jean Kane under the supervision of Professor James G. Clawson. The case was written as a basis for class discussion rather than to illustrate effective or ineffective handling of an administrative situation. Copyright © 1997 by the University of Virginia Darden School Foundation, Charlottesville, VA. All rights reserved.

involved in every aspect of the business. First, he initiated measures to modernize, reorganize, and expand Stewart Glapat. He modified the factory to increase the safety and comfort of employees. He installed a modern computer system to improve communications, business planning, and engineering. He held frequent management meetings and instituted procedures for setting and meeting firm delivery deadlines. He sought expansion by training engineers, aggressively searching for new markets and products, and designing new advertisements. Eventually, Stewart created a second shift, which he himself supervised, to fulfill the new orders that these efforts had won for the company. (See the Stewart Glapat A–F case series, Darden School OB-0348-0354, for details of the challenges Stewart faced when he returned to the family business.)

The results of these changes were mixed. Many of them were not as well accepted as Stewart had hoped they would be. The changes were a source of frustration for many of Stewart Glapat's 30 employees. Some of the employees missed the family spirit that they felt had pervaded the company under his brother Charlie's more relaxed management. These employees found Bill overly involved and directive. They believed that he set unrealistic goals and ignored the suggestions that he frequently solicited. In short, some of the workforce thought that Bill was probably a fine teacher, but he was not an effective manager.

On the other hand, the financial results of these efforts were impressive. Stewart Glapat's average monthly level of sales rose from $282,000 in 1984–1985 to $800,000 for the period 1988–1989.

PRODUCTS

Stewart Glapat specialized in adjustable, cantilevered, telescoping conveyor systems. These systems consisted of a moving conveyor belt running over an adjustable boom

**William T. Stewart
PH. D., P.E.
President and COO**

**Charles T. Stewart, Jr.
Chairman and CEO**

that could be extended and retracted by a single operator while he or she loaded and unloaded large truck trailers. Each system typically had a series of button controls at both ends that controlled speed of the belt, and the length and angle of boom extension. The company had been marketing such equipment under its trademark, "Adjustoveyor," since 1946 (see Exhibit 16-1 for a page from a company brochure). Telescoping conveyor belts such as the

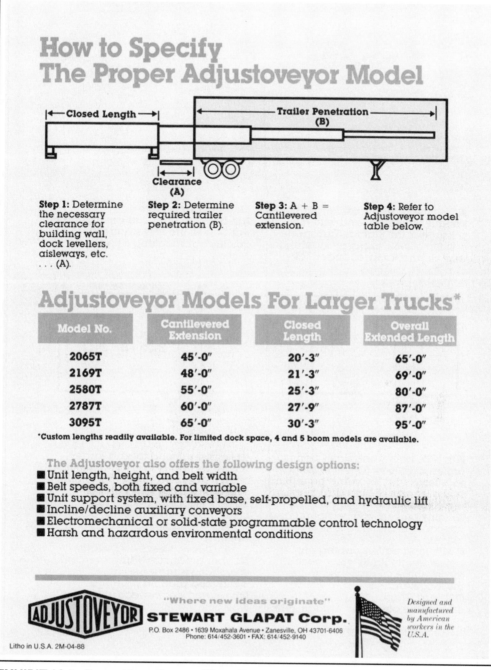

How to Specify
The Proper Adjustoveyor Model

|←——— Closed Length ———→| |←—————— Trailer Penetration —————→|
(B)

Clearance
(A)

Step 1: Determine the necessary clearance for building wall, dock levellers, aisleways, etc. . . . (A).

Step 2: Determine required trailer penetration (B).

Step 3: A + B = Cantilevered extension.

Step 4: Refer to Adjustoveyor model table below.

Adjustoveyor Models For Larger Trucks*

Model No.	Cantilevered Extension	Closed Length	Overall Extended Length
2065T	45'-0"	20'-3"	65'-0"
2169T	48'-0"	21'-3"	69'-0"
2580T	55'-0"	25'-3"	80'-0"
2787T	60'-0"	27'-9"	87'-0"
3095T	65'-0"	30'-3"	95'-0"

*Custom lengths readily available. For limited dock space, 4 and 5 boom models are available.

The Adjustoveyor also offers the following design options:
■ Unit length, height, and belt width
■ Belt speeds, both fixed and variable
■ Unit support system, with fixed base, self-propelled, and hydraulic lift
■ Incline/decline auxiliary conveyors
■ Electromechanical or solid-state programmable control technology
■ Harsh and hazardous environmental conditions

ADJUSTOVEYOR   "Where new ideas originate"
STEWART GLAPAT Corp.
P.O. Box 2486 • 1639 Moxahala Avenue • Zanesville, OH 43701-6406
Phone: 614/452-3601 • FAX: 614/452-9140

Designed and manufactured by American workers in the U.S.A.

Litho in U.S.A. 2M-04-88

EXHIBIT 16-1   Excerpt from Stewart Glapat Brochure

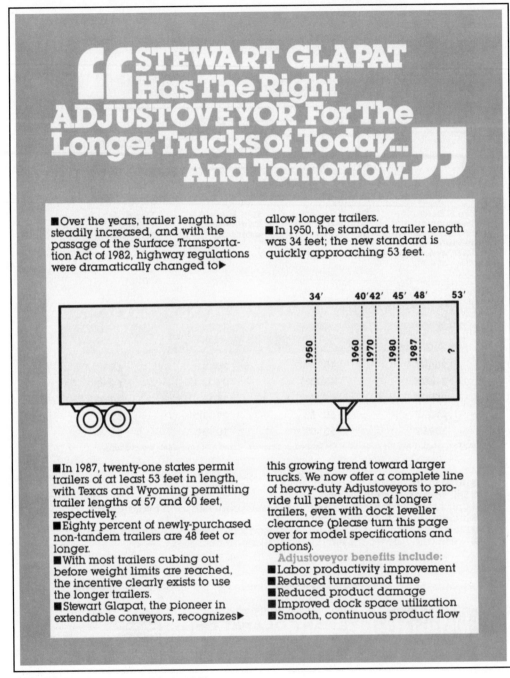

"STEWART GLAPAT Has The Right ADJUSTOVEYOR For The Longer Trucks of Today... And Tomorrow."

■ Over the years, trailer length has steadily increased, and with the passage of the Surface Transportation Act of 1982, highway regulations were dramatically changed to▶ allow longer trailers.

■ In 1950, the standard trailer length was 34 feet; the new standard is quickly approaching 53 feet.

■ In 1987, twenty-one states permit trailers of at least 53 feet in length, with Texas and Wyoming permitting trailer lengths of 57 and 60 feet, respectively.

■ Eighty percent of newly-purchased non-tandem trailers are 48 feet or longer.

■ With most trailers cubing out before weight limits are reached, the incentive clearly exists to use the longer trailers.

■ Stewart Glapat, the pioneer in extendable conveyors, recognizes▶ this growing trend toward larger trucks. We now offer a complete line of heavy-duty Adjustoveyors to provide full penetration of longer trailers, even with dock leveller clearance (please turn this page over for model specifications and options).

Adjustoveyor benefits include:
■ Labor productivity improvement
■ Reduced turnaround time
■ Reduced product damage
■ Improved dock space utilization
■ Smooth, continuous product flow

EXHIBIT 16-2 Effects of Federal Changes

Adjustoveyor helped load and unload material, usually boxes, that was being shipped from truck trailers. With a telescoping conveyor, dockworkers could keep the conveyor belt next to them and transfer boxes to and from the moving belt without repeatedly getting in and out of the vehicle. Telescoping conveyors made loading and unloading much faster and safer.

Telescoping conveyors were usually divided into two major categories: long and short. Short conveyors extended to a maximum of about 20 feet and typically were made from formed steel, meaning the steel parts of the system were made by bending or forming steel sheets into C-shaped pieces that could then be assembled into the boom for a finished conveyor system. Because formed steel was too weak and malleable to support longer booms, longer telescoping conveyors (extending 20 to 55 feet) generally were made from structural steel, which was rolled into strong shapes (usually "I" beams) during production. Producing telescoping conveyors out of structural steel units was a more complex and labor-intensive process, but its capital costs were comparatively low.

Stewart Glapat produced both types of telescoping conveyors, but specialized in building long conveyors made from structural steel with reinforced, heavy-duty flanges. The cantilevered design of the Adjustoveyor resembled a diving board in that no part of the extending boom touched the floor. The strength of the structural steel components along with Stewart's engineering designs allowed Stewart Glapat to build systems with 25-foot boom sections that could extend up to 55 feet, unsupported. The larger units weighed as much as 6 tons and created a "footprint" of 25 feet by 5 feet fully retracted.

The company sold conveyor systems ranging in size, design, and strength, for prices ranging from $15,000 up to more than $75,000 for the largest units. Customized designs were more expensive. Ninety-seven percent of the firm's sales were made in the continental United States. This was in part due to the cost of shipping the heavy units and to Stewart Glapat's history and tradition. The company marketed to customers in industries that depended on trucks for shipment: trucking firms, newspapers, fast-freight and postal delivery services, general retail distributors, meat packers, automobile manufacturers, and integrated systems providers. Stewart Glapat served the international market in a limited way, shipping a few systems to customers in Canada, Mexico, Brazil, and the Pacific Rim. The company sold almost no conveyors in Europe, where narrow, winding roads tended to limit truck lengths.

CUSTOMERS

The Trucking Industry

In the early 1980s, the Reagan administration deregulated U.S. transportation industries. In addition to removing guidelines for truck and air transport rate structures, the federal government allowed longer trucks on highways: Trailer length limits were extended from 40 feet to 48 feet and 53 feet (see Exhibit 16-2 for examples). Use of the 40-foot van, historically the largest and most common truck on the highway, gradually decreased as the trucking industry responded to deregulation.

As the result of deregulation, there were two major truck configurations operating by the early 1990s: long, single trailers and tandem trailers, or "PUPS," which piggybacked two 28-foot trailers behind one tractor. The large retail companies, such as Wal-Mart and J.C. Penney, tended to use the long, single trailers, and general-purpose freight companies such as Roadway Package Service and Yellow Freight favored the PUPS. Some firms, such as United Parcel Service (UPS), used both configurations.

The new regulations on trailor length tested the abilities of the telescoping conrequired conveyors that reached farther into their vehicles. During the early 1980s, no company had been able to meet the technical challenges of producing a unit that would extend 55 feet unsupported from its base. Stewart Glapat's accumulated skill in the design and manufacture of cantilevered structural steel conveyor systems put the company at a distinct advantage over firms that used formed-steel processes.

In 1985, Stewart Glapat built the Adjustoveyor Model 2580T, the first telescoping conveyor that could extend a full 55 feet, all the way to the end of the new, longer trailers. The first Model 2580T was installed in the J. C. Penney Distribution Center in Columbus, Ohio, just 45 minutes away from Zanesville and Stewart Glapat headquarters. Bill Stewart began taking potential customers to Columbus to see the new unit in action. He noted, "Once people saw it in operation, they naturally wanted it as it was clearly more productive than a shorter unit." The advantage of the 2580T was clear: With shorter units, employees had to walk 10 to 12 feet from the end of the conveyor to the front of the trailer for each package; with the 2580T, the conveyor followed them all the way to the front wall of the trailer. The longer extension of the model 2580T did require a longer "footprint" on the loading dock, but most newer warehouse buildings built with the standard 40 feet between support pillars easily allowed for this extra space. As a result of the popularity of longer trucks, the new Adjustoveyor model became the industry's best-selling unit. By 1990, the model 2580T accounted for 60 percent of Stewart Glapat's sales.

The Newspaper Industry

Newspaper companies represented a modest customer segment for Stewart Glapat. Most newspaper companies used shorter conveyors for their truck loading, as they commonly relied on 18- to 24-foot trucks to deliver papers on narrow city streets. In smaller cities, papers even used vans to drop off loads within their service areas. Only large newspapers such as the *Washington Post* or the *New York Times* used large trucks for deliveries to their satellite areas. Furthermore, newspapers began to experiment during the 1980s with wheeled carts and pallets to ship bulk loads to such satellite distribution centers. A standard pallet, which measured 4 feet square when loaded with tied or shrink-wrapped bulk items, was too large and heavy for handling by conveyor. The use of pallets further decreased the newspaper industry's need for long conveyors. "Sometimes, we will get an order for 12 to 24 units, and it is a nice chunk of business," Bill Stewart remarked. "Then we might go 9 to 12 months without an order." Stewart Glapat's success in this industry depended primarily on system integration of mailrooms, a major investment for newspapers. During the late 1980s and early 1990s, the newspaper segment comprised less than 15 percent of the company's sales.

Fast Freight and Postal Services

Fast-freight carriers, on the other hand, were a major part of Stewart Glapat's business. These companies had grown and thus expanded their materials handling needs during the 1980s. With the advent of overnight delivery services, UPS, which had specialized in truck shipment, began to ship by air, as well. Federal Express, which had specialized in air delivery, expanded into the overland shipping segment. By 1992, however, the U.S. express delivery market had become very competitive and was suffering from recession. The search for other market opportunities, particularly in Europe, led UPS to enter the air-freight market there at the same time that Federal Express was retreating from this market—where it had incurred heavy losses.

Stewart Glapat had been a key supplier for the U.S. Postal Service since the 1960s. Over the years, the company added UPS, Purlator, Federal Express, and Airborne to its list of fast-freight customers. For its first contract with Federal Express, in 1988, Stewart Glapat installed a telescoping conveyor in FedEx's Dallas Airport facility. As Federal Express expanded into truck delivery, Stewart Glapat became its sole supplier of expandable conveyors. According to Bill Stewart, Stewart Glapat "enjoyed a favored status" with Federal Express during the late 1980s and early 1990s. In 1988, shipping services accounted for 35 to 40 percent of Stewart Glapat's sales, a segment that continued to grow through the 1990s. Fast freight and mail service was clearly Stewart Glapat's dominant market segment.

THE CONVEYOR INDUSTRY

Stewart Glapat was the leading company in this industry. The firm had pioneered dependable designs in the structural-steel-telescoping segment of the industry. Further, its experience with structural-steel designs had allowed the company to take advantage of the change in regulations that allowed longer trucks. Because several competitors' efforts to build long, formed-steel conveyor systems had failed, Bill Stewart had concluded that no formed-sheet-metal manufacturer would be able to produce a cost-effective, durable conveyor able to extend 55 feet, and that he had secured a stable, secure, profitable niche in the industry. Stewart Glapat pursued a pricing strategy that allowed the company to sell its long, structural-steel conveyors at a premium over the company's cost structure while keeping the price lower than that of less-effective and shorter formed-steel units.

Integrated-Systems Suppliers

Integrated-systems suppliers were companies that purchased various kinds of equipment from several vendors and marketed a "single-stop shopping" solution to companies that wanted simple, installed, turnkey processes for handling their materials and finished products. These companies included parts and raw-materials-handling equipment in their designs, as well as loading docks and their related machinery. Stewart Glapat sold Adjustoveyors of varying sizes and capacities to many of these systems suppliers, and at times they were a significant part of Stewart Glapat's overall business volume.

COMPETITION

During this period, Stewart Glapat had two major competitors in the United States, Portec and Machine Design Services, and several smaller competitors, such as WASP. Stewart Glapat's only major foreign competitor was Caljan, a Danish firm.

Portec

Portec, a large, international industrial group, specialized in railroad equipment, construction machinery, and materials-handling activities. In the mid 1980s, in order to augment its product line, Portec began to build extendable conveyors at its small Flomaster Division in Colorado. Portec chose to manufacture such new products to avoid buying them from other companies. By building the units themselves, the company could offer more complete turnkey systems to its customers. Portec focused on the general retail market, acquiring customers such as Target Stores and K-Mart.

Portec had had some difficult experiences recently in the telescoping-conveyor market. Unlike Stewart Glapat, Portec used formed steel in the construction of its telescoping conveyors. Portec built formed steel units for Target, but found that they were neither cost efficient nor reliable in the longer lengths—so much so that Portec could not fulfill its contract with Target. This large customer then sued its supplier. Subsequently, Target replaced Portec's equipment with conveyors built by Stewart Glapat. Federal Express also used Portec, along with Stewart Glapat, as a supplier, but the well-known delivery service was dissatisfied with Portec's equipment and soon discontinued using it.

Machine Design Services

Machine Design Services (MDS), also located in Colorado, sold integrated manufacturing systems to the newspaper industry. In providing such equipment to newspapers, the company took turnkey responsibility for procuring and installing complete materials-handling systems. MDS entered the extendable conveyor market solely to meet the needs of its existing customers, who primarily needed short conveyors for their shipping systems.

MDS had captured about 30 percent of the U.S. market share in the newspaper industry with the shorter, formed-steel conveyors that belonged to its integrated systems. This strategy, however, kept MDS from selling telescoping conveyors to other integrated-systems firms that served the newspaper industry, such as Quipp, Inc., Hall Processing Systems, and IDAB, Inc. These companies viewed MDS as a competitor and purchased telescoping conveyors for their handling systems from Stewart Glapat.

WASP

WASP, a Minnesota firm, built a customized, short, formed-steel conveyor for UPS in the mid 1980s. To become a second supplier to UPS, Stewart Glapat had also modified its conveyor design for UPS use. From 1987 through 1989, Stewart Glapat and WASP were United Parcel Service's key suppliers for truck-loading conveyors. Forced to compete on price for this customer, however, Stewart Glapat gradually stopped bidding on UPS contracts.

Caljan

Located in Denmark, Caljan successfully served the European extendable-conveyor market. Like Stewart Glapat, the company specialized in telescoping conveyors. It had focused on supplying short, formed-steel conveyors to postal services throughout the Common Market. In the late 1980s, Caljan began to sell short conveyors in the United States, as well. Airborne, the fast-freight company located in Wilmington, Ohio, bought conveyors from both Caljan and Stewart Glapat and used them side by side. As Caljan began to sell more equipment in the United States, its engineers attempted to develop designs suited to the longer American trucks.

CALJAN'S ENTRY INTO THE UNITED STATES

In the early 1990s, Caljan hired a consultant in Virginia to do a market analysis of the North American market for extendable conveyors. The consultant found that there was a lucrative and solid long-term market in North America, especially with the elimination of tariffs at the borders between Mexico and Canada and the United States brought on by the North American Free Trade Agreement (NAFTA). His research showed that more freight would be moving throughout the continent. Furthermore, as the United States emerged from its most recent recession, services in materials handling, logistics, and distribution would grow to meet continental needs. Finally, the report noted that in entering a strong potential market for long conveyors, Caljan would compete with only one viable, long-term manufacturer: Stewart Glapat.

In response to this report, Caljan's management hired the consultant as the president of North American operations and decided to build a plant in Hampton Roads, Virginia, which opened early in 1992. Initially, the plant functioned as an assembly facility for heavy parts manufactured in Denmark, although the law allowed Caljan to claim that its conveyors were "made in America." Later, Caljan began to integrate vertically and finally to manufacture fully its various parts and subassemblies in Virginia.

COMPETITION FROM CALJAN

Prior to his conversation with the FedEx purchasing agent, Bill Stewart had considered Caljan a competitor for shorter units— as Airborne's purchases indicated—but had never experienced any competition from Caljan in the long-conveyor segment. Because the longer designs were predominant in the industry at the time, Stewart Glapat did not view Caljan as a major threat to its business.

Bill Stewart was astonished to learn, therefore, that after 5 years as Federal Express's sole supplier, Stewart Glapat was now faced with a competitive bid from Caljan. He also realized that because many of his customers understood and would respond to competitive bidding, this method of doing business could well become the standard in a niche in which Stewart previously believed he enjoyed a favored status.

After his phone conversation with the Federal Express buyer, Bill searched for answers. "What was Caljan's strategy?" he wondered. "How do they compete? What kind of financial backing do they have? Where will they attack next? How could this have happened without our being aware of it? How good are they? Do they really have a comparable product? What other products do they have?" Finally, he concluded, "They can't be as good as we are!"

Nevertheless, Bill didn't hesitate. Seeking answers to his questions, he began to research Caljan. He obtained a 10-minute tape that described the company. He studied Caljan's history and products.

Seeking to restore Stewart Glapat's favored relationship with Federal Express, Stewart hurried to schedule an appointment with members of FedEx's Memphis staff. In his meeting with Federal Express procurement agents and engineers, Stewart asked for explanations. "Can Caljan make a unit that competes with ours technically?" he asked.

"Yes, and it works quite well," replied a Federal Express manager. "And to be frank with you, Mr. Stewart, the way this is going to play out is in a competitive bid, predominantly based on price."

Stewart saw the writing on the wall: Caljan had launched a pricing war against Stewart Glapat. A small family business with limited financial resources, Stewart Glapat would have to fight an international corporation whose financial resources could be vast. Stewart had to devise a strategy fast or his family business could be ruined on his watch. ■

Case 17   Jiffy Lube International, Inc. (Abridged)

In November 1988, Jiffy Lube's chief executive officer (CEO), Jim Hindman, was pondering the future of his company from his offices at the company's Baltimore, Maryland, world headquarters. Less than 10 years ago, he had purchased this tiny franchise chain of retail fast-oil-change centers and turned it into the internationally recognized industry leader. In fact, the industry had literally grown simultaneously with his company. Jiffy Lube International (JLI) now boasted about 1,000 mostly franchised centers and reported more than $250 million in systemwide revenues (including those of its franchisees) during the fiscal year ended March 31, 1988.

Despite its phenomenal growth and the fact that JLI now had about three times as many centers as its closest competitor, the company was under considerable pressure from the financial community and the press. The price of JLI's common stock was at its lowest point ever, and the business press had been increasingly negative in its assessment of JLI's financial condition. Moreover, a Washington-area TV station (located next door to JLI's headquarters) had recently broadcast a damaging news segment that suggested that consumers were taking considerable risks by having their cars serviced at local Jiffy Lube centers, and a Philadelphia TV station was planning a five-part segment there soon.

During the last several months, Hindman and his senior management team had formulated a new strategy to take Jiffy Lube through its next phase of development. The emphasis was to shift from growth to consolidation. Because the elements of this new strategy had not yet been widely communicated outside the company, Hindman thought now would be a useful time to consider where the company was going, in light of where it had been.

THE JIFFY LUBE SERVICE CONCEPT

Jiffy Lube emphasized preventive automotive maintenance rather than repair. At its drive-up centers, it offered a complete fluid-maintenance service for all types of automobiles, vans, and light-duty trucks. Customers needed no appointment, and most centers were open between 8 A.M. and 7 P.M., Monday through Saturday. The standard 14-point service was advertised to take only 10 minutes. For an all-inclusive price averaging about $22, the "J-Team" would:

- change the oil (with a well-known brand, usually Pennzoil)
- replace the oil filter
- lubricate the chassis
- check and top off all other fluids:
  transmission fluid
  brake fluid
  power-steering fluid
  differential fluid
  windshield washer fluid
  battery fluid
- inflate the tires to proper pressure

UVA-BP-0417

This case was abridged by Professor L. J. Bourgeois. The original case was prepared by Kathryn Breen (MBA 1989), under the supervision of John L. Colley, Jr., Almand R. Coleman Professor of Business Administration, and L. J. Bourgeois, III, Associate Professor of Business Administration. Copyright © 2000 by the University of Virginia Darden School Foundation, Charlottesville, VA. All rights reserved.

- examine the air filter (for excessive dirt)
- vacuum the interior of the vehicle
- examine the windshield wiper blades
- clean the windows (or wash the car, where available)

For an extra charge, Jiffy Lube provided ancillary services and products, including flushing and filling the radiator; gearbox service; recharging air-conditioner Freon; changing automatic transmission fluid and filter; and installing new air filters, breather elements, windshield wiper blades, and radiator coolant. These add-on services increased the average ticket by about $6.

The typical Jiffy Lube center looked distinctly different from a gas station. It was clean (with no grease spots or dirty tools lying about) and efficiently designed, and it had a comfortable waiting room for customers. Exhibit 17-1 shows the layout of a Jiffy Lube center with two service bays, each capable of accommodating two cars simultaneously (some centers had three bays and/or a car-wash facility). Cars were driven into one of the bays, entering from the back and exiting to the front. This drive-through design significantly increased the center's capacity as compared with a traditional service station's drive-in/back-out design. Also, JLI centers had a bi-level layout: The floor had an open pit through to the basement over which the car was positioned for servicing. This setup allowed one "lube tech" working below the car to drain the oil and check the chassis and transmission lubrication while two others worked simultaneously at floor level replacing the oil filter, adding new oil (from pull-down hoses), vacuuming the interior, and so on.

While the car was being serviced, customers could relax in the waiting room with free coffee and an assortment of magazines or watch the lube techs work through the

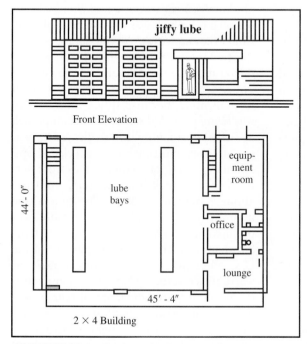

EXHIBIT 17-1   Design of a Typical Jiffy Lube Center
Source: JLI drawing.

window. When servicing was complete, the lead technician gave the customer a personal explanation of the exact services performed, at which time the technician could point out any problems and offer ancillary services that could be done on the spot. To encourage repeat business, Jiffy Lube either left a card in the car (noting the mileage at which the next service should be done) and/or mailed a reminder to the customer's home at the appropriate time.

Jiffy Lube's service objectives were modeled after those used by McDonald's: quality, service, cleanliness, and value. To those four, Hindman added another for JLI: convenience. As he often said, "We're selling convenience, not oil." JLI attempted to provide consistent quality across its nationwide system, but visits by this case writer to two centers suggested that service quality varied considerably and that the standard service sometimes took longer than 10 minutes.

THE QUICK-LUBE INDUSTRY

The quick-lube (also known as fast-oil-change) industry was one segment of the automotive aftermarket, which included muffler shops (e.g., Midas), transmission specialists (e.g., Aamco), tire/brake centers (e.g., Goodyear), and so on. Like them, quick-lube centers specialized in one service to focus their message to consumers and achieve operational efficiencies.

The growth of automotive specialty repair/maintenance firms had resulted largely from a steep decline in the number of full-service gas stations over the last 15 years. The oil price shocks of the 1970s drove many gas stations out of business, and most of the remainder dropped repair services to become gas-only outlets. According to information obtained by JLI, there were 226,000 service stations in the United States in 1972, 90 percent of them full-service outlets. By 1986, there were about 110,000 ser-

vice stations, less than 30 percent of them full service.

Despite the decline in the number of service stations, there were more automobiles on the road than ever before, and people were keeping them longer. The number of autos and light-duty trucks grew from 102 million in 1972 to 160 million by 1986, and their average age increased from 5.7 to 7.2 years. The increase in two-income families had also led people to spend money to save time and hassle in getting their cars serviced.

Car owners had several options for obtaining regular fluid-maintenance service. Auto dealers and independent repair shops were available but required that the car be left for a day while this minor work was squeezed in between larger jobs. A local full-service gas station normally charged a lower price than Jiffy Lube for a basic oil change (averaging $12 to $15), but the service required an appointment and took longer (about 45 minutes), because the car had to be raised and lowered twice on the lift. Finally, a car owner could change his or her own oil, which was messy and took time from other activities.

In late 1988, the United States contained more than 3,500 quick-lube centers. The exact number of operators was difficult to determine, because quick-lube service was being provided not only in centers such as JLI's, but sometimes in dedicated bays at gas stations and other auto service shops. About 5 percent of all oil changes were performed by quick-lube centers, up from about 2 percent in 1982. The quick-lube industry was expected to grow rapidly over the next several years, with potential market share as high as 35 to 40 percent of the U.S. oil-change market. Longer new-car warranties offered by U.S. auto manufacturers, which required evidence of regular service, might also contribute to growth. Moreover, there was thought to be a large, unfilled market of consumers who did not change their oil as often as they should.

JIM HINDMAN

Hindman was the prime motivator in the JLI organization. Jiffy Lube's culture had been shaped by his personal code of ethics, which he communicated often and consistently. In "Ain't It Great!" a bound collection of his personal philosophy as delivered in letters to franchisees and in speeches to training classes, he said, "With the wrong attitude you can do everything right and fail, but with the right attitude you can do everything wrong and still succeed." For Hindman, the right attitude was "We're here to help . . . do what's right and reasonable, even when no one is looking . . . fairness to the customer . . . and always work harder than the next guy."

Hindman's background illustrates his self-reliance and drive to achieve. He described himself in a Jiffy Lube public relations release as having been "a strong-willed kid and a street fighter. You'd have to kill me to whip me." He spent part of his childhood in a boys' home, caring for himself and two younger brothers. He put himself through college and graduate school, spent 9 years as a hospital administrator, later formed a partnership that built and operated 32 nursing homes, and bought several other businesses. By 1970, at age 35, he was a millionaire.

As he became successful in business, Hindman began to devote time to his college sport, football. In 1977, he became head football coach at Western Maryland College, working without salary and helping to finance the team by buying equipment and funding scholarships. During his 4 years as head coach, Hindman turned a losing team into a winning one with an overall record of 21-7-8. He said in a JLI publication:

I believe firmly in the importance of the old-fashioned American work ethic and the team spirit. This was the philosophy that helped our football team achieve success, and the disciplines that it takes to be a success in football are the same ones it takes to be successful in business.

THE BIRTH OF JLI

When a Western Maryland College student complained about the lack of opportunities for young people to make a million dollars today, Hindman was so incensed that he bet the student that he (Hindman) could do it again. He later explained that JLI "was born as a personal challenge to the negativism that runs rampant through much of our society. And the growth, success, and health of the chain proves that opportunity is alive and well today."

In mid 1979, Hindman's partnership purchased the trademark, logo, and franchise agreements of a nine-outlet fast-oil-change company in Salt Lake City named Jiffy Lube. He renamed it Jiffy Lube International, Inc., envisioning that JLI would expand to national and even international prominence.

Initially, Hindman both developed company-owned centers and sold franchises, many to his friends and associates. In 1982, however, he decided JLI didn't have the resources to be in both types of business, because a large network of company centers required a large corporate staff to manage it. That year, JLI sold all of its stores to franchisees and focused on selling individual new franchises. When Hindman purchased JLI in 1979, his major objective was to reach 100 centers, considered a critical "level of respectability" for a franchisor. It took Jiffy Lube 5 years to reach that goal.

GROWTH STRATEGIES

After reaching 100 stores in fiscal 1984, Hindman set a new goal of 1,000 centers by the end of (March 31) fiscal 1989. His strategy was to preempt significant competition before it could get started, and to achieve a wide enough scale to support a national advertising effort. (National advertising was considered critical to maximizing daily car counts and establishing Jiffy Lube as the industry leader.) So, the 1,000-store goal became JLI's overriding strategic objective, and it affected almost every action the company took through the end of fiscal 1988.

To accelerate growth, in 1984, JLI began selling area-development rights, which granted an investor the exclusive right to develop and operate Jiffy Lube centers within a particular Area of Dominant Influence (ADI), an advertising term of the Arbitron Rating Service that referred to population centers. The area developer paid a negotiated, nonrefundable fee up front that varied by the potential number of centers to be built, the demographics of the area, and the difficulty of development there. The area developer's continuing right to exclusivity depended on opening a specified number of centers within each year of its 5-year contract; in practice, JLI usually granted extensions. The rights to virtually all of the top 30 ADIs had been sold by the end of fiscal 1987.

The area-development program spurred fast growth in the number of franchised Jiffy Lube centers, and area-development fees became an important source of revenue for JLI. However, JLI discovered that area developers were investors rather than operators, who relished "doing deals" over managing their stores and ensuring proper customer service. Hindman believed that this characteristic was a prime reason for the lack of franchisee profitability in some areas, and this problem was to be explicitly addressed in his new strategy.

JLI had also grown by acquiring smaller chains and converting independents to the Jiffy Lube system. In its acquisitions, price had been less a concern than store location and competitive position, because Hindman believed that quick-lube shops would only become more valuable as the industry grew. Most stores JLI acquired were later sold to franchisees, and some acquisitions were made directly by franchisees but financed by JLI. The company also added centers by convincing independent quick-lube operators to become JLI franchisees. Jiffy Lube converted 26 such independents during fiscal 1986, 75 in fiscal 1987, and 83 in fiscal 1988. To encourage these conversions, JLI had sometimes waived initial franchise fees, offered reduced royalty rates for a year or two, and/or provided funds to enable the physical conversion of the centers. JLI rarely built new company-owned centers.

Jiffy Lube's strategy for organizing this growth was to concentrate its centers in the largest (metropolitan) ADIs in order to reach national advertising scale quickly. Furthermore, JLI built "clusters" of centers within each ADI, rather than individual stores in outlying areas, to enhance consumer awareness of both the quick-lube concept and of Jiffy Lube. JLI wanted its name to be the first thing that came to mind when consumers thought about getting an oil change. Clustering was also thought to preempt local competition, and it clearly offered economies of scale in local advertising, distribution of product to the centers, and store management. The distribution of Jiffy Lube centers across the country in June 1988 appears in Exhibit 17-2.

During this high-growth period from 1984 through early 1988, JLI had pursued several goals simultaneously: expanding to 1,000 centers as quickly as possible, increasing daily car counts across the system, and improving the quality of Jiffy Lube service to the consumer. As the summary operating data in Exhibit 17-3 show, the results were impressive. By November 1988, JLI had more than 1,000 stores, systemwide revenues increased from $28 million in 1984 to $252 million in 1988, and the average daily car count rose from 35.9 in fiscal 1984 to 43.1 in fiscal 1988. The break-even car

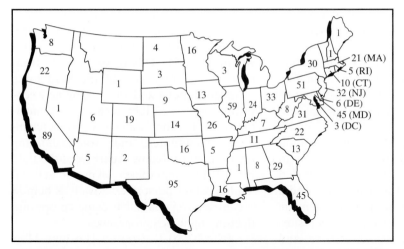

EXHIBIT 17-2 Distribution by State of Centers Open at June 30, 1988
Source: JLI map.

	Fiscal Year Ended March 31				
	1988	*1987*	*1986*	*1985*	*1984*
# Centers Open					
Co.-Owned	71	29	14	21	1
Franchised	737	532	334	187	119
International	15	—	—	—	—
Total	823	561	348	208	120
# States with					
JL Centers	44	39	33	28	23
System Sales	$252,082	$151,590	$91,201	$48,750	$27,762
Avg. Ticket Price/					
Vehicle Served	$27.63	$27.78	$27.01	$26.24	$24.86
Avg. # Vehicles/Day	43.1	42.2	41.8	44.0	35.9
Eff. Royalty Rate	5.2%	5.3%	4.6%	4.6%	4.8%

JLI Corp. Employees			
	4/30/88	*4/30/87*	*4/30/86*
Senior management	16	15	14
Management and professional	77	69	24
Field operations	55	40	25
Clerical	128	81	51
Co.-owned centers	855	351	146
Total	1,131	556	260

Source: JLI stock offering prospecti (1986 and 1987) and 3/31/88 *10-K* report to the SEC.

EXHIBIT 17-3 Summary Operating Data for Fiscal Years 1984–1988

count (systemwide) was about 35 cars per day, but some centers regularly serviced more than 100 a day.

From the beginning, Hindman had dreamed of expanding overseas, which he did in 1988. By March 31, JLI had opened nine stores in Canada, five in Europe, and one in Australia and had another 33 under development abroad. JLI's international strategy was to find local companies to assume a Master License, which entitled them to receive initial franchise fees and a share of the royalties of operating centers. In effect, the Master Licensor was a subfranchisor, investing its own time and money to develop the area. JLI provided support in training, standards, and operating methods and received lower royalties than in the United States because of its reduced role. Elf France, a division of Elf Aquitaine (France's largest oil company), had obtained a direct license for most of Western Europe, and JLI had established an office in Paris to manage its international expansion effort.

MANAGING GROWTH

The Role of JLI Corporate Headquarters

As a franchisor, JLI's most significant responsibilities were assisting its franchisees in developing and operating their centers, maintaining systemwide operating standards, and managing the national marketing effort.

Jiffy Lube provided *development assistance* by helping franchisees select sites, manage construction of the centers, and locate financing. All sites had to be approved by JLI, which generally used the criteria listed in Exhibit 17-4. The company also supplied franchisees with standard center designs and operating procedures, and it trained new franchisees and store managers.

To provide *operating assistance,* JLI maintained a field force of district managers

(DMs). There were 20 DMs in the field to service 753 franchised centers in fiscal 1988; by the end of fiscal 1989, JLI projected it would have 34 DMs to service 970 franchisees. The functions of the field force included training and supervising new center managers and lube techs, communicating JLI's operating standards and merchandising techniques, and troubleshooting operational problems. Apart from the field force, JLI headquarters staff provided training for center personnel, as well as help in organizing regional advertising co-ops and fleet-maintenance programs.

In 1983, JLI acquired Heritage Merchandising to achieve economies of scale through centralized purchasing of non-oil products. As a wholly owned subsidiary, Heritage supplied both franchisees and company-owned centers with 90 percent of their oil filters and air filters, as well as other operating supplies and equipment. From its national network of eight public warehouses, Heritage could reach almost all centers within 48 hours. Heritage also distributed various products to outside customers.

If a franchisee had financial or operational problems, JLI might elect to assist in several ways: arranging additional financing, facilitating a transfer of the license agreement to a new franchisee, extending payment terms on accounts and notes due to JLI, or as a last resort, repurchasing the franchise rights. In such circumstances, JLI had repurchased franchise rights to 16 centers in fiscal 1987 and 41 centers in fiscal 1988. Historically, JLI had been quite successful in buying back financially distressed centers, turning them around, remarketing them to new franchisees, and recovering at least its acquisition cost.

Maintaining standards. The relationship between JLI and its franchisees was like a partnership, because the company did not enjoy direct authority over franchises. Under its franchise agreements, JLI could, however,

The following preferred site parameters are used in the selection of freestanding sites and shopping center pad locations.

Location
- corner: most desirable
- inside: preferably with left-hand turn
- near shopping center and major food stores
- near other successful services and fast-food restaurants
- good visibility from both directions

Property Size
- range: 10,000 to 15,000 square feet
- a smaller size may be acceptable, depending on other characteristics of the site
- with common ingress and egress, as little as 4,000 square feet can be utilized

Standard Building Size

building	size	square feet
2 × 4	46 × 48	2,208
1 × 3	34 × 61	2,074
3 × 6	46 × 61	2,806

Zoning
- local zoning that will allow a fast-lube center or that can be rezoned

Traffic
- 20,000+ cars per day
- two-way, undivided traffic
- traffic speed of 35 mph or less

Area
- population of 60,000 within a 3-mile ring
- median income of $21,000

Terms
- lease
- purchase
- build-to-suit

Price
- the prevailing price per square foot or front foot in the market area

Source: JLI pamphlet for prospective landlords.

EXHIBIT 17-4   Preferred Site Parameters for Center Locations

inspect franchise centers at any time to ensure that employees were using approved products and following Jiffy Lube procedures. The company used both field personnel and "mystery shoppers" (who posed as customers and reported back to headquarters) to monitor franchise operations. If a franchisee failed to operate a center according to JLI's standards, the company had the right to revoke the franchise rights and obtain control of the center. This step had been taken for the first time only recently; in its quest for growth, JLI had not always enforced strict adherence to its operating policies.

In mid 1986, JLI made a substantial effort to encourage improved service quality throughout the system. To focus its efforts, the company introduced the "Zero Defects Program" around which to rally franchisees and store managers as they worked toward the stated goal of 100 percent defect-free performance for every customer. To convey this new attitude to customers, a plaque containing the Jiffy Lube Pledge of Quality was displayed prominently in every store; it encouraged customers to contact JLI headquarters directly if dissatisfied with their service. JLI also developed a computerized tracking system to follow and analyze defects when they did occur.

To help support this renewed focus on quality, JLI significantly expanded its training programs. Previously, the company had offered only a 2-week program for franchisees and store managers at headquarters; at this time, it introduced standard training consisting of vidoetapes and workbooks to "certify" lube techs at the individual center sites.

JLI also expanded its field force, recruiting people who were particularly suited to lead franchisees in the quality-improvement effort. The field force, which in fiscal 1987 consisted of only nine DMs covering 545 franchised centers, was given responsibility for performing the newly introduced operational audits; under this system, DMs formally measured centers on 150 attributes of service. Finally, JLI established a Customer Service Department to follow up on every complaint received at headquarters. During 1988, the number of complaints averaged about 100 a month; the most common was that the customer didn't get the full 14 points of service.

Marketing. Jiffy Lube was the only quick-lube chain with a national advertising effort. Each center contributed 3 percent of gross revenues to a National Ad Fund, which was used to produce commercials, buy media time, and create signs and other materials for systemwide promotions. The fund's expenditures had grown dramatically, from $510,000 in fiscal 1985 to $8.1 million in fiscal 1988. The fund's emphasis

had been on TV commercials featuring well-known TV personalities (Dick Van Patten and family, Sally Struthers, Sherman Helmsley) using the theme: "We treat you like family." Over and above its contribution to the National Ad Fund, each franchisee was required to spend 5 percent of gross sales on local and regional advertising, often through co-ops arranged by JLI.

FINANCING GROWTH

Development of Centers

In 1988, developing a new Jiffy Lube center from the ground up cost about $500,000, as shown in Exhibit 17-5. Franchisees had always been responsible for financing the development of their own stores, but to spur growth of the system, JLI assisted wherever possible. Sometimes the company helped franchisees negotiate "build-to-suit" leases, especially in the early years. It also helped franchisees find construction loans (sometimes providing them itself) and helped arrange permanent financing of real estate and construction expenditures from mortgage lenders with which it had developed relationships. With respect to real estate, JLI had come to prefer owning or leasing center sites and buildings itself and subleasing them to franchisees, which was thought to provide better control over the use of these properties. It also allowed JLI to profit on the spread between its mortgage/lease cost and rental revenue. A significant proportion of franchise sites were now subleased from the company, as shown in Exhibit 17-6. Another way JLI helped its franchisees develop centers was by providing acquisition financing for the purchase of competing stores in their territories. Finally, JLI had often provided loan and lease guarantees of franchisee debt to third parties.

JLI Corporate Financing History

JLI's need for capital was driven by its decision to help finance the growth in centers,

	Estimated Range	
	Low	*High*
Type of Expenditure		
Purchase real estate	$100,000	$350,000
Site improvements/ construction	225,000	250,000
Start-up operating costs:		
License fee	15,000	35,000
Equipment/fixtures	38,000	78,000[a]
Initial inventory	17,500	17,500
Working capital/prepaid expense	35,900	43,400
First month's rent	4,000	5,000
Total start-up cost	110,400	178,900
Total to Develop Center		
	$435,400	$778,900

[a]Includes $40,000 for car-wash facility.

Source: JLI 3/31/88 *10-K* report to the SEC.

EXHIBIT 17-5   Costs to Develop a New Center in 1988

which it considered vital. During the early years, JLI had literally lived from hand to mouth, stretching payments and patching together loans from unlikely sources. In 1981, Pennzoil had provided a crucial $1 million when it bought preferred stock with warrants (which Hindman later repurchased) for 30 percent of JLI. In 1985, its major source of mortgage loans (Old Court Savings & Loan) was closed by federal regulators, which precipitated a crisis in funding completion of several centers then under construction. Until as late as 1986, Hindman himself often lent the company large sums of money, and he sometimes waived his salary.

In December 1985, JLI privately placed a $10.5 million loan (with warrants) with Bridge Capital Investors, a well-known New York investment company. This mezzanine financing introduced Jiffy Lube to Wall Street and lent the company an aura of legitimacy to help prepare it for going public. Seven months later, in July 1986, JLI had its initial public offering of common stock on the NASDAQ, which netted the company $28 million and introduced both the quick-lube concept and Jiffy Lube to the investing public. The offering price was $15 per share, but investor interest pushed the price to $21 later that day; it later settled in at about $17.[1] In March 1987, the stock price peaked at $49, when it was split 2-for-1. During the next quarter, the stock hit an all-time high of $25 1/4 (adjusted for the split), but it had dropped by the time JLI completed its second offering in June 1987. At an offering price of about $15 per share (adjusted), the company raised $34 million. Since that offering, the stock had declined steadily, and it currently traded around $6 to $7 per share.

JLI Operating Performance

As shown in the financial statements in Exhibit 17-7, JLI's corporate revenues were

[1]"Striking It Rich," *Warfield's Magazine* (Baltimore), October 1986.

FYE 3/31/86

	Operated by:		
	Company	Franchisee	Total
Sites			
Owned by company	3	33	36
Leased by company[a]	11	54	65
Owned/leased by franchisees	0	247	247
	14	334	348

FYE 3/31/87

	Operated by:		
	Company	Franchisee	Total
Sites			
Owned by company	8	49	57
Leased by company[a]	21	113	134
Owned/leased by franchisees	0	370	370
	29	532	561

FYE 3/31/88

	Operated by:		
	Company	Franchisee	Total
Sites			
Owned by company	14	84	98
Leased by company[a]	57	220	277
Owned/leased by franchisees	0	448	448
	71	752	823

[a]Includes sites where company owns buildings and improvements.

Source: JLI stock offering prospecti (1986 and 1987) and 3/31/88 *10-K* report to the SEC.

EXHIBIT 17-6   Ownership of Center Locations During Fiscal Years 1986–1988

derived from four general areas. Revenues from *operations* represented sales of the company-owned centers. *Franchising* revenues included area-development and Master License fees, initial franchise fees, and royalties. Initial franchise fees were earned when a new center was opened and varied according to each franchise agreement. JLI's average initial franchise fee had been rising; it was $20,900 during the 2-year period including fiscal 1987 and 1988, up from $17,300 during fiscal 1985–1986. Royalties, earned monthly, were usually 5 percent of each franchise's gross revenues during a store's first year of operation and 6 percent thereafter. Revenues from *distribution* represented sales of supplies and equipment by Heritage Merchandising to franchisees and outside customers. *Real estate* revenue was rental income JLI earned by subleasing properties to franchisees. Over the years, JLI had recorded significant income from *other sources,* including gains on the sale of real estate and company-owned centers and interest on short-term investments and notes receivable from franchisees.

During the past several years, nonrecurring revenues (such as area-development fees, initial franchise fees, and gains on the sale of real property) had contributed a significant portion to total revenues. However, these revenues were expected to decline in relative importance as growth

Income Statement	6 mos. 9/30/88	1988	1987	1986
Revenues				
Sales-company stores	12,556	18,974	8,079	7,825
Initial franchise fees	1,631	4,706	3,327	2,490
Area development fees	46	5,719	4,481	2,150
Franchise royalties	8,518	12,133	7,551	3,847
Heritage merchandising	14,657	21,490	13,505	8,792
Rental income	10,216	14,048	6,495	4,288
Other operating revenue	639	1,132	732	59
Total Revenue	48,263	78,202	44,170	29,451
Expenses				
Company stores	15,168	18,739	7,331	6,548
CGS-products	11,727	16,993	11,217	7,492
Rental props.	7,534	10,397	5,259	4,065
S, G & A	13,574	21,447	13,029	9,281
Prov. bad debt	1,260	1,391	681	271
Total Expenses	49,263	68,967	37,517	27,657
Operating Income	(1,000)	9,235	6,653	1,794
Other Inc./(Exp.)				
Other income	2,741	4,947	1,940	824
	(2,604)	(2,138)	(1,362)	(1,197)
Minor int. in loss	0	(132)	(213)	41
Total Other	137	2,677	365	(332)
Income Before Tax	(863)	11,912	7,018	1,462
Income Tax Expense	(448)	5,003	3,333	720
Inc. Bef. Extr. Items	(415)	6,909	3,685	742
Extraordinary Items				
NOL carryfwds.				470
Debt extinguish			(219)	
Total After-tax	0	0	(219)	470
Net Income	(415)	6,909	3,466	1,212

Balance Sheet	Interim 9/30/88	1988	1987	1986
Assets:				
Cash & S-T invest	2,146	3,497	1,277	2,474
Accts & fees rec.	23,919	19,753	7,584	6,771
Notes receivable	13,318	11,844	4,682	1,811
less allowance	(2,551)	(2,054)	(935)	(299)
Net receivables	34,686	29,543	11,331	8,283
Inventory	4,973	4,932	1,217	752
RE held for resale	0	0	0	2,719
Other CA	3,339	1,742	1,130	258
Total current assets	45,144	39,714	14,955	14,486
Accts & fees rec.	1,135	1,185	933	783

(continued)

EXHIBIT 17-7 Financial Statements for Fiscal 1986–1988 and Interim 9/30/88

Stores held-resale	11,376	4,644	2,663	0
Notes receivable	25,715	22,668	9,616	3,181
Inv/adv-affiliates	3,875	2,138	2,217	237
FA leased to franchisees				
Constr. advances	5,460	15,860	8,592	0
Land	22,066	16,654	8,966	3,613
Bldgs. & equ.—gross	17,338	9,840	9,807	9,299
Financing leases	77,136	61,624	26,658	7,694
Constr.-in-progress	13,171	14,617	4,298	0
Gross	136,171	118,595	58,321	20,606
Less accum. deprec.	N/A	(1,222)	(938)	(885)
Net	136,171	117,373	57,383	19,721
Net prop. & equip.	21,246	15,329	1,885	4,271
Intang. assets (net)	13,032	14,783	9,104	6,227
Other assets	7,281	7,929	3,687	1,787
Total Assets	264,975	225,763	102,443	50,693

	Interim			
	9/30/88	**1988**	**1987**	**1986**
Liabilities:				
Accts. pay/acruals	11,755	10,045	6,926	3,905
Income tax pay.	0	125	2,241	0
Notes payable	0	0	1,981	2,403
Constr. adv.—				
RE held for resale	0	0	0	2,331
CMLTD	10,589	17,561	1,047	1,355
Total current liabs.	22,344	27,731	12,195	9,994
Long-term debt	91,927	74,911	21,797	9,971
Sub. debentures	19,309	4,299	4,887	9,736
Cap. leases	48,456	36,130	18,969	9,586
Def. tax/Other liabs	1,126	1,805	1,054	504
Def. franch. fees	1,306	1,500	872	4,131
Total L-T liabs.	162,124	118,645	47,579	33,928
Total Liabilities	184,468	146,376	59,774	43,922
Minority interest	0	0	3,173	10
Common stock	381	380	294	180
PIC	77,513	75,979	39,479	10,222
Retained earnings	6,217	6,632	(277)	(3,467)
Less due for CS	0	0	0	(175)
Less treas. stock	(3,604)	(3,604)	0	0
Total Equity	80,507	79,387	39,496	6,760
Total Liabs. + Equity	264,975	225,763	102,443	50,692

Source: JLI *Annual Reports* and 9/30/88 *10-Q* report to the SEC.

EXHIBIT 17-7 (continued)

slowed. Rental income would become more significant, because JLI had bought many properties during the past 2 to 3 years; lease rates on new centers were typically low in the early years and rose as the centers matured. Also, area-development revenues had been dramatically reduced by a recent order of the Securities and Exchange Commission requiring JLI (and all franchisors) to recognize area-development fees over the term of a contract rather than in current income, as previously done.

The largest drain on JLI earnings was from company-owned centers held for resale. Exhibit 17-8 shows data on the growth and operations of company-owned centers over the last few years. JLI intended to keep some stores in order to remain knowledgeable about center operations and to test new methods. Over the last 2 years, however, it had purchased a substantial number of distressed centers to turn around and remarket. At the end of fiscal 1988, JLI classified 34 of its 71 centers as held for resale. During fiscal 1988, operating losses on such centers totaled $950,000.

During the second quarter of fiscal 1989, losses from centers held for resale caused Jiffy Lube to post its first quarterly net loss since going public. For the 6 months, JLI reported a loss of $415,000 on revenues of $48.3 million. During the same period a year earlier, revenues had been 39 percent lower, but net income was $3.3 million. Systemwide sales for the first 6 months of fiscal 1989 were $172.8 million, up 50 percent over the previous year. During those months, JLI had acquired 70 centers intended for resale.

| | *Interim* | | | |
	9/30/88	*3/31/88*	*3/31/87*	*3/31/86*
# Co.-Owned Centers at End of Period:				
To keep	25	37	8	14
Held for resale	81[a]	34	21	0[b]
Changes in # Centers During the Period:	—	—	—	—
Acquisitions	34	88	61	1
Centers built by co.	21	9	0	0
# Centers sold/leased	(20)	(55)	(45)	(8)
# Centers closed	0	0	(1)	0
Net change in centers	35	42	15	(7)
Centers Held for Resale ($000):				
Assets (year end)	$11,376	$4,644	$2,663	N/A
Results of Opns.				
Sales	$6,783	$6,664	$2,951	N/A
Operating Exp.	$9,650	$7,614	$3,282	N/A
Operating Loss	$(2,687)	$(950)	$(331)	N/A
Gain—Sale of Centers	(7)	$1,242	$1,000	$317

[a]Twenty-eight of these centers were located in Houston, Texas.
[b]Before FY 87, JLI did not classify centers as held for resale.

Source: JLI stock offering prospecti (1986 and 1987), 3/31/88 *10-K,* and 9/30/88 *10-Q* reports to the SEC.

EXHIBIT 17-8   Data on Company-Owned Centers

JLI FINANCIAL CONDITION

JLI's assets consisted primarily of accounts and notes receivable from franchisees, and real property (most of which was leased/subleased to franchisees). Accounts receivable encompassed all amounts currently due from franchisees, including initial franchise fees on a quarterly payment plan, royalties, rents, and Heritage receivables. A small portion was area-development fees. Notes receivable represented amounts due from franchisees, of which 50 percent represented financing of franchisees' acquisitions and 30 percent working-capital financing for stores in the early stages of growth.

Fixed assets consisted mostly of land and buildings. Assets leased to franchisees in fiscal 1988 were about $117 million, of which $85 million represented land and buildings owned by JLI; the remainder was mostly leased property that was subleased to franchisees.

Jiffy Lube had assumed considerable debt in its acquisition of real estate and operating centers. At the end of fiscal 1988, total long-term debt and capital leases of $129 million balanced equity of $79 million.

THE PENNZOIL STRATEGIC ALLIANCE

In March 1988, JLI signed a 20-year Strategic Alliance Agreement with Pennzoil Products Company, which, with 21 percent of U.S. motor oil sales, was the leading motor oil company in the United States. The agreement continued the close reltionship the two companies had developed over the years. Pennzoil promised to discontinue financing new, independent quick-lube operators and to assist JLI in converting as many of its 750 qualifying independents as possible to the Jiffy Lube system. Pennzoil also committed to make equipment loans to all new franchisees approved by JLI. Moreover, Pennzoil agreed to contribute $0.20 for each gallon of motor oil purchased by the Jiffy Lube system to JLI's National Ad Fund; this contribution would equal about $4 million in fiscal 1989. Finally, Pennzoil agreed to pay JLI an "administrative fee" of $.05 per gallon sold through the JLI system.

For its part under the Strategic Alliance, JLI agreed to pay Pennzoil 25 percent of the royalties it would collect from Pennzoil independents who converted. (These independents would pay no initial franchise fee.) JLI also committed to designate Pennzoil as the Jiffy Lube system's "oil of choice," use its best efforts to persuade all JLI franchisees to use it (more than 80 percent of the system already did), and feature Pennzoil in its national ads. Finally, JLI promised to place the Pennzoil logo on its own private brand of oil filters and pay Pennzoil $0.04 per filter sold.

The conversion of Pennzoil independents was progressing slower than planned. JLI had hoped to convert 350 operators during fiscal 1989 but had converted only 100 by November 1988. The company changed the projection to about 100 a year for the next 2 to 3 years.

QUICK-LUBE COMPETITION

Jiffy Lube was the market leader in both sales and number of centers, as the list of major competitors in Exhibit 17-9 shows. Like Jiffy Lube, most of the large national chains were affiliated with one of the top motor oil marketers. Minit Lube, the second-largest chain (about 300 stores), was owned by Quaker State, which had about 17 percent motor oil market share. Minit Lube was the only major chain with a strategy of growing through company-owned stores instead of franchises. The third-largest chain was Instant Oil, at about 178 stores; it was owned by Ashland Oil, whose Valvoline motor oil had about 13 percent market share. Instant Oil had been attempting to grow through acquisition of smaller chains and construction of company-owned stores.

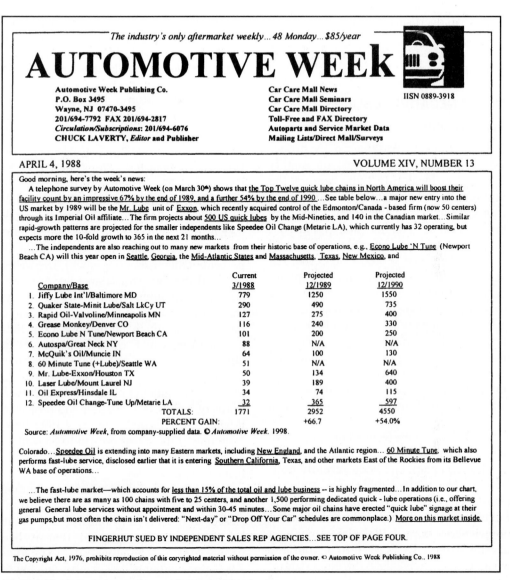

The industry's only aftermarket weekly... 48 Monday... $85/year

AUTOMOTIVE WEEk

Automotive Week Publishing Co.
P.O. Box 3495
Wayne, NJ 07470-3495
201/694-7792 FAX 201/694-2817
Circulation/Subscriptions: 201/694-6076
CHUCK LAVERTY, Editor and Publisher

Car Care Mall News
Car Care Mall Seminars
Car Care Mall Directory
Toll-Free and FAX Directory
Autoparts and Service Market Data
Mailing Lists/Direct Mall/Surveys

IISN 0889-3918

APRIL 4, 1988   VOLUME XIV, NUMBER 13

Good morning, here's the week's news:
  A telephone survey by Automotive Week (on March 30th) shows that the Top Twelve quick lube chains in North America will boost their facility count by an impressive 67% by the end of 1989, and a further 54% by the end of 1990...See table below...a major new entry into the US market by 1989 will be the Mr. Lube unit of Exxon, which recently acquired control of the Edmonton/Canada - based firm (now 50 centers) through its Imperial Oil affiliate... The firm projects about 500 US quick lubes by the Mid-Nineties, and 140 in the Canadian market... Similar rapid-growth patterns are projected for the smaller independents like Speedee Oil Change (Metarie LA), which currently has 32 operating, but expects more the 10-fold growth to 365 in the next 21 months...
  ...The independents are also reaching out to many new markets from their historic base of operations, e.g., Econo Lube 'N Tune (Newport Beach CA) will this year open in Seattle, Georgia, the Mid-Atlantic States and Massachusetts, Texas, New Mexico, and

Company/Base	Current 3/1988	Projected 12/1989	Projected 12/1990
1. Jiffy Lube Int'l/Baltimore MD	779	1250	1550
2. Quaker State-Minit Lube/Salt LkCy UT	290	490	735
3. Rapid Oil-Valvoline/Minneapolis MN	127	275	400
4. Grease Monkey/Denver CO	116	240	330
5. Econo Lube N Tune/Newport Beach CA	101	200	250
6. Autospa/Great Neck NY	88	N/A	N/A
7. McQuik's Oil/Muncie IN	64	100	130
8. 60 Minute Tune (+Lube)/Seattle WA	51	N/A	N/A
9. Mr. Lube-Exxon/Houston TX	50	134	640
10. Laser Lube/Mount Laurel NJ	39	189	400
11. Oil Express/Hinsdale IL	34	74	115
12. Speedee Oil Change-Tune Up/Metarie LA	32	365	597
TOTALS:	1771	2952	4550
PERCENT GAIN:		+66.7	+54.0%

Source: Automotive Week, from company-supplied data. © Automotive Week. 1998.

Colorado...Speedee Oil is extending into many Eastern markets, including New England, and the Atlantic region... 60 Minute Tune, which also performs fast-lube service, disclosed earlier that it is entering Southern California, Texas, and other markets East of the Rockies from its Bellevue WA base of operations...

  ...The fast-lube market—which accounts for less than 15% of the total oil and lube business – is highly fragmented...In addition to our chart, we believe there are as many as 100 chains with five to 25 centers, and another 1,500 performing dedicated quick - lube operations (i.e., offering general General lube services without appointment and within 30-45 minutes...Some major oil chains have erected "quick lube" signage at their gas pumps,but most often the chain isn't delivered: "Next-day" or "Drop Off Your Car" schedules are commonplace.) More on this market inside.

FINGERHUT SUED BY INDEPENDENT SALES REP AGENCIES...SEE TOP OF PAGE FOUR.

EXHIBIT 17-9   Information on Quick-Lube Industry
Source: Reprinted with permission of Automotive Week.

It recently announced an intention to concentrate on franchising, however, with a goal of 1,500 franchised centers by 1995.[2] The fourth-largest quick-lube chain, Grease Monkey, had about 120 stores and was independent of any oil company. Its stores were virtually all franchised and were located mostly in the western states in a shotgun pattern, often near Jiffy Lube centers.

  Smaller local and regional quick-lube chains abounded, some with fewer than ten stores. New independents seemed to be springing up all the time. These competitors often attempted to steal Jiffy Lube's cus-

[2]"Ashland's Valvoline Plans to Franchise Quick-Lube Outlets, Stepping Up Rivalry," Wall Street Journal, October 24, 1988.

tomers by advertising 15-, 16-, or up to 21-point services; claiming to take 9 minutes instead of Jiffy Lube's 10; and circulating discount coupons.

RECENT NEGATIVE PUBLICITY

Service Quality

In the then-recent Washington TV broadcast, a two-part news report on quality problems at local Jiffy Lube centers, the reporter elicited on-camera horror stories from consumers. In one, Jiffy Lube had drained a car's old oil but hadn't replaced it with new oil. Later, the engine seized and had to be replaced at a cost of $3,500. JLI responded to these allegations by explaining that out of the thousands of cars serviced daily, very few had such problems; furthermore, the company had promptly paid for those that did occur. The reporter conceded that area consumer protection agencies had received few complaints against Jiffy Lube, but pointed out that the centers hired unskilled labor, training them with a series of videotapes and workbooks. "After all," Jiffy Lube says, "lube technicians don't have to be mechanics."[3]

The company had been recently notified of the Philadelphia TV station's planned five-part news segment on Jiffy Lube on "The Consumer's Friend" portion of their show. In early 1987, the former area developer there had agreed to discontinue what the Pennsylvania Attorney General charged were deceitful sales practices.[4] Employees had been selling unnecessary transmission and differential fluid changes by showing customers a sample of their car's "dirty" fluid compared with one of new, "clean" fluid; in fact, automobile performance was not affected by the color of these fluids. Since then, JLI had instructed all its centers to stop showing such "comparisons" to customers and had repurchased this area from the developer.

Financial Condition

In August 1988, the *Wall Street Journal* titled its "Heard on the Street" column "Jiffy Lube Raises Some Eyebrows with Loans to Its Franchisees for Their Up-Front Expenses." The article reported that the stock, then trading at about 9½, had "plummeted nearly 50 percent from its 52-week high of 18¼," and that the outstanding short position was 2.4 million shares (about 16 percent of all outstanding stock). The writer asserted that investor concern over financial interdependence between JLI and its franchisees had caused the decline. He cited one case of a troubled franchisee, Lone Star Lubrication, which owned 67 centers in Texas and Oklahoma. Lone Star had lost $4.2 million during fiscal 1988 and owed a total of $9.5 million in long-term debt (two-thirds of it to JLI). Lone Star had projected it would turn profitable in fiscal 1990, however, only if there was growth to 85 centers and an increase in its average car counts from 27 to 49 per day.

JLI responded in the article by noting that most of its loans and leases to franchisees were secured by real estate in prime locations, and it explained that it had financed the franchisees in order to build its 1,000-store nationwide network quickly to win market share before competitors did.[5]

JIFFY LUBE'S NEW STRATEGY

The planned shift in strategic emphasis from growth to consolidation focused on improving the quality of service at Jiffy

---

[3]"Jiffy Lube Auto Shops Accused of Inefficient Services," *Eyewitness News,* WUSA Television, Washington, D.C., October 17–18, 1988 (from a transcript provided by Radio-TV Monitoring Service, Inc.).
[4]"Quick-Grease Artists: Fast-Lube Shops Slip into Area Market," *Washington Post,* April 27, 1987.
[5]*Wall Street Journal,* August 29, 1988.

Lube centers and increasing individual franchisee profitability. Financially, JLI would step back from direct financing of franchisees and attempt to facilitate third-party financing. JLI planned also to cut $3 million in sales, general, and administrative expenses to help offset current losses.

To increase franchisees' profitability, Hindman set a goal of 65 cars per day systemwide. The company had analyzed historical center data that showed that systemwide car counts increased with the age of a center. However, the Jiffy Lube system was still young: In May 1988, 72 percent of centers were less than 3 years old, 58 percent were less than 2 years old, and 32 percent were less than a year old. Exhibit 17-10 shows a graph of the trend in Jiffy Lube center car counts over the past 4 years. Exhibit 17-11 shows that, during fiscal 1988, every age cat-

egory experienced higher daily car counts than during fiscal 1987. JLI's growth was built on the premise that car counts would continue to increase over time.

Other Operational Plans

JLI planned to make a major effort to recertify all lube techs at Jiffy Lube centers. With the relatively high employee turnover typical of a mostly teenaged workforce, the company had found it difficult to maintain its earlier certification program. Jiffy Lube also intended to commission a time-and-motion study to reexamine car-servicing procedures (unchanged since the early days of the chain) and to test the 10-minute claim. JLI would continue to expand its field force and reduce the number of centers per DM in an effort to enforce its operating standards more diligently than in the past.

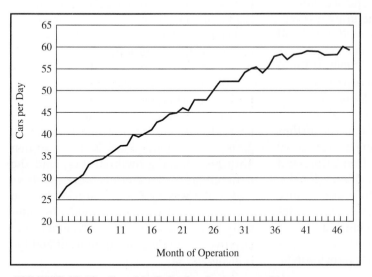

EXHIBIT 17-10   Trend in Daily Car Counts over Time

The strength of the Jiffy Lube center and the system is measured by a center's ability to grow its car count. On average, center car counts in their first 48 months of operation climb to approximately 60 cars a day, translating into a compounded annual growth rate of 23.4 percent. As the system matures and a greater number of centers are 48 months or older, the Jiffy Lube systems' average car count per day will rise.

Source: JLI internal analysis.

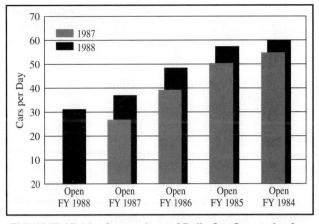

EXHIBIT 17-11 **Comparison of Daily Car Counts by Age Category Fiscal Year 1987 vs. 1988**

Financial Restructuring Program

JLI had recently announced a program to reduce its financial leverage. The first element involved replacing some short-term debt with long-term debt. The second element of the financial restructuring was selling assets. The company planned to sell and lease back its new $10 million headquarters building, purchased in April 1988. JLI also hoped to sell $15 to $20 million of other real estate (store sites to franchisees) and some of the $30 million of notes receivable.

Third, JLI planned to control further increases in debt by initiating an aggressive accounts-receivable collection effort and restricting financing of franchisees. Finally, the company would seek to become more effective at helping franchisees find independent sources of financing. JLI had recently hired a manager who had experience in this area with another franchisor.

QUESTIONS TO CONSIDER

Hindman wondered whether the new strategy had addressed the most important issues facing his company and whether the plan would satisfy the concerns of the financial community. How would he manage the franchisees differently now? What was the impact of the large number of company-owned centers?

Would the new plans help JLI maintain its market position? Hindman was convinced that the JLI service concept, if properly implemented, would work in all parts of the country. Thus, he believed that both his earlier growth strategy and the national advertising effort were justified. Jiffy Lube was by far the largest chain in the quick-lube industry. Could the company sustain competitive advantage and improve profitability for both itself and the franchisees? ■

# PART 4

INTERPERSONAL INFLUENCE

Case 18   Alvarez (A)

Pinto, the assistant plant manager, arrived earlier than usual on Monday morning. Last Friday, he, the plant manager, the personnel manager (Caesar), the maintenance engineer (Mike Stone), and the majority owner, Bellini, had met to decide what to do about the situation that Alvarez was creating in the plant. They discussed Alvarez's career, his past contributions to the company, and the plant's policies, but they did not reach a conclusion. In the end, they had decided that whatever had to be done, Pinto had to decide.

CANALVEN

Canalven was originally a subsidiary of Canadian Aluminum Company (CANAL), but nationalization plans in Venezuela had required all companies to have 51 percent of their capital Venezuelan. At that time, a wealthy family, the Bellini family, acquired the required 51 percent from CANAL, and the company became Canalven. Canalven produced standard and customized window rails and frames and a line of roofs. At the time of the case, Canalven was facing difficult foreign exchange rate differentials and stiffening international competition. The company was also expanding its foundry facilities to cope with the shortage of some raw materials and to increase production. Canalven was also adding a finished line of products to its historical semifinished aluminum products lines. The new finished products were either painted or anodized (a process that polishes the previously extruded aluminum ingots). To perform these operations, two new process lines had been added to the existing production lines. Part of the new machinery for the foundry had to be ordered from foreign companies to be built on site by Canalven personnel, but some of the minor machinery (such as a crushing machine for the silicon that was added to the aluminum alloy) was built and designed at Canalven.

Mike Stone supervised construction of all these new production lines and the assembly of the imported machines. Cerruti was in charge of the quality-control department and supervised all the finished products. She and Stone worked together closely in the design and improvement of many technical aspects of the factory. Because the Bellinis were cattle owners and did not have any experience in the aluminum business, the owners delegated all responsibility and plant-related decisions to the plant manager. He, in turn, delegated all responsibility for the new processes to Stone and Cerruti.

From the point of view of Stone and Cerruti, Canalven did not have enough engineers to implement all the new required processes for their new line of products. They had to assemble all the imported machinery based on blueprints, and they

UVA-OB-0660

This case was written by Ingrid Celis, MBA, International University of Japan, under the direction of Professor James G. Clawson while he was a visiting professor at IUJ. Copyright © 1998 by the University of Virginia Darden School Foundation, Charlottesville, VA. All rights reserved.

had to run tests on the equipment. They also had to supervise the new layout. All these activities were very technical and required engineers. Like Stone and Cerruti, Pinto also thought that engineers had to look after the business from now on if management wanted the plant to continue to be competitive. Times had changed, and well-prepared people had to be in the key positions.

One of Canalven's main labor policies was "promotion from within." Only when nobody from within could qualify for a job would the company hire someone from outside. Canalven also sent well-performing workers for training so that they could be promoted.

PLANT MANAGEMENT

The plant manager was an engineer, but his diploma was not valid in Venezuela. He had experience in several countries and knew the international business scenario of the aluminum industry well.

Pinto had become assistant manager 5 years previously. He had started working in Canalven 20 years ago and had spent his entire career there. Unlike the plant manager, he was not an engineer, but he had completed many specialization programs in the United States in aluminum processes. Pinto was respected by the workers because of his open attitude toward them. He believed he also had influence over the union. Six years ago, the previous plant manager had implemented some measures that created unrest with the workers, and a series of strikes had undermined Canalven's productivity. Pinto had controlled the problem without further strikes and implemented further measures that benefited the plant. The plant manager called him the "charismatic man."

Mr. Stone, the maintenance engineer and a Canadian, had been working at Canalven for a year. He was in charge of

maintenance and repair of the existing production lines, as well as development of new production lines. The previous maintenance engineer had returned to his country, and the plant manager had wanted for the job a young engineer with experience in the maintenance of industrial equipment, so Stone was chosen. Upon graduating in mechanical engineering, Stone had worked in a thermoelectric plant for 10 years. He decided to take the job at Canalven because it represented a promotion and because the working conditions in his previous job had required him to work different shifts, which he didn't like anymore.

PROBLEMS IN THE PLANT

When Stone arrived, he was placed in charge of 20 skilled workers—electricians, welders, and mechanics. Alvarez, the oldest of his subordinates and a Colombian, was a "career man" within Canalven. He was 55 years old, very energetic, and very proud of his job. He had worked at Canalven for 25 years and was 5 years away from retirement. His career was a vivid example of the "promotion-from-within" policy: He started as an unskilled worker and was trained and given additional experience. Only the assistant manager had been with Canalven a comparable length of time. Many workers disliked Alvarez for being a "full-time grumbler."

Stone and Alvarez had problems from the beginning. Alvarez would not accept Stone's authority, and he commented to other workers, "That young engineer, he thinks he knows everything. He doesn't know the machines; he hasn't been here for a month and is already changing things that had worked for years. Only God knows what will happen to this factory."

Apart from the usual maintenance work, Alvarez designed and built machines for Canalven. His machines were of good quality and accomplished the job, and although such equipment did not require high technology, it required talent and cleverness. He knew his job and did it well and proudly. He was so proud of it that he printed in bright yellow on every machine that he finished, for everybody to know: "Designed by Alvarez for Canalven."

The first time Cerruti visited the factory, this printing on the machines had caught her eye. Stone disliked the practice and wanted to dissuade Alvarez from doing it on the new machinery for the foundry. Because Alvarez would not accept that decision, Stone complained repeatedly to the assistant manager about it.

> It is just unacceptable! His machines are part of Canalven's assets, and I can't stand seeing his name all over the place in yellow. He even has a template with the inscription ready to use at any time! He demoralizes other workers and tells them that what I'm doing is wrong. They don't trust me. I think that Alvarez is just getting old and can't stand a new generation of people working in the plant.

Stone also commented, "The previous maintenance engineer let Alvarez have his way on the printing and didn't care about it. The two of them worked together for many years, and they had in common that they were foreigners. He also delegated to him too much authority over the workers."

THE FURNACE INCIDENT

One of the machines imported was a furnace the size of a big truck. It arrived in pieces and had to be assembled according to the blueprints the U.S. company sent (in English). It required lots of welders and mechanics. Stone supervised the construction of the foundations for the furnace, the rails for the cars that carried the aluminum ingots into and out of the furnace, and the subsequent assembling of the furnace. He had a hard time reading the blueprints because of their complexity and lack of clarity. During the process of assembling, he made some mistakes; the pieces had to be welded again, and the job was delayed.

Alvarez ignored the orders Stone gave him during the furnace assembly and placement. He believed that what Stone was doing was wrong. He did not like Stone to call for opinions from other engineers in the plant, because they were neither related nor experienced in the building of such machinery. He thought that they were interfering with his job. Stone also found out that the workers were following Alvarez's orders instead of his during the assembling of the furnace. Once one of the welders asked Alvarez if he wasn't afraid of being fired, and Alvarez said:

> Me? Fired? They would never do such a thing! I am part of the history of this plant. I've been here longer than Pinto. Mr. Bellini knows me. He knows I'm a hard worker. Look around! My name is on every piece of equipment here! I know these machines better than anyone. Fire me? They can't do without me!

THE FRIDAY MEETING

Stone had complained about the situation with Alvarez several times, but when he went to the assistant manager once again, Pinto called for a meeting with the plant manager, the personnel manager, and Alvarez to sort out the problem. At the meeting, Stone complained that Alvarez did not ask for his advice, that Alvarez countered his orders to the workers, and that Alvarez grumbled all the time, but most of all, Stone was irate about what he called "Alvarez's mania" for printing the yellow lettering on every piece of equipment he built. After Alvarez left, Stone commented to the other three, "What Alvarez wants is to be able to build the furnace himself so that he can print his lettering on it."

The assistant manager asked Alvarez's opinion about the situation. Alvarez said that he did not like the way things were being done at the factory since Stone arrived. He thought Stone should ask him for advice. He also reminded them of his long experience at Canalven. Before leaving he said:

> I know how to do my job better than anyone! I do not have to take orders that I know are wrong! Sooner or later, his [Stone's] mistakes will be evident, and the job will have to be done all over again. He made mistakes before! If he had asked me, he would be on schedule, ah . . . but he is the manager and we have to follow his orders!

At six o'clock, the quitting bell rang. Alvarez said that he had to go and left. The assistant manager reminded them of Alvarez's long career and how he was an example for the other employees. He noted that his work was of high quality and unquestioned. The assistant manager also commented that he did not like the "Made by Alvarez" letterings either and that this affected his feelings toward Alvarez. He said that Alvarez was not liked by many workers and that many complained of his grumbling.

Pinto asked the plant manager about the possibility of firing him, but the personnel manager reminded them that Alvarez was only 5 years away from retiring and if they fired him now, they would have to pay twice his social benefits at severance. (This was established by the labor law.) Pinto asked them to consider what the effect of his firing would be on the workers and the problems that would arise for Alvarez with the difficult economic times. With the current unemployment rate, it would be difficult for Alvarez to find another job.

The plant manager said that whatever had to be decided should be decided during the weekend and that the decision would be Pinto's. He said he would be home if Pinto needed him, and left. ■

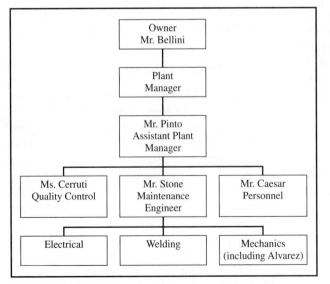

EXHIBIT 18-1   Abbreviated Canalven Organization Chart

Case 19   Great Expectations (A)

Mr. Y. Hiraki, construction section chief of International Urasa Consulting Engineers Company Limited of Japan (IUCEJ), was enjoying a drink in the small bar in Nibuwatar, the site of the Second Kulekhani Hydroelectric Project in the small Himalayan country of Nepal. He had left Tokyo 2 days earlier, had a hurried briefing session in the firm's Kathmandu office before leaving for the construction site, arrived less than a half an hour ago, and was overcome with jet lag.

Hiraki relaxed for a while and went through the list of his responsibilities. He was a bit confused and surprised to find out that in addition to his technical responsibilities, he was expected to mentor his subordinates—the Nepalese engineers, supervisors, and assistants, who were to be assigned to IUCEJ by the Project Office.[1] Hiraki was to supervise the construction work in English through the team of Nepalese engineers, supervisors, and assistants with one senior Japanese supervisor, Mr. S. Suzuki. He hoped that the Project Office would assign good, experienced engineers and supervisors to the project. He had seen Nepalese engineers working when he was involved with the first Kulekhani Project and had concluded that they were generally good.

Hiraki was excited to be given the responsibility of managing and teaching the Nepalese engineers. After all, he thought, he was to receive more than twice the number of engineers and a large pool of supervisors for this project, much more than IUCEJ's usual allocation of manpower for similar jobs.

Later, as he tried to relax in his quarters, Hiraki reviewed the situation and began to lay out his plan of action. Then, wearily, as he went to sleep, he thought, "What a fortunate man I am! God has been good to me! If I can manage the team well, and I know I will, I will have a lot of time to play tennis and relax in the sun."

BACKGROUND

Established in 1954, International Urasa Consulting Engineers Co. Ltd. of Japan was recognized by the World Bank as one of the world's leading engineering consulting firms. IUCEJ was active in many sectors including hydroelectric plants, agricultural developments, and power transmission cable work. Known for its steady management policy, IUCEJ had head offices in Tokyo, Japan, and overseas offices in Manila (Philippines), Jakarta (Indonesia), Nairobi (East Africa-Kenya), and Kathmandu (Nepal). Their main projects were consulting in domestic urban development projects and international infrastructure projects like the construction of hydroelectric plants, irrigation canals, and roads.

UVA-OB-0739

This case was written by Mohan Das Manandhar, MBA International University of Japan, under the direction of Professor James G. Clawson while he was a visiting professor at IUJ. Copyright © 1992 by the University of Virginia Darden School Foundation, Charlottesville, VA. All rights reserved.

[1]According to the contractual arrangement, the Project Office was the office representing the employer, the Electricity Department, Ministry of Water Resources, His Majesty's Government of Nepal [the Ministry]. The Project Office was to monitor the progress of the work, coordinate the consultant, contractors, and various related government ministries and departments, approve invoices and forward them to the related banks or funding agencies for payments, and perform other related administrative work.

IUCEJ entered Nepal in 1960 as a consulting engineer for the prefeasibility study of the Karnali Hydropower Project. In 1977, IUCEJ established an office in Kathmandu to supervise the design and construction of a major irrigation project in eastern Nepal.

In 1979, the Ministry of Water Resources, His Majesty's Government of Nepal awarded IUCEJ a contract to supervise the engineering and construction of the Kulekhani Hydroelectric Project. This project, which consisted of constructing a 107-meter rock-fill dam and a 7.1-kilometer tunnel with an underground powerhouse, was successfully completed within the scheduled time in December 1983. Subsequently, the Ministry awarded IUCEJ the second phase of the Kulekhani Project (SKHP). Construction was started in January 1984.

SKHP consisted of a headworks (a 14.5-meter weir and sand settling basin with head pond), a tunnel (5.85 kilometers long and 2.50 meters in diameter), and a subsurface powerhouse scheduled for completion in December 1986. The site was remote, surrounded by the mountains, 200 kilometers away from the capital, Kathmandu.

Housing for the workers was organized into two main areas. First, there was a large construction camp, which was divided in two by barbed wire, one side for IUCEJ personnel and the other for Ministry personnel. The brick houses in this camp were small. Second, temporary contractor camps were located about 2 kilometers away. There were four contractors: a civil works contractor from Japan, a electromechanical contractor also from Japan, an equipment supplies contractor from China, and a transmission line contractor from India. The civil works contractor had set up a single, small medical clinic. Except for one tennis court and a small bar inside the IUCEJ compound, there were no places to go for sports activities or for entertainment.

Y. HIRAKI

Mr. Y. Hiraki, 35, section chief of the Construction Section of IUCEJ, was responsible for supervising the civil works personnel for SKHP. After graduation from Kyoto University with a civil engineering degree, he joined IUCEJ in 1974 and was assigned to a design section. In late 1979, he was assigned to overseas projects. Hiraki was surprised to find out that he was assigned as a construction engineer for the Kulekhani Project in Nepal. He felt strange and agitated; he left his family behind when he went to Nepal.

During his work on the Kulekhani project, Hiraki had little chance to come in contact with the Nepalese engineers because he was quite busy with the supervision of the tunnel workers. The only things he enjoyed about Nepal, especially the project site, were the sun and drink. The locals made wine, called "Chhang," that was sweeter and stronger than Hiraki's favorite sake, "Nihonshyu."

After the Kulekhani project was completed in mid 1983, Hiraki felt relieved and excited; he was given a one-month vacation as a reward. He spent two weeks on a jungle safari in the Chitawan National Park in Nepal and the rest with his family back in Tokyo. He was also able to save a substantial amount of money. Hiraki mused that if he had another chance to work overseas, he would be able to buy a small and beautiful house on the outskirts of Tokyo.

Four months later he was again assigned to an overseas project. Fortunately or unfortunately (he was not quite sure), it was in the same remote place as before. Hiraki was promoted to construction section chief for the SKHP and left Japan on March 10, 1984.

THREE MONTHS LATER

The rainy season that year was long and unprecedented in its strength. The rains destroyed many roads and temporary working camps. During the summer, Hiraki was busy assessing the damages caused by the rain and rescheduling the work plan. Officials at IUCEJ reviewed the damage and the construction schedule and submitted a new project completion date to the Ministry for approval. When the Nepalese engineers assigned to the project (contractually called "counterpart engineers") began to come in, Hiraki assigned them a few jobs but did not discuss his plans nor seek the engineers' views.

Then, on August 12, 1984, Hiraki summoned all the counterpart engineers together to discuss the project. He allocated work to each engineer and asked them to honor IUCEJ's system and carry out their duties. (The project organization chart is shown in Exhibit 19-1.)

COUNTERPART ENGINEERS' JOB DESCRIPTION

The counterpart engineers as well as other supporting staff were assigned to the various sections that reported to IUCEJ's project office. During the first week of their assignments, the counterpart engineers were given the technical specifications of the project to read. Then, they were taken to the various sites for a tour. Afterward, Hiraki explained IUCEJ's organization of the work, method of reporting work progress, and other related matters.

The counterpart engineers who were assigned in the Construction Section were responsible for monitoring work progress and managing their subordinate staffs.

There were two shifts on the underground tunneling work but only one day shift in the powerhouse and headworks. The shifts ran from 8:00 to 8:00. Each shift supervisory staff consisted of two supervisors and four assistants at each site. Each shift supervisor was to report to the site engineer in writing daily. The first shift supervisors had to report work progress the next day at 8:00 A.M. before going back to work. The second shift supervisors were required to report work progress between 8:30 and 9:00 A.M. right after completion of their shift. (Except for a few supervisors, the shift staff could barely write in English.) Four-wheel-drive vehicles carried the shift workers to and from the residence camps and the work sites.

THE PROBLEM

Hiraki and his colleagues were troubled by the new counterpart engineers sent by the Project Office. Only two incoming counterpart engineers had worked on the first Kulekhani Project; the rest were all fresh graduates and not familiar with tunnel construction procedures. One counterpart had graduated with a specialty in skyscraper construction and was not even familiar with the language of hydraulics and geotechnical[2] construction. He was assigned, for instance, to an Adit[3] but did not understand what it was.

IUCEJ officers tried to persuade the Project Office to send experienced engineers, but the Project Office argued that they were sending those fresh graduates not only to work but also to be trained. According to the contract, IUCEJ had the

---

[2]In tunneling work, geotechnical and hydraulic knowledge is extremely important.
[3]Adits were access tunnels to the 5.84-kilometer main tunnel. Adits were clustered into three groups: Adit No. 1: 0.0 kilometers to 1.8 kilometers, Adit No. 2: 1.8 kilometers to 4.2 kilometers, and Adit No. 3: 4.2 kilometers to 5.84 kilometers.

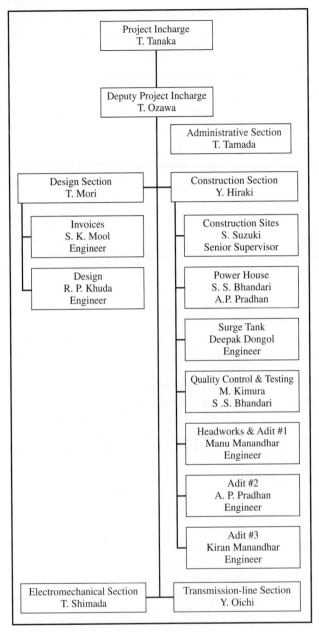

EXHIBIT 19-1 IUCEJ Second Kulekhani Hydroelectric Project, Nepal Organization Chart

obligation to train them as well as involve them in the work.[4]

AN ENCOUNTER WITH COUNTERPART ENGINEERS

Hiraki was quite busy in rescheduling the work plan when the counterpart engineers began to arrive and did not have time to attend to their assignments. After the Japanese fashion, Hiraki arranged the counterpart engineers assigned to him in orderly rows in the same room with him so he could monitor their work constantly. He gave them the project's technical specifications to read and told them to visit the construction sites frequently. There was not much effort required to do either. The plans were straightforward and construction was halted due to the rain.

At first, the counterpart engineers read quietly. However, as the days passed, they started talking with each other in low voices. This annoyed Hiraki because he was used to working in a quiet place and could not concentrate on his work. Even more frustrating was the fact that he could not understand their language. Hiraki knew that the Nepalese had a habit of talking and socializing in the office while they were working, but he assumed that the counterpart engineers would soon understand IUCEJ's working methods and change their ways, so he tried not to make a fuss about it. The talking, however, became more distinct and loud.

In the weekly review meeting with Mr. Tanaka, the man in charge of the project, Hiraki explained the problem he was facing with the counterpart engineers' behavior and asked whether he could take action. Tanaka cautioned him, saying that Hiraki could only instruct them not to talk because IUCEJ did not have authority over them. He explained that IUCEJ could not take any action against the counterpart engineers and that IUCEJ could not send them back, except in extreme cases, even if they were incompetent.

THE FIRST INCIDENT (DECEMBER 20, 1984)

Hiraki was inside the tunnel on this day when he got a call from Tanaka instructing him to come to the office as soon as possible. Hiraki hurriedly completed his work and came out of the tunnel. When he reached the front door of the office building, Hiraki was virtually dragged into Tanaka's room by the design section chief, Mr. Mori. In the room, Mr. Kimura, the quality engineer, was waving his arms and explaining something in Japanese to Mr. Tanaka. The atmosphere was tense. At first, Hiraki could not understand what Kimura was saying. Then, slowly, it became clear:

> Yes! He said exactly those words. It was at 11:30 when I saw Mool. He was taking pictures of the concreting process in the powerhouse foundation level. I was surprised to find him there. I went to him and asked him why he was there. I told him he was assigned to the design section and not to the construction section for the supervision of work in the powerhouse. So, I instructed him to go back to the office and get to work. Then, he stared strangely at me and shouted, "Who are you to order me? Who the hell do you think you are?" It angered

---

[4]In the contract, it was clearly specified under the Transfer of Technology clause that IUCEJ would train the counterpart engineers by involving them in the design and construction work. The clause further stated that the dispatched counterpart engineers would be treated the same as the IUCEJ staff and that counterpart engineers would report to their superiors in IUCEJ but that the total liability and responsibility for the counterpart staff would lie with the Project Office.

me, but I did not shout back. I just told him to go back to the office. That's all I said. But sir, I could not understand why he was allowed to go to the powerhouse without prior permission from his section chief, Mr. Mori.

Mori replied that Mool did not have his permission, that he had not even informed him of where he was going, and added that Mool was not at work that afternoon.

Mr. Tanaka called in Mr. Ozawa, the deputy project chief, who suggested that IUCEJ should take disciplinary action against such insubordination. However, Tanaka pointed out the fact that they could not take disciplinary action; all they could do was send him back to the Project Office. Before doing so, Tanaka said he would consult with the Project Office. He said he did not want to hamper relations with the Ministry. Subsequently, Mool stayed on the job.

THE SECOND INCIDENT (DECEMBER 25, 1984)

Hiraki had noticed during the last week that one of the counterpart engineers, Mr. Manu Manandhar, was not punctual. Hiraki was annoyed with the counterpart engineer's carelessness. That day, too, he had come late. It was 8:54 when Manandhar entered the office. Looking at Manu, Hiraki pointed his finger toward the wall clock without saying anything. Manu just shrugged. Hiraki felt offended by his behavior, so he told Manu that he was late and that he would not tolerate such carelessness. He asked Manu to clarify why he was late. Surprising Hiraki, Manu asked why he should come to the office at 8:00. As far as work was concerned, Manu went on, he went to the site last night. Further, Manu argued that his duty was to manage the site and supervise the construction work, not write reports, so there was no reason why he should be at the office exactly at 8:00. He added bluntly that he hated routine desk work.

Hiraki, finding this conversation too unorthodox, cut it short inadvertently by growling in *Nihongo* (Japanese). Manandhar became furious. He looked around and found that everyone in the room was looking at them. Manu walked back to his desk and slammed his helmet on the desk. Then Hiraki realized that he had made a mistake by speaking in Japanese. He had wanted to threaten Manu, but his anger had caused him to forget the English words.

THE THIRD INCIDENT (JANUARY 2, 1985)

During the New Year's celebration party organized by IUCEJ (at which the participation from the Nepalese side was virtually nil), one of the civil contractor's engineers cautioned Hiraki in Japanese that the night shift staff was making trouble on the site. He went on to say,

> In one instance, the [Nepalese] night shift supervisor, obviously drunk, stopped my jeep and ordered me to take him back to the colony. My night shift staff had complained many times about the misbehavior of the supervisors and assistants, but I told them that they [the supervisors] were representing the employer's side as well as IUCEJ's side and to just tolerate it. If the supervisors had been only your staff, Hiraki-san, I should have asked you for a stern action a long time back. But we don't want to destroy our relationship with the employer [the Ministry]. That's why we've been treating this carefully.

Hiraki had assured him that he would consider the matter and discuss it with Tanaka.

THE FOURTH INCIDENT (JANUARY 9, 1985)

Over the previous 5 months, there were many times when at least one of the counterpart engineers had been absent. Hiraki had asked why and always gotten the same reply, "official work." Every week, it seemed, there would be one counterpart engineer who was assigned to go to Kathmandu for some official work for 4 to 5 days. Then, after lunch on January 9th, three counterpart engineers, Manu Manandhar, Kiran Manandhar, and Deepak Man Singh Dongol, came to Hiraki and asked him to sign a form permitting them to go on the food stuff van. The food stuff van was scheduled to bring groceries from Kathmandu for the Japanese expatriates twice a week on Wednesdays and Fridays. The form was designed for use by IUCEJ's local administration [Nepalese] staff. The local staff were required to get written permission from their section chief to go to Kathmandu in the food stuff van.

Hiraki told them it was not possible. Without a word, they went out of the room. After an hour Manu came back to Hiraki asking him to consider it again because they had important things to do in Kathmandu. Hiraki was furious by now. Angrily, Hiraki asked what was it in Kathmandu that was more important than the work.

MANU: We have to be home tomorrow. We have a religious festival, and it is important.

HIRAKI: But then, who will take responsibility for your work? I am sorry, I cannot let you go. As you know the concreting in the headwork has already started, and we are facing trouble in the penstock tunnel! It is a crucial time. If you don't supervise the contractor's work now, you will not be able to control the quality later on. And. . . . .

MANU: Forget it! Last Saturday! What happened in Headwork? Do you remember when I rejected the batch? I rejected that batch of concrete because it was already 90 minutes past due. As per the specification, the concrete should be poured in the site within 90 minutes after it has been mixed in the batching plant. But the contractor's site supervisor (Japanese)

did not listen to me! Instead, he called you. It was you who told me that if the concrete seems OK, then I should allow them to use it. How the hell you expect me to know whether concrete seems OK? I go with the specification: If it is written 90 minutes, so be it! Not a single minute's delay!

HIRAKI: But . . . It is not realistic, you see. You have to judge whether the concrete is good or not. I know that the specification does not allow it. But why don't you understand? The weather is cold. It takes more time to set. You should be a little flexible in these kinds of jobs.

MANU: Then why did you put down that clause in the first place? And also how much flexibility I should allow? One more hour? Anyhow, I am not the only one facing this problem. Anyway, I don't want to discuss this matter now. I want to know whether you are permitting us to ride in your so-called food stuff van or not.

HIRAKI: But who gave you permission for a leave of absence? I can't give you any kind of vacation now!

MANU: I am not going on a leave of absence; neither are the others. We are going to Kathmandu for official reasons. We have already been instructed to go. I am here not asking for your permission to leave. I am here for the permission to ride in that van.

HIRAKI: But it is not true! You have already told me that you are going home for your own reasons. How can you possibly relate it to the official work? I have not given you any such work.

MANU: Formally speaking, I am on official work. I want you to know the truth because I want you to understand our system. Do you think I can swallow this place? No where to go except the tunnel, and no entertainment either! I will go nuts if I don't go to Kathmandu once a month! And to put it clearly, I am not responsible to you! I am an employee of the Electricity Department, not IUCEJ! You do not have any authority to approve or disapprove my leave of absence of any sort! As far as the work of supervision is concerned, Suzuki is there to look after it. Even if you do not permit us to go in that van, we will arrange the trip ourselves! We *will* go today and will be back after 5 days, that is, on January 14, 1985. . . .

HIRAKI: Why can't you understand my position? I rely on you people. You have to take the work seriously. Work is more important than family affairs.

MANU: No . . . no . . . it may be important for you, but not for us and certainly not for me. My family comes first. *Then* work!

HIRAKI: Ok! Let me think. Let me talk with Tanaka. Come back after an hour. The food stuff van is scheduled to leave at 4:00. It's only 2:30.

Manu left, informing Hiraki that he had to finish some Project Office-related work. After Manu left, Hiraki reviewed the conversation he had had with Manu. Now, he understood the "official work" excuses they had been using when they were away. So, that was it! The "official work" was recreation time! He hated their insubordination—and the worst thing was he did not have any authority to take action.

Hiraki looked at the wall clock. It was 3:00. He had to think fast; he had to decide. He had to do something. Given the fact that the construction work was progressing faster than expected and Suzuki alone would not be able to handle it, he had to handle the situation cautiously. In addition, he had to think about the shift staffs, too. He tensed.

Hurriedly Hiraki went to discuss this matter with his boss, Mr. Tanaka. At the end of the meeting, Tanaka concluded:

Hiraki, it is up to you now. If you think we should take action against Manu, it's OK by me. But think again. It may destroy the morale of others. And as far as bringing in more expatriates is concerned, contractually, I can request to Tokyo (headquarters) for only one additional construction engineer or supervisor, that's it. You have a limited choice. Remember, the construction has just started. If you cannot handle them properly now, we may face trouble in the future. ■

Case 20   Crossroads (A)

Roy Pemberton was not a happy man. He had just returned to his company's headquarters in London after a 6-week period of absence (the result of a riding accident) and was still not quite fully recovered. However, as the most senior partner of Pemberton, Merton-Briggs, Limited, he found himself faced with a decision that would affect the future of the company. The situation concerned Michael Grant, the vice chairman of the firm's U.S. subsidiary. The management committee had recently concluded a meeting at which Grant had presented a strategic plan for the U.S. subsidiary that would also affect the London office. The partners had discussed the plan that morning at the partners' meeting, but the vote had been split almost evenly for and against accepting it. Pemberton had asked for a 30-minute adjournment to consider his position before voting. As the largest shareholder, his vote would be conclusive. If the proposal was turned down, Grant was bound to resign from the firm. Pemberton liked the plan personally, but other aspects had to be considered.

THE INDUSTRY

The securities industry in 1991 served an important role in the flow of capital within an industrialized economy. First of all, it provided a means of channeling funds from the savings sectors of the economy to the investing sectors. Second, the industry facilitated the trading of securities between buyers and sellers, and thus influenced the abilities of industries and firms to expand and diversify. Finally, the industry provided investors with a wide range of investment vehicles with various degrees of liquidity and risk/return characteristics. These functions were carried out through two types of activity: the issuing and placement of new issues of stock, and the transfer of previously issued securities. These functions were carried out by various securities companies, or investment banks. The companies provided brokerage services, underwrote corporate and government securities, and dealt in the securities markets. Some investment banks also provided a wide range of financial advisory services to both corporations and investors.

THE COMPANY

Pemberton, Merton-Briggs, Limited (PMB), incorporated in 1970, was a privately owned investment-banking boutique,[1] headquartered in London, with small branch offices in Paris and Brussels. The firm focused its efforts on the banking and real-estate industries, and its main objective was to sell

---

This case was prepared by Tunde Onitiri, a student at the International University of Japan in Urasa, under the direction of James G. Clawson while he was a visiting faculty member there. The case was written as a basis for class discussion rather than to illustrate effective or ineffective handling of an administrative situation. Copyright © 1999 by the University of Virginia Darden School Foundation, Charlottesville, VA. All rights reserved.
[1]A small, specialized securities firm dealing with a limited clientele and offering a limited product line.

the stocks of European and American companies in these industries to institutional investors on both continents. The firm also provided corporate finance services to companies within these two industries. The company was owned by five partners, all of whom were British. Richard Merton-Briggs, Charles Griffith, Roy Pemberton, Edward Grenville, and James Meyers-Brown had all studied at Cambridge together in the 1950s, and had all subsequently worked with related real-estate/brokerage companies in Connecticut in the 1960s. (Please see Exhibit 20-1 for management committee membership).

PMB had two subsidiaries: US Pemberton, Merton-Briggs, Inc. (USPMB) and International Political Risk Analysts, Inc. (IPRA). IPRA was involved in selling country-risk research to international banks and multinational corporations. IPRA headquarters were adjacent to the parent company's offices in London, and the subsidiary also had offices on four continents. IPRA was headed by Meyers-Brown, who was also a managing director (and the second-largest shareholder) of PMB. JMB, as he was known in the firm, had once been a PMB bank analyst; as the firm expanded its operations, he came to focus his efforts on running IPRA, while leaving the day-to-day management of PMB to Merton-Briggs and Pemberton. JMB retained a keen interest in the field of investment research, however, and he enjoyed talking with analysts, both in New York and London, about their current recommendations. He often had to travel to New York to visit with major U.S. clients and to oversee the operations of the IPRA New York office, and he would take such opportunities to meet with the analysts in the PMB office. He would also stop by the controller's office to discuss the finances of USPMB.

USPMB was organized along the same functional lines as the parent company,

Partners' Committee
Roy Pemberton
Richard Merton-Briggs
James Meyers-Brown
Edward Grenville
Charles Griffith
Management Committee
Roy Pemberton
Richard Merton-Briggs
James Meyers-Brown
Edward Grenville
Charles Griffith
Michael Grant
Derrick Walton

EXHIBIT 20-1   Membership of the Partners' and Management Committees

but it concentrated its sales efforts on American institutional investors. The firm's offices were located in Manhattan, with a small branch in Stamford, Connecticut. In the 1970s, the parent company, lacking any trading operations in New York, had made an arrangement with two American brokerage houses through which its U.S. transactions could be U.S.-made. One of the PMB partners, Charles Griffith, had moved to Stamford to act as a liaison between the London office and the two brokerage houses. After a few years, this relationship went sour, however, and in 1980, PMB set up a full-fledged subsidiary in New York. Griffith moved to New York to open the new subsidiary.

The subsidiary initially had a staff of four: one trader, one salesman, and two research analysts. Later, a small office was opened in Stamford, simply because the real-estate research analyst initially hired lived in Stamford and did not want to move to New York. Over the next 8 years, annual revenues grew to $12 million and total staff to 40. (See Exhibit 20-2 for the organizational structure of the New York office.) An

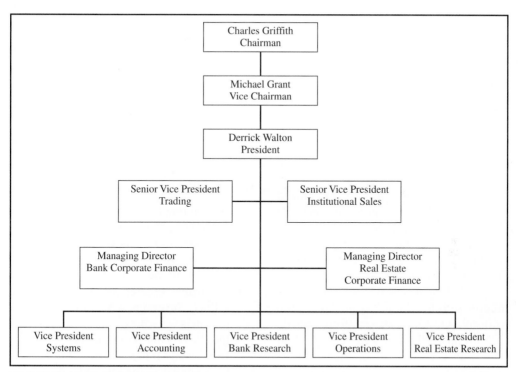

EXHIBIT 20-2 USPMB Organizational Chart

IPRA office, opened later in New York, occupied offices adjacent to USPMB.

USPMB OFFICERS

Charles Griffith

The chairman of USPMB, Charlie Griffith, was an excellent salesman who was responsible for about 40 percent of the commissions of the New York office. Griffith was an introvert and did not interact much with members of the staff outside the Sales, Trading, and Research Departments. He did not like administrative work and preferred to sit on the trading floor, even though he had his own office. (He went into his office only for confidential meetings or to sign administrative documents.) As a result, the office was under very loose man-

agement, which incorporated flexible financial control systems. This approach had not affected the firm's profitability much during the bull market, but after the stock market crash of 1987, management found it necessary to keep better track of the flow of funds within the office. Griffith thus decided to hire someone to take over his administrative duties so that he could concentrate on sales and trading. Derrick Walton, a 35-year-old Englishman, was employed to do this job.

Derrick Walton

Walton had the titles of president and chief executive officer. His contract was tentatively for a 2-year period, with a review due after the first year. His duties were to oversee all the administrative matters in the company and to supervise the sales force. Walton had been highly recommended to the firm by one of its clients; he had organized a powerful sales force at a large British brokerage house. His edge as a salesman was that he knew more about Euroequities than most of his clients. As far as U.S. equities were concerned, however, his knowledge and analytical ability were limited, and he proved to be an ineffective salesman.

Although Walton effectively organized the sales force, he could not cope with the administrative duties required of him. Furthermore, he did not command the respect of his peers and his subordinates. In fact, he was often the subject of jokes among the clerical staff of the firm. Hence, 9 months into his tenure as president, the firm decided to hire someone from outside with administrative experience on Wall Street to act as vice chairman. An executive-recruitment firm was engaged for this purpose, and through this process, Michael Grant was hired.

Michael Grant

Grant, a graduate of the Wharton School, was a well-known analyst on Wall Street. He had made his name during a 10-year stint at a major Wall Street firm where he had been a vice president and head of financial institutions research. During this period, he had been named to the Institutional Investor All-American Research Team several times. He then had spent time at two other large investment banks, in such capacities as senior vice president of mergers and acquisitions and partner in charge of mergers and acquisitions.

Grant had a reputation on the street for being a "difficult" man. The rumor was that he had not been made a partner at his first firm because of this trait. Nevertheless, the partners of PMB had done business with Grant for almost 20 years and were pleased to have him accept their offer.

MAJOR CHANGES AT USPMG

Over the next few months, Michael Grant undertook a comprehensive streamlining of the firm's operations. For this purpose, he spent a week working with the heads and senior members of staff of each department. The major changes implemented were as follows:

- Accounting and financial reporting procedures were computerized, and new systems for tracking the performance of analysts, traders, and salespeople were implemented.
- The firm's research products were refined. Several new analytical products were designed, such as the PMB Bank Index and the PMB Real Estate Index. These systems were similar to the research products at Grant's previous firm. The analytical methods, writing styles, and presentations of research analysts were altered to conform to the new research products. In addition, the Research Department's compensation scheme was adjusted to be tied directly to the performance of recommended stocks.
- The Corporate Finance Department was expanded. One junior associate was hired for the bank corporate finance area, and a real-estate corporate finance area was established. Two former managing directors at Paine Webber were hired to head this area. Grant actively used his contacts in the business to pursue more corporate finance deals. The bank and real-estate research analysts also became more involved in the evaluation of potential corporate

finance deals. As a result of these efforts, PMB was named underwriter for a private placement[2] for a Florida bank. (This deal, although potentially lucrative, proved to be a drain on the resources of the firm, however.)

- The Sales Department was expanded by the addition of three salesmen, and the sales force was reorganized along client geographical location lines, as opposed to the previous product-oriented arrangement. In order to enhance this new scheme, the Stamford office was closed, and the salespeople there were required either to move to New York or be in the New York office at least 3 days a week (with the firm covering only a fraction of commuting expenses). Jerry Thom, who had been the director of sales in the Stamford office, became codirector of sales in the New York office.
- The compensation structure in the Sales and Trading Department was also altered. Grant believed the sales force was being paid too much. A new scheme was instituted whereby, on a monthly basis, the salespeople and the traders would review the trades for the month and negotiate the distribution of commissions based on the relative efforts of each department. These meetings were usually highly charged and ended with the final "decision" coming from Grant himself.

- An investment account was created to put the firm's capital into bank stocks. This account was managed by Grant and proved to be very profitable. Grant also received commissions on profits generated by this account. An arbitrage[3] account was also established to invest the firm's capital in potential takeover stocks. The first major trade in this account proved to be a minor disaster. On Grant's recommendation the firm acquired a block of shares (at $70 per share) in a North Carolina bank that was a takeover candidate. Within 3 weeks, the price had dropped to $20 per share, and USPMB lost $0.5 million in the transaction.
- A time-card system was instituted whereby the administrative secretary in each department would record the arrival/departure times of each employee in the department, including senior management. This system was said to be for real-estate purposes, and it greatly improved punctuality. Employee fringe benefits were more strictly regulated than in the past. Employees had previously been able to sign off on company limousine vouchers. (If an employee stayed in the office until 7:00 P.M., he or she was allowed to take a limousine home.) This rule was changed to require pre-approval from the respective department head.

---

[2]Securities placed directly with an institutional investor, such as an insurance company, rather than sold through a public issue.

[3]Arbitrage in this context refers to an activity carried out when an acquisition was announced at a higher price than the current stock price of the target firm. The Risk Arbitrage Department of an investment bank would then decide whether to buy the stock to take advantage of the higher offer price.

- A new image was created for the firm. An interior decorating company (run by Grant's wife) was hired to redesign the office. New furniture was acquired, and the walls of the office were repainted. Grant even suggested having the receptionist wear a bowler hat to underscore the fact that PMB was British. Another designer was hired to come up with a new layout for research reports. Initially, Grant used the office reserved for Griffith and the services of the secretarial staff of the Trading Department. He later moved into an office of his own and hired a private secretary. This office was furnished with a $10,000 antique desk (paid for from personal funds) and several framed English prints. The adjacent room, fitted with a mahogany conference table and new chairs, was used as a private conference room. These rooms had been previously occupied by the Real-Estate Research Department. USPMB rented additional floor space on the same floor to accommodate this department. The sales and trading area was also redesigned. The walls separating Griffith's office, which was adjacent to the trading floor, were taken down in order to add extra floor space to this area.

Grant's name was actively used in the marketing of USPMB's products and services. As a result, the firm's client base increased significantly, including the addition of some large, "blue-chip" institutional investors. Also, for the first time, the firm's Bank Research Department was ranked in *Greenwich Review,* a well-known publication that evaluated Wall Street research products.

SIDE EFFECTS

The atmosphere at USPMB changed noticeably within a few months after the start of Michael Grant's tenure at the firm. Grant had a hard-driving personality and an authoritative management style. He liked to have things done his way and would often threaten to fire those who persistently disagreed with his opinion. As a result, he was disliked and feared by most members of the staff. The mood in the office was much more relaxed whenever he was away on business trips.

A month after joining USPMB, Grant took on the additional title of chief executive officer, while Derrick Walton remained president and director of the sales force. (Soon after the Stamford office was closed, Jerry Thorn, senior vice president of institutional sales, had left the firm to open his own brokerage house in Boston.) Because Grant took a personal interest in the sales and trading activities of the firm, however, Walton, despite his title, effectively had no power. The two men did not get along, and other members of USPMB firmly believed that Walton's contract would not be renewed. Three months before his contract was due to expire, Walton left the firm. At this point, Grant took over the day-to-day management of the sales force.

Grant was well liked by Roy Pemberton, and the two men had a good working relationship. Pemberton was pleased with the results of Grant's operation and believed the firm was in a much better position than it had been to compete in the volatile business environment of Wall Street. Pemberton would often invite Grant to London for 2-day trips to discuss firm strategy for the New York subsidiary. Richard Merton-Briggs, who did not have much contact with Grant, also had a strong liking for him and had been particularly pleased with the improvements in the financial conditions of the New York office.

On the other hand, an intense animosity existed between Grant and James Meyers-Brown. Grant resented JMB's coming into the New York office to "nose around," and he had told JMB so to his face. Nevertheless, JMB maintained his habit of dropping into the controller's office at USPMB whenever he was in New York. JMB regarded Grant as uncouth, but, in light of the increased profitability since Grant had come aboard, was prepared to tolerate his behavior.

Edward Grenville, the managing director in charge of the London corporate finance office, did not get on well with Grant either. After making several trips to the London office in connection with a cross-border corporate finance transaction, Grant had suggested applying the same cost-cutting strategy to parts of the London operation as was done in New York. Grenville strongly resented this idea.

Griffith, although he had been visibly upset about the large trading loss in the arbitrage account, showed a neutral attitude toward Grant. The two men worked together closely and often traveled together on client visits.

Over the 2 months following Grant's changes, one salesman and three research analysts left the firm. The employees who resigned had been with the firm for at least 5 years each and had been well-liked and respected by other staff members. Morale in the office suffered, and speculation about further resignations increased. Several members of the Research and Sales Departments were suspected to have their resumes "out on the street." USPMB was finding it difficult to hire qualified people to replace the lost staff. A number of offers had been made to some senior employees of large Wall Street firms, but so far, they had all been rejected.

Griffith was increasingly worried about the atmosphere in the New York office, and he intended to raise the issue at the forthcoming partners' meeting in London. Grant, for his part, focused on drafting a set of proposals concerning the general strategy of USPMB, which he intended to present at the management committee meeting that would directly precede the partners' meeting.

GRANT'S PROPOSALS

At the quarterly management committee meeting in London, Grant presented the following proposals:

- A complete review of the salary scales in the New York office and an increase in the budget for this purpose. Although this proposal had originated with the heads of the Real-Estate Research and Bank Research Departments, Grant agreed that, in general, salaries in USPMB were not competitive with those in other Wall Street firms.
- The establishment of a full-fledged Euroequities Department in New York, through which the research efforts of the London office could be marketed in the United States and the firm could offer its American clients a full range of European equities. Two or three specialized salespeople would have to be hired for this purpose.
- Transfer of the management of the entire corporate finance operations of the parent company to the New York office, where it would be headed by Grant (because of his track record in the field).
- Complete autonomy (for Grant) for setting the strategy of the New York office and for administering finances.
- Increased emphasis on corporate-finance deals, with an increase in capitalization of the New York

subsidiary for this purpose. Establishment of merchant banking[4] activities.

- In the light of his performance so far, an increased equity stake in the company for Grant.
- Promotion of Grant to full partner status in the parent company.

The PMB partners were strongly in favor of the salary-scale review. They believed that their difficulty in attracting staff from other Wall Street houses had been a result of this factor. The other proposals were received neutrally. A few questions were asked by Pemberton and Merton-Briggs for clarification purposes, but the others did not say much. The meeting ended with Pemberton assuring Grant that his proposals would be further discussed in the partners' meeting the next day and that a swift decision would be made.

Grant flew out of London on the same evening. He decided to go fishing in Antigua over the weekend before returning to the New York office the following week. Before leaving, he called New York and spoke with the head of bank research. Grant told him that things had gone well in London and that he would have good news for everybody when he got back to New York. Griffith stayed behind in London for the partners' meeting.

During the 30-minute adjournment that he had requested, Roy Pemberton reviewed in his mind the events of the last few months. Clearly, the firm was at a crossroads, and at this moment, he was in the driver's seat. The fact that his fellow partners would respect any decision he made did not make him feel any more comfortable. Which way should he go? ■

---

[4]In the context of U.S. investment banking, merchant banking refers to activities in which a firm commits its own capital to a transaction, as when making equity investments in a company.

Case 21   Peninsular Insurance (A)

Patrick Wale stood in the conference room staring in amazement at the chairman, Tan Sri Ibrahim Nassan. Ibrahim Nassan, the titular head of Peninsular Insurance, had just taken charge of Wale's planning meeting with an interruption that Wale saw as an attempt to subvert his authority with his managers. By the looks on their faces, Wale surmised that his managers were just as surprised as he by such an overt power play. With the 1985 Malaysian economy in recession and company revenues sliding, now was not the time to play politics. As his adrenalin began to flow, Wale was at a loss as to how to regain control of the meeting and, by implication, of his Malaysian insurance organization. As his mind raced, he thought, "All I know is that whatever I do next, it's going to have to be played by the Malay rules: respect for elders and 'saving face'. The question is whether I can show one without losing the other."

BACKGROUND

Patrick Wale had arrived in Kuala Lumpur ("KL," capital of Malaysia) almost 3 years previously to oversee the merger of the wholly owned Malaysian subsidiary of New Zealand Insurance Corporation (NZI) with the Malaysian-majority-owned Peninsular Insurance. He should have been finished within the first 12 months. In fact, however, after the first 2 years, he had barely scratched the surface of a project that was becoming more Byzantine by the week.

Wale considered himself good at adapting and working with other cultures. His work for NZI had taken him to Nigeria, South Africa, India, and, in his last position as branch manager, to Hong Kong, NZI's largest branch in Asia ($8 million in annual sales). (See Exhibit 21-1 for a profile of Wale and other key executives.)

Wale had felt at home in the freewheeling, business-first culture of Hong Kong. The absence of political barriers allowed him to concentrate on "getting on with business" without the worry of government regulations. But when the NZI general manager of International Operations called to offer him the position of chief executive officer of the Malaysian joint venture, Wale jumped at the opportunity.

The combination of NZI's $12 million subsidiary with its 49 percent owned, $4 million Peninsular would be double the size of the Hong Kong division in staff and sales. The task was an unusual one, because Wale would be wearing two hats—as the head of the NZI subsidiary reporting to the home office in New Zealand, and as general manager of Peninsular reporting to the local board. That situation would change, however, when the merger went through and the combined ($16 million) entity would be 74 percent owned by NZI and working under a single management.

NZI, LIMITED

"New Zealanders pride themselves on their self reliance . . . it's called kiwi ingenuity."[1]

NZI was a diversified financial-services company based in Auckland, New Zealand. One of the country's largest companies,

UVA-OB-0416

This case was prepared by James M. Berger, Darden 1992, under the supervision of Professor L. J. Bourgeois.
Copyright © 1992 Darden Graduate Business School Foundation, Charlottesville, VA. Rev. 2/98.
[1]Annemarie Orange, Darden 1992, native of New Zealand.

Central Characters

Patrick Wale
Age 42

After dropping out of high school in New Zealand, 16-year-old Patrick Wale began work in 1961 as an office boy with NZI. He studied in night school for 3 years to complete the insurance exams and began to move up the corporate hierachy. In 1966, he was offered a position with the overseas staff.

A self-described "adventurer," Wale accepted transfers to offices around the world, including Nigeria, India, South Africa, and Hong Kong. Each move improved his position within the corporation and finally led to his present appointment as CEO of the NZI joint venture with a Malaysian partner.

Married in 1969, Wale met his wife in Calcutta, where she was working for the British High Commission. Their two children, a 14-year-old son and 13-year-old daughter, had recently been sent to boarding schools in England.

Nigel Fisher
Age 57

Fisher had been employed by NZ since 1942; he was appointed to a senior position with the home office in 1960 after a series of international transfers. His progress within the company appeared stalled after the 1981 merger produced a surfeit of middle managers, but he was appointed general manager of the international group in 1985 after its previous 2 years of results fell well below corporate expectations for the Asian operations. Fisher was due to retire in June of 1986.

Fisher was described by a colleague as possessing strong analytical but weak interpersonal skills and having a "dour" personality.

Tan Sri Haji Ibrahim Nassan
Age 73

Tan Sri Haji Ibrahim Nassan Bin Haji Ibrahim Siddiq[a] (his full name) had had a prominent civil-servant career with the Malaysian government, culminating as Secretary General of Internal Affairs, responsible for Police, Justice, and Immigration. Retired at age 55, he was quickly invited to sit on several company boards and had been Peninsular Insurance's chairman since 1967. He was required to retire from all but Peninsular's board at age 70.

Nassan was known as a man who paid strong attention to detail and required a high level of protocol at all times. He was married with five sons.

---

[a]A convention in Malaysian names and titles conveyed social and political rank, lineage, and Muslim pilgrimage: "Datuk" was a title conveyed on men of accomplishment. "Tan Sri" was a higher honor, fewer in number. It was given by the Sultan, usually for public servants of high rank. "Tun" was the highest honor possible in Malaysia, short of royalty. "Haji" indicated that the individual made the pilgrimage to Mecca. "Bin" meant "son of."

EXHIBIT 21-1 **Peninsular Insurance Employees**

NZI was formed in 1981 from the merger of New Zealand Insurance (founded in 1859) and South British Insurance Company (founded in 1872). The result was a multinational corporation operating in 24 countries through hundreds of offices.

Revenues of the merged company had reached $630 million in 1982, with a reported net income of $28 million. The international divisions of NZI's General Insurance Group contributed 35 percent of divisional income. (See Exhibit 21-2 for organization of NZI.) Each of the seven divisions of the company was run as a profit center.

NZI had concentrated its foreign business in the Pacific Rim and Africa and adopted a strategy of growth through local offices in order to gain a balance in both operations and the product mix offered by the company. NZI had recently been riding a tremendous wave of new business brought about by booming regional economies and an aggressive new corporate style of management that expanded the company's business into previously unconventional areas. NZI had also concentrated on shifting power to the local offices in order to encour-age growth, and the new strategy called for equally aggressive management by NZI's field managers, who were afforded a large degree of autonomy by the "Home Office." Within the Pacific and Asia regions'

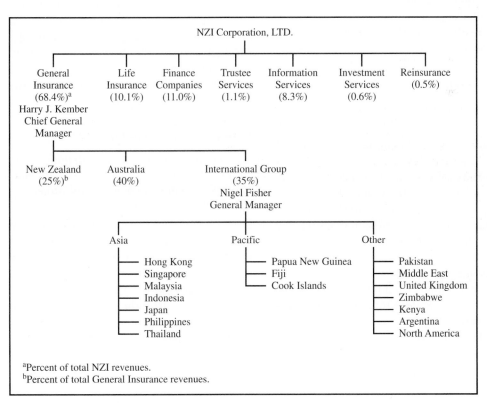

^aPercent of total NZI revenues.
^bPercent of total General Insurance revenues.

EXHIBIT 21-2   NZI Organization in 1985

financial-services industry, NZI was considered to be one of the most aggressive in its mix of markets, products, and technologies.

NZI held interests in two key Malaysian operations. NZI Malaysia was a branch network offering the full range of insurance services and accounting for $12 million in revenues. Peninsular Insurance Company, with $4 million in revenues, was 49 percent owned by NZI, with the remainder owned by Malaysian nationals. Peninsular had been formed by NZI in 1967 with the ultimate aim of controlling all its business interests in Malaysia, in line with government policy of local incorporation of foreign branches.

Weak profits in an otherwise-growing economy had led to a decision in 1982 to consolidate all Malaysian operations in order to reduce costs and provide for a more coherent strategy. An agreement was reached that Peninsular Insurance would merge with NZI Malaysia in a pooling-of-interests transaction.

MALAYSIA

The Federation of Malaysia was a peninsular country located at the southern tip of Thailand, with two Malaysian states located several hundred miles across the South China Sea on the island of Borneo. Following independence from the United Kingdom in 1957, the federation was established in 1963. Malaysia was a constitutional monarchy with a parliament and prime minister. The king (the Yang di Pertuan Agong) was elected for a 5-year period by a council of nine ruling sultans from nine of the 13 federated states. (Federally appointed governors headed the four other states and the federal territory.)

Natural Resources and the Economy

Malaysia had a population of 14.8 million people, with the capital of Kuala Lumpur housing 938,000. The country held a dominant world position in rubber, palm oil, pepper, tin, and tropical hardwoods; these and other abundant natural resources had given Malaysia one of the highest annual growth rates per capita in the world: growth at 4.5 percent per year since 1965 and per-capita gross national product of more than $1,555 by 1985.

The government had been aggressively pushing the economy toward a manufacturing base since the 1970s. Emphasis was on building the travel and communication infrastructure necessary for industrial growth, and the government maintained a policy of encouraging rapid population growth in order to stimulate domestic demand. The policy appeared to be working: Manufacturing began to overtake agriculture as a percentage of gross domestic product and, by the 1980s, was the main source of economic growth. The unemployment rate was 5.6 percent in 1985, and the inflation rate was 3.7 percent.

Political Aspects and the "NEP"

"It's not a law, it's a government policy, and it is really like shadow boxing because you never really know quite where the target is."[2]

Because Malaysia was a multiracial society, friction generated by the different cultures was the most important aspect of Malaysian politics. Political parties were based primarily on racial lines; the United Malays National Organization was the largest, but shared power in a broad-based coalition with the Malaysian Chinese Association,

---

[2]Interview with Patrick Wale.

the Malaysian Indian Congress, and several other, smaller parties. Malays made up about 50 percent of the population, Chinese about 35 percent, and Indians about 10 percent. The three ethnic groups spoke different languages and followed different religions. While Malays were the most powerful politically, the Chinese controlled most of the nation's economy and owned a large proportion of Malaysia's businesses.

After a violent race riot in 1969, the Malaysian government established the "mitigation of inequity between races" as the overriding goal for the government. As a response to this goal, the New Economic Policy (NEP) was established in 1970. NEP was established to help the "bumiputra" (Malay for "son of the soil"), which refers to native Malays, who were considered the main beneficiaries of the policies. One way the NEP attempted to reach its goals was through increased spending on education and basic services. Public enterprises such as the Trust Council for Indigenous Peoples were chartered to finance native Malay businesses and to provide advice to prospective Malay businesspeople.

The government also had set a goal of increasing native Malay ownership in the corporate sector to 30 percent by 1990. All other Malaysians were designated 40 percent corporate ownership, and foreign-owned stakes were to have access to the remaining 30 percent. In addition, foreign-owned companies were required to restructure equity so that at least 70 percent was held by Malaysian investors.

According to Wale, at the time of his arrival in 1982, the government was putting extra pressure on foreign firms to "domesticate" their firms and to increase their local share holdings. One way of applying this pressure was to grant limited-term work permits. Government regulations in 1982 required all foreign nationals to apply for a Visitor's Work Visa, usually for 12 months. But when pressure on a company was desired, only 3 or 6 months were given, and the threat was always present that a visa would not be renewed. As Wale described this threat, "I had no idea whether I would be here for the full 5 years of my assignment or I would be on the plane in a month's time. They were playing the game with all insurance companies here that the best way to make foreign companies take on local partners was to mess around with their work permits."

Another important factor in the Malaysian political structure was the presence of the military. In the early years of the federation, in a period known locally as "the emergency," the country was plagued by civil war. Not until the middle 1970s did the threat from the communist insurgents greatly lessen. The product of the civil war was a virulently anticommunist government that retained full constitutional control of the professional military force.

THE NZI MALAYSIAN STAFF

"Well it's all very much tied into the Asian face thing, that you don't just say what's on your mind to the guy in case you offend him."[3]

Not long after taking over as general manager of Peninsular, Wale established good working relationships with the management and board. (Wale was appointed to the board in March 1983 as an alternate for

---

[3]Interview with Patrick Wale.

Harry Kember, a board member based in New Zealand.) The foremost figure of the company was the local chairman of the board, Tan Sri Ibrahim Nassan, a prominent citizen in Malaysia who had once served as a high-level government official in the Interior Department (see Exhibit 21-1).

Wale soon realized that the chairman was remote from any real decision making for Peninsular; he served in a mostly ceremonial role. The chairman would show up at board meetings, start the occasion with a brief speech (usually written for him), and then leave management to discuss the mundane operational issues. Wale found the chairman to be a supportive gentleman; he allowed Wale to go about the business of modernizing the company's operation and organizing the mechanics of the merger, and he was particularly helpful in the area of smoothing over potential problems with the government. Immigration had been one of the departments under the chairman's supervision, and he several times expedited Wale's reapplication for a work permit.

The 73-year-old chairman, at 5'7", was quite a contrast with Wale who, at 42, was 6'4" and 250 pounds. Recently, Nassan had been forced to leave most of his other board positions because of the mandatory retirement age written into most public companies' bylaws. Peninsular, as a private company, did not have such a rule. The chairman was thought to be well off financially, although Wale had also heard that he recently had been involved in some rather unfortunate investments, probably in the volatile Malaysian stock market.

Since the early, supportive days, Wale had found himself on occasion becoming annoyed by the chairman's tendency to bypass Wale and call the corporate secretary, Goh Lai King, when he wished to check on the business or consult with a manager. King had been with Peninsular for almost 15 years, and the chairman had formed a separate line of communication with him. Wale believed that as a matter of protocol, the CEO should be the first to be consulted for advice or questions, but he had also recognized how petty it would be to try to cut off this communication. (See Exhibit 21-3 for Peninsular organization.)

Wale had also quickly formed a close working relationship with the Malaysian operations manager, Tan Peng Soo. Tan was particularly knowledgeable about the daily workings of Peninsular, and Wale relied on his judgment about how best to implement the new training and computerization programs that would bring Peninsular's operations up with the rest of the NZI organization. Because Wale expected to move on when the merger was consummated, he began grooming Tan Peng for the CEO position. Wale understood that Tan's strong business acumen and Malaysian nationality would make him a natural choice to run the merged company.

MEETING WITH THE CHAIRMAN

The question was whether the merger would ever come to fruition. Wale had become increasingly frustrated by the torturously slow nature of Malaysian business dealings, particularly those with the vast government bureaucracy. Two years had already passed, and almost nothing had been accomplished. He spent most of his time waiting months for written replies from government officials, replies that would have taken days in Hong Kong.

During this first 2 years in Malaysia, Wale occasionally visited the chairman at his home in a wealthy KL neighborhood to update him on the progress of the merger and discuss how the business was doing in general. Wale had arranged such a meeting to discuss the slow replies of the government and an upcoming board meeting with the visiting directors from New Zealand.

As a courtesy, Wale had always visited the chairman at home, but he was becoming

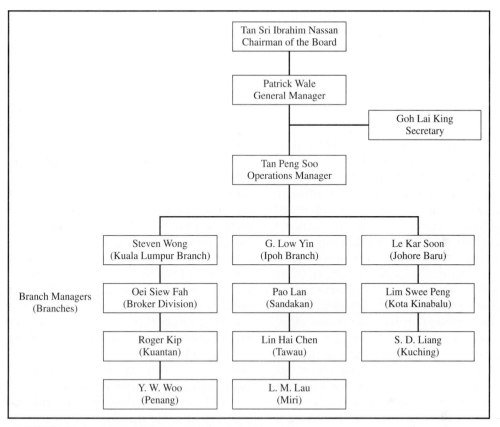

EXHIBIT 21-3 Peninsular Organization in 1985

increasingly uncomfortable with the practice. He had noticed that while they were seated in the chairman's sitting room discussing business, the chairman's wife would be sitting in the adjacent room apparently listening in on their conversation. She would often make an excuse to come in and interrupt and would then linger on during the discussion. The chairman's wife was quite a bit younger than he, probably 15 or 20 years. Wale recognized that she was a strong-willed woman, and perhaps this trait, combined with her ability to make her presence felt and known, was what made Wale uncomfortable.

On this humid July 1984 day, the chairman seemed to have little to offer in regard to the government delays. Wale then asked,

"Well, sir, do you have any suggestions on where we may want to host the dinner for our visiting board members? I thought that your club did a superior job on the last occasion."

The chairman leaned forward, "Yes, well, I believe . . ."

"The club? Certainly not the club!" His wife suddenly emerged into the room. "Why don't we try the Rasa Sayang for a change? I think the gentlemen from the home office would much prefer that."

Wale observed the chairman as his wife continued telling them where the meeting should be and what should be on the menu. The chairman was obviously a bit taken aback, and Wale realized that he probably had the same expression on his own face.

Driving back to his office that afternoon, Wale decided to discontinue the practice of going to the chairman's house to talk business. Perhaps he was being silly, but the wife's interference was bothersome.

NIGEL FISHER VISITS

Several months later (February 1985), Wale received a call from Nigel Fisher in the New Zealand office telling him that Fisher would be visiting the Malaysia office in 2 weeks. Fisher was the newly appointed general manager in charge of International Operations, the third general manager in as many years. Fisher had worked with Wale before, and Wale looked forward to being able to discuss with him the reasons for the merger's slow going. Wale hoped to receive the level of support from the home office necessary to accelerate the merger.

A few days before Fisher's arrival, the chairman called Wale to his office. He requested that Wale arrange for King, the company secretary, to be present at Nassan's meeting with Fisher "just in case there is anything that I would like to put on the record." Wale checked with King later that day to arrange for him to attend the meeting.

The day before the meeting, King approached Wale and asked whether it was really necessary for him to attend. King said, "I am very sorry, but I realized that I have a prior appointment with the Tax Department and think that it oughtn't be broken." Wale readily agreed that the appointment was important and promised that, if necessary, he would take notes. Wale assured King that the chairman would not mind.

"Well, the chairman did bloody well mind," Wale recounted later. Before the meeting with Fisher, Wale went to the chairman's office and asked whether he would like for Wale to sit in and take notes on the meeting. "No, I would prefer this meeting to be one on one," the chairman responded. The meeting lasted almost an hour, and

immediately afterward, the chairman called Wale into his office. "Where was Mr. King?" he asked as Wale took a seat. "I instructed you to have him here to take notes."

"Yes, he came to me yesterday and informed me that he had a previous engagement with the Tax Office. I told him to carry on with his meeting and that I would take any notes if you wanted. But obviously you . . ."

"This is very upsetting, Patrick. Why did you countermand my specific instructions for the secretary?"

Wale had never heard this kind of tone from the chairman, who was always scrupulously polite. "I must apologize if it seems that way. It was a genuine misunderstanding on my part. I had thought that under the circumstances he should carry on with his meeting and I could take notes."

"The circumstances were that I gave specific orders and you saw fit to ignore them. If you ever countermand my instructions again, I will call the home office to have you removed from Malaysia."

Wale left the office feeling confused and a bit angry at the chairman's behavior. It was becoming apparent that he would have to start keeping his eyes open to what was a changing situation at Peninsular.

Soon thereafter, Wale asked Fisher about what had transpired during the meeting. Although Wale had never particularly got on with Fisher, finding Fisher's style too aloof for his tastes, he was confident that Fisher was sufficiently loyal to him not to discuss things with a local chairman behind Wale's back. Fisher said, "Oh, we mostly discussed the mechanics of the merger, the pricing of the shares, and that sort of thing. I told Tan Sri Nassan that NZI believes in keeping an arm's-length relationship with our foreign offices. Said we would act as corporate advisors and assured him that we wouldn't steamroll the minority stockholders." When Wale brought up the timing of the merger and his troubles with the bureaucracy, however, he was frustrated by Fisher's lack of support.

"I'm sure you will get things moving along. You're just going to have to stop spending so much time dealing with the politics," Fisher said, smiling weakly.

Wale understood that his point was not getting through. If he had learned one thing from his 2½ years in Malaysia, it was that business *was* politics here.

THE ANNUAL PLANNING MEETING

"I guess I was fairly stunned."[4]

In the next 6 months, the two companies made some real progress toward merger. Wale met with the corporate attorneys, who calculated that at the negotiated pricing, NZI should control 76 percent of the new entity, which would afford the company similar representation on the board. However, the company planned to keep the present four-to-four ratio of NZI representatives and local board members to keep up the appearance of a joint venture.

For the moment, Wale was concerned with the annual planning meeting scheduled for the end of September. During the meeting, the managers of each of Peninsular's 12 regional branches would present their individual financial plans and their strategies, staffing, and support needs for the coming year. As Wale described it, "We would put all these into the melting pot at this workshop and then come back about a month later with a finalized plan on a countrywide basis. This was the start of that cycle—asking each territory to stand up for 15 to 20 minutes and give a rundown on their major objectives for the year, their strategies, and where their strengths and weaknesses were. Normally, it would be the practice of two or three of us at the KL office to ask probing questions of the branch manager." The managers were encouraged to try out new ideas and to question each other or Wale

about operational practices. Wale saw this open forum as serving two purposes: It encouraged branch managers to think beyond their own office's needs, and it could anticipate many of the questions that would come from the home office when budget requests were reviewed.

This year, Wale was particularly concerned about the downturn in the Malaysian economy and wanted to keep the next year's costs to a minimum. (Peninsular was projecting a small loss for the year. See Exhibit 21-4.) As he always did, Wale asked the chairman if he would like to address the meeting before morning tea. The chairman agreed and accepted Wale's offer to write a brief speech on the state of the company.

The meeting was held in the board room; the large, adjustable table was that day configured in an open square, at which sat the 12 branch managers, the corporate secretary, the technology manager, Operations Manager Tan, and Wale, and the chairman (seated next to each other). The morning started normally enough. The chairman offered his welcome to the branch managers and read Wale's opening statement. After the morning tea, Wale called the meeting to order. To his surprise, the chairman had not slipped out as he normally did but had come back to his seat next to Wale.

During the second presentation by the Sandakan branch manager, Wale interrupted to question the manager's figures:

WALE: "Mr. Pao, I'm not sure I see the basis for your staffing requirements. What are the growth projections that you are using for your figures?"

BRANCH MANAGER: "We are forecasting a 15 percent growth in sales and revenues."

WALE: "From what I have seen of your present operations, I would say that you already have the excess staffing necessary

---

[4]Interview with Patrick Wale.

New Zealand Insurance, Ltd. (NZ$millions)			
	1982	*1983*	*1984*
Revenues	630	752	805
Net Income	28	18	49

Peninsular Insurance (NZ$millions)[a]			
	1982	*1983*	*1984*	*1985(e)*
Revenues	5.6	4.9	4.8	4.2
Net Income	0.3	0.6	0.4	(0.04)

[a]Converted at NZ $1.00 = 1.17 Malaysian Ringitt.
In 1985, NZ $1.00 = US $0.468.

EXHIBIT 21-4 Financial History

to support even a 15 percent growth, which is certainly aggressive. From a cost basis, I do not see how you can justify that many more people. Do you suppose . . ."

CHAIRMAN: "Hold on, Patrick. It is very easy for you managers in the central office to look at numbers and question them. But this man is dealing with the reality of working in the field and seems to have very good reasons for his staffing numbers. You always expect these poor chaps in the branch to meet the targets, but then they never get the proper support from you. Now they cannot even get the staff they require to do their job correctly."

WALE: (After pausing for a moment) "Mr. Chairman, perhaps we should take a look at this situation after the meeting. I'm sure we can discuss this and have it sorted out very quickly."

CHAIRMAN: "The issue is certainly an important one. I believe that all of the branch managers would like clarity about the signals they are getting from the central office in Kuala Lumpur. Mr. Pao's projections seem perfectly reasonable, and I know from my long association with Peninsular Insurance that his office is one of the finest in this organization. Mr. Pao,

please continue with your excellent presentation. And Patrick, I will be happy to discuss this with yourself and Mr. Tan at the end of these proceedings."

The chairman waved his hand at Mr. Pao as a signal for him to continue. The branch manager stammered to a start and quickly moved on to a new topic.

Wale did not hear a word of it. The chairman's outburst had come as a complete shock, and Wale was trying to gather his wits and consider what his next move should be. He scanned the faces around the table as the managers quickly switched their eyes from him and back to the speaker. Tan returned his gaze with a look that was both stunned and quizzical, and Wale knew that they were thinking the same thing: "What is the old bugger up to?"

Wale was not about to stand aside. For the rest of the day, he continued to facilitate the meeting, but there was almost no free exchange of ideas from the managers from that point on. Everyone seemed to be concerned about saying something that might lead to another controversy. Meanwhile, the chairman continued to chime in, making it perfectly clear who he thought was in charge of the proceedings.

Wale wondered what his next move should be. He wondered what the chairman's next move would be. The man did have connections, and the merger was 6 months, at least, from completion. Having a retired bureaucrat who knew nothing about business attempting to run the show certainly was not going to help things along. Also, what about the other managers? Wale had never considered questioning their loyalty, but this episode put everything in a new light. ■

Case 22   Making the Tough Team Call (A)

Gudrun Dammermann-Priess was stunned after this latest round of project presentations. In the 9 years since the international management program (IMP) began, she never had a project so bad that she considered not allowing the project to go forward. With only 6 weeks until the final project deliverable in mid May 2000—a 15-minute presentation in front of 100 top executives at Continental AG, including the CEO and at least four other members of the Vorstand—the "software team project" was a potential embarrassment in a high-stakes environment.

The CEO's concluding remarks from last year's IMP-1999 echoed in her ears. "I would like all my top managers to take notice. If only your presentations were as good as those we have seen this afternoon." The IMP program had risen substantially in stature and useful strategic output over the last several years, and the risks of presenting a poor project were, for Frau Dammermann, acutely felt.

From literally the first module of IMP-2000 in November 1999 when teams were put together and matched to mentors and projects, the three members of this project were in complete disagreement about almost every aspect of the project and its development. They disagreed on what the mentor wanted them to accomplish and how they might begin to approach answering the key questions. Furthermore, even though there were some personal interest overlaps, the styles of two of the team members mixed like oil and water. Despite repeated conversations and interventions to help the team gain momentum, the team floundered and its work languished. It was painfully obvious to Frau Dammermann that the team had made little progress in the last several months.

The decision about just what to do weighed heavily on her mind. If the team went ahead and presented a poor project in May, Frau Dammermann's credibility as director of the training program and her oversight of the project work could be negatively affected. Ending the project now meant that the senior line manager who had paid DM 35,000 for this investigation had wasted his time and his money. Adding to the complexity, one of the project mentors was a senior executive at TEVES, the newly acquired subsidiary of Continental, and this was Conti-Teves's first project in the program.

If she were to intervene with the team, what would she do? Realistically, there were only 6 weeks remaining, the team was not functioning well at all, one of the members would be traveling for his regular job assignment for three of those weeks, and another team member would not even be in Germany. The remaining German team member seemed less than engaged in IMP and the project.

Frau Dammermann knew she needed to deal with the situation immediately. But how? The decision she would make had implications not only for the software team but also for the five other projects this year and any future projects in upcoming years.

UVA-0B-0705
This case was prepared by Associate Professor Lynn A. Isabella. This case was written as a basis for class discussion rather than to illustrate effective or ineffective handling of an administrative situation. Copyright © 2000 by the University of Virginia Darden School Foundation, Charlottesville, VA. All rights reserved.

CONTINENTAL AG

We make individual mobility a whole lot safer and more comfortable. As manufacturer of components, modules, and systems we are the backbone of the global automotive industry. We establish international standards and help automakers make good on the promises they've made with respect to their products.

Our Tire, ContiTech, and Automotive Systems product areas pool their high-tech potential. This broad synergistic approach provides the basis for technically and economically attractive solutions. Our goal is the development and production of promising systems in the areas of brake technology, vehicle dynamics control, tires, and energy management.

— STEPHAN KESSEL, CHAIRMAN OF THE
EXECUTIVE COMMITTEE, 2000

Continental AG had undergone significant transformation since its humble 1871 beginnings in Hanover, Germany, as a joint stock company manufacturing soft rubber products, rubberized fabrics, and solid tires for carriages and bicycles. Its earliest history was crammed with technology successes and tire firsts [e.g., first German company to manufacture pneumatic tires for bicycles (1892); world's first tire with patterned tread (1904); inventor of the detachable rim for saloon cars (1908); and processed first synthetic test tires from vulcanized specimens of synthetic rubber (1909)]. As the company evolved, Continental prided itself on its German heritage, its technological expertise, and its standing as a member of the Lower Saxony community. See the company Web site for a complete history (www.conti-online.com).

Through a series of acquisitions, Continental began to build a platform for global expansion in traditional and new markets outside Germany. In 1979, with the takeover of the European tire operations of Uniroyal, Inc., USA, and four production plants in Belgium, Germany, France, and Great Britain, Continental gained a wider base in Europe. In 1985, Continental took over tire operations of the Austrian company Semperit and acquired General Tire Incorporated of Akron, Ohio just 2 years later, giving Continental four plants in the United States and two in Mexico, as well as participation in South America, Africa, and Asia.

The takeover in 1989 to 1990 of National Tire Service Limited NTS, second-largest tire dealer network in the United Kingdom, gave Continental 400 outlets, which subsequently grew to about 3,000 retail and franchise outlets in Europe. Continental and the Portuguese company, Mabor, set up a joint venture for the production of tires in Lousado/Oporto, Portugal, in 1993, and with the takeover in 1992 of Nivis Tire, the Swedish tire manufacturer, with its Gislaved and Viking brands, Continental had a global tire portfolio.

The most major acquisition to date, however, came in 1998 when Continental bought ITT Automotive Brake and Chassis unit from ITT Industries, Incorporated, USA, for US $1.93 billion. This globally recognized auto industry partner for brakes and chassis management systems had more than 10,000 employees, many headquartered in Frankfurt. The new unit, which included 23 plants, research centers, and test tracks, was integrated into the Continental Automotive Systems Group as Continental-Teves.

Thus, by 1999 Continental AG was a global systems supplier to the automotive industry and the number four player in automotive tires. The then-current Continental organization consisted of Continental Passenger Tires, Continental Commercial Tires, Continental General Tire (the North American operations), and Continental-Teves Automotive Systems. It also operated a highly profitable division, ContiTech, which housed a conglomeration of 21 smaller businesses, with products loosely tied to rubber and rubber technology. See Exhibit 22-1 for recent financials.

INTERNATIONAL MANAGEMENT PROGRAM (IMP)

The International Management Program, known within the company as IMP, was designed for high-potential managers. The intent was to challenge these individuals with strategic projects of importance to the corporation and to observe how they handled themselves and the project itself. Sponsored and guided by a senior line manager (the mentor) with a burning strategic problem or question (the project), participants worked in cross-functional and cross-national teams to provide answers and advice. For many participants, this program provided a first business cross-cultural experience—Germans with non-Germans and vice versa, an opportunity to work in English (the corporate business language, but for only a few their native language), and a platform for broader general management skills.

Participants were carefully selected and screened from nominations by bosses, superiors, and human resources staff. Being chosen to participate was a great honor. The program had been in existence long enough to produce a string of success stories. One past participant now sat on the Vorstand, the German equivalent of the board of directors, and quite a few former participants, because of their senior management status, were now mentoring projects themselves. One participant every several years was chosen to be an assistant to the CEO, a fast-track position for heading up a business unit. For those participants who rose to the challenge, IMP could be their ticket into higher management.

IMP had a reputation of being tough. The program required participants to devote

7 months, in addition to their regular jobs, to their project. Participants were intentionally matched with projects outside their area of experience, expertise, or influence. This strategy allowed participants to learn about other parts of the corporation and gain exposure to different executives and their ideas. Every 6 to 8 weeks over the 7-month period, participants gathered for weeklong intensive modules. During these modules, they received content input of value to their project and got hands-on coaching and consultation to move the project forward.

One standing expectation of any project was the need to collect "1,000 pieces of data." In between formal modules, participants were expected to advance their project through interviews with Continental managers and/or outside customers, design and distribute questionnaires, read and decipher company reports, construct spreadsheets, formulate recommendations and implementation strategies—whatever it took to fully and completely answer the question posed by the mentor. There were also regular meetings with mentors and the expectation that each participant would keep his or her direct supervisor apprised of progress. The program ended with a final presentation, attended by the CEO, other board members, mentors, and selected senior executives, and a 3 to 5-cm-high written report, which was posted on the company's Web site and avilable on CD-ROM.

The strategic project was at the core of IMP. Projects represented demanding business or strategic issues for the company as a whole or for individual business units. Mentors of the projects agreed to pay DM 35,000, which contributed to the financial base to run IMP, in addition to all the direct expenses of the team members. Frau Dammermann estimated that on average the expenses charged back to the mentor were DM 30,000 per project. Lodging, meals and travel for participants during the weeklong modules were to be covered by participants'

Amounts in Millions of EUR	1995	1996	1997	1998	1999
Sales	5,242.0	5,333.1	5,719.4	6,743.2	9,132.2
Earnings before interest and taxes	198.2	268.0	320.4	380.3	511.3
Net income	79.4	98.4	164.5	138.2	234.7
Dividend	24.0	29.0	41.0	47.0	58.8[a]
Cash flow	378.2	416.5	490.9	567.0	849.7
Debt ratio	2.7	2.0	0.6	3.4	2.0
Capital expenditure on property, plant, and equipment	302.3	282.0	282.6	416.3	581.5
Depreciation, amortization, and write-downs[b]	282.6	311.5	306.8	395.7	576.5
Shareholders' equity	866.9	951.2	1,381.8	1,329.1	1,760.6
Equity ratio in %	25.3	27.8	35.3	19.6	23.8
Employees at year-end[c]	47,918	44,767	44,797	62,357	62,155
Share price (high) in EUR	12.0	14.6	26.0	31.9	27.0
Share price (low) in EUR	9.6	10.4	14.1	16.8	18.0

EBIT by Division

in % of sales	1998	1999
Automotive Systems	−0.8	2.3
thereof Teves before Goodwill	5.5	6.3
Passenger Car Tires (EU)	10.1	10.6
Commercial Vehicle Tires (EU)	6.5	5.4
Continental General Tire	5.1	4.9
ContiTech	4.6	7.6
Consolidated EBIT	5.6	5.6

ROCE by Division

in %	1998	1999
Continental Automotive Systems	−0.2	2.7
thereof Teves before goodwill	3.8	17.7
Passenger Car Tires (EU)	16.1	17.7
Commercial Vehicle Tires (EU)	8.6	7.2
Continental General Tire	5.9	5.7
ContiTech	9.8	15.7
Consolidated ROCE	5.6	6.9

[a]Subject to the approval of the Annual Shareholders' Meeting on May 19, 2000.
[b]Excluding write-downs of investments.
[c]Excluding trainees.

EXHIBIT 22-1   **Continental AG: Recent Financial Performance and Company Statistics**

home departments. Five off-site modules, including travel, room, and board, were not insignificant expenses.

Strategic projects were much like consulting projects. Most projects were rarely scoped out cleanly by the mentors. In fact, much of a team's work over the course of the first several months was to specifically identify what question(s) were to be addressed by the project, balancing what the mentor said he or she wanted with what the mentor needed. In a number of cases, part of the team's work was to convince their mentor(s) that the scope of the project needed to be altered or expanded.

In 1997, the lead internal sponsor, Gudrun Dammermann, invited two faculty members from a leading Eastern business school to work as cofacilitators in IMP. It was hoped that the academics would bring business content expertise, classroom facilitation skills, and an international business perspective to an already-strong program design. Working together, the academic facilitators and Continental consultants crafted a tightly constructed, "just-in-time" program, integrating content inputs with where the project would be in its evolution.

Continental had every reason to feel proud of this program. The program now attracted much more strategic and complex problems, and the results offered the company significant opportunities. For example, just recently ContiTech and Otis Elevator, a subsidiary of United Technologies, announced an alliance that brought the most significant technological innovation in 150 years to the elevator industry. That alliance began as the "lifting belt project," in which three IMP-1997 participants explored how to utilize Conti's conveyor belt technology vertically instead of horizontally. As part of their IMP project, the "lifting belt" team explored market feasibility, assessed potential partners, and made the initial contacts with Otis. The market potential for Continental as a

result of the project-turned-alliance was a new $300 million business.

Up through 1999, all projects were connected to Continental AG in Hanover. With the acquisition of Teves from ITT and the desire to more fully integrate Teves, IMP 2000 included two projects from the Teves side of the business. Having not been members of the Conti organization until recently, Teves's managers were unfamiliar with the IMP and the benefits the program could offer. Frau Dammermann had worked hard to convince Teves's top managers that sponsoring an IMP project was a valuable activity. Frau Dammermann was well aware that the quality of any deliverable on a Conti-Teves project would most likely have post-acquisition implications. Given that the acquisition was only 18 months old, the companies and managers were still finding their optimal working relationships and synergies.

IMP 2000

Module 1

Module 1 was held in Hamlin, Germany, the week of November 13. In this first module, participants got to know each other and learn more about the IMP process and project expectations. The six projects for this year's IMP were introduced and teams of participants formed by the facilitation team (two internal Conti facilitators and two outside academics). Mentors arrived midweek to describe the projects personally, meet their project teams, and allow the teams to meet them and discuss the project. By the end of the week, teams were expected to have a written contract with their mentor on the broad project deliverables. Input sessions focused on identifying and refining the key question(s) and subquestions each project must answer.

The Software Project The title of this project, as crafted by the mentors, was

"Software—Product or Service." The project mentors, two senior managers in the automotive systems side of the business, had in mind a project that explored this notion: Was the pricing of the software embedded in brake systems possibly an independent stand-alone product or was it essentially a service that went with the hardware? See Exhibit 22-2, which lays out the questions to be tackled and the outcomes outlined by the mentors at the project's beginning.

The project question for the software project was a challenging one indeed. As automobiles and automotive systems became more complex, electronics, governed by software, played an increasingly important role. What the customer saw as a brake system was much more than the metal hardware. Sophisticated software was integral to brake system operation. Industry estimates suggested that by 2020, 40 percent of a car would be electronics and software would be the integrating core.

These IMP 2000 participants were assigned to this project:

Herr Doctor Klaus Meier: Dr. Meier was a German Ph.D. engineer (age 38), married with one child. He came to Continental in January of 1998 as marketing manager for a Czech subsidiary. His project work involved managing a staff of 12 people, finalizing projects totaling U.S.$40 million, and conducting negotiations with Eastern European stakeholders. In addition, he was associated with a key project in a newly created division of Continental in Hanover. Before Continental, Meier had worked most recently with a consulting group that specialized in training materials.

Herr Werner Winkel: Herr Winkel was a German attorney (age 32), single, specializing in alliances and partnerships. He joined Continental's Legal Department, located in the main headquarters building in Hanover, in January 1996, most often working solo and without direct reports. He had full negotiating responsibility for several key, multimillion projects of the company. After receiving his law degree in 1991 from a law school in the United States, Winkel had worked for several German companies as a negotiator, as well as for a large, New York City–based law firm.

EXHIBIT 22-2 Project Description—IMP 2000

Software: Product or Service?

Target: To develop a business concept for selling software
1. Which problems/issues have to be tackled?
   - Why does software cost money?
   - Portion of software products in passenger cars (development over time and future prognosis)
   - Substitution of hardware by software
   - Carwide system approach
   - Risk analysis
   - How is Continental Teves affected by the technology trends?
   - Which dependencies exist for an automotive supplier?
   - Customer sights and interests
   - How to earn money with software products?
2. Outcome
   - Strategies for the marketing of Continental Teves software products

Mr. John Caldwell: Caldwell was an American-born accountant (age 28) and single. He received his accounting degree from a college in southwest Virginia. He worked for Continental's U.S. operations since September 1994 as a financial analyst, project manager, and most recently accounting manager in Conti's Charlotte facility. IMP represented his first international trip and first to corporate headquarters. Before Continental, Caldwell worked as a restaurant manager.

Key Module 1 Interactions The project did not get off to the smoothest start. The following interactions were indicative of the team's initial encounters:

- Just after the teams were announced and the projects assigned, Winkel approached one of the facilitators to say that he was completely dissatisfied with his team and wanted another team or project. While his arguments were heard, he was told changing projects and teams was not possible.
- Meier and Winkel were at odds over the project direction and question. Meier wanted to take the idea into the future; Winkel wanted to literally answer the questions proposed by the mentor. Caldwell acted as a mediator, yet agreed more closely with Winkel's way of thinking.
- Winkel announced he had a 3-week vacation scheduled in Thailand, a piece of information not even known to Frau Dammermann. Because of that holiday, Winkel doubted he could put any energy into the project until February. Winkel's two team-mates were not happy.

- Toward the end of the module, each team was asked to discuss their individual answers to three questions. Those questions and each team's response are included in Exhibit 22-3.
- Winkel did not attend the historic tour of Hamlin with the rest of IMP, citing a need to catch up on his sleep. Facilitators did notice that he fell asleep most mornings in class. He also spent most of his break time reading his tourist books on Thailand.
- After meeting with their mentors, the software team classified their project as "highly unstructured." In working with their mentor, Caldwell commented that they had no problem communicating. "Our mentor is an inventor; he doesn't have a structured background."
- Teams ended the module with a brief presentation containing their current understanding of what their project was about. The Software team states that their key question is "How to achieve maximum profit with chassis control software." Their subquestion is a detailed follow-up.

Module 2

Module 2 was held December 16 to 18 in Frankfurt, Germany. This short module concentrated on priming projects for the necessary data-gathering efforts. Input sessions focused on refining the key questions and subquestions and linking those to the kinds of data needed. Data-gathering techniques were explained, and each team received individualized consultation on data-gathering techniques of relevance to their project. The teams were asked to begin the process of storyboarding the logic behind their final project.

	Meier	Winkel	Caldwell
What do I personally want to work on during IMP?	• To work on a challenging project with a focus on business. • Preferably no "Hanover" issues.	• A business project that requires me to work on a problem outside of my current field of experience.	• I want to expand my vision. I need to open my mind and explore different ways to solve problems. • I want to take advantage of the opportunity to network with others.
What skills and abilities do I bring to IMP?	• Experience working in (and with other people from) other cultures—apart from various educational skills.	• Logical thinking, experience with projects/ joint ventures. • I like to discuss with/convince people. • I like to bring things forward and act.	• Strong ability to communicate with others. • To perform different roles within a team. • My drive and commitment assure my full devotion.
What drives me crazy about working with other people?	• If people do not do their necessary homework before the teamwork starts.	• People not listening to arguments. • People dominating a process. • Being interrupted when talking/arguing.	• Unproductive meetings. • Team members not contributing.

EXHIBIT 22-3   Initial Questions to Participants

245

Key Module 2 Interactions

- The initial status presentation of the project looked similar to where the project was at the end of Module 1.
- The team did not sit with one another, and they didn't interact outside their group meetings. Caldwell has been the only team member to present so far. In fact, Caldwell seems to be the only team member who interacts with the larger IMP group during social times.
- The team assignment was to storyboard the final presentation; team repeated information the mentor gave them.
- The team asked several of the facilitators to help them. One facilitator spent an hour with the team trying to surface their differences and get them moving positively. The team appeared stuck in its way of thinking and no one individual wanted to "give in" or change or approach the situation from another's point of view. Each wanted certainty that the direction taken would be fruitful and not wasted time. Winkel did not share his view.
- At the end of the module, teams were asked to rate themselves on a 1 to 3 scale (3 being a great team). The software team gave themselves a 1. When asked to visually demonstrate the team dynamics, Caldwell stood at the front of the room, Winkel sat in his chair, and Meier stood in the back of the room, striking a "nose-in-the-air" pose.

Module 3

Module 3 was conducted on February 6 to 10, 2000, in Charlottesville, Virginia. Input in this module focused on the strategy, marketing, and financial basics participants might utilize for their projects, as well as their future career development. An additional resource of this module was the archival data research made possible at the university library. For a number of participants, this module represented a first trip to the United States.

Key Module 3 Interactions

- The team had several conversations with facilitators about what to search for in the library databases. They expressed frustration regarding what companies to benchmark or where to look. Because there did not seem to be any directly similar companies or situations, generalizing posed problems for the team. The facilitating team provided suggestions. One facilitator even conducted some sample searches.
- The team met with a marketing faculty member who told them, "You have a really interesting and extremely difficult problem. If I can help, let me know." Caldwell followed up on this offer, but scheduling even a brief phone conference proved impossible.
- While the other five project teams were working well together and engaging in sport and other outside activities, this team split apart at every opportunity. Rarely were they seen talking to each other. Rarely were they seen mixing with other participants, with the exception of Caldwell, who remained quite social with other participants.

Module 4

Module 4 was held from March 28 to 31 in Stadtoldendorf, Germany. This module focused on change and change implementation processes. It was expected that by this point in the project process, most, if not all, data had been collected and preliminary conclusions reached. Therefore, formulating recommendations and implementation strategies of those recommendations became a major module component.

Key Module 4 Interactions

- The software team was the first to present the status of their project at the beginning of the module. Caldwell discussed several interviews they had. Informal chatter among other participants suggested that the team was not far along. It was common knowledge that the team was having problems. Their loud arguments did not go unnoticed over the last 2 modules. The facilitation team noted that the presentation was identical to that given in Module 3.
- Caldwell shared with the facilitators some of the work he had done since Module 3, talking to managers at Texas Instruments and Teves (Auburn Hills) about software issues. He had also made a benchmarking contact at SAP.
- The team got ready for the "killer questions" exercise, in which other teams asked questions with the express purpose of finding the holes and weaknesses in the project.

WHAT NOW?

The software team had just finished (rather endured) the killer questions exercise. It was apparent to all, facilitators and other participants, that this project was in serious trouble.

After the participants left the room to continue to work on their projects before lunch, the facilitating team huddled with Dammermann. Clearly something needed to be done and soon.

What were the options? How would any of those options be executed? Although the facilitating team had different viewpoints on next steps, all agreed that whatever they decided needed to be done quickly and decisively—in fact, that day! ∎

Case 23   GE FANUC North America (A)

Marybeth Sullivan-Rose sat in her office just off the production floor at GE FANUC Corporation's world headquarters in Charlottesville, Virginia. As Human Resources manager, she was responsible for the company's High Involvement Work Force (HIWF) programs. This responsibility included managing the training of and relationships with the 42 HIWF teams that were on their way to becoming highly efficient and highly productive contributors to GE FANUC's bottom line.

The progress that had been made was formally recognized in October 1992 when *Industry Week* magazine named GE FANUC one of America's top 10 plants. According to *Industry Week,* the award represented "what can be accomplished when managers and employees take up the quest for continuous improvement and world-class manufacturing."

In a month, Sullivan-Rose would be taking maternity leave. When she returned, she would be in a different role at the plant. Her successor, Cheryl Platte, who had been transferred from Finance, had been working with Sullivan-Rose for the past several weeks, "learning the ropes." Sullivan-Rose was straddling a fine line: "I want Cheryl to have a clear sense of what is going on here. There are a number of reasons for HIWF. All of us in management have our own theories about this program (see Exhibit 23-1), yet I want her to draw her own conclusions about where we are."

GENERAL ELECTRIC CORPORATION (GE)

Thomas Edison's General Electric Lighting Company, which had started in Schenectady, New York, in 1868, had grown into one of the largest businesses in the world.

Few corporations are bigger (298,000 employees); none is as complex. GE makes 65-cent lightbulbs, 400,000-pound locomotives, and billion-dollar power plants. It manages more credit cards than American Express and owns more commercial aircraft than American Airlines. Of the 7 billion pounds of hamburger Americans tote home each year, 36 percent keeps fresh in GE refrigerators, and after dinner, one out of five couch potatoes tunes into GE's network, NBC.[1]

GE had always been an innovator: It was on the leading edge of management organization (Strategic Business Units (SBUs) were a GE idea); it constantly created new ways of assessing its profitability and its markets (Activity Based Costing was born at GE and market research was another GE initiative); and its products were new and bold (lighting, turbines, aircraft engines). Nevertheless, by the late 1970s the company had grown into an unwieldy behemoth whose brains were isolated from its muscles by as many as nine layers of management.

UVA-OB-0437

This case was prepared by Ted Forbes and Lynn A. Isabella, Associate Professor of Business Administration. This case was written as a basis for class discussion rather than to illustrate effective or ineffective handling of an administrative situation. Copyright © 1993 by the University of Virginia Darden School Foundation, Charlottesville, VA. All rights reserved.

[1]Thomas A. Stewart, "GE Keeps Those Ideas Coming," *Fortune,* August 12, 1991.

Bob Collins, CEO, GE FANUC North America

"We used to have a 'traditional' management here. We would put people into boxes and say 'this is your job.' In essence, we were also saying 'this is not your job.' As we became more global and found competitors we never knew we had, we had to manage differently. The rules of competition changed; we could no longer compete on just quality or delivery time. Those became given; we had to compete on price, too. That meant that productivity was key. We are careful to have everything driven by the market, so people perceive these changes as a viable reason and way to sell HIWF. HIWF is a way to cut costs. We're inventing this on the fly, but the process is inherently correct; we've done so little wrong that the process must be correct. It has been hard to link some shop-floor jobs directly to profit, but it is profit that is the bloodstream of the business. It is profit that generates cash."

Bob Wayand, senior vice president, Manufacturing

"We got into HIWF for three reasons. First, we needed something to sustain the 6 percent productivity growth we had been realizing. Second, we were just running out of time. We couldn't micromanage any longer and we needed to get those resources out there, those people, to pick up more responsibility. Third, there is nobody that knows their job better than the one who is doing it. With 35 years at GE, HIWF was a tough idea for me. Some would say I held it up for 6 months, but I wanted to be absolutely sure that we did this thing right."

Tim Smith, plant manager

"I enjoy seeing changes. It is easy to ask someone a question and stand there and wait for an answer. They don't always like it, but I am trying to get people to think. We are really trying to empower people here. For example, I am not aware of a single request for tools or process improvement that has been turned down. It is so rewarding to see people having excellent conversations; they are focusing on positive things and getting them done. And I just walk away from those conversations feeling really good."

Donald C. Borwhat, senior vice president, Human Resources

"From a performance standpoint, GE FANUC was strengthened by our efforts to empower our workforce through HIWF. The process was designed to maximize inputs from our production associates and to put management in the role of enablers—counseling teams, eliminating barriers, and encouraging them to win and be successful in their intellectual efforts. HIWF is designed to draw our production associates into the decision process via problem solving. Continual improvement of our manufacturing processes is our main focus. HIWF's goal is to continue to improve GE FANUC's productivity and allow us to compete in a new, ever-changing world economy."

Marybeth Sullivan-Rose, manager, Human Resources

"When I present the process to customers, I use HIWF as a selling tool. I tell them that what is in it for them is less cost. Why do we do HIWF? It is the right thing to do for people, but let's also be realistic, we do this to make ourselves better and we do it to make the customer better.'"

EXHIBIT 23-1   Management Perspectives

In 1981, Jack Welch became GE's chief executive officer (CEO). His strategy for the increasingly global arena of the 1980s was simple and straightforward. GE would only be in businesses that were number one or two in their markets and that could win in an increasingly competitive global environment. Those that could not succeed would be fixed, closed, or sold. As a result, Welch led the divestiture of $10 billion in assets and acquired $19 billion in new, world-class businesses. GE consolidated 350 product lines and business units into 13 key business areas (Aerospace, Aircraft Engines, Appliances,

Financial Services, Industrial and Power Systems, Lighting, Medical Systems, NBC, Plastics, Communications and Services, Electrical Distribution and Control, Motors, and Transportation Systems). Twenty-nine pay levels were compressed into five broad bands, and 100,000 jobs were eliminated. The results were impressive. Market capitalization increased by 450 percent and, by 1990, sales had reached $58 billion with a net profit of $4.3 billion.

THE FACTORY-AUTOMATION PRODUCTS DIVISION

A key aspect of Welch's strategic vision during the early 1980s was a future in which factories would be heavily automated. As part of a campaign to grow GE's "high-tech" reputation, Welch assembled the company's best resources and people and invested $500 million to start a new division in Charlottesville, Virginia. Welch viewed the Factory-Automation Products division as a complete source for the robots, controllers, software, motors, sensors, and other machinery that would drive the "factory of the future." This division aimed to overtake FANUC, the Japanese company that dominated the world ($1 billion in sales) in industrial robotics and machine-tool controllers.

For a variety of reasons, Welch's ambitious goals did not pan out. Robots proved to be more difficult to incorporate into existing plants than anyone had thought. Even the simplest robot had to be custom fitted for each client's needs. In addition, the recession of the early 1980s had depressed capital expenditures. By 1985, GE had lost $200 million in Charlottesville and had gained little, if any, ground on FANUC. The Charlottesville plant was in disarray; morale was low, and a constant parade of executives had failed to turn the business around. The global market for robotic production never materialized, and American machine-tool manufacturers were rapidly losing ground to Japan, where more efficient, flexible, and price-competitive machines were being made. In 1987, Welch chose a new strategy.

GE FANUC JOINT VENTURE

Today the factory of the future looks different than Welch's 1981 vision of it. Robots have not replaced humans, but automated technology is a critical component of every manufacturing process. The machine tools, lathes, and presses used to punch, drill, cut, mill, and form raw materials into salable products are now directed by combinations of small computers and software programs that drastically reduce variability and increase efficiency. The "brain and nervous system" of the tool is a Programmable Logic Controller (PLC) or a Custom Numerical Controller (CNC). General Electric and FANUC have made both. In 1987, the leading-edge work on CNCs was being done by FANUC in Japan; the leading-edge work on PLCs was being done by GE in the United States.

In January 1987, Jack Welch of GE and Dr. Seiuemon Inaba, CEO of FANUC, which had formerly been GE's chief competitor, announced the creation of a joint venture known as GE FANUC. The two parties agreed to capitalize on their individual strengths; GE gave up CNCs, FANUC gave up PLCs, and the firms agreed to share their markets. Ownership of the GE FANUC holding company was split evenly; there were three divisions: GE FANUC North America, GE FANUC Europe, and FANUC-GE Asia. Operating control and size of the three divisions varied (see Exhibit 23-2).

GE FANUC North America's new CEO, Robert P. Collins, enthusiastically predicted 1987 annual sales of $250 million, a 20 percent increase over the combined product-line performance of each party in the venture. The joint venture was an exciting development that coincided with a radi-

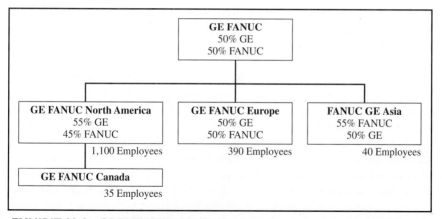

EXHIBIT 23-2   **GE FANUC Worldwide Organization: Structure, Ownership, and Size of GE FANUC Joint Venture**

cal new strategic initiative that Welch had launched at GE.

WORK-OUT

Welch conceived Work-Out on an airplane in September 1988, and it was initiated corporatewide in January 1989. Designed to get useless and unnecessary work out of the system (hence the name "Work-Out") and encourage people to work more closely together, Work-Out represented a radical assault on traditional canons of management. According to Welch's view of the 1990s, "a corporate Gulliver is doomed without the Lilliputian virtues [of] speed, simplicity, and self-confidence." Aided by outside consultants and academics, GE began to change the way business and management were conducted at its many locations, including GE FANUC. The 1989 GE Annual Report summed up Welch's vision:

Work-Out is a fluid and adaptable concept, not a "program." It generally starts as a series of regularly scheduled "town meetings" that bring together large cross sections of a business—people from manufacturing, engineering, customer service, hourly, salaried, high and lower levels—people who in their normal routines work within the boxes on their organization charts and have few dealings with one another.

The initial purpose of these meetings is simple—to remove the more egregious manifestations of bureaucracy: multiple approvals, unnecessary paperwork, excessive reports, routines, rituals. Ideas and opinions are often, at first, voiced hesitantly by people who never before had a forum—other than the water cooler—to express them. We have found that after a short time, those ideas begin to come in a torrent, especially when people see action taken on the ones already advanced.

With the desk largely cleared of bureaucratic impediments and distractions, the Work-Out sessions then begin to focus on the more challenging tasks: examining the myriad processes that make up every business, identifying the crucial ones, discarding the rest, and then finding a faster, simpler, better way of doing things. Next, the teams raise the bar of excellence by testing their improved processes against the very best from around the company and from the best companies around the world.

The individual is the fountainhead of creativity and innovation, and we are struggling to get all our people to accept the counter-cultural way. Only by releasing the energy and fire of our employees can we achieve the decisive, continuous productivity advantages that will give us the freedom to compete and win in any business anywhere on the globe.

We have seen, with the demolition of the control superstructure we once imposed on our business, and we are beginning to see even more clearly, as Work-Out starts to blossom, that controlling people doesn't motivate them. It stifles them. We've found that people perform better, even heroically, when they see that what they do every day makes a difference.

WORK-OUT AND HIWF

GE FANUC was, in many ways, a microcosm of the efforts Welch was making across the entire corporation. In Charlottesville, sharp distinctions existed between management and workers, and this situation led to an atmosphere of mistrust and suspicion. Mounds of paperwork and Byzantine mazes of approval processes were necessary to get things done and were overseen by a bloated middle-management layer. The initial reaction to Work-Out at GE FANUC was less than enthusiastic. Many viewed it as just another management initiative that would run its course and go away.

At the end of the initial Work-Out process, the workforce had identified more than 200 projects that, when completed, would reduce unnecessary work and contribute to the corporate goals of speed, simplicity, and self-confidence. By 1990, Work-Out was finished, and by 1991, most of the projects were completed.

Donald C. Borwhat, senior vice president of Human Resources at GE FANUC, recalls:

We had built up tremendous momentum with Work-Out. We had gained a new level of trust with the workforce. The real challenge was what to do with all of it. We had already been thinking about some kind of work-team idea—self-directed, high involvement, and so on but we didn't know how to do it. We kicked the idea around for several months and then decided to move on it.

The momentum was sustained through a new initiative known as the High Involvement Work Force (HIWF).

THE HIWF PHILOSOPHY

The HIWF goal was to create a facility that was the most efficient and productive possible and that enjoyed the best-possible quality of work life. The basic premises of HIWF were: Everyone is a potential contributor; those closest to the work influence decisions; and employees are empowered to influence results. These premises inverted the traditional organizational pyramid, where communication and decision making flowed down from the top and where upper management formulated strategies and handed them to middle managers, who in turn worked through supervisors who oversaw the workers who actually did the work.

HIWF envisioned a new workplace where employees had significant impact on their jobs; where planning was as important as production and thinking was a key part of the job; and where people were treated as professionals and were recognized, appreciated, and proud of a job well done. As a symbol of this new vision, senior management elected to extend "dress-down Fridays" throughout the workweek. CEO Bob Collins recalls, "Suits and ties implied a class distinction. We wanted to break this barrier down, because it was a real impediment to what we were trying to do."

The new HIWF culture meant a flatter organization with management as a shared function (see Exhibit 23-3). Everyone was empowered and *expected* to contribute, and the role of the manager/supervisor was one of leader and developer. Finally, the entire initiative was built on the concept of goal-directed, highly communicative, involved, and consensus-oriented teamwork.

THE HIWF ROLL OUT

GE FANUC hired a consultant to assess the company's readiness for a work-team structure. The consultant spent 2 days in Charlottesville during January 1991 interviewing key management personnel and a random cross section of hourly workers. He also spent a great deal of time surveying the work-flow process and the physical plant. A week later, he submitted a report outlining his observations and conclusions, which cited a number of factors as either conducive or detrimental to the HIWF effort (see Exhibit 23-4). Overall, however, he suggested that GE FANUC was ready. Borwhat and his team now had to design an implementation strategy.

From Borwhat's perspective, it was critical that HIWF roll out right the first time. He sent Larry Jones, a Human Resources manager and a key team member, on a tour of several production facilities that were using work teams. Jones benchmarked the best practices at these plants and brought them back to Charlottesville. Realizing that the pace of unfolding such a significant change, which would alter the entire culture, would be hard to predict, Jones outlined an ambitious time line for implementation of HIWF (see Exhibit 23-5). Jones remembers, "We were really shooting from the hip on this; Collins thought it would take 6 months, Borwhat said a year, and I thought several (years)."

EXHIBIT 23-3   GE FANUC Merger Organization Chart Inverted Pyramid

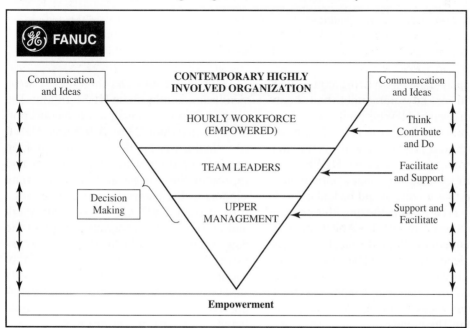

Factors That May Help HIWF Rollout

- Top management support
- Steady projected business growth
- Workforce size and physical layout conducive to team interactions
- Attractive wage-and-benefits package
- Well-regarded plant manager
- Flexibility in labor costs
- Workforce desirous of greater responsibility and autonomy
- Workers motivated to do a good job
- Workforce generally satisfied with employment at GE FANUC
- Excellent training facilities

Factors That May Hinder HIWF Rollout

- Previous top-management turnover
- Mixed perceptions of the history of and motivation for the joint venture
- Uncertainty about financial-measurement status (cost center or profit center)
- Discrepancy in educational achievement
- Past history of layoffs at Charlottesville plant
- Differences among supervisory styles and uses of rewards and punishments
- Extraordinary division between technicians and "pool-grade" levels
- Strong desire to see immediate impact
- Shift in strategic focus from product to customer
- Perceived favoritism and inconsistent application of policies and procedures, especially in hiring processes
- Past negative experiences with "open communication"
- Inordinate amount of "turf building"
- Virtual absence of goals and measures
- High level of anxiety about and potential resistance to change, especially at the middle- and low-management ranks
- Concern that employee-generated process improvements could cost jobs

EXHIBIT 23-4 Consultant's Findings

By early 1991, a steering committee composed of key personnel had been formed to oversee HIWF's implementation. HIWF soon faced its first test when business conditions required layoffs at the factory. In order to allay fears that HIWF was a rubric for cost cutting, management had promised that no one would be laid off as a result of HIWF. Recognizing the critical nature of this promise, GE FANUC made a new decision. For the first time, the layoffs were made at the salaried level, rather than at the hourly level. This action proved to be a key factor in gaining the employees' trust and commitment to the HIWF goals and philosophy. The momentum was gathering.

November and December 1991 were significant months in the HIWF rollout. The Human Resource function was reconceptualized (see Exhibit 23-6). A full-time HIWF coordinator was hired to be a champion on the factory floor who could solidify and represent the process and offer real-time support to the teams. The governing structure of the HIWF teams was established, and an orientation program to explain the new systems was held for the entire workforce. Training programs were begun to acquaint the team developers (formerly supervisors) with new skills, such as meeting facilitation and group goal setting. Finally, the hourly workforce was organized

GE FANUC Automation N.A., Inc

Team Responsibilities
Time Phased Objectives

Teams Fully Responsible For				
6 Months	12 Months	18 Months	24 Months	Longer

• Establish Teams
• Everyone on a Team
• Effective Meetings
• Communications Across the Organization
• Receive Training for:
  –Meeting Skills
  –Facilitation
  –Goal Setting
  –Problem Management
	• Establish and Maintain Team Goals
	• Measure Work Performance
	• Setting/Scheduling Work Priorities
	• Identify, Analyze and Solve Problems Effectively
	• Operate in Cooperation/ Conjunction with Other Teams
	• Scheduling Personnel
		• Scheduling Overtime-Vacation, etc.
		• Interview and Hire Team Members
		• Resource Allocation (People)
		• Selecting Leadership Roles (Team Leaders)
			• Area Cost Responsibility
			• Administer Approval Authority
			• Anticipate and Compensate for Peak Work Loads
				• Peer Appraisals
				• Salary Allocation
				• Budget Achievement
				• Multi-Skilled Cross-Trained

Teams Participate in (Making a Significant Contribution)				
• Formulation of Internal Policies/ Procedures • Implement Work, Improvements & Changes — Workout	• Meeting Operating Goals of the Business • Formal Communications Programs	• Handling Discipline • Developing/Conducting Training • Staff Evaluations	• Team Design/Redesign • Investment Decisions • Research New/Improved Work Concepts (Work Simplification) • Evaluate Other Teams	• Managing the Manufacturing Process • Administer Workforce Fluctuations • Pay Delivery Redesign

(continued)

EXHIBIT 23-5   Implementation Timetable
Source: GE FANUC

into 42 teams of ten to 12 people (see Exhibit 23-7). Each team consisted of "Normal Work Units," people who now worked together in the same general area. According to Borwhat, "None of us got a whole lot of sleep those months!"

The workforce strategy was to provide a series of incremental training opportunities that would offer specific skills roughly in the sequence and time in which the groups needed them. In January 1992, to coincide with the first HIWF meetings, formal training in team-meeting skills was provided for all of Manufacturing. In February, management-skills training began. Over the period of March through September 1992,

workshops in goal setting, conflict management, and problem solving were conducted. HIWF at GE FANUC was underway.

HIWF IN ACTION

Each HIWF team met once a week for an hour. Most meetings were held in one of the many conference rooms in the HIWF area, an entire floor in a building allotted exclusively for team meetings and HIWF activities. Three roles were important to team functioning. Each team chose a team facilitator (responsible for orchestrating the meeting's agenda and facilitating the discussion), a production communicator

		1991				

FANUC

HWIF

Name	Dates	Sept.	Oct.	Nov.	Dec.
		3 10 17 24	1 8 15 22 29	5 12 19 26	3 10 17 24
Create Steering Committee	9/3/91 - 9/3/91	●			
Get Coordinator on Board	9/3/91 - 11/4/91	▬▬▬▬▬▬▬▬	▬▬▬▬▬▬▬	▬▬	
Orient Steering Committee	9/3/91 - 9/3/91	●			
Steering Committee Site Visits	9/3/91 - 10/14/91	▬▬▬▬▬	▬▬▬		
Draft Charlottesville Factbook	10/1/91 - 10/1/91		●		
Draft Comm. Plan for Change	9/11/91 - 9/11/91	●			
ID Equipment Needs Meeting Places	10/4/91 - 10/4/91		●		
Train the Trainers	11/11/91 - 11/12/91			□	
Preliminary New Org. Chart	11/13/91 - 11/13/91	▬▬▬▬▬	▬▬▬	○	
Review Org. Chart-Strong Comm.	11/13/91 - 11/13/91			○	
Review Org. Chart-Outside Group	11/13/91 - 11/26/91			▭	
Complete Comm. Plan for Change	11/15/91 - 11/15/91			○	
Complete Orientation Non-Mfg.	12/4/91 - 12/4/91				○
Complete Orientation Mfg.	12/5/91 - 12/5/91				○
Reexamine Super Roles/Titles	12/11/91 - 12/11/91				○
Final New Org. Chart	12/13/91 - 12/13/91				○
Define Measurement Areas	11/27/91 - 11/27/91			○	
Create Team Rosters/Leadership Role	12/13/91 - 12/13/91				○
Create Team Meeting Place/Time	12/20/91 - 12/20/91				○
Quantify Measurement Areas	12/27/91 - 12/27/91				○

(continued)

EXHIBIT 23-5 (continued)
Source: GE FANUC

(responsible for overseeing actual production responsibilities), and an administrative coordinator (responsible for keeping meeting notes and minutes).

In addition to these internal roles, each team was overseen by a team developer. The developers, formerly supervisors, were responsible for insuring that the teams were evolving in an effective and efficient manner. Developers were themselves members of a team that met on a weekly basis to provide support and advice to one another.

At first, HIWF was difficult for everyone involved. The team developers were specifically instructed not to interfere with the team process. People struggled with the idea of unlearning well-established work routines and replacing them with new ones. In the ensuing months, some teams picked up the process quickly, while others floundered. Sullivan-Rose became concerned that the effort was in jeopardy: "I felt like things were hitting the wall. We started off with a hands-off approach, but it became clear that we were going to have to get more involved. We had teams coming to us begging for help."

In the summer of 1992, GE FANUC instituted the "support-a-team" concept. Various employees from the salaried ranks volunteered to serve as external-support resources for all teams. Support-a-team members attended meetings and offered in-meeting and out-of-meeting advice and counsel. Moreover, the team developers were asked to take a more active role in facilitating the growth and learning of their teams.

GE FANUC

HWIF

Name	Dates	1992 Jan.				Feb.				Mar.	
		7	14	21	28	4	11	18	25	3	10
Coaching/Counseling F/Exempt	1/6/92 - 1/23/92										
Stake Driving Event HWIF/WOII	1/10/92 - 1/10/92										
Complete Charlottesville Factbook	1/10/92 - 1/10/92										
First Meeting for Teams	1/13/92 - 1/13/92										
Complete Meeting Mgmt. Training	1/13/92 - 2/21/92										
Leadership Role Trng./Clarification	1/21/92 - 1/30/92										
Pulse Check Supervisory Roles	2/4/92 - 4/24/92										
Complete Goal Setting Training	3/2/92 - 4/23/92										
Complete Conflict Mgmt. Training	3/3/92 - 11/12/92										
Complete Problem Solving Training	3/3/92 - 11/12/92										
Create App'd Plant/Team Goals	4/13/92 - 5/14/92										
Create Team Improvement Procedure	4/15/92 - 4/15/92										
More Advisor/Leader Training	6/1/92 - 6/1/92										
Create Feedback Process	6/1/92 - 6/25/92										
Blow-Time	6/1/92 - 6/25/92										
Document 1st Team Gen'd Imp	7/1/92 - 7/1/92										
Design New Employee Orientation	8/10/92 - 9/10/92										
Create Compensation Program	3/1/93 - 3/1/93										

EXHIBIT 23-5   (continued)
Source: GE FANUC

By the spring of 1993, the process was running more smoothly, and Sullivan-Rose was due to leave in April. Some teams were performing in an exemplary fashion and were even asked to make presentations to the entire workforce at the monthly operations meetings. Nevertheless, some teams were still struggling with issues that had nagged them from the start. With her maternity leave coming in just a few weeks, Sullivan-Rose felt pressed to get Cheryl Platte ready for the challenges she would soon face. Clearly, the disparity of performance among the teams was a perplexing issue. Sullivan-Rose had some ideas about what made a team perform well or poorly, but she reflected, "I think it is critical to Cheryl's success in this process for her to make her own deductions." ■

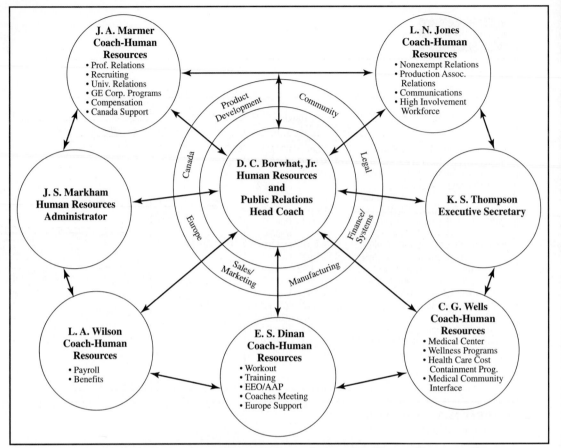

EXHIBIT 23-6 HR Organization Chart Wheel GE Fanuc Automation Human Resources Team

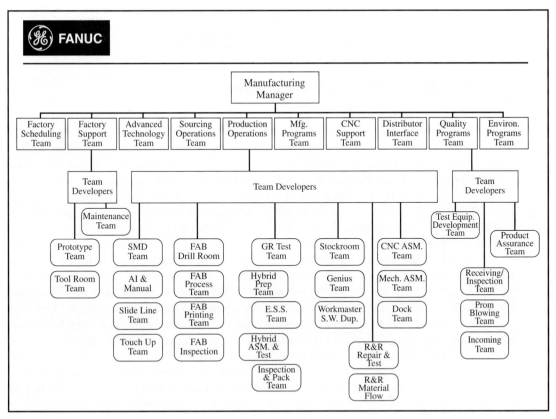

EXHIBIT 23-7   GE Fanuc Merger Organization Chart HIWF Teams

Case 24   FMC Aberdeen

Kenneth Dailey, site manager for FMC Corporation's Green River, Wyoming, facility, leaned back in his seat in the conference room near his office. He was listening to a team of employees tell him about their visit to FMC's Aberdeen, South Dakota, plant and the unusual operating procedures they had observed there. Dailey was intrigued with the results that Roger Campbell, plant manager at Aberdeen, and his predecessors had been able to achieve at the plant, and he had sent his team to see it and make recommendations about whether or not it would work at Green River. He wondered if the Aberdeen system would work for his operation as a whole, in part, or not at all; if there were parts that might work, he wondered what they were and how to implement them.

Dailey knew that his operation was different from the Aberdeen plant in a number of significant ways and that these differences would make his deliberations difficult. First, Aberdeen had only a single customer, but Green River had more than 100 and distributed its products worldwide. Second, the Aberdeen facility employed only 100 people; Green River had 1,150. Third, Aberdeen produced basically a single product, but Green River had several product lines. Fourth, Aberdeen had been a new start-up 5 years ago, and the first of the several Green River plants was begun in 1948. Dailey was supervising the start-up of three new plants in his complex this year, though,

and recognized that similarity. Fifth, the two units functioned in very different industries—Aberdeen in defense and Green River in chemicals. Finally, Aberdeen had no union, but the Green River site worked with the United Steel Workers of America.

Despite these differences, there were several features of the Aberdeen management approach that were either appealing to Dailey or suggested that the Aberdeen approach might fit his operation. Operating under FMC corporate guidelines, both management teams enjoyed, along with the other 87 FMC North American sites, considerable flexibility in how they ran their businesses. Both units also had a common link to the FMC corporate image and objectives and thus had some similar operating values and systems. Dailey also knew that productivity in the Aberdeen plant had grown dramatically since its opening and that costs had continued to drop. Finally, Dailey felt that the principles and values upon which the Aberdeen system were built aligned well with his own. As Dailey listened to his team describe the Aberdeen system, he continued making mental notes and questions about the system and its applicability to the situation in Green River.

FMC CORPORATION

FMC Corporation was a Chicago-based conglomerate with $3.4 billion in 1989 sales

UVA-OB-0385

spread over five major businesses: Industrial Chemicals ($975,000), Performance Chemicals ($566,000), Precious Metals ($190,000), Defense Systems ($900,000), and Machinery and Equipment ($783,000). The company's products included military equipment (including the Bradley Fighting Vehicle); a variety of industrial chemicals; gold and other precious metals; agricultural chemicals and a variety of specialty chemicals; and a broad range of specialized machinery and equipment for the materials-handling, petroleum, and food industries. When FMC's Naval Systems Division (NSD) won a secondary sourcing bid with the U.S. Navy to supply them with surface-ship missile-launching canisters, many factors pressed NSD management to consider a new plant to fill the contract.

Headquartered in Minneapolis, Minnesota, NSD was a large facility with more than 40 acres under factory roof and more than 3,000 employees. Its primary product was naval surface-ship gun mounts, large systems that were produced at the rate of about one per month. The smaller ($2' \times 2' \times 20'$) missile canister could be produced at the rate of about two per day and was viewed by NSD as a volume product that required a different production approach from that of the gun mounts. NSD executives also noted that because the canisters contract was a fixed-price one, the new operation was much more like a "commercial" operation than the cost-plus government contract under which NSD usually worked. Furthermore, recent investigations of the local business environments suggested that the tax regulations, community support, and available labor pools and wage rates were more favorable in nearby South Dakota than in Minnesota.

With these factors in mind, NSD's director of manufacturing, Ron Weaver, chose Bob Lancaster as the manager for a new plant. Lancaster had been plant manager in FMC's construction equipment division's Bowling Green, Kentucky, plant when Weaver had been director of manufacturing for divisional headquarters in Cedar Rapids, Iowa. While in Bowling Green, Lancaster had captured Weaver's attention with his unorthodox managerial style and ability to raise plant productivity some ten to 15 points higher than the parent Cedar Rapids facility. In the fall of 1984, Weaver and Lancaster chose Aberdeen from among many aggressive offers as the site for the new facility. Aberdeen was a town of about 30,000 people located 90 minutes flight time southwest of Minneapolis. The Aberdeen Development Corporation had offered to build a building to FMC specifications, to give FMC favorable tax status, and to assist in whatever way possible in return for the selection. FMC negotiated a 7-year lease on the new building, with options to renew annually thereafter.

Although NSD had seen the missile canisters as a natural extension of its work with other naval surface-ship weapons systems, the new product was different in many ways and surprisingly complex. First, the canisters had to be strong enough to withstand the tremendous heat and explosive force of the ignited rocket engines that propelled the missiles. A structurally failed canister could endanger the entire ship and the lives of its crew. The missiles used were powered by solid-propellant engines that, once lit, could not be shut down. If a missile failed to launch, the canister would have to contain and control the engine until it burned out. For this reason, the canisters were fitted with a controllable fire extinguisher system that could flood the entire canister.

The tubes also were fitted with launching electronics that armed the missiles' warheads and ignited the engines. The insides of the tubes were lined with a system of rails and flanges that guided the missiles out of the tubes on a straight course and allowed their folded guidance fins to extend properly. The inside of the top part of the tube also was covered with a shock-absorbing material to ease the impact on the warheads of any inadvertent bumps from loading or the rigors of sea passage. The entire canister had to be clean and relatively free of dirt to minimize the possibility of malfunction. The tubes also were fitted with an antielectromagnetic shielding system that shielded the missiles and their launch electronics from any disruptive electromagnetic force. The top of the canister had to have carefully designed, tearable membranes to keep the tube clean and yet allow free and easy passage once the missile was ignited.

Also, amid the extremely corrosive conditions of sea life, the canisters had to be completely rust proof. Pinpoint-sized holes in the rust-proofing paint on the canisters would begin to run and wear through in as little as 2 weeks at sea. The canisters were designed and built to fit in eight-tube modules in large holes in the decks of missile cruisers and frigates. Consequently, they also had to have armored, watertight, and carefully synchronized sections of decking with a hatch for each tube to be secured in place after the loaded tubes were lowered into the decks of the ships.

NSD also knew that modifications of the present tube design were coming soon. New prototypes probably would include stronger structural components, heat-sensitive and flame-retardant paint materials that would immediately well to 32 times their normal size in case of a fire, and more sophisticated electronics subassemblies. Consequently, if the new facility were to survive, it would have to have the capacity of responding to and contributing to these new designs as they came along.

BOB LANCASTER

Lancaster was known throughout FMC as something of a maverick. As the plant manager at Bowling Green, he had tried several new approaches to management, most of which were based on principles of participative management, trust of production workers, and respect for the individual. One Lancaster story originated when he worked where they built cranes in Bowling Green. One young man from a poor family came and asked for the blueprints to the company's crane. He said he was going to build a scale model, sell it, and then go to college. Lancaster gave him the blueprints. Several months later, the boy returned with a remarkable working scale model of the crane. Lancaster asked him how much it was worth. The boy said $5,000. Lancaster paid him $20,000 and installed it in front of the office building as a marketing tool. The divisional controller expressed serious concern with Lancaster's action. Lancaster persisted, though, knowing that he was paying for the boy's college education.

Stories like this about Lancaster circulated through the company. One time, Lancaster had told his employees that they knew what needed to be done and he expected them to do that without bothering him. If they needed something they couldn't get, he remarked offhandedly, then steal it. The next morning as Lancaster arrived in his office, he noticed that his water cooler was gone; he later found it in the welding bay. Recognizing this as a test of his commitment to his ideas, he left the cooler where it was and did without himself. Another time, Lancaster had a customer who was complaining about late delivery of parts. When another order for a small part came in, Lancaster had a parachutist carry the part and jump into the customer's backyard. Then he called to see if that was fast enough service. Once he had been pressing divisional leadership for a new, retractable factory door that would accelerate the flow of materials. The division had balked at the cost and refused. Lancaster then began encouraging an employee to drive his forklift truck through the wall, saying that it was the only way they could get through the bureaucracy. At first, the employee resisted but finally gave in and destroyed the wall in question. Lancaster got his retractable door.

Roger Campbell, the first quality manager at Aberdeen and later plant manager, explained one of Lancaster's central beliefs:

> He had a saying, "What's the worst they can do to me?" And then he'd sit and tell you the worst. "The worst they could do is kill me, right? And as long as I'm OK with dying, I'm OK. I've made my peace with dying. What is it that's gonna stop me?"

In his negotiations with Ron Weaver, Lancaster had said that at Aberdeen he wanted to build a participative-management system on the principle of trust, involving self-directing work teams that would eliminate fear from among all employees. In January 1985, Lancaster began to assemble a team to build and manage the new plant. He wanted people who were open to new ideas, who had a history of participative-management interests, who were dedicated to serving the customer, and who were not only willing but eager to create something new—something outside the mainstream of current management practice. He chose five men, four of whom had grown up in the South Dakota area and who therefore wanted to live in the Aberdeen area for more than professional reasons. During this recruitment period, Lancaster also began to formulate the basic principles that would govern the new plant. He printed these up for all to read and to use in training his new team (see Exhibit 24-1).

Lancaster's desire to create a new management system at Aberdeen presented something of a problem for the plant's only customer, the U.S. Navy. Navy contracts required adherence to MIL-Q-9858, which specified inspection systems, supervision, and other quality-control processes that would not be manifestly visible at Aberdeen. Roger Campbell explained that:

Bob Lancaster was a master at sitting down with other human beings and talking about what it is that's important and what isn't. He spent a lot of time with the local NAVPRO [U.S. Navy purchasing department] folks telling them that he considered them his customer, and that he was going to do what was necessary to make sure that he kept them satisfied with what was going on there. He convinced them that participative management and the quality standards were not mutually exclusive. He spent a lot of time doing just that. This is the "commercial mentality" we were trying to get. Commercial people are businesspeople.

Having selected his leadership team and cleared the way with the Navy, Lancaster began organizing his staff and teaching them the principles that would govern the plant. The entire organization would be built on trust of every employee: They would eliminate fear altogether; they would eliminate supervisors and foremen by organizing self-directing work teams; they would expect people to assume and exercise responsibility; they would pay everyone a salary based on their ability to contribute; and they would maintain high standards of quality and service. Lancaster began meeting with his staff every night after work in Minneapolis for extended dinner discussions about how they should organize the plant. These sessions often lasted for 3 hours and extended over a 3-month period. Out of these meetings and Lancaster's values statement, the group developed the initial concepts that were to become the Aberdeen Credo shown in Exhibit 24-2.

EMPLOYEE SELECTION

Employee selection for the Aberdeen plant became a rigorous process that focused on a 4-hour assessment-center activity. Lancaster

Robert F. Lancaster, Plant Manager
01 Jan 85

The Aberdeen plant will operate on policies and procedures that come from a foundation of "TRUST." This is in line with modern American business practices and certainly encouraged by FMC Corporation. For clarification, I quote from "Building Trust in the Workplace" by Gordon F. Shea:

> America is undergoing a social revolution as profound as its technological one. The transformation, as far-reaching as any in history, is as fundamental as the emergence of democracy and self-government, the growth of public education, or the rise of capitalism.
>
> This benign overturning is in the way people interact with one another for mutually beneficial ends. And the business community has positioned itself at the forefront of the revolution, though sometimes unknowingly.
>
> Never before have we seen such a pervasive interest in participative management, quality circles, union-management committees, work teams, quality of work life programs, and the like. At their core, each of these innovations draws on the power of mutually beneficial interaction.
>
> And this unleashing of the human potential, a great resource indeed, will continue to shape our future. Across America, individuals are increasingly searching out, informally, through their churches, schools, and institutions of higher learning, human relations skills to improve the quality of their personal, family, and organizational lives. These efforts to become more effective, to develop problem-solving skills, and to operate more productively in organizations signal a new era of human growth.
>
> How do you identify these "budding revolutionaries?" As Caesar's spies knew, when ferreting out early Christians, you note the words they use, the deeds they do, the ideas they express, the locations they frequent, and with whom they associate. From these, you can ascertain their beliefs and guiding philosophy. As with those earlier, gentle revolutionaries, many of our "new breed" have chosen the inner way and are therefore difficult to discern.

During the past 10 years with FMC, I have explored many of the concepts and practices of working together, with common goals, in an open communications environment. I have found these concepts to be much more productive than our historical "win-lose" approach, which invariably results in "lose-lose" outcomes.

Quality

Product quality is *everyone's* concern! The plant is to function with a total quality concept where each piece part is to be known to meet specification and each operation is performed in a manner known to produce the specified result. Defects (which can cause expensive rework and scrap) are to be *prevented* by focusing on process control inside the plant and vendor manufacturing techniques for buy parts.

Design Engineering, Manufacturing Engineering, Production employees, and Quality Control employees are to work as a team to identify and solve quality problems. Responsibility for documentation and follow-up of these activities rests with the Quality organization.

Customer Relations

Customers (the U.S. Navy) are not adversaries—they are the people we intend to please. We will interface openly, with integrity. We will provide *all* appropriate information in an accurate and timely manner. We will assume that the customer is the final authority on what is required and make every effort to accommodate his wishes.

(continued)

EXHIBIT 24-1   Aberdeen Plant Philosophy and Policies

Community Relations

This Plant is a corporate citizen of Aberdeen, South Dakota. It is concerned about the environment and will take appropriate action to assure its preservation. It will financially participate in community activities, and its employees will be encouraged to take active leadership roles in civic, charitable, political, social, educational, and religious activities.

Employee Relations

All employees will be on the salary payroll and will share the same benefit programs. A highly productive, disciplined work environment will be maintained. All employees will be treated fairly, thereby making Unions unnecessary.

Health and Safety

FMC is particularly concerned about the physical and mental well-being of its employees. Every employee will be asked to participate in maintaining a safe, healthy, and pleasant environment.

Cost Containment

This Plant represents a large investment by FMC Corporation as well as the city of Aberdeen. The product for this Plant was competitively bid, and future contract awards depend on our ability to remain competitive.

Opportunities for product cost reductions should be sought and cataloged so that proposals can be made at the appropriate time. Individual productivity must be maximized to reduce labor and overhead costs. All expenditures should be tested for their value added to the business.

Systems

Systems are to be kept simple! Current technology makes it possible to handle large amounts of information very efficiently. Since our plant is quite small we will emphasize the use of micro-computers using commercially available software. All personnel will need an understanding of these devices in order to effectively participate in the business.

Organization

Job titles and labor grades will be developed to accurately reflect the unique circumstances at Aberdeen. Because of the size, each job title will have a broad job description which may include the combining of functional responsibilities in nontraditional manners.

EXHIBIT 24-1   (continued)

hired a consultant to lead his team through a 2-day seminar that identified the kind of employee that would thrive in the new environment. Their underlying philosophy was that technical skills were more easily taught than personal and interpersonal skills and attitudes. Once the group had agreed on what those skills were, the consultant developed four group exercises for use in identifying those skills. The skills and attitudes targeted by the workshop were group skills, communications skills, personal skills, problem-solving skills, results orientation, and leadership skills. These were the same criteria that the company determined to use in performance evaluations.

The recruiting assessment centers typically were conducted on Saturday mornings, in which 12 applicants were divided equally into two groups, each with two assessors. As the groups worked on the various problems and tasks given them during the morning, the assessors would observe and rate each applicant on the key dimensions. Each assessor used a 1 to 7 rating scale in which 4 was the average acceptable level of that skill in that assessor's view. After each task, the assessors and applicants would rotate to

---

Quality: Everyone is responsible for quality in everything we do.

Customers: We will willingly satisfy our customer through honesty, integrity, cost, and quality.

Community: As citizens of Aberdeen, we will actively promote and participate in community activities and work to protect the environment.

Employees: Employees are treated fairly and trusted to actively participate and communicate in achieving objectives.

Health and Safety: Safety and health is everyone's responsibility to each other and must not be taken for granted.

Cost: All employees continually strive for the most productive use of labor, money, and materials to ensure our future.

Systems: Systems will be kept simple and understandable while remaining efficient and effective.

Organization: Broad jobs necessitate nontraditional, creative methods. All employees creatively define their responsibilities and work beyond job title and salary grade boundaries.

EXHIBIT 24-2   The Aberdeen Credo

give the assessors each a chance to observe all of the applicants. When the applicants had been dismissed at noon, the assessors would remain to compare notes and ratings, to generate a composite score for each applicant, and to make hiring decisions. Typically, only four of the 12 applicants would meet the assessors' minimal standards. The opportunity for assessors to review hiring criteria and values and to reach consensus on what they looked for in candidates was a significant culture-building aspect of the assessment center.

All of the exercises in the assessment center were designed to highlight aspects of group-versus-individual behavior. The goal of the first exercise was to have each and every member of the team construct a completed square from parts of squares given to each team member. The second was a survival exercise in which team members had to rank the importance of a list of items left to them in the midst of a life-and-death emergency (like being shipwrecked at sea, crash landed in the subarctic, or stranded on the moon). The third exercise was a hiring decision that had to be made by a leaderless group. Many of the "candidates" were minorities. The fourth exercise was a problem-solving situation in which each of the team members had important but disparate clues to the solutions.

By 1990, this recruiting-and-selection process had produced 100 Aberdeen employees, 74 of whom worked in production. The administration manager commented that they had 30 percent women plantwide, and about 8 percent minorities, primarily American Indians. He noted that the goal of the plant was to have 50 percent women.

TRAINING

Lancaster and his staff expected that in order to make the experiment work, employees in the facility would need to have introductory and ongoing training. They began with an orientation to the philosophy of the Aberdeen plant in which the idea that everyone was responsible for the success of the facility was presented. If this were to work, management noted, there could be no game playing and no withholding of data in plant relationships. Lancaster and his team told the new employees that they were to be included in the decision-making process and they were to be trusted with all relevant management information. Furthermore, employees were taught how to give and receive information about each other as data rather than as judgments or criticisms.

Fear of every kind, especially fear of failure, Lancaster noted, also had to be eliminated. Failure was sometimes the result of taking good risks and usually had a positive effect on learning and growth. People should not be held at risk for making honest mistakes and for learning from them. He stressed that the usefulness of any innovation was limited to the time when a better idea came along and that every employee should be seeking new innovations constantly. The management team taught that the "invented here" mentality caused people to stop looking for and accepting new solutions. They stressed that there were no job definitions in the plant and that therefore *everyone* was responsible for making top-quality canisters profitably. The management team also discussed their own willingness to share power and to include all employees in the decision-making process. Fear and trust, they said, could not survive in the same environment. People had to be free to do the right thing and to make decisions without fear of reprisal and arbitrary anger and dismissal. Lancaster knew from his previous experiences that the new employees would test these ideas before accepting them fully.

Lancaster and his staff retained a consultant from New Jersey to conduct three 9-day seminars divided into 3-day segments in topics like personal growth, accepting responsibility, interpersonal skills, nurturing fellow employees, giving clear and descriptive feedback, causation, a sense of "family" at work, and team management skills. These sessions were called "Mastery Training" and included the idea that people were perfect as they were, and therefore employees had no need to try to change others. In Mastery Training, useful feedback consisted of relating data and facts, including how one felt about those facts. The sessions were intended to point out that these ideas were not simply nice, abstract ideas, but the values upon which Aberdeen would operate. By 1990, three groups of 15 employees had been through the full 9 days of Mastery Training. They had been encouraged to pass on what they had learned to those who had not yet gone. At least one employee interviewed claimed that these seminars changed her entire outlook on life and work.

In the emerging Aberdeen culture, criticism and allegation were replaced by direct feedback. Campbell explained:

> We talk about feedback being neither positive nor negative; it's only feedback. That's an important piece of what we do in the evaluation system. When you're giving somebody feedback, you're saying this isn't negative or positive; it's just feedback. For example, "I notice you were late days last week. When you were late, that caused me to work harder; I noticed I was pretty irritated about that." People talk about how this training helps them in their families. We talk about the plant being a family. As a result of being here, people should be doing better with their lives and taking more responsibility for their lives.

TEAM ORGANIZATION AND MANAGEMENT

The fundamental work unit of the Aberdeen organization was the work team. Teams ranging in size from three to 16 managed virtually every aspect of the plant's work and reporting. Teams scheduled work hours, purchased materials and tools, planned work schedules, coordinated with other teams, evaluated team members' performance, recommended salary increases, generated reports, and dealt with virtually every problem that arose in the running of the plant.

Every employee at Aberdeen was assigned to a team. A team leader was chosen by the team from among volunteers. The team decided how long team leaders would serve; this tenure varied from a few weeks to 2 or more years depending on the team leader's willingness and perceived competency. Each team also selected a supply person, a safety person, and a quality person to pay particular attention to those areas. Teams met as needed to discuss and resolve issues that confronted them. A team member of the Deck and Hatch team (responsible for assembling the decking and hatches that covered a pod of eight canisters) who had been with the company 5 years and in manufacturing environments for 19 years, commented:

We have 13 on our team now. When we have problems, we don't wait for a meeting. If our leader met with [the plant manager] about a schedule or something, he'd come back and holler, "Come on over! We need to talk for a few minutes." And we would get things ironed out right away. That really helps. We do not wait for pay evaluation time to talk. If we have problems, we take care of them right away. It is so much easier that way. If you have something on your mind that you are going to talk to this person about, go see them now. If you do, a month from now, that person might have realized what he was doing and have changed it. The problem is, if you don't get it out and talk about it, it just keeps getting worse and worse. Our people have learned that.

Each employee's work schedule at Aberdeen was administered by his or her team. One team member outlined the system:

On a normal week, our average hours are 6:00 to 4:30. We say you have to call in if you're not there by 8:00. Eight o'clock is late, but unless it really disrupts the function of another station or

another team or something, anything between 6:00 and 8:00 is OK. We work 40-hour weeks, 4 or 5 days a week. If our schedule is good, some of the teams may work four 10-hour days and then they have Friday, Saturday, and Sunday off. Then the rest of us use Friday for any kind of catch-up paperwork or updating manufacturing procedures or anything like that that has to be done. Working 50 hours a week is pretty normal out here. This year we have cut down a lot compared to the last few years. We work the overtime to insure our jobs. We'd rather work overtime than to have more people hired so that we were working an even 40 hours and then sometime in the future have a layoff. Now, we would just cut back to 40. It helps keep our jobs secure.

The plant manager added:

The interesting thing is that the teams will make it OK for people to work different hours. Mothers out here with young children are allowed to work around baby-sitting schedules. When people have baby-sitter problems or things like that, the team will figure it all out and still get the work done. I couldn't administer that. Nor could anybody else. They can administer that so much better than anything I could do.

Team leaders were an important part of the Aberdeen team organization. Donna Cwikla, a former team leader for more than 2 years, described the role:

Team leaders facilitate. If you see a problem, you call them together. If someone comes to me and says, "I have a problem," you don't solve it. You say, "OK, let's get a meeting." You keep things going if meetings get sidetracked. If they get into personal fights or just talking, the team leader has to get them back on track. Team leaders are responsible. You've got to make schedule, so you can suggest this and that. But it is up to the whole team what your schedule is, what your hours are, and what we do. Team leading is facilitating mostly.

I think the hardest thing for me [as a team leader] was to step back and stop taking responsibility. If the team failed, I would take it as if I had failed. That was really hard to get over. But once I realized that it was going to be the team's responsibility, whether I was a member or the team leader, it took a lot of the pressure off.

The importance of selecting the right kind of people to fit the system was highlighted by this team member:

One thing that works against us is people who withhold from actually involving themselves or people that just don't want that responsibility. There are very few of those people. Most people enjoy the fact that they can be responsible and take responsibilities easily. But there are a couple of people that I have worked with that said, "I don't really need this job; I don't really have to participate and be responsible; my husband has a better job and we get by, or I am just working here because xyz." That makes it hard.

The team will sit down and counsel that person, if they are like late for work, if their quality is bad, or whatever the problem may be, just their attitude, or getting along with other people. At any given time, your team or a team member can ask for an evaluation of you. If the team feels that it is necessary to have it documented and put it into your personnel file, they will bring in Sheila [human resources manager] and sit down and go around the room and say, "This is what I feel, and I don't think you are living up to what the expectations are of this place, and we either feel that you should

conform or else find another job." They are usually given a choice and a time limit to how long they think that it should take a person to come around. Usually people react fairly well. There have been a few people who have just left; they just didn't like it. And they just didn't fit in. Some people who just didn't like working indoors.

One team member talked about program innovations that teams made:

We are responsible to keep our own area clean. There for a while, it had gotten so that production was really heavy, and the people weren't caring about the way the place looked as much as what they had when I had started. I have always been kind of picky about that, because I knew how good and clean the place can look, where other people if they come in and it is halfway dirty they never realize that. So, I went out and purchased two signs that said "Cleanest Area in the Plant," one for the plant and one for the office. We rotate them on Mondays. The last team to receive it will go around, survey the plant on Monday morning before the 8:00 plant meeting, and then come in and give it to another team to keep for a week. It's an honor and lots of fun. We used to have a Pig Pen award, but the negative began to outweigh the positive. We usually concentrate heavily on the positive. Negative just shows up. You don't have to try to find it. And people bring it from other plants, other jobs, their home life, whatever. You don't have to work to make negative feelings happen.

INFORMATION

Managing at Aberdeen required individuals who were willing to share information. Campbell held plantwide meetings Monday and Thursday mornings involving all

100 employees; these meetings were a primary means of communication in the Aberdeen plant. Roger Campbell described these meetings:

[Thursdays] We talk about schedule; we talk about quality; we talk about customer questions and what's going on with the competition. About costs, about our new budget, about overtime, productivity—all those things. We talk about the contract: "Here's the contract, and here's the contract delivery requirement. Here's how we think we have to smooth this work to make this factory work and help the contract schedules. Here's how each team has to interface with each other team in order to get this flow going so that it gets through the assembly in the time it's supposed to. Here's when we are going to start ordering materials and tooling." We run that meeting as a group. Then people go off in their teams and talk about whether or not this makes sense, and can we live with this schedule, and maybe we ought to move this to there, and so on. So, when they're done, it's their schedule; it's not mine.

On Monday, we open it up; we talk about everything. We talk about the company picnic, about the fishing trip, personal sorts of things that go on. We talk about anything that anybody wants to know about—softball games and who went fishing last week. We make that a time when people get together and talk about what needs to be talked about. See, my perception is that it'll happen anyway. I'd just as soon have it done there where you aren't asked six different times to tell the story over and over. Observers who just spend a day in the plant won't see that time savings. They'll just say, "Gee, you guys spend a lot of time in meetings." Thursday's meeting is more focused toward the plant, the schedule: Who

needs help; what are we going to do about this weekend?

Two large charts in the cafeteria provided focal points for these discussions. One was a diagrammatic layout of the plant with movable stickers showing each canister's location in the manufacturing process. The second was a large table showing productivity measures for each department in the plant. Because these charts were updated weekly, anyone in the room could easily see what was going well and what needed further attention.

With regard to management information, Campbell described the custom-built Aberdeen system:

We built a customized dBase system in this plant. The neat part of it is that it fills the demands of the new government requirements, materials-handling requirements, and accounting system, including the ten key elements. We think that $200,000 systems don't do the things that ours does. We tie in and integrate shop-floor control systems with the purchasing and quality system. And we run all that off the master schedule. For $30,000. That was a part of our credo. We keep things simple.

REWARDS

The Aberdeen reward structure was unusual in a number of ways. First, all employees at the Aberdeen plant were referred to as technicians and were paid on a salary basis. Those who were production technicians also were paid overtime for any hours worked beyond 40 per week. There were no annual bonuses, no profit-sharing plans, no stock-option plans. Elaine Jensen, a team member, described one reward the teams had in addition to salary:

We do have a thing going right now where if we can keep four or five factors, including productivity, sick time, our downtime, and our absenteeism, at certain rates, we get a day off around the Fourth of July. So, it's sort of like a bonus or an incentive-type day.

The evaluation system included a continuous peer-review process. Team members were expected to give accurate and timely feedback to their team members on their work on an ongoing basis. When evaluation time came around, the team decided whether or not a team member had learned enough and contributed enough to deserve a pay increase.

QUALIFICATION STANDARDS

At Aberdeen, each team member was expected to learn all of the jobs associated with his or her team so that if one person were gone, others could fill in. This was done on a voluntary basis at a self-determined pace through a certification process. Team members who were certified on each set of tasks assigned to the team were expected to respond to requests by other team members for coaching, training, and eventual certification.

People were paid according to the number of skills, called "qualification standards," in which they were certified. Each skill had a number of points assigned to it according to the contribution it made to the plant's work. The more jobs a person could do, the more valuable he or she was as an employee and the more he or she was paid. The plant had guidelines for how long a person had to work with a particular skill before being eligible for that pay level. Overall, though, a person could move to the top of the five-step pay scale within 2 years. An outline of the pay system and the related qualification standards appears in Exhibit 24-3.

Certification for each of the qualification standards involved four basic, agreed-upon steps. First, an employee had to find a coach who was willing to teach the set of skills to him or her. Then, the aspirant would observe the certified coach perform the task to see how it was done correctly. Third, the person would perform the task under the supervision of the coach until the coach was satisfied that the person had learned the skills. Finally, the person would perform the tasks alone for subsequent review by the coach. When the coach was satisfied that the person could perform the task in the skill set independently and properly and with high quality, he or she would sign a certificate indicating that the person was "certified" in that skill set. Roger Campbell described this as "watch while I do it; do it while I watch; do it alone; follow up."

Elaine Jensen described her experience learning new skills:

> When I came out here, the only thing I knew about welding was that you weren't suppose to look at it because you would go blind. We lived on a farm, and my dad told me. I went into receiving, but I wanted to learn to weld. I worked hard on those certifications. To me, it was like going to trade school. That's what this whole shop is. People are not hired on their technical skills; they are hired on their behavioral factors. We make our salary and are still being taught a skill that we can take with us the rest of our lives. I think it is fantastic!

> Every Monday and Wednesday, we had a class, on our own time. We came out here, and we welded. They've changed that now to get more people certified because of the demand for welders. So they pay them during the regular hours now. I learned how to machine parts and to paint. Some of those skills you can take with you no matter where you go. Once you learn them, it's great.

LAYOFFS, TURNOVER, AND MORALE

There had been only two forced terminations at Aberdeen in recent history. In both

The Aberdeen FMC employee skill-based pay/evaluation system is based upon two criteria: (1) technical competence and (2) social/interpersonal skills. The employee attaining the subsequent step in pay must complete both criteria.

Technical Competence

Technical competence is demonstrated by means of a series of qualification standards. Qualification standards have their roots in the "Nuclear Navy" and are based on demonstrated skill in particular areas of plant operations. For example, an employee would have to demonstrate competence in operating a forklift (including safety and maintenance requirement), slinging, lifting, etc., to be qualified in material handling. These skills are demonstrated by a plant employee that has been identified as qualified in that particular area. Completion of a qualification standard is indicated by the qualified "signer" signing off on demonstration indicating satisfactory completion.

At the Aberdeen plant there have evolved approximately 70 qualification standards. These standards range in length from several sign-off lines to as many as 30. Each qualification standard, when complete, indicates attaining skills in a particular area of plant operation.

Generally there is a qualification standard for each work area in the plant, mandatory areas such as safety, hazardous materials, material handling, etc., and "elective" qualification standards such as Lotus, dBase, Multi-Mate, Assessing, etc.

A point value is assigned for each elective and plant work area qualification standard. This plant value is based upon complexity, skills required, and duration to complete. At the Aberdeen plant a group of Shop Technicians and Office support personnel review the standards and establish point values. This group will generally meet annually for this purpose. At that time any requirement for new standards will be established, if necessary.

The point designation is used as a basis to determine when an employee is eligible to be considered for a pay increase. At Aberdeen, the employee review group is integral to the process of determining what the point requirement is in order to be eligible to progress to the next pay level. For example, there are approximately 700 points available, 400 points required to reach the top of the pay scale (fifth step), and 40 points to be eligible for the first pay evaluation.

Social/Interpersonal Skills

Upon completion of the technical requirement the employee will petition the team he/she is working with for a pay evaluation.

In this process the team members and any plant employee that has input will evaluate the employee. All data is acceptable with certain "ground rules" being observed:

• Whatever is said with the employee out of the room must be said with the person in the room.
• Employees giving input must speak for themselves and in the first person. Example: "I notice that you are very competent in your grasp of the first station assembly requirements."
• Give straightforward feedback. Use examples to illustrate points. State facts and tell how you choose to feel about the stated action. Example: "I noticed that you were late coming back from break three times last week. That causes me to work harder to make schedule and I feel angry when that happens."
• Do not attack the human being. Follow the precept that all human beings are perfect and there may be behaviors that the person may choose to alter. Come from the position that everyone wants to work and do a good job.
• Establish eye contact.
• Keep the comments serious. Joking causes confusion about whether you mean what you say.
• Feedback is neither positive nor negative. Data given is merely data and the person may choose how he/she interprets the feedback.
• Demonstrate care and concern for the employee.

Based upon completion of technical requirements and acceptable social/interpersonal skills, the team members determine by consensus if the employee is entitled to the pay increase.

(continued)

EXHIBIT 24-3   Skill-Based Pay System

Most pay evaluations end positively. The session is training in the art of feedback and straight-forward talk. The pay increase is often secondary to the feedback session. That gets everyone on the team "flat" with each other and gives a forum to get personality and habit differences on the table before they get out of proportion. It also establishes the legitimacy of an evaluation or feedback session whenever it is required.

It will typically take 18 to 30 months for an employee to get through the five pay steps. In order to accomplish this the employee will have to pass through four of the seven teams.

A monthly point system was established for positions in the plant that did not allow for completion of qualification standards or where longer time in the job is desirable. Examples would be maintenance and the receiving area. At Aberdeen, we determined that 10 points per month for a maximum of 24 months was a norm for those positions.

The employee acceptance of this pay/evaluation system has been extraordinary. They have a stake and responsibility in the pay system and an influence in the outcome. The feedback sessions generally have a positive outcome and the employees normally are relieved to hear honest comments from their peers.

At Aberdeen, we incorporate the same evaluation system for office support and staff personnel. Employees have the opportunity to evaluate the plant manager in the same fashion as their peers.

Positions Earning Points by Month

The following positions are treated as exceptions to the Pay Progression System.

Since these team members are expected to stay in these positions for a minimum of one (1) year (and more than likely longer), they will accrue qualification points per month at the rate listed below. The maximum number of points that can be acquired by working in any of the jobs that have monthly points is 240. Once 240 points have been earned, through one or more of the jobs listed below, no additional monthly points are earned.

Points per Month	*Position*	*Team*
10	Material Coordinator	ASSY
10	Material Coordinator	CCA
10	Material Coordinator	D&H
10	Material Coordinator	WELD
10	Machining Expert	MACH
10	Maintenance	WELD
10	Maintenance	FINISH
10	Category H	CCA
10	Category D	CCA
	Total People	9

Pay Progression Criteria
First Step

- Accumulate 40 qualification points.
- Complete all mandatory qualification standards.
- Obtain team consensus in formal meeting that pay increase is warranted.
- Complete one welding certification or a soldering certification.

Note: All Shop Technicians are expected to progress to the first step in 3 to 12 months after hire. Shop Technicians will be counseled by their respective team and management if they take longer than 6 months.

(continued)

EXHIBIT 24-3 (continued)

Second Step
- Accumulate a total of 95 qualification points.
- Complete one elective qualification standard.
- Complete one weld certification and one soldering certification, or two welding certifications.
- Obtain team consensus in formal meeting that pay increase is warranted.

Note: All Shop Technicians are expected to progress to the second step in 6 to 24 months after hire. Shop Technicians will be counseled by their respective team and management if they take longer than 12 months.

Third Step
- Accumulate a total of 205 qualification points.
- Complete two weld and one solder certifications, or three welding certifications.
- Complete a total of three elective qualification standards.
- Obtain team consensus in a formal meeting that pay increase is warranted.

Note: All Shop Technicians are expected to progress to the third step in 12 to 36 months after hire. Shop Technicians will be counseled by their respective teams and management if they take longer than 18 months.

Fourth Step
- Accumulate a total of 300 qualification points.
- Complete a total of five elective qualification standards.
- Obtain team consensus in formal meeting that pay increase is warranted.

Fifth Step
- Accumulate a total of 400 qualification points.
- Complete a total of seven elective qualification standards.
- Obtain team consensus in formal meeting that pay increase is warranted.

Note: The team consensus meeting required at each pay progression step is an opportunity for the team and management representatives to give that individual feedback both positive and negative on their performance.

The individual desiring a pay increase will ask his/her team leader to schedule the meeting. At this point the team leader should check with the Human Resources Rep to see if all requirements have been met (number of points, mandatory and elective quals, certs). Schedule the meeting with Human Resources Rep and Plant Manager or designate.

The team and management representatives will meet prior to inviting the individual to join them to develop a consensus as to whether the individual should receive a pay increase based on that individual's performance and behavior.

Qualification Standard Listing

Qual #	# Points	Description	Type
10	15	Assy Station 1	A
12	10	Safe & Arm Drilling Station 2A	A
45	10	Assembly Inspection	A
54	15	Assy Station 5	A
79	0	Blue Print Assembly Mk14	A
11	15	Assy Station 2	A
42	20	Final Acceptance Test	A

(continued)

EXHIBIT 24-3 (continued)

46	10	Safe & Arm Assembly	A
78	0	Blue Print Assembly MK13	A
9	95	Totals	
48	10	Soldering Cable Conduit Assembly	C
56	15	Test and Wrap Station	C
58	10	TB2/J2/J1 Assembly	C
60	10	J3 MK14 CCA	C
62	5	Box Build-Up Mk14	C
34	5	Pre-Assemble Box MK13	C
55	5	J-1 Kit Assembly	C
57	10	W2-W3 Sub-Assembly	C
59	10	P1 MK14 CCA	C
61	5	P2 MK14 CCA	C
63	10	Final Box Assembly MK14	C
11	95	Totals	
70	15	Hatches Sub Assembly	D
72	20	D&H Assembly I	D
74	15	D&H Test	D
81	20	D&H Assembly IV	D
83	15	Elevator Door/Cyl Brack/Adjust	D
93	10	Inspection/Close Out	D
71	15	D&H Assembly II	D
73	20	D&H Assembly III	D
75	5	D&H General	D
82	10	Mechanical Sub Assembly	D
84	5	Deluge	D
11	150	Totals	

(continued)

EXHIBIT 24-3 (continued)

cases, the employee's team members concluded that the individual did not fit temperamentally with the management concepts at Aberdeen. One individual, described by several Aberdeen employees, simply wanted to be told what to do and not have to accept responsibility to find out what to do.

Turnover at the Aberdeen plant, at 5 to 10 percent annually, was not unusually high or low. Most people who left the plant did so because they did not like the independence of the working culture, because they had found better-paying work elsewhere in the country, or because they were going back home.

A team member noted:

We've had maybe 5 percent turnover since I started, I think. I think that is fair to say. I have been working on the [company] newspaper lately and, on the last three issues, I have gone back through all the people who had started out here and the people who have left, trying to track down everybody that has moved on to other things. What I have found is

Qualification Standard Listing

Qual #	*# Points*	*Description*	*Type*
16	0	Receiving	E
22	0	Plant First Aid	E
25	0	Computer-DBase III	E
29	0	General-Assessment Center	E
32	0	General-Public Relations	E
37	0	General-Group Facilitator	E
39	0	General-Consensus Building	E
98	0	Station Training Requirements	E
9	0	Gage Calibration	E
17	0	Just in Time	E
24	0	Computer-Lotus	E
26	0	Computer-Word Processor	E
30	0	General-Career Development	E
35	0	General-Group Problem Solving	E
38	0	General-Training	E
99	0	Misc	E
16	0	Totals	
7	20	Finishing-Ablative/Autoclave	F
14	15	Finishing Inspection	F
36	10	Finishing-Interior Paint	F
47	5	Finishing Receiving Inspection	F
77	0	Blue Print Finishing MK14	F
6	10	Finishing-Exterior Paint	F
8	10	Finishing-Surface Prep	F
23	10	Finishing-RTV-Baseplate	F
44	15	Flame Spraying	F
76	0	Blue Print Finishing MK13	F
10	95	Totals	
15	20	Machining Inspection	K
49	25	MK13 Machining	K
51	10	Tool Set Up	K
80	0	Blue Print Machining	K
66	55	Launcher Cable Prints	K
5	15	Deburring	K
31	20	Machining-Cincinnati	K
50	25	MK14 Machining	K
53	10	De-Grease	K
8	125	Totals	

(continued)

EXHIBIT 24-3 **(continued)**

Qual #	# Points	*Qualification Standard Listing* Description	Type
65	40	Launcher Cable Manufacturing	L
67	5	CCA & L. Cable Safety/Quality	L
68	5	CCA & L. Cable Hand Tools	L
69	5	CCA & L. Cable Automatic Tools	L
5	110	Totals	
13	0	Quality Program	M
19	0	Manufacturing-Material Handling	M
21	0	Manufacturing-Safety	M
33	0	General-Employee Orientation	M
18	0	Shop Floor Control	M
20	0	Manuf-Hazardous Material	M
28	0	General-Plant Security	M
64	0	Employee Expectations	M
8	0	Totals	
1	10	Longeron Fabrication	W
3	15	Shell Fabrication	W
27	5	Weld-General	W
41	15	Leak Check/Path Weld	W
52	15	NCI Inspection	W
2	15	Panel Fabrication	W
4	15	End Casting Welding	W
40	15	Pad Welding	W
43	15	Welding Inspection	W
9	120	Totals	

Type Codes

(E)—Elective
(M)—Mandatory
(W)—Welding
(K)—Machining
(L)—Launcher Cables
(F)—Finishing
(A)—Assembly
(D)—Deck & Hatch
(C)—Cable Conduit

Source: FMC Aberdeen internal document.

EXHIBIT 24-3 (continued)

that everybody has really done great with their lives. Everybody seems to be really happy, really content with what they have done and that leaving FMC was a good decision for them. FMC does not discourage that.

Roger Campbell also commented on turnover:

I don't want you damaged when you leave here. If it doesn't look like you fit into this organization, then it's time now for you to go find a job someplace else where you'll be happier and more comfortable. There's a lot more responsibility here than at most places. Are people going to stay here for money? No, probably not. They stay because they're in control of their lives, their destinies here. The idea of having people walk around with smiles on their faces while they're doing their job seems like it's foreign to many people. And you spend half of your life here [at work]! People at work ought to be happy.

Morale was consistently high. People commented on how much they appreciated being trusted by management; having management's help in times of need; having a management who listened to their concerns; and having control over their work environment, pace, and structure.

MANAGERIAL STYLE AND ORGANIZATIONAL CULTURE

Dailey's team noted that a key balance in self-directed systems was the amount of upper-level involvement in planning and implementing such systems. For some, this was a paradox. Mark Scherschligt, manager of administration, commented on the importance of the business leader in making a system like the one at Aberdeen work:

I truly believe that this has got to come from the guy at the top. You could pro-

nounce that, "yeah, there is no fear, everything's on trust." But if you don't act like that and *really* have a commitment to it, it won't work. It *is* a commitment. You've got to let people make mistakes. We see that when people from other FMC plants come to visit, that the guy at the top says, "yeah, I want this to happen, but I'm not willing to give up any of the power that I've got to make it happen." I see that so much when people come visit here. That's the thing that's got to be changed, that unwillingness to give up their so-called power.

Given this emphasis on the leadership of the operating officer, Dailey's team had asked Campbell about his managerial style:

I am not going to run off and fire you or take disciplinary action against you for telling me how you feel about something. Now, if they can tell me how they feel, it also follows that I get to go out and tell people how I feel about what they're doing. One of the rules we've got here, and we've got damn few of them, is you don't attack the human being. We try to run this place like a family. Once people come in here, they're OK like they are. We don't go around trying to change human beings. And what the heck, I'm too tired and too busy to go off and try something impossible like change human beings anyway. So, I'm OK with people being like they are. Once in a while, there are some things that I point out to them and ask them to consider changing.

Now, this isn't a democracy. There are certain things that we do here, and we decide as a group, as a plant, what's unacceptable behavior. I usually sit and talk to every person that gets hired here and spend some time with them. I tell them that I don't want them to lie, cheat, or steal, and I want them to understand that they're responsible for their own actions in this place. Once I get people to nod their head that they agree with that—that's about the only rule we need to put into place. Lancaster expanded it and said that you could run an entire plant based on the Ten Commandments. That's probably true, but I've got it down to you can't lie, cheat, or steal. That's what we ask people to do when they come to work here. Don't lie, cheat, or steal, and be responsible for your own behavior.

I tell them, "I want you to run this like it was your own business; I want you to help me manage it. If you know the right thing to do, by all means, do it." We give the team leaders, for instance, purchasing authority to $500. You hear horror stories about people who need six signatures to get a wrench. We tell them to go to the store and buy a wrench, and we sign the invoice when it comes through. New employees always test us on this. They'll come in without exception and ask about buying something. And I ask them, "Is it something you need for the business? Would you do this if this were your business?" If the answer to that is yes, then I ask them, "Why are you asking me about it then?"

We allow for some mistakes. We consider it a learning experience. I could tell an example about myself. We have to vacuum out these canisters about four times, and it is hard on vacuum cleaners. I came up with the idea that a sump sucker [a large machine used to clean out the sumps of oil-cooled machine tools] would work like a huge vacuum cleaner and cut the vacuuming time in half. It was a good idea in theory; however, a sump sucker doesn't work very efficiently if you don't have it in liquid. And the hoses are really bulky and hard to haul around. So, I went out and bought one of these things for $12,000, and it didn't work

well. So, I sent it back, and I took some pretty good ribbing from people. People don't walk around saying, "I wonder if I'm going to lose my job" about things like that. They don't wonder if they're going to get sat down and hear the riot act. We tolerate honest mistakes all the time here.

A variety of social activities also helped build the family culture at Aberdeen. The plant sponsored softball teams, basketball teams, fishing tournaments, and an annual all-employees meeting. Donna Cwikla explained:

They make a point of it. When the plant started, family activities were everything. They had swimming parties, roller-skating parties; the whole point wasn't how many canisters you were going to get off that week; it was: We are going to be a family. We are going to do things together. And it is still that way; that's as important as anything else.

The annual off-site all-employees meeting provided another example of employee involvement. Before 1990, these meetings were often seen by employees as boring and dry, filled as they were with overhead transparencies, charts, statistics, and long recitations of the past year's events. In 1989, the employees came to management and asked if they could plan the day. Given the chance, a team took responsibility for the entire event. They planned the day around the credo, dividing the group up into teams who made presentations and led cheers on each element in the credo. Six months later, photos of the event still hung in the main corridor of the plant and people still talked with enthusiasm about what a good experience it was.

When asked if they thought the Aberdeen system was a durable one, Dailey's team reported that Campbell expressed confidence that the Aberdeen system was well in place and that even if a more traditional, authoritarian manager were to replace him, the system would carry on. "I don't think you could change it if you wanted to. It's down the path now," he had said. He also expected that he would have some say in who the next plant manager would be and that he would try to make sure that a person with values consistent with the Aberdeen culture would be selected.

ABERDEEN STRUCTURE AND ORGANIZATION

The organizational structure at Aberdeen was simple. The plant manager had a staff of four: a quality and engineering manager, a purchasing manager, a production manager, and an administration manager. None had a secretary. One office technician answered the phones and greeted people at the front door. Campbell commented that if you wanted a letter typed, you learned how to use a word processor (listed, by the way, as one of the skills on the qualification-standards list).

It was clear at Aberdeen who the plant manager was, but the usual trappings of executive title were missing. Campbell usually wore boots, jeans, and an open-necked shirt to work. He parked in whatever slot was left open. He did have a nice, new, expensive laptop computer on his work counter in the plant manager's office, but he noted that anyone who needed it could come in and use it.

ABERDEEN AND FMC

The Aberdeen facility was a cost center for accounting purposes within FMC. Initial engineering and product designs came out of NSD in Minneapolis, as did sales and marketing support and government liaison. At the same time, Campbell noted, the plant's products were built, tested, inspected,

shipped, and invoiced from Aberdeen, so that the Navy began to look at the plant as its primary contact for the canisters. Aberdeen did not maintain its own general ledger but consolidated with NSD. In absolute terms, the Aberdeen plant was not a major contributor to FMC. FMC's defense segment was about 30 percent of overall sales, and Aberdeen's part was only 3 percent of the defense business.

The plant manager reported to two people at NSD—one a dotted-line relationship to the program director for vertical launch systems and the other a solid-line relationship to the site manager at NSD. This was a change from recent history when the Aberdeen plant manager reported directly to the vertical launch systems' program director. The plant manager was evaluated on meeting production schedule, on controlling costs, and on the quality of the product. Human resource activities for the plant were managed locally.

MANAGEMENT SUCCESSION

After 2 years, Bob Lancaster had established with great care and consistency the operating culture outlined here. At that time, he returned to NSD headquarters in Minneapolis, where he began teaching similar principles to the larger installation. Then one day, he complained to his wife of chest pains. She called an ambulance and when it arrived, accompanied her husband to the hospital. As she stepped out of the ambulance at the emergency room, she collapsed and died. Lancaster passed away 2 days later. When Lancaster had left Aberdeen, he was replaced by Jeff Bust.

JEFF BUST

From the description by those who worked for him, Bust, who graduated from the U.S. Naval Academy and had an M.B.A. from the Amos Tuck School at Dartmouth, really lived the Aberdeen philosophy. Sheila Quinn, the human resources manager, described his style:

> He would try to get you to think about things differently. He would go around to the plant and spend a lot of time just talking with folks trying to get them to see things a little differently. Jeff actually lived it. He would go out and actually work in an area. He would go out and work with the welders, and he lived there and learned how things were going by actually spending time with the teams. Even as plant manager, he would go weld. Both he and Bob would get to where they wanted to get you to go. Bob would talk about it a lot longer; Jeff wouldn't. Bob would bend your ear for 2 hours, where Jeff would take 30 minutes. Roger's more easygoing than both of them.

Elaine Jensen, a member of the Cable Conduit team, added her description:

> Jeff Bust was always in here with his worn-out, steel-toe work boots on. He always wore these shabby, shabby coveralls that we always begged him to get rid of, but he would spend more of his time, I would say he spent 60 percent of his time if not more, out on the shop floor. He would weld, he would grind, whatever awful job needed to be done, he would walk around and say, "Well, where are you having a problem in your team today?" It meant a lot to the people out on the floor, because here was the plant manager, this was the guy that was our role model, and he was coming out here. Nine times out of ten he got the real rotten jobs, the jobs that everybody would kind of leave to the last, or the dirtiest, or, you know, the heaviest. That meant a lot.

ROGER CAMPBELL

Roger Campbell became the third Aberdeen plant manager in 1988. He had received his bachelor's degree from South Dakota State University in mechanical engineering and gone to work for FMC directly out of school. He had worked in the Construction-Equipment division and observed Bob Lancaster as he managed the Bowling Green plant. When he heard that Lancaster was putting together a team to start a new plant in Aberdeen, South Dakota, he had contacted Lancaster and convinced him to let him join the team. Although he knew that Lancaster's approach was not his own style, he was intrigued by Lancaster and welcomed a chance to live near the area in which he grew up. He started out as the quality manager for Aberdeen, then went to manage production, and finally became plant manager. By 1990, he was 41 and had two children.

Campbell wasn't sure how people would describe him but offered that he was pretty easygoing about most things. The thing that made him angry was:

> Dishonesty is probably the biggest one. People not taking responsibility. And people who quit without giving me notice.

With regard to his future, Campbell mused:

> I'd like to go run another plant someplace; maybe start one up again. If I went to work in Chicago [at company headquarters], I'd probably have to get an M.B.A. before I did that. My challenge is to go find another place to work and let somebody else come in here. That's a responsibility I've got to the folks in a plant this size.
>
> If I went to another plant, I'd do the same thing I'm doing here. It would take

longer. There's a magic number in the world someplace, and I haven't found it, that says this is the optimum size of factories. Maybe it's 200, maybe it's 500, I don't know. It's not 2,000, I don't think. It's easier if you've got fewer numbers of people because you can sit everybody down in one room and talk to everybody at once. They all get the same story; they all get a chance to get out what they've got on their minds.

I came out of a traditional UAW [International Union, United Automobile, Aerospace and Agricultural Implement Workers of America] shop with the yelling and screaming, "Do it this way," and all that. It doesn't really work. If you're desperate, for a short term, you could get 10 more points out of this plant in productivity. You go around and rant and rave and scream and fight. But it doesn't last. Here we "benchmarked" the standards. We work on learning curves. We're working on a 79-percent learning curve here on decks and hatches. We think that's about 6 points better than Minneapolis was doing.

Mark Scherschligt, the manager of administration, described Roger:

I've known Roger for a long time. I knew him back in a previous life in Cedar Rapids, and he's changed a lot. Roger's changed an awful lot. He was kind of authoritarian, and he's changed into a people-type person now. In fact, when he first started, he had a lot of doubts about this philosophy and how this thing would work. Through his involvement and just working on it over time and since becoming plant manager, he's switched 180 degrees from where he was before. He really believes in it, really feels that it's important to push responsibility down to the lowest level, and he supports it all the way through. I think the swing for Roger

took a couple of years, to really sign up for it and to live it.

Elaine Jensen commented on the change in management:

I had a lot of problems dealing with the change in management. Bob was like my father. He was the man that gave me all the encouragement and support and the nurturing that my own father hadn't given me in a completely different adult life relationship. And then Jeff Bust—he was a young, highly intelligent, brother type of a guy, and when he left and Bob left, I felt really alone. A lot of the people I had started with have left. When Roger came, he was okay, but he was very traditional—up until last November, when Roger finally just kind of *got* it. He realized he was more empowered by releasing his powers than by dictating. It really empowers the people to release your power. He had no idea, I think, how powerful he really became after that.

CAREER DEVELOPMENT AT ABERDEEN

The topic of management succession stimulated Dailey to ask about career development at Aberdeen. He could see how the rotating training was a career development of sorts, but with a flat organization, there wasn't much room to move up. On the rotating assignments, the team reported on Elaine Jensen's experience:

I started out here in November 1985, right after the grand opening, doing a little bit of receiving. That was before any teams were really born. Then I became a member of the Weld team. Then I went into the Finishing team and was team leader there. Then I went into Assembly. I worked there for quite a long time, and finally into the Cable Conduit team. I am still a member of the Cable Conduit team, but I work outside of the team as a material coordinator for the cables, doing a lot of receiving of their supplies and whatnots. So, I have kind of circled the place and come back to receiving, which has changed a lot.

What about quiet people? Some people when they come into a team are quiet. But the more you get to know people, the more they come out of their shell. They do open up. They do take responsibility. On every one of the teams, we have a supplies person, a safety person, a quality person, and we have a team leader. Everybody gets a chance to take on one of those responsibilities. So, being a team member responsible for an area encourages that person to grow. I have seen massive growth in people that before would have had a real tough time just speaking in front of a group. We do that, too; we take turns. In the Thursday plantwide meeting, we take turns standing up and conducting the meeting.

VISITORS TO ABERDEEN

The unusual nature of the Aberdeen operation had, as Bob Lancaster predicted, made it something of a model to be studied by others. In fact, interest was so high that observation teams, like the one from Green River, came through at the rate of about two per month. Roger Campbell commented:

People come to visit and walk away from here a little disappointed because I don't give them a cookbook about how you do this. There is no magic to it. If you *really* believe that people want to do a good job, and that's a well-worn thing, but if you believe that and that they're intelligent, sensitive human beings, and if you just get out of their way, they'll do the job for you; then I guess it's all pretty easy.

It's the middle managers that are stopping this whole thing from going on in the whole country. They're the ones that don't understand about sharing their power. For years, you were taught: When you get promoted, you've got a little more authority. Then, the game is to go collect all the authority you can and all the power you can, and keep it. Try it the other way. Go get all the authority you can, then walk around and give it away to people, and see how it works. It's amazing how it works.

We've got folks that offer, and they've done it, to get in a car, drive to Indiana, and pick up 10 gallons of adhesive because we're out of it, and we couldn't figure out how to get it here any faster. No one told them to do that. And if you would have, they'd have thought you were crazy. They wanted to do it because that's how you get the product out of the door. They come up with stuff in this place on a monthly basis that amazes me. All this by just saying, "Now, if this was your business, what would you do?"

There are some people in the world, a few of them—two that I can think of—that came through here, that leave because they don't like this management style. They want to come in here in the morning and be told what to do, be watched, make sure they did it right, and then go home with their minds shut off. They are absolutely miserable here.

One team member who had been at Aberdeen for 5 years and working in manufacturing for 19 years before that reflected on one visiting team meeting he had participated in:

I have talked to people out of a Wyoming plant, out of an Idaho plant, out of a West Virginia plant. I have talked to people out of San Jose and all over who came here and looked at our system.

They come thinking "It ain't going to work, it ain't going to work!" and by the time they leave, they're convinced. They go out and see how happy and cheerful the people are that are working here. The best part is we are building quality product, and we are moving it fast. So they say, "Maybe this will work." By the time they leave, they have gotten an idea. And lo and behold, they get back and start talking about this to other people.

But to take it into a union? I shouldn't say it, but I got my foot in my mouth one day. I was in a meeting of some men that worked in the soda ash plant in Green River, Wyoming. I was saying to them, "I don't think I have worked in a union job before." I said, "I don't think that you could take this kind of a management system into a full-blown union shop." My team member kicked me under the table, and I told him, "I don't care. I want everybody at the table to hear it." I didn't know who they were. It was the union president.

They were opening new sections to their plant, but it was still management against workers.

Sometimes Aberdeen employees were invited elsewhere to explain the system to others. In one such trip to another FMC facility in Minneapolis, Elaine Jensen explained the plant and then fielded questions. One listener, referring to Roger Campbell's trips to Washington, said:

"Well, if you guys are so equal, why is Roger in D.C. and you're here?" They had asked me so many questions, I felt like I had really been prosecuted by noon. They were asking me all these questions, and I answered them basically as honest as I could, and when Roger came back from Washington at noon, this man asked Roger the same questions. It was as if Roger and I had sat down and had planned this all out, had it all written down, 'cause his answers were almost word for word what I had said. It was funny. And people had actually come up to me afterwards and apologized for being rude and disbelieving. I think it is a philosophy that we truly believe in. We have the credo that we have written and we work by it; we live by it. I think if you ask anybody out there [in the plant], they all know. It's a way of life; it's nothing special, we just do it. It is easy to have the same answer to come out of 20 people, because that's just the way it is. It's nothing special to us. It's a way of life.

RESULTS

The results of the Aberdeen experiment through the end of 1989 were dramatic. Productivity had been increasing steadily at a fast rate, costs had been decreasing consistently, and employee morale continued unabatedly high. Employees were learning a variety of new skills that they could use, enjoyed a variety of tasks and assignments, were listened to in all employee and team meetings, and felt and behaved as if they were colleagues with the management group.

Pride in the plant's work and in being a part of the team was high among employees. Campbell relayed one incident in which some used canisters came back to the plant for refurbishing. The Navy said that they didn't want them cleaned up, just made functional again for further test launches. The factory employees could not tolerate returning the canisters in their dirty state. Unasked, they vacuumed, scrubbed, and touched up the old canisters so that they went back looking almost as good as brand new ones. That kind of pride in quality and reputation, Campbell noted, came along with giving employees all the business data so they knew who their customers were and so that they realized they were part of the success or failure of the plant.

Campbell said he also often sent shop technicians ["hourly workers," in the usual parlance] to visit dockside at the naval yards so they could talk to the sailors and get the real story on how their canisters were performing. Campbell thought that they learned more from those conversations than from the managerial-level discussions. This policy also contributed to the high level of employee morale.

Enthusiasm for the Aberdeen way was perhaps best exemplified by this team member's comments:

I love everything about this place. It's hard for me to get that across to people; I haven't worked that many places. I am so young, but it's just when people ask me about this place, it's like I just can't tell them enough. I mean, it's the most incredible thing! I can't believe it works. I guess the hardest thing to think is it works without supervisors and stuff, but the thing I like about the plant most, I guess, is what it does for the person. Everything you get done is going to be self-motivated. I think that every person that works here, even if they didn't come in growing or self-motivated, that's the way they are going to get around here. It took me a while to realize when I first started. I was so happy to get the job, because I went from a minimum-wage job working in a jewelry store to this, and it was all completely new. I was getting a lot of money, and they trust me! I have been here a year and a half, and the money doesn't even impress me anymore. In a way, that's not why I am here. I'd give up everything; I'd give up the great benefits and everything to be able to work in a place like this.

FMC GREEN RIVER

As Ken Dailey listened to his team present the major features of the Aberdeen system, he outlined in his mind the major characteristics of the Green River facility. The large underground mine employed 400 people and produced about 5 million tons of trona ore (a mixture of bicarbonate of soda and soda ash) a year. The first plant, begun in 1948 and completed in 1953, produced about 1.3 million tons of various grades of soda ash a year. The second refining plant, completed in 1970, turned out 1.5 million tons of a single grade of soda ash; Green River also had the largest sodium tri-polyphosphate plant in the world. The power plants for the complex relied on the coal and natural gas that were abundant in the high Wyoming/Utah/Idaho basin. The refineries were organized by the steel workers' union. Dailey was supervising the construction of three new, smaller plants, one each for 60,000 tons annually of sodium bicarbonate, 30,000 tons of sodium cyanide used in refining precious metals, and 60,000 tons of caustic sodium hydroxide.

Dailey had been in Green River for 18 months. Previously, he had been an operating supervisor at another FMC chemical plant, the plant manager of FMC's coke plant, manager of the environmental compliance project at the company's Pocatello, Idaho, facility, and most recently, development director at the Alkali Division headquarters.

The Green River complex was a part of the Alkali Chemicals Division of FMC that supplied sodium-based chemicals to the detergent industry, the glass industry, and large commercial chemical plants. Each day, the complex would send out an 80- to 100-ton hopper car train full of product. Much of the bicarbonate went out in 50- or 100-pound bags. Green River sent about 10 percent of its products by truck to different railheads in an attempt to spread out its distribution costs to different railroads. For most of these products, freight composed 25 percent of the final cost. Some 25 percent of Green River's revenues came from overseas. FMC competed against Texas Gulf, General Chemical, Rhone-Poulenc, and Tenneco (owned 20 percent by Japanese interests) in these markets. Dailey believed that the market for his products was strong over the next 10 years.

Dailey had recently reorganized the facility. Historically, there had been separate managers for the mine and for the surface plants. Now, he had a manager for the soda ash business in both below-surface and surface facilities, one to oversee the three new plants under construction, and one to look after all of the services required by the plants.

Recruitment in Green River was surprisingly easy. Green River itself was a town of only about 15,000, but for the last ten openings that FMC had advertised, more than 300 applicants, from as far away as Colorado and Alaska, had applied.

Dailey thought that his management style was interactive, with a high level of trust for people; he was relatively open, was willing to pass out information, and was eager to drive decision making down into the organization. He believed that the company's ability to share information was limited by its computer systems.

Dailey thought that the union was a progressive one that still labored under old standard job descriptions. He believed he would receive their support in seeking more flexibility in applying those job descriptions. He also noted that the Green River force earning $18 per hour was the highest paid among all FMC employees. Mine productivity, too, he noted, had doubled in the last 8 years, despite a decline in the size of the workforce.

As he thought about the Aberdeen system and whether or not it would work at Green River, he wondered about the huge infrastructure already in place in Green River and did not know if he could change it quickly. He also realized that the plants, built 20 and 40 years ago, contained isolated workstations with little opportunity for groups of people to interact.

As Dailey wondered if the special characteristics of the South Dakota plant were what made it possible for the Aberdeen system to work so well, his team reported the comments of one Aberdeen team member:

I personally feel that you can do this anyplace in the country. I know we have had groups from all over the country in here. I think the biggest factor that you will find is the trust level. You can initiate trust simply by eliminating fear. When I started up here, there were only six of us technicians out here. Bob Lancaster was our plant manager, and he told us to do what we needed to do. I wasn't used to having freedom to just do whatever I wanted: If you need it, go buy it. It just amazed me, and I still had a lot of fear about that. He says, "How about if I tell you this? No matter what you do," he says, "as long as you don't perform an unsafe act toward yourself or a fellow employee, I promise you you won't lose your job. You do what you want to, you do what you need to, to get this product produced at this set time. But other than that, however you want to go about getting it done, just go do it." ■

Case 25 The Department of Work and Family Life at Marriott Corporation (A)

Donna Klein, director of the Department of Work and Family Life at Marriott Corporation, faced a major challenge in April 1989. Since the founding of the department in January, Klein had gathered considerable information regarding the work and family needs of Marriott employees. This information revealed a wide variety of concerns, such as locating adequate and affordable child care, balancing commitments to career and family, caring for elderly parents, and so on. Klein was charged with the task of designing a comprehensive set of programs that would respond to these needs. This task was complicated not only by the nature of the needs expressed by employees, but also by the sheer size of Marriott, which operated more than 3,800 units and had more than 200,000 employees representing numerous ethnicities and cultures and speaking 26 different languages. Furthermore, Marriott was a highly decentralized organization, in which unit managers made nearly all operational decisions and were held accountable primarily for generating revenues and holding down costs. Designing and delivering programs that would appeal to this diverse workforce and would be accepted and encouraged by highly autonomous unit managers would be an enormous undertaking.

COMPANY BACKGROUND

In May 1927, J. Willard and Alice S. Marriott opened a nine-seat root beer stand in Washington, D.C. With the approaching winter months, Mr. and Mrs. Marriott added hot Mexican food, prepared from recipes borrowed from a chef at the Mexican embassy. They dubbed the small restaurant the "Hot Shoppe." Over the next 10 years, the business expanded with the opening of more Hot Shoppes and the hiring of additional employees. In 1937, Mr. Marriott noticed Hot Shoppe customers buying box lunches to take on flights out of Washington's Hoover Airport and, based on this, pioneered the airline catering business. In 1939, Marriott revolutionized the food-service industry by providing food-service management to businesses and institutions. By 1941, Marriott had opened 18 Hot Shoppes, with 14 located in Washington, two in Philadelphia, and two in Baltimore. During the next 10 years, Marriott opened units at the rate of six per year, totaling more than 80 by 1952. In 1957, the company opened its first hotel, the Twin Bridges Marriott on the Virginia side of the Potomac River, which became an instant success.

In 1964, the founders' son, J. W. Marriott, Jr., was named president of the company. At

UVA-OB-0425

This case was prepared by Jeffrey R. Edwards and Colleen R. Logan. Information for this case was obtained from interviews with Marriott personnel, company documents, and published material in the public domain. Copyright © 1992 by the Darden Graduate Business School Foundation, Charlottesville, VA.

that time, Marriott Corporation consisted of 77 restaurants and four hotels, with more than 9,500 employees. In 1967, Marriott Corporation acquired the Los Angeles-based Big Boy restaurant chain, and 1 year later opened its first Roy Rogers fast-food restaurant. Marriott continued to expand, and by 1970, employment had grown to 26,000 and annual sales had exceeded $300 million. In 1972, J. W. Marriott, Jr. became chief executive officer, and by 1980, Marriott Corporation had expanded to include a workforce of 67,300, with sales of approximately $1.2 billion.

The 1980s marked a decade of accelerated growth for Marriott (see Exhibit 25-1). As of 1980, Marriott operated or franchised 65 full-service hotels with about 30,000 rooms. By the end of 1989, the hotel division consisted of 539 hotels with more than 134,000 rooms, including 208 full-service Marriott Hotels and Resorts, 140 moderately priced Courtyard hotels, 148 Residence Inns for extended stays, and 43 Fairfield Inns in the economy segment. The contract services division had also grown considerably, and by 1989, provided food-services management to 2,200 clients; custodial and housekeeping services to 550 clients; food, beverages, and associated merchandise in 52 airports and numerous travel plazas on 14 major highway systems; and living quarters and health services to senior citizens in 13 retirement communities. Total sales in 1989 were more than $7.5 billion, with 47 percent from the hotel division and the remaining 53 percent from the contract services division. The Marriott workforce exhibited similar growth, increasing to approximately 230,000 by 1989. Throughout this period of tremendous growth, Marriott consistently maintained a return on equity above 20 percent and led the lodging industry in customer service, receiving more Mobil and AAA awards than any other lodging chain.

CORPORATE CULTURE

The corporate culture at Marriott was characterized by three basic principles. The first was concern for all employees. This was exemplified by Marriott's "Guarantee of Fair Treatment" policy, an internal, decentralized means for all employees to express problems and have them resolved in a timely manner. As part of this policy, managers were expected to communicate regularly with employees; get to know their aspirations, ambitions, home life, and work motivations; and involve employees in decisions that affected them. Through this, it was believed that employees would be more motivated and enthusiastic about their jobs, happier in their work, and ultimately more effective. In addition, managers were encouraged to fulfill basic employee needs, such as providing clean uniforms and proper equipment, based on J. Willard Marriott's philosophy that if you "take good care of your employees . . . they'll take good care of the customers." Managers also were expected to develop employees who were friendly, hard working, and interested in helping others, and recognize good work with sincere, regular feedback.

The second principle characterizing Marriott's culture was hands-on management. This involved setting an example for employees, showing them the benefits of making their work a high priority. As expressed by J. Willard Marriott:

> The price of success is hard work—not just 8 hours 5 days a week, but nearly all our waking hours. At least that has been my experience. When I started, it was about 62 days and nights a week for many years. But it paid off. I set an example for others and gave many who were willing to pay the price for an opportunity to grow and have the good things in life.

Hands-on management also meant being involved in the details of the operation,

	1989	1988	1987	1986	1985	1984	1983	1982	1981	1980
Summary of Operations										
Sales	$7,536	$6,624	$5,846	$4,654	$3,611	$2,875	$2,378	$1,992	$1,448	$1,210
Earnings before interest expense and income taxes	483	448	425	357	304	236	196	163	134	121
Interest expense	185	136	90	60	76	62	63	72	52	47
Income before income taxes	298	312	335	297	228	174	133	91	82	74
Income taxes	117	123	148	139	99	74	55	35	31	30
Income from continuing operations	181	189	187	158	129	100	78	56	51	44
Net income	177	232	223	192	167	140	115	94	86	72
Cash Flow Information										
Cash from continuing operations	423	411	326	287	257	217	198	158	105	97
Proceeds from asset sales	1,390	1,016	675	365	302	204	–	184	110	71
Capital expenditures	1,368	1,359	1,053	821	911	627	462	433	317	220
Cash dividends and share repurchases	306	381	446	78	19	105	11	9	7	190
Capitalization and Returns										
Total assets	6,496	5,981	5,371	4,579	3,664	2,905	2,501	2,063	1,455	1,214
Total capital	5,080	4,689	4,248	3,562	2,861	2,331	2,008	1,635	1,168	978
Long-term debt	3,050	2,499	1,663	1,192	1,115	1,072	889	608	537	
Shareholder's equity	628	710	811	991	849	676	628	516	442	312
Return on average common shareholder's equity	23.8%	30.4%	22.2%	20.6%	22.1%	22.1%	20.0%	20.0%	23.4%	23.8%
Per Common Share and Other Data										
Earnings per common share:										
Continuing operations	1.62	1.59	1.40	1.16	.96	.74	.56	.41	.38	.32
Net income	1.58	1.95	1.67	1.40	1.24	1.04	.83	.69	.64	.52
Cash dividends declared	.25	.21	.17	.14	.11	.09	.08	.06	.05	.04
Common shareholder's equity	6.11	6.53	6.82	7.59	6.48	5.25	4.67	3.89	3.22	2.49
Market price at year-end	33.38	31.63	30.00	29.75	21.58	14.70	14.25	11.70	7.18	6.35
Common shares outstanding (in millions)	102.8	108.7	118.8	130.6	131.0	128.8	134.4	132.8	130.8	125.3
Hotel rooms:										
Total	134,349	117,789	102,893	77,730	67,034	60,873	54,986	49,432	40,419	30,169
Company-operated	109,561	94,253	81,244	64,502	55,920	50,930	45,909	41,126	33,088	23,704
Employees	229,900	229,600	210,900	194,600	154,600	120,100	109,400	109,200	81,800	67,300

Dollars in millions, except per share amounts. *Source:* Information obtained from company annual reports.

EXHIBIT 25-1   Selected Financial Data

delegating responsibility, and following up to make sure that work was performed correctly.

The third principle was an unrelenting commitment to meeting customer needs through excellence in quality, service, and hospitality. During his tenure as president, J. Willard Marriott read thousands of customer response cards and personally introduced himself to customers, asking them what they liked or disliked about their experience. J. W. Marriott, Jr. continued this tradition, visiting Marriott operations daily, meeting with employees, and talking with customers to measure their reactions to the quality of their experience. From the beginning, this commitment to the customer was part of the Marriott culture, which explicitly emphasized keeping units clean and attractive at all times, being courteous and helpful to the customer, and providing the best products possible. These efforts paid off for Marriott, resulting in customer service ratings that routinely topped the lodging and food-service industries.

THE ESTABLISHMENT OF THE DEPARTMENT OF WORK AND FAMILY LIFE

Various forces contributed to the establishment of the Department of Work and Family Life at Marriott. One force was the changing demographics in the workforce. In 1989, Secretary of Labor Elizabeth Dole reiterated the results of the Workforce 2000 report by forewarning that two thirds of the new entrants into the workforce between 1990 and the end of the century would be women. Most of these women would be of childbearing age and would bring with them a new set of personnel issues, such as the desire for child care, flexible work schedules, and parental leave. This trend was evident at Marriott, where more than half of the entire workforce and 40 percent of management were female. Lifetime expectancies were also increasing for both men and women, which would make elder care an issue for employees in coming years. Employers who were not sensitive to these issues might fail to attract and retain valuable employees.

Another force was the growing concern for work and family issues among American corporations in general. In 1989, about 20 large American corporations had established departments devoted to family concerns. By 1990, this number had doubled and included such highly visible companies as IBM, Honeywell, and Xerox. This signaled that corporations throughout the country were beginning to recognize the importance of the complex and costly relationship between work and family issues.

A third force was the growing cost to U.S. corporations of personal and family problems. These problems often caused employees to arrive late, leave early, miss work entirely, and resign during summers when children were home from school. Even while at work, employees were often preoccupied with concerns regarding their children and families, causing them to perform at suboptimal levels. It was estimated that in 1991, lost wages and productivity attributable to these problems reached $137.6 billion.

DONNA KLEIN

In January 1989, Donna Klein was asked to spearhead the newly founded Department of Work and Family Life. As director of the department, she would report to Kathleen Alexander, vice president of Personnel Services. Alexander, in turn, reported to Clifford J. Erlich, senior vice president of Human Resources and a corporate officer for Marriott. Klein was responsible for designing programs and services to deal with a broad array of work and family issues, communicating the benefits of these programs and services throughout Marriott

Corporation, and ensuring that they were effectively implemented.

Before becoming director of the Department of Work and Family Life, Klein had worked at Marriott for about 2 years as manager of training and development. Klein's background included a bachelor of arts in psychology from the University of Akron, postgraduate work in counseling psychology, and nearly 20 years experience in training, development, and other human resource management positions, mostly with the B. F. Goodrich Company in Akron, Ohio. Along with other companies in the "smokestack" industry, Goodrich had experienced major financial difficulties in the late 1970s that resulted in severe budget cuts, reductions in benefits, and massive layoffs. Following these traumatic events, Goodrich felt a need to "reinvent" itself by closely examining its remaining resources, including its employees, and developing programs to put those resources to their most effective use. Throughout this process, Klein had played a key role. To Klein, some of these issues seemed directly relevant to her current challenges of responding to the diverse work and family needs expressed by Marriott employees.

MARRIOTT EMPLOYEES VOICE THEIR CONCERNS

Soon after the department was formed, Klein organized focus group meetings in Washington, D.C., Los Angeles, and Chicago. These meetings were intended to verify anecdotal information regarding work and family needs, and to raise any other work and family issues of concern to employees. During these meetings, employees at all levels openly discussed the tough issues they faced. For example, many hourly employees described difficulties in locating adequate childcare:

It's very hard for me — very, very hard. When my husband leaves for work,

about 4:30 in the morning, I wake up and get my little ones dressed. Then I take them to my baby-sitter, who lives not too far away. She walks one to school, but I don't know what she does with the baby when she does that.

If I'm supposed to be at work at noon, I have to leave at 10 o'clock in the morning to get [my child] to the other destination. I have to take two buses, and that hurts my time a lot.

If something was to happen to one of my kids, as far as leaving them by themselves in the house, I would not come back to work because I couldn't deal with it. I'm barely dealing with it now. If something would happen, I would just quit.

One hourly employee described her 2-hour commute to and from work, which required several bus and subway transfers. Because of the complexity of these connections, she dropped off her infant son at a baby-sitter on Monday morning but could not pick him up until Friday evening:

My kid stays at the baby-sitter's home all week, because it's very hard to just pick him up when I get off in the evening . . . the only time I get a chance to see him is on the weekend . . . it's very depressing . . . it's heartbreaking.

Even when adequate child care could be located, many hourly employees reported that the price, in terms of time, finances, and stress, had stretched them to their limits. Some also worried that spending time away from their children would damage the parental bond they had tried to develop:

I'm afraid that my daughter, since she's so young and she'll be with my Mom all the time, that she's going to call her "Mom," and I'll just be the stranger next door, because I just bring her home, feed her, and put her to bed.

Hourly employees also described how balancing career and child-care concerns had placed great strain on their relationships with their spouses:

> When I was working weekends and my husband was home baby-sitting, we didn't have any lifestyle as far as a marriage, let alone a family life, was concerned. He baby-sat on his days off, and I did the same on mine. It was a struggle trying to have time for each other. I mean, what's more important, working more and having no family, or working less and having more of a family? You wonder about that.

Other hourly employees indicated that the requirements of caring for their children interfered with their chances for recognition and advancement:

> We have a program in our shop, "Employee of the Month," and none of the mothers win this because they always miss [work] at least once or twice every month because of their kids.

> If you want to go for crew chief, or shop trainer, as it's put, it's very hard, because I'd like to spend more time with my baby in his tender years, until he goes to school.

Work and family problems were not limited to hourly employees. For example, managers within the hotel and contract services divisions also raised numerous concerns. Some of these concerns, such as those involving difficulties in obtaining promotions, paralleled those of the hourly workers:

> There was a position that came up at our account that would have put me into a higher management position, but it turned out that I ended up not even going for it because there had to be, on certain days, someone working 9:30 to 6. But since I have to travel quite a bit to get to day care, which closes at 6 o'clock—when I'd still be working—I couldn't take the job.

> I've turned down positions already because the next step up for me in my position would mean shift work. But I don't think my daughter's old enough to handle me working shifts. She's 9 now, and I'll probably want to wait until she's about 15 so I'll feel safe with her being alone until 11 P.M.

> I jeopardized my career because of my children a couple of times. I mean, it was my choice and I realized that eventually I would get to where I wanted to go, but I think I put myself back a couple of years. I missed opportunities because of child life and home life—just trying to juggle it all. That was the decision I made all the time.

Other concerns expressed by managers reflected an underlying friction with hourly employees:

> I think that the hourly employee has a tendency to take off for less crucial instances than what a manager may take off. I mean, I have a staff person calling in sick saying, "My daughter's got a bad cough. I need to stay home with her." Whereas, I don't think managers have the same option to be able to just call up the district manager and say, "Hey, my daughter's got a cough. I can't be in today." It just doesn't seem to work the same way.

> We're open 24 hours a day, 7 days a week. We're never closed. And, it's like family doesn't matter. Sales is the name of the game. And I know, more than likely, come Christmas night I won't have a second shift, and I'm going to have to go, because I won't have anybody. The district managers, the regionals, all the corporate people, where are they? Home with their families.

Comments from other managers reflected the belief that family concerns were not sufficiently recognized:

> Marriott does a great job touting itself as a family oriented company, but in practice that is not the case, it's just lip service. In practice, Marriott's attitude is very much like the old army sergeant— "If the army had wanted you to have a wife, we would have issued you one." If you choose to have a family, that's your responsibility, and it's your problem. It better not affect your work, because you'll pay for it. And that's very much the attitude.
>
> When I told them I was pregnant, I asked them what the policies were at what happens from here. And they said, "Well, look at it like being sick." I said, "What do you mean?" And they go, "Well, if you have a lot of sick days, then you're OK. If you don't have a lot of sick days, then you don't get any pay." So my first thoughts were negative.

Corporate staff members also voiced numerous concerns. A number of these concerns reflected the tension created by attempting to remain dedicated to both work and family:

> When 20 people are coming in for a big Sunday meeting, you kind of feel a little bit reluctant to raise your hand and say, "I've got something planned with my kids that day, and I would rather not come."
>
> It's an internal struggle—you want to do a good job, but you're forced to make a decision between your family and your work, and yet you're very much committed to both. But I don't think that you can relieve the pressure from the family side. I mean, you can't get the kids not to be sick. The bottom line is that somebody's got to watch the kids.

Other comments seemed to reflect the view that the demands created by raising a family had not been adequately acknowledged:

> I truly feel that because I have children, it's particularly difficult at Marriott. It's a real negative thing, and they would rather see me move to another department rather than to see me move up in my department, because I'm a risk. My kids will get sick. I will miss time.
>
> You have to work twice as hard and arrange to come in on Saturdays and do other things to prove to them that you're worth keeping. And yet I feel that by not securing your job when you're out on maternity, that kind of makes you very, very vulnerable in your position.
>
> Before I went on maternity leave, I asked for a day shift opening. They said they didn't have one. And then when it was almost time to go on maternity leave, they hired a computer operator in the night shift. That means I lost my job.

Taken together, the concerns described by employees in the focus groups indicated a pervasive and fundamental conflict between the commitments of work and family. According to Klein, this confirmed what was occurring in society in general regarding the effects of work on the children of employees and what employees themselves must go through just to survive:

> For us, the *real* question is what are we doing to the next generation of children, and where does our responsibility as a company lie?

EARLY INITIATIVES OF THE DEPARTMENT OF WORK AND FAMILY LIFE

Following the focus group meetings, Klein's first step was to implement section 129 of the federal tax code. Section 129 allowed employees to deduct up to $5,000 from their annual income to apply toward child care and elder care. This not only reduced personal income taxes paid by employees, but also decreased payroll taxes paid by Marriott, creating funds that could be used to finance the operation of the department.

Klein also organized a nationwide survey of Marriott employees. The survey was intended to supplement information obtained from the focus group meetings by providing a more comprehensive assessment of work and family concerns of Marriott employees. The survey contained questions regarding the number and ages of dependents, type and cost of current child care, lateness and absenteeism due to breakdowns in child care arrangements, and related issues. A total of 1,600 randomly selected employees in Boston; Atlanta; Chicago; Washington, D.C.; and Los Angeles were surveyed, 85 percent from field locations and 15 percent from corporate headquarters in Bethesda. Of these employees, about one third were exempt and two thirds were nonexempt. About 35 percent had children under 12, 15 percent had children under 5, and 25 percent expected to have children within the next 5 years. In addition, 15 percent of the employees had dual-dependency concerns, involving both child care and elder care.

The survey generated several important findings. For example, of the employees at corporate headquarters, 51 percent reported significant difficulties in managing work and family responsibilities, as compared to 22 percent of field employees. Also, on the average,

employees with children under age 12 were absent 4 days and tardy 5 days per year due to child-related issues. Furthermore, during the previous year, nearly one third of employees with young children took 2 or more days off work when their existing child-care arrangements fell through. About 20 percent of those surveyed had left a previous employer due to work and family concerns. Finally, 58 percent indicated that they would like help from the corporation in locating adequate and affordable child care.

As Klein carefully considered the information from the focus group meetings and the employee survey, she reached six broad conclusions. First, the demands of employees' personal lives had a direct impact on job performance. Second, time appeared to be the most crucial issue in balancing work and family. Third, balancing work and family roles was of equal concern to men and women. Fourth, problems with child-care arrangements created stress among employees and limited their ability to work certain schedules and overtime hours. Fifth, elder-care concerns were on the increase. Finally, managers who were supportive of personal concerns were apparently essential to a positive working atmosphere. Based on these conclusions, Klein turned her attention to the formidable task of developing a set of programs that would meet the diverse work and family needs of Marriott employees throughout the entire corporation, as well as the mechanisms required to deliver these programs on an ongoing basis. ■

Case 26   Organizing the Comanche Program (A)

In March 1991, Bill Wesley, Martin Marietta Corporation (MMC) program manager for the Comanche light helicopter program, approached Dr. Don Kelly, the technical director for the project, and requested a start-up organizational plan for the program. All indications were that the prime contractors working with MMC, Sikorsky and Boeing, were about to receive the government contract for the next-generation light attack helicopter, so Wesley wanted a plan for development and production of the system as soon as possible.[1] This start-up plan was to give a detailed outline of the steps that the MMC Comanche team would take in order to fulfill the contract in the now-likely event that it were won. Kelly's assignment from Wesley was straightforward:

> You can assume now that MMC will get this program about May 1, so we need to know, in terms of facilities, people, and organization, how we will develop these systems and produce them. And by the way, make sure that you include concurrent engineering principles in your plan.[2]

Wesley and Kelly both knew that although the company had begun to experiment with concurrent engineering princi-

ples in some of its current programs, this would be the first effort at organizing a major program from start to finish using those principles. Both Wesley and Kelly were concerned that the effort be well planned and executed.

Martin Marietta Corporation

Martin Marietta Corporation was a diversified corporation engaged in the electronics, information management, aerospace, and energy industries. MMC's lines of business included guided missiles and space vehicles, search and navigation equipment, computer-integrated systems design, office machines, prepackaged software, space propulsion units and parts, radio and TV communications equipment, and to a lesser extent, crushed and broken limestone. The company was well known throughout the defense industry for fire control systems, night vision targeting and acquisition systems, and nap of the earth navigation systems. Given the enormous cost and danger associated with many of its products and services and the subsequent need to do things right the first time, MMC had accumulated a strong technical staff and developed a reputation for meticulous planning. In the MMC system, most managers were engineers and expected to

UVA-OB-0432

This case was written by Catherine Alexander and James G. Clawson. The case was written as a basis for class discussion rather than to illustrate effective or ineffective handling of an administrative situation. Copyright © 1992 by the University of Virginia Darden School Foundation, Charlottesville, VA. All rights reserved.

[1]Defense company program teams often worked for years on preliminary designs for systems before a government contract was awarded. In the case of the Comanche, the real need to organize to produce the systems intended for the helicopter did not come until 8 years after MMC began working on them.

[2]The Request for Proposal for the Light Helicoptor/Attack from the Department of Defense included, for the first time, a requirement that the company winning the contract use "concurrent engineering," a relatively new approach to organizing and managing product design and development.

know most of the intricate details of their programs.

Electronics, Information, and Missiles Group

Martin Marietta Electronics, Information and Missiles Group (EIMG), headquarted in Orlando, Florida, designed, developed, and produced electronic systems for precision guidance and air-defense programs, electro-optical target acquisition, designation and navigation systems, missiles and missile-launching systems, computer-based information systems for civil and military applications, simulation systems, automated equipment for high-speed mail sorting, and military ordnance. EIMG comprised four companies: Electronic Systems, Missile Systems, Information Systems, and Martin Marietta Ordnance Systems. The Light Helicopter/Attack program, dubbed Comanche, was a part of the Electronic Systems organization. The company had been successful to date and was, in the

words of one senior officer, good at "nurturing an idea into an engineering concept: "That's what we do and that's what the customer likes."

Programs like Comanche were enormous undertakings with many complex organizational and technical challenges. Department of Defense (DOD) officers would outline a capability that they would like to have in the field and then invite private contractors to suggest ways of achieving that capability. The DOD often awarded competitive developmental contracts to fund design bids from different contractors in an effort to find the best possible design. Development time on projects could take years and because of the complexity of the projects, involve many subcontractors, each working on various subsystems. A copy of a poster showing the related Comanche subcontractors appears in Exhibit 26-1. When a design was finally selected, a production contract would be awarded, and the prime contractor and related subcontractors

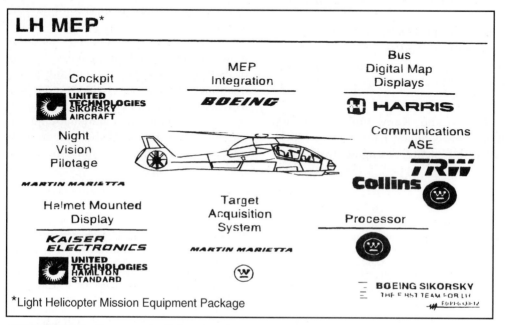

EXHIBIT 26-1   Commanche Subcontractors

would gear up to produce the design in quantity. Producers also had to support their products in field operations, often under demanding environmental conditions like severe heat, cold, or weather. Support, maintenance, and parts were a large portion of such contracts. The success of a product in the field significantly affected a contractor's reputation with DOD. The practicality of the design significantly affected the contractor's ability to make the designs at a profit.

In order to manage the huge costs associated with researching, developing, and producing systems that could meet the exacting goals of the DOD officers, defense and aerospace firms were forced to develop new organizational forms that minimized redundancies and their related costs. The matrix organization, common by 1990, was such a form. Typically, a matrix would have functional departments (like design, engineering, preproduction engineering, production, marketing, procurement, quality assurance, maintenance, etc.) on one side of the matrix and program managers with budgets to manage on the other.

THE TRADITIONAL SYSTEM DEVELOPMENT PROCESS

Until the late 1980s most defense contractors went through a common sequence in developing new systems for DOD. Doug Groseclose, director for Staffing and Development at EIMG, described the sequence of steps that a defense contractor had to work through on a typical program:

First, an idea is nurtured into an engineering concept. Then, we obtain [contractual] funding for advanced development and concept demonstration. Once the idea is shown to have potential, we receive a Request for Proposal (RFP) from the customer. The RFP will take one of two possible tracks. It could request only that a demonstration of the value of the concept be generated and proven, or

it could require the development of a prototype.

In a development or prototype program, the company just shows that the concept will work. Usually the item [at that stage] is not producible in quantities greater than one. The fundamental technology for the Comanche project had already been demonstrated with the Apache helicopter. Therefore, the new RFP required that the project's goal be to create a *manufacturable* prototype—that is, when all the individual pieces of the project [from the various subcontractors] come together, the product needs to work without significant engineering design changes, *and* be able to be mass produced.

MMC's Historical Approach

At EIMG, the process of conceiving an idea, developing a design, building and testing a prototype, and manufacturing the final product had been, for the most part, successfully accomplished within the existing framework of the group's operating procedures. EIMG, and indeed most of MMC, had for many years mirrored the strict, hierarchical, military-like organizational structure of its DOD clients (the Armed Forces). Each organizational unit had a clearly designated leader and a specified task. See Exhibit 26-2 for a typical program structure. Projects were organized in a careful, step-by-step approach that proceeded logically and sequentially through each functional group. This sequence of functions usually included technical operations, production operations, product support, product assurance, procurement, business operations, and business development and is outlined in Table 26-1. Several MMC managers termed this the "stovepipe" approach because there was little communication between the various functions at anything but the highest levels. Each function would perform its task on the project and then pass it on to the next. People assigned to a function sat

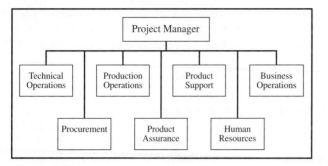

EXHIBIT 26-2   Typical Program Structure

physcially with that function despite EIMG's use of modular office furniture.

This approach had worked well for a number of years, but recently both MMC and DOD observers were increasingly concerned that the approach was not functioning as well as it could. They noted that MMC's experience with the Target Acquisition and Detection System (TADS) and Low Altitude Navigation and Targeting Infra Red system (LANTIRN) programs were examples that pointed toward a need for a better organizational approach.

TADS. MMC had experienced some problems with the Target Acquisition and Detection System developed for the Apache attack helicopter. The system was unable to meet the required technical specifications when it went into production. In essence, it was physically impossible to manufacture the system from the engineering drawings.

TABLE 26-1 Sequential Engineering Common at MMC Before Comanche	
Step	*Sequential Engineering*
1. Concept Definition	• Initial system performance objectives established.
2. Demonstration/Validation	• Performance specifications finalized. • Model built to demonstrate performance feasibility.
3. Full-Scale Development	• Design specifications finalized. • Engineering prototypes built. • Initial performance tested using a development model.
4. Low Rate Initial Production	• Redesign for production and support. • Performance tested/verified. • "Build To" package delivered.
5. Full Rate Production	• Final production configuration delivered. • Reliability growth curve achieved. • Field repair capability verified. • Manufacturing process verified. • Problem correction very costly.
6. Maintenance and Field Services	• Field data collected and analyzed. • Field repair operations. • Problem correction very costly.

As a result, as many as 600 design changes a month over the course of several months were required to make the system manufacturable. These changes, each one costing MMC an average of about $10,000, occurred while the system was waiting on the production floor. As a result, the contract slipped more than a year beyond the due date and well over budget. One EIMG manager estimated that engineering design changes at the concept level cost about $1, at the preliminary design stage about $10, at the drawing stage about $100, at the advanced drawing stage about $1,000, at the hardware production stage about $10,000, and about $100,000 to $1 million after a product was operational in the field.

The TADS problems existed partially because the field engineering design team was different from the production design team. There was little integration or coordination in the design process between the two. Further, the design team was comprised primarily of design engineers so that the team did not enjoy a sensitivity to production issues or other functional points of view. Consequently, little thought was given to the producibility of the TADS design early on.

LANTIRN. Another example of the need for change was the Low Altitude Navigation and Targeting Infra Red system (LANTIRN) built for the Air Force F-15 and F-16 fighter aircraft. LANTIRN consisted of two long, cylindrical pods, one for a navigational system and the other for a targeting system. With LANTIRN, a pilot could set the altitude at a few hundred feet above the earth and fly automatically at high speeds, even at night. As the project progressed, it was clear that the development of the navigation pod was on schedule and within budget but that the development of the targeting pod had many of the same cost, design, and time overrun problems as did the TADS system.

Key members of EIMG recognized the need to improve the group's ability to man-age the system-development process from development right through to production and maintenance much more smoothly. The high cost of modern program development also was putting strain on an already-overburdened DOD budget, and this increased pressure on EIMG to find ways to design, develop, and produce new systems more efficiently. Additionally, there was no guarantee that the DOD would be able to continue to fund the kind of unexpected overruns that occurred with the TADS and LANTIRN programs.

In the attempt to respond to these concerns, EIMG had developed the Program Management Plan (PMP). This was a document intended to outline in some detail the steps and activities that had to be completed at each stage of a program over the course of its life. Early PMPs focused on simply improving the effectiveness of disseminating information about the program in hopes that this would improve the coordination among functional areas working on a program. All Electronics Group program managers used a program development manual that offered the program manager and each functional representative options on how to develop their phase of the project. One functional manager would receive the booklet, check off the items that applied to that particular subsystem, and pass it on to the next person.

Kelly's goal for the development of a new Comanche PMP was to standardize the operating procedures (specifically regarding the development process) and to minimize the options (variability of the process from project to project). Even so, the PMP was recognized to be a living document requiring frequent updates. At the time, though, the PMP was the primary device used to coordinate the various functions for a particular program.

Concurrent Engineering

In 1988, the Office of the Assistant Secretary of Defense—concerned about defense system cost overruns, midstream design changes, late delivery of systems, and awkward maintenance procedures and costs—commissioned the Institute for Defense Analyses (IDA) to study and report on the role of "concurrent engineering" (CE) in weapons system acquisition. Industry officials assisted the IDA in defining CE as:

> . . . a systematic approach to the integrated, concurrent design of products and their related processes, including manufacture and support. This approach is intended to cause the developers, from the outset, to consider all elements of the product life cycle from conception through disposal, including quality, cost, schedule, and user requirements.[3]

According to the IDA report, concurrent engineering was characterized by (1) a focus on the customer's requirements and priorities, (2) a conviction that quality was the result of improving a process (rather than a product), and (3) a philosophy that improvement of the processes of design, production, and support were never-ending responsibilities of the entire enterprise. The integrated, concurrent (or simultaneous) design of new products and processes was at the heart of the concept of concurrent engineering. In this philosophy, representatives from the customer, design, tooling, procurement, manufacture, service, and any other related function would all be involved in the design of the product or system from the outset. In essence, an isolated, independent design engineering function was eliminated as all "downstream" processes were co-designed toward a more cost-effective design that optimized not only function, but also production, maintenance, and upgrad-

ing. IDA asserted that this approach would help avoid the kind of costly and delaying redesign work done on systems like TADS and LANTIRN (although DOD was having similar difficulties with many suppliers, not just MMC). This emphasis on overall cost efficiency was brought to the fore by the end of the Cold War.

For 40 years, U.S. strategic policy emphasized maintaining a technological edge. Now, President Bush plans to reduce long-range nuclear arsenals, potentially eliminating some of America's most advanced cold-war weapons. With Russian President Boris Yeltsin's agreement to cooperate in making deep nuclear cuts, there's no need to rush new weapons into the field. Instead, the Pentagon will spend more time and money developing and testing weapons without committing to full production. "We will focus on research and development to create a storehouse of technology, which we can use when needed," says Defense Secretary Dick Cheney.[4]

Although the concept of concurrent engineering was not new, there were several reasons why many defense companies had not adopted it by 1992. First, CE demanded that traditionally organized companies make fundamental, wrenching, and far-reaching changes in their structures, systems, methods of management, style, and cultures. This much change was expensive, disruptive, and uncomfortable to managers who had learned a different system. Additionally, in the companies who pioneered the use of CE, it was clear that CE was not a magic formula for success; many other factors including the talent of personnel and their interpersonal styles and skills were also critical. In addi-

---

[3]Winner, Robert I. et al., *The Role of Concurrent Engineering in Weapons System Acquisition, IDA Report R-338,* Institute for Defense Analyses, 1988, 11.
[4]*Business Week,* February 10, 1992, 27.

tion, many firms experienced initial *higher* expenses as they adapted CE processes, even though they hoped costs over whole programs would be lower. Further, some companies had misconstrued CE to be the arbitrary elimination of a phase in the existing, sequential, feed-forward engineering process and therefore were not really able to develop a true CE process.

Given the government's searching for methods that would assist in reducing contract overruns, the Army required that its next big program, the light attack helicopter replacement program, Comanche, be developed using CE processes, and that contractors prove that CE processes were in fact being used. With defense budgets shrinking and the rest of the industry making significant adjustments, Kelly knew that EIMG had to do something different not only to ensure its own survival, but also to position itself as a long-term competitor. CE seemed to provide a means to do that.

Don Kelly's Challenge

In thinking through his assignment to organize the Comanche program, Kelly faced some real challenges. Following the guidelines outlined by the IDA report for the DOD and suggestions from Sandy Friedenthal, who was assigned overall responsibility for implementing CE through EIMG, Kelly realized that he had to pattern an organization that would run in parallel at reduced cost. MMC's organizational culture, however, worried him. The way that EIMG had done things in the past had been a source of strength, but Kelly knew that the traditional hierarchical structure would be a hindrance to organizing the Comanche program. As he began to draw a traditional organization chart (See Exhibit 26-3), he knew that it wouldn't work under the new RFP guidelines. Kelly knew that his Comanche organization would have to grow as much organizationally as it would technologically. Although the functional approach had created a clear understanding of who was responsible for an area or function, it also created barriers to communications between and among functions. These barriers had become all too evident in the TADS and LANTIRN programs. As Kelly tinkered with the lines and boxes of the current organization chart, he couldn't figure out how to make the organization reflect CE principles.

Kelly realized that in order to implement an effective concurrent engineering program with the Comanche project, communications between the various functional groups usually associated with a program would have to improve dramatically. Without this, there would be no way of reducing the number of engineering change requests. Kelly needed an organization and culture that would encourage open communications and exchange of ideas at every step of the process.

Kelly also knew that most of the senior EIMG officers had been with the group for most of their careers and therefore were steeped in the traditional MMC way of doing things. Many of these managers relied heavily on the personal relationships they had built up over the years to help them manage their projects. Through these relationships, they could gather information, work toward consensus on various program issues, talk over ideas, and seek support for their programs' needs. This network of relationships had assisted greatly in managing MMC's matrix organization.

The Comanche Program

In 1983, Boeing and Sikorsky had asked MMC-EIMG to begin design work on a night vision system for the next generation of the Army's attack and reconnaissance light helicopter. The new system would replace current MMC systems on the Apache helicopter and would allow pilots to see images much more clearly at night and from a farther distance than was previously possible. MMC engineers expected that pilots using

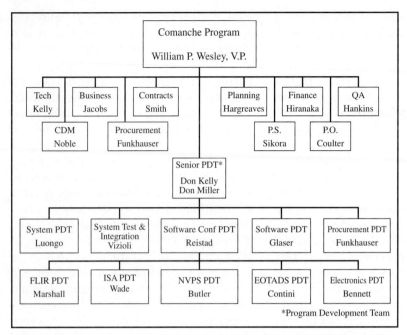

EXHIBIT 26-3   The Traditional Comanche Organization as of March 1991

the new Comanche night vision and target acquisition systems would be able to see terrain in any direction up to 6 miles with the same clarity (although in black and white) as they could during full daylight.

The Comanche program was an important one for MMC. The initial contract was worth $300 million but had the potential to generate $3 billion for MMC by the year 2010.[5] This stream of revenue was important in light of impending severe defense budget and military program cuts following the end of the Cold War. Like most programs, Comanche had many critical subsystems as shown in Table 26-2. Each of these subsystems was being designed by specialist engineers. Kelly estimated that the program would grow to be between 600 and 1,500 hourly workers and from 50 to 150 salaried workers at its peak. Kelly had the idea that

he needed to form program development teams (PDTs) to organize all of these people and activities, but he couldn't figure out how these teams were going to work or who should be on them. Exhibit 26-4 shows the way Kelly began to assign managers to each team and other necessary functions that he knew he needed on the program.

Don Kelly's Approach

Shortly after Don Kelly met with Bill Wesley, he contacted Jim Deese, the engineering scheduler for the Comanche program, and Sandy Friedenthal, the director of Concurrent Engineering for EIMG, to begin discussions on how they should proceed to organize the Comanche program. Deese provided a basic chart of how the program should progress as shown in Exhibit 26-5.

---

[5]See the *Orlando Sentinel,* September 10, 1991, C6.

TABLE 26-2 Key Subsystems on the Comanche Program	
Project Development Area	*Purpose*
Electro Optic Target Acquisition Detection Sys. (EOTADS)	Design EOTADS peculiar hardware, software, and tooling/test equipment. Generate the software and tooling/test equipment. Perform EOTADS unit integration in preparation for mission equipment package integration.
Opto-Mechanical	Design the optical system/elements and housings for the infra red, TV and Laser paths. Generate engineering drawings in support of fabrication/procurement. Create assembly and test procedures. Define the TV and Laser components. Integrate subunit and prepare for EOTADS unit.
Structures	Design mechanical structure for mounting optics, electronics, mechanisms, dewar, TV, Laser, and cooler. This includes the design of the elevation mirror, fine line-of-sight stabilization mechanism, and cooling air venting. Prepare assembly and test procedures. Integrate subunit and prepare for EOTADS unit integration.
Forward Looking Infra Red (FLIR) Electronics	Design the FLIR video electronics. Define the detector/cooler and thermal reference sources. Generate assembly and test procedures. Integrate subunit and prepare for EOTADS unit integration.
Power Supply/Amp	Design the power supplies and power amp cards required for the EOTADS unit. Prepare assembly and test procedures. Integrate into subunits.
Servo	Design the servo loops for the elevation mirror, fine line-of-sight stabilization, and other mechanisms. Generate the software and analog electronics required for the loops. Specify motor/torques, resolvers, gyros. Prepare assembly and test procedures. Integrate subunits in preparation for EOTADS unit integration.
Digital Electronics	Design all processors, serial communication links, electronics, and software. Design the video data link and controls to the MMC. Prepare assembly and test procedures. Integrate subunits in preparation for EOTADS unit integration.
Packaging	Design electronics packaging for all schematics. Generate assembly and test procedures. Provide integration support during subunit integrations.

Kelly then asked Friedenthal to help him figure out what concurrent engineering (CE) was and how it would apply to the Comanche program. His primary areas of concern were "producibility," meeting tactical requirements, insuring little or no need for redesign work, low unit cost, and meeting budgetary cost constraints.

Next, Kelly met with Doug Groseclose, senior vice president of EIMG's Staffing and Development office, to talk about how to organize the new program. Groseclose recommended that Kelly take four steps to define the start-up process:

1. **Establish the Program Mission.** Groseclose noted that the mission statement should have (a) clarity, (b) brevity, and (c) power. Kelly noted that the Comanche team's stated objective was:

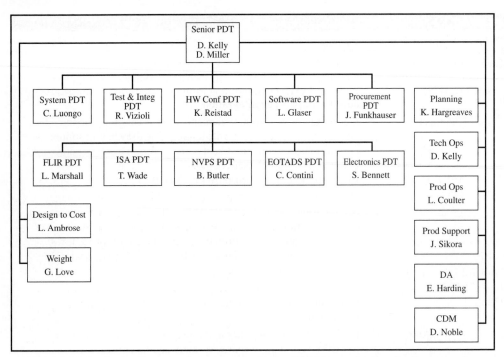

EXHIBIT 26-4 **Senior Program Development Team (PDT) Organization for Commanche**

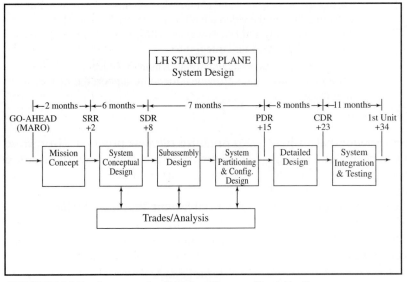

EXHIBIT 26-5 **Commanche Program System Start-Up Sequence**

to develop and prove out a tactical light helicopter night vision design that would be ready for production and operationalization and that would insure MMC's competitive position for follow on long-range initial procurement program.

2. **Establish Strategic Tasks.** Groseclose suggested that these should be made up of two primary parts: first, long-term goals that defined the primary (highest priority) accomplishments needed to assure the system's ability to accomplish its stated mission, and second, core competencies that defined those skills in which the program staff must have superb expertise. Groseclose and Kelly agreed that these two pieces of the Comanche plan should be initially defined by the senior management of the program, and then refined and finalized during the early phases of the program by program staff.

3. **Determine Core Values and Guiding Principles.** Groseclose also said that it was important that the program team define what values and principles would be central to how they behaved, both internally among each other and externally in relationship to the rest of the company and other "outside" constituents. He also referred Kelly to the small card that summarized several aspects of EIMG management principles. (See Exhibit 26-6.)

4. **Define Rules of Engagement.** Groseclose offered that the core values would then provide a means of defining a clear set of behavioral expectations for team members in terms of what they could expect from the directors, the staff, each other, and in their dealings with groups/individuals external to the program.

Groseclose commented on the importance of these four steps:

These four items together could comprise a framework for individual and collective action on the Comanche program. We rarely define any of these as a normal part of doing business at Martin Marietta, yet since the vast majority of problems and issues we can expect to encounter on this program are not technical but relationship oriented, this approach seems appropriate. With this framework defined, accepted, and a process in place to assess its effectiveness, relationship problems should be minimized, and the energy normally channeled to them can be redirected toward the technical challenges of the program.

SENIOR MANAGEMENT'S VIEW

Dick Cook, president of the Electronic Systems Group (see MMC organization chart in Exhibit 26-7), had been with the group for 3 years. His coming had signaled a change in the groups' management style. Cook had observed high-performance work teams while he was assigned to the Denver group, and he felt that similar concepts could be transplanted to the Orlando group. Additionally, he saw that in light of the defense budget downsizing, the company had to change the way it did business. Cook felt that MMC should not necessarily attempt to capture market share, but seek to make quality and process improvements first. He decided to attempt to apply the complete process to the Comanche project.

Cook was hoping to develop a model success story with the Comanche project, but he realized from observing similar efforts at companies like DEC, IBM, and Ford that it could take 10 years to realize the

Core Values

- Customer satisfaction
- Excellence in everything we do
- Integrity and ethical behavior
- Teamwork based on openness and trust
- Respect for dignity of the individual
- Meet commitments
- Simplify, simplify, simplify
- Grow our business through performance and technology

Principles

- Give people benefit of the doubt—employee best interest is the tie breaker
- Achievements are to be publicly congratulated; criticism of employees in public or criticism of one employee to another is not acceptable
- You will participate in decisions that affect your work
- You should have informal one-on-one conversations with your supervisor once a week; work group once a month.
- You will participate in quarterly goal reviews and task development sessions.
- When adding a major task, management will review your workload to fit the resources and time available.
- Essential decisions will not be deferred.
- If a task seems impossible, supervisors will work with employees for a mutual solution.
- Work will not be rescheduled nor overtime added without an explanation.

Vision

To be recognized as the best electronic systems company in the world by our employees, our customers, and our competitors.

EXHIBIT 26-6 **Martin Marietta Electronic Systems Core Values, Principles, and Vision**

benefits of the program. He observed that American industry was caught up in the search for quick fixes to returns on investment (ROI), but he felt that a culture change was necessary for real, lasting, enduring financial improvement to take place:

I need to get CE embedded in the culture by first developing an atmosphere and environment of openness and trust, where people are willing to step up and be different.

Reception of the proposal to change to and integrate CE was cool among other senior managers, however. Many wanted to wait and see if the government would mandate CE before they went headlong into it; others felt that it was too costly or too

timely a process to undertake at that time. Cook saw himself as a change agent, champion, and role model in attempting to break down communications barriers and in introducing CE core values and guiding principles among senior management. He hoped his senior colleagues would see the value of CE and follow his lead.

Back to Don Kelly

Meanwhile, Don Kelly condensed and listed the challenges he faced in implementing a new organizational design and a new development process in the Comanche program. He noted that he had to:

- Oversee the definition and tailoring of the pilot CE program in MMC.

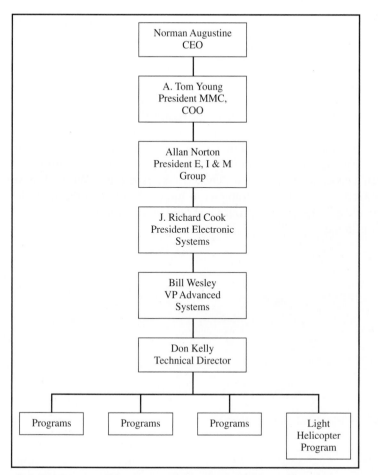

EXHIBIT 26-7   MMC Basic Organization Structure Through EIMG

- Translate the new organizational structure ideas into the reality of a viable working organization.
- Engender more than a verbal commitment to the success of CE from top, middle, lower and functional personnel.
- Obtain complete and substantive upper management understanding and support.
- Make the changes as substitutes for previous practices without *adding* process requirements.

- Help MMC Comanche personnel see and support the need for change. He worried that few saw the crisis as clearly as he did. Too many thought, "We've always done it this way and survived. Even with cost and time overruns, the government has come through with the additional financing."
- Help change company policy. Those who control and implement the policy must sign on to the change and its enforcement.

- Stick with CE principles throughout the life of the project and make them a living process that would be open to updates and changes as the company grew.
- Develop education and training programs at all levels of the organization.
- Instill a sense of ownership of the process into every person associated with it. It's easier to ditch a process or project if you don't own it.
- Insure that the group made a long-term commitment to continued improvements.

Kelly reviewed the grounds for making a change in the way the group did business. Despite the enormity of the changes being anticipated, he had two strong factors in his favor: In the attempt to avoid the overrun problems associated with LANTIRN and TADS, the Army this time had *stipulated* that CE be used and that proof of implementation be provided and the enthusiasm and encouragement from the group president, Dick Cook, be evident. With all these thoughts in mind, Don wondered how the program should be organized. ■

Case 27   U.S. West: The Case of the Dinka Letters (A)

In January 1988, Judi Servoss, vice president for Public Relations and Advertising at U.S. West, Incorporated, was reading through a packet of clippings and unedited correspondence she had received in the mail from the Minnesota Women's Consortium just before Christmas 1987. The letters and newspaper articles revealed that the top management and an employee of Fallon McElligott (FM), the advertising agency with which U.S. West worked, had displayed offensive sexist and racist behavior.

U.S. West was one of a dozen telephone spin-offs established in 1983 after the divestiture of the Bell system from the American Telephone & Telegraph Company (AT&T). Early in U.S. West's history, management realized that the company's workforce, which was predominantly white, male, and middle-aged, did not reflect the changing trends in the country's demographics. The company was aware that it would soon lose its corporate competitiveness if it did not change with the times. It began a concerted effort to diversify its workforce to better mirror its market base, where the percentage of white males was declining and the numbers of Hispanics, African Americans, Asians, and women were increasing. As one employee noted, pluralism at U.S. West was taken seriously by everyone in the com-

pany. Pluralism was not a program with a start and a finish; it was an ongoing process of changing the makeup of U.S. West to reflect the "melting pot" of U.S. society and the needs of the country's diverse people.

Servoss was disturbed that a vendor hired to work with the U.S. West image did not share the same concerns about diversity. Now that U.S. West was in the midst of restructuring, Servoss would have to reevaluate the company's advertising. She wondered whether a sound business judgment would be to continue the relationship with FM or to seek a new agency.

U.S. WEST

U.S. West was established on January 1, 1983, as a result of the AT&T divestiture. The company owned Mountain Bell, Northwestern Bell, Pacific Northwest Bell, U.S. West Direct (a yellow-page company), and subsidiaries in other related communications services. U.S. West served 14 states including Colorado, Idaho, Iowa, and Utah. The company faced difficulties realizing profits at levels comparable to other "Baby Bells" because of its sparsely populated and outspread geographic region. The company's primary business, local phone service, was growing at only 3 percent to 5 percent

UVA-0B-0436

This case was written by Lynn A. Isabella, Associate Professor of Business Administration, with the assistance of Tya Daud. Copyright © 1993 by the University of Virginia Darden School Foundation, Charlottesville, VA. All rights reserved.

annually.[1] The stagnant economies in the region U.S. West served were not likely to see dramatic growth in the near future.

Jack A. MacAllister, chairman of U.S. West, Inc., had from the beginning challenged the breakup agreement with AT&T. Nevertheless, he was not disheartened by the situation. He contended that in order to survive, the company had to compete with rivals such as private transmission carriers, computer-equipment suppliers, and cable-TV providers. He argued that U.S. West should be able to freely price new services, such as cellular phone business, central-phone switching, and private lines. Due to his efforts, some 11 states had loosened their regulations, allowing U.S. West to price its services competitively. In 1984, the company established U.S. West Financial Services to provide diversified financial services and leasing. Other new subsidiaries included Beta West Properties (1986), a developer of commercial real estate, and Applied Communications (1987), which provided software to the banking industry.[2] By the end of fiscal year 1986, sales had totaled $8,308,000. (Refer to Exhibit 27-1 for summary financial information.)

Before being chosen to head U.S. West, MacAllister had been president of Northwestern Bell since 1975. After graduating from the University of Iowa in 1950, he started his career in the phone business working as an underground cable installer. His career progressed quickly in the phone business, culminating in his position as chairman and chief executive of U.S. West, a company worth more than $7 billion.

MacAllister's management style was greatly influenced by his past life experiences. One of his characteristics was intolerance for discrimination. MacAllister grew up in a small town in Iowa during the Depression. Once, while visiting his grand-

	Annual Growth (%)	1984	1985	1986	1987
Sales ($ million)	5.5	7,280	7,813	8,308	8,445
Net income ($ million)	6.5	887	926	924	8,445
Income as % of sales	—	12.2	11.8	11.1	11.9
Earnings per share ($)	7.1	2.31	2.42	2.43	2.66
Stock price—high ($)	—	17.72	22.25	31.00	30.13
Stock price—low ($)	—	13.91	17.13	20.81	21.25
Stock price—close ($)	—	17.63	22.25	27.00	25.56
P/E—high	—	8	9	13	11
P/E—low	—	6	7	9	8
Dividends per share ($)	6.2	1.35	1.07	1.50	1.61
Book value per share ($)	4.5	17.25	18.24	19.16	20.09
Employees	(1.0)	70,765	70,202	69,375	68,523

Source: Hoover's Handbook of American Business.

EXHIBIT 27-I   U.S. West Financial Summary

[1] U.S. West, Inc., *Hoover's Handbook of American Business,* The Reference Press, Inc., December 31, 1992.
[2] *Ibid.*

mother, who lived in a bigger town than he did, MacAllister went to see a softball game. He recalled that when the stands were filled, someone in the crowd demanded, in graphic language, that a young black man vacate his seat for a white man: "I must have only been 5 years old, but I remember the hurt in that man's eyes. I can almost picture his face. I felt that hurt with that individual."

MacAllister felt that making a blanket categorization of a person because of his or her color or gender was unacceptable from a moral perspective and was also a loss from a human-resources perspective. Holding back minorities and women from certain jobs cut off human resources that could be made available to help the country, companies, and communities become greater.[3]

His strong feelings about discrimination led MacAllister to introduce innovative programs as early as the 1970s at Northwestern Bell. MacAllister then took these programs with him when he became head of U.S. West. His efforts to introduce pluralism gradually evolved into a comprehensive set of programs that affected hiring, promotion, and the day-to-day activities of the company's employees.

One unique example, found only at U.S. West, was the company's Women of Color Project that, as of 1988, was still in the works. In 1985, employee-resource groups took a close look at the career paths of the women of color in the company. Juanita Cox-Burton, director of leadership succession for the company, explained the project's origin:

Although there was equal opportunity for the 65,000 employees, the resource groups felt management's definition of women and minorities extended to white women and black men, and that women of color—black, Hispanic, and Asian—were overlooked for promotion. The resource groups predicted that by the year 2000, 70 percent of the civilian labor force would be made up of women and people of color. If the company was truly serious about recruiting these workers of tomorrow, it needed to have role models to ensure recruiting and keeping the best people.[4]

The company identified women of color who had the greatest potential to become leaders in the organization. These women would be armed with the knowledge and the resources necessary to succeed in a major corporation. The final selection included performance appraisals by corporate and senior management of the candidates' on-the-job competence. The women chosen would be trained in conflict resolution, managing diversity, and the intricacies of power and influence. Each participant would receive feedback and would be expected to develop specific career objectives. After completing the program, participants would be given challenging job assignments and placed with supervisors and mentors. Contrary to many people's assumptions, these women were not given special privileges; rather, they would probably be facing numerous challenges they had not considered before. They would have to face not only the obstacles common to most upwardly mobile individuals, but also hurdles specific to upwardly mobile women.

On an even larger scope, U.S. West initiated the Accelerated Development Program.

---

[3] "For U.S. West's Jack MacAllister, Doing Good and Doing Business Go Hand in Hand," *The Denver Business Journal*, April 24, 1989.

[4] Diane Feldman, "Women of Color Build a Rainbow of Opportunity," *Management Review*, August 1989.

It was hoped that by April 1993, each of the company's 65,000 employees would have taken part in the training, which focused on the challenges of future leadership. The progressive approach U.S. West took to sensitize its workforce helped the company learn how to better satisfy its customer base, which was as diverse as its employees. Company management believed that pluralism made good business sense.

FALLON MCELLIGOTT

Fallon McElligott, a Minneapolis-based advertising agency, was established in 1981 by Thomas McElligott, Patrick Fallon, and Nancy Rice (who left in 1985 to open her own agency, Rice & Rice). Since its inception, the agency had earned a sterling reputation for its breakthrough creativity, and billings went from zero to more than $100 million in a 6-year period. The agency had succeeded in capturing virtually every advertising award in the industry in the previous few years while strategically building its clientele to include companies like U.S. West, The Wall Street Journal, Porsche U.S.A., Federal Express, Timex, and Lee Jeans.

Throughout its prosperity, the Fallon McElligott agency earned a reputation for being an enviable place for educated, talented, ambitious professionals of both sexes to work. Women outnumbered men, 71 to 53. More than half of the managerial and professional positions were filled by women. Women headed several departments, two management supervisors were female, and 31 out of 37 people promoted to professional positions were women. Furthermore, the agency appeared to be a model of equal employment and tolerant accommodation to personnel's family and flextime needs. The agency also cultivated a high community profile by doing pro bono advertising campaigns for a number of Minnesota organizations, including the Minnesota Women's Fund and the Children's Defense Fund.

THE DINKA LETTERS

The incident in fall 1987, however, blemished the agency's reputation. The controversy began when Charles Anderson, a partner in FM's subsidiary, Duffy Design Group, led a statewide conference on marketing higher-education services. In his presentation, Anderson used visuals and language that workshop-participant Dr. Neala Schleuning found inappropriate, offensive, and sexist. FM had created a print advertisement for a Chicago television station promoting its syndicated "Dynasty" broadcasts. Above photographs of the show's three female stars was the headline "Bitch, Bitch, Bitch." Anderson had used this advertisement and slides of cancan dancers labeled "whores" to emphasize that marketers should not "prostitute" themselves for their customers. Said Schleuning:

> I got tired of listening for nearly an hour to how it "takes balls" to design an aggressive marketing program . . . no one element [of the presentation] was offensive in itself. It was the totality, the steady onslaught of stag-party language and sex-object symbolism. I decided it was worth a letter expressing my annoyance at the male-gonad style of business the agency perpetuates in its promotional literature.

Schleuning, director of the Women's Center at Mankato State University, Minnesota, decided to send a complaint to Anderson. (See Exhibit 27-2 for an excerpt of the letter.)

Much to Schleuning's surprise, Anderson's reply had nothing to do with the issue Schleuning raised. Instead, Anderson suggested in his letter that if Schleuning was committed to changing unacceptable behavior, she should visit the Dinka tribe in East Africa and put a stop to their social practices. Included in Anderson's response was a picture of a Dinka boy licking a cow's anus

> While I was generally impressed with the creative level and quality of the work of your organization, I would like you to know that I was both annoyed and offended by the persistence of negative stereotypes of women in your AV presentation. I appreciate your personal apologies and discomfort with that material, but it somehow didn't make up for the references to "bitches," "whores," and, in particular, your company's interest in perpetuating what I will forevermore think of as the male-gonad style of doing business.
>
> While you may dismiss my complaints as those of a "feminist," I would also like to point out to you the irony that a company which prides itself on new images and creativity must continue, for some strange reason, to perpetuate such base and offensive stereotypes in its promotional literature. It's a shame that you have to. . . .
>
> *Source:* Betty L. Harragan, "The $10 Million Blunder," *Working Woman,* May 1988.

EXHIBIT 27-2   Excerpt of Dr. Schleuning's Original Complaint

as part of a traditional ceremony. (See Exhibit 27-3 for an excerpt of the reply.) Schleuning remarked:

> I couldn't believe that a complaint about sexism would be answered by racism. That's when I sent a copy of the correspondence to the Minnesota Women's Consortium, asking, "Is this their stock response when they get criticism about sexist stereotypes?"

The Minnesota Women's Consortium was founded in 1980 and was run by a paid staff of experienced business and political specialists. The consortium had a membership of 170 established organizations that were managed by experienced and salaried executives. Individuals represented within these organizations included a high proportion of Minnesota's women doctors, lawyers, teachers, nurses, business owners, politicians, lobbyists, communications specialists, union organizers, and many others. The main interest of the parties involved was some aspect of equal rights for women.

In response to Schleuning's letter, Gloria Griffin, coordinator of the St. Paul-based Women's Consortium, sent copies to FM's founding partners and chief officers. Tom McElligott and Pat Fallon did not respond to Griffin's letter, but instead wrote directly to Schleuning (see Exhibit 27-4 for excerpts of their letters). McElligott's letter, which was accompanied by a pith helmet and mosquito net, thanked Schleuning for

> As the enclosed photo clearly illustrates, The Dinka tribe of East Africa has a rather barbaric ritual that has apparently been going on for centuries. I know you'll find it as deeply troubling as we do, but I pass it along to you believing that you will be able to deal with these people in the same firm, yet even-handed manner in which you dealt with us. Won't you please write them (or better yet, visit them), and put an end to this horrible practice, Doctor?
>
> Again, thank you for your letter. We will eagerly await to hear your response to the Dinka problem.
>
> *Source:* Betty L. Harragan, "The $10 Million Blunder," *Working Woman,* May 1988.

EXHIBIT 27-3   Excerpt of Anderson's Reply

In any event, we're all extremely pleased to hear about your gracious offer regarding the Dinka problem. Let's face it, Doctor, the Sudan is not exactly Cannes. Getting volunteers for this mission—especially appropriate volunteers—hasn't been easy.

So, while last week you may have been just a strange, anonymous person whose amusing letter entertained 150 people around the company bulletin board, today you are our brave missionary to the Dinkas. Needless to say, you've made all of us here very, very happy.

Godspeed, Doctor.

Excerpt of Fallon's Reply

Charles should obviously have sent you not just one photo, but the entire Dinka story. How else could he expect you to be prepared for your trip to the Dinka tribe of East Africa, after all? Moreover, Charles didn't even offer to help defray your expenses, or provide you with a map! Again, I'm appalled.

Anyway, on behalf of this entire organization, I'd like to apologize for Charles' behavior and set things right. Therefore, I have enclosed the whole Dinka story (copied from the December 1992 issue of *Life* magazine). I've also enclosed a map of Africa to help prepare you for your trip. And, finally, Dr. Schleuning, realizing that this public service effort on your part will not be cheap, all of us here have agreed to pay half of your travel expenses to Africa (or full expenses, one way).

Source: Betty L. Harragan, "The $10 Million Blunder," *Working Woman,* May 1988.

EXHIBIT 27-4   Excerpt of McElligott's Reply

entertaining everybody around the company's bulletin board. Fallon's reply was accompanied by a map of Africa with a promise to pay half a round trip or "full expenses, one way."[5]

Once again, Schleuning shared her letters with the consortium. After consulting with consortium members knowledgeable about or active in the private industry, the consortium decided to take the issue to people they thought would take the incident seriously: FM's clients. One week before Christmas, 35 packets of the entire correspondence were sent out to a selected list of FM clients. Kay Taylor, legislative coordinator, commented:

We didn't editorialize at all. We merely noted that this correspondence had come to our attention and we thought

they might be interested because of their personal or business dealings with this group of Minneapolis businessmen.

CONCLUSION

Servoss thought back to when she first received the packet. It was hard for her to believe that FM could be responsible for such apparently thoughtless behavior:

They have done an extremely effective job for 4 years to establish U.S. West as a separate entity . . . no one here has ever seen them exhibit any sign of the attitudes revealed in the Dinka letters in their personal behavior or their professional work.

Nonetheless, Servoss placed numerous calls, both to Fallon and to McElligott,

[5] Betty L. Harragan, "The $10 Million Blunder," *Working Woman,* May 1988.

expressing her and other U.S. West executives' strong disapproval. Says Servoss, "I had many conversations with Fallon over that Christmas week."

On New Year's Eve, Fallon sent a letter of apology to Schleuning. Many people who knew about the situation were not surprised when FM offices were besieged with phone calls and the agency's cash flow came under threat.

So far, the controversy had appeared in only local Minneapolis-St. Paul newspapers. Servoss felt, however, that U.S. West employees would soon hear of the incident. Several FM clients were quoted in the media about FM's behavior (see Exhibit 27-5 for quotes). Was this incident an isolated case that would not be repeated in the future?

Concomitantly, U.S. West was in the process of restructuring, and Servoss had to review the company's advertising and which agency would be handling it. She had to decide if the "Dinka Letters" were a strong enough reason to terminate the company's $10 million relationship with FM.

Servoss weighed her options. Changing agencies would demand an enormous commitment of time and cost to build a strong relationship. In addition, U.S. West had no guarantee that another agency would be as effective as FM or would be more thoughtful than FM in its behavior. On the other hand, how would U.S. West, a company known for its commitment to pluralism, look if it maintained business relations with FM? How would U.S. West employees expect their company to respond? Would it be more realistic to assume that the incident would blow over and would not have a damaging effect on U.S. West?

Servoss realized this was not a lightly made decision, and having used the Christmas holiday to look at the problem from all angles, she knew she could no longer delay making a decision. ■

Kent Brownridge, General Manager, *Rolling Stone Magazine:*
I know these guys and they are not sexist, not bad, evil, or discriminating. It was just a dumb move on their part.

Spokesman for *Wall Street Journal,* quoted in that paper:
The behavior was clearly inappropriate . . . they publicly and privately apologized, as indeed they should have.

Editorial in *Advertising Age,* the leading journal in the trade:
How can Fallon free itself from the Dinka Curse? . . . For some time to come, at every client meeting, at every new business pitch, someone will be making a mental note that this agency suffered a monumental lapse in judgment. That in choosing or sticking with Fallon, the company shoulders part of the burden of that mistake.

Source: Betty L. Harragan, "The $10 Million Blunder," *Working Woman,* May 1988.

EXHIBIT 27-5   Excerpts from FM Clients

Case 28   James Carroway (A)

Three weeks after Tara Pauwels had been promoted from Latin American sales representative to the new coordinator for Strong Tubing's Billingsgate initiative, she and Jack Blackmore, European sales manager, were reviewing candidates to fill the position she was vacating with Sven Bjorkman, the director of International Sales, and Bob Ebbett, vice president for Special Projects. In the minds of Tara and Jack, James Carroway was head and shoulders above the other candidates for the position. After a lengthy discussion, however, Sven proclaimed,"James may be the best candidate, but we are going to hire Karen. Bob and I are just not comfortable with hiring James."

Jack Blackmore sat in disbelief. After weeks of interviewing candidates to replace Tara Pauwels as Strong Tubing's sales representative for Latin America, Sven Bjorkman had effectively told them that the leading candidate would not be offered the position because of his race. Jack and Tara were not prepared for Sven's final decision. They left his office and went to the conference room to discuss what had just happened.

BACKGROUND

Strong Tubing was the leading producer of steel pipe and tubing in the United States. The company was founded in Kansas City in the mid 1960s with a single tube mill on the north side of the city. Since that time, Strong Tubing had expanded its production to 17 roll-forming mills in six states east of the Mississippi. In 1988, the company was acquired by Hollis Incorporated, a British steel conglomerate owned by Sir Nathan Paulson, a driven, self-made man who had recently become the world's newest billionaire. Since being taken over by Hollis, the Strong Tubing name had grown to be synonymous with the highest-quality structural tubing around the globe.

In 1996, Strong Tubing signed an agreement to lease production time from Billingsgate Tube, a small, regional producer in Indiana, with an option to buy the facility. Tara Pauwels was tagged to head up the management of the new initiative. She was to begin her new responsibilities immediately, while maintaining her old responsibilities until a replacement could be found.

TARA PAUWELS

Tara came to Strong Tubing in 1994, straight from her undergraduate work at the University of Kansas. She was hired over other, more experienced candidates both because of her facility with the Spanish language, and the endorsement of Sven's wife, who had worked with Tara's mother for many years. She immediately distinguished herself as an astute salesperson with a natural ability to build relationships with customers. Within 6 months of arriving at Strong, Tara was promoted from trainee to full sales representative status. During her tenure she built a presence for the company in Colombia, Chile, and parts of Central America, while establishing Strong as the preeminent supplier of steel tubing to Mexico. The relationships she forged with the key customers in each market were

UVA-OB-0688
This case was prepared by Eric Anderson under the supervision of James G. Clawson, Associate Professor of Business Administration. Copyright © 2000 by the University of Virginia Darden School Foundation, Charlottesville, VA. All rights reserved.

strong enough to discourage competitors from attempting to enter those markets.

At Billingsgate Tara would be in charge of scheduling production time on the mills, expediting raw material delivery, executing coil conversion orders, expediting shipment of finished goods, and generating new business. It was an opportunity to operate a small business inside a large corporation without much of the risk involved. It was a full-time job that would keep her in the office for 10 hours a day, 6 days a week. This placed urgency on hiring and training a replacement to take over her old duties in international sales.

In finding a replacement for Tara, it was important that the transfer of accounts went as smoothly as possible. Strong was in a dominant position in Latin America, but it was tenuous. Success in the industry was based on the strength of relationships with distributors. Both Mexican and U.S. competitors were eager to take market share in the region. If customers did not feel as though Strong was adequately serving them, they could shift all of their business to competitors within 3 months. With this in mind, it was imperative to bring in a candidate who was already fluent in Spanish, had an outgoing personality, could be a salesperson and a partner to the distributors, and could cope with the pressure and uncertainty that comes with shipping break bulk[1] products internationally. It was important that her replacement could step in and quickly establish relationships with valuable customers who were concerned that Tara was the only one who could serve them. The transition would have to be seamless.

As soon as Tara's impending transfer was announced, Sven charged Tara and Jack Blackmore with finding a replacement who was fluent in Spanish and could hit the ground running. Jack contacted Polly Robeson of Human Resources to set the ball rolling.

THE HIRING PROCESS

Strong Tubing conducted a fairly simple hiring process. Once a position description was received, the Human Resources department would post the opening on the bulletin board at each facility, in the leading local paper, American Metal Market newspaper, and, depending on the nature of the position, at local universities and technical colleges. Human Resources collected resumes and conducted first-round interviews to screen out unqualified candidates. The resumes of applicants that passed the initial screening were then forwarded to the department with the opening. The hiring lead in the department would determine which candidates would be invited for the second round. In most cases, the second round consisted of at least two separate interviews, and, in the case of international sales, an intensive language skills interview. The top candidate would come back for a final interview with the department head. A candidate that made it to the final round would usually be offered the position.

Strong Tubing had no formal employee-training program. An entry-level sales hire began with the title of product representative trainee. They were assigned customer accounts on their first day and engaged in on-the-job training. The trainee was introduced to new customers via telephone by the outgoing sales rep or department manager. An experienced sales rep sat with them until they became comfortable with the company's information systems and customer service procedures, usually less than 1 week. The new employee was then assigned a desk next to an unofficial mentor,

---

[1]*Break bulk* is a shipping term for products that cannot be shipped in traditional containers. These products are usually large and heavy and can be transported only by railcar, flatbed truck, or in the hold of an oceangoing vessel.

who was there to coach the trainee and answer any questions that arose. If the employee progressed as expected, they were promoted to the position of product representative after 6 months and their customer account base was expanded.

The international department was slightly different. Because of the resources of the department and the demands of the position, trainees were given a full account base on the first day. They were required to learn not only the responsibilities of their job, but also the intricacies of the entire manufacturing process. The trainee would spend a second week doing daylong rotational assignments in finance, scheduling, purchasing, and shipping. This was followed by a 2-day plant tour in the third week.

Once a trainee was deemed to have reached a functionally independent level, they received a double promotion to the international sales representative position. This meant that they would receive commissions on new business and could travel to visit customers abroad.

In the case of the new candidate for Latin American sales representative, Tara would have limited time to train and mentor the new hire. Jack Blackmore would be responsible for the candidate's initial training and ongoing mentoring. The new hire would report directly to Jack, but would formally report to Sven Bjorkman.

INTERNATIONAL DEPARTMENT

Jack joined Strong Tubing in January of 1995, after graduating from Washington University. Sven hired him to replace Rose Kelly, a Strong Tubing veteran who was taking over a newly created position as corporate logistics manager. Rose had led the formation of the international department 6 years earlier and had come to embody the spirit of the department. Her combative nature and acerbic personality had earned her no friends in the company, but had allowed her to create a new program from the ground up. Unfortunately, her social skills ultimately held back the department because she had to be insulated from customers through the use of outside sales agents, and her list of enemies at Strong had created an anti-export sentiment within the company.

Jack was hired to turn the program around. Unlike Rose, he could converse in other languages and had the type of consensus-building skills that could move the department forward. After settling in and becoming familiar with the responsibilities of the position, Jack began a campaign across the company to increase the reputation—and thus effectiveness—of the department. He published four issues of a newsletter designed to inform the entire company about what was involved in selling, producing, and shipping for export customers. He also spent time with influential personnel, explaining to them why Strong Tubing must export and what it meant to the bottom line.

Once Jack had built support, he aligned with Frank Grady, vice president of Materials, to create an interdepartmental task force on export business. Over the next 3 months, the task force enacted sweeping changes that shrank customer lead times from 6 months to 4 weeks.

Jack then took on the market. He traveled to Europe to meet major customers face to face. No direct employee of Strong Tubing had ever done this; customers only knew the faces of the outside sales agents. He convinced customers that the company had made vast improvements and that it was in their best interest to increase their business with Strong.

Jack came back from that trip with enough orders to surpass all of the previous year's export business in just one business quarter. Most importantly, the orders were filled as promised, and business took off.

Jack gradually phased out all outside sales agents, establishing strong relationships directly with customers.

Because of the demands created by the increased business, Jack could no longer adequately service the few customers that Strong had in Latin America. Tara was hired and trained by Jack by the fall of 1995. Within a few months, business in Latin America took off.

Because of the success of the international department since Jack and Tara arrived, they had developed significant informal influence within the company. They were widely respected throughout the company, a status that Sven Bjorkman had never enjoyed.

SVEN BJORKMAN

Sven Bjorkman was hired in late 1993 by Tony Ponte, then vice president of Special Projects, to take over Tony's responsibilities for international sales. Tony was one of the most well-liked and influential executives in the company. Six months after hiring Sven, Tony left Strong to take over the management of another company in the Hollis Group.

Sven came to Strong after a highly successful career selling defense-related equipment for the world's most successful builder of fighter jets. With the defense industry slowing down, Sven decided to look for an international sales position with a smaller manufacturer. Strong Tubing fit the profile of the type of company and position he was seeking.

Besides being a successful salesman, Sven spoke Danish, Norwegian, German, and some Japanese. He had an incredible ability to gather important information from customers and competitors. As the new manager of a small department, he focused on handling direct sales to the Pacific Rim region, and he took a hands-off approach to managing his team.

From the day he was hired, Sven had serious problems with Rose Kelly, who believed that she should have been given the position of international sales manager. Rose, as the source of all information, made Sven's life difficult. Sven pushed hard for her reassignment to another department. Six months later, when Jack was hired, she was removed from the department.

Unfortunately for Sven, he had never learned the intricacies of Strong's manufacturing process. This led him to make promises to customers that could not be kept, forcing various departments to jump through flaming hoops on a number of occasions. These things did not endear him to the rest of the management team or to plant management.

Because of this, Sven relied heavily on Jack, and later Tara, to be his eyes and ears within the company, providing him with information that he needed to provide good customer service and warning him when things looked like they were going to get hairy. After gaining confidence in them, Sven began to rubber-stamp any suggestions that Jack and Tara made, effectively letting them lead the department. Only later, when it appeared that Jack and Tara were now regarded by the rest of the company as the real managers of the department, did Sven begin to take a more active role in leading the department.

JAMES CARROWAY

More than 50 resumes were reviewed for the Latin American sales position, and 10 candidates had been chosen for second-round interviews. In the end, one candidate emerged as the clear choice for the job. James Carroway was a recent graduate of St. Louis University. He had gained fluency in Spanish while studying abroad in Seville, and he was also conversant in French. He had graduated near the top of his class and came with unusually strong references. Most importantly, James was emotionally stable and detail oriented, two things that were crucial for success in exporting. On top of all this, James was a genuinely affable person that Jack felt would be able to win over the customers right away.

When Tara and Jack presented James as their choice to Sven Bjorkman, he seemed receptive. Sven agreed that James's resume was strong, and he was impressed by the quality of his recommendations. James's final interview was scheduled with Sven for the next day.

BACK TO THE DRAWING BOARD

The next afternoon, Sven walked into Jack's office.

SVEN: "Could you give me the name of another candidate? I am not sure James is the right person for the job."

JACK: "What's wrong, did James blow the interview?"

SVEN: "No, James is a fine young man. I just do not believe that the customers would react well to him."

JACK: "How so?"

SVEN: "It's a feeling, just get me another candidate."

Jack related his conversation with Sven to Tara, who was surprised that Sven had not agreed that James was the obvious choice for the position. They agreed that all the other candidates were far less suited for the position, but decided to give Sven two other names.

JACK: "I think that after Sven interviews these other two candidates, he will see that James is the clear choice. In the meantime, I'll try to get a better idea why Sven feels uncomfortable with James."

TARA: "You're right, Jack. Karen and Jim are not even in James's league. I am sure

Sven will realize that and we can get James in here soon. Pedro at Grupo Ortiz is anxious to find out who his new sales rep will be."

GETTING NOWHERE

The next afternoon, after Sven had interviewed Karen Zaloom and Jim Tremblay, he stopped by Jack's office.

SVEN: "Do you have any more candidates?"

JACK: "Sven, the quality of candidates drops off even further after Karen and Jim. What did you think of them?"

SVEN: "Well, Karen is bright, but I am not sure that she has the right temperament. Jim has a successful track record, but he doesn't seem to have a good grasp on what it takes to do business internationally. I like the fact that he has recently learned Spanish, but he makes exporting sound like going to an amusement park."

JACK: "What about James?

SVEN: "He has all the tools, but I discussed it with Bob, and we are not sure how customers will react to having an African American as their sales rep. It might hurt business, especially in Latin America."

JACK: "Sven, our Latin American customers do not care who our sales rep is, as long as they do a good job. Look at how well Tara did. As a young woman straight out of college, she gained their respect immediately. They recognized what an excellent businessperson she is. I had similar success. Don't you think James would have the same success?"

SVEN: "I don't think that the company can afford to take the chance. That market has become such an important part of our business. The situation just isn't the same as when we brought you and Tara in."

Sven walked out of Jack's office with the entire stack of resumes that had answered the sales rep opening. Jack knocked on the window separating his office from Tara's and motioned for her to come in.

JACK: "So I found out why Sven doesn't want to hire James."

TARA: "Did he blow the interview?"

JACK: "It's because he is African American."

TARA: "You're kidding. That is the biggest load of crap I have ever heard. Our customers don't care whether James is black, white, green, or purple."

JACK: "He discussed it with Bob."

TARA: "That doesn't surprise me, but Bob probably has no idea how well qualified James is for the job."

JACK: "Let's go talk to Bob."

MEETING THE VICE PRESIDENT

Robert "Bob" Ebbett was the vice president of Special Projects for Strong Tubing. Since Strong Tubing bought Bob's former employer, de Maurier Tubes of Canada, in 1986, Bob had served as Canadian sales manager, sales manager for Pipe and Fabrication, and vice president of Marketing. He was widely considered to be second in command at Strong. He was a talented executive who had an unmatched knowledge of the industry. In his newest position, Bob worked on strategic acquisitions, new product development, and putting out whatever fires the president dropped in his lap. He had a fiery temper and always believed that it was his way or the highway. Bob was famous for pulling people into his office, shutting the door, and reducing them to tears. However, Bob was respected for his ability to make the right move every time.

JACK: "Bob, do you have a minute?"

BOB: "What's up?"

JACK: "Tara and I wanted to talk to you about James Carroway."

BOB: "Shut the door."

JACK: "Bob, we've interviewed all of the candidates for Tara's job, and we think that James Carroway stands head and shoulders above everyone. Sven seems to agree that James is well qualified, but he thinks that customers will not react well to having an Afro-American sales rep. What do you think?"

BOB: "I've seen James's resume. Tara, do you think that Enrique Ortiz is going to be comfortable dealing with a young black man straight out of college?"

JACK: "Yes."

BOB: "So do I, but I'm not sure. Are you sure? Longhorn Tube is building a new tube mill near the Mexican border. We already know that they have been knocking on Grupo Ortiz's door. We've spent 4 years building a strong relationship with them. We can't afford to take any chances. James appears to be well qualified for the job, but if we lose the business, what good is it?"

TARA: "Bob, I can see your point, but if we lose their business for that reason, was their business really worth having in the first place?"

BOB: "Come on Tara, you are not that naïve. Grupo Ortiz controls 70 percent of Mexico's steel distribution and is one of our 10 biggest customers. We cannot afford to lose four railcars worth of shipments a month. As long as they pay their bills and keep buying tubing, they will be our customer. Their politics are none of our business."

JACK: "Tara, Bob has a point. Wherever we do business abroad, we have to respect the cultural norms of our customers. We are shipping product every month to people whose politics are different than ours. Not all of our customers can be our best friends. We have to be sensitive to their differences. However, Bob, I think that in this case it makes no difference. What is important here is what is right in our society, legally and morally."

BOB: "I can't disagree with you, Jack. But, as a director of Strong Tubing, I have to look out for what is in the best interests of our company, the owners, and everyone who works here. If we lose the Grupo Ortiz business, not to mention Juan Perreira and Super Steel's business, it is going to affect the bonus of each and every employee in this company. I appreciate your concern, and I have heard what you have to say. I'll speak with Sven."

CHECKING ON THE CONCERN

With that, Bob picked up the phone and barked some instructions to his assistant. Tara and Jack walked out more confused than ever. Bob had made some good points. As a manager, Jack had to look out for what was in the best interest of the company and all its employees. If they lost the Grupo Ortiz business, they would be virtually locked out of Mexico, which had proven to be a resilient and profitable market over the past 4 years. However, it was also his responsibility to hire the best candidate for every position.

Just after 6:00 P.M., Jack grabbed Tara on her way out the door.

JACK: "Do you think you could find out how Grupo Ortiz and our other Latin American customers would feel about working with an Afro American, without tipping them off to what is going on?"

TARA: "Sure, I guess I could find a way to get that info."

JACK: "Good. Tomorrow morning I want you to get me a list of the reactions of the top two customers from each country."

TARA: "You'll have it by lunch."

REPORTING THE RESULTS

Late the next morning, Tara and Jack walked into Sven's office with the results of her research in hand.

JACK: "Sven, Tara has done some checking, and not a single one of our top 15 customers in Latin America would see any problem in working with an Afro-American sales rep."

SVEN: "Whom did you speak with?"

TARA: "Of course I spoke with our main contact at each company. Don't worry, though. I handled it in casual conversation, so they have no idea what is going on."

SVEN: "Did you speak with Enrique Ortiz or any of the other top guys?

TARA: "No, that would not have been appropriate."

SVEN: "Hold on." Sven picked up the phone and dialed Bob's office. "Bob, can you come to my office for a minute?"

BOB: "Sven, I'm kind of busy, what's up?"

SVEN: "Jack and Tara are in. . . ."

BOB: "I'll be right there."

Jack related the same information to Bob, and a lengthy discussion ensued. It became clear that unless they were able to confirm that the key decision makers at each of the top 10 customers were OK with it, they were not going to take a risk on hiring James. Everyone agreed that it would be impossible to get this information without alerting the customers to what was going on. The customers were already concerned with losing Tara; it would not be prudent to risk upsetting them further.

"I'll be sending this out after lunch." Sven handed Jack an offer letter to Karen Zaloom. "James may be the best candidate, but we are going to hire Karen. Bob and I believe that it is our responsibility to insure the success of Strong Tubing. Karen is the most appropriate candidate for the job. I am sure that you understand." They had already made their decision. With that, Tara and Jack were excused, and the door shut behind them. They went directly to the conference room to talk about what had just happened.

WHAT TO DO?

Tara and Jack could not believe what had just happened. Bob and Sven had agreed that James was a well-qualified candidate, and they didn't have anything against him personally. However, they were not willing to take a chance that foreign customers might respond negatively to an African-American sales rep. Both of the executives had hired minority candidates before, so their personal feelings didn't seem to be an issue. They just wanted to look out for the company's best interests.

However, Jack and Tara kept coming back to the fact that what was happening was wrong—James was the best candidate, so he should be offered the job. They discussed their options and wrote them in a list:

1. Drop the whole thing and work hard with Karen Zaloom to ensure her success.

2. Go to the president, Frank Bayer, and blow the whistle on the whole thing. However, Frank was out of town for the rest of the week and would be difficult to contact.

3. Contact Jerry Jones-Henry and get her reaction. However, Jerry would handle everything officially. She would make it a point to inform Sven and Bob that they had contacted her.

4. Talk to Polly Robeson. Polly, an African American, had taken a special interest in James's candidacy, and she also felt that he was the leading candidate. If she found out that he wasn't being offered the job, she would want to know why. Polly was not the type of person to handle things quietly.

5. Alert James to what was going on. This would probably blow up on the legal side, something that none of them wanted. ∎

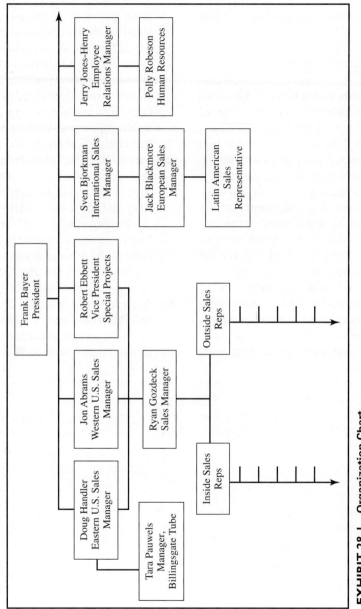

EXHIBIT 28-1   Organization Chart

324

Case 29   John Franklin

Late in the evening, John Franklin sat down to talk with the interviewer about the time he had spent in the Middle East and his current position with Major Construction Company, Incorporated. Franklin had recently returned to the United States after working in Saudi Arabia for 3 years and said he felt as if his "defense mechanisms" were starting to return.

John Franklin was a black American; after growing up and working in the United States, the differences in cultures that he had seen in Saudi Arabia were dramatic. Life in Saudi Arabia had a tremendous effect on him. He had worked with a number of different people from a variety of nations, but he had not experienced the racial prejudices he had felt in America. Upon his return to the United States, Franklin noticed that he felt more cautiousness toward his white counterparts than he had in the Middle East, and he recalled having had this same feeling prior to going to Saudi Arabia. Thinking about this feeling and reflecting on his experiences, he considered the question, "What was it like being a black American in Saudi Arabia and how was it different from being black in America?"

BACKGROUND

Franklin was currently a project manager with Major Construction Company in the United States. For the previous years, he had worked for SEI Engineering, a Saudi Arabian construction company. Franklin had traveled to Saudi Arabia after working for 4 years on various construction jobs in the Sunbelt region. He was born and raised in Tennessee, but had worked throughout the states and had traveled previously to Saudi Arabia while working for another U.S. company. He remembered his visits to the Middle East as enjoyable. "Americans were well respected for their ingenuity," he told the interviewer.

The move to the Middle East was prompted by the vast financial opportunities offered there. "The 1981 Reagan tax plan eliminated or reduced taxes for Americans working outside of the United States, making it much more attractive," Franklin commented. "This was the major incentive for most of the expatriates in Saudi Arabia—the money!" Highly regarded for their skills, Americans also were paid a premium to work in Saudi Arabia. Benefits paid by companies operating in Saudi Arabia included medical, housing, automobiles, and education and travel expenses.

Franklin's job with SEI Engineering had consisted of managing a variety of construction projects in and around the capital city of Riyadh. SEI, which was owned by an American-educated Saudi, built facilities for Saudi royalty and government ministries. Projects included sports complexes, hospitals, dormitories, and office buildings. Franklin went to SEI as a construction

UVA-OB-0382

This case was prepared by Bryan W. Smith under the supervision of James G. Clawson, Professor of Business Administration. This case was written as a basis for class discussion rather than to illustrate effective or ineffective handling of an administrative situation. Copyright © 1990 by the Darden Graduate Business School Foundation, Charlottesville, VA. All rights reserved. Rev. 12/00.

manager and was promoted to the position of director of Construction Management after a year and a half. His duties included the management and supervision of engineers from countries such as Korea, the Philippines, India, Denmark, England, Scotland, Sweden, and the United States. A variety of religious backgrounds was also represented, as Muslims, Hindus, Buddhists, and Christians were included among the workers. Construction projects progressed much more slowly in Saudi Arabia than in the United States, partly because of owner fickleness and partly because of logistical problems associated with obtaining building materials. Another key obstacle was communications; although English was the business language in Saudi Arabia, communicating with various laborers was a challenge: "You would quickly pick up certain words to communicate with the laborers. Showing emotion was important. We also used hand signals to a great extent," Franklin explained.

REFLECTIONS ON SAUDI ARABIA

Managing in a foreign country was a unique experience for Franklin. It was important for him always to try to see things from the laborer's perspective. Managing workers who were from so many diverse backgrounds exposed him to the vast differences among people. Although the cultural differences were clearly evident, there were few conflicts. All foreign workers in Saudi Arabia were "invited" to work there; you could not enter the country unless you had government authorization and were sponsored by a Saudi representative. Because of this climate, all expatriates were given equal treatment. Racial and religious factors seldom came into play. The government considered foreign workers to be in the country for a specific purpose and treated them accordingly. This environment suited John Franklin well: "I felt like I was

free, or rather, equal . . . at least accepted as an equal for my abilities. If someone did not like you, it wasn't because of your race or religion."

In addition to respecting his educational background, the Saudis trusted Franklin, in part because of his being a black American. The black American was thought to be an underdog, and the Saudis felt they related to the experiences of black Americans. White Americans were thought to be a part of the "system." Franklin recalled that the Saudis would often confide in him regarding business proposals:

> When putting a proposal together or presenting a competing bid, often after the meeting the Saudis would ask what I really thought about the negotiations, even if I was involved in the bid. They would ask, "Is this guy giving me a fair shake; are they being honest with me?" They felt more comfortable with me. They felt they could trust me. This wouldn't happen in the States.

Franklin believed that the great variety of cultures found on the construction sites in Saudi Arabia made race/cultural relations easier than if only a few cultures had been represented. In addition, because so many of the workers were foreigners and were isolated, there was a comradery that bound them together and made working together easier: "It was nice . . . it was nice not being a minority."

Franklin indicated that management problems that existed in the United States also were present in Saudi Arabia, but the preconceived notions that were common in the United States were not present there. He admitted that there were prejudices, but they were not related to racial differences. The prejudices that he had seen were related to social, cultural, and religious differences that existed primarily in the Middle East. Franklin felt that in Saudi

Arabia he was allowed to manage based on his abilities, not the color of his skin. He believed that white Americans had more difficulty adapting to the Saudi culture:

> The biggest difference you notice is in the dealings with a white American when he realizes that for the first time he is a minority. It's a big change for him. When he's sitting in a meeting and we're all black [Saudis or Americans]— that was interesting.

CONTRASTS

Franklin noted particular contrasts between how people were treated in the United States and in the Middle East. He had returned to the United States because he wanted to raise his daughter here. His job as a project manager with Major Construction Company had responsibilities that were similar to those of his previous job in Saudi Arabia, and he felt comfortable with the types of projects that Major Construction handled. The relaxed racial atmosphere that he had experienced in Saudi Arabia, however, did not exist in the States. Franklin felt that here he was always on guard around his coworkers, and he believed that they always second-guessed his judgment. He felt tension in social settings as if his peers were being especially careful not to tell offensive jokes or make derogatory comments around

him. In Saudi Arabia there had been no pressure to conform, and Franklin felt confident and self-assured about his abilities. He recalled:

> Here everything is based on color. Being used to that caught me off stride in Saudi Arabia. There, the race issue never crosses your mind. But it doesn't hit you all at once; it's gradual. You gradually go from one extreme to the other. Whereas in the States you're always on guard, in Saudi Arabia I relaxed and lost that guarded feeling— that "sixth sense" that all black Americans have. It was a good feeling.

The relaxed racial climate that Franklin experienced in Saudi Arabia made coming back to the United States difficult. He knew that the conditions in Saudi Arabia could be attributed to many different factors, but he wondered whether this climate could be duplicated here. At Major Construction Company, Franklin supervised workers that were both black and white. He wondered how his prejudices would affect his supervision and whether his "defensiveness" toward whites affected his performance. In considering what he could do about his prejudices, he decided to begin looking for answers in his experiences in Saudi Arabia. ■

Case 30   Jeri Caldwell at MOEX, Incorporated (A)

The church sermon had been inspiring. The choir had most of the congregation rocking and clapping in their seats. However, Jeff Fairbanks was less focused on the discerning of the spirit than on the activity that was to follow. He approached his next stop with some trepidation. Fairbanks had been the vice president for Strategic Human Resources at the MOEX Corporation for 2½ years. The previous day he had received a call from Jeri Caldwell in which she relayed to him the details of what she called the "Friday blowout." She had been passed over for promotion—a third time. During a meeting with her manager, she found herself yelling in frustration and then storming out of his office. She asked Fairbanks to meet with her to discuss what she should do next.

Under normal circumstances, Fairbanks would not informally meet with an employee at the center of such a volatile situation. Within the hierarchy of MOEX, there were three layers of management between Jeff and Jeri's manager. It would have been more appropriate to have one of Fairbank's subordinates manage the situation. However, Fairbanks didn't feel that these were normal circumstances. He felt compelled to meet with Caldwell out of a sense of responsibility for her well-being and success. Because he had lived the story before with countless other employees, he knew the tale Caldwell would reveal, and he knew

he supported her. He didn't know what to do about it, though.

MOEX

In 1966, an ambitious young Californian, Desmond Morris, dropped out of the engineering school at the University of California at Berkeley to start up a computer electronics supply company in Oakland, California. Morris Electronics, Incorporated (MOEX) grew rapidly from a small supplier of computer mainframe components to a leading company in the design, development, manufacturing, and marketing of computer components and peripherals, including printers, fax/copiers, scanners, calculators, and a host of components and related products at numerous levels of integration. More recently, MOEX developed a line of personal digital assistants (PDAs) and was aggressively pursuing audio product development to leverage the increasing popularity of MP3 technology. In addition to its commercial products, MOEX also produced embedded products for communications, industrial equipment, and the U.S. military. MOEX's sales rapidly expanded during the late 1970s as it supplied semiconductor memory for large computers. By the mid 1980s, the firm's diversified product line and reputation for high-quality products secured MOEX's position as an industry

UVA-OB-0691

This case was prepared by Gerry Yemen under the supervision of Martin N. Davidson, Associate Professor of Business Administration. The authors thank Rachel Bagby, James Clawson, Joseph Harder, and C. V. Harquail for their helpful comments. This case was written as a basis for class discussion rather than to illustrate effective or ineffective handling of an administrative situation. Copyright © 2000 by the University of Virginia Darden School Foundation, Charlottesville, VA. All rights reserved.

leader. The company's annual sales rose from $400 million in 1989 to more than $2.5 billion in 1998.

MOEX had a reputation for having a congenial and pleasant climate in which to work. The culture was one in which employees tended to be cordial and collegial with one another. High value was placed on teamwork and collaborative learning; MOEX was one of the few companies that genuinely rewarded employees for effective teamwork as well as for individual accomplishment. For example, a work team could receive team bonuses if the innovative product maintained a baseline of sales volume over its first 6 months on the market. When conflict arose, MOEX employees were expected to resolve the differences professionally and amicably.

As MOEX expanded both domestically and globally, senior management became increasingly aware that a varied set of skills and perspectives would be necessary to shepherd this growth. Already MOEX's competitors had outbid them in securing lucrative contracts in Japan, China, Ghana, and Brazil. Top management suspected that its managers were somehow a step behind in managing key relationships in these negotiations and that its managers and representatives would need to cultivate greater skill in its global interactions. Alarmingly, MOEX's inability to garner key contracts was not restricted to the international front. MOEX had been denied a key government contract because it had failed to meet the most basic affirmative action guidelines that would apply to U.S. government contractors.

The company had been founded and its ranks dominated by white males in their late 30s born in the U.S. (mostly in northern California). However, the labor pool of talented engineers and technicians in the West and Southwest included increasing numbers of Asians and Asian Americans, African Americans, Latinos, and Native Americans. Moreover, MOEX had serious concerns that competitors would have the advantage in attracting these engineers and technicians. MOEX had never been an industry leader when it came to attracting and retaining talented minority and international candidates. The company was perceived as conservative in its culture relative to other high-tech firms, and it had developed a reputation in communities of color as being unsupportive and, in isolated situations, hostile to people of color. Fairbanks felt the criticism was patently unfair, but it was a fact of life.

The company was not passive toward its public image. In fact, MOEX had taken several steps toward change. The firm actively tried to recruit from Historically Black Colleges and Universities (HBCUs) like Florida A&M, Southern, and Howard University. MOEX paired employees with high school students from the public school district, which was 80 percent nonwhite. The company even received a letter commending its efforts from the National Societies of Black and of Hispanic Engineers in the Western States region. Yet despite the concerted endeavor to attract new talent, recruitment numbers were modest compared to industry norms. Even more alarming was the observed trend of attrition of talented African American and Asian American engineers from MOEX over the past 10 months. Peremptory exit interviews offered little insight into why this trend was emerging.

JEFF FAIRBANKS

Jeff Fairbanks had been an employee at MOEX for 18 years. He started in 1982 as a technician setting up new computers, and he had risen through the ranks to become the first African-American vice president at the firm. He was familiar with the "first" or "only" situation minorities often faced in corporations. He was one of a small number of black executives who made substantial personal sacrifices in order to succeed in corporate America:

The interesting thing I found out in MOEX when it came to race is that not just in corporate America but in a lot of different arenas, being black is a liability—"last hired, first fired," "gotta be better than the best," all of that. And with my white counterparts it was just opposite, they thought that me being black was an advantage. So I spent a lot of time in those kinds of discussions and they would say, "Well, you know MOEX is going to promote blacks and that's going to happen to you because you're black." But when you look at the numbers, you see the reality. But it was always that feeling that you're treated especially well, given extra breaks because you're black. So I think that where it shows up the most was that I felt like I had to adopt certain work ethics that were associated with whites, and put up with certain kinds of behaviors that were associated with being "in" with whites. I very quickly said that if I'm going to be successful, I can't necessarily associate them with being white, but I have to associate them with being successful.

Even so, Fairbanks was proud of MOEX's attempts to recruit talented minority candidates and its overall concern about becoming more diverse.

As the choir closed, singing a spiritual chocked full of hallelujahs, Fairbanks still thought about Caldwell. Perhaps talking to her would give Fairbanks an opportunity to understand more deeply what caused the more recent spate of departures of talented people from MOEX.

JERI CALDWELL

Jeri Caldwell was smart, young, and ambitious, and anyone who spent a few minutes with her knew it. She had a quality of quiet dynamism about her that was both appealing and sometimes mysterious. Jeri gradu-

ated from MIT in 1996 in the top 5 percent of her class. People who knew her mused at how she seemed to defy the stereotype of MIT engineers as nerdy white guys with pocket protectors. She had a tremendous interest in applying her intelligence and training to the private sector and envisioned her career as a fast-moving executive in a high-tech firm. When she landed an entry-level position in product design at MOEX in the fall of 1996, she felt she was right in the career track she wanted.

Jeri worked hard in her new position, and although the tasks at hand were challenging and fun, at times she had difficulty connecting with her colleagues. She had always been a little introverted and had struggled to cultivate close relationships with people. The people with whom she worked at MOEX were extremely nice and helpful to her. A couple of the more experienced design technicians made a special effort to show her the ropes when she first arrived. Her coworkers' attitudes made her feel supported in her first days there. However, as time progressed, she never felt like the connections she was making were sustained. People were never mean or impolite to her. Rather, they seemed to be more and more pleasantly indifferent. Jeri found this odd but she didn't dwell on it. The bottom line was that she loved what she was doing, and she was optimistic about her prospects for advancement at MOEX.

IN THE KITCHEN

Jeri pulled the mugs down from her cupboard, five total. She seemed somewhat distraught as she measured out coffee from the can to the pot. She only had about 20 minutes before a few friends and colleagues from work would arrive at her home to help her sort out how she should handle the repercussions from the "Friday fallout." Jeri always saw herself as easy-going and friendly, and a little conflict-avoidant. So she was as surprised as anyone to find herself standing in Frank Tanner's office, yelling at the top of her lungs. Tanner, her manager for the past 3 months, had asked Jeri to come to his office to discuss her candidacy for a promotion to product manager. When he informed her that she had been denied the promotion, she could not contain her disappointment. She lost it and stormed out of Tanner's office and out of the building.

So on this Sunday after the confrontation, she waited to talk with four key people she trusted—Bonita Harriman, C. J. Roberts, Raeford Marshall, and Jeff Fairbanks. The group sat comfortably around the round kitchen table. A boxed coffee cake lay open in the table center. Caldwell poured both the coffee and her troubles . . .

Jeri Caldwell: I don't know, the scenario felt like déjà vu. I had been passed over before for a similar promotion, even though at the time I thought I was ready for it. I had studied hard and gained a good working knowledge of the product line. I had tried to cultivate positive relationships with my peers. So when my boss explained that the person who got the position had more experience, as well as stronger relationships with several key internal clients, I was disappointed. But after some reflection I admitted to myself that I could have used more seasoning.

Fairbanks shifted his weight from one side of the chair to the other. He wouldn't have been there save for family friendship shared by the Fairbanks and Caldwells. Fairbanks harbored fond memories of time spent with "Gram Caldwell," Jeri's grandmother. She had baby-sat Fairbanks, Jeri's dad, and several of the other kids from the neighborhood. If he tried hard enough, he could still smell the aroma of homemade bread that flowed from Gram Caldwell's kitchen. When Jeri's father died in 1993,

Fairbanks took it upon himself to watch out for Jeri. He wasn't a guardian or even a mentor in the professional sense. Yet he felt it was important to support her as much as possible. In essence, she was family.

However, he was less than comfortable with the others in the room. He gazed past Caldwell, at the rest, hoping to gauge their reactions to the discussion so far. Bonita Harriman was one of Caldwell's contemporaries at MOEX, bright and industrious, but a little overbearing. She was the kind of person in whose presence Fairbanks had to stifle a cringe because she often would say something that he found inappropriately candid. In her youthful exuberance, Fairbanks reasoned, she hadn't learned to temper her behavior . . .

Bonita interrupted Jeri:

Bonita Harriman: Give me a break, will you! You can call it "more seasoning" but every one of us sitting here knows what's going on. You were getting into the office at 6:30 in the morning and going home well past the rest of the managers. You worked hard, you produced, and you know full well that if you had been one of the white boys in that place, we would be sitting here excited for you over your next promotion. We all know there is only one way to win in that place. Act white, act mannish. If you don't want to play that game, don't even pretend that you'll move up there. Period!

Jeri and Bonita had met during orientation at MOEX and instantly hit it off. She knew she could trust Bo to bring a breath of the outside world to any situation. Jeri generally appreciated Bo's attitude, even though she was sometimes annoyed by it. Jeri went on:

Jeri Caldwell: Well, rejection is a painful process, so I decided to get something out of it. I remembered this study on marine species we talked about in E-school at

MIT. You know, the group of scientists studying marine life behavior. They built a tank with a transparent, but impermeable, barrier down the middle. On one side of the wall the scientists placed food and then proceeded to place different marine creatures on the foodless side of the tank's wall. The researchers observed various types of marine animals and their behavior, one by one.

A carp was the first creature placed in the tank. It swam around and around going after the food. The carp kept hitting its head on the wall but couldn't get the food, so it gave up and swam away. A shark was placed in the tank next. It too swam around and around and charged after the food. The shark hit the wall and, although slightly stunned, it backed up and hit the wall harder and harder again several times. Finally the shark gave up. It was a bloody mess and still hungry. The last species observed was a dolphin. Like the carp and shark, it swam around and then went after the food. The dolphin also hit the wall over and over. But it never hit the wall in the same place twice and finally jumped over the wall. I decided I would get over the wall, too. I would never accept being an "outsider."

Feeling like an outsider himself, Fairbanks tried not to look at Raeford Marshall as he gulped down the last of his coffee. Marshall had joined MOEX before Fairbanks but never advanced past the lower echelons of management. He once told Fairbanks that the stereotyping, good ole boy's jokes, and condescending attitudes pained him too deeply to keep networking in that circle. If that was the only way up, he refused to bend over or even slightly lean toward sacrificing his blackness for a chance at advancement. Fairbanks circled the top of his coffee cup with his index finger, round and round and round and listened . . .

Jeri Caldwell: So, this time I knew I was ready for the promotion. I had positive feedback from subordinates who described my leadership style as flexible enough to direct or delegate when appropriate. On more than one occasion I was thanked for encouraging participation and enhancing other people's sense of efficacy. I could feel genuine excitement about their work on certain projects. So when Tanner gave me the news that I had been passed over once again, it was like he had stuck a fork in my heart. He said that my proficiency was top notch, but despite the progress I had made, my leadership and teamwork skills left something to be desired. I was seething—it just wasn't true! I lost control of my emotions when I let Tanner have it.

Marshall accidentally knocked the spoon off his plate. The white, ivy-bordered enamel tabletop rang tinnily with the bump of the dinnerware. Marshall hopelessly shook his head as he spoke slowly and softly.

Raeford Marshall: And that there is probably the gravest mistake you made, Jeri. You are not allowed to get pissed off. I thought you understood that. It's all right for some folks to get angry and throw chairs but that does not include you. You are allowed to be "disappointed." That's it.

Bonita Harriman: Maybe so, maybe not, Raeford. Jeri losing it might not be as big a problem for her as it would be for you or me. I have always maintained that if I make an error, folks will just say "that figures." I graduated as an engineer from a "black college" so that somehow makes me less qualified and bound to make mistakes. Even though we were both on the dean's list, Jeri's mistakes are construed as bumps along the path, isn't that right 'Mr. VP?' she said, giving Fairbanks "the look."

No, Jeri is just "developing" or "training," not making fatal mistakes. I heard one of the industrial technician managers talk about how Jeri had made it through MIT and he had not been able to cut it. That Jeri was really qualified as opposed to those of us who went to Howard! I bet Tanner could be convinced to see this as a spot in Jeri's maturity phase, not as a character flaw in an emotional black female.

Jeri Caldwell: I wondered whether being a double minority had something to do with continually being passed over. I had discounted people's grumbling in the past—you included Bo—because I can't stand the victim mentality. But it seemed like I had conquered one layer of the decision-making process only to discover another one emerged that effectively blocked my advancement. I just couldn't believe it had come to because I thought I could move up the ranks of a high-performance, dynamic firm. When I arrived, only 3 years ago, if you had asked me about whether I would be taking my place as an effective leader in the company, I would have answered with a resounding "Yes!"

It was C. J. Roberts who spoke up next. Roberts was several years older than Caldwell and had joined MOEX a few years after Fairbanks. She had experienced barrier after barrier to advancement at MOEX and knew that being black and being a woman was a combination that held her back. She rarely blew her stack at hints of aspersion but simply preferred to resort to facts.

C. J. Roberts: Jeri, the way I see it you have run up to a tree that you just can't climb. You have to understand something, sweetheart. Corporate America was not designed to be an institution for you. I don't say this with any malice—it's simply fact. If you are white, male, and speak the King's English (or maybe I should say Desmond Morris's English), then you have a chance. If you are black and female, you think in one direction and one direction only. Go to places like MOEX, learn what you can about operating in the business world, acquire capital, and always plan your exit strategy so that you can start your own enterprise. Don't get caught up in the illusion that you can ever really be a part of a place like MOEX.

It was with that statement that the odd array of coffee drinkers collectively looked at Fairbanks, the one who had made it. He started out tentatively, searching for the right words, "OK, you don't see anybody before me in MOEX that looks like us, do you? I'm not blind to that fact. But I am not yet in a position . . ."

Before he could finish his defense, Bonita, who could generally manage to convey her distain with a glance, burst out, unable to constrain herself, "Oh, get off it Jeff! How long are you going to put up with this mess! What are *you* going to do?"

Fairbanks sat silently. In that moment, the variety of challenges was apparent to him. He was the vice president of Strategic Human Resources and one of the most powerful people in MOEX. He believed deeply in the importance of fairness in the workplace, both because it was good business and because it was the right way, the spiritual way, to treat people. No situation in which people are treated unfairly can be tolerated. In addition, he was the highest-ranking African American executive in MOEX and felt a responsibility to younger black employees to help eliminate the barriers that had confronted him in his career development.

He also knew that in just 36 hours, he would be face-to-face with the seven members of the executive leadership team. Prior experience made it clear that raising issues of fairness and diversity in this group would be controversial. He just didn't know how much influence and goodwill he would sacrifice if he really pushed the diversity issue. He knew that at least a couple of his colleagues would question whether he was raising this as a tactic to deflect attention from the shortcomings of the HR Department. He also wondered if he could develop the systems necessary to tackle these problems effectively.

Fairbanks had to decide what to do. ■

Case 31   Robert Jones

The autumn sunshine streamed into Robert Jones's office as he sat working through his mail. It had been a good year thus far, and he was busy, humming through his afternoon routine, when there came a loud knock on his door. Before he could speak, the door opened and in stormed an angry woman. He thought he'd seen her somewhere before but wasn't quite sure. His confusion cleared when she announced that she was the wife of one of his immediate subordinates, George Ellis. George was an auditing engineer who traveled from plant to plant in the company reviewing and auditing engineering procedures and practices; he also visited various customers' construction sites, providing an engineering consultation service to them.

"Mr. Jones," the woman said, with obvious indignation, "the situation with my husband and his new trainee is absolutely intolerable! It is obvious that the woman has not had proper training as a young child, and I find it completely unacceptable that she be not only allowed but *encouraged* to travel with my husband in the way she is now! Given that she hasn't received the training that she should have, I would be happy to pick up the motel and traveling expenses in order for me to travel with them and act as a mother for this young woman and give her the proper training for how she should conduct herself in society!"

Mr. Jones was taken aback at the suddenness and the vehemence of Mrs. Ellis's comments. As she stood before his desk, her hands on her hips, glaring at him, he struggled to put the situation into context.

Background

C&B Industrial Products, Incorporated, manufactured a variety of metal parts and subassemblies for a wide range of industrial customers. The company also provided a range of engineering consultation services to its customers with regard to its products and their relation to their customers' specific needs. C&B maintained manufacturing plants throughout several states in the southeastern United States. At the time Mrs. Ellis came in to see Mr. Jones, about 3,200 employees were working for C&B.

As head of Engineering Services, Robert Jones had two jobs. First, he periodically reviewed and made recommendations for the improvement of various engineering techniques and procedures that the company used in its plants. Second, he supervised visits to customer work sites to assist in the design of the parts and subassemblies that they wanted C&B to manufacture and to consult with them on various aspects of their operations. This on-site service saved both the customer and the company much time and expense, all of which meant that George Ellis traveled a lot to the company's plants to conduct the "engineering audits," assessing the effectiveness and efficiency of the procedures used throughout the company, and to customers' sites and facilities.

Mr. Jones thought back quickly to the company's recruiting season the previous spring. He had been heavily involved with attempts to find a new engineer to travel with George Ellis and the other engineering auditors. Mr. Jones was delighted when the

UVA-OB-369
Prepared by James G. Clawson. Copyright © 1988 by the Darden Graduate Business School Foundation, Charlottesville, VA.

state university's engineering department had produced several candidates he thought could fill the job. He was equally excited when he discovered that without any compromise in technical standards, he could contribute to the firm's Equal Employment Opportunity goals by hiring a woman, Deborah May Jackson. He remembered his interviews with Deborah, her assertiveness and buoyant personality. He found her engaging and well-trained, if a little young and inexperienced, and he was enthusiastic about her joining his department and learning the auditing job from Mr. Ellis. He expected that she would be able to take on additional responsibilities in the near future.

The Immediate Problem

Mr. Jones's mind snapped back to the present; he refocused on the face of the woman standing before him. He knew that Mr. and Mrs. Ellis had been married for more than 20 years. He believed the couple to be faithful and devoted to each other in their marriage. Mr. Ellis was a long-term and valued employee of C&B. Mr. Jones's thoughts were interrupted by the insistent voice of Mrs. Ellis:

> About a year ago, while I was visiting my sister who was sick and dying with cancer, George called on several occasions to tell me that the company had decided to hire a female engineer. I was surprised at the time as to why he was so concerned about this, but the more he called and talked to me about this situation, the more I began to understand. He was concerned that they might hire a black female engineer and wondered what it would mean for him to be traveling with this person on field trips. Most of the field trips, as you know, are in rural settings and down country roads wherever the next project might be. George was afraid that people might start calling him names, and he didn't like it.
>
> A few weeks later, after you all had hired this Jackson woman, she and

George were on one of their first trips, a 3-day trip, this time to Pennsylvania. He brought her by the house to pick up his suitcases. I was lying in bed feeling ill with a backache. As we were talking, I realized that this *female* traveling companion, in her immaturity, was walking down the hallway taking her own tour of the house. I said something to her, and George got mad at me for being short about the situation. He told me to take her out to the living room and entertain her and talk with her while he was packing. Which I did.

> Mr. Jones, you know that George has a physical condition that requires that he take long walks on a daily basis. Well, when they got to the Pennsylvania hotel and after they had finished dinner, he said "goodnight" and went out for his evening walk. She apparently called after him and said "Oh, wait, let me go with you; I'll go on a walk, too." During this whole time, my husband was *very* uncomfortable, and he was wondering how other people were viewing them.

> That's *another* thing, Mr. Jones! I know the corporation has an expense account, and I find it very distasteful that my husband will be taking this young woman to relatively expensive restaurants at the company's expense and having dark, candlelight dinners with her. I just don't think that's right!

> *Then,* on another trip, when they checked in to the hotel, the clerk looked at one, then looked at the other and said, "The bill will be $60. Who will be paying for it?" He apparently believed that it was going to be the two of them staying in one room for some kind of *tryst* rather than a business meeting! My husband was embarrassed for himself *and* for this female. He asked for two rooms, and they went their separate ways. But when he returned he was disgusted, and he told me that he refused

to travel with her anymore. Frankly, Mr. Jones, I agree with him. I will not stand by while my husband is entertaining and traveling with young, immature women who don't know their place!

And do you know *what?* I understand this woman came to work the other day with a new bumper sticker on her car which read "This Profession Does It with Precision." I like to died! This is absolutely deplorable, and it's indicative of the kind of character that this woman brings to work!

A *further* thing, Mr. Jones! Here's a picture from a local newspaper. It shows the changes in events that have taken place at [the state university] and a picture of several university officials and students. One of the student leaders, the president of student council, is a male, and the other four or five of the officers—including those of the Engineering School—are women! This just goes to show you how the *boys,* and I do mean *boys,* 'cause we certainly can't call them "men," are allowing the aggressive, young, immature females to take over all the positions of power both at the university and now increasingly in business. We personally have decided not to contribute any more funds to the university in order to demonstrate our protest at this deplorable change in behavior. Although times are changing, the Bible says that God has always been and will be the same, forever, and it is not appropriate for young women to be pursuing jobs like this that will allow them to seduce people's husbands at the office and ruin other women's lives and marriages!

Mr. Jones listened patiently while Mrs. Ellis continued:

On another occasion, when they went to dinner, my husband paid the bill. That's the way that other traveling men

do this; they trade off when they travel. No one ever worried about who was paying more or who was paying less, because it all evened out in the end. However, when he picked up the bill, he noted that while *he* had only had one beer for the evening, *she* had had *three* cocktails. George thought that was an unusual expense. Don't you?

Before Mr. Jones could answer, she went on:

The next night, she didn't pick up the bill, so George thought things were getting out of hand here. So, the next night, before dinner, George gave her his pocket change and told her that if she was going to live in a man's world, she would have to behave like a man, and so *she* was to pay the bill. He said that she looked a little surprised. George has told me that many of his colleagues feel the same as he does and that they won't travel with this woman either!

Now then, what are *you* going to do about this?

Mr. Jones knew that Mrs. Ellis was a professional woman, a social worker, respected in the community, and that she and her husband had two grown sons and a daughter, all of whom had graduated from the local state university. He also knew that the firm enjoyed a good relationship with the school and had hired many engineers from it. As he considered all that Mrs. Ellis had told him, his mind searched frantically for what he might say to her. How accurate were Mrs. Ellis's descriptions of the events? How many of his employees felt the same way as she did, whether or not her husband felt as she did? And what were the general trends and feelings in the community in which the corporation operated?

Then he opened his mouth to speak. ■

Case 32   Kellogg-Worthington Merger

Looking over downtown Battle Creek from his office in Kellogg's headquarters, John D. Cook was anticipating the new direction that his next steps would take his company. Mr. Cook had been in his position as executive vice president of the Kellogg Company and president of Kellogg North America for only 9 months. Yet this was a point that could start a transformation at Kellogg. Tomorrow, October 1, 1999, Kellogg was announcing its acquisition of Worthington Foods, Incorporated, a vegetarian and health food manufacturer based outside Columbus, Ohio.

Cook had known what he was getting into, from a business perspective, when he accepted the offer to leave McKinsey & Company, Incorporated and join Kellogg. He knew and understood the pressures facing food manufacturers. After all, as the leader of McKinsey's Midwest Consumer Goods Practice, he had helped multiple companies understand, adapt to, and profit from the same trends Kellogg was facing. Yet he knew that this coming challenge was going to be formidable.

Kellogg was the recognized "King of Breakfast." Yet its dominance in the breakfast market was eroding, and most of its recent strategic initiatives had been unable to stem the tide. The company's share of the cereal market was shrinking; its previous acquisition, Lender's Bagel, was a $180 million disaster, and the company's highly anticipated Ensemble foods line was being removed from shelves at this very moment. The company needed to pursue a direction that would both halt the company's struggling performance and accelerate its growth.

Cook thought he had found it. Worthington Foods could be a first step: It seemed to be a perfect fit, with its nutritious products, common distribution, and presence in a growing (albeit niche) market.

Cook had been the prime advocate for acquiring Worthington. Kellogg was paying an estimated $307 million in cash for Worthington, 15 times Worthington's operating income. Accordingly, the company would recognize close to $200 million in goodwill, a hefty premium.

Worthington could provide the growth Kellogg was searching for. Unfortunately, it could do little to stop the deterioration in the company's cereal business. All Cook had to do was find roughly $200 million in benefits to break even on the Worthington deal and turn around the other Kellogg businesses. He just needed to decide where to start.

GENERAL HISTORY

Kellogg Company was founded in 1906 in Battle Creek, Michigan, by Will Keith (W. K.) Kellogg. W. K. and his older brother, Dr. John Harvey (J. H.) Kellogg,

UVA-BP-0426

This case was prepared by Luis Franco, MBA '00, and Margaret Cording, Ph.D. candidate, under the supervision of L. J. Bourgeois, Professor of Business Administration. Support was provided by PricewaterhouseCoopers and the Batten Institute. Copyright © 2001 by the University of Virginia Darden School Foundation, Charlottesville, VA. All rights reserved.

discovered flaked wheat and corn cereal while running the Battle Creek Sanitarium in 1894. The sanitarium was an internationally known Seventh Day Adventist hospital and spa that treated patients using exercise, fresh air, and strict diets prohibiting caffeine, alcohol, tobacco, and meat.

The Kellogg Company has had a focus on nutrition since its founding. J. H. Kellogg and his wife, Ella Eaton Kellogg, and Mary Barber, the founder of the Seventh Day Adventist Church, were early proponents of the nutritional qualities of grain-based foods and improving the health of the American public. W. K. Kellogg split with his brother and the sanitarium after philosophical disagreements on whether or not whole-grain cereal should be a mainstream or niche product. After the split, W. K. created the Battle Creek Toasted Corn Flake Company, the predecessor of the Kellogg Company.

W. K. Kellogg and the Kellogg Company continued to promote the importance of nutrition after separating from the sanitarium. The company, in fact, set the industry standard for nutritional focus in the growing cereal industry. Kellogg was the first company to hire a professional nutritionist, restore cereal nutrient content to whole-grain levels, and print nutrition information on cereal packages.

Kellogg continued to build on its nutritional food heritage with the development of its fortification capabilities and a new emphasis on "functional foods." Functional foods were intended specifically to benefit health, as the understanding of the impact of diet on leading causes of death such as cancer, diabetes, and cardiovascular disease increased.

Following the death of W. K. Kellogg in 1951 and until the present, the company attempted to broaden its product portfolio. New cereal brands were added in addition to noncereal products, such as Kellogg's Pop-Tarts, which were introduced in 1964.

The company also effectively used advertising to accelerate its growth from the time it was founded. Kellogg was able to capitalize on the newest and most popular media at the time, making the progression from print to radio to television advertising. The company was the first to place a full-page ad in the *Ladies Home Journal.* The Kellogg Singing Lady was a popular radio personality who "enchanted young children with songs, verse, and fairy stories."[1] In addition, Kellogg sponsored radio programs such as Wild Bill Hickok, Tom Corbet, and Space Cadet, later moving to television with sponsorships of *Rin-Tin-Tin*, the *Partridge Family*, and the *Woody Woodpecker Show.* Kellogg also relied on innovative promotions, such as a national contest for the "best ear of corn," for which the company paid the winner $1,000.

The early importance of advertising developed one of the company's principal strengths, the Kellogg brand in cereal. Kellogg's icons—such as Tony the Tiger®; Toucan Sam®; and Snap,® Crackle,® and Pop®—were among the most recognized in advertising (see Exhibit 32-1).

By 1999, Kellogg was the world's leading producer of ready-to-eat cereal and a leading producer of grain-based convenience foods. The company's cereals and convenience foods were manufactured in 20 countries on six continents and sold in more than 160 countries around the world. Its product portfolio included ready-to-eat cereal, cereal bars, toaster pastries, and, until recently, frozen bagels.

COMPANY PERFORMANCE

Recently, Kellogg had been struggling. In 1998, the company reported sales of $6.76 billion, down 1 percent from 1997 and

---

[1]History exhibit, Kellogg's Cereal City, Battle Creek, Michigan.

Cereals	Cereal bars (Apple Cinnamon)
Apple Jacks	Cereal bars (Mixed Berry)
Frosted Flakes	Cereal bars (Strawberry)
All Bran	**Pop-Tarts**
Raisin Bran	Frosted S'mores
Cocoa Krispies	Frosted Wild Berry
Product 19	Strawberry
Crispix	Blueberry
Corn Flakes	Pastry Swirls (Apple Cinnamon)
	Pastry Swirls (Cinnamon Creme)
Eggo	Snack Stix (Cookies and Creme)
Buttermilk Pancakes	Snack Stix (Frosted Strawberry)
Low Fat Nutri-Grain Waffles	**Rice Krispies Treats**
Nutri-Grain Waffles	Peanut Butter
Toaster Delights	Chocolate
Waf-Fulls	Original
Blueberry Waffles	Cocoa
Nut and Honey Waffles	
Nutri-Grain	
Twists (S'mores)	
Twists (Strawberry and Blueberry)	

EXHIBIT 32-1   Kellogg Company Product and Brand Portfolio

3.5 percent below 1995's sales level of $7 billion, its best year ever.

Kellogg's profit performance also had been deteriorating. The company's operating and net margins each fell close to 20 percent from previous-year levels. In addition, since 1994, Kellogg's operating margin had declined at a compound annual rate of -4.3 percent. The decline in margin was reflected in the company's earnings per share (EPS). Kellogg's 1998 EPS fell to $1.35 from $1.70 a year earlier, marked by four consecutive quarters of lower earnings. Only recently had the slide abated, with second-quarter 1999 earnings per share exceeding the same previous-year period by $0.01 ($0.35 versus $0.36). (See Exhibits 32-2 and 32-3 for financial highlights.)

The decline in financial performance was driven largely by weakness in Kellogg's core cereal business. Growth of the flagship cereal brands had been minimal and the company had been unable to compensate in other areas. The company's global cereal volumes fell by close to 2 percent, offsetting the gains of global convenience foods. Although Kellogg led the industry with an estimated 38 percent share of worldwide cereal volume, it was a decrease from 44 percent in 1992.[2] Table 32-1 shows the company's unit volume market share by region.

Kellogg's problems had not gone unnoticed in the market, with investors showing little confidence in the future prospects for the company. In 1998, the stock underperformed the S&P 500 by 58 percent and the S&P Food Index by 21 percent. That difference grew to 159 percent and 97 percent, respectively, when compared over the

---

[2]Kellogg Company, "We See the Cereal Bowl as Half Full Rather than Half Empty," Salomon Smith Barney, January 15, 1999.

	1993	*1994*	*1995*	*1996*	*1997*	*1998*
Income Statement						
Net Sales	$6,295	$6,562	$7,004	$6,677	$6,830	$6,762
Cost of Goods Sold	2,724	2,695	2,919	2,871	3,000	3,022
Depreciation	265	256	259	252	270	261
GROSS PROFIT	3,306	3,611	3,826	3,554	3,560	3,480
Margin	*52.5%*	*55.0%*	*54.6%*	*53.2%*	*52.1%*	*51.4%*
SG&A Expense	838	942	1,028	1,018	933	1,105
Advertising & Promotions	1,340	1,435	1,467	1,357	1,310	1,270
Other	59	72	72	84	123	139
OPERATING PROFIT	1,069	1,163	1,259	1,095	1,193	966
Margin	*17.0%*	*17.7%*	*18.0%*	*16.4%*	*17.5%*	*14.2%*
Interest Expense	33	45	63	66	108	120
Other Income/(Expense)	(2)	12	21	2	4	7
PRETAX INCOME	1,034	1,129	1,218	1,031	1,089	853
Taxes	353	424	456	380	384	304
Extraordinary Items	(6)	0	271	120	159	46
NET INCOME	686	705	490	531	546	503
EPS—Cont. Ops	$1.46	$1.57	$1.74	$1.53	$1.70	$1.35
EPS—Reported	1.47	1.57	1.12	1.25	1.32	1.24
Dividends per Share	0.66	0.70	0.75	0.81	0.87	0.92
Balance Sheet						
Total Assets	4,237	4,467	4,414	5,050	4,877	5,052
Long-Term Debt	1,713	1,808	1,591	1,282	1,415	1,614
Shareholders' Equity	522	719	718	727	998	890
Cash Flow						
Net Income	$681	$705	$762	$651	$705	$549
Depreciation & Amort.	265	256	259	252	287	278
Deferred Taxes	9	(13)	(79)	58	39	46
Chg. Working Capital	(37)	62	84	(77)	(10)	(136)
Operating Cash Flow	918	1,011	1,026	884	1,021	738
CAPEX	(450)	(354)	(316)	(307)	(312)	(374)
Dividends Common	−(305)	(314)	(329)	(344)	(360)	(375)
Free Cash Flow	154	330	460	175	310	(11)
Share Repurchases	(548.1)	(327.3)	(374.7)	(535.7)	(426.0)	(239.7)
Proceeds from Divestitures	114.6	101.8	6.3	11.6	5.9	6.8
Acquisitions	0	0	0	(505.2)	(25.4)	(27.8)
Cash Available for Debt	($271)	$117	$13	($796)	($98)	($272)

(continued)

EXHIBIT 32-2 Kellogg Financial Highlights (in millions)

(Net Inc. + Dep.)/Share	$2.04	$2.14	$2.33	$2.12	$2.40	$2.04
EBITDA/Share	$2.88	$3.16	$3.46	$3.17	$3.58	$3.07
Ratios						
Long-Term Debt to Total Capital	338%	251%	222%	176%	142%	181%
Return on Assets	16%	16%	11%	11%	11%	10%
Return on Equity	131%	98%	68%	73%	55%	57%

EXHIBIT 32-2 (continued)

	1993	*1994*	*1995*	*1996*	*1997*
North America					
Revenues	$3,782	$3,853	$4,085	$3,780	$3,968
Operating Income	658	709	768	635	742
Operating Margin	*17.4%*	*18.4%*	*18.8%*	*16.8%*	*18.7%*
Europe					
Revenues	1,541	1,684	1,824	1,745	1,705
Operating Income	245	288	332	281	278
Operating Margin	*15.9%*	*17.1%*	*18.2%*	*16.1%*	*16.3%*
Other International					
Revenues	965	1,037	1,096	1,147	1,161
Operating Income	166	167	159	179	173
Operating Margin	*17.2%*	*16.1%*	*14.5%*	*15.6%*	*14.9%*
Ready-to-Eat Cereal					
Sales	5,046	5,466	5,584	5,277	5,098
Growth	—	8.3%	2.1%	−5.5%	−3.4%
Operating Profit	875	987	1,016	862	885
Operating Margin	17.3%	18.1%	18.2%	16.3%	17.4%
Convenience Foods					
Sales	1,249	1,096	1,420	1,400	1,732
Growth	—	−12.3%	29.6%	−1.5%	23.7%
Operating Profit	194	175	244	233	309
Operating Margin	15.5%	16.0%	17.2%	16.6%	17.8%
Total Kellogg Sales	6,295	6,562	7,004	6,676	6,830

EXHIBIT 32-3 Kellogg Segment Financials (US$ millions)

previous 5 years. No analysts were currently recommending the stock, and the average rating of the stock was slightly below "underperform" and above "sell." The following chart illustrates the relative performance of Kellogg stock.

Meanwhile, Kellogg continued to pay dividends to shareholders. Dividends were increased in 1998, for the 42nd consecutive year, to $0.96 per share. Forty-five percent of the outstanding shares were held by the W. K. Kellogg Trust (33 percent) and one

TABLE 32-1 Ready-to-Eat Cereal Regional Volume (units) Market Share

Region	Volume Market Share 1998	1997
North America	33%	34%
Europe	43%	44%
Asia	43%	43%
Latin America	61%	60%

Source: Salomon Smith Barney, January 1999.

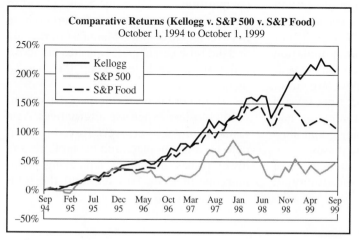

Source: Bloomberg.

director (12 percent). Other officers and directors held 1.5 percent.

Kellogg had been able to maintain the increase in dividends due to its continued strong cash flow. Since 1990, the company averaged close to $850 million in annual operating cash flow. In 1993 to 1998, Kellogg generated after-investing, after-dividend operating cash flow averaging close to $290 million. This was despite a negative year in 1996. The strong cash flow had been supplemented with an ongoing commercial paper program and worldwide credit facilities to provide ample liquidity to meet annual operating needs. Although cash flow levels had also begun to decline, cash flow was expected to remain a strength of the company even with diminishing margins and operating pressure, due to the company's operational efficiency.

Kellogg's struggling performance led to significant changes in Kellogg leadership in 1998 and the first 6 months of 1999. Carlos M. Gutierrez, appointed president and chief operating officer in 1998, became chief executive in early 1999, replacing longtime CEO Arnold Langbo. Each of the company's four major global sales regions was under new leadership, two of which came from outside Kellogg. These changes reached beyond the executive suite as managers throughout the company were reassigned or replaced.

INDUSTRY DESCRIPTION

The global ready-to-eat (RTE) cereal market was estimated to be a \$12 billion market.[3] Prior to 1994, cereal consumption had grown on average 4 percent annually. Since 1994, annual cereal consumption growth slowed to 1 percent. It was expected that cereal consumption growth would not return to rates greater than population growth (estimated at 1.5 percent) in the near future.[4] Correspondingly, in 1994, 66 cents of each dollar spent on breakfast went toward RTE cereal. By 1998, that amount had fallen to 62 cents. The following graph illustrates the decline in cereal purchases.

Several factors fostered the decline of the RTE cereal market: the substitution of "deskfast" for breakfast and the introduction of less expensive and more convenient cereal alternatives, retailer consolidation, and the introduction of private label cereals.

The RTE cereal industry was one of the most competitive food industries. There were four major branded competitors including Kellogg: General Mills, Post (a division of Kraft/Philip Morris), and Quaker Oats (see Exhibit 32-4 for competitor financials).

During the period of steady growth, competition traditionally took place in advertising, as the large manufacturers chose not to compete on price. Manufacturers could and did raise cereal prices at rates far above inflation, which helped keep RTE cereal margins healthy.

High cereal prices helped drive consumers to less expensive alternatives. As a result, manufacturers were forced to compete by offering increased promotions and lower prices, ultimately squeezing profit margins. In 1996, Post led, and the RTE

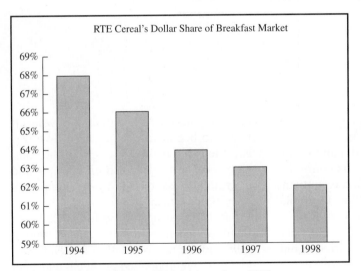

Source: Kellogg Company, PNC Advisors, June 1999.

---

[3]Ibid.
[4]Kellogg Company, PNC Advisors, June 14, 1999.

Income Statement	Philip Morris Companies, Inc.			General Mills			Quaker Oats Co.[b]		
	1996	1997	1998	1997	1998	1999	1996	1997	1998
Net Revenues	$69,204	$72,055	$74,391	$5,609	$6,033	$6,246	$5,199	$5,016	$4,843
Cost of Goods Sold	26,560	26,689	26,820	2,328	2,538	2,594	2,808	2,565	2,374
Excise Taxes on Products	14,651	15,941	16,578	0	0	0	0	0	0
Gross Profit	27,993	29,425	30,993	3,281	3,495	3,652	2,392	2,451	2,468
Operating Income	11,769	11,663	9,977	1,042	950	1,017	411	512	595
Net Income	$ 6,303	$ 6,310	$ 5,372	$ 445	$ 422	$ 535	$ 244	$ 253	$ 280
EPS	$ 2.57	$ 2.61	$ 2.21	$ 2.82	$ 1.33	$ 1.74	$ 1.80	$ 2.10	$ 2.04
Ratios									
Long-Term Debt to Capital	91%	83%	78%	309%	859%	1,038%	357%	389%	526%
Return on Assets	11%	11%	9%	11%	11%	13%	6%	11%	11%
Return on Equity	44%	42%	33%	90%	222%	326%	20%	111%	185%

[a]Philip Morris and Quaker Oats report results on a calendar-year basis; General Mills's fiscal year ends May 31.
[b]Quaker Oats's 1977 operating income and net income results are before a $1,486 pretax charge for restructuring, asset impairments, and losses on divestitures.

EXHIBIT 32-4 Competitor Financial Information Fiscal Years Ended 1996, 1997, and 1998[a] (US$ in millions, Except per share data)

industry followed, a 20 percent reduction in cereal prices. Manufacturers sought to create alternative products to compensate for the loss of cereal sales. As a result, costs for research and development, testing, and new product rollouts increased dramatically.

New competitors—namely national retailers and private label cereals—also emerged and intensified the pressure on branded RTE cereal manufacturers. By 1999, private label cereals controlled 8 percent of global RTE cereal volume, up from slightly greater than 5 percent in 1994. Private label cereals were a compelling value proposition for consumers: Despite recent reductions in branded cereal prices, private label cereals remained on average 40 percent less expensive than branded varieties.

One of the more dubious effects of the growing preference for private label cereals was the commoditization of branded products. Many manufacturers' product lines consisted of brand extensions or varieties of core products. The substitutability of private label products for branded products reduced the value of the brand and ultimately rendered the branded product a commodity, entitled to little or no premium due to brand.

National supermarket chains, such as Kroger and Safeway, were increasingly consolidating smaller retailers, while large discount stores, most importantly Wal-Mart, were increasingly moving into the grocery business. The five largest food retailers controlled greater than 35 percent of food store sales. Kroger and Wal-Mart alone controlled 20 percent.[5]

Lastly, time-pressured consumers were increasingly inclined to skip breakfast altogether or replace it with a snack consumed at a more convenient time, such as in the car or at one's desk. As a result, more convenient breakfast alternatives had seriously eroded the breakfast market share of RTE cereals.

RECENT STRATEGIC INITIATIVES AND RESULTS

Kellogg management had made attempts to bolster and accelerate the company's market growth and financial performance, albeit with varying results. Kellogg was one of the first food companies to expand internationally, and, until recently, it had been the unchallenged leader. Although the company's products were consumed in 160 countries worldwide, 70 percent of Kellogg cereal volume was sold in the United States, the United Kingdom, Mexico, Canada, Australia, Germany, and France. There was considerable potential in international cereal markets as the market was estimated to top $12 billion.[6] A list of the company's historical international expansion can be found in Exhibit 32-5.

In 1990, General Mills, Kellogg's principal U.S. competitor, teamed with Nestlé in a 50-50 joint venture known as Cereal Partners Worldwide (CPW). CPW was focused entirely on acquiring international market share and its volume grew dramatically, often directly at the expense of Kellogg. The graphs on page 348 illustrate the deterioration of Kellogg's international market share since the formation of CPW.

Given the slowing growth of the RTE cereal category, Kellogg launched new products as line or brand extensions and as entirely new products. Unfortunately, the results of these attempts had not been consistent.

Kellogg enjoyed some success introducing new products, primarily in the convenience foods category. Since the introduction of Pop-Tarts in 1964 and Eggo waffles

---

[5]"Packaged Food, Who's Next? For Food Makers, the Mating Dance Gets Serious," Bear Stearns, May 2000.
[6]"Kellogg Company," Salomon Smith Barney.

1906	United States
1914	Canada
1924	Australia
1930–1939	United Kingdom
1940–1949	South Africa
1950–1959	Mexico
1960–1969	Colombia, Venezuela,
	Brazil, Denmark, Japan, Argentina
1970–1979	Spain, Guatemala
1980–1989	South Korea
1990–1995	Italy, Latvia, India, China
1997	Thailand

Source: Salomon Smith Barney.

EXHIBIT 32-5   Kellogg International Expansion Time Line

in 1970, the company successfully followed suit with Nutri-Grain cereal bars in 1991 and Rice-Krispies Treats in 1993. Recently, the company had capitalized on these strong brands with Pop-Tarts Pastry Swirls and Nutri-Grain twists.

Some of Kellogg's new cereal introductions also sought to combine the company's brand equity with new ideas; Kellogg's Raisin Bran Crunch and Kellogg's Special K Plus were excellent examples. Other new cereal initiatives included current attempts to target upscale consumers who preferred premium products. For instance, the company's recent introduction, Country Inn Specialties cereal, was priced at $4.49 for a 10.5-ounce box. This was a substantial premium, averaging 65 percent, over the average cereal.[7] This strategy was successful in the company's 1998 introduction of Kellogg's Smart Start but the company was still awaiting the results for Country Inn Specialties.

However, these successes were infrequent and had been offset by disappoint-ments. The most recent setback for Kellogg was the poor performance and rollback of the recently launched and much-hyped Ensemble line of cholesterol-lowering products. The Ensemble products contained psyllium, which had been proven to lower cholesterol and was approved by the U.S. Food and Drug Administration. The Ensemble line of functional foods encompassed seven categories and included frozen entrees, bread, dry pasta, baked potato chips, frozen breakfast and dessert mini-loaves, and cookies, not to mention cereal.

These products were in test marketing and were planned to expand the company's vision of providing nutritious products to also providing health benefits. At that time, the national rollout for Ensemble was in doubt, as it appeared that the test products were being pulled from shelves and there was speculation that the line might be discontinued only 1 year from its launch.

Kellogg also placed increased emphasis on operational and financial management

[7]Kellogg Company, PNC Advisors.

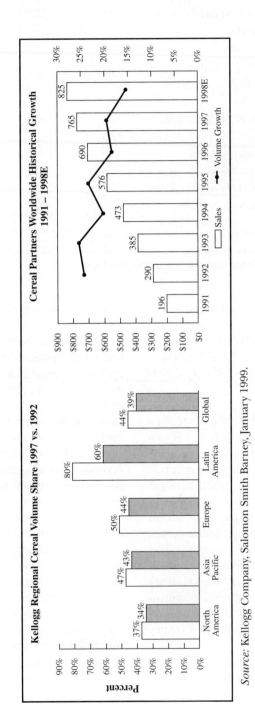

Kellogg Regional Cereal Volume Share 1997 vs. 1992

Cereal Partners Worldwide Historical Growth 1991 – 1998E

Source: Kellogg Company, Salomon Smith Barney, January 1999.

to bolster its performance. In August, Kellogg announced the closure of the south operations of its hometown Battle Creek cereal production facilities. The closure was expected to result in the loss of at least half of the 1,100 hourly and salaried positions at the plant. Although Kellogg's efficiency focus had not been isolated to the United States (Kellogg was pursuing similar supply chain efficiency in Europe), the action had a heightened effect in its backyard.

Acquisitions were another method of creating new growth opportunities for Kellogg. However, Kellogg had not frequently used acquisitions for growth in the past. Prior to 1996, the company's last major acquisition was Mrs. Smith's Pies in 1976. Furthermore, Kellogg's most recent acquisition was a considerable disappointment and was largely considered a failure.

LENDER'S BAGEL BAKERY, INCORPORATED

"Next to Quaker's acquisition of Snapple, Kellogg's acquisition of Lenders is the worst food acquisition of the 1990s."

— JOHN MCMILLIN, A FOOD ANALYST WITH PRUDENTIAL SECURITIES, INCORPORATED

"The fast growth of the segment is not for the part they bought."

— KEN HARRIS, PARTNER, CANNONDALE ASSOCIATES.

ANALYSTS' REACTION TO KELLOGG'S SALE OF LENDER'S BAGEL BAKERY, INCORPORATED.

> In 1994, the Quaker Oats Company agreed to purchase the Snapple Beverage Company for $1.7 billion. This acquisition was similar to the situation facing Kellogg. Quaker was a massive food products company, well known for its oatmeal, cereal brands, and Gatorade sports drink, whereas Snapple was a small and high-flying beverage company. Conflicts in culture, distribution channels, and strategy, and changes in the competitive environment never allowed Quaker to realize the benefits it sought. Quaker sold Snapple in 1997 for $300 million.

In November 1996, Kellogg acquired Lender's Bagel Bakery, Incorporated from Kraft Foods, a division of Philip Morris, Incorporated, for $466 million. Lender's brought to Kellogg a new breakfast franchise to support its floundering cereal business. The acquisition was touted as the perfect complement to Kellogg's convenience-food business.

However, the trumpeted benefits of acquiring Lender's never materialized, and the company and its investors were left to revisit the assertions of the transaction's critics. Many had questioned the acquisition, not for its strategy but for the product selected.

Bagels were the fastest-growing segment of the breakfast market at the time and Lender's was the unquestioned leader of the $218 million frozen bagel market with 73 percent share.[8] Unfortunately, the company had overlooked the fact that this growth was originating in the fresh bagel market and that the market for frozen bagels was declining. In 1995, the total bagel market was approximately $2.3 billion, and it grew to $2.5 billion in 1996.[9] During the same period, the frozen bagels share of the market was falling from 11 percent to slightly more than 8 percent.[10]

Now Kellogg had another product with declining sales. Kellogg attempted to salvage the brand through increased advertising and the introduction of new products. However, by the end of 1998, Lender's was

---

[8]Stephanie Thompson, "Kellogg's Lender's Buy: The Right Category?" *Brandweek,* December 2, 1996, 14.
[9]"Kellogg Enters Bagel Arena," *Prepared Foods,* January 1997, 98.
[10]Ibid.

estimated to have lost 17 percent of its grocery share.[11]

Kellogg's attempts to incorporate and grow the Lender's Bagel business ended when it agreed to sell the business to Aurora Foods, Incorporated, a firm that had success in acquiring and revitalizing struggling brands, for $275 million. The company expected to take close to $180 million in charges relating to the divestiture of Lender's.

The disappointment of Kellogg's Lender's Bagel experience would color the company's approach to acquisitions for some time. When asked to describe Kellogg's approach to acquisitions after Lender's, Steve Benoit, vice president for Natural and Functional Foods, said, "It affects you psychologically . . . 'don't screw it up' [is how you feel the next time] . . . we don't know everything."

WORTHINGTON FOODS

Worthington Foods, Incorporated, located in Worthington, Ohio, was a leading manufacturer and marketer of healthy food products, including meat alternative and zero cholesterol products. The company offered more than 150 products including veggie burgers, meatless sausages, and chicken. A list of the company's brands and products is found in Exhibit 32-6. Financials are shown in Exhibit 32-7.

Similar to Kellogg, Worthington had ties to the Seventh-Day Adventist Church. The original company, "Old Worthington," was founded in 1939 to produce nutritious and vegetarian foods for the church. Miles Laboratories purchased the company in 1970. A management buyout in 1982 returned the company to independence.

Since 1983, the company enjoyed a compound annual growth rate of 12.5 percent, leading to $140 million in sales in 1998. During that time Worthington used acquisitions to fuel its growth. The company acquired LaLoma Foods, Incorporated and the Loma Linda brand in 1990, followed by the Harvest Burgers brand of meat alternatives in 1998.

SEARCH PROCESS

The pressures of the market had forced Kellogg to search for growth opportunities outside its traditional businesses. The company began to search for a suitable addition to its product portfolio. This process included considerable internal and external research and development, fact finding, and surveys to determine what food areas the company should go into. Ultimately, Kellogg's management concluded that the natural foods market provided the greatest potential for growth. Kellogg could capitalize on and expand the market with its established infrastructure and operating experience.

Kellogg management's decision to enter the natural foods market reflected lofty expectations. Driving these expectations were the company's own standards of performance and the urgency dictated by market conditions. Kellogg's objectives included $500 million in natural foods sales within 3 years, yielding a business with 20 percent annual growth.

These high expectations required Kellogg to acquire one of the existing market participants. Three players, Worthington Foods, Gardenburger, and Boca Burger, dominated the veggie foods category in the natural foods market. According to Benoit, "We evaluated all three natural foods competitors. We didn't have time to build, and scale of operations was a concern." Ultimately, Worthington's product portfolio and research and development capability

---

[11]"Kellogg Company," Salomon Smith Barney.

Morningstar Farms

- Garden Veggie Patties
- Spicy Black Bean Burger
- Oven Roasted Veggie Burgers
- Grillers™
- Garden Grille®
- Better'N Burgers®
- Harvest Burgers®, 4 flavors
- Quarter Prime
- Hard Rock Café®
- Veggie Burgers
- Chik Patties®
- Chik Nuggets™
- Meat-Free Buffalo Wings
- Veggie Dogs
- Meat-Free Corn Dogs
- Mini Corn Dogs
- Stuffed Sandwiches, 3 flavors
- Scramblers®
- Better'n Eggs
- Breakfast Patties
- Breakfast Links
- Breakfast Strips
- Breakfast English Muffins
- Ground Meatless
- Burger Style Recipe Crumbles
- Sausage Style Recipe Crumbles

Worthington

- Frozen Items
- Dry Burger Alternatives
- Frozen Breakfast Items
- Canned Vegetarian Meat Alternatives

Natural Touch

- Veggie Burger Kits
- Dinner Entree
- Fat-Free Vegan Burger
- Vege Frank
- Garden Vege Pattie
- Kaffree Roma
- Roma Cappacino
- Lentil Rice Loaf
- Okara Pattie
- Nine Bean Loaf
- Spicy Black Bean Burger
- Vegan Sausage Crumbles
- Vegan Burger Crumbles
- Natural Touch Roasted Soy Butter
- Entree Mixes

Loma Linda

- Canned Vegetarian Products
- Canned Entree Mixes
- Gravy Quik® Mixes

EXHIBIT 32-6 Worthington Foods Product and Brand Portfolio

| Income Statement | Full Year Ended December 31— | | | 6 mos. Ended June 30[a] |
	1996	1997	1998	1999
Sales	$109.1	$117.9	$139.5	$82.7
Gross Profit	43.1	48.7	60.3	36.0
Operating Income	12.8	14.0	15.3	7.7
SG&A Expense	(29.0)	(33.3)	(43.4)	(27.4)
Net Income	7.4	8.0	8.0	4.2
Earnings per Share				
Basic	0.65	0.70	0.70	0.37
Fully Diluted	0.63	0.67	0.67	0.35

[a]Figures for the 6 months ended June 30, 1999, are unaudited.

EXHIBIT 32-7 **Worthington Financial Highlights (in Millions of U.S. Dollars)**

were determined to be superior to its peers. Additionally, Worthington's strength in developing foods with suitable texture would fit nicely with Kellogg's expertise in food flavoring.

MOTIVES FOR THE ACQUISITION OF WORTHINGTON FOODS

Acquiring Worthington seemed attractive in light of various considerations:

- **Growth opportunity.** The market for vegetarian foods was expected to reach $600 million by 2000. There were an estimated 20 million vegetarians in the United States in 1998, and that number was growing at a rate of 20,000 new vegetarians per week.[12] An increasing number of consumers were reducing their consumption of meat and other high-cholesterol and fatty foods and replacing them with healthier alternatives.[13] Worthington's sales had increased 13.5 percent annu-

ally over the last 3 years, and this growth was expected to continue.

- **Complementary capabilities.** Cook believed that the business mix of the two companies complemented each other in terms of: research and development (Worthington's strong capabilities in researching and developing new products was evident in their 150 products and leading position in the vegetarian and health foods market); marketing (Kellogg was a successful and experienced marketer, with its ability to build, profit from, and expand brand equity); distribution (Kellogg had the resources and leverage to increase the reach of Worthington's products both internationally and within the grocery channel, while Worthington's work with food service organizations such as restaurants could open other avenues for Kellogg); supply-chain management; and operations

---

[12]Worthington Foods, Inc., Form 10-K, 1998.
[13]Ibid.

(Kellogg offered best practices in international and large-scale manufacturing).

- **Synergies.** Cook and his staff had identified several possible opportunities to cut costs. Distribution and warehousing were the most obvious. Kellogg would be able to increase the reach of Worthington's products with its distribution infrastructure, and they could provide much-needed brand and sales management expertise. Kellogg's extensive infrastructure also would allow for the consolidation of redundant facilities. Administration and support would be another likely source of savings. Cook believed Kellogg's resources in Battle Creek were sufficient to incorporate all functions supporting Worthington. Cook and his staff also were anticipating sizable revenue enhancements from the acquisition of Worthington. Kellogg's ability to support increased advertising and promotions was expected to accelerate the growth of Worthington's sales. Additionally, Kellogg's size brought leverage with retailers that increased the likelihood of premium placement of Worthington's products on shelves.

ACQUISITION RISKS

Events at Kellogg and trends in the industry raised several possible hurdles in the acquisition of Worthington. These included the following:

- **New management.** Eight of the 10 top Kellogg executives, including Mr. Cook, and 21 of the 35 top North American managers had been in their positions for 1 year or less.[14] While all were accomplished performers, few had worked together before and several were new to the company (see Exhibit 32-8). It could take time for this group to work well together.

- **Poor acquisition history.** Kellogg lost close to $180 million in its acquisition of Lender's Bagel. Most managers were not involved with the disaster of Lender's Bagel, but it was widely accepted that acquiring and integrating companies was not a capability of the company. However, the new managers were expected not to duplicate mistakes made in the Lender's acquisition, and the scrutiny of their actions would be more intense than under the Lender's acquisition.

- **Increased competition.** Competition in the natural foods category in which Worthington operated had become intense and was continually increasing. Competition that was once small and fragmented had become stronger. In addition to increased resistance from cooperative groups supporting comparable meat items, several smaller meat-alternative food manufacturers received support from larger, well-funded organizations. The U.S. food company, Heinz, recently announced its acquisition of a 19 percent stake in the organic group Hain. As the market for vegetarian, low-fat, and low-cholesterol products continued to grow, this segment would remain attractive to new entrants.

---

[14]"Kellogg Company, Meeting with Management," Credit Suisse First Boston, April 4, 2000.

Executive	Position	Appointed[a]	Joined Kellogg[a]
Carlos Gutierrez	CEO	Apr '99	1975
John Cook	EVP and President, Kellogg USA	Feb '99	Feb '99
Jacobus Groot	EVP, President Kellogg Asia-Pacific	Jan '99	Jan '99
Alan Harris	EVP, President Kellogg International	Mar '97	1984
Janet Kelly	EVP, Corp. Development, General Counsel	Jul '99	Jul '99
Donna Banks	Sr. VP, R&D	Jul '99	1983
Joseph Stewart	Sr. VP, Corporate Affairs	Sep '88	1980
James Larson	VP, Human Resources	Mar '99	1997
Gustavo Martinez	President, Kellogg Latin America	May '99	1982
Michael Teale	Sr. VP, Global Supply Chain	Feb '99	1966
[Within Kellogg USA:]			
Steve Benoit	VP, Natural and Functional Foods	Jun '99	1997
Jeff Montie	VP RTE, Cereal		1986
John Forbis	VP, Convenience Snacks	1998	1998
Open	VP, Food Service		

[a]*Source:* Kellogg Web site.

EXHIBIT 32-8   Kellogg Company Management

- **Conflicting cultures.** Kellogg had 1998 sales approaching $6.8 billion compared to Worthington's $139.5 million. Worthington had strong products, research and development, and entrepreneurial spirit, but also an underdeveloped infrastructure. In contrast, Kellogg was a massive organization with established policies and processes supported with the staid and conservative culture built over time. (A chart comparing the two cultures can be found in Exhibit 32-9. The organization charts of Kellogg Natural and Functional Foods Division and Worthington Foods are shown in Exhibits 32-10 and 32-11.) The success of the acquisition would be predicated on uniting the two organizations without destroying the characteristics that were the basis for their success.

- **Accelerated deterioration of cereal.** The anticipated success of Worthington was contingent on Kellogg's increased investment in advertising, promotion, and so on. Further loss of cereal market share despite higher marketing and operations costs could lessen the resources available to support Worthington.

INTEGRATING WORTHINGTON

Acquisition and integration capability are not the strengths of the company. We have limited acquisitions processes and nothing for integration. Bringing in Worthington will [hopefully] help us learn to develop these capabilities.

—STEVE BENOIT, VICE PRESIDENT OF NATURAL AND FUNCTIONAL FOODS, WHEN ASKED TO DESCRIBE THE STATE OF KELLOGG'S ACQUISITION CAPABILITIES.

There were a number of factors that Cook needed to consider in integrating Worthington into Kellogg. Integration planning was step one. Among other things, he had to consider which executives from each of the two organizations to include in the transition team. However, Worthington was a Kellogg acquisition, and much of the value of the acquisition lay in the transfer of Kellogg's attributes and knowledge to Worthington. Cook needed to ensure that these benefits were realized. ■

	Kellogg	Worthington Foods
Strategy/Planning/ Implementation	• Formal and accepted strategic planning processes and outputs. • Rigorous and regimented planning and implementation process. • Weak generation and product concepts, but strong follow-through. • Cross-functional and integrated processes and teams. • Strong and consistent monitoring systems are in place. • Accountability is well defined. • Beginning to be customer oriented. • Broad-based national and global customer orientation. • Customer knowledge through rigorous research, competitor and brand analysis, etc.	• Few formal and accepted strategic planning processes and outputs. • Short-term, seasonal strategy. • Strong idea generation and product concepts, but weak follow-through. • Teams are not cross-functionally integrated (productions, sales, marketing, etc.) resulting in frequent product launch delays. • Accountability is unclear for planning, implementation, monitoring, and improvement. • Customer oriented based on personal relationships and informal data gathering. • Targeted/niche and local customer orientation.
Decision Making	• Distributed power through management by organization. • Strong delegation and empowerment by leadership. • Strong process orientation. • Enterprise wide processes/procedures. • Methodical, analytical processes. • Great employee involvement and awareness of key issues. • Distributed influence and accountabilities. • Decentralized. • Matrix decision making, cross functional. • Strong supervisory skills. • Strong delegation and assigning of ownership and accountabilities.	• Power and control resides with the few at the top. • Highly centralized, top down. • Paternal view of employees. • Minimal documentation or procedures. • More functional focus, less enterprisewide focus. • Minimal employee involvement and awareness of key issues. • Functional decision-making responsibilities. • Supervisors have poor managerial/people skills.

(continued)

EXHIBIT 32-9   Culture Comparison

Values	• Results and the bottom line are primary values. • Management-by-organization-oriented. • Changes, improvement, and higher results are highly valued. • May be perceived as aloof and impersonal.	• Highly values driven. • Company as a family, a neighbor in the community. • Altruistic—focusing on giving back to people, community. • May be perceived as folksy and impractical. • GRIP (*G*ood taste, good nutrition; *R*espect for our employees; *I*ntegrity is more important than profits; *P*eople are whole beings).
Performance Management and Reporting	• Strategic objectives are aligned with individual objectives. • Strong link between performance and incentives. • Performance the driving factor in incentives. • Strong process orientation. • Enterprisewide processes/procedures. • Methodical, analytical, fact based. • Rigorous and strong financial reviews and projections from planning to implementation. • ROI analysis is a formal process.	• Lack of alignment between strategic objectives and individual objectives. • Minimal link between performance and incentives. • Seniority a factor in incentives. • Strong entrepreneurial spirit. • Minimal documentation or procedures. • More functional focus, less enterprisewide focus. • A trial-and-error approach to new product introduction. • Ad-hoc financial analysis and go/no-go decisions, usually after product launch. • Limited ROI analysis.

(continued)

EXHIBIT 32-9   (continued)

People Practices	• Technologically oriented. • Most unionized. • Strong skill sets (especially general business skills, finance, project management, supervisory and technical skills). • Larger Fortune 500 mindset—from dress to mannerisms, "corporate" stereotype. • Performance-based promotion. • Formal investment and practices in training and development.	• Manual systems, low technology utilization. • Half unionized. • Weak skill sets (especially general business skills, finance, project management, supervisory skills). • Strong loyalty and commitment to the organization. • Seniority a key criteria for promotion of the internal candidates. • Minimal nonconsistent training and development investment and practices. • Mainly on-the-job training.
Diversity	• Few women or people of color in key positions. • Recognized weakness. • Beginning corporatewide policy and business practice.	• Few women or people of color in key positions. • Not identified as a business imperative.
Information Access and Communication	• Frequent, ongoing, mass distribution. • Multiple channels (people, electronic, written). • Key philosophy—"A basic business tool." • Ongoing cross-functional communication.	• Infrequent, consistent void, hearsay. • Limited channels (mainly gossip/hearsay). • Key philosophy—"On need-to-know basis." • Top down, often does not reach everyone. • Inefficient cross-functional communication.

Source: Company documents.

EXHIBIT 32-9 **(continued)**

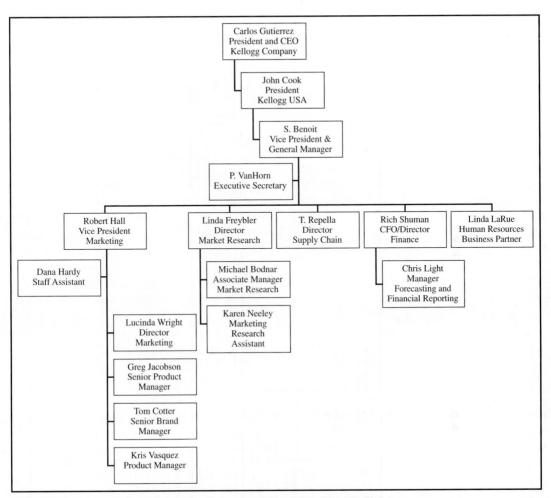

EXHIBIT 32-10   Kellogg Company Natural and Functional Foods Division

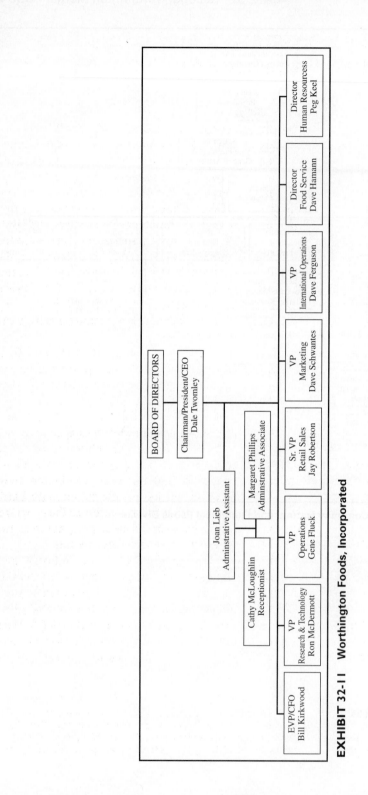

EXHIBIT 32-11 Worthington Foods, Incorporated

Case 33 Louis Gerstner and Lotus Development (A)

On June 12, 1995, Louis Gerstner, chairman and CEO of International Business Machines (IBM), was on stage for a presentation at Wang Auditorium in downtown Boston. IBM had just taken over Lotus Development Corporation; in fact, it was only the day before the boards of both companies had approved the $3.5 billion deal.[1]

The saga began on June 5, when, for the first time in its history, IBM made a hostile bid to take over another company.[2] Having learned that there was no apparent "white knight" — a company interested in stepping in to buy Lotus in a "friendly" transaction — Jim Manzi, CEO of Lotus, opened conversations with IBM. The takeover of the Massachusetts-based software firm concluded in a somewhat friendlier manner than it had begun.

IBM AND THE COMPUTER INDUSTRY

Thanks to the enormous success of the proprietary mainframe computer System/360 launched in 1964, IBM once enjoyed a virtual monopoly of the computer industry. As the challenges from competitors both foreign and domestic intensified, holding the dominant position in its flagship mainframe market gradually became tough for "Big Blue." Meanwhile, the birth of the personal computer in the late 1970s brought a drastic change to the industry.

In 1981, IBM entered the emerging market of personal computing. To develop competitive products quickly, IBM decided to use key components developed externally for the first time in its history. Intel provided the processor chip, and a small start-up called Microsoft provided the MS-DOS operating system. Though not the first personal computer on the market, the IBM-PC was an instant success, due in part to the legitimacy of the IBM brand. However, the decision to rely on external suppliers later enabled competitors to build hardware compatible with the IBM-PC ("clones") by sourcing the same key components from the same suppliers.

The success of the IBM-PC and IBM clones opened up a huge window of opportunities for the software industry. It provided a common platform to the fragmented personal computing world and created a big market for packaged software. The common hardware platform led to the emergence of "killer applications," software programs that not only dominated their markets, but led people to purchase hardware in order to have access to the program. VisiCalc, a spreadsheet program, was the one of the first such software hits.

During the 1980s, the industry also witnessed another trend — networking. Individual small computers (clients) were linked with larger computers (servers) that literally served in the background. With the development of powerful workstations, the client/server-computing model gained

UVA-OB-0696

[1] Doug Garr, *IBM Redux* (New York: HarperCollins, 1999), 218. Doug Garr, a former IBM speechwriter, is a business and technology journalist.
[2] Ibid.

popularity because of its openness, flexibility, and cost effectiveness compared to traditional proprietary mainframe systems. PCs also could be connected to a server to form local area networks (LANs) so that people could share information as well as resources like printers and data storage.

Two revolutions in the 1980s—first the PC and then client/server networking—completely changed the way people viewed, purchased, and utilized information technology. The history section of IBM's official Web site explains the 1980s as a time of struggle for the company: "Businesses' purchasing decisions were put in the hands of individuals and departments—not the places where IBM had long-standing customer relationships. Piece-part technologies took precedence over integrated solutions. The focus was on the desktop and personal productivity, not on business applications across the enterprise."[3]

IBM experienced "near death," partly because of these fundamental shifts in the industry, as well as failed strategy, bad management, and stifling bureaucracy. Under the leadership of John Akers, the predecessor to Louis Gerstner, the company posted record profits in 1990 but lost $2.9 billion the following year. This was only the beginning. Annual net losses reached $8.1 billion by 1993 despite cost management and restructuring efforts to decentralize the company. During the same period, about $6 billion in shareholder value disappeared as a result of a 75 percent drop in the stock price from its peak in 1987. (See Exhibit 33-1.) The morale of employees was at an all-time low, and valuable talent started to leave the company. Leadership was lost.

LOUIS GERSTNER AND IBM'S TURNAROUND

Louis V. Gerstner, 51 years old, was brought into IBM as chairman and CEO in March 1993 from RJR Nabisco, with a 9-year contract, a $4 million signing bonus, and options on 500,000 shares. Unlike any of his predecessors, he was not an internally grown IBM'er. He was the first outsider to run the 70-year-old company. Nor was he an industry expert. Instead, customer-oriented sensitivity and strategic-thinking expertise were what made Gerstner an ideal candidate.[4] After receiving his MBA from Harvard, Gerstner started his career at McKinsey & Company. He became the youngest principal in the company's history at 28 and later became one of its youngest directors at 33. He then joined American Express as executive vice president and head of the charge card business at age 35. After his 12 years of service at Amex, he was invited to RJR Nabisco Holding Corporation as CEO by Kohlberg, Kravis, and Roberts, shortly after their infamous $25 billion leveraged buyout.

Gerstner was known as a classic McKinsey type with passion about management and business. He was a perfect model of the intense urgency—he was known for the ability to outwork practically anybody.[5] Doug Garr wrote in his book *IBM Redux:*

> Gerstner is not a casual guy. He doesn't go onstage in khakis and a sweater. He is wearing a perfectly pressed dark suit, white shirt, beige print tie. His suit coat is buttoned, and it will remain that way until he sits on a stool.[6]

Because of his style and personality, a number of people thought Gerstner was a

[3]IBM Corporate site, *About IBM,* www.ibm.com/ibm/, data taken March 2000.
[4]Gerstner was the fourth pick after such candidates as Jack Welch, CEO of General Electric; Lawrence Bossidy, CEO of Allied Signal; and John Young, retired CEO of Hewlett-Packard.
[5]Stratford Sherman, "Is He Too Cautious to Save IBM?" *Fortune,* October 3, 1994, 84.
[6]Garr, *IBM Redux,* 2.

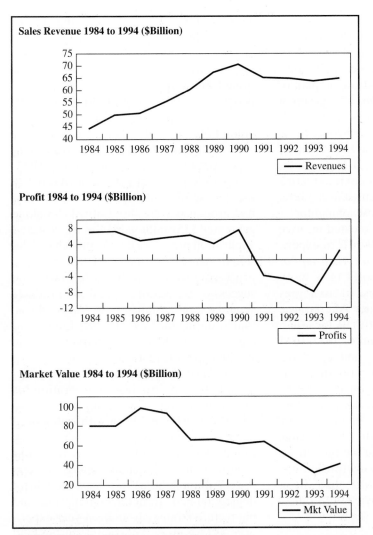

Sales Revenue 1984 to 1994 ($Billion)

Profit 1984 to 1994 ($Billion)

Market Value 1984 to 1994 ($Billion)

EXHIBIT 33-1   IBM Financial Indicators

hard-hearted, arrogant person. Gerstner once said about this reputation:

> I'm intense, competitive, focused, blunt, and tough, yes. That's fair. I'm guilty. Quite frankly, I am not very comfortable in chitchat. When I go to board meetings, I arrive 2 minutes before and leave when it's over. I don't stay for lunch or go early and have coffee. But if arrogance means pride, wanting to take credit for everything, not seeking others' advice, I don't think those are fair characterizations.[7]

Gerstner had to quickly stabilize the company that he thought was in some kind of death spiral. His challenge included

---

[7]Betsy Morris, "The Holy Terror Who's Saving IBM," *Fortune,* April 3, 1997, 70.

cutting back the workforce, reducing costs, and rebuilding various product lines, as well as encouraging people and restoring morale. Within a couple of months, he officially abandoned Akers's strategic plan of splitting IBM into "Baby Blues," a group of smaller companies, believing that IBM's strength was in providing integrated solutions for customers. Later it was said to be the most critical decision he made at IBM. Gerstner then initiated more than 30 discrete reengineering projects to cut expenses to the level comparable to IBM's toughest competitors.

At the same time, he executed massive layoffs that IBM had never before experienced. This contrasted with IBM under Akers, who managed layoffs in a more piecemeal way—a few thousand employees at a time. Surprisingly, under Akers three times more employees lost their jobs than under Gerstner.[8] By the end of 1993, IBM finally stopped losing money and reported a small gain in the fourth quarter of that year. Gerstner continued to work on accelerating product development process, rebuilding product lines to compete in the rapidly changing market. As a result, 1994 became, as Gerstner put it, "the year we proved we could survive."[9] IBM's workforce, once peaked at 406,000 in 1985, had been trimmed down to 219,000 by 1994.

LOTUS DEVELOPMENT AND THE PC SOFTWARE INDUSTRY

Lotus Development Corporation, headquartered in Cambridge, Massachusetts, was best known for the success of its earlier "Lotus 1-2-3" application software, an integrated spreadsheet program. Mitch Kapor, a charismatic juggler who preferred Hawaiian shirts to business suits, founded Lotus. The name *Lotus* came from the language of Transcendental Meditation, a movement Kapor was involved in at the time.[10] Kapor, inspired by VisiCalc (the previously mentioned killer application that encouraged people to buy the hardware to run the software), developed the original 1-2-3 program. Lotus 1-2-3 was launched in January 1983 and quickly became the de facto standard spreadsheet program for the IBM-compatible platform (thus contributing to the demise of VisiCorp, the company that had produced VisiCalc). Lotus 1-2-3 alone generated $157 million in sales by 1984, and application programs like Approach (a relational database) and AmiPro (a word processor) were introduced following the success of 1-2-3. Lotus's desktop products gained a large installed base and loyal customers during the 1980s. In 1989, Lotus 1-2-3 enjoyed nearly 90 percent market share on IBM-compatible platforms.

In April 1986, knowing that Lotus had already become too big a corporation for him, Kapor turned the company over to Jim Manzi, who had been with Lotus since 1983 and served as president since 1984. Manzi, who was only 34 at that time, was known as an intelligent and energetic executive. Although he did not have a graduate degree, he had strengths in marketing and big-picture strategy from his 4-year experience at McKinsey. An example of the kind of person Manzi was is that he dressed in drag and sang Aretha Franklin's hit "R-E-S-P-E-C-T" to celebrate the 10th anniversary of Lotus Development. Doug Garr wrote, "Manzi could be charming and witty or crude and nasty, depending on the day. Manzi's sense of humor was sly and subtle; those who liked him were extremely loyal."[11] Manzi knew little about software technolo-

[8]Garr, *IBM Redux,* 63.
[9]A part of Gerstner's annual worldwide speech to employees, January 1997.
[10]Lotus Corporate Home, *Lotus Story,* www.lotus.com/home.nsf/welcome/corporate.
[11]Garr, *IBM Redux,* 214.

gies; instead, he relied on two extraordinary talents of the industry—John Landry, a highly respected technology officer, and Ray Ozzie, one of the industry's software superstars.

In May 1990, Microsoft launched Windows version 3.0, the first MS-Windows program that proved to be practically useful. Microsoft started aggressive marketing of its Word and Excel application programs for Windows, bundling these products as an integrated "office suite." Office suites quickly became the latest trend in the industry and put significant price pressures on stand-alone programs. Lotus launched a Windows version of Lotus 1-2-3 in 1991, but unfortunately, most analysts found this product to be disappointing and buggy.[12] Lotus's position in desktop applications had clearly eroded. Even Lotus 1-2-3 had become a distant number two in market share to Microsoft's Excel. A stock price that once reached $85 had fallen to $32.

Meanwhile, a new concept called "groupware" was emerging, corresponding to the client/server, networking revolution. Groupware was a type of software that worked in a client/server environment and focused more on the productivity of groups than individuals. Lotus had made its early entry in this field with software called Lotus Notes. Notes was a sort of flexible database platform for groups on which people could collaborate, share and circulate documents, keep track of discussions, and manage electronic messages.

Development of Lotus Notes started back in 1984 under the leadership of Ray Ozzie. Ozzie had gathered the best of the best talents of Lotus to his group called Iris, and worked exclusively on Notes development. People at Iris were treated differently from the rest of the company; they even had separate stationery, business cards, and generous benefit packages. Iris preserved the strong start-up culture that had somehow already faded at the Cambridge headquarters of Lotus. Knowing that desktop products were maturing, Manzi had poured $100 million generated from the desktop products group into Notes development in hopes of making it the next generation of killer applications. In the meantime, the company had continued to grow; by December 31, 1994, Lotus Development employed 5,522 people, of which 1,811 were outside the United States.[13]

Despite the fact that Notes was considered a product with huge potential and was recognized as a technology leader of this segment, by 1994 it had yet to generate any significant profits for Lotus (See Exhibit 33-2). In addition, it was clear that competition in this segment would intensify in the next few years. Microsoft, no longer a small company, had revealed its intention to enter the groupware market with a program called Exchange, which was expected within a year. Rumor was that Microsoft was considering bundling the Exchange client software with the new Windows 95 operating system, thus ensuring a steady base of customers.

IBM TAKING OVER LOTUS

J. P. Morgan and Company first pitched the Lotus-IBM merger idea to both companies during the fall of 1994. Lotus's software revenues were down 15 percent in the previous year, and the stock price was now hovering around $40. The logic of the plan was (1) Lotus could benefit from IBM's marketing power and deep pockets to promote Notes before Microsoft would come in, and (2) the addition of Lotus would

---

[12]J. Walk and Associates, *The Spreadsheet Page,* www.j-walk.com/ss/123/index.htm.
[13]Lotus Development Corp., Form 10K, 1994.

strengthen IBM's client/server and networking segment of the business, which had never seemed successful. Manzi was not convinced or interested in this idea; however, IBM continued further studies under John M. Thompson, an IBM executive vice president who was leading IBM's software group and had put together a software task force.

IBM had never been known for its software and had just experienced a devastating failure in its operating system, OS/2.[14] J. P. Morgan further pointed out IBM's weak-

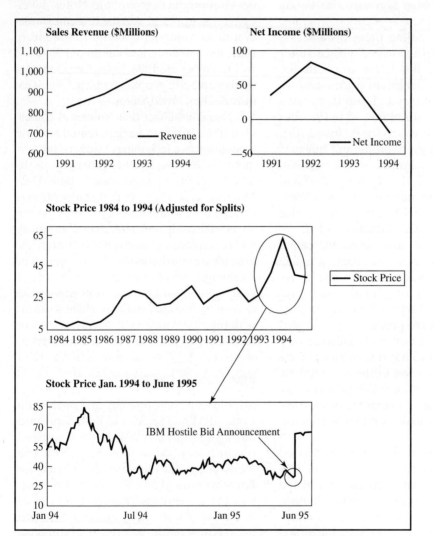

EXHIBIT 33-2 **Lotus Development Corporation Financial Indicators**

---

[14]OS/2 was meant to be a replacement for MS-DOS, and IBM initially worked together with Microsoft. This IBM-Microsoft relationship did not last long, because of the frustration of Bill Gates with IBM's bureaucracy. Gates pushed for the development of Windows simultaneously. Although OS/2 was more reliable than early versions of Windows, it could not gain market share vis-à-vis Windows version 3.0, released in 1989. By 1994, IBM had captured less than 5 percent of the operating system market.

ness in client/server database, workstation, and server businesses; network collaboration software; and data networking infrastructure, and suggested acquisitions in each segment.[15] The Lotus takeover fit into this big picture. Thompson's software task force at IBM concluded that Lotus's desktop products would be a nice addition to its product portfolio, and Notes was a must have to develop a networking presence.

In May 1995, IBM's board approved the hostile bid against Lotus Development Corporation. On Monday, June 5, Gerstner called Manzi precisely at 8:28 to tell him a fax was on its way to his office. The fax message Manzi received 2 minutes later said IBM was making a bid for $60 a share for Lotus. Five hours later, Gerstner held a press conference in New York City and announced its intention to acquire Lotus. He stated that IBM could take advantage of Lotus's product line, while IBM could provide financial and marketing muscle. Gerstner never used the word *hostile* during the conference.[16] Manzi was upset about this sudden move of IBM. Apparently, though several software agreements were on the table, the merger between IBM and Lotus had never been discussed before this moment.[17] Manzi frantically tried to find someone to save Lotus but only learned in the process that there was no one willing to go up against IBM. By Tuesday afternoon, June 6, Manzi opened a direct conversation to negotiate better terms.

During the negotiations, Manzi concluded that Gerstner was "totally clueless" about what he was about to purchase. Manzi believed that a software company was like a baseball team, with star players who needed to be treated well. Manzi knew the people were the most important assets for a company like Lotus, and he knew who the star players in his organization were. However, he suspected that Gerstner did not have the slightest idea who one of his superstars, Ray Ozzie, was. Manzi arranged a meeting between Gerstner and Ozzie. Gerstner, wondering what he could offer to entice Ozzie to stay, proposed what was to IBM a prestigious package, an IBM Fellowship. IBM Fellows received a salary and a budget and the opportunity to sit around a lab and think for a living—with no agenda other than pure research. However, Ozzie had made a lot more money than IBM Fellows did and already had a bigger staff. Gerstner apparently missed the fact that if there were anything that would motivate Ozzie to stay, it was likely to be his commitment to the Notes project he had been involved in for 10 years.

The larger merger agreement was finalized only 6 days after the initial hostile bid, at a price of $64 per share. Manzi was to remain as Lotus CEO and become an IBM senior vice president. Previously announced plans for cost cutting and layoffs at Lotus would proceed, with $50 million to be cut from the budget and managerial ranks to be trimmed by 15 percent. Finally, IBM promised Lotus autonomy in running its business.

GERSTNER'S SPEECH TO LOTUS EMPLOYEES

As he prepared to make his statement about the merger to Lotus employees, Jim Manzi and John Thompson joined Mr. Gerstner on stage. There were some 2,500 people in the audience, mostly Lotus

---

[15]According to *IBM Redux,* J. P. Morgan suggested Sybase, Sun Microsystems, Lotus, and LDDS/Cable and Wireless.
[16]Garr, *IBM Redux,* 220–221.
[17]Ibid., 221.

employees from the Cambridge headquarters. Manzi spoke first. In his remarks, he said, "In this agreement with IBM, I can honestly tell you without reservation that we've taken care of our employees, our shareholders, and our customers, and now I can tell you it is time that we take care of Microsoft." After his speech, Manzi introduced Gerstner to the audience.

Gerstner began to speak, "Thank you, Jim. Thank you very much. . . ." ■

Case 34   Bank One Corporation and the Park Cities (A)

Senior Vice President C. O. "Buck" Horn looked out across downtown Dallas toward the Park Cities from his office at Bank One, Texas-Dallas. After unprecedented change in the 1980s, the Texas banking industry was preparing itself for the 1990s and the twenty-first century. Acquisitions and mergers had been prolific as holding companies sought to strengthen their presence and increase their market share. In December 1991, efforts at Bank One, Texas to centralize banking operations and achieve economies of scale were being completed. For example, Bank One, Texas-Dallas was the regional headquarters for an area that included the "Park Cities." It handled many of the Park Cities' customers through its recently centralized operations.

A recent 60-second radio commercial from a competitor, however, raised serious concerns in Horn's mind. Although the commercial did not explicitly address Bank One's Park Cities' branches, it did harp on the many changes that Bank One had been going through. It began:

FEMALE: Welcome to Bicker and Dicker National Bank.

MALE: I thought you just changed your name to Co-Ambivalent Bank and Trust.

FEMALE: Oh, we haven't been Ambivalent for several weeks.

MALE: Yeah, but all my checks still say First Foggy Bridge Bank.

FEMALE: Oh, that was two or three names ago.

MALE: Two or three names ago . . .

FEMALE: But don't order any checks yet, sir.

MALE: Really?

FEMALE: (Kind of whispers.) There's a rumor going around that we'll be Comatose National any day now.

The commercial continued:

ANNOUNCER: With all the confusion in banking today, it's difficult to remember who your bank is. But one bank hasn't changed. Capital Bank is still Capital Bank. Still locally owned and operated . . . for over 20 years. Still independent. And still located at Central and Mockingbird, and Mockingbird and Central. If you want a bank that you can depend on, call Capital.

MALE: So, you're no longer Co-Ambivalent?

FEMALE: Right.

MALE: You're Bicker and Dicker?

FEMALE: Right.

MALE: Well, can you cash this check from Foggy Bridge?

FEMALE: No. We don't cash checks from other banks.

MALE: It's your bank!

FEMALE: Look! We hate to bicker at Bicker and Dicker but . . .

UVA-OB-0444

This case was prepared by Eric Colsman under the supervision of Jack Weber, Associate Professor of Business Administration. This case was written as a basis for class discussion rather than to illustrate effective or ineffective handling of an administrative situation. Copyright © 1993 by the University of Virginia Darden School Foundation, Charlottesville, Virginia. All rights reserved. Revised March 1994.

INTERCOM BUZZES TWICE

FEMALE: Oh, okay . . .

MALE: What was that?

FEMALE: We just became Comatose!

MALE: Oh no . . .

ANNOUNCER: Capital Bank. To be independent, you need Capital. Member FDIC.

All morning Horn had been reviewing past events carefully. He summarized the situation as follows:

> Our competitors are doing a terrific job—at our expense! They are leaving banking specialists, such as lending, trust, and mortgage officers, right in their bank in the Park Cities. As independent banks that are not part of a holding company, they do not face the centralize/decentralize issue. They are particularly good at providing full service. They are using this as a competitive advantage against us by saying, "You have to go downtown to get anything done at other banks." The bank from this morning's commercial is building a whole campaign around this theme. The bottom line is that we are losing market share.

Horn thought about the marked decline in deposits for Bank One's Park Cities branches. Both he and Tyree "Ty" B. Miller, chief executive officer of Bank One, Texas-Dallas, believed market share was slipping, though they could not verify their suspicions for two reasons. First, although separate Park Cities' numbers could be calculated with much effort, the rapid growth through acquisitions made period-to-period comparisons difficult. Second, the newly centralized Management Information and Control System (MICS) did not provide separate profitability figures for the Park Cities' branches. Adding to this latter problem was the fact that income from the trust, mortgage, private banking, small business,

and securities businesses was reported through separate systems respective to their own organizations. Horn grew frustrated and concerned as he recalled the high level of service that he had provided to the Park Cities in the mid 1980s as president of Preston State Bank.

Horn also reviewed the myriad management issues that engulfed most of Texas banking and that made it difficult to analyze and assess the situation in the Park Cities. The last 10 years saw the birth of branch banking in Texas with all of its complexities, the Texas banking crisis and related failures, and a host of acquisition activity that Horn, Miller, and the rest of the Bank One, Dallas management team had been directly involved with. At the same time, MCorp acquired the premier bank in the Park Cities, the Preston State Bank, through its acquisition of Southwest Bankshares Company. In 1987, branch banking was legalized in Texas. Two years later, Banc One Corporation acquired MCorp. In the midst of all this activity, various internal issues such as integrating and centralizing operations, how to go about implementing branch banking, and how to manage systems through this sea of change blurred banks' focus—including Bank One, Dallas—on customer service issues.

As he looked toward the Park Cities, Horn wondered how he could restore customer service to the level of the early 1980s when the Preston Branch had been known as Preston State Bank, *the* community bank in the Park Cities.

PARK CITIES AND BANKING IN TEXAS

The Park Cities was a lucrative market. In 1991, it was viewed by some members of management as the market with the greatest potential in Texas, and perhaps even in the entire southern United States. With Bank One deposits of approximately $650 million, Park Cities was a pocket formed by two independent cities, University Park and Highland Park. Completely surrounded by the city of Dallas, the two cities bordered each other and were nicknamed the "Bubble." Residents of the Park Cities did not pay Dallas taxes and maintained their own roads, fire department, and police department. The combined population of the two cities was approximately 28,500, with between 15,000 and 18,000 households. High-income families, average home prices of $450,000, Southern Methodist University, and a superior secondary-school system defined the neighborhoods. The Dallas areas bordering the Park Cities were similar in nature.

Banking in Texas had remained a highly regulated industry because branch banking had been prohibited in Texas up until the late 1980s. Of the 16,000 banks in the United States, 1,600 were in Texas. With the exception of Illinois, all other states had permitted branch banking during that period. Although holding companies were legal and existed in Texas, each bank was required to operate as a separate institution with its own charter, board of directors, and set of financials. This system was terribly inefficient from a capital standpoint.

During the late 1980s, the banking environment in Texas changed dramatically. In 1985 and 1986, Texas passed a branch-banking law, which came into effect in 1987. Throughout the rest of the decade, most of the existing bank-holding companies consolidated operations in an effort to increase efficiency and profitability. At the same time, Texas banking underwent a massive restructuring as most bank-holding companies, both inside and outside Texas, rushed to build a branch-banking network in Texas through mergers and acquisitions.

BUCK HORN'S CAREER PRIOR TO 1987

Horn began his career at the First National Bank of Dallas in 1967. He progressed from the executive development training pro-

gram to a position as vice president, where he was responsible for the Executive & Professional Lending Department. From 1975 to 1982, he managed the Dallas region market for Texas Commerce Bankshares by serving as CEO of six north Dallas community banks. Horn joined Preston State Bank in 1983 and was named president 2 years later by Preston State Bank's holding company, Southwest Bancshares Company.

HORN'S STYLE AT PRESTON STATE BANK

Located in the Park Cities, Preston State Bank had been a large, stand-alone, full-service bank through the mid 1980s (see Exhibit 34-1). It had been largely consumer oriented, offering credit cards, home-mortgage lending, and consumer-lending services. The bank sold Treasury bills and bonds and had a Trust Department. In addition, Horn and his predecessor began to add small business services—primarily commercial lending and private banking—that catered to executives, business owners, and entrepreneurs.

Horn's management style had always been customer driven. He was people oriented and cared about his personnel. He delegated often and allowed subordinates plenty of leeway to accomplish the tasks assigned to them. Two of Horn's great strengths were his ability to work with different groups without offending anyone and his ability to encourage groups to work together for the good of the whole. Because he was a team player, he expected others to be team players, too.

Horn's friendly, outgoing nature was a hallmark of his personality and management style. In many ways, his style reflected Preston State Bank's style, which was characterized by direct customer involvement. Preston State Bank staff, including Horn and other senior officers, were in the lobby and behind the teller line in the natural

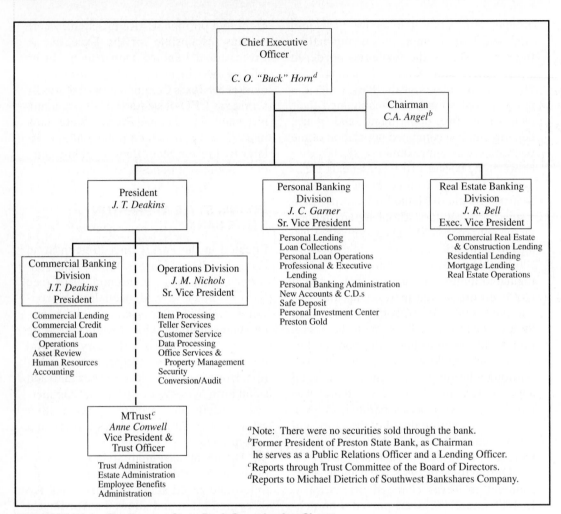

EXHIBIT 34-1 The Preston State Bank Organization Chart[a]

course of their daily schedule. They welcomed customers, asked how customers were, and said, "Glad to have you in here today." "This was everyone's role," explained Horn, "and senior officers played it and younger officers learned it. It was just part of the fiber of the bank and everybody did it."

All of Preston State Bank's customer service happened naturally: No one stepped forward to announce customer service performance goals. The evolution of customer service may have been connected to the fact that many people in Dallas perceived the Park Cities as being "different" and referred to the Park Cities as the "Bubble." As some people would say:

They breathe different air over there in the "Bubble." You know, the rich people want it different. They have their own schools, you know. There's competition among athletic teams. People in Dallas love to beat Highland Park. I can't tell you how competitive it is . . .

Customer service also may have been motivated by the fact that many customers were older individuals, many of whom were wealthy. They liked to come to the bank: a visit to Preston State Bank was part of their weekly activity, if not their daily routine.

Whatever the reason, Preston State Bank was sensitive to customer needs. Horn summarized, "Problems were solved quickly. Every complaint was considered an important complaint and was acted on very quickly." Although separate departments existed for trust, home-mortgage lending, real estate, and consumer and commercial loans, customers were treated with such care that these boundaries were for all practical purposes nonexistent. All departments appeared to be one seamless entity to customers: Preston State Bank.

In the customer's eye, Preston State Bank was clearly a "total bank," a "full-service community bank." Customers were attracted to the bank by its name and reputation. Clearly, Preston State Bank had no strong suburban competitors. Running the bank was a matter of continuing the successes of the past by constantly focusing on improving customer service. At a time when a return on assets (ROA) figure of 1.0 percent in Texas banking was excellent, Preston State Bank's ROA, which fluctuated between 1.70 percent and 1.85 percent, was extraordinary.

BANC ONE CORPORATION PRIOR TO 1989: MORE THAN 120 YEARS OF GROWTH

Banc One's roots reached back more than 120 years to City National Bank in Columbus, Ohio. By early 1989, just before it acquired MCorp, Banc One had become one of the most profitable bank-holding companies among the 50 largest American banks, as measured by ROA. By January 1989, Banc One had a total of 56 affiliates with 566 offices: Banc One Ohio had 26 affiliates including banks in Ohio, Michigan, and Kentucky; Banc One Indiana had 11 affiliates; and Banc One Wisconsin had 19 affiliates. Banc One Corporation presided over 18,000 employees and $23.7 billion in assets. Exhibit 34-2 shows financial figures for Banc One from 1982 to 1992.

Growth through acquisitions had been and continued to be the strategy behind Banc One's success. In 1968, the small City National Bank merged with the even smaller Farmer Savings and Trust, which had $55.2 million in deposits, to form the First Banc Group.[1] From 1968 to 1980, the First Banc Group acquired 22 banks. Anticipating changes in the interstate banking laws, competition from other financial institutions, and limitations to growth, CEO John B. McCoy registered the name "Banc One" in every state in the late 1970s. By the early to middle 1980s, changes in state banking laws allowed Banc One to purchase out-of-state banks. Banc One's acquisitions included midsized banks throughout Ohio, Indiana, Kentucky, Michigan, and Wisconsin.

A synopsis from a Banc One annual report provided insight into Banc One's philosophy of growth:

Banc One Corporation is structured around our bank and nonbank affiliates, and all activities are designed to support their individual efforts.

The word *affiliated,* as opposed to *acquired,* was an early distinction, separating Banc One from most other bank-holding companies. The word *affiliated* to Banc One means "partnership." As a matter of fact, the very basis of our culture is steeped in what we call an "Uncommon Partnership" philosophy.

---

[1]The spelling *Banc* cleverly circumvented an Ohio state law that prohibited nonbank institutions from including the designation *Bank* in their names.

10-Year Performance Summary
(unaudited)

| Year | Total Assets | Income and Expenses | |
		Net Interest Income	Net Income
1992	$58,249	$3,240.1	$781.3
1991	33,861	1,838.5	529.5
1990	27,654	1,309.3	423.4
1989	25,518	1,193.7	362.9
1988	23,484	1,142.0	340.2
1987	17,538	907.3	208.9
1986	16,299	830.4	199.8
1985	9,539	523.2	130.4
1984	8,088	448.6	108.0
1983	6,153	311.6	83.3
1982	4,511	230.4	57.5
Annual Growth:			
1992/1991	72.02%	76.24%	47.55%
Compound Growth:			
5 Years	27.13	28.99	30.19
10 Years	29.15	30.26	29.81

Data per Common Share

Year	Net Income	Cash Dividends	Stock Price	Total Market Capital ($ millions)
1992	$3.28	$1.22	$53.15	$12,331
1991	2.91	1.05	47.85	8,833
1990	2.51	0.95	25.23	4,408
1989	2.29	0.86	26.76	4,239
1988	2.15	0.76	18.39	2,876
1987	1.64	0.68	18.04	2,360
1986	1.60	0.62	17.19	2,082
1985	1.51	0.52	17.59	1,491
1984	1.31	0.45	11.67	929
1983	1.16	0.39	10.66	802
1982	1.00	0.33	10.63	655
Annual Growth:				
1992/91	12.71%	16.19%	11.03%	39.60%
Compound Growth:				
5 Years	14.87	12.40	24.11	39.19
10 Years	12.61	13.97	17.46	34.11

(continued)

EXHIBIT 34-2 Selected Banc One Financial Data, 1982 to 1992

	Operating Ratios		
Year	Return on Average Assets	Net Interest Margin	Net Income per FT Equiv. Employee
1992	1.34%	6.22%	$23,912
1991	1.56	6.09	21,449
1990	1.53	5.33	19,871
1989	1.42	5.20	20,388
1988	1.45	5.42	20,166
1987	1.19	5.80	15,064
1986	1.23	5.73	15,790
1985	1.37	6.22	15,167
1984	1.33	6.30	13,666
1983	1.35	5.78	12,001
Average:			
5 Years	1.46%	5.65%	$21,157
10 Years	1.38	5.81	17,747

	Equity Ratios		
Year	Return on Common Equity	Long-Term Debt to Common Equity	Total Return Net Income
1992	16.26%	24.2%	13.9%
1991	16.58	19.8	95.0
1990	16.24	20.2	(2.0)
1989	16.69	16.5	50.5
1988	17.69	18.8	5.8
1987	15.12	17.9	8.6
1986	16.49	13.6	0.8
1985	17.77	11.9	56.1
1984	17.84	15.7	14.1
1983	18.42	19.7	4.0
Average:			
5 Years	16.71%	19.90%	28.22%
10 Years	16.92	17.83	21.53

EXHIBIT 34-2   (continued)

We believe this philosophy is one of the cornerstones of our success. It drives almost every aspect of our business, including the way we operate; which banks we affiliate with; and the kind of banking company we want to be in the future. This philosophy is based on three principles: decentralizing the people side of business; centralizing the paper and electronic transaction sides of the business; and operating under a superb financial management system, which continuously measures and reports the success of our efforts.

Each affiliate bank has its own charter, board of directors, and chief executive officer, formulates its own business plan, controls all personnel and lending functions, and determines all product pricing and marketing, based on local market conditions. The 18 banks which comprise Bank One, Texas were consolidated into one company under ownership of the FDIC. They remain under one charter, but are operated and managed as separate banks like all other affiliates. Each affiliate bank reports to a state holding company . . . which in turn reports to Banc One Corporation in Columbus, Ohio. New state holding companies are formed as Bank One presence reaches a significant asset level in the state. Until that time, banks in a new area report to one of the closest existing state holding companies. Authority and responsibility is clearly defined at each level of the Company. . . .

Key elements of our behavioral differences include the fact that our organizational structure centers on our individual affiliate banks operating in individual markets, rather than regions or districts. The clarity of our decision-making authority is high. We focus on process and financial measurement, which have a major link to incentives and performance. And our commitment to customer service keeps us focused on what is most important to the success of any company.

BANC ONE'S SYSTEMS FOR GROWTH

As Banc One grew, it implemented systems that successfully integrated new banks into the "Bank One way." Exhibit 34-3 details the structural elements provided by Banc One Corporation, the state holding companies, the affiliate chief executive officers, and the systemwide committees.

The state holding company structure was born in 1987 as the complexities of mul-

Banc One Corporation *provides:*
- Systems and operations development, direction, and support
- Treasury management
- Financial monitoring and control
- Mergers and acquisitions
- Corporate marketing
- Legal and compliance administration
- Cross fertilization of ideas across affiliates

State Holding Companies *provides:*
- State financial analysis
- Goal setting, measurement and compensation

Affiliate Chief Executive Officers:
- Function as independent CEOs of banks
- Choose to use optional central resources

Systemwide Committees:
- Develop standardized products
- Share best practices
- Establish human resources policies

EXHIBIT 34-3   Banc One Structure
Source: Banc One Corporate Annual Report.

tistate operations became apparent. This structure permitted many responsibilities, products, resources, and services to be centralized. New affiliates could be easily integrated and local management talent could be nurtured under this new structure. In addition, centralized efforts could provide expertise and policy guidelines in a cost-effective manner. For example, in the summer of 1988, Banc One reduced the number of financial products offered by all of its affiliates from 63 to 10. By standardizing features, marketing efforts, product terms, and product conditions, decisions about pricing, marketing, and operations became easier. Bank One also began to save $5 million annually as a result of its central-office materials-procurement program.

In 1988, Banc One went a step further in providing structure by creating the Banc One Services Corporation. Its goal was to handle all operations for all affiliates, including information technologies, computer systems, programming and develop-

ment, check processing, and credit-card processing.

As the state holding structure proved itself by successfully addressing the complexities of multistate operations, the second reason for its implementation—nonbanking operations such as mortgage, securities, and trust services—grew in importance. By the end of the 1980s, Banc One decided to do more than verbally acknowledge the effect on bank strategy of this growing influence.[2] In 1990, a new organization was formed, Banc One Diversified Services Corporation.

Paul Walsh, chairman of Diversified Services, used a chart showing estimated financial services revenues from U.S. households (see Exhibit 34-4), together with the following data, to explain the rationale for the formation of the new company:

> From our research, we've determined that roughly $400 billion is paid out by U.S. households for retail financial services. About 25 percent is in the traditional

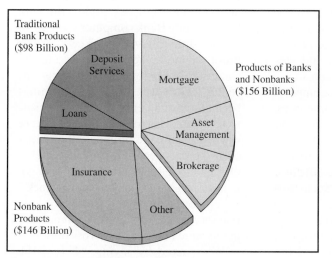

EXHIBIT 34-4   Bank One Diversified Services Corporation

---

[2]For detailed insight on the competitive forces shaping Banc One's future, see case number EVE-BP-0335, "Bank One Corporation: Diversified Services," the University of Virginia Darden School Foundation.

product area of bank-deposit services and consumer loans. The rest is in the nontraditional area that encompasses the services we're offering.

Six individual companies constituted Banc One Diversified Services Corporation. Banc One Investment Advisors created and managed a variety of investment products including mutual funds and tax-exempt funds. Banc One Leasing Corporation provided leveraged, middle-market, municipal, and vendor leases to the commercial market. Banc One Mortgage Corporation provided residential mortgage products in 12 states through its own offices, through the Banc One affiliates, and through correspondents. Banc One Securities Corporation sold and marketed both Banc One and other institutions' financial-securities products through its 100-person sales force in Banc One branch offices and its toll-free telephone service. Banc One Financial Services, Incorporated provided home equity loans and refinancing of residential real-estate loans. It was headquartered in Marion, Indiana, had 78 offices in 13 states, and envisioned creating a national network. Banc One Insurance Group offered life, health, and reinsurance services and was headquartered in Milwaukee, Wisconsin.

Most of the Diversified Services employees worked for their respective companies. Thus, an affiliate bank could easily have an independent Diversified Services banker under its roof. For example, a securities officer would not report to the affiliate bank but rather to Banc One Securities Corporation's reporting structure.

All of these structures, including Banc One Diversified Services Corporation, Banc One Services Corporation, and the state holding companies, fulfilled Banc One's acquisition strategy. These structures also continued to shape Preston Bank's service to the Park Cities after Banc One acquired Preston Bank in 1989.

PRESTON STATE BANK AND MCORP FROM 1984 TO 1989

In 1984, as the Texas bank branching law was being passed, MCorp acquired Preston State Bank with its holding company, Southwest Bankshares Corporation. When the branch-banking law went into effect in 1987, MCorp and all other bank-holding companies rushed to consolidate operations. Branch banking in Texas had begun.

Throughout the 1980s, the Texas banking industry, including MCorp, centralized operations. Many activities in small banks were removed. In order to consolidate resources, improve asset utilization, cut costs, and improve profitability, Preston State Bank became MBank Preston Branch. It also lost many of its in-house, specialized services. Trust, mortgage, private banking, real-estate, and data-processing operations were all centralized at MBank's downtown Dallas headquarters. Horn described the situation at Preston State Bank as follows:

When the branch-banking law changed, we began to hand things off to the other departments. For example, the old Preston State Bank computer went away. So we didn't have bookkeeping and proof anymore. We gave that up to the computer operation and the operations center for MCorp. Those sort of things began to have an effect on customer service. When an error was made or there was a problem, the problem often didn't occur here. It occurred somewhere else. One had to tell the customer, "We've got to check on it for you and call you back." When you were an independent bank, that's a change. You know, the item is not in the same building, it's across the city.

We reacted by saying, "This is the way things are going to be." I think there was this feeling of, "This is what branch banking is." It's more efficient to do these things this way because we're consolidating everyone's back room into a common back room. That is going to be far more efficient, and it is going to help profitability for the holding company.

In December 1987, Horn, president of the MBank Preston Branch, was transferred to the downtown Dallas headquarters. His new responsibilities included managing MCorp's 10 Dallas banks and converting them to a branch-banking system.

BANC ONE ACQUIRES PRESTON BANK, 1989 TO 1991

In July 1989, Banc One Corporation acquired the Deposit Insurance Bridge Bank, a 20-bank subset including the Preston Branch, of MCorp's failed operations. Banc One agreed to pay between $375 and $510 million over the ensuing 5 years, depending on the bank's financial performance, to the Federal Deposit Insurance Corporation (FDIC). (The FDIC had created the Bridge Bank from a subset of MCorp's assets.) Thus, with Banc One's purchase of the Deposit Insurance Bridge Bank, Banc One bought the third-largest bank in Texas. It held $13.1 billion in assets and had 65 branch offices spread across the state.

Banc One worked to integrate MCorp into its structure and systems using the Banc One strategy of centralizing paper and processes. At the same time, Banc One executed an acquisition plan. Banc One was concerned that Dallas was severely "under branched,"[3] so the company set out to acquire other banks and savings and loans in the Dallas area. During 1990, Bright Savings and three independent banks were acquired. Within 18 months of acquiring Deposit Insurance Bridge Bank, Banc One added 21 offices to its Dallas network. Two

of these offices were in the Park Cities. Thus, through greater presence and market share, Bank One immediately strengthened its newly acquired retail business in Dallas.

Each acquisition brought its own culture with it. Each needed to be assimilated. While Banc One Corporation had a strong culture, no Bank One, Dallas managers had any Banc One Corporation experience. They were creating a new culture blended from their respective histories, Banc One Corporation, new acquisitions, and the branch-banking developments in Texas.

By 1991, Horn's responsibilities had grown and reflected the array of management issues that Bank One, Dallas management was addressing. The original 10 MCorp branches had now grown to 36. Suddenly branch training, branch support, and teller support surfaced as urgent issues. Financial planning and reporting took on new proportions and complexities. Operations, including deposit operations and conversions, were being conducted on a much larger scale than before and demanded a new approach.

Moving quickly to adjust, Horn organized his senior vice president, branch management position's responsibilities as per Exhibit 34-5. The 36 branches were divided into five geographic areas. To manage each area, a new position was created, called area manager. The five area managers reported directly to Horn.

Horn also held the position of acting executive vice president, Dallas Retail Division. With mass distribution being a key element to branch banking, he and Bank One, Dallas management organized this position as per Exhibit 34-6. As more banks were acquired and converted to branches, a Branch Operations and Support Department was created.

---

[3]Banc One had 52 branches in Indianapolis and 45 branches in Columbus at the time of the MCorp acquisition. Both regions had less than half the population of Dallas.

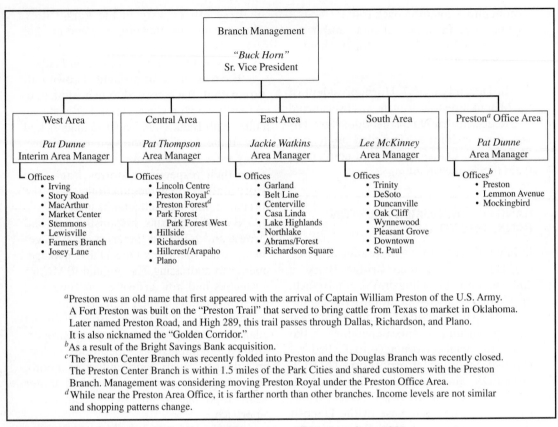

EXHIBIT 34-5 Bank One, Dallas Branch Management Structure, Late 1991

Similarly Consumer Lending/ Acquisitions, Small Business Lending, and Financial, Planning, and Reporting Departments addressed the needs of branch banking.

From 1989 to 1991, Horn and Bank One, Dallas management worked to realize a branch-banking network and make Bank One, Dallas a success. This was a period of constant growth and change. For example, the acquisition of Bright Savings Bank included offices in the Park Cities called Preston Center and Douglas. These were closed soon after the acquisition. Chuck Eikenberg, who was the branch manager for Bright Savings, became a Bank One, Dallas senior vice president and was charged with the responsibility of streamlining consumer

lending operations by leading the new Consumer Lending/Acquisitions Department as shown in Exhibit 34-6. Also, area managers and upper management held lengthy discussions as to where to draw the boundaries between the five areas in Exhibit 34-6. A case in point was the Lemmon Avenue Branch that was moved from the Central Area to the Preston Office Area. Thus, the organizational chart in Exhibit 34-6 was in a constant state of flux.

CREEPING CRISIS AT PARK CITIES?

In 1991, members of Bank One, Dallas management began to refocus on the Park Cities as one of the bank's most promising

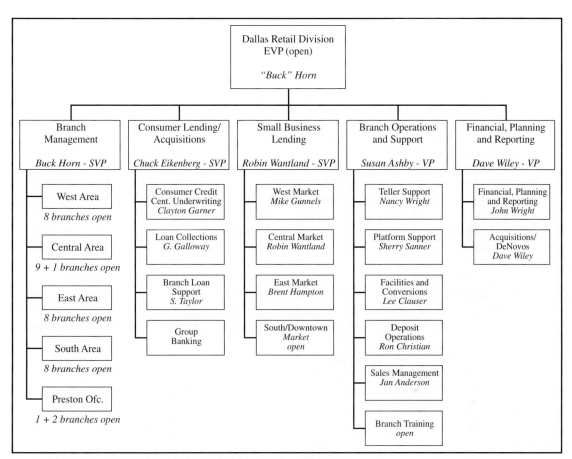

EXHIBIT 34-6   Bank One, Dallas Retail Organization Chart

Date	Preston	+Bright S&L P/C
10/87	$629	
	−170[a]	
4/90	459[b]	$559
6/91		$520

[a]Deposit loss from reorganization and failure of MCorp:

Failure-all CDs	$95 MM
School Fund Contracts	25 MM
Credit Card Banks	25 MM
Internal Transfers R/E	22 MM
Credit Card Merchants	3 MM
TOTAL	**$170 MM**

[b]Includes the $100MM acquisition of Bright S&L office in Park Cities

EXHIBIT 34-7   Bank One, Texas-Preston Deposit Trend (in millions of dollars)

markets. At the same time, Horn and Miller recognized that they harbored an uneasy feeling about Bank One's performance in the Park Cities and that this feeling had been growing, rather than subsiding, during the past months.

Bank One, Dallas had three branches located in the Park Cities in late 1991. They were being managed under the Preston Area, one of five areas on Exhibit 34-6. Based on number of branches, the Preston Area was the smallest area. Branches included Bank One–Preston (situated in the Preston Building, the original Preston State Bank building), Bank One–Mockingbird, and Bank One–Lemmon.

Market share appeared to be slipping. The Park Cities' deposits were clearly down although acquisition activity made the analysis difficult to follow as Exhibit 34-7 shows. Furthermore, it was uncertain whether or not this was a result of lost market share or of lower interest rates that caused customers to withdraw their deposits, especially CDs, to invest in higher-yielding investments. Disintermediation was one of many management issues that vied for management's attention. Profitability figures for the Park Cities were difficult to obtain because Bank One's MICS aggregated the Dallas market and did not provide separate Park Cities numbers.

Both Horn and Miller were quick to recognize the growing competitive threat. At least three independent banks had emerged as strong competitors during the past few years. Capital Bank's advertisement on the radio certainly did not help matters. The question remained: At what point was action warranted? Besides, there were branch banking issues, merger and acquisition activities, and efforts of assimilating all units into a cohesive Bank One, Dallas operation that warranted management's full attention.

By now many services had been withdrawn from the Preston Building and were centralized in downtown Dallas, far removed from the customer. The customers were separated by a long, inconvenient drive from many of the decision makers in mortgage lending, trust, private banking, securities, and small business.

Both Horn and Miller lived in Park Cities. They not only thought as professionals about how all these changes adversely affected service, but they also experienced this adverse effect through friends and neighbors. Conversations in Park Cities' social settings included comments such as, "I liked it [Preston Bank] better the way it was," and "Why do you have to go downtown for everything?" People even used the Preston State Bank of the 1980s as a benchmark: "I understand that that new First National Bank of Park Cities is trying to act like another Preston." These comments cropped up at cocktail parties, church, and high school football games. Many were direct and hurt, such as "Y'all don't do things like you used to," and "I'm looking for somebody that did it like y'all used to and I think I'm going over to North Park."

In light of all the changes brought on at the Preston Bank Building in the last few years, from bank branching to Bank One's acquisitions, Horn wondered what action should be taken to restore Bank One's competitive advantage in the Park Cities. ■

Case 35 Two Big Banks' Broken Back Office

Megan stared at her computer screen in disbelief. The bank's vice chairman had responded to her e-mail with a curt message: "Megan—I don't want to hear it." What was going on around here? Megan wondered. Ever since Megan's bank merged with the bank literally across the street, her customers complained continuously about an erosion in service. Megan had simply reached out for help—and had her hand slapped. How was she going to maintain her current business—not to mention grow it—and the morale of the salespeople who worked for her under these circumstances? Was this nightmare ever going to end?

Megan began with the bank as a management trainee right after completing business school. Over the years, she had held several positions in the bank and was well respected. Megan was a survivor of several previous mergers (a so-called "best of the best" because she had never been laid off as a result of merger redundancies) and was impressed with how management had handled those mergers: careful planning, solid execution, strong communication and—perhaps most importantly—a transparent integration from the perspective of the customer. This merger was a radically different experience.

In her current role as managing director in charge of Foreign Exchange Sales, Megan had spent the past 6 months engaged in three principal activities: soothing angry customers, counseling discouraged salespeople, and working with the Operations Department to work toward a solution to improving the bank's back office system. None of these activities led to a growth in her profitability—the principle measure against which Megan was evaluated and compensated.

THE FOREIGN EXCHANGE BUSINESS

Foreign exchange was perhaps the only true global trading market. A highly liquid market, more than $1 trillion a day was traded in the FX market. Trading activity began in London, moved with the clock to New York, then to Tokyo, and back to London. The price of currency—always expressed as one currency in terms of another (i.e., the price of British pounds per U.S. dollar, or the price of Japanese yen per German mark)—was highly volatile. Despite its liquidity, the foreign exchange market often experienced moves of more than 3 percent in a matter of minutes. Megan's bank was a leader in both "market making" (continuously offering a price at which it would buy

UVA-BP-0432

This case was written by Margaret Cording, doctoral candidate, under the supervision of L. J. Bourgeois, III, Professor of Business Administration. The authors gratefully acknowledge the financial assistance of the Darden School's Batten Institute. Copyright © 2001 by the Darden Graduate Business School Foundation, Charlottesville, Virginia. All rights reserved.

or sell currency) and in hedging vehicles (products such as forwards and options designed to minimize the risk of adverse price movements for its clients). A highly profitable business, Megan's bank consistently ranked among the top three global foreign exchange players.

Banks traded foreign currency for two reasons: to take a proprietary position in the hopes of turning a profit and to provide a service to customers. Customers, in turn, could be broadly segregated into two categories: those seeking to speculate in the foreign exchange market and those whose currency needs arose from doing business internationally. An example of the first instance would be a large hedge fund seeking to take a large position in, say, the Turkish lira. The fund manager would look to Megan's bank to provide competitive prices, valuable market intelligence, and fast execution. Also valued was a quiet execution, so that other market players were unaware of the hedge fund's position, minimizing competing activity that might bid up the price of the currency. Corporations of all sizes—from a small Italian shoe importer to a large multinational—needed to manage the foreign currency risk that arose from revenue earned or expenses incurred in a currency other than their home currency.

The transaction did not end, however, with agreement between the bank and its counterpart as to the terms of the trade. Equally important as price, execution, and market analysis was the ability to deliver the promised currency to its designated destination on the appropriate day. This massive movement of money around the globe required a sophisticated back office system. Automation of as many functions as possible was important to minimize error and keep costs low. An ideal system, for instance, would not require human intervention from the moment a trader or salesperson input the trade (paper "tickets" no longer existed in large trading rooms) to the time the money arrived at its required destination.

Tradition in the securities industry required the managerial separation of trading and sales and that of the back office—or the operations function. This was designed for two principal reasons: One, the managerial talent required for the two functions was substantially different, and two, it minimized the risk of fraud and embezzlement. (N. B. Nicholas Leeson of Barclay's Bank was in charge of both areas, which facilitated his ability to exceed corporate limits on his trading activity. His speculative activities led to the insolvency of Barclay's in 1996.)

The problem Megan was wrestling with concerned the bank's back office system. Quite simply, money was not arriving in a timely manner at its specified destination. As a result, customers did not have access to the funds when and where they thought they would. Chief financial officers, treasurers, and cash managers confronted problems that were a direct result of the bank's incompetence. The phones never stopped ringing with yet another problem.

THE MERGER: PEOPLE AND SYSTEMS DECISIONS

Both prior banks were significant players in the foreign exchange market, and the merger presented an opportunity to extract cost savings as well as the opportunity to create a world-class team. Immediately after the merger announcement, top management began to consider who would run the new bank's businesses as well as which back office systems would be selected. Quick decisions in both areas were required but for two different reasons. The "people" decisions would help minimize uncertainty, which helped reduce potential losses of productivity and a lack of focus on the business. An early decision on the system was desirable because of the complexity of changing and integrating computer systems. As much advance planning as possible would lead to a smooth transition.

Having selected the team that would run the new bank's foreign exchange business—dominated by managers from Megan's bank—the vice chairman turned his attention to the selection of the back office system and the managers who would run the operations area. This was a difficult trade-off between the regional computer system Megan's bank employed, which was highly automated and efficient, and the other bank's system, which was global, enabling the systematic aggregation of information across all of the bank's trading activities and locations. This latter consideration was important not only because it was cost effective but, perhaps more importantly, because it also facilitated the management of global market risk across a wide array of products and locations.

The vice chairman in charge of global capital market activities (in addition to other functions) had one concern that kept him up at night: What market position, in what location, would blow up and negatively affect earnings? Commercial and investment banks tended to suffer from a relatively low price/earnings (P/E) ratio, due to the volatility and risk of their capital markets product revenue streams. One mistake could wipe out an entire quarter's earnings for the whole bank. The vice chairman was well aware of his obligation to maintain a steady and consistent earnings record to facilitate an increasing price and P/E ratio for his bank's stock.

Given this information requirement and the fact that the trading and sales managers were largely from Megan's bank, the vice chairman selected the other bank's computer system. The other bank's senior back office executive was placed in charge of the area in the new bank. Under him, Sam was selected to run the New York back office. Sam was a 20-year veteran of Megan's bank

and had played a pivotal role in developing that bank's back office system.

THE NEW BANK'S BACK OFFICE

Megan and Sam had worked together for years and had a comfortable working relationship. Megan paid close attention to the manner in which Sam engaged his new responsibilities. The first thing Megan noticed was Sam's lack of enthusiasm and commitment to the other bank's system. Every time they talked, Sam was filled with negativity about the system's capabilities. Early on in the integration process, Sam was plotting scenarios about how to get the decision reversed. Megan began to have a sense of doom: Did Sam, consciously or unconsciously, hope that the system would fail?

Nonetheless, Sam worked diligently toward building a team and transferring data to the new system. On "Day One"—the first day of the newly combined bank—things went relatively smoothly. Traders could view their currency positions; salespeople had access to customer records. Although there was some confusion over how the system worked, Sam made sure that qualified people were close by to answer any questions and quickly resolve any problems.

The situation, however, quickly deteriorated. Several days later, the trading floor was in chaos. Salespeople were getting calls from customers, saying that currency was not delivered. The back office staff was unable to provide an explanation. No one seemed to know what was going on.

A high-level task force was quickly put together to assess the situation. The vice chairman headed this team, and they met weekly to discuss three key issues: What were the problems, what were the solutions, and who was responsible for implementing them? A member of the task force, Sam grew more despondent every day.

A month into the merger, Megan invited Sam to have drinks after work. During this conversation, Sam reiterated a remark Megan had heard often in the months leading up to the bank combination: "I just don't understand why we don't switch to our old system, Megan, it is far superior." On several occasions during the conversation, Megan thought she saw tears in the corners of Sam's eyes.

CLIENT MANAGEMENT CONCERNS

In addition to the close working relationship between product areas such as Foreign Exchange and the Operations Department, other interdependencies existed that had to be managed. The most important of these for Megan was the relationship her department had with the "client managers"—generalists who were responsible for managing an overall relationship between the bank and its clients.

For new business generation, these "client managers" were Megan's front-line marketing resource. Megan and her team depended on the client managers to pitch the bank's foreign exchange capabilities and try to secure a meeting between one of Megan's salespeople and officials at the company. In one sense, therefore, a bank client manager was as much a client as, say, a chief financial officer. Megan spent a significant amount of time managing these relationships, as she competed with all of the bank's other product areas for the client managers' time and attention.

As these client managers began hearing about the foreign exchange delivery problems from their corporate clients, they became increasingly skeptical about the department's ability to provide a world-class service. Megan was aware that this perspective would survive long after the back office was fixed, potentially affecting her ability to grow the business for years to come.

Attempting to minimize the damage, Megan spent a significant amount of time communicating with client managers. The vice chairman of Client Management was Max, also from Megan's prior bank. Max knew well the strong foreign exchange capabilities of the prior bank and had confidence in the product. However, the recent problems had worn on Max as well as on the executives under him. He and Megan had reached a short-term decision: now was not the time to pitch the bank's foreign exchange (FX) services to new clients. Max was increasingly concerned, however, about how the current problems were affecting existing relationships, and he was increasingly angry about the amount of time his client managers were devoting to FX problem resolution. Compounding this distress was Max's historical rivalry with the vice chairman in charge of Global Capital Markets—Megan's boss.

ORGANIZATIONAL STRUCTURE AND INTRABANK DEPENDENCIES

As a large global institution, Megan's bank required its managers to work adroitly across organizational lines. Given the complexity of the client base and product portfolio, one's daily contacts spread throughout the organization. In many cases, the only common point of management was the office of the chief executive officer.

In terms of the Foreign Exchange Department, Megan had a peer who was responsible for the group's trading activity. She also had numerous colleagues who managed the sales function of other capital markets products. This group of sales managers would meet routinely to share experiences, best practices, and client information. It represented a support network of managers who were dealing with problems similar to those facing Megan (although none had experienced the broken back office that Megan was dealing with).

More broadly, however, Megan worked with numerous other personnel. In addition to the client managers described above, she depended on the Credit Department, the Market Risk Management Department, the Operations Department, and other support areas. Exhibit 35-1 presents a partial functional organizational chart of the various functions.

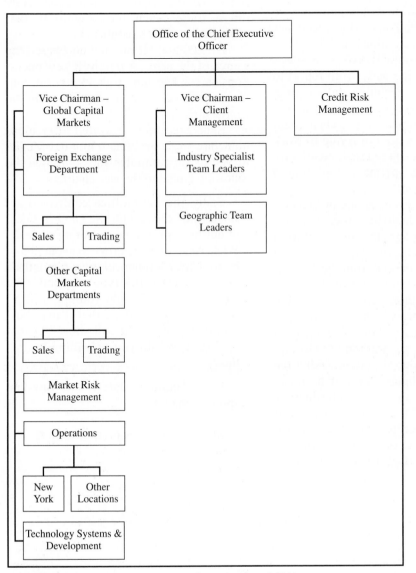

EXHIBIT 35-1   Partial Functional Organizational Chart

TODAY'S PROBLEM

It had been a long 6 months since the banks merged. Although progress with the back office system was being made, errors still occurred at a rate far above what was acceptable. Megan was tired. She was tired of listening to angry customers. She was tired of trying to tell salespeople to hang in there—that a solution would emerge. She recognized the challenges that faced her staff: How can one enthusiastically sell a product that one knows is broken? She was tired of looking at her daily profit report to see the numbers declining rather than increasing. She was tired of explaining the department's incompetencies to client managers. She also was tired of trying to work with Sam and his team to create temporary band-aids, pending a permanent solution to the computer system.

At 8:00 in the evening, one of Megan's salespeople walked into her office. Terrance had been working late on a proposal for a large potential client. He was livid. He had just received a phone call from the CFO of one of his largest multinational clients. During this telephone conversation, the CFO asked Terrance why his bank thought it necessary that the chief financial officer of a *Fortune* 100 company was required to confirm a trade of under $1 million. Didn't the CFO have better things to do with his time?

Customary in all securities businesses, before the end of the trading day, a staff member of the operations area telephoned a contact person at the customer firm to confirm the details of a transaction conducted earlier in the day. This procedure ensured that (a) the terms of the trade were accurate and any errors were discovered as early as possible, and (b) fraud had not occurred. Usually, this conversation occurred between operations personnel at the bank and at the customer firm. Many multinationals stipulated the contact level as a function of the size of the transaction; rarely did a trade reach the magnitude that required the CFO to confirm it.

By 9:00 P.M. Megan had uncovered the source of the error. A relatively new operations person had simply glanced at the contact list and called the CFO to confirm the transaction.

Exhausted and frustrated after a 14-hour day and a grueling 6 months, Megan turned to her computer and composed the following e-mail to the vice chairman:

Sadly, the back office confirmed a small trade today with the CFO of one of our most profitable corporate clients. While we have made progress in our ability to deliver foreign currency, 6 months into this merger this type of mistake is still occurring. Thought you might like to know. I also believe that it may be useful if you would call the CFO to apologize. Would you be willing to do this?

Thirty minutes later, the one-line response came:

Megan—I don't want to hear it. ■

Case 36   Brubaker: A Guide for Viewing, Understanding, and Applying the Film

Brubaker describes an actual event of 1971 to 1972 in which Henry Brubaker (Robert Redford) is appointed the new warden of Wakefield State Prison. In order to learn about the prison, Brubaker arranges to be admitted in disguise as a prisoner. The film depicts his attempts to reform the institution.

Brubaker provides an excellent vehicle for highlighting the factors that influence the success of organizational change efforts and for examining the managerial role in those change efforts. We will stop the film at several points to ask questions and to generate discussion on those topics and others. The pages that follow include discussion questions for some of the major stopping points of the film. Please do not read ahead, but wait until asked to turn to the next page.

Because the film depicts prison life and attempts to do so realistically, it includes strong language, some graphic violence, and brief nudity. We hope that this will not obstruct your ability to see the change processes at work in this situation and to learn from them.

Even though they are often referred to as such, corporations are not prisons. Yet many of the motivational and leadership issues that arise in organizations are apparently more extreme and therefore more clear in prison settings. By observing the obvious, we can be better equipped to observe and manage the more subtle. As you watch the film, think of the organization with which you are most familiar and try to see the subtle, psychological parallels to the physical events that take place in the prison. In the first segment, keep watch for the prison's objectives, structure, culture, ways of socializing new members, rules, punishments, and their impact on the prison's motivational climate.

As the film begins, please review the list of major characters. Do not turn ahead further.

Some of the Central Characters in *Brubaker*

Eddie Caldwell	Trustee with navy cap and rifle
Henry Brubaker	New warden
Huey Ross	Head trustee
Dickie Coombes	Black trustee with shotgun
Pinky	Cafe owner in town
Carol	Pinky's sister, Huey's girlfriend
Bullen	Habitual criminal, Pontiac lover
Roy Purcell	Clerk trustee
Floyd	Trustee with plaid cap

(continued)

Captain Renfro	Outgoing warden
C. P. Woodward	Community lumberyard owner
Willits	State employee
Abraham Cook	Old black man
Lilian Gray	Brubaker's sponsor on the prison board
John Deech	Prison board chairman (17 years)
Charles Hight	Senator

BRUBAKER: ASSIGNMENT 1

By the time the death row inmate threatens Bullen's life and Brubaker tells him that he is the new warden, we have learned something about the process by which people enter the organization and something about the way in which newcomers are taught lessons about the rules of the organization, and we have some idea about the culture of the organization. All of these elements have a great influence on the motivation of the newcomers.

Please write down the major elements of your organization on these dimensions:

Describe the process by which people enter your organization:

How do newcomers learn the rules of your organization?

List the major rules of behavior in your organization and the penalties for breaking them:

BRUBAKER: ASSIGNMENT 2

By the time Brubaker meets the contractor, Woodward, he has encountered a variety of people whom he must manage in order to succeed. These include his bosses (Lil, the prison board and its chairman, John Deech, legislators, and the governor), peers in the community (business people like Woodward and citizens who either supply the prison or buy from it), and subordinates (including the rankmen, the death row inmates, the trustees, and the guards.) This CONSTELLATION OF KEY RELATIONSHIPS points out how much Brubaker relies on people all around him for success and how much each group is different in terms of what motivates them and what leadership style they are likely to respond to.

In the following space, diagram the constellation of relationships upon which you depend for success in your present (or last) job:

BRUBAKER: ASSIGNMENT 3

When Brubaker forms the newly elected inmate council, he clearly has an objective in mind. He is trying to help the men learn that their opinions, thoughts, beliefs, and values count. His theory is probably something like, "If I can get them to believe that they are worth something, there is a higher probability that they will grow here on the inside and therefore a higher probability that they will be able to succeed on the outside."

Please list the ways that you encourage your subordinates to grow in their self-image, their skills, and their abilities to contribute to the real objectives of the organization:

Now list some additional ways that you might do this:

BRUBAKER: ASSIGNMENT 4

When Brubaker faced the senator's offer of financial support and freedom to reform the prison if he stopped digging for corpses, he faced a major dilemma. On the one hand, if he accepted, he might be able to make a significant difference in the prison's facilities. We don't know if later on the senator might have said to Brubaker what Huey said to Pinky earlier in the film: "Sorry, Pinky, I just couldn't come up with two sides of beef this time, but I'll make it up to you." We also don't know how the rankmen would have responded to the knowledge that Brubaker had made a deal.

On the other hand, if Brubaker refused the deal, his job and career were in great jeopardy, and he might have been constrained from making any further impact on the penal system in the state.

List one or two experiences you have had when you had to decide between the desires of senior management and the desires of your subordinates. What did you do? What was the impact on both groups? What was the impact on you? What would have happened if you had done the other thing?

BRUBAKER: ASSIGNMENT 5

As Brubaker is driven out of Wakefield Prison, we are left wondering what will happen. Coombes once accused Brubaker of starting wars and letting other people fight them. Now, Brubaker is leaving, and the new warden, Roy Polk, is making his introductory remarks.

What do you think will happen? Why?

BRUBAKER: ASSIGNMENT 6

As you reflect on the film, summarize below the major principles or ideas you have gleaned about how to manage change. What seems most important to remember about managing change in business organizations? ■

Case 37   Chicago Park District (A)

In the spring of 1993, Mayor Richard M. Daley of Chicago called his former chief of staff, Forrest Claypool, into his office and offered him the job of general superintendent of the city's park district. Claypool had become familiar with the park district while working in the mayor's office and was concerned about the magnitude of the job that attempted to serve the recreational needs of the 8.6 million people who lived in the Chicago area. He also knew that a local advocacy group, Friends of the Parks, had recently graded the district a "D-" because of "deeply rooted and long-standing problems that result in poor service to citizens."

Mayor Daley's request came at a time when the park districts of other major American cities were facing major financial difficulties. County supervisors in Los Angeles had just proposed closing 24 parks in their system along with massive personnel layoffs. New York City officials had already cut their park system to half what it had been in the 1960s (from 4,500 employees down to 2,500), so that one official noted that trying to make any more cuts would be like "giving liposuction to a skeleton."[1] A 1993 study of cities across the country showed that state and local park administrations had faced budget shortfalls of more than $37 billion collectively between 1987 and 1993.

BACKGROUND

The Chicago Park District (CPD) was an enormous organization. By 1993, CPD had grown to include 550 parks on 7,400 acres with 259 field house/recreation centers, 191 gymnasiums, 90 indoor and outdoor swimming pools, 850 baseball and softball diamonds, thousands of game courts and playgrounds, two conservatories, one internationally known zoo, a major league sports stadium, an underutilized and underperforming concession business, a $500,000 annual revenue parking operation, and six golf courses, as well as 31 miles of waterfront recreation facilities with few amenities, and commercial locks on the Chicago River that fed into the second-largest harbor system in the United States. In all, CPD assets totaled $2.3 billion at this time, some of which were unique in the country. For instance, Chicago had a uniquely accessible harbor system, managed by CPD, in which a person could leave work in the financial district and be on his or her boat in less than 10 minutes headed for Lake Michigan. Sixty million people a year used the waterfront recreation facilities alone; this yielded about $30 million in concession revenues — and 8 million pounds of garbage. CPD also maintained a variety of historical buildings, monuments, and statues and owned an airport, Meigs Field, on a landfill island near downtown that it leased to the city. One of the largest CPD facilities, Soldier Field stadium, home of the Chicago Bears of the National Football League, also hosted a variety of public events and was slated to handle World Cup soccer games in 1994 as well as concerts by the Grateful Dead and the Rolling Stones. CPD was truly a huge, and hugely important, Chicago asset.

UVA-OB-0618

This case was prepared by James G. Clawson. Copyright © 1996 by the University of Virginia Darden School Foundation, Charlottesville, VA. All rights reserved. The Darden School expresses its thanks and appreciation to the officers of the Chicago Park District who made this case possible.

[1]Charles Mahtesian, "The End of Park-Barrel Politics," *Governing,* January 1995, 38.

The CPD story began in the late 1800s when Chicago citizens, notably Jane Addams and Jens Jensen, began building a grand vision of how neighborhood parks and recreation facilities could simultaneously provide anchors to the local, often ethnic, neighborhoods and a means of binding together the city as a whole. They envisioned a system of attractive green neighborhood parks encircling the city that would give respite from the harsher side of urban life by providing affordable recreation and leisure activities. This system of parks, it was thought, would be the "lungs of the city, offering breathing room to millions of nature-starved urbanites."[2] Addams and Jensen along with other interested civic leaders organized efforts to build parks in neighborhood centers here and there around the Chicago area. The era's most famous landscape architects, Frederick Law Olmsted, Daniel Burnham, and others, joined in the work.

Twenty-five years later, in 1907, Theodore Roosevelt said that the CPD was the most notable civic achievement he had seen in a modern American city. At the same time, the various completed parks had not yet been molded into a single system. The Chicago Park District Act of 1934 consolidated the neighborhood parks into a single system and gave the CPD authority to levy property taxes for their support independently from other tax measures.

In subsequent years, however, the CPD became a growing case example of the dark side of government and its related bureaucracy, a classic patronage system. CPD officers gave park management and supervisory positions to their friends and family members. Community-oriented programming and activities planning declined. Monies allocated to maintenance and improvements were siphoned off into personal accounts.

With independent authority to levy and a close affiliation with the appointments process in city government, management of the CPD increasingly lost contact with the original purpose and intent of the park system—to provide leisure and recreation—so that service to the various communities deteriorated. By the early 1990s, this course had produced a park district that was enormous in its scope and complexity, but a glaring example in the public eye of government run amuck. One CPD official noted that the system "served CPD employees and politicians, but not the public." One reporter summed it up:

> Even though the Park District [was] legally a separate entity with its own budget and taxing authority, a succession of mayoral appointees managed to commandeer the district and bloat the payroll with thousands of patronage workers, almost all of whom came equipped with a letter from their ward committeeman and an attitude not especially conducive to public service. The legion of politically connected employees had little incentive to respond to the communities they served. Their jobs, for the most part, depended more on voter turnout than on park user turnout.[3]

Claypool understood that the mayor was asking him to clean up the CPD and manage it back to its founding mission and purpose. Claypool also knew that there had been many attempts in recent history to improve the situation at CPD. First, Ed Kelly had supervised CPD for 13 years, then Jesse Madison had tried, and finally Bob Penn, whom Mayor Daley had hired to run CPD after a national search, had given his best efforts. Although each had made some progress, each found the system

---

[2]Ibid., 34.
[3]Ibid.

unyielding to their efforts; not much change had taken place. Each successive unsuccessful attempt had further eroded CPD morale and reputation.

PROBLEMS AT THE CPD

Given the lack of change up through the 1990s, local reporters, citizens' groups, and advocacy groups had begun to focus on CPD. Newspapers and television stations ran features periodically highlighting the poor CPD service. In 1990, the *Chicago Tribune* sent reporters to visit 30 CPD facilities. Their investigations and those of other interested citizens brought examples of CPD's ineptness to public light:

- People reported that it took up to 4 days simply to register for a class being offered by CPD. One study concluded that it took *on average* 29 hours to register for a CPD class.
- Many of the classes and recreational programs were poorly attended or utterly unattended because they were never advertised. "The park programs were secret and basically designed for people who were in the club and who knew about them, but not for the general public who were paying the freight for those programs," said one well-informed observer.
- Parks were referred to as "ghost towns" by the *Tribune.*
- Property taxes levied by the CPD had increased significantly each year in recent times to cover deficits.
- A woman who called the CPD office to find out if a class she wanted to take was being offered was told, "That's confidential

information. It can't be given out over the phone."[4]
- One CPD facility began to offer boxing programs. When the people in the neighborhood said that most of their children were little girls and that they wanted ballet instead of boxing, the answer came back, "We're doing boxing!"
- Many citizens went to CPD facilities at the times announced to attend classes and found the buildings closed and dark. One study showed that CPD classes occurred on average only 56 percent of the scheduled times. Reasons for this included instructors absent (34 percent of the time), no enrollment (19 percent), schedule changed (13 percent), building closed (8 percent), outside event (5 percent), program cut (3 percent), no supplies (2 percent), and no explanation (9 percent).
- A taxpayer took his family to a CPD pool and was disgruntled to discover that the staff closed the pool every hour for 15 minutes in order to "check the chlorine." During this time, swimmers had to leave the pool, dress, and wait outside chain link fences before being re-admitted to the pool. Furthermore, swimmers could not leave the pool during the 45-minute swimming period because the staff padlocked the pool gates.
- Children in one field house were not allowed to play on the gym floor because, the supervisor said, they might "scuff the floor."
- In one widely discussed incident, a CPD officer visited a field house anonymously and, observing trash

---

[4]Maureen Ryan and David H. Roeder, "Glasnost at the Park District," *Chicago Enterprise,* May/June 1994, 17.

around the entrance, went in to see the manager. Seeing a person behind the counter with his feet up watching a football game on television, he asked about the trash outside the door and was told, "I don't know. That's not my job." When the officer asked what the person's job was, he replied, "to sit here and collect a paycheck."[5]

This last anecdote became a rallying point in the city for demands for changes in the patronage system at CPD. But the public association of poor service with the patronage system did not adequately describe the condition of the underlying systems within the CPD organization.

Human-Resource Concerns

First, no one could tell how many people CPD employed; some estimated several thousand, as many as 5,000, but it was not clear. It *was* clear, though, that CPD employees were represented by 37 different trade unions—although roughly two thirds of them were members of the largest of these, the Public Employees Service Union. One union leader said that the problem with CPD was not the employees, but management. Absenteeism among CPD employees (which included trade and operations people, attendants, cultural instructors, physical instructors, and park and playground supervisors) was high and viewed as one of the worst characteristics of the patronage legacy. (Absenteeism was later discovered to be about 16 percent, three times the local private industry average and well above the national average of 9 percent). The way the system worked was explained inadvertently and eloquently one evening at a public retirement dinner for a senior park official,

when one of his subordinates made the following statement:

> Twenty years ago, when I was a young clerk in the system, I used to roll out of bed when I rolled out of bed; go to work when I felt like it. Usually arrive about 11 o'clock. Make a couple of phone calls, go out to lunch, come back, make a few more personal phone calls, and go home. [The retiring senior officer] was great. He covered me for all those years.[6]

Subsequent analysis[7] revealed that firing a nonperforming worker like this required 84 administrative steps and more than a year's time, but then an appeals process took effect, so that practically speaking, one could not *be* fired from CPD. Consequently, poor performers were simply transferred around the system. One park's castoff became the next unsuspecting park's nightmare.

One reason for this kind of result was that most of the decisions regarding CPD activities were made in the district's headquarter offices at the north end of Soldier Field on McFetridge Drive. Previous administrations had recognized in part that this centralization was inefficient and had tried to push decision making out to the parks. The present administration, for instance, had organized the district into clusters—groups of parks with a central "host park"—and, on paper, decentralized control of decisions affecting the parks. In reality, though, it was generally recognized that all of the major decisions still came from headquarters. Park supervisors were told they were responsible for their local park's activities and condition—but also that they had no say in the budgeting process, that they were not allowed to choose what programs

---

[5]Forrest Claypool, "Remarks to the Chicagoland Chamber of Commerce," January 27, 1994, 1.
[6]Mahtesian, 36.
[7]"Subsequent analysis" was performed by the new, incoming CPD management team.

and/or classes they would offer, and that they had little say over who their staff was to be. Park supervisors could hire some of their staff but only from a list of approved candidates circulated by the head office, and it took literally 38 administrative steps to do so. Four to 10 people were involved in the hiring decision, so that a low-level personnel specialist isolated in headquarters, in effect, had more say than the park supervisors. Even then, no one seemed to be responsible for decisions that were made.

There were 13 divisions reporting directly to the general superintendent including two deputy general superintendents of Finance and Parks, superintendents of General Services and Engineering, as well as offices of the General Attorney, Secretary, Investigations, Labor Relations, Budget and Management, Employment, External Affairs, Communications, and Research and Planning. Of the 13 divisions that reported to the general superintendent, only one focused on parks and recreation, the core mission of the CPD. The superintendent's energy was scattered. In addition, there seemed to be no sense of core mission in the previous administration. Attention on the daily business of running the parks was diverted regularly to special services having nothing to do with parks, such as Soldier Field, parking garages, and golf courses. An organization chart showing the 1993 organization appears in Exhibit 37-1.

Over the years, the central bureaucracy had grown, and grown more ineffective, while the local parks were neglected. Neglect had, in turn, led to alternative influence, and by 1993, several of the city's parks were known locally to be "run" by the neighborhood gang. One interviewee compared the CPD to the old Soviet Union: "No

accountability, no sense of needing to work hard."[8] Claypool himself had noted that "the old bureaucracy was run like the Kremlin. And it was equally ineffective."[9] Another independent organization, the Civic Federation, had labeled the CPD as "dysfunctional," and another called it "a patronage system for jobs, not citizens."[10] Media interest in the district had became so intense that CPD employees avoided any contact with reporters or disgruntled citizens for fear of appearing in negative press. Morale at the CPD was low, and few employees had a sense of pride in their organization or work.

While the CPD had many real human resource problems, Claypool was also aware that there were many excellent employees who delivered on the district's mission—in spite of the system. He called these people *renegades* because they had gone around the system to deliver services. John Duda, the Mozart Park supervisor, for example, had an annual budget for cleaning and recreational supplies of only $1,500. He said, "I'm the type of supervisor who will take a rule and bend it 'til it frays. I won't break it."[11] With limited budgets, supervisors had to use their own funds, work out trade deals with other parks, and/or find other ways of covering the costs of necessary items. Two employees on the South Side, for instance, had built a music studio with their own money and resources when their request for a new studio, approved, had gotten lost in the system. Another trying simply to get 15 aerobic steps for her aerobics class gave up after many attempts at working through the system and got 15 friends to test drive new cars at a dealership where the owner was advertising a free aerobic step with each test drive. These

---

[8]Ryan and Roeder, 18.
[9]Mahtesian, 36.
[10]Claypool, 1.
[11]Ryan and Roeder, 19.

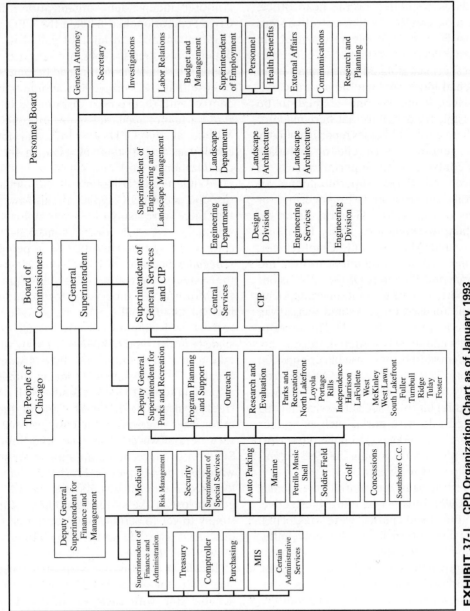

EXHIBIT 37-1   CPD Organization Chart as of January 1993

398

employees, stellar though they were, received no recognition or additional compensation. Hourly wages for typical CPD employees were $9.70 without medical benefits; park supervisors made about $35,000 a year. Yet, somehow, there were those who believed in the mission of the district enough to continue to sacrifice their own resources for the good of their customers.

One example of a dedicated employee who came into the system *not* through the patronage system was Roger Konow, who had been with CPD for 20 years. As one of 15 children, Konow used the Chicago park system extensively when he was growing up. He began working for the district while in high school as a landscape aide in the mayor's Summer Program, picking up trash papers in the parks. Then he became, in succession, a summer day camp leader, weekend recreation leader, physical instructor (no benefits, just hourly wages), and then, after taking the civil servants' examination, playground supervisor, park supervisor, a host park supervisor, and finally a cluster manager in the organization set up by the current superintendent. In the meantime, he earned his bachelor's degree part time from the University of Illinois in Parks Recreation, Physical Education, and Business Management.

Race relations had not gone well at CPD, either. In 1983, the federal court system had ordered CPD to remedy a pattern of racial discrimination in its organization and services. In the years following, CPD spent $50 million on facilities in minority neighborhoods in an attempt to rectify the situation, but later, many agreed the sum had been spent foolishly. Although the buildings were put up, the central office still controlled the programming assets so that many new buildings had few staff or programs. As a result, minority communities continued to suffer inadequate recreational facilities. One observer noted that Latino children were playing soccer on a softball field in part because the CPD seemed to be locked into a 1940's view of the world.

Facilities Concerns

Facilities management and maintenance in general was also a disaster at CPD. Supervised parks in the CPD system were denoted as either A, B, C, or D facilities. "A" facilities were full-service sites, and "D" facilities had an on-site supervisor and a few programs. Green spaces with park benches and grass but no staff, regardless of size (some were 15 acres), were not rated. For all of these, there were few preventative maintenance programs in place. Instead of inspecting roofs on a regular basis, for instance, CPD staff used a "repair-by-exception" approach and would wait for a roof to leak and ruin the hardwood gym floor beneath before sending in a repair team. At one location, the floor was so badly damaged that the gym had been locked shut, even though exercise classes had been scheduled and announced for it. One winter when the temperature dropped to 25 degrees, ill-maintained heating pipes in the Garfield Park Conservatory broke and hundreds of rare plants on display died shortly thereafter; 80 percent of the conservatory's tropical plant collection was destroyed.[12] At Soldier Field, a painting crew painted the lines on the grass for football games on Mondays. The grass was watered on Tuesdays. The paint crew returned on Wednesdays to repaint the lines. Elsewhere, a gold dome roof had been leaking rainwater onto an expensive, ornate marble floor for more than 5 years, leaving it stained and ugly. According to one observer, park employees would be advised of the district management's park inspection schedule in advance and spend 2 weeks prior to inspection readying each site on the schedule. When

---

[12]Mahtesian, 36.

the management team incumbent at the time came around, chauffeured in Lincoln Continentals, the parks looked "fine," yet for the rest of the year, the parks fell into disrepair.

New facilities projects were also having major difficulties. Building and contractor relationships with management were in disarray. One observer noted:

> The accounting books and records were in horrible shape. The capital projects—you never knew what was started, what was finished. They did a very, very poor job dealing with the contractors. Nobody really cared. I don't know if it was a bad round of patronage or whatever, but whatever a contractor wanted, they got. It didn't matter how many change orders there were or what percent of the contract it was, if they said they needed more money, if they said they needed more time, they got it, and nobody questioned it. . . . Nobody was watching the bottom line. So, when they decided to relocate Lake Shore Drive, which was a $90 million project, the Park District agreed. Oh sure! We'll do the trees, we'll do this, we'll do that. In fact, it went so far that when there were hurricanes down south, they volunteered our pumps. Take them down south to help, you know, with disaster relief—which is a very admirable thing to do, but then when we had problems here in Soldier Field, we weren't able to address them because all of our equipment was elsewhere!

Financial Concerns

Management of the CPD's financial resources seemed anarchic. Although specific figures were never reported, observers suspected huge cost overruns on capital improvement projects that sometimes never seemed to be completed. CPD had recently committed to $60 million in capital improvements projects, but no one seemed to know how they were to be paid for. The building design and execution process, managed by CPD's Capital Improvement Division, was loose: A division of engineering design drew up blueprints and passed the design on to another division, which made alterations and passed the plans on. After three or four iterations of this, the plans eventually got to a contractor, who never spoke to any of the design teams. Waste was often the result. The Mozart Park building, completed in 1991, had a roof that "leaked like a sieve."[13] One project, the Don Nash Center on the south side, was a year behind schedule and $1 million over budget, yet when one visited the building site, it looked like little more than a bombed-out shell. One consultant described the process as "professional anarchy."[14] Some also thought that the Soldier Field complex was losing several million dollars a year.

The purchasing department took 6 to 9 months to deliver on requests, so most people at CPD had begun to circumvent the department, ordering instead on vouchers. This meant that vendors were presenting bills for payment when CPD management had no idea of the amount of outstanding bills. One officer reported that after receiving a bill from the "T" company with a 100 days overdue notice attached, he called down to accounts payable and asked when this bill was going to be paid. He was told that the person was paying bills in the "G's" and wouldn't get to the "T's" for some time: Invoices were not paid based on age but were paid in alphabetical order. This same officer also had discovered that for an orga-

---

[13]Ryan and Roeder, 19.
[14]Ibid., 17.

nization with a $400 million annual budget, the Accounting Department was only keeping track of a single expense account, "expenses." At the same time, however, the CPD's tax levy had increased 40 percent since 1987.[15]

A concise summary of the problems facing CPD had begun to emerge from the various groups examining the CPD. This list is presented in Exhibit 37-2. This litany of concerns comprised the situation facing Forrest Claypool as he considered the mayor's request.

FORREST CLAYPOOL

Claypool had no previous park management experience. He had been a political consultant, a congressional campaign press secretary, and deputy commissioner of the Cook County board of tax appeals prior to coming to the mayor's office as his chief of staff. Following that position, Claypool was deputy state treasurer and then a member of the treasurer's office staff when Mayor Daley called him in. Claypool had been raised in a small town of 1,300 in southern Illinois and graduated from high school there in 1975. After graduating from law school, Claypool began working for a large Chicago law firm. By 1993, he was married and had one child. He commented on his interests:

I'd always had a lifelong interest in politics, worked in campaigns, cared about public issues, so I had done some work for different elected officials, and I had a series of government jobs in management progressively at the local, county, and state levels. I was a deputy state treasurer. And I was Mayor Daley's chief of staff in his first term.

By 1993, Richard M. Daley had been in the mayor's office for 6 years. He had served part of one term and been elected to his own second term. As for why the mayor would request such a change in CPD at this time, one CPD manager explained:

I think he's committed to having a city that runs well and where the quality of life is high. I think he was frustrated with the parks. You know, the parks are not high tech. It's not rocket science. . . . When you talk about the patronage [system], you know the rule [now here in Chicago] is, you have to do your job and you have to do it well.

Another CPD officer said that she thought the mayor's goal was to "turn the empty [CPD] buildings into teeming community centers." When asked why he would even consider Mayor Daley's request, Claypool responded:

For a lot of reasons. One is it's the ultimate management challenge, a classic turn-around situation. You couldn't really have a more dysfunctional bureaucracy. The editorial boards of the major papers in town and the civic federation had for years chronicled the abuses and problems of the Park District. You know, Friends of the Parks had been formed precisely to try to *monitor* the abuses. The Park District had been held in contempt by the federal courts for race discrimination in the '60s and the '70s and was actually under a consent decree for some time. So, they're really intractable problems in an intractable culture. But more importantly, I think, from the positive side, the Park District in Chicago is unique in the nation. We have more facilities here than any other program park system in America. ■

---

[15]Ibid., 16.

This report is the result of intensive investigations into current management practices, analysis of services provided, and spot visits to various parks throughout Chicago. Eight formal employee teams participated in the process, with input from their colleagues and countless park users. A strategic plan is being developed to respond to major findings. That plan will be revealed next month.

THE CHICAGO PARK DISTRICT IS NOT CONSUMER FOCUSED.

There is no systematic or aggressive market research to understand our communities and their needs.

- Facilities and employees are often not available during peak hours.
- Hiring decisions made downtown prevent park supervisors from staffing to meet community needs.
- Coordination with other community organizations is sporadic.

Information about programs and activities is inconsistent.

- Marketing efforts to inform the public on programming, facilities, and events are limited.
- Programs are not eliminated if interest and attendance are low.
- No consistent program schedule information exists.
- There is no standardized registration process.
- It takes an average of 29 hours to register for a class, because knowledgeable staff is not available.

PARK OPERATIONS ARE UNRELIABLE.

Scheduled programs are only available on average 56 percent of the time.

- Front-line employees are absent from their jobs 16 percent of working hours (corporate average is 5 percent).
- Total paid leave allowance is close to 30 percent higher than the national average for parks and recreation departments.
- Citywide tournaments and repair work often disrupt or halt local park programming.

Park usage and attendance rates are low.

- Of nearly 200 instructional programs observed at 80 parks, the average number of participants is nine.
- In one region, it was as low as six.

PARK RESOURCES ARE INEFFICIENTLY ALLOCATED AND MANAGED.

Financial resources are not allocated to effectively support the parks' core mission.

- Only 15 percent of the total 1993 budget went directly to parks and recreation.
- As much as 32 percent of the total 1993 budget went for administration.
- 42 percent of the total 1993 budget went to maintenance and improvements to facilities.

Park staff cannot easily get the supplies they need.

- The purchasing process takes approximately 20 steps, requires at least nine approvals, and requires roughly 8 weeks to process an order.
- Park supervisors and instructors often have to purchase recreation and art supplies out of their own money.
- There is no discretionary funding for supplies at the park level.
- Park staff do not understand or have ready access to the lengthy and complicated central purchasing process.
- Park supervisors and instructors are pulled away from their parks to pick up supplies at the storehouse (the storehouse is located up to an hour away from many parks).
- Trades workers, paid at high salaries, waste time picking up their supplies at the storehouse.

(continued)

EXHIBIT 37-2   The Chicago Park District's Case for Change[16]

[16]Chicago Park District, "The Chicago Park District's Case for Change" (undated).

Repairs and landscape maintenance at local parks are not efficiently managed.

- The work order system allows for favoritism and a "squeaky wheel gets the grease" approach to service delivery.
- There is no planning or preventative maintenance program.
- Approximately one third of work orders for repair and maintenance take longer than 3 months to complete.
- Repairs are driven by complaints or repeated requests and there is no way to assure equitable distribution of maintenance resources.
- Nonemergency work orders are traditionally handled only the first 3 days of every month, often causing park supervisors to wait a month just to have their work orders reviewed.
- Many nonemergency work orders are handled as emergencies at a greater cost to the district.
- Central administration prioritizes and controls all work orders with little knowledge of parks' actual needs.
- Trades work is not sufficiently coordinated with programming schedules: often ball fields and outdoor pools are not ready for use at the start of the season.
- Trades workers waste time responding to work orders that have already been completed because work orders are not taken off the list.
- Trades workers arrive at parks ill-equipped to handle work orders because the work descriptions they have received are incomplete or insufficient.

The current budget process does not include modern accounting practices.

- No attention is given to increasing revenues for the Park District.
- There is no opportunity for budget planning by field or park staff.

EMPLOYERS AND MANAGERS ARE NOT GIVEN THE TOOLS THEY NEED TO DO THEIR JOBS EFFECTIVELY.

There are no systems to evaluate, discipline, or reward employees.

- Employees are not evaluated against defined performance standards.
- Poor supervisors and instructors are often transferred from park to park rather than terminated.
- Good employees are frequently promoted and transferred out of their parks and into administrative positions. There is no career path for them in the parks.

Personnel policies consistently detract from park performance.

- The termination process, without appeals, requires 84 steps and more than a year to complete.
- Filling a park staff opening requires 38 steps (with as many as 10 employees involved in these steps), four approvals, and anywhere from 10 to 30 weeks to complete.
- High turnover and frequent employee transfers lead to a lack of continuity in local park staffs and hampers the development of stable community relationships.[a]

[a]In the Chicago Park District, 40 percent of the park supervisors have been in their positions less than 2 years.

EXHIBIT 37-2 **(continued)**

Case 38   NYT PubCom (A)

In February 1988, Robert Bellhouse was promoted to general manager of the Public Communications Department at NYNEX's subsidiary, New York Telephone (PubCom), the part of the company responsible for the firm's thousands of New York City public telephones. At the time, PubCom was facing a serious array of problems. Mired in severe service problems that left it highly vulnerable to new competitors, the department was experiencing rampant vandalism and phone fraud; employee morale was low; and although subsidized, PubCom had been losing significant amounts of money for many years. Mr. Bellhouse noted that "The public-telephone business in the New York Telephone Company was generally considered to be a backwater, leave-it-alone, laissez-faire operation." One colleague said, "We happen to have New York City, which is the most difficult place in the country to do business in pay telephones."

Bellhouse had been assigned to lead a 1986 task force charged with reviewing PubCom's operations. When he was promoted at the end of the task force's work, Bellhouse was told he had 3 years to turn the business around.

COMPANY BACKGROUND

In 1982, AT&T signed a consent decree with the U.S. Justice Department in which it agreed to divest its local communications networks by January 1, 1984. The divestiture spawned seven new regional Bell operating companies (RBOCs), which were indepen-

dent companies but held joint and equal ownership in Bell Communications Research, AT&T's former laboratory research division. NYNEX Corporation, one of the seven new RBOCs, provided local service and access to long-distance carriers in the New York and New England regions. Independent companies that had not been part of the AT&T system, such as Southern New England Telephone Company (SNET), continued to operate within the NYNEX service area.

In 1988, NYNEX was organized into 11 principal subsidiaries. New York Telephone Company provided telecommunications services within the state of New York, and New England Telephone and Telegraph served New England. Other major groups included NYNEX Science & Technology, NYNEX Worldwide Services, and NYNEX Mobile Communications. For financial reporting purposes, revenues and expenses were grouped into five segments. Although New York Telephone information is buried in the totals, Exhibit 38-1 contains financial data for NYNEX for the period 1985 to 1987.

THE PUBLIC COMMUNICATIONS DEPARTMENT

Prior to the divestiture of AT&T, the pay-telephone business was a "regulated stepchild" of the former Bell System companies, according to John Chichester, a PubCom district manager. Chichester explained, "The word profitability never came [across] the

UVA-OB-0591

The original case was written by William F. Allen, MBA 1992, under the supervision of Alexander B. Horniman and Robert D. Landel, Darden School, University of Virginia. This version was edited by James G. Clawson. Copyright © 1995 by the University of Virginia Darden School Foundation, Charlottesville, Virginia. All rights reserved. Revised March 1996.

(In millions, except per share amounts)	For the year ended December 31, 1987	1986	1985
Operating Revenues			
Local service	$ 5,613.1	$ 5,593.7	$ 5,283.3
Network access	1,333.5	1,254.3	2,558.1
Toll service	3,132.5	2,978.8	1,236.1
Other	2,004.6	1,514.3	1,206.1
Total operating revenues	**12,083.7**	**11,341.1**	**10,313.6**
Operating Expenses			
Maintenance	3,239.9	3,258.4	2,119.5
Depreciation	2,030.7	1,640.7	1,433.2
Taxes other than income	969.4	926.6	985.7
Marketing and customer services	1,261.1	1,291.9	1,030.9
Employee benefits	—	—	681.5
Other	2,190.7	1,707.9	1,752.7
Total operating expenses	**9,691.8**	**8,825.5**	**8,003.5**
Operating income	2,391.9	2,515.6	2,310.1
Other income—net	70.7	88.7	97.9
Earnings before interest expense and income taxes	**2,462.6**	**2,604.3**	**2,408.0**
Interest expense	507.9	499.3	516.9
Earnings before income taxes	**1,954.7**	**2,105.0**	**1,891.1**
Income taxes	678.2	889.7	795.8
Net Income	**1,276.5**	**1,215.3**	**1,095.3**
Earnings per Share	**6.26**	**6.01**	**10.85**
(In millions, except per share amounts)			
Weighted average number of shares outstanding	204.0	202.4	101.0
Assets			
Current assets:			
Cash and temporary cash investments	$ 358.2	$ 232.8	$ 170.8
Receivables	2,241.8	2,201.2	2,072.1
Inventories	381.9	330.5	202.5
Prepaid expenses	202.0	182.1	153.3
Deferred charges	343.9	396.3	396.2
Total current assets	**3,527.8**	**3,342.9**	**2,994.9**
Property, plant, and equipment—net	18,531.0	17,903.5	17,106.7
Other assets and deferred charges	947.0	558.2	498.1
Total Assets	**23,005.8**	**21,804.6**	**20,599.7**

(continued)

EXHIBIT 38-1 NYNEX Income Statements

Liabilities and Stockholders' Equity			
Current liabilities:			
Accounts payable	2,289.9	2,383.8	2,259.6
Short-term debt	111.8	20.0	9.2
Other current liabilities	523.5	458.4	377.3
Total current liabilities	**2,925.2**	**2,862.2**	**2,646.1**
Long-term debt	6,269.9	5,475.6	5,403.4
Deferred credits:			
Deferred income taxes	3,638.9	3,593.2	3,213.6
Unamortized investment tax credits	841.3	935.5	958.7
Other	134.0	69.7	29.1
Total liabilities	**13,809.3**	**12,936.2**	**12,250.9**
Commitments and contingencies			
Stockholders' equity			
Preferred stock—$1 par value,			
25,000,000 shares authorized	—	—	—
Common stock—$1 par value,			
250,000,000 shares authorized	204.4	202.7	101.1
Additional paid-in capital	5,779.6	5,776.7	5,774.4
Retained earnings	3,406.9	2,889.0	2,473.5
Total stockholders' equity	**9,390.9**	**8,868.4**	**8,348.8**
Total Liabilities and Stockholdlers' Equity	**23,200.2**	**21,804.6**	**20,599.7**

Source: Company Annual Reports.

EXHIBIT 38-1 (continued)

lips of anyone. That's the way AT&T worked. They just poured money into us as they did the many other units within the Bell system. They took it from their profitable entities and put it into the nonprofitable entities. They would just force-feed you with money. . . . It was something in those days they felt they had to do; they had to provide the public with pay telephones. Most regulatory agencies would have crucified them if they ever attempted to stop [providing pay telephones]."

At the time, public telephone stations and booths were placed to provide public service; no consideration was given to strategy or profitability. Key telephone operations were divided among other larger departments, which operated basically without any budget constraints.

PubCom was not formally organized as a unified department until late 1978. According to Staff Manager Susie Satran, "One of the problems in the beginning was getting other groups, even within the telephone company, to recognize our existence and our worth." In particular, technical assistance from other departments was difficult to obtain.

Bellhouse commented,

Morale suffered because the department had been neglected in terms of the resources provided to it. [And] There had been no formal training curriculum for public telephone operations in almost 20 years.

INTRODUCTION OF COMPETITION

In 1985, the Federal Communications Commission (FCC) decided to allow private ownership of public telephone stations. Later that year, the Public Service Commission of New York State passed an enabling act that cleared the way for competition in the public telephone business beginning in 1986. A number of competitors quickly entered the business.

By 1988, these competitors, which serviced customer-owned, coin-operated telephones (COCOTs), had captured roughly 14 percent of the New York public telephone market. In many instances, these companies promised to proprietors higher commissions than New York Telephone. The COCOT vendors also generally enjoyed a cost advantage by employing nonunion labor and using cheaper phone equipment. At the same time, COCOT vendors were experimenting with state-of-the-art technology in a few of their stations, which offered many features unavailable at New York Telephone stations.

The COCOT vendors were required, however, by regulation to maintain the basic 25 cent local call, but unlike New York Telephone, the COCOT vendors could set their own rates for such classes of phone calls as cross-city and long-distance overtime and operator-handled calls. In addition, the COCOT vendors aggressively pursued new locations, often finding profitable spots that had been neglected by New York Telephone.

In response, New York Telephone had simply continued its past practices. According to Chichester, "We had the Bell mentality that said 'No one can come in and take this over from us. We're too good. We know what we're doing. We're the best.'" Bellhouse stated, "We knew competition was occur-

ring, and we didn't know what to do about it." Because of the lack of information on revenues and expenses, PubCom had no idea how much it earned or spent. The department focused mainly on repairing and installing phones. The sales effort consisted of waiting for the phone to ring with new orders. As already noted, the COCOT vendors had made significant inroads into PubCom's business. Chichester noted that the COCOT vendors "were here to stay and have made our lives very interesting."

THE BELLHOUSE TASK FORCE

In June 1986, George Barletta, New York Telephone's vice president of Customer Services, assembled a six-person task force to examine the feasibility of creating a divested, lightly regulated public telephone subsidiary. Bob Bellhouse was brought in to lead the team, which included three people on loan from other departments and two permanent PubCom assignees.

For more than a year, the team conducted an iterative business case analysis of the public telephone business. They consistently concluded that the cost of taking the business out on its own was too high and that the public telephone business was too tightly entwined with the New York Telephone network to separate it.

TAKING ON THE VANDALS AND THIEVES

These days, New Yorkers who want to use a pay phone to reach out and touch someone usually end up wanting to punch someone.

DON BRODERICK, *NEW YORK POST,*
APRIL 18, 1990

The temptation posed by millions of dollars worth of quarters sitting on the streets of New York had proved to be irresistible to New York's highly creative criminal element. Chichester estimated that between

150,000 and 200,000 acts of pay telephone vandalism were committed each year, with roughly 15,000 stations accounting for most of the damage. Thousands of phone stations were blown up beyond recognition. According to Bellhouse:

> The deteriorating service of public telephones wasn't because New York Telephone was not fulfilling its responsibilities. It was largely because there was an organized group of people who were vandalizing the phones to get the money out of them or to keep our phones in poor working condition.

Virtually all of New York Telephone's public telephones were Western Electric 1C/2C electromechanical sets, which were equipped with mechanical coin chutes. These chutes were highly susceptible both to failure and vandalism. For example, after the 1987 release of a popular movie that included a scene showing people how to make free calls by grounding the phone with a pin pushed through the transmitter, New York Telephone was replacing handsets at the rate of 190,000 per year at $30 per piece. New York Telephone could not afford the investment necessary to replace the Western Electric sets entirely with new technology offered by the COCOT vendors. Unfortunately, no off-the-shelf technology existed to upgrade the New York Telephone pay phones.

Enterprising thieves also were making up to $2,000 a day stealing calling-card numbers and selling time to people who wanted to make international calls. Places such as Grand Central Station and Port Authority bus terminals were ideal for the operation because they were air conditioned, well equipped with phones, and had lots of transient traffic. Some people would bring their families to these locations and spend the day making illegal calls to relatives overseas at well below market rates. Other criminals discovered how to dial into the switchboards of large New York City businesses and then get an outside line to make long-distance calls.

LABOR DIFFICULTIES

Relationships with the International Brotherhood of Electrical Workers and the Communication Workers of America, which represented approximately 35,000 New York Telephone craft people, were also difficult at this time. The main stumbling block in contract renewal negotiations involved employee contributions to medical benefit plans. The company was concerned that the negotiations might end in a strike. Incidents of violence and vandalism began to punctuate the growing rift between management and union members.

Bellhouse recognized that he had a tremendous employee morale problem on his hands:

> Morale in the department had suffered greatly over the years. It was poor when I arrived because of isolation, stagnation, and weak leadership at the upper levels of the department. Morale also suffered because the department had been neglected corporately in terms of the resources provided to it. There had been no formal coin-telephone training curriculum for that business in almost 20 years.

At the time Bellhouse began his administration, several anonymous allegations of wrongdoing by members of his department were submitted to the Office of Ethics and Business Conduct. Bellhouse observed:

> There were a lot of investigations going on at that time—really unpleasant stuff. While we began trying to fix the service and improve the department, others were making anonymous accusations that could quite literally destroy people's careers.

MR. BELLHOUSE'S BACKGROUND

Mr. Bellhouse had a military background:

Some people misread that. A lot of people think I went to West Point. I did not. I graduated from Hofstra's ROTC program.[1] My military background does play a big part, but in a way that a lot of people don't know, because I don't talk about it very much. When I was a second lieutenant in Germany, I was a platoon leader in an armored cavalry division. I made a lot of really big mistakes; no one got hurt, but I made a lot of mistakes that, when I look back on them now, I feel ashamed. I can put it in perspective. My college education did not equip me for that, so I made mistakes and as a result I was transferred out of that unit to a headquarters organization. At headquarters, I did very, very well. I stayed in the Reserve program and have had a great military career. It was a good learning environment, because while I made mistakes there, I was allowed to get past them and grow. I didn't have to carry them with me. Aside from that, I think my military experience keeps my head clear, because it gives me a separate organizational environment in which to participate. ■

---

[1] Reserve Officers Training Corps.

Case 39   Big Sky, Incorporated: The Magasco Paper Mill (A)

Big Sky was an integrated forest-products company headquartered in the Northwest with operations throughout the United States and Canada. Founded when two well-established lumber companies merged operations, Big Sky was a young organization by industry standards. The company manufactured and distributed paper and paper products, office products, and building products, and owned and managed timberland to support its operations. In 1990, Big Sky reported sales of $4.5 billion and earnings of $275 million. Paper and paper products accounted for $2.5 billion in sales and represented 70 percent of the company's operating income and 55 percent of its revenue. Office and building products accounted for the balance.

During the fiscal year 1990, Big Sky invested a company record $750 million in the expansion, modernization, and improvement of its plant and facilities. The majority of these improvements were made at the company's paper-manufacturing facilities. Most of these operations were located in the Pacific Northwest, the Southeast, and the Northeast. Because papermaking requires vast amounts of lumber, the majority of Big Sky's paper mills were located in rural timberlands. Big Sky manufactured a broad range of products, including uncoated white papers for printing and general business use; newsprint; and uncoated groundwood paper for the manufacture of such products as paperback books, coated paper for magazines and cata-

logs, containerboard used in the construction of corrugated containers, and market pulp that was sold to other manufacturers.

Paper operations at Big Sky were divided into two primary groups: P-Three and Plain Paper. The P-Three Division was responsible for producing three primary paper products—newsprint for publishing, linerboard for packaging, and marketable pulp. The Plain Paper Division was responsible for producing all other products, including business forms, envelopes, and carbonless and copier papers.

THE PAPER INDUSTRY

The practice of papermaking dates back to at least the third millennium B.C. when the Egyptians first recorded their activities on pounded papyrus stalks. Although not as ancient as papyrus, the basic process of changing wood chips into pulp and then drying and pressing the pulp into paper sheets had not changed much over the last several hundred years. By 1990, however, papermaking had evolved into a highly capital-intensive and technology-driven industry. As a result of the introduction of modern information systems and computer-aided manufacturing, papermaking was an increasingly efficient and sophisticated process.

Because of the nature of the extensive plant and equipment required to operate a modern paper mill, the cost structure of papermaking was heavily weighted toward

UVA-OB-0396
Prepared by F. B. Brake, Jr., under the supervision of Alexander B. Horniman, Professor of Business Administration. Copyright © 1991 by the University of Virginia Darden School Foundation, Charlottesville, Virginia. All rights reserved. Revised September 1994.

fixed costs. In 1990, a single paper machine capable of producing 500 tons of paper a day was estimated to cost in excess of $500 million. The raw-material cost of timber and labor costs—the two primary variable costs— had traditionally received little attention.

Historically, the papermaking industry had close ties to the lumber industry. In fact, many companies such as Big Sky were direct descendants of lumber companies. Because of the paper industry's dependence on timber as a raw material, most paper companies were vertically integrated and owned or closely affiliated with timber operations in order to reduce their exposure to commodity price fluctuations. Culturally, the paper industry shared the Paul Bunyan mystique of the timber industry. Papermakers, like lumberjacks, were often characterized as "macho" and "tough, rugged individualists." Because of the manual nature of the work, both industries were known for their high incidence of injury. The Occupational Safety and Health Act (OSHA), passed by Congress in the 1960s, cited the forest-products industry, including papermaking activities, along with more celebrated industries such as meatpacking, as the focus of OSHA's early efforts to reduce work-related injuries and deaths.

Large, organized labor groups such as the United Paper Workers International represented much of the industry's workforce. At some mills, workers in different industry trade groups represented workers in various functional areas—the machinists, who were responsible for performing the maintenance function, or the paper-machine operators. Over the years, these groups had negotiated lucrative contracts for their members. In addition to wages that were comparable to those paid in the steel industry, the industry trade representatives had negotiated for a number of concessions that were commonly found in the timber industry. For example, lumber companies and the sawmills they owned typically operated on a 40-hour workweek, closing on weekends and holidays. Because these operations were so labor intensive, this was considered an acceptable practice. Many union representatives at paper mills had successfully negotiated similar "cold shutdowns" at their locations. Because of the high fixed costs associated with running a paper mill, however, this practice was extremely costly to the paper companies. One mill manager estimated that a cold shutdown for a 3-day holiday weekend had cost his mill almost $6 million.

In addition to wage and benefit concessions, the unions had been successful in negotiating for restrictive work practices that specifically defined individual work practices and job assignments. Restrictive work practices often precluded qualified personnel from performing tasks at different locations within the mill or on different mill machinery, regardless of the employee's ability to perform the job. Management was often unable to deploy its workforce efficiently as a result of these work practices. Mill managers regularly compensated for the inflexible nature of their labor agreements by simply hiring additional employees. Many of the restrictive work practices and spiraling wage costs were tolerated by management because the industry had traditionally considered wage costs to be just a fraction of the total manufacturing cost.

Throughout much of the 1970s, demand exceeded supply in the industry, and papermakers were reluctant to close their mills over strikes for wage concessions they knew they would not have to absorb. A company executive addressing an industry gathering explained this logic:

From the mid-60s to the mid-70s, we found it much easier to simply let union representatives dictate conditions to us without offering much resistance, perhaps believing—or hoping—that things would correct themselves. . . . Often we were fairly certain that many of the conditions demanded—whether they related to work practices or wage and benefit rates—were not in the best interests of our operations or our employees long term, but it was simply easier, less hassle, to acquiesce to union demands and then simply pass on increased costs to the customer. We had a business environment that allowed us to do that.

By the late 1970s, however, the situation had clearly gotten out of control. "We found ourselves in a fight for the very lives of our companies—and the jobs of our employees," said another executive. The industry was facing increasingly stiff competition from foreign manufacturers, particularly from Scandinavia and South America. Most foreign manufacturers had substantially lower labor costs than U.S. papermakers and were receiving assistance from their home governments in the form of subsidies and import restrictions.

Because demand for domestically manufactured paper products had historically exceeded supply, most U.S. manufacturers had traditionally operated at, or near, capacity. Many consumers would accept virtually any product shipped from the mill, so most manufacturers had adopted a manufacturing philosophy based on quantity as opposed to quality. As a direct result of encroaching foreign competition, however, capacity throughout the United States was on the rise. For the first time in recent memory, supply exceeded demand. At the same time, foreign manufacturers were also introducing higher-quality products. Consequently, domestic consumers of paper products were increasingly demanding in terms of the quality they expected from U.S. manufacturers. As a result of increased industry capacity and the relatively low rate of annual inflation during the early 1970s, however, manufacturers were unable to pass along cost increases associated with the quality programs they needed to initiate in order to remain competitive. Industry profitability thus declined throughout the late 1970s.

In order to increase efficiency and productivity, in the late 1970s and early 1980s, many companies attempted to introduce new, more relaxed work practices when bargaining with unions. As one industry executive stated, "We needed to be substituting more flexible work practices for antiquated work rules that, over the years, had virtually immobilized many of our operations in a web of inefficiency and lowered productivity." Many industry observers were convinced that fierce foreign competition, increasing customer demands, rising labor costs, and restrictive labor practices would force many mills out of business.

In response to dwindling profits, more and more companies were willing to operate mills during strikes, a practice long avoided by the industry. In some extreme cases, when striking employees refused to return to work, they were replaced. Despite these apparent hardball tactics, most experts agreed that concessions would be required of everyone; something serious had to be done. In response to critics who claimed that the paper companies were just trying to drive out the unions, one industry veteran offered the following response:

> None of these tactics were meant to bust the union as some would suggest. Rather, they demonstrated our increased willingness to maintain commitments to our customers and to the communities who depend on the successful operation of our facilities.

THE MAGASCO MILL

The Magasco Mill, a member of Big Sky's Alpine Division, was located in an area commonly known as Texarkana, where the borders of Texas, Arkansas, and Louisiana converge. Because of the proximity of vast pine groves and a temperate climate that accommodated accelerated tree-growing cycles, the area was ideal for papermaking. Opened in the early 1970s, Magasco was one of the first mills actually built by Big Sky. Most of the company's other paper-making operations had been acquired through various mergers and acquisitions. The mill was equipped with the latest technological innovations, including three cutting-edge paper machines capable of producing in excess of 1,500 tons of newsprint and linerboard a day.

When plans for the Magasco Mill were originally announced, Big Sky stated that it intended to introduce state-of-the-art management practices at the new facility. The hope was that the *de novo* effort would enable managers to introduce new work practices free from the influence of established cultures found at facilities purchased by Big Sky. The company hoped Magasco would serve as a model for other company mills as well as the rest of the industry.

Although many other new mills in the South were discouraging the formation of unions at their mills, Big Sky invited organized labor into the Magasco Mill. They anticipated that this action would foster a cooperative environment and reduce the possibility of future conflicts between labor and management.

None of the approximately 500 skilled laborers, all of whom were represented by the Amalgamated Paperworkers Union (APU), or 150 managers and engineers was required to use a time clock. Management perceived the absence of a time clock, a symbolic gesture, to be a token of the trust between management and labor. The concept of "multicraft" also was introduced to provide flexibility in the maintenance functions. Multicraft required each employee to be skilled in and perform multiple tasks rather than discretely defined job functions. At the time, these practices were considered to be revolutionary by industry standards.

Magasco, like most other papermaking operations at the time—with demand exceeding supply—was profitable even in the start-up years. The fact that the mill opened in the middle of a recession had little bearing on its initial performance. Despite early financial success, little headway was made, however, with management's attempt to institute what some observers considered to be the most progressive work practices in the industry. After 5 years of Magasco operation, it was clear that despite a contractual agreement between the APU and management, a functional craft distinction had evolved and the multicraft initiative had failed. Time clocks also appeared, at the APU's request. The union claimed that without time clocks, its members were not being equally compensated for overtime.

As was the case at many other mills, management found complying with labor's demands easier than following through on its own initiatives. Despite hopes for a mutually cooperative work environment, an adversarial relationship between labor and management soon established itself at Magasco. The mill quickly developed a reputation throughout the industry as a labor-relations hotbed. Part of the reason for this reputation stemmed from a much-publicized strike at Magasco in the early 1970s.

The primary catalyst for the strike was management's unwillingness to grant further concessions in the area of restrictive work practices. The strike involved so much violence at the mill that a judge issued a permanent restraining order restricting picketing activities from anywhere within sight of the mill gate. As one employee said, "This place had a reputation in the industry as the Alamo. . . . It was a place you were sentenced to." Another employee related an incident in which, when he was introduced to a group of executives from competing mills at an industry gathering and it was announced that he worked at Magasco, the group erupted in laughter.

In addition to continued labor strife, the Magasco Mill faced a number of other challenges during the late 1970s. As a company, Big Sky, like many other major corporations, had adopted a corporate strategy of diversification during the 1960s. Before long, the company found itself managing operations ranging from South American cattle ranches to Caribbean cruise lines, in addition to its core businesses, the paper operations. Operations at Magasco were largely ignored by the corporate staff throughout this period, as more attention and resources were directed toward the company's other businesses.

As a result of the declining profitability of the paper industry (as well as a number of its diversified holdings), Big Sky experienced some dire financial problems in the mid to late 1970s. In an attempt to save the company from financial ruin, executives at corporate headquarters began to exert significant pressure on individual operating units. As a result, mill managers throughout the company were forced to surrender much of their autonomy.

Not surprisingly, Magasco experienced a tremendous amount of management turnover during this time. Some Magasco veterans claimed that the only constant at the mill was the union representatives who sat down at the bargaining table every 3 years to negotiate a new contract. As one longtime employee said, "There are a lot of management teams buried in this mill." The high attrition rate in the managerial ranks at the Magasco location was widely acknowledged not to be necessarily attributable to the quality of mill managers. "It was," as one employee said, "as if they were facing insurmountable odds."

Throughout the late 1970s and early 1980s, management attempted to introduce a number of new initiatives and mandates. The APU, however, was extremely reluctant to comply with any of management's change initiatives, because the union had come to understand the short-lived nature of most of management's proposals. Many employees shared the following story: No sooner would a change be initiated at the mill than a Big Sky corporate jet would fly over the plant with a representative from headquarters on board and land at the small municipal airport outside of town. Before the plane took off at the end of the day, the change would be reversed.

The mill's problems during the late 1970s and early 1980s were not solely financial. Despite the presence of safety procedures—warning signs and posters located throughout the facility promoting safe work practices—the mill had a dismal safety record. Two people were killed at Magasco in industrial accidents during 1 year, and every year a number of others were disabled so badly they could not return to work. As one employee said, "It wasn't a big deal for any number of people to be so severely injured that they never came back to the mill after being hurt on the job." In addition to the tremendous pain and suffering incurred by the injured employee and his or her family, these accidents directly influenced the mill's financial performance. Under state worker's compensation regulations, Big Sky could be required to set aside as much as $300,000 immediately following an accident for future payment to a disabled employee.

"TIMES, THEY ARE A-CHANGING"

Jock Duncan joined Big Sky as the director of human resources at Magasco a few months before the mill management was set to negotiate its 3-year contract with the APU in the summer of 1983. Duncan had come from the chemical industry, where he had nearly 2 decades of experience in human resources. Initially, he was surprised by the restrictive nature of the work practices in the paper industry. He quickly concluded that relations between management and the union employees at Magasco were adversarial at best. "The workforce here at the mill was much more compliant than those in the chemical or petroleum industries at that time," Duncan later recalled.

Duncan was disturbed by the assumptions made by management and labor about the role hourly employees should play in the workplace. He knew these assumptions were the result of years of behavioral observation and reinforcement. As illustrated in Exhibit 39-1, in a mutual compliance organization such as Magasco, management, based on behavioral observations, assumed employees were antagonistic and apathetic. Systems and work technologies were eventually developed on the basis of these assumptions. This approach often resulted in fragmented work assignments and constant supervision by management. Employees, perceiving management as adversarial and nontrusting because of the work practices instituted, often responded by exhibiting apathetic and antagonistic behavior, thereby reinforcing management's original perception.

Despite Big Sky's original expectations, by the time of Duncan's arrival, the Magasco Mill, along with most of the company's other facilities, was characterized by poor labor relations and hazardous working conditions. The mill also was losing nearly $35 million a year. Magasco's newsprint machines were operating at just over 80 percent capacity, and the linerboard machines were producing at just over 90 percent of total capacity. As a result of increased competition and increasing capacity, the market price of the mill's paper was falling at a rate of 9 percent a year, while its total manufacturing cost per ton was increasing by 9 percent. Duncan and the other senior members of the mill's management team believed that the mill's survival hinged on the successful introduction of some significant changes at the upcoming labor negotiations.

The discreet work assignments that had developed over the years as a result of various managements' reluctance to aggravate labor had put a choke hold on the mill's ability to produce paper efficiently and affordably, particularly in the face of foreign competition. Management concluded that more flexible work practices had to be introduced. Although recent labor agreements had clearly defined step-by-step job descriptions and work assignments for the APU members at the mill, Duncan and the other managers proposed new language that would provide management with greater discretion in defining and assigning work. Duncan knew from past negotiations that a change in the wording from one contract to another of this magnitude was serious enough to instigate a walkout.

In order to facilitate the change to a more flexible work environment, management planned to introduce the team concept. This approach represented a radical departure from the mill's traditional work assignments and was reminiscent of the multicraft concept originally introduced at the mill nearly a decade earlier. In the team approach, the mill would be divided into three primary functional areas: the paper machines, the pulp mill, and the wood yard. Whereas each area might have previously had anywhere from 10 to 15 individual jobs, it was proposed that these jobs be divided into three or four clusters or teams consisting of three to four jobs. Teams of employees would be assigned to a particular cluster, and each employee would be expected to perform every job in the cluster on a rotating basis. This process would broaden the skill base of every employee and provide management with greater flexibility in developing work assignments.

The rationale for introducing the team concept was described in the proposed contract as follows:

> The team concept is designed to improve the efficiency and competitive position of the mill [by] providing for the flexible

utilization of production and storeroom personnel. The elements of the team concept are considered essential to the survival of the mill.

Mill management was acutely aware of the sensitivity of the proposed changes but believed that a crisis situation had developed and that without tremendous change the mill might go under. As Duncan noted, "We knew we were introducing a tremendous amount of change, but it had to be done."

In an attempt to alleviate some of the anxiety regarding the proposed changes, management assured the APU that no union jobs would be threatened as a result of the introduction of the team concept. In the preamble to the proposed labor agreement, management included the following statement: "No current employee will lose his employment or suffer a reduction in his wage rate due to the implementation of the team concept. . . ."

THE WALKOUT

Unfortunately, it came as no surprise when the APU representatives recommended a walkout at the beginning of the talks. "Change requires loss," said Duncan, a key figure in the negotiations, "and the union representatives realized that they were being asked to make sacrifices—sacrifices they felt they could not make." While the union members walked out of the mill, management was determined to keep the mill up and running. For what may have been the first time in industry history, the salaried staff of a paper mill actually took over running the paper machines.

In the weeks leading up to the contract negotiations, Duncan and the other members of the staff had been preparing for the logistical nightmare that would follow in the wake of a walkout. In order to keep the mill operating, Big Sky was prepared to keep the production facilities fully staffed. A camp was set up on the mill property, and salaried employees from throughout the company were ferried on commercial airlines as needed in order to meet the mill's production schedule. One participant likened the experience to a military airlift.

In another break with tradition, management made every effort to keep all employees, including those on strike, as well as the community, abreast of the ongoing negotiation. In the past, Magasco had left it up to the union to keep its members informed. This time, however, management wanted to ensure that everyone knew what was happening. In addition to establishing a hotline that any employee could call to get daily updates, mill management worked closely with the press to keep the community informed. As managers of the largest employer in the surrounding three-county area, Magasco Mill management also met regularly with community and business leaders to keep them up to date on the situation.

About a month into the strike, when little progress was being made and both parties appeared to be deadlocked over the proposed changes in the contract, the federal mediators who had been called in to oversee the negotiations announced that the talks were at an impasse. Management developed a replacement strategy.

In accordance with its contingency plan, mill management began interviewing prospective applicants to replace the striking workers. Because the country was still recovering from a recession, Big Sky had no shortage of qualified applicants from which to choose. Unemployed papermakers drove in from as far away as Ohio and Maine to be processed. Throughout this time, tensions continued to rise as some of the striking employees realized that they might soon be replaced. Acts of violence and harassment, including instances of gunfire, were reported at several of the assessment centers Big Sky had established around Magasco for the processing of applicants. Several of the incidents were captured on videotape. The situation became so charged and received so much attention that the site was visited by the FBI and the Bureau of Alcohol, Tobacco, and Firearms.

Despite these incidents, management was determined to keep the mill running and continued to process applicants. Finally, Big Sky announced that it would implement all changes outlined in its proposed labor agreement during the first week of November, 2 months after the contract had originally been proposed, and any striking employee who wished to return to work at that time would be welcomed; those who did not would be replaced.

The day before the changes were scheduled to go into effect, the mill was contacted by the office of the governor-elect, who had strong ties to labor and felt a moral obligation to lend his assistance. He asked Big Sky to delay action for 24 hours while he personally attempted to resolve the situation. Big Sky agreed to postpone its initiative, but informed the governor-elect that it would agree to no concessions and would institute the changes as outlined in its original proposal regardless of the outcome of his discussions. To the surprise of many observers, the governor-elect was able to reach an accord with the union and informed Big Sky that the striking employees would come back to work with no conditions. They would accept the originally proposed labor agreement, including the contested team concept.

Despite the governor-elect's assurances, when Duncan and the rest of the negotiating team met with the APU representatives to ratify the contract, the APU suddenly demanded a condition. Specifically, the union asked for amnesty for those employees captured on videotape during the conflicts that erupted at the processing centers. The mill manager was furious with the APU's lack of good faith. He was not about to begin bargaining at that point, and he informed the governor-elect that the union representatives had not followed through on his promise. The governor-elect responded with tremendous disappointment and told management to do what it had to do.

During the strike, a phone bank had been established at the mill to inform applicants of Big Sky's decision to hire them as replacements in the event an agreement between Big Sky and the APU could not be reached. As the meeting broke up in downtown Magasco, Duncan prepared to drive out to the mill to initiate the replacement process. When he arrived at the mill and began to gather the team to phone, he was informed that the union representatives had changed their minds and would not request any concessions.

The news hit Duncan like nothing he had ever experienced. Now what would he and the mill manager do? Was it possible to create a "new Magasco mill"? Was it possible to transform all the negative energy that had been focused on the strike to building a totally different organization? These questions and what seemed like hundreds of other ideas flooded his mind. What was possible? How should the journey start? ■

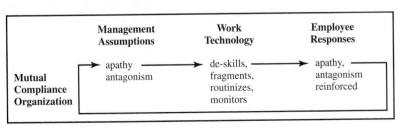

Mutual Compliance Organization	Management Assumptions	Work Technology	Employee Responses
	apathy antagonism	de-skills, fragments, routinizes, monitors	apathy, antagonism reinforced

EXHIBIT 39-1   Mutual Compliance Model

Case 40   Marsha Harris (A)

Marsha Harris drove in the quiet, predawn dark to a local restaurant where she was to meet her new subordinate, Jerry Crittenden, for breakfast. It was October 1, her first day as the chief financial officer (CFO) for the Sales and Distribution Department of the Appliances Division of the Winston Electric Corporation (WEC) in Charlotte, North Carolina. She had won the job in a competitive interviewing process that had included Jerry, a long-time WEC employee and the acting CFO for the past 6 months, and she believed that talking with Jerry before going to the office was important. She knew that he believed he should have gotten the job. After Marsha found Jerry and ordered breakfast, they began to talk. Jerry began the conversation:

> Well, you will find me a very candid person. The general consensus says the only reason you were hired is because you are a woman. So, you are walking into a situation on Day One where you have to decide how you are going to deal with it.

One year later, Marsha was in her office wondering what she should do. Sluggish sales, declining margins, and overly ambitious forecasts had taken great tolls on her organization, and she was now faced with one of the toughest decisions of her career. Her boss had ordered her to reduce her organization of financial professionals by 47 percent. Marsha knew that her decisions would mean that many people would start their Christmas holiday involuntarily unemployed—at the end of their careers at WEC.

MARSHA'S BACKGROUND

Marsha Harris grew up in Wisconsin with four sisters. Her father was a surgeon, and her mother was an occupational therapist by training but a full-time homemaker. All of her sisters found their careers in medicine. Reflecting on her early years, Marsha noted:

> My parents impressed upon us the teaching that we could be whatever we wanted to be as long as we were willing to produce and apply ourselves. There has always been that fundamental achievement drive in me. Overall, I feel quite good about my youth.

Marsha went to public high school in Madison, Wisconsin, and proceeded to get double undergraduate degrees in journalism and economics. Immediately after her graduation, she started working for Winston Electric, where her first assignment was in the finance-training program in Nashville, Tennessee. After a 3-year development program, she became a general-accounts manager. Shortly thereafter, she accepted a position with WEC's corporate audit staff. She did auditing for 4 years and traveled to about 30 states in the United States as well as to South America and the Far East. Later, she was appointed chief financial officer for WEC's semiconductor affiliate in Singapore. After 2 years of working abroad, she was asked to redesign WEC's financial-management program back in the States from ground zero. Her work in revamping the training program was well acknowl-

UVA-OB-0562
This case was written by Maki Depalo and James G. Clawson. Names have been disguised. Copyright © 1994 by the University of Virginia Darden School Foundation. All rights reserved.

edged when WEC's chairman asked her to manage worldwide recruiting for WEC.

Two years later, she saw an opportunity to return to the field in a job opening for a functional CFO position in an operating company within WEC.

The interviews for this position were held with the vice president of Sales, the CFO for Appliances, the vice president of Marketing, and the human-resources director. I was to have the CFO responsibility for the functions of Sales, Marketing, and Distribution. In addition to myself, there would be a CFO for Engineering and another for Manufacturing. The position appealed to me on a couple of counts. First of all, WEC Appliances is a consumer-product business, and I could identify with the products. Secondly, I was impressed with the vice president of Sales, who would be one of my dotted-line bosses for this position. [She also would have a dotted-line responsibility to the vice presidents of Marketing and Distribution.] I also had had a previous association with the CFO for the whole division. He was also the group manager of Finance to whom I would be reporting directly. On top of all that, the opportunity to be the first woman CFO of an operating company in WEC played to my ego. When the group CFO extended me an offer, I accepted it on the spot. Even though nobody had clearly articulated the job's goals, my understanding of the job in terms of providing the financial services to a business unit and attending to its fundamental routines and controls was absolutely clear.

ORGANIZATION'S BACKGROUND

WEC sold about $5 billion worth of appliances ranging from air conditioners, washers, dryers, and refrigerators to microwaves and ovens. Given the product line, the $5 billion in sales flowed through the system in $200 increments. Marsha's organization kept track of margin profitability for every single product and product type. In refrigerators alone, WEC had 285 different kinds of products.

When Marsha arrived in Charlotte in October, she was responsible for 385 people (see Exhibit 40-1). Of these, the largest group (250 people) was in the Credit-Collection Department, which had one credit-collection-center manager and seven layers of management between the manager and the front-line collectors. WEC Appliances sold through a dealer network and to contractors so that normally customers would order appliances from WEC by the truckload. Dealers placing an order would have to be credit approved before WEC would ship. The Credit-Collection Department was in charge of credit approvals. If, after the appliances were released, the dealer was slow in paying the bill, the Credit-Collection Department would attempt to secure payment. The department was also involved in financing (selling) some of the dealer receivables to finance companies.

Marsha had five direct staff members: managers of Customer Financial Services, Field Analysis, Headquarters Analysis, Distribution Financial Support, and Business Analysis. The manager of Customer Financial Services, Harvey Winthrop, had been a credit-collection professional for his entire career at WEC. He was in his fifties, well recognized in his discipline, innovative in dealing with credit collection, and a real gentleman. From a technical point of view, Marsha noted that Financial Services ran on its own with him at the helm. Despite his success at innovating his organization's information system, however, his extremely traditional management approach had restricted his taking full advantage of the interactive nature of this system. Marsha characterized his approach as "my way or the highway."

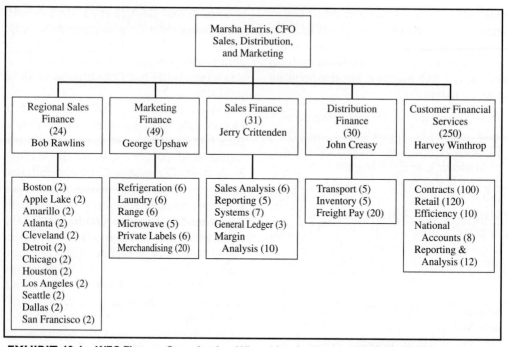

EXHIBIT 40-1   WEC Finance Organization When Marsha Assumed Responsibility

Bob Rawlins, in his early forties, was the head of Field Analysis. Marsha and Bob were contemporaries; she had once worked for him when she audited the company. Marsha thought he was a tactical person in his work style and approach. His detail orientation made him helpful in implementation but left him struggling with the big picture at times.

When Marsha arrived in October, John Creasy, who headed Distribution Financial Support, had already announced his retirement in December. Marsha had seen this development as her first opportunity to hire her own staff.

Jerry Crittenden was in charge of preparing analyses required by corporate headquarters. The incident at the first breakfast meeting with Jerry made it easier for Marsha to know how best to approach him. Hoping to gain his confidence, she tried to show her appreciation of his capabilities by constantly asking his opinion. She noted that his wealth of knowledge far surpassed what she could acquire within the time she expected to be in her position. She also valued the fact that he had the allegiance of the finance people in his department, who had spent their entire careers in the industry. Even though she found it frustrating "to play Sally Numbnuts" (i.e., stupid), as she put it, Marsha predicted to herself that her efforts would definitely bear fruit in terms of Jerry's growing loyalty to, and confidence in, her.

George Upshaw, however, was difficult for her to deal with, and the "Sally Numbnuts" approach was definitely inappropriate. He managed Business Analysis, which covered pricing analysis, merchandising, and marketing support. Moreover, he and Jerry were rivals. George's ego drove him always to try to retain more staff members than Jerry. To George, having more staff meant more responsibility. George frequently referred to Marsha as "the little lady," which Marsha interpreted to mean, "Isn't she cute trying to pretend she is a finance manager?"

In retrospect, Marsha believed she was naive about the conditions of the business itself. Not until she got involved with the management team and got a better perception of the financial services required by the business did she have a full appreciation of what was happening there. During October and November, as she worked her way into the position, she became familiar with the scope of the position, the management team involved, and the problems facing the unit. These problems were severe enough that by the end of the year, the vice president of Sales found it necessary to consolidate: He closed 6 of the 12 regional sales offices. The accompanying layoffs affected Marsha's staff because the 12 analysts that worked in or supported the redundant field offices lost their jobs. Marsha was not personally involved in the layoffs because the positions cut were those attached directly to the sales offices' senior management. Nevertheless, this reorganization was the first to hit the ranks of management. Marsha commented:

I guess the backhand [of this situation] was that ... salaried people got their first taste of being impacted by a lay-off. I think that previous layoffs had pretty much focused on manufacturing people.

THE NEXT FISCAL YEAR

Following the consolidation—and after 2 months of getting acquainted with people and obtaining more knowledge and information about her organization—Marsha believed that she was well on her way to success as the first woman CFO at WEC. She organized frequent meetings involving people from all five of her subdepartments to address issues such as getting management to focus on margins, improving the efficiency of process-information reporting,

and eliminating some of the 2,000 reports that her people generated each month. Unlike her peers, Marsha included a mixture of secretaries, clerical staff, managers, and analysts in the meetings, depending on the subject matter. She included the secretaries because she believed they were flow points for a lot of relevant organizational information. Marsha knew that even though most management people were inclined to believe that secretaries did not read all correspondence, they did, so she encouraged secretaries to give their insights about how to make things run more efficiently. She also made it a point to keep an unpredictable meeting pattern to avoid a sense of routine.

Marsha and her fellow managers knew that the fiscal year would be a difficult one:

Our volume, as we headed into the new year, was sluggish. Our margins were being squeezed. We decided to attempt a price increase around May. We took the lead in the marketplace with about a 6 percent price increase. Our intelligence told us that our competitors were suffering from the margin squeeze as much as we were. Therefore, we were fairly confident they would follow our price-raising policy. It turned out they did not. Our sales volume started to tumble, and this caused additional pressure on our income commitments to the corporation. By October, it became too serious to let it continue; we were losing market share quickly. We finally decided to abandon the price increase and try to get market share back at all costs. Changing our pricing policy toward regaining market share certainly made the salespeople happy. We asked them to sell at whatever price they could get in order to raise our volume and retrieve our market share. This was a mistake. Although our market share came back, the volume did not improve our margin. Instead of expanding our margin [during that period], we lost two points from where we started.

During this period, Marsha was keeping a rigorous personal schedule. Her typical day would start at 4:30 in the morning. She would use a treadmill and do light weightlifting until about 5:30, then have some coffee and breakfast, take a shower, get dressed, and go to work. She was at the office from about 7:30 in the morning until about 8:00 at night. Her day would conclude with a light dinner, after which she would go directly to bed. She was not married and her weekends were spent walking, shopping (Marsha noted that she enjoyed spending money), dining with friends, and watching movies and TV shows.

During the first part of the new year, Marsha had to make several more reductions in her staff. The closing of the six sales offices had resulted in the layoff of 12 of her people; subsequently, one analyst in each of the remaining six offices was let go, reducing her staff by six. Marsha then decided to (1) merge the merchandising- and purchasing-services departments (−20 people); (2) hire an outside firm to process freight payments (−20 people); (3) transfer some legal work to an outside firm (−8 people); and (4) increase the productivity of the Collections Department through increasing individual authority levels and loosening the write-off policy (−67 people). These changes resulted in a net employee base of 252 people in Marsha's group and a reduction in management layers from seven to five (see Exhibit 40-2).

By September, however, Marsha and her peers realized that they were not likely to make their annual income commitments to the corporation. In addition, they had just projected the forecast for the following year and concluded that they would have to make another layoff. According to Marsha, her group manager of Finance, Leo Hines,

decided to go "front and center" with this information and demonstrate to his management team that they could reach their corporate commitment. After scheduling a meeting with his staff, he called Marsha into his office and said, "Marsha, you have got the largest employment base within WEC Appliances, so you and I are going to do what it takes to make the organization as small as we possibly can." He noted that he had assigned the business an overall goal of a 5 to 10 percent cut in expenses in order to reach its annual contributory-profit goal. Before the meeting, he said he needed to come up with an outline of how many employees would be necessary to keep the finance organization going. He asked Marsha to ascertain the minimum number of controller-related employees needed for the market/sales distribution function. Leo said he wanted "no fancy analysis, no proactive involvements in business, just enough staff to keep us out of jail."

Walking out of Leo's office, Marsha realized that this effort to cut base cost would again hit the salaried ranks directly, and that the first layoff had merely been a prelude for what she would have to go through now. Although the previous layoff had been a function of offices being closed and thus relatively impersonal, Marsha knew that this effort would require her direct involvement and would likely be much more difficult.

MARSHA'S DILEMMA

Looking for an answer to her boss's demand, Marsha decided to take an auditor's approach. She concentrated on the numbers to see where the company was at risk in terms of financial controls and routines that would cause a loss of cash or property to the company. She went through each of her organizational areas and determined that a minimum number of 132 people—92 in Credit Collection and 40 in Headquarters

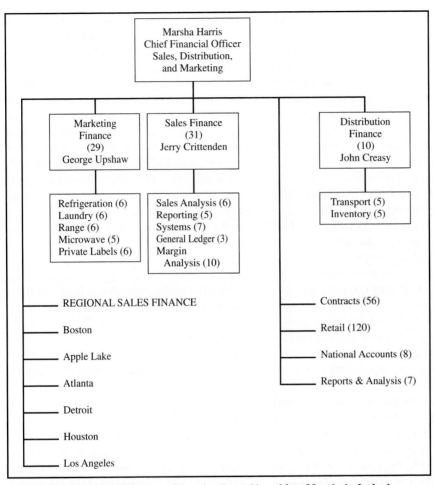

EXHIBIT 40-2   WEC Finance Organization 1 Year After Marsha's Arrival

Analysis—were needed to control warehouse inventory, monitor the merchandising programs, and control the major risk areas.

She knew that this figure was well below what would be needed to prepare financial statements and other business analyses that supported management's decision-making processes. Although Marsha arrived at this figure totally on her own, she felt confident that this minimum number would give her boss a bare-bones baseline from which he could determine what additional staff he would need to give senior manage-

ment the kind of information support they would need to run the business.

She submitted her analysis to Leo and began to wait. She was anxious to learn what his assessment would be of the total additional staff he would ultimately allocate to Marsha's function in order to support management's decision-making needs.

While she waited for Leo's answer, Marsha prepared to manage the layoff process for whatever his final number would be. Given the size of the businesswide layoffs, the law required that the company give its employees 3 months' notice. Marsha also knew she needed to have specific names identified by the end of December in order to set up liability accruals for the lay-offs and still be able to book those costs in the current year. Without the individual names, the labor costs would fall into next year's books, and her organization would miss its profit goals for this year. She also knew she would need to notify the affected staff as early as possible because they would be gearing up for Christmas and fully expected to be with WEC next year.

Two weeks after Marsha had given Leo the bare-bones number, she got an answer from Leo by electronic mail at her computer terminal: "Lay off your staff down to 132 people." Leo had used the same number she had given him as the target! Furthermore, even though he had used her basic audit-control number, Leo communicated that he still assumed her organization would maintain full service to the operating divisions. (Marsha's organization provided information to both the vice president of Sales and the vice president of Marketing.) She could not believe what she was reading. She would have to talk with the two vice presidents immediately, explain what she had been asked to do, and declare that it would not be possible to maintain the same level of support that they had enjoyed in the past. Marsha imagined what they might say.

While all this was happening, Harvey Winthrop, the head of Customer Financial Services, announced that he had found a new job in California. Moreover, George Upshaw had just discovered that he had a brain tumor and would need an operation immediately. He would not be able to come back to the office for 3 to 6 months. Marsha was confronted with a major dilemma, and two key management positions were suddenly vacant. With these two managers gone, Marsha was now faced with 12 instead of five direct reports.

Marsha put her head in her hands and wondered:

> How do you take an organization that— given the scope of analytic effort and the size of the business—certainly was not fat to begin with and shrink it 45 percent? Especially when you can't turn to your boss, the person who *gave* the order, and say, "By the way, you don't get any analysis anymore. From now on, we can only count beans!"

Marsha knew her decisions would mean that many of her employees would be unemployed by Christmas. She also wondered how she should organize the effort. Should she use the calculations she had originally done or some other method? What about morale? ■

Case 41   Battalion Chief James Scott of the Lynchburg Fire Department

When you get on the fire ground and we ask somebody to do something—you do this, you do that, a direct-order kind of thing—they know it is a life-threatening situation. There's no hesitation; It is done immediately without question . . . It's almost like you're operating in two different worlds and you have to switch gears.
—COMPANY COMMANDER FITZGERALD

How do I run my station? I do what I'm supposed to do and hope I've trained the firefighters to do what they're supposed to do, and I just monitor it and if I see that they have a problem, or if the workload gets to a point where they have a problem . . . we just work as a team, and they know that if we have a lot of calls, there's a lot of paperwork to do . . . and they realize that they've got a little extra work, and they don't mind doing it. If we get overburdened a little bit, it's very simple. Work and teamwork and working as a team . . . It just makes things a lot easier, and you feel if you need help, somebody will help you. It makes the stress level lower when you feel you can do a better job when you do go out on the street.
—COMPANY COMMANDER DAVIS

In the spring of 1997, James Scott, battalion chief of the Lynchburg, Virginia, Fire Department, was getting ready to retire. During his 25 years of service, Scott witnessed many changes in the fire department, and in his years as sector commander had worked to institute methods to make the department more efficient. Now that he was preparing to leave, Scott hoped those changes would continue, but he wondered if his successor would see their value.

Early on the morning of July 9, 1996, a newspaper carrier delivering papers in the southern end of Lynchburg spotted flames shooting through the roof of a duplex and quickly made an emergency call to 911.

In Station One of the Lynchburg Fire Department, the Shift A firefighters were asleep in the dormitory just behind the large bay where the fire trucks were parked. Alongside the bunks sat their rubber boots, fire-retardant pants tucked inside them. At 4:46 A.M., the emergency command center sounded a tone, alerting them to the fire. The firefighters jumped out of bed, stepped into their boots, and pulled up their pants. Within 45 seconds, they and the ambulance, ladder truck, engine company, and squad units were speeding out of the station.

Just think about it now—you're in bed sound asleep at 4 o'clock and a minute later you are barreling down the highway. And you arrive on the scene, there's a man saying "My 3-year-old is trapped in the house." Smoke is coming out, fire is coming out, you've never been in that house before, you have no idea where the bedrooms are, or steps are, and you know you've got to do everything in your power. Somehow go into a zero-visibility, hostile situation.

UVA-OB-0625

This case was prepared by Sheila McMillen under the supervision of Theodore M. Forbes III, Instructor in Business Administration, and Lynn A. Isabella, Associate Professor of Business Administration. Copyright © 1997 by the University of Virginia Darden School Foundation, Charlottesville, Virginia. All rights reserved.

It's hot, the temperature is in excess of a thousand degrees; and you have to get in there and find that child.

Before James Scott became a firefighter, he served as a noncommissioned officer in the Marine Corps, reaching the rank of sergeant before returning to civilian life. When he first came to Lynchburg, Scott hoped to become a policeman, but the fire department was looking for minority candidates, and he was asked to take the firefighter's test. "I lucked up and passed the test," he said. "And I do mean lucked up, because it was tough." He went to work for the Lynchburg Fire Department on April 17, 1971.

At that time, Scott had a GED but in his years as a firefighter, he received an associate's degree in applied science, a certificate in fire science, a certificate in fire inspection, a bachelor of arts in public service, and a master of science in public administration. He attended school at night and on weekends, and at one point was enrolled in both undergraduate and graduate school.

In 1971, the firefighter's job was much simpler than it became later. "All we did was put wet stuff on the red stuff and go home," Scott reminisced. "But now the fire department is involved in figuring hydraulics involved with water systems and stuff like that, the stresses on materials when they burn, how long different types of structural material will last . . . stuff we never concerned ourselves with when I first came here."

The chain of command was also much different, both in the firehouse and on the fire ground. The practice in the past was for the firefighters to arrive at the fire ground and wait for the battalion commander to arrive. "We lost a lot of property that way," Scott said. "We were frightened to do things because we might do something wrong." As commander, Scott now expected the first unit on the scene to take action.

Don't wait for me . . . I may be on the other side of the city . . . I've got two engines who within a couple of minutes are going to be there. If they are standing around waiting for me to make a decision, then we've got problems . . . So, they make their own decisions. They make them and because I train with them, . . . I trust that they're going to do the right thing and I back it . . . I assume the responsibility for their actions because they've demonstrated that they have what it takes to do it.

As the trucks rushed toward Wards Road and the scene of the fire, the officer in charge of each truck ran through a quick mental checklist, considering the location of the fire and any hazards the fire department might expect to encounter. Where would the hydrants be located? What kind of structure was it? Had any of the firefighters been there before? What other information could the dispatcher give them about where they were going and what they were getting into? Because they knew the territory of the city well, the firefighters had a good image of the fire's general location, but they didn't know what kind of fire they'd find.

You're sizing the situation up as you go. You're considering the weather, the time of day, day of the week, and so forth. What's likely to be going on there? Are there people there? Are they going to be in bed asleep? Are the kids in school? Is it afternoon; are they liable to be at home?

If first on the scene, the battalion chief decided procedure; otherwise, the officer of the first unit arriving took charge until the battalion commander arrived. This first unit had to assess the fire and quickly devise a strategy to extinguish it.

You've got a chain of command. You've got an officer on the truck, and when you leave that door, the officer is in control and responsible for what happens on the fire ground. So once you leave this door and get to the fire scene, you've got to tell each individual not so much what to do, because if you're trained as a team you know what they're doing, but the conditions on the fire ground are not like in the station. I can control the conditions here. I can't control them on the fire ground.

James Scott's methods of running his sector were shaped by his background as a firefighter. His own boss had tended to make every decision for him, but Scott realized he didn't want to be that kind of manager. "I'm not interested in power," he said. "I'm interested in results . . . I don't need to tell people to do things . . . I need to get things done, because that's what I was hired to do."

In his first assignment as sector commander, Scott made a choice: "I could go in and be a ramrod and spend all my time trying to convince them that I was smarter than them, or I could take advantage of the fact they had . . . knowledge and experience, and put it to work for me." Scott valued the skills of the people actually doing the fire fighting. "When we have a big, successful fire fight," he said, "and we save a building, I get the credit, but I'm not the one who did it. The ones who did it are the women and men who went in and took care of it." Consequently, he decided the most efficient method of managing his sector was to use the talents of his people in as many areas as possible.

I just know I've got a bunch of smart people and I don't have a lot of time and most things they know. So I utilize their intelligence. All I do is make certain that they know what they're doing . . . I empower them to do their job by telling them what I want done . . . I've got a new officer that turned out to be worth the trust to let him go, instead of having to spend a lot of time with him. The first

few weeks, I realized that he was capable and that I could trust him to do a job and so all I do now is assist him. In fact, that's all I do with all of them . . . assist them with whatever they need. If they need something and they need me, fine. If they don't need me, I go by and just talk with them, and the rest of the time I don't bother.

Within minutes the firefighters were on the scene, but the one-story brick duplex was completely engulfed in flames. A neighbor ran out to the firefighters, saying he and his son had been awakened by a noise and a flash. He too had called 911, and then ran to the burning house to bang on the door and warn his neighbors. But the door was so hot he could not touch it. A family of five lived there, he shouted. He was pretty sure they were trapped inside.

The firefighters spread out, the officer in charge making the initial "size-up." If he made a mistake, the fire would become much bigger and more dangerous. With portable radios, the firefighters reported back to the officer coordinating their activities. Once the officer chose a plan of attack, all the firefighters on the fire ground would share a common purpose: to rescue the endangered people, find the fire's precise location, confine the fire, attack and extinguish the flames. The "incident commander" controlled the staging and operation of the fire fighting itself, as well as acting as liaison with the police and utility departments. The commander also had to weigh the possibility of chemical hazards, a danger increasing so rapidly that the fire department kept hazardous-response books on the engines.

The incident commander, whoever he or she may be, has all that responsibility. He may not do as well as a seasoned officer will, but still he's got those basics that he's got to do. You might pull up and start an action plan and get into it and holler at the crew, "What do you think? We're doing something wrong here; we've got to do something else." Every fire I've been to, I've never seen one that I expected this to happen and that's the way it happened and we put it out and we've come back to the station. Something always happens that you never expect. You have to be flexible enough to say, "Hey, we have to do something else."

At the same time that Scott worked to involve his firefighters in decisions and trusted them to make the right ones, he also recognized that limits were necessary, especially on the fire ground, where the situation was dangerous and unpredictable. "Once it [the fire] gets going," Scott said, "the only team is at the command post. All the rest of them are work groups . . . whose function is to carry out some specific aspect of that operation." In a fire or rescue emergency, there was no place for what the firefighters called "freelancers"—people going off on their own. "You can't operate a team at that point," Scott explained. "Too many extraneous factors . . . That's how people get killed."

The firefighters were fully geared up, wearing their air packs and their fire-retardant suits. Their faces and skin were completely covered against the intense heat. They needed to wait a moment for water in the hose line, because what they were about to do would make the fire worse. With no time to lose, they broke through the front door with their axes. This was perhaps the most dangerous part of the entire job, for the sudden ventilation provided openings to allow hot air and toxic products of combustion to escape. If done correctly, ventilation could save the building, but when it was done incorrectly, the sudden addition of fresh oxygen could intensify the fire and cause an explosion. Black smoke billowed out the opening into the air. Hose lines in hand, the firefighters crawled in low, both to search for the family, who might be unconscious on the floor, but

also because of the heat: The temperature inside near the ceiling was more than 1,200 degrees. The heavy smoke made it impossible to see; the firefighters felt their way into the interior of the house.

You get to the point where when you start sweating and the sweat pops out, it immediately turns to steam, and you get steam burns, and feel how hot it can get. A lot of times, especially at night, you don't really know who you're working with. Maybe they've got on protective clothing. You might run up on somebody that's got an air pack on, and you have no idea who it is.

It took more than an hour to bring the fire under control. A short while later, the firefighters found the family of five in the den— two adults and three children, all of them dead in their nightclothes. In all likelihood, the family was already dead by the time the fire department arrived. Still, it was the experience each of them dreaded. As one of the firefighters explained later, "This is a feel good/feel bad job. You can help people and that feels great, but then terrible things happen. You're on a real roller coaster—up and then down, real down."

Though the cause of the fire wasn't immediately apparent, it looked as though it had started in the living room, adjacent to the two bedrooms, and spread slowly for several hours. The family must have awakened and found the front and back doors blocked by the fire. They tried to escape down a hallway into the den. A cracked window in the den near the bodies suggested that the family might have tried to break through it but were overcome by smoke. In the water-drenched hallway, the firefighters found a smoke detector; it had melted in the fire, but the wiring was recovered. As Deputy Fire Marshall John Jennings commented later, "I've got serious doubts whether the detector worked or not. If the family had known there was a problem, they should have gotten out."

Because there were deaths involved, the fire department and the police department would work together to discover the cause of the accident. The bodies were sent to Roanoke for autopsies—also standard practice in the case of death during a fire. The fire was the worst in Lynchburg in more than 25 years. "I don't remember anything this bad ever happening in the city," said Fire Marshall Wayne Saunders.

The loss of life in the Lynchburg fire that morning was, unfortunately, not an unusual circumstance in the United States. Fire fighting and fire prevention were important community resources for the protection of life and property; and with more than 30,000 fire departments across the nation, nearly every community in the United States had its own fire department. Even so, the rate of fire-caused deaths in the United States was higher than in any other industrialized nation. For example, Chicago, half the size of Hong Kong, had three times as many deaths by fire. Similarly, Baltimore, the same size as Amsterdam, had 13 times as many fire-related deaths. Nearly 2.5 million fires occurred each year in this country, resulting in more than 6,000 deaths, countless injuries, and billions of dollars in property damage.

All of the firefighters in Lynchburg were professionals, a portion of the more than 260,000 paid firefighters working in the United States. The profession was a dangerous one. In 1994, 95,400 firefighters were hurt while working, and 104 firefighters died. Firefighters also suffered a higher rate of cancer, lung disease, and heart attacks than the national average.

You go from a relaxed atmosphere like we are in now, no pressure, and when that tone goes off, you don't know what you're getting into. The most stressful fire I ever went to, you arrive on the scene and you hear a child screaming inside and there's nothing that we can do. We could not rescue the child or we'd perish. I can see and relive that like it was yesterday. Fire fighting is one of the most dangerous occupations. We just had two people in Chesapeake killed a couple months ago, two firefighters there . . . We lost a total of 20 people, I think, within this department.

Another thing on the back of our minds more and more is the hazardous materials that we're coming in contact with. I'm not talking about going out to a tractor-trailer accident; I'm talking about going in your house when it's burning. The toxic chemicals used in plastics and so forth are affecting us in record numbers right now. The chance of you coming down with cancer is 25 times greater than if you are somebody working out on the streets. A lot of things out there jump up and bite you and they don't have to get into your lungs; they just get in contact with your skin through your clothes.

Fire fighting as a profession has grown increasingly more difficult, complicated, and stressful. "As new flammable synthetics proliferate, firefighters must be part physicist and part chemist. On emergency medical calls or prolonged extractions—when people are not just injured but often panicked—firefighters are both doctor and shrink . . . Gone are the days, if they ever existed, when the only requirements were strength and grit."[1] See Appendix A for a history of fire fighting in the United States.

The first unit arriving on the scene that morning was also the last to leave, for it was responsible for gathering the information needed to fill out a fire report (see

---

[1]Steve Delsohn, *The Fire Inside: Fire Fighters Talk About Their Lives* (New York: Harper, Collins, 1996), 4.

Appendix B). When the fire was finally extinguished, and the trucks and firefighters returned to the station, the shift sat down for an extensive debriefing with the sector commander. Everyone critiqued the station's performance in the fire—what they did right, what wrong, was there anything else they might have done to save the family? Was there anything they could learn from the experience for the next time? This session was candid; rank was not a factor in who spoke or what was said.

About 6 or 8 years ago, everything was authoritarian through the station. The firemen had very little input into anything. If you've got a better idea and it was mentioned to the captain, he got a little upset and said that's the way we do it and that's the way we're gonna do it. You didn't ask why either. But I know this department's changed a lot in that respect over the years . . . especially with the battalion chief we've got [James Scott]. He's definitely on the team approach and having committees, and we've heard every idea that comes up in the city now. It's mainly through the team comprised of supervisors and officers. He's put everything to the team approach. I feel it's finally getting down to the ranks. Even the firefighter on the bottom is now a member of the team and knows what's going on. He or she was made a part of it and is more ready to go along with the decision that was made.

In the past, sector commanders had usually been authoritarian, both at the station and the fire ground. Scott recognized that this style might work well at a fire, but not at the station.

What I say is simply this: Commander, if you will run your station, I'll run your sector. It's that simple . . . I don't interfere in operations at the station unless they ask me to or if there is something egregiously wrong. If I go in and there's something so blatantly wrong that as the sector commander I can't ignore it, I have to address it. But otherwise, there might be things that I see—uniform issues and all kinds of things that should be addressed—but the commander knows what the rules are. The commander knows what goes on. If it makes this station run smoothly and it doesn't interfere with fire-department operations overall, then so be it. I let the commanders manage their own people . . . and we are all more productive by far.

However, making these changes and getting his firefighters to think differently had not been easy for Scott. Initially, his employees didn't trust the new method.

They didn't think I knew my job, basically. And if you ask them, they'll tell you that. They think that the reason I'm asking them to decide what to do is because either I don't want to or I don't know how to do it, instead of my needing to get them thinking for themselves. Once they got to doing that and then a few things happened and they realized I was completely aware of that, I was monitoring what was going on, then the respect starts to set in, and they understand, "Hey, wait a minute, he's not ducking anything, he's asking me to do the job I get paid for." And then, surprisingly when people do that, they all of a sudden take off and they change direction.

When the debriefing ended, the shift inventoried all the equipment and made sure that everything, such as air packs, was on the equipment and ready to be used. Each of the firefighters was working for 24 hours, eating and sleeping at the station (though ready to respond to a call) and then everyone had 48 hours off. One hallmark of the firefighters' world was the close proximity in which they spent their working day with others on

*their shift. Many of the firefighters acknowl-
edged that the level of mutual trust necessary
for successfully fighting fires was built up
over the years of such close contact.*

We are a whole lot different from other
working environments in that we live
here at the station. Every third day we
come in at 7:30 in the morning and
we're with the same group of people till
7:30 the next morning. We share in
what's going on in their lives, we eat
three meals a day together, we have
recreation together, and then we sleep
in the same bedroom. So it's like a family here.

*At the beginning of each shift change,
the captain made sure all the equipment was
manned, then the station was cleaned up and
the equipment wiped down. Once a week
there was an in-depth maintenance check.
People knew at the beginning of the shift
what their jobs would be.*

We've got greater flexibility at the station. Things are pretty relaxed. At first
it's hard to make that switch from station to fire; it's still autocratic there. It
used to be much more autocratic in the
station as well, iron fist, telling everybody what to do, [an] absolutely regi-
mented schedule with no flexibility.
Nobody in the past was given credit for
knowing what they're doing. Now it's
more hands off. Better training makes
people competent, and superiors trust
them more. If people are trusted, they're
going to do a better job.

In our line of work, team management works around the station and during training exercises, but on the fire
ground you have to be more authoritarian. But give everybody an input if
you've got a task to do . . . If we don't
have any trucks on a fire call, then we
prefer to work as a team. We have to
know what the other person is doing

and their level of training and competence, or else we can get into trouble
right quick if we don't. So, if you try to
have a crew and don't train it as a team,
you're not only hurting yourself, you're
hurting them.

*In preparing equipment for the next fire,
everyone knew the routine. With the equipment ready, the firefighters were ready for
the next call.*

The tones will go off and everybody
immediately stops what they're saying. If
the TV's on, radio's on, they all have to
be shut off and we listen to what's going
on first. It may be an announcement saying a street's closed, or it could be a fire
call. You develop a sixth sense . . . you
just have a feeling when it goes off,
before they ever start speaking, you just
know whether it's going to be a fire.

"I solve problems," Scott said, talking
about the challenges of his job. "And that's
why I like where I'm at, because I solve
problems. I love problems. I do puzzles and
games and things because I like to work with
problems, anything new." But as much as he
loved solving problems, Scott was willing to
step aside and let his firefighters solve them,
too. "They don't have to come to me and say,
'We have a problem.' They share with me
that there is a problem, and they're going to
address it, if it doesn't need me. And if they
need me, they tell me." He appreciated the
trust and resourcefulness of the people who
worked for him, their willingness and ability
to take the initiative in a crisis:

I had a fire on Main Street a few months
ago and I missed the call because my
radio malfunctioned. Not a single command officer was on that call, but they
called the ladder truck, set it, fought the
fire, and by the time I got the call and got
there, they were taking the truck down,
had put the fire out and everything. And
these were acting command officers who

handled this entire thing from beginning to end, and all I did was get there and praise them for what they had done. They weren't afraid they weren't going to get backed if something went wrong, that they weren't going to be supported. They were making their best effort. I owe them that and they, in turn, gave me that.

As he looked back on his career, Scott wondered how he could describe what he had done as sector commander. What, in fact, had he accomplished? ■

--------------- A P P E N D I X   A ---------------

Fire Fighting in the United States[1]

In the mid 1600s, the first fire laws in this country were passed in Boston and New Amsterdam (later New York). These laws banned the construction of wooden chimneys and thatched roofs and required residents and business owners to keep their chimneys clean of soot. New Amsterdam also appointed four fire-safety inspectors called "the Worshipful Fire Wardens." These men didn't fight fires; instead they enforced the law and collected fines from people unlucky enough to have their homes or businesses burn. The money the fire wardens collected in New Amsterdam purchased the first municipal fire equipment—fire ladders, hooks, and leather buckets. In 1664, when the British acquired New Amsterdam, laws were enacted requiring every resident to place three buckets of water on his doorstep at sunset in case of fire during the night.

As the colonies grew, so did the volunteer fire companies, as well as fire laws and fire departments. Many of the founding fathers of the country served on volunteer fire brigades. Benjamin Franklin founded the Union Fire Company in Philadelphia in 1736. George Washington joined the Alexandria, Virginia, fire department in 1750 as a volunteer. Most American fire departments began as volunteer organizations for their neighborhoods; however, this fragmented system resulted in turf rivalries, in which the departments arriving at the scene of a fire sometimes fought each other instead of putting out the fire.

A number of devastating fires toward the end of the 1800s led to a growing awareness that fire costs were losses not only for an individual, but for the community as a whole. With this awareness came the establishment of paid fire departments. By the early part of the twentieth century, all-professional fire departments had become the norm in most large American cities. Gradually, this model spread throughout the country.

A major concern for communities was ensuring that their firefighters be well organized, trained, and disciplined. To this end, New York appointed General Alexander Shaler, a veteran of the Civil War, as fire commissioner in the late 1860s. Shaler instituted more rigorous training along military lines and divided the department into divisions and battalions similar to those he had known in the Union Army. Shaler also established a strict chain of command throughout the department, and the use of standard uniforms and ranking for the firefighters. The heads of the engine and ladder companies were called "captain"; the men just below them were "lieutenants." Under Shaler's command, firefighters were graded by length of service, experience, and meritorious service.

After the Great Chicago Fire of 1871, the city hired General Shaler to reorganize

---

[1]John V. Morris, *Fire and Fire Fighters* (Boston: Little, Brown and Company, 1955).

its fire department, and he made changes similar to those he had established in New York. Shortly after this, Boston also reorganized its fire department using the Shaler method. Gradually this pattern spread to other cities, and then to the country as a whole. To this day, a quasi-military structure remains the basic organizational pattern in most fire departments.

-------------- A P P E N D I X B ---------------

The Lynchburg Fire Department

The Lynchburg Fire Department has eight stations (see Appendix C). Station One on Clay Street serves as headquarters and is the largest station, housing not only the firefighting unit but the administrative offices for the department as a whole and the 911 emergency command center. Within the section used by the Fire Department are a variety of facilities: a dorm for sleeping, a kitchen, a weight room, a classroom, offices, and a four-story tower in which wet hoses are dried out after a fire.

The department has three different shifts (A, B, and C), and each shift has a sector commander. Each shift works for 24 hours, eating and sleeping at the station (though ready to respond to a call), and then has 48 hours off. The total workweek is 56 hours. (See Appendix D for work schedule.) Each firefighter contributes $5 per day for food; cooking and cleaning responsibilities are shared. Each person also contributes to a station fund that pays for cable TV, towels, and a telephone for private calls.

The Lynchburg Fire Department has six sector commanders, with two serving on each shift—one for Stations 1, 2, 4, and 5; another for Stations 3, 6, 7, 8—and the Airport Safety Public Safety Office. The sector commanders report to the chief of operations, who is directly under the fire chief, who reports to the city manager. (See Appendix E for organizational chart.)

There are four levels of firefighter in Lynchburg: Fire Fighter One, Fire Fighter Two, Fire Fighter Three, and Commander. Certain skills are required to move up from one level to another, but there is no formal testing necessary for promotion. Fire Fighter Three is reserved for those who have served 15 years or who have made a particular contribution to the department.

Uniforms for all firefighters are the same except for the collar insignia and helmets—officers wear white helmets; everyone else wears a yellow helmet. Each helmet has the firefighter's name on it, so they can recognize each other at a fire when they are wearing air packs, which cover the face.

In 1995, the Lynchburg Fire Department responded to more than 3,400 calls, including building and vehicle fires, as well as rescue and other calls. Fire damage amounted to more than $3.2 million, and the firefighters suffered more than 40 fire-related injuries.

BECOMING A FIREFIGHTER

Anyone wanting to become a firefighter in Lynchburg must first fill out an application and take a written test. Those who pass the test then take a test of physical strength and agility, and the score of these two tests is combined to give an eligibility rating. The process is usually very competitive.

Although the state of Virginia has a training center for firefighters, Lynchburg conducts its own training of new employees both in-house and at the department's nearby training center. Occasionally, several companies in the city get together for hazardous materials training. Many of the state fire instructors work at Lynchburg, so the department is confident its level of training is high. Training is conducted every weekday morning from 9 to 11, except on Friday, which is special maintenance day. New firefighters are trained in all areas, but their first assignment is riding on the ambulance and learning to set up the first-aid station. The first year is a probationary period.

EQUIPMENT IN LYNCHBURG

The basic equipment for fighting fires in any industrialized nation is the fire engine, or "pumper," equipped with hose, water tanks, and pumps. This truck and the firefighters operating it are known as an "engine company." The ladder truck is another crucial piece of equipment, and its crew is known as the "ladder company."

An engine company consists of three people: a driver/operator, an officer, and a person on the back who operates the hoses. If a fourth person is available, he also works on the back.

The ladder company also requires three people: a driver, an officer, and a tillerperson at the back to help steer the equipment. If a fourth person is available, she serves in the jump seat on the side. Each engine and ladder company in Lynchburg has a commander who shares the duties of the station, including responsibility for the squad unit.

The National Fire Protection Association recommends five people per engine company, with a bare minimum of three. In the past, the Lynchburg Fire Department had five people on each engine and ladder company, but in recent years, as a result of budget cuts, this number has been cut to three people per engine company or ladder company.

When I first joined the department, they'd always have four firefighters on an engine like this. In fire season when nobody's on vacation, in the wintertime, you'd have five. You had a lot of people there to take care of a situation. Now most of them get three, so you've got situations you've got to be able to handle with less personnel. Things have gotten more technical with chemicals we've got to deal with now.

When I first joined the department, we didn't go to car wrecks or . . . heart attacks . . . Now we all train as EMTs [emergency medical technicians] and we respond to heart attacks and car wrecks . . . There are just more things that we're responsible for and there are more laws we have to comply with. Now there are only three people on the engine and the officer has to chip in and work just like everybody else . . . That's how you start earning respect. The guys know if he tells them to do something, he's not telling them to do something he wouldn't be willing to do himself.

A fire alarm in Lynchburg receives a standard response: two engine companies, a ladder company, a squad unit, and a medic unit. The exception to this standard is in Response Zone One, which consists of Lynchburg's downtown. In that area, the city's most densely populated, the standard response is three engine companies. For any fire, though, the first company on the scene was responsible for completing a fire report.

-------------- **A P P E N D I X C** --------------

Equipment and Stations in the Lynchburg Fire Department

Station 1 (Headquarters): largest station with engine company, ladder unit, medic unit, squad unit

Station 2 (Grace Street): engine company

Station 3 (Fort Hill): engine company and medic unit

Station 4 (Rivermont): engine company and medic unit

Station 5 (Boonsboro): engine company

Station 6 (Miller Park): engine company and medic unit

Station 7 (Lakeside Drive): engine company, squad unit, sector commander, ladder company and reserve medic unit (unmanned except in emergency); a tanker and truck for places with inadequate water supply

Station 8 (Old Graves Mill Road): engine company

-------------- A P P E N D I X   D --------------

Work Schedule for Lynchburg Fire Department 1996

1996

January

S	M	T	W	Th	F	S
	A 1	B 2	C 3	A 4	B$ 5	C 6
A 7	B 8	C 9	A 10	B 11	C 12	A 13
B 14	C 15	A 16	B 17	C 18	A$ 19	B 20
C 21	A 22	B 23	C 24	A 25	B 26	C 27
A 28	B 29	C 30	A 31			

February

S	M	T	W	Th	F	S
				B 1	C$ 2	A 3
B 4	C 5	A 6	B 7	C 8	A 9	B 10
C 11	A 12	B 13	C 14	A 15	B$ 16	C 17
A 18	B 19	C 20	A 21	B 22	C 23	A 24
B 25	C 26	A 27	B 28	C 29		

March

S	M	T	W	Th	F	S
					A$ 1	B 2
C 3	A 4	B 5	C 6	A 7	B 8	C 9
A 10	B 11	C 12	A 13	B 14	C$ 15	A 16
B 17	C 18	A 19	B 20	C 21	A 22	B 23
C 24	A 25	B 26	C 27	A 28	B$ 29	C 30
A 31						

April

S	M	T	W	Th	F	S
	B 1	C 2	A 3	B 4	C 5	A 6
B 7	C 8	A 9	B 10	C 11	A$ 12	B 13
C 14	A 15	B 16	C 17	A 18	B 19	C 20
A 21	B 22	C 23	A 24	B 25	C$ 26	A 27
B 28	C 29	A 30				

May

S	M	T	W	Th	F	S
			B 1	C 2	A 3	B 4
C 5	A 6	B 7	C 8	A 9	B$ 10	C 11
A 12	B 13	C 14	A 15	B 16	C 17	A 18
B 19	C 20	A 21	B 22	C 23	A$ 24	B 25
C 26	A 27	B 28	C 29	A 30	B 31	

June

S	M	T	W	Th	F	S
						C 1
A 2	B 3	C 4	A 5	B 6	C$ 7	A 8
B 9	C 10	A 11	B 12	C 13	A 14	B 15
C 16	A 17	B 18	C 19	A 20	B$ 21	C 22
A 23	B 24	C 25	A 26	B 27	C 28	A 29
B 30						

July

S	M	T	W	Th	F	S
	C 1	A 2	B 3	C 4	A$ 5	B 6
C 7	A 8	B 9	C 10	A 11	B 12	C 13
A 14	B 15	C 16	A 17	B 18	C$ 19	A 20
B 21	C 22	A 23	B 24	C 25	A 26	B 27
C 28	A 29	B 30	C 31			

August

S	M	T	W	Th	F	S
				A 1	B$ 2	C 3
A 4	B 5	C 6	A 7	B 8	C 9	A 10
B 11	C 12	A 13	B 14	C 15	A$ 16	B 17
C 18	A 19	B 20	C 21	A 22	B 23	C 24
A 25	B 26	C 27	A 28	B 29	C$ 30	A 31

September

S	M	T	W	Th	F	S
B 1	C 2	A 3	B 4	C 5	A 6	B 7
C 8	A 9	B 10	C 11	A 12	B$ 13	C 14
A 15	B 16	C 17	A 18	B 19	C 20	A 21
B 22	C 23	A 24	B 25	C 26	A$ 27	B 28
C 29	A 30					

October

S	M	T	W	Th	F	S
		B 1	C 2	A 3	B 4	C 5
A 6	B 7	C 8	A 9	B 10	C$ 11	A 12
B 13	C 14	A 15	B 16	C 17	A 18	B 19
C 20	A 21	B 22	C 23	A 24	B$ 25	C 26
A 27	B 28	C 29	A 30	B 31		

November

S	M	T	W	Th	F	S
					C 1	A 2
B 3	C 4	A 5	B 6	C 7	A$ 8	B 9
C 10	A 11	B 12	C 13	A 14	B 15	C 16
A 17	B 18	C 19	A 20	B 21	C$ 22	A 23
B 24	C 25	A 26	B 27	C 28	A 29	B 30

December

S	M	T	W	Th	F	S
C 1	A 2	B 3	C 4	A 5	B$ 6	C 7
A 8	B 9	C 10	A 11	B 12	C 13	A 14
B 15	C 16	A 17	B 18	C 19	A$ 20	B 21
C 22	A 23	B 24	C 25	A 26	B 27	C 28
A 29	B 30	C 31				

------------- **A P P E N D I X   E** -------------

Lynchburg Fire Department Organization Chart

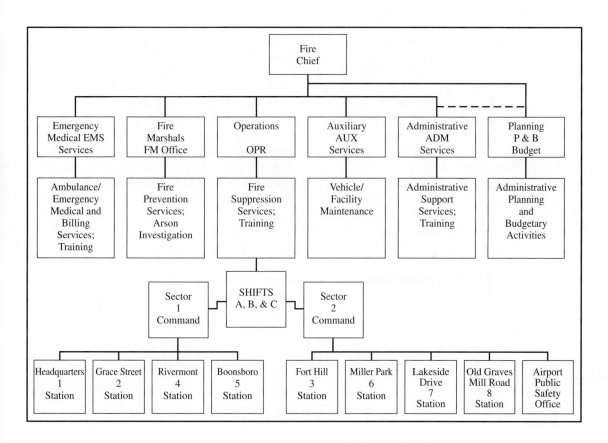

Case 42   Goodwin House, Incorporated

In the fall of 1999, Marvin Ogburn reflected on some of the issues he faced as the president of Goodwin House, Incorporated (GHI). Mr. Ogburn had served as a consultant to GHI for several years before accepting the chief executive's job in 1994. GHI had been a growing, successful Continuing Care Retirement Community (CCRC), yet Mr. Ogburn knew that he must find solutions to several problems if the organization was to continue to thrive. As the heavy traffic on nearby I-395 in Alexandria, Virginia, just south of Washington, D.C., droned on, he reflected on the strategic challenges facing GHI.

"Marketing," said Mr. Ogburn, "is my number one priority." Occupancy rates in two recently completed facilities were lower than anticipated, and Mr. Ogburn was concerned about how slowly the unoccupied units were filling. Mr. Ogburn also faced significant financial concerns. On the one hand, increasing commercial competition was putting pressure on fee structures; competitors were offering à la carte and lower initial fee programs, contrasting with GHI's relatively inclusive long-term fee structure. Although GHI had selected a relatively upscale market, the organization had a stated mission to serve a broad constituency. At the same time, the costs of improving services and paying wages[1] that inched ever higher pressured his margins. Meanwhile, residents were always requesting better services. Further, his new chief financial officer had just announced plans to leave the orga-

nization after only a year of employment. The CFO's work to organize the institution's books and accounting systems was potentially jeopardized by the transition to a new, as-yet-unfound CFO.

Mr. Ogburn also recognized some difficult organizational problems. First, jealousy between GHI's two main facilities, Goodwin House East (GHE, the original facility) and Goodwin House West (GHW), was affecting coordination and employee morale. Even the residents felt some tension between the two communities, located only 3 miles from each other. Organizational variations at both facilities meant that members of Mr. Ogburn's staff had different responsibilities, further fueling the feelings between them. Just recently, Mr. Ogburn had organized regular management committee meetings and separated out the corporate office space from the GHE office suite. He wondered if these changes were helping as much as he had hoped. Finally, several of Mr. Ogburn's staff had mentioned concerns for his "participative" leadership style—a style Mr. Ogburn felt helped develop stronger subordinates, but which apparently left some of them feeling confused about direction and priority.

Mr. Ogburn wondered how GHI could best achieve its responsibilities to its residents and the broader community and its founding institution, the Episcopal Church, in the face of these challenges. Some members of management wondered whether GHI should expand its role and find a way

This case was prepared by James G. Clawson, Randolph New, and Greg Bevan. This case was written as a basis for discussion rather than to illustrate effective or ineffective handling of an administrative situation. Some names have been changed at the request of the subjects. Copyright © 2000 by the University of Virginia Darden School Foundation, Charlottesville, Virginia. All rights reserved.
[1]Current wages paid at GHI were thought to be lower than wages for similar organizations in the area.

to serve new markets outside the I-495 Washington beltway. Mr. Ogburn felt a strong commitment to working with the board of directors, who also were concerned about the strategic issues facing the organization. The weight of these issues settled into the wrinkles on Mr. Ogburn's face as he stalked the hallways at GHI, greeting residents, chatting with the employees, and wrestling with what to do next.

Senior Living: The Continuing Care Retirement Community (CCRC) Industry

Since the 1960s, the senior living industry had been growing rapidly in the United States. As the physical distance separating parents from adult children began to grow in a more mobile society, and as more pension and other retirement income became available to retirees, demand for senior living facilities and related long-term care had increased significantly. A Price Waterhouse study of the investment potential of senior living and long-term care properties highlighted three trends: (1) the senior housing market was expected to grow in a linear fashion through 2010 (from 1.78 million to 2.18 million), then grow exponentially from 2010 to 2030 (to 3.7 million); (2) the gross capital size of the marketplace was estimated to grow from $86 billion in 1996, to $126 billion in 2005, and to $490 billion in 2030; and (3) the stability of future seniors' housing demand, as the population aged, was expected to be independent of economic and business cycles.[2] Exhibit 42-1 provides further detail regarding estimated growth in the senior population.

As the demand for senior living grew, many different combinations of shelter, care, and services became available. The largest increase in the number of CCRCs occurred during the 1980s. By the end of the millennium, there were an estimated 700 to 1,500 such facilities.[3] Continuing Care Retirement Communities provided a continuum of housing, services, and health care within a single community. These typically included three levels of care: independent living, assisted care living, and continuous care living. Residents who joined a facility in an independent arrangement typically were expected to move to the succeeding care levels as they aged and required more help.

When a new resident joined a CCRC, the agreement between the resident and the provider was intended to last the resident's lifetime, with living arrangements evolving with the resident's needs. Exhibit 42-2 shows one categorization of senior living arrangements, including sample monthly fees and types of services provided. The exhibit utilizes two major groupings of care provided: assistance with Activities of Daily Living (ADLs) and assistance with Instrumental Activities of Daily Living (IADLs). ADLs were the physical activities that an elderly person might need help with such as walking, dressing, bathing, eating, toilet use, and administering medication. IADLs were more complex, combined mental/physical functions, and included meal preparation, shopping, telephone use, and money management.[4]

The many types of CCRC agreements differed in two major ways: the amount of health care included in the agreement and

---

[2]The Investment Case for Senior Living and Long-Term Care Properties in an Institutional Real Estate Portfolio, prepared by Price Waterhouse LLP for the National Investment Conference for the Senior Living and Long-Term Care Industries, date unknown, 199_, pages 13 and 19.
[3]Price Waterhouse, ibid. The difficulty in determining what various facilities do creates the large range in the estimate.
[4]Price Waterhouse, ibid, p. 27.

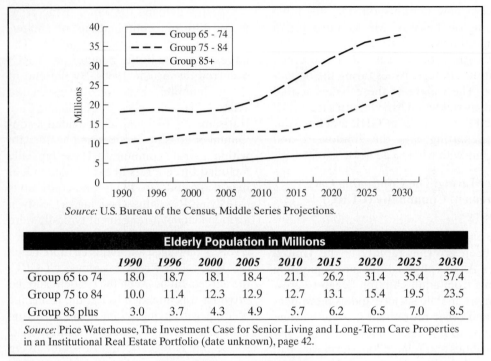

Source: U.S. Bureau of the Census, Middle Series Projections.

Elderly Population in Millions

	1990	1996	2000	2005	2010	2015	2020	2025	2030
Group 65 to 74	18.0	18.7	18.1	18.4	21.1	26.2	31.4	35.4	37.4
Group 75 to 84	10.0	11.4	12.3	12.9	12.7	13.1	15.4	19.5	23.5
Group 85 plus	3.0	3.7	4.3	4.9	5.7	6.2	6.5	7.0	8.5

Source: Price Waterhouse, The Investment Case for Senior Living and Long-Term Care Properties in an Institutional Real Estate Portfolio (date unknown), page 42.

EXHIBIT 42-I   Elderly Population Estimates 1990 to 2030

how payment was made. Three types of health care coverage were common: extensive, modified, and fee-for-service. Similarly, there were three common types of financial arrangements: entry fee plus monthly fee, rental, and ownership or equity.

GOODWIN HOUSE'S HISTORY

The Episcopal Diocese of Virginia created in May 1955 a corporation, eventually named Virginia Diocesan Homes, Incorporated (VDH), to purchase and operate a home for the aged in Richmond, Virginia. The Cary Montague Home was opened in 1957, providing residential care for 30 women, men, or couples. In 1962, a parcel of land in Alexandria, Virginia, was given to the Diocese on condition that a "life care"

home would be constructed. In August 1967, Goodwin House was opened as a nondenominational[5] CCRC on the traditional model: entry fee plus monthly maintenance fee, with no additional fee when nursing unit admission was necessary. The Cary Montague Home was closed the same year, and its residents were given the option to enter Goodwin House or find other accommodations. During the following years, VDH also decided to join its Presbyterian counterpart to establish a number of other new homes in Virginia. The first of these, "Westminster Canterbury Houses," was established in Richmond, and later in Irvington, Winchester, and Charlottesville.

GHI received limited financial support from VDH, the parent organization. GHI was classified as a charitable organization

---

[5]By 1999, 43 percent of the residents were Episcopalian.

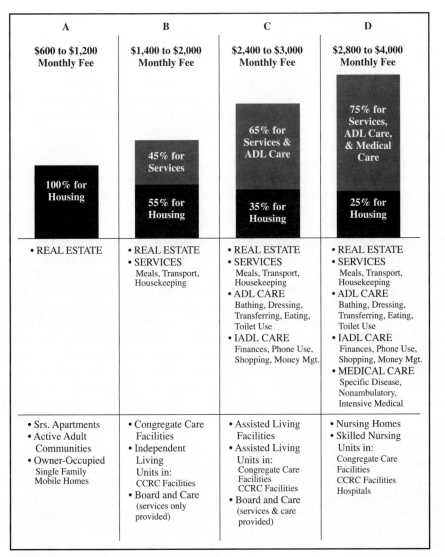

A	B	C	D
$600 to $1,200 Monthly Fee	**$1,400 to $2,000 Monthly Fee**	**$2,400 to $3,000 Monthly Fee**	**$2,800 to $4,000 Monthly Fee**
			75% for Services, ADL Care, & Medical Care
	45% for Services	65% for Services & ADL Care	
100% for Housing	55% for Housing	35% for Housing	25% for Housing
• REAL ESTATE	• REAL ESTATE • SERVICES Meals, Transport, Housekeeping	• REAL ESTATE • SERVICES Meals, Transport, Housekeeping • ADL CARE Bathing, Dressing, Transferring, Eating, Toilet Use • IADL CARE Finances, Phone Use, Shopping, Money Mgt.	• REAL ESTATE • SERVICES Meals, Transport, Housekeeping • ADL CARE Bathing, Dressing, Transferring, Eating, Toilet Use • IADL CARE Finances, Phone Use, Shopping, Money Mgt. • MEDICAL CARE Specific Disease, Nonambulatory, Intensive Medical
• Srs. Apartments • Active Adult Communities • Owner-Occupied Single Family Mobile Homes	• Congregate Care Facilities • Independent Living Units in: CCRC Facilities • Board and Care (services only provided)	• Assisted Living Facilities • Assisted Living Units in: Congregate Care Facilities CCRC Facilities • Board and Care (services & care provided)	• Nursing Homes • Skilled Nursing Units in: Congregate Care Facilities CCRC Facilities Hospitals

EXHIBIT 42-2   Senior Living Categories

under Section 501(c)(3) of the U.S. Tax Code. As applied to homes for the aged, this meant that it "operates in a manner designed to satisfy the three primary needs of aged persons, namely housing, health care, and financial security." As a result, the organization was exempt from federal and state income taxes, and Virginia sales, real, and property taxes. In 1992, GHI formed a separate entity, Goodwin House Foundation,

to hold and receive charitable contributions and bequests. In 1999, Ms. Stephanie Reponen was responsible for the activities of the foundation. The goal of the Goodwin House Foundation was to raise charitable funds to cover the cost of financial assistance to residents and to support other charitable programs.

GHI began as a single facility in Alexandria, Virginia. The original structure was completed in 1967 and had 224 units. The building was expanded in 1976 to extend the capacity to 278 units. The facility included a small exercise pool, workout room, beauty salon, convenience shopping store, library, cafeterias (one for residents and one for employees), chapel, several reading areas, and large foyer/reception area. When the facility opened in 1967, none of the units had been pre-sold. Over the years, many apartments were combined, reducing the number of units to 169. Mr. James Meharg served as president of the new organization from 1974 to 1994. He had a reputation as an "old school," very direct, autocratic, and forceful leader. The new GHI venture enjoyed considerable success to the point that the board of directors approved the design and construction of a second unit.

Construction of Goodwin House West (GHW), located only 3 miles away from GHE, began in 1985 and was completed in 1987. GHW was a 12-story, brick building with 258 residential units licensed to house 500 residents. (See Table 42-1 below for details.) According to the current GHW executive director, GHW was run at that time as a "wing" of Mr. Meharg's central organization. GHW residents soon developed an interest in the financial health of the organization in order, they said, "to protect their investments," a concept with which Mr. Meharg, who thought they were customers, not investors, did not agree. Nevertheless, residents became increasingly interested in the management of the new facility and demanded regular financial updates. When Mr. Ogburn arrived with a more "open" management style, GHI departmental control over GHW declined.

Meanwhile, at GHE, the original facility, a major renovation had been completed in 1999. This renovation included refurbishing in the original wing and the construction of a new, adjacent 15-story tower that added 131 units. When the new tower was finished in March 1999, after 2 years of construction, approximately 55 percent of the new units had been reserved. By January 2000, this had moved up to 75 percent at GHE and 90 percent at GHW. (See Table 42-1.)

The majority of residents who moved to GHW and GHE paid a one-time entry fee and monthly fees. In return, they received a range of services (outlined in a resident care agreement) that included lifetime use of a living unit, meals, housekeeping, maintenance, and health services. In addition, residents secured lifetime assisted living and nursing services at no cost beyond the monthly fee. Many residents equated the entry fee with the purchase of real estate, although they gained no equity or ownership position. Under its continuing care contracts, GHE and GHW provided the following services: utilities, meals (food service was subcontracted to Marriott), transportation (additional cost to residents), linen with laundry, housekeeping, maintenance and repair, mail service, social and other

TABLE 42-1 Residential Units Capacity and Occupancy as of January 2000				
	Goodwin House East		**Goodwin House West**	
Unit Size	*Capacity*	*Occupied*	*Capacity*	*Occupied*
Studio	72	50	15	11
One Bedroom	86	79	103	91
One Bedroom/den	29	22	35	35
Two Bedroom	80	62	85	80
Three Bedroom	30	10	13	11
Total	297	223	251	228

programs, and various arrangements of medical and nursing care.

Various payment plans were available for entrance and monthly fees. Table 42-2 shows the fees for a selected sample of units for "standard" and "refundable"[6] payment plans. Assisted care and health care unit charges were additional to the basic rates.

Company Governance, Organization, and Key Personnel

A board of trustees (BOT) governed GHI. The board had 17 members, 15 of whom were appointed by VDH and two of whom were appointed by the foundation. None of the management staff served on the board. The BOT viewed their role as legally representing the organization, establishing broad policy for governing activities carried out by management, and insuring management succession and sound financial management. The BOT delegated the operations of day-to-day business to the president of GHI. The board was organized by committee. The standing committees, Executive, Finance (with Audit and Investment Subcommittees), Community Relations, and Nominating, oversaw the key functional areas of the institution. The board also organized ad hoc committees to address temporary strategic issues of the organiza-tion, which in 1999 included Development, Study Committee for a Western Community, and Marketing. Although the board oper-ated by consensus, full provision was given for the hearing of any dissenting vote.

Edward Wilson had served as chair of the board for approximately 2 years and had recently agreed to serve another 1-year term. He received his undergraduate degree from the University of Virginia and his law degree from Georgetown University. Mr. Wilson had served as associate counsel to the pres-ident of the United States, general counsel for the Office of Administration, acting general counsel for the Office of the Treasury, and most recently as partner in several Washington, D.C. law firms. He later attended the 6-week-long Executive Program (TEP) at the Darden Graduate School of Business at the University of Virginia. Hyde Tucker, vice chair of the board, also attended the The Executive Program. Mr. Tucker had served for 40 years as an executive at Bell Atlantic in a wide variety of jobs, including president and chief executive officer of Bell Atlantic Interna-tional, before retiring.

GHI was organized in the fall of 1999 as shown in Figure 42-1. Mr. Ogburn had sev-eral direct reports including the executive directors of the two main facilities, the

TABLE 42-2 Common Fee Structures for GHI

| Type of Unit | Goodwin House East | | Goodwin House West | |
	Standard Plan	Refundable Plan	Standard Plan	Refundable Plan
Studio	$66,950	$91,750	$79,500	$109,000
One Bedroom	124,630	170,750	122,000	167,000
One Bedroom/den	206,000	282,250		
Two Bedroom	200,430	274,500	191,000	261,500
Three Bedroom	370,000	505,500	285,500	391,000

---

[6]If an incoming resident selects the refundable plan, they pay an entrance fee that is higher than established by the standard rate schedule, in exchange for a refund option at an amount not less than 50 percent of the entrance fee paid. The refund entitlement is determined by the months of residence since initial occupancy, times a percentage that ranges from 1 to 4 percent depending on whether termination was made by resident, GHI, or death.

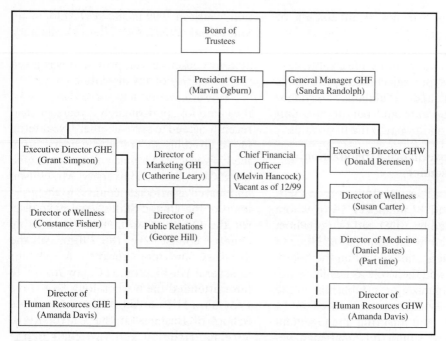

FIGURE 42-I   Goodwin House Organization Chart, Fall 1999

director of marketing, the director of public relations, and the GH Foundation. Marvin Ogburn had been president of GHI for more than 5 years; he had graduated from the University of Maryland with a degree in business and then gone to work for one of the large public accounting firms. Serving as a consultant to GHI, he was offered the president's job. Mr. Ogburn was a tall, slender, mild-mannered man who worked at a fast pace and with a humanistic style. One of his direct reports referred to him as a "nice Type-A manager." Mr. Ogburn, commenting on the CCRC industry, said, "This is one of those businesses where to stick with it you really need to love what you are doing—serving the residents."

Grant Simpson, 38, was executive director of Goodwin House East. He had first become acquainted with GHI as a student intern 15 years earlier and had joined the staff at Goodwin House West after graduation in May 1985. Mr. Simpson arrived at

GHW about a month before it opened, so he had seen the whole history of that organization. Mr. Simpson dressed carefully and managed his appearance with care. Working in the same building with Mr. Ogburn, he sometimes felt that the division between the corporate offices and GHE were not as clear as they might be. Mr. Simpson had also presented himself as a candidate for president when Mr. Ogburn was hired.

Donald Berensen, 60, executive director of Goodwin House West for the past 6 years, had joined GHI 11 years ago. Mr. Berensen graduated with a bachelor of arts from the University of Massachusetts and a masters of business administration from George Washington University in Washington. He had served in the U.S. Air Force as a Medical Service Corps officer. Mr. Berensen was a Fellow in the American College of Health Care Executives, a licensed nursing home administrator, and nursing home administrator preceptor in the Commonwealth of Virginia.[7] Mr. Berensen had a direct leadership style; at least one of the GHI staff referred to him as an "autocrat" who did not "buy in" to Mr. Ogburn's participative leadership style.

Melvin Hancock, certified public accountant, had been chief financial officer for a little more than 1 year. He was hired in part because of his 13 years of prior experience with two other Episcopalian CCRCs. When he came to GHI, Hancock was surprised by the disarray of the organization's financial accounting and bookkeeping systems. He had been working hard for more than a year now to get the systems "in shape." He noted that the CCAC accreditation review was approaching, and he was working hard to insure that GHI would pass that review. He reported that "The industry has become increasingly competitive, and survival requires that we keep improving the effectiveness of systems and practices in all areas, including finance and accounting, marketing, and human resources." He previously had worked with a Big Eight public accounting firm and a real estate development firm after graduating from Radford University with a degree in business administration.

Catherine Leary had been senior vice president for Admissions, Marketing, and Residence Issues for nearly 10 years. She had joined GHI as a secretary 33 years ago and then progressively moved into positions of administrative assistant, director of admissions, and vice president of Admissions and Marketing. She had received her Nursing Home Administrator's License 25 years ago. She had also served as recording secretary of the Virginia Diocesan Homes, Incorporated, and for the GHI board of trustees. For the past 10 years, she had been serving as the assistant secretary to the GHI board of trustees.

Amanda Davis had been human resources director since 1991. Prior to this, she had worked at other nursing homes and with a building contractor. She felt that one of the key challenges facing the company was finding and training the right people to deliver GHI's services.

George Hill had been director of Public Relations for 1 year, having worked as a marketing associate at GHI for the previous 5 years. Mr. Hill was concerned that the company was running at the "speed of a turtle," that technological changes, including the Internet, were creating more competitive challenges for the firm, and that in general, GHI needed to be more responsive in its market.

Constance Fisher was director of Health and Wellness. Ms. Fisher had bachelor of science and master of science degrees in nursing administration from George Mason University. She had joined GHI in 1987.

Susan Carter was also a director of Health and Wellness. She was a licensed nursing home administrator, as well.

The medical directors for GHW and GHE were physicians who served on a part-time basis as outside medical consultants for those facilities. Mr. Ogburn estimated that these positions occupied a little more than 10 percent of each of their total medical practices.

Governance procedures used by these managers to run the organization clearly revolved around and reflected Mr. Ogburn's acknowledged participative style. During the early part of Mr. Ogburn's administration, most decisions were made in consultation with individuals on the management staff. In the spring of 1999, however, Mr. Ogburn instituted a series of new management meetings. The first of these was an executive management committee meeting

---

[7]The Commonwealth of Virginia requires this license to manage a licensed nursing home, and one floor of GHW is licensed and operates as such.

designed to meet every 2 weeks. Members of the executive management committee were Mr. Ogburn, the two executive directors, the vice president of marketing, the chief financial officer, and the directors of wellness from both facilities. Mr. Ogburn did not lead these 90-minute meetings; rather, he chose to rotate the meeting leadership with the aim of developing the leadership capabilities of his staff. According to one committee member, the few meetings that took place had minimal agendas usually initiated by members of the staff around issues they were personally interested in (wellness programs, for instance), and the rest were similar to previous meetings where updates were heard from each functional manager on their responsibilities.

At the next level, each executive director held a weekly staff meeting that also included the vice president of marketing. A senior leaders' meeting gathered the management and supervisors of both facilities monthly for informational, educational, and new policy discussions. The semiannual objectives meeting convened twice a year to review annual goals and objectives with current operating and fiscal results. These four meetings constituted the principal governance forums of the organization.

Observations from One Executive Committee Meeting

The new executive committee meetings were often held in a conference room in the newly organized corporate office suite on the bottom floor of the GHE complex. At one meeting held in August 1999, one of the wellness directors conducted the meeting. After a short team-building exercise, the wellness director began with the meeting's agenda. The first item was whether or not the organization should support tuition for employees at professional conferences. The conclusion was that two of the committee's members would provide "more data" on the topic for the next meeting.

The next item on the agenda was a review of health insurance benefits. It was noted that there were only four major insurers available nationally, that 90 percent of employees covered were women, and that the highest cost benefits were psychological, OB/GYN, and pharmaceuticals. Some discussion ensued about reducing the utilization of the coverage, perhaps by raising the deductibles. One person said, "We should be supporting families." At the end of a lengthy discussion, the president announced that he and the CFO would decide what should be done at a later date.

The third item discussed was what the organization's stance about possible union organization should be. It was noted that the local union was interested in organizing more CCRCs and that with relatively low wages, they were ripe for union attention. Without resolution, the meeting moved on when the president raised some strategic issues.

The president noted that he saw "four major, long-range planning" issues: (1) employee retention by the year 2005 to deal with nursing staff shortages, (2) social accountability and community service goals, (3) developing guidelines for financial assistance programs for new residents, and (4) developing a refundable plan that balanced out actuarial expectations versus experience in longevity versus annuity planning. Two members volunteered to put together an initial plan for staffing to be presented at the November meeting. Two members volunteered for the social accountability initiative, three for the financial assistance subcommittee, and three for the devising of a refundable plan.

The group then discussed potential alliances with a vendor on various human resource plans including education and training, payroll and benefits, a joint pharmacy for all facilities, and benchmarking between facilities.

The wellness director then asked if there were any agenda items for the next meeting and if so to send them in advance. Then she asked who would chair the next meeting. During the closing minutes of the meeting, comments were made that there were resident councils in place in both facilities, that the organization needed some supervisory training for registered nurses, and that some were still worried about the local union.

Company Strategy and Planning

The Vision and Mission Statements for GHI had been developed by Mr. Ogburn and his staff, and approved by the board of trustees in 1995; these are shown in Exhibit 42-3.

The initial long-range plan for GHI developed under Mr. Ogburn's direction was adopted by the board of trustees in 1994 and included six key goals: (1) improve financial performance (by adding 80 to 100 residential units, enhancing current facilities and adding amenities, improving occupancy rates), (2) strengthen the nonprofit mission of service (increasing the amount of finan-

cial assistance available, providing services in a more humanistic and individualistic manner than competitors, serving as a community resource facility more frequently), (3) enhance programs offered to residents, (4) implement a quality improvement program, (5) strengthen ties to Diocese and northern Virginia parishes, and (6) plan for new CCRCs to meet needs of growing elderly population in northern Virginia.

In November 1998, Mr. Ogburn provided a 5-year report to the board of trustees in a four-page memorandum. He stated that quality had improved for residents as a result of the 4-year-old quality improvement initiative, *Quality Now,* which was based on delegation and empowerment of the front-line staff. In the report, he noted a major challenge in this area as reducing employee turnover, through such means as "increasing compensation, continuation of our education and training, recognition, building trust, management training, and

---

OUR MISSION

We are a community service organization established in 1955 as a nonprofit charitable Virginia Corporation. Goodwin House, Incorporated, derives its mission from the Episcopal Diocese of Virginia. Its officers, trustees, and staff are committed to providing, where needed in northern Virginia, the highest-quality retirement housing with continuing care services. We are dedicated to promoting each resident's dignity, privacy, and individuality.

VISION STATEMENT

Goodwin House, Incorporated, will continue to provide retirement housing with continuing care services. The organization will be known for the highest-quality services and for its lifetime commitment to its residents. We will be "customer-driven" and encourage persons to live at their highest level of independence through wellness and noninstitutional health settings. Residents, through their active, independent councils and participation at meetings of the volunteer board of trustees, have voice in the community. Innovation and creativity will be encouraged. We will maintain a quality workforce while recognizing the advantages of cultural diversity among employees. Our retirement housing and services will serve as wide a population as possible through our financial assistance program. Goodwin House, Incorporated, will maintain close ties to the Episcopal Diocese of Virginia in its northern Virginia parishes. We will be a resource for the community and will build relationships with educational institutions. Goodwin House, Incorporated, will continue to be financially stable and meet future needs through the development of additional retirement communities in northern Virginia.

EXHIBIT 42-3   Goodwin House Mission and Vision Statements

motivating staff." He reported on the expansion of facilities and services, especially the repositioning of the Goodwin House facility, renovation of GHW, and adding or enhancing services such as dining, wellness and fitness, and transportation. The report also included comments on significant enhancements of communications between the board, residents, and management. He reported a shift in board focus from evaluating operating policy to a more appropriate focus on strategic matters. He reported "outstanding" financial results, including net assets increasing more than $1 million per year, debt reduction from $12 million to zero, substantial operating losses at GH forecast to be positive beginning in 3 years, and annual increases in resident fees below the medical cost of living. Finally, he reported enhanced service to church and community with the doubling of financial assistance (given an increase in foundation assets from $3.5 million to more than $8.0 million) and new communications and educational programs ready to be implemented.

In the fall of 1999, the board and Mr. Ogburn were engaged in developing a new strategic plan. As part of that process, the board had been provided with a summary of progress toward goals in the first strategic plan, and a survey to complete regarding board and CEO performance and soliciting input for the next strategic plan. In brief, Mr. Ogburn's summary of progress stated that the physical plant, programs, and service components of Goal 1 had been met but that marketing had been a problem during the renovation process and should be "the number one management objective for the next several years." The report stated that Goals 2 and 3 had been achieved, and that much of Goal 4 had been accomplished but that maintaining a highly qualified and motivated staff might be the biggest challenge of the next 5 years. Progress was reported on Goal 5, with the acknowledgement that "We will always

have much more to do to strengthen our relationship with the church and surrounding community." Finally, it stated that GHI's market area had been defined, and possible expansion beyond the two Goodwin houses was a key strategic issue for the next 5 years.

In advance of the 1999 summer meeting of the executive committee of the BOT, Mr. Ogburn provided members with a summary of the surveys completed by board members (15 had responded) about board and management performance and ideas for the next strategic plan. The schedule called for adoption of broad strategic goals by the executive committee before the end of the current year and approval of a 5-year plan by the next meeting of the board in March.

Financial Structure and Operations

Mr. Ogburn's goal was for both GHW and GHE to be self-sustaining as soon as possible. The operating results of both communities were combined for purposes of external financial reporting because the corporate entity, GHI, was responsible for the payment of all debts and meeting all commitments to residents. Melvin Hancock, the CFO, noted that financial reporting for CCRCs was a somewhat misleading proposition from a generally accepted accounting principles (GAAP) point of view, in that many of the CCRCs did not use universally consistent principles in their actuarial tables and projections. The details of residential contracts, the assumptions made in the actuarial projections, and the ways that these were reported all made it difficult to compare one CCRC with another.

Typically, a CCRC will operate at a deficit for a significant period of time after opening based on GAAP. This phenomenon is due to the large amount of depreciation expenses and also the method of recognition of deferred revenue from entry fees. Financial performance must be evaluated by review of cash flow results and actuarial status, as well as the income statement.

At GHI, the monthly financial results were used internally by management to evaluate whether each community was meeting financial goals and targets, and quarterly results were reported to the finance committee of the board and shared with residents through their council. The financial statements were reviewed annually by outside auditors, and the annual report was distributed to the board, residents, governmental agencies, financial institutions, prospective residents, donors, and other third parties.

GHI was making long-term commitments to residents, including, in effect, the financial protection of unlimited long-term care "insurance." This benefit was a significant portion of the corporation's liability to provide future services to residents. The average life expectancy of residents was approximately 12 years, although some would live more than 25 years. The financial reporting for GHI was made on an accrual basis. Entry fees received from residents were reported as a liability to provide future services. Revenues were reflected on the income statement based on contraction in the life expectancy of each individual resident (adjusted annually). Exhibit 42-4 shows a recent balance sheet and income statement.

GHI Strengths

Despite the challenges that Mr. Ogburn faced, he knew that GHI was essentially a sound organization with many strengths. One person mentioned how well the organization had adapted to change with the industry as it evolved, its emphasis on staff development, and quality of service to residents. Many staff members commented on the basic desire at GHI to put residents first. Mr. Berensen, executive director at GHW, cited degree program affiliations with many local colleges and noted that

GHI had the best educational programs for residents and employees in the area.

Current Issues

During the summer and early fall of 1999, researchers interviewed most of the senior staff at GHI. Meanwhile, the BOT was preparing for an August assessment of management. The board reviewed 11 aspects of GHI management and summarized their perspective in the ratings and comments shown in Exhibit 42-5. Comments from the staff interviews are summarized later.

Clarity of GHI Strategy   Mr. Ogburn was concerned about the strategic future of the institution. As one of the exercises he undertook in preparation for the August board meeting, he prepared a document outlining key trends and several strategic assessments including the traditional SWOT (strengths, weaknesses, opportunities, and threats) analysis shown in Exhibit 42-6. Mr. Ogburn also made an assessment of the key trends and their implications for the strategy of the organization, and he solicited the feedback and reaction of a group of residents at Goodwin House West. The summary of that effort is shown in Exhibit 42-7.

Several members of the management team were concerned about the lack of clarity in GHI's strategy and future vision. One senior member said that he felt that the mission of the organization was not clear enough. Further, he was not sure if the organization had the right structure if the strategy *were* clear. Strategy questions that came to his mind included whether or not GHI should branch out into a wider area in soliciting residents, whether GHI should be more active in outreach programs that would raise occupancy rates but hinder revenues, and how they should think about competing against major forces in the industry like Hyatt and Marriott. This manager also felt that the organization was on

Assets

Current assets:

Cash and cash equivalents	$3,148,558
Current portion of assets whose use is limited	7,465,298
Accounts receivable:	
Residents	568,006
Medicare and Medicaid	239,620
Entry fees	33,300
	840,926
Notes receivable	100,000
Accrued investment income	528,659
Prepaid expenses and inventory	277,412
Total current assets	12,360,853

Assets whose use is limited:

Externally restricted under bond indenture agreement (held by trustee)	34,688,105
Externally restricted under residency agreements	2,040,424
	36,728,529
Less amounts available for current liabilities	7,465,298
	29,263,231
Beneficial interest in split interest agreements	1,134,548
Investments	13,511,633
Property, plant, and equipment, less accumulated depreciation of $18,253,022	55,255,756

Other assets:

Notes receivable	85,359
Deferred financing costs, less accumulated amortization of $39,018	1,533,432
Deferred marketing costs	277,396
Total other assets	1,896,187
Total assets	$113,422,208

(continued)

EXHIBIT 42-4 Income Statement and Balance Sheet 1998

the precipice of major change and had to resolve some serious issues, including how to balance corporate business goals with maintaining the "trust" the company had with its current residents. He noted that a resident survey, for instance, was not consulted during the recent renovation and construction at GHE. Currently, the staff was generally close to residents, and he felt that focusing more on "business" goals could harm that relationship and erode the quality of living at GHI.

Governance and Leadership Several interviewees expressed concerns about the current leadership climate at GHI. One noted that the challenge was to balance the demands of the corporate structure with the demands of the two operating units. Questions raised here included, "Do the

Liabilities and net assets

Current liabilities:

Current portion of long-term debt	$570,112
Accounts payable	390,301
Deposits:	
Deposits for expansion units	1,831,135
Health care center deposits	96,264
	1,927,399
Construction costs	3,982,462
Interest payable	1,151,701
Other accrued expenses	1,262,074
Total current liabilities	9,284,049
Long-term debt, less current portion	59,198,096
Entry fees and deposits:	
Entry fee deposits	129,050
Refundable entry fees	226,545
Deferred revenue from entry fees	34,550,270
	34,905,865
Annuities payable	135,142
Total liabilities	103,523,152
Net assets:	
Unrestricted	7,623,840
Temporarily restricted	1,134,548
Permanently restricted	1,140,668
	9,899,056
Total liabilities and net assets	$113,422,208

EXHIBIT 42-4   (continued)

president and executive directors have the right balance of authority?" and "Does the corporation have too much power?"

Commenting on Mr. Ogburn's style, one member of the staff echoed others' concerns about Mr. Ogburn's highly "participative" style by saying:

He has great potential as a leader. He wants to bring everyone into the decision making, but he needs to know when to say "no" and he needs to hold people accountable. He only listens; he doesn't take action. We look to him to make the tough decisions. I'm not afraid to make a decision, but there are people in the company under Marvin who are very autocratic and are destroying the company. Marvin doesn't agree with them, but he doesn't do anything. He just says "yes, yes, yes" to everyone.

Another of his direct reports said that Mr. Ogburn was "in line with management style nowadays" in that he focused on developing his people through education and internal promotion, on providing quality service to residents, and he was committed to improving. His "open door policy" allowed people to go straight to the top,

Scale: 1 to 5 where 1 is high and 5 is poor	Average Rating	Range
Management Performance		
Achieving goals from last 5-year plan		
financial performance	3.0	1–4
mission and fund-raising	2.1	1–3
expansion of programs	1.8	1–3
quality improvement	1.9	1–3
closer ties to Diocese	2.9	2–4
plan for expansion	2.8	1–5
Communications/relations with board	2.1	1–4
Communications/relations with residents	1.8	1–3
Managing staff and employee relations	2.3	1–4
Quality of services	1.9	1–3
Staff development	2.0	1–3
Awareness/planning for new trends	2.1	1–4
Meeting budgets	3.0	2–4
Managing cash flow and investments	2.2	1–4
Capital improvements meet market expectations	2.1	1–4
Public and community relations	3.2	2–4

Average of all averages = 2.3

Comments by Board Members Regarding Management Performance
Limit spending for GH III until existing facility is on solid financial footing.
We are doing great things for residents and employees.
We should be commended for accomplishing major goals over the past 5 years.
We should develop closer ties to diocese.
Residents are not persuaded about the rationale for expansion.
Foundation and fund-raising results were very good.
Key is marketing, marketing, and marketing.
I don't know whether GH Tower meets market expectations.
We must enhance revenue through improved marketing.
Need strong public relations plan that has support of board, management, and finances.
The expansion at GH was unnecessarily ambitious.
We must improve quality of services in health care.
GH East is overstaffed, far ahead of occupancy.
One of the great challenges is retaining staff given current low unemployment rate.
We need to enter new areas of community service.

EXHIBIT 42-5 **Board of Trustees Evaluation of Management Performance**

Strengths

Thirty-year record of service.
Reputation for quality service.
Strong sponsorship.
First-class buildings with a broad array of unit sizes and levels of care.
The Foundation and tax exemption enhances financial security.
The population of persons over age 75 is growing rapidly.
We have stability of staff, management, and board.
We have vitality through cooperate effort and sharing of decision making among board,
    residents, and management.

Weaknesses

We have negative operating results due to renovation and expansion costs at GHE.
We have current levels of occupancy substantially below our 90 percent target.
Our public relations and marketing programs have historically not been strong.
Our communities are located in neighborhoods that some perceive as declining and are
    attractive only to persons within a 5-mile radius.
The low unemployment in the area and our low compensation levels will increase our costs
    faster than inflation.
Size of the properties limits expansion at existing two communities.

Opportunities

Expand our mission to serve a greater number of low- and moderate-income elderly.
Expand our mission to serve persons living outside the beltway.

Threats

Poor real estate markets resulting in difficulty in marketing.

EXHIBIT 42-6   Mr. Ogburn's Preliminary SWOT Analysis

"which could be a problem." In the end, he said, this came back to lack of clarity about the mission of the organization. Without clarity on that, it was hard to know whether they should branch out more or not.

This person was also concerned about the social responsibility of the organization and how they could preserve their tax exemption status and yet compete with the high-end providers. He felt that they needed to appoint staff specialists to watch and protect the tax status of GHI. Finally, he expressed concern that most of the staff had been overworked during the recent construction period. He hoped that with the renovation completed, staff would be able to breathe easier and work more normal schedules. He expressed concern that they were unable to hire enough staff to insure reasonable work schedules. Part of the problem, he offered, was the overly participative management style of Mr. Ogburn. He opined that this was a natural result of a desire to move away from the more centralized control of his predecessor, but that the pendulum had swung too far the other way. The CEO's desire to develop people from within created a strong sense of loyalty; however, he felt the organization did not have the depth of skill necessary in human resources, marketing, and accounting that the size of the organization currently called for.

When asked what Mr. Ogburn might do differently, one manager expressed a desire that Mr. Ogburn would make more of the lingering, unanswered strategic questions so that they could achieve more clarity about

Demographics

Key Trends	Implications for GHI	GHW Residents' Response
(a) Inside the beltway, population is growing rapidly, especially among those 85+; (b) among households 75+, 66% have annual incomes over $25K and 45% over $50K, and number over $50K and over $75K is expected to double and triple, respectively, from 1990 to 2003; (c) outside the beltway, population 75+ is expected to double from 1990 to 2003, which is about double the growth rate inside the beltway.	Market size will continue to grow, with fastest growth among population 85+; upper-income market is growing at a strong pace; however, greatest need is among the one third of population with income under $25K; there is rapidly growing market outside the beltway.	Better marketing should keep both houses filled; as we age in place, we will attract more of the older old, but marketing focus should be on attracting younger, active 70- to 82-year-old segment; always huge need for affordable housing for low-income elderly, but is GHI the organization to provide it? GHI should complete goals with current housing prior to considering expansion; let VDH worry about needs in other geographical areas.

Desires of Seniors

Key Trends	Implications for GHI	GHW Residents' Response
(a) Seniors desire independence, staying involved in world around them, control of their lives, choices, fitness, wellness, financial protection, transfer of assets to future generations, and lifelong learning; (b) occupancy at both GHW/GHE is below 95%; (c) assisted living and nursing care at GHI will be almost fully occupied exclusively by residents from the apartments, i.e., very few direct admissions; (d) the asset levels of GHW residents have declined from 5 and 10 years ago; (e) residents want a strong voice; (f) GHW/GHE are not attractive to persons living outside the beltway (i.e., we are too urban); (g) many new services are now in place to support the desire of most of our residents to "age in place."	GHI must continue to adjust programs to the marketplace and offer greater options; marketing and PR will be high priority for next several years; GHI will not be able to respond to requests for admissions to assisted living and nursing care, which can create negative publicity with church and community; with several newer communities in our competitive area, we may be attracting less affluent residents; strong communications with residence is essential; we have an opportunity to serve persons living outside the beltway; we must sell the advantages of moving to GHI and overcome objections of the "not ready yet" market.	GHW does not need to buy adjacent property to expand amenities/services—"we like it the way it is"; marketing is the highest priority and better marketing should give 95% occupancy; are we certain assisted living and nursing care capacities are adequate to meet current residents' needs as they age in place? Resident asset levels should have recently increased with rise in stock market; agree absolutely that strong communications are essential; GHI should not try to serve persons outside the beltway; counter "not ready yet" with more contact between residents and prospects.

(continued)

EXHIBIT 42-7   Mr. Ogburn's Assessment of Key Trends and Implications with Resident Responses

Mission

Key Trends	Implications for GHI	GHW Residents' Response
(a) Our current programs are focused around serving middle- and upper-income persons, (b) the GH Foundation is funding 100% of financial assistance, and expects to be able to increase support at least to match inflation; (c) governments are challenging real estate tax exemption and nonprofit status, and the board and Foundation have a continuing debate regarding the importance of social accountability; (d) many consumers desire to age in place and have services that are provided in their existing homes.	We need to be sure that we are meeting "real" needs and not just running a business; the Foundation is a great strength and over the past 30+ years a resident has never been asked to leave due to lack of financial resources; the board must provide direction regarding meeting the needs of and being a resource for the northern Virginia community, and clarify the goals and roles between the Foundation and GHI; we have an opportunity to provide community-based services (i.e., in-home).	We are meeting real needs of upper-income sector; fundraising has been successful, but can't brag of never asking a resident to leave for financial reasons, since that is IRS requirement for nonprofit status for CCRCs; Foundation could help fund some community programs; explore possible joint venture for in-home care with Foundation and VDH.

Relationship with the Church

Key Trends	Implications for GHI	GHW Residents' Response
(a) employees and residents perceive that being a faith-based community is important, (b) religion is of increasing importance to many of the current group of retirees, (c) parishes have a need to address issues of aging.	Opportunity to build human resources through communications of our values; opportunity for chaplaincy and CPE to be an important part of residents lives; CPE program and other resources along with support from the seminary could be used as springboard for education programs.	Most residents are not Episcopalian, so do not overdo role of chaplains outside the HCU and avoid creating a "churchy" atmosphere; education on aging issues could be useful in community and churches; many residents feel CPE program should be entirely church funded, not resident funded as it is now.

Human Resources

Key Trends	Implications for GHI	GHW Residents' Response
(a) GHI workforce will continue to be very diverse, (b) 90% of GHI employees are female, many are single heads of households, (c) compensation levels remain below many other industries and employers in the area.	Education and training will continue to be essential; we should explore new benefits such as child day care; levels of compensation may need to increase faster than inflation.	Agree; have we surveyed workers about need for day care? Maybe.

EXHIBIT 42-7   (continued)

their direction, and that leadership would be more assertive in putting the right people in the right jobs, rather than waiting too long past the point where lack of performance was long since evident. He felt the organization needed a chief operating officer (COO).

The issue of leadership had come up in an off-site executive team meeting held in March 1999. At that meeting, executives of the organization said that they "expected, from Marvin" the following: active listening, leadership, vision, direction, consistency, making tough choices, dealing with issues, involvement in all decisions, balanced input, honoring his commitments, clear communication, support, recognizing the value of managers, appropriate delegation, sense of humor, sense of fair play, autonomy, practicing what you preach, and appreciation of a job well done. This was one of the longest lists developed in that retreat, and it included some contradictory expectations. One interviewee said that she felt the company needed three things: a strong CEO, a senior human resource executive, and a willingness to make decisions.

Finances Current financial data for both GHE and GHW reflected a decline in net operating income, a fact that concerned Mr. Ogburn and members of the BOT. See Exhibit 42-8 for a summary of these data and the projections that management made about future financial results.

Another senior manager was concerned about several things. From a financial point of view, he said, there was an imbalance in GHI: "GHW was carrying the load." The obsolete technology the company was using also hindered its ability to track and manage its finances in a modern

way. His second major concern was the lack of training in the people who held senior positions. He expressed concern about marketing, information systems, and human resource functions. While these people were clearly loyal to the company and long-term employees, they were not, in his estimation, prepared for the demands of their jobs. "In today's environment," he said, "it is a competitive business and we can no longer afford to maintain the 'family feeling.'"

Another manager expressed some concern that Mr. Ogburn was not involved more in the details of the financial side of the business. Further, Mr. Ogburn's participative leadership style was frustrating; he felt the organization needed more direct leadership. The "decision by committee," as he put it, took too long and too many decisions were getting reversed, depending on who had talked with the president most recently. He was concerned about the soft agendas in their new management meetings and even whether or not they had the right people in that meeting. He also commented on the lack of coordination across functions at GHI: "Key people are often left out of important meetings. How can marketing plan for the future without input from information systems and finance and the other functions? The people here don't want to make the tough decisions," he said, "so we've got too many staff."

The CFO expressed some concern about GHI's ability to manage its costs. Reporting that the organization was at about 79 percent occupancy rate, he noted that this measure needed to be significantly higher. He also mentioned that one measure of efficiency in the CCRC business was the number of full-time-equivalent employees to residents.[8] In many organizations like this, he said, a full-

---

[8]He noted that one could subtract the independent living residents because they needed much less attention than the others.

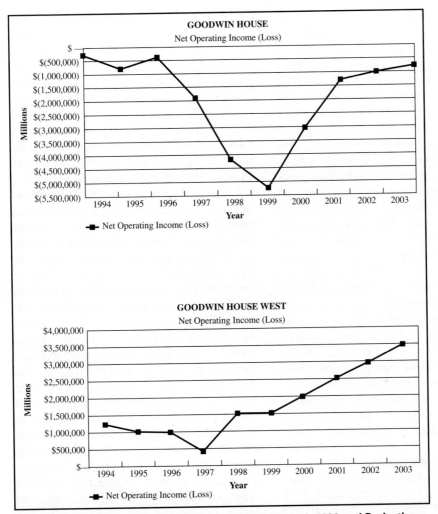

EXHIBIT 42-8   Net Operating Income Results Through 1998 and Projections

time employee/resident (FTE/RES) ratio would be about 0.40, but at GHI it was closer to 0.81. Clearly, he said, GHI needed to either greatly increase the number of residents or reduce its cost structure, and neither seemed to be happening quickly. In summary, the CFO noted that he thought the key issues at GHI were, in order of priority, the Marketing Department; managing costs, including payroll and benefits; and developing operating efficiencies in the internal systems.

One manager, when asked what he thought should be done differently, suggested that the Marketing Department needed to be reorganized, that the CFO's office needed more resources, that the president should take a more direct stand in making decisions, that the organization needed to get highly qualified people in the right positions, and that financial considerations needed to be taken into account more frequently in decisions throughout the organization.

GHW Versus GHE Several senior staff members expressed concern about the relationship between GHE and GHW. Part of the problem was their proximity: Both communities drew from the same potential pool and in some sense were competing not only with other organizations but also with each other. One staff person saw evidence of a growing jealousy between the two. This jealousy had grown to the point that hallway talk included comparisons about which tower had been completed on time and in budget and which had not, which had a better resident council, which had higher occupancy rates, and which had the better human resource and pay systems.

Catherine Leary felt that the two towers needed to have their own identities. GHW, she said, was developing a fine arts identity based on the eight professional artists who lived there, while GHE's tower was newer, more luxurious, and somewhat better appointed. She hoped that prospective residents would visit both facilities before deciding. Another manager mentioned that the two facilities seemed to want to operate independently and that this contributed to inconsistencies in several key policies (including compensation) between them.

Marketing Several staff members mentioned their concern about the marketing function at GHI, particularly in view of the lower occupancy rates. During 1999, Catherine Leary, senior vice president of Marketing, noted that she had used several approaches to building the occupancy rates. First, she was using a direct mail campaign to reach people in the surrounding region. Second, she had a modest advertising budget in which she was emphasizing "the Goodwin House family of communities," and third, she had given a number of speeches to churches in the community, hoping to draw from their membership.

Organization Many staff also commented on GHI's organization. One person men-tioned that the current organizational struc-ture with the two executive directors and the vice president of Marketing all report-ing to the president created some confusion and friction. Another noted that the organization was growing so rapidly that Marvin could only stretch himself so far and that he needed more functional specialties than before—a move that might be construed as a return to a more centralized structure like under Mr. Meharg. Further, there appeared to be some confusion about reporting lines. The executive director (ED) at one facility felt like the HR function reported directly to the president (and should report to the ED), but the HR director felt like she reported to the ED and needed to report to the president. One observer noted that the president's staff were not "walking the participative talk," that the organization had become too bureaucratic and complicated, and that as a result even the BOT was beginning to take a functionally specialized interest in the operating affairs of the organization. One manager seemed confused when he noted, "Marvin seems to be behind the idea of making more decisions at lower levels in the organization, but does the organization reflect this? Is this a flat organization or a pyramid?" Policies, according to one manager, had become more clear in the last 2 years but were still confusing because financial and HR policies seemed to emanate from the corporation while other policies were left up to each of the facilities.

Human Resources Under its previous president, GHI had a single human resource (HR) director. One manager felt this had contributed to a "hierarchical" structure that overemphasized the employ-ees at the expense of the residents' needs. The corporate HR director had left after Mr. Ogburn became president, and Marvin left the office open under some encour-agement from the BOT to reduce adminis-trative overhead. Currently, there were two

HR directors, each reporting directly to Mr. Ogburn with a dotted-line relationship to the executive directors (see Figure 42-1). To some, this approach created unnecessary confusion between the two organizations in compensation and other human resource management policies and procedures. Several interviewees expressed a concern about the HR function and recommended that a senior HR executive be hired to manage the function for the whole organization.

Meanwhile, one of the HR directors said she felt that HR was "not sold" to the management team and that she got too little support and too little staff (one assistant) to do her job—which included all interviewing, benefits work, training, and managing an 18-month-old pay-for-performance system, employee recognition programs, and compliance with the plethora of government employment regulations. She felt underrecognized and noted that "No one higher up knows all the little jobs I have to do." She suggested that management staff needed a recognition program, too. "HR is a no-win situation," she said, "You're going to be the bad guy because we're only there to hire and fire. HR needs to be on the executive committee and it's not."

Finding and retaining people in the Washington, D.C., area at this time was difficult. The fast-food chains often paid higher wages than GHI. One HR director noted that employees stay not because of the money but because of their dedication to the residents. She noted that turnover was below industry averages and morale was high, but that turnover was still costly and higher than it "needed to be."

One senior executive commented that he thought the organization needed a more sophisticated human resource function. He noted that there was a lack of performance management or management by objectives, that pay scales were out of date, that pen-

sion accruals seemed inadequate, and there was no apparent succession plan or leadership development program in place. He was concerned that the number of people reporting to the president was too high. The two most pressing problems he saw were the lack of a succession plan and slow sales of units.

Community Service and Outreach Finally, one senior executive commented that GHI needed to be doing more community service work, particularly among the middle- and upper-income segments. Historically, he noted, the churches had done most of this work, and now the commercial organizations like Marriott were doing more. Now, he noted that the organization was not serving as many of the elderly as it used to when entrance fees were not so high.

The President's View

The president of the organization commented on his major priorities. "Marketing," he said, "is my number one priority." He noted that GHI was in the process of working with a consultant to develop a branding process for the organization. He noted that GHI had never had a hard marketing strategy and that it needed one now. The changing marketplace was a threat, and he thought that increasing the occupancy rate should be a "slam dunk," but it was not. He noted that they had stopped admissions during the renovations and that perhaps that had been a mistake. He also noted that the organi-zation was building resident pro-grams (tours, exercise, development, and learning programs) that were unique. With regard to finances, he noted that he did not worry about finances, believing that if the organization took care of services for the residents, finances would take care of themselves. He expressed confidence in the CFO.[9]

---

[9]This comment was made before the CFO announced his departure effective the end of 1999.

Mr. Ogburn also expressed concern that many concerns of the BOT and others were too short term in nature. He hoped that both his staff and the BOT would develop a stronger sense of vision as they moved ahead. Marvin also felt frustrated with his management staff: He wanted them to take more responsibility for decision making and they did not seem to want to. "They are not impassioned. They want to be managed, not led," he said. "The residents want what they want when they want it. You have to empower the staff to do what it takes and management doesn't seem comfortable with that." He also noted that part of the "problem" was that many of the residents came from an age of authoritarianism and they wanted the staff to be "whipped into shape."

Mr. Ogburn also was concerned about finding good employees. It was hard, he noted, to find people who excelled at customer service. He acknowledged that the organization had no methodology for finding these people and added that the training, wage structure, pay system, and evaluation systems currently in place were all "brand new." Mr. Ogburn felt some relief that buildings and resident programs were much improved now that both towers had been completed and renovated recently.

With all of these concerns rolling around in his head, Mr. Ogburn stopped in the foyer to greet a resident. After inquiring how she was doing and sending her on her way with a smile, he turned and said, "To succeed in this business you really have to care for the people. It has to come from your heart." ■

Index